Penguin Books
Thirteen against the Bank

Norman Leigh was born in London in 1928.
Conscripted into the army in 1946, he served as
an interpreter for three years, and then joined his
father in the hotel business. In 1955 he joined a
company in Bournemouth and it was there that
his study of roulette began. He settled in
Twickenham in 1965 and a year later formed the
team which is the subject-matter of this book.
His other interests are political philosophy,
history and the arts.

Norman Leigh

Thirteen against the Bank

Penguin Books

Penguin Books Ltd, Harmondsworth,
Middlesex, England
Penguin Books, 625 Madison Avenue,
New York, New York 10022, U.S.A.
Penguin Books Australia Ltd, Ringwood,
Victoria, Australia
Penguin Books Canada Ltd, 2801 John Street,
Markham, Ontario, Canada L3R 1B4
Penguin Books (N.Z.) Ltd, 182–190 Wairau Road,
Auckland 10, New Zealand

First published in Great Britain by
Weidenfeld & Nicolson 1976
Published in Penguin Books 1977

Copyright © Norman Leigh, 1976
All rights reserved

Made and printed in Great Britain by
C. Nicholls & Company Ltd
Set in Monotype Times

This book is dedicated to Dianne Roberts, a great lady who stood by me in my hour of need, and to the twelve gallant and courageous men and women without whom this book would not have been possible.

Foreword

This book is a true and detailed account of how a lifelong obsession led me to achieve what all expert opinion holds to be impossible – beating the table at roulette. I have changed certain names and places to protect the innocent – and the guilty. I fully expect a great deal of hostility, both from 'experts' and from an industry which needs no lessons in ruthlessness, as you can judge for yourself from what happened in casinos in London and France to the group of law-abiding English people I brought together to 'break the bank'. Our only crime – to win methodically and consistently at roulette.

If I have found the perfect system for beating the wheel, why should I wish to reveal it to the whole world? Why am I not seated even now at the table before a vast pile of chips and plaques, turning myself into a millionaire? You will understand the answer to the question when you have read this book. Let me make it clear – my system is not a secret formula for winning easy money, far from it. It is damned hard money.

The events described here took place in 1966. Why have I waited so long to write about them? Simply because it did not occur to me until one evening in a hotel bar in Hampshire when I was describing my roulette adventure to a friend, Derek Solity, a jewellery representative. He said it would make a marvellous book. The more I thought about it the more I had to agree. But even then I hesitated. There is a dark side to the mythology of casinos, strange stories of disappearances and the like, death and rumours of death. After all, the gambling industry is not run on the same lines as the Church of England and has vast profits to protect.

Inevitably, attempts will be made to discredit both my system and my character. Certainly I am no candidate for canonization. I have served a term of imprisonment because of incidents totally unconnected with roulette. Some two years after my return from Nice I set up a property consultancy in Twickenham and subsequently became involved in an alleged fraud case, for which I was sent to prison. This in turn merged into a criminal libel prosecution regarding material I published concerning a policeman. Rightly or wrongly, I elected to defend myself at the Old Bailey rather than be represented by counsel. I received an acquittal on the major charge but was convicted on a count of what amounted to publishing matter which could have resulted in a breach of the peace. For this I was sentenced to a subsequent term of imprisonment. Let me make one obvious point – one would not expect to find a lifelong obsession with gaming at a professional level in a lay preacher. To some extent my compulsion to make roulette history has been a jagged reef on which my life several times came near to foundering.

While a certain sleight-of-hand has been used to dramatize events, I should stress that real names have been changed to protect the members of my team. In getting cash out of France we committed an offence against that country's currency laws, and as members of an organized syndicate they would have had tax problems in Britain.

However let me assure the reader – I am willing to accept, in advance, *any challenge whatsoever* to the feasibility of my method for winning large sums at roulette, which I call the Reverse Labouchère system.

I put myself at no risk – thirteen of us proved that my method works and we proved it at the table, with real money.

NORMAN LEIGH
Hants, 1975

Currency Exchange Rates

In 1966, when most of this story took place,
the following currency exchange rates were in effect:

13.7 francs = 1 pound
 4.9 francs = 1 dollar
1 pound   = 2.8 dollars
1 shilling = 14 cents
£90 = $250 (staking capital at the Regency Club, London)
2,600 francs = £190 ($525) – maximum stake at
   Casino Municipale, Nice

Throughout the book, figures have been rounded off.

Chapter One

By 2 p.m. on that searingly hot September day on the Côte d'Azur, under the bluest of all blue skies, the thirteen of us had assembled at pavement tables outside the Café Massena.

'It seems that everybody is present and correct, Mr Leigh,' said Oliver Blake in his twenty-two-carat Etonian accent. 'Is there anything you wish to say to us before battle commences?'

Despite the usual small-talk about their respective journeys from London, I could see clear signs of tension on the faces of my little assortment of unmistakably English men and women. Diagonally across the square, only fifty yards away, was the dull ochre building which housed the Casino Municipale in Nice. In sixty minutes the *tourneurs* would spin the brass spokes of the roulette wheels to open the day's gaming, and we would be staking the first chips of our attempt to break the bank.

Around us local habitués of the café were deep in their never-ending games of dice. In front of us the pavement was thronged by the cosmopolitan crowd endemic to the south of France – Germans, Americans, Italians, Scandinavians, Arabs; the young and beautiful, the smart and the innocent. Few gave our little party a second glance. We fitted no obvious category and had little in common except our Englishness. The youngest of us was twenty-six, the oldest sixty. Our clothes ranged from the ostentatiously correct to the downright dowdy. Our accents covered the social scale from Oliver Blake's clipped Etonian drawl to working-class London. We included an office clerk with acne, a wealthy businessman, a very glamorous housewife, a minor civil servant, a timid widow who had never travelled abroad before, and a Londoner whose passport described him, rather inaccurately, as a clerk.

If the cynical locals around us had been told that we proposed to take on the unlimited reserves of the casino with a capital of

11

only £90 ($250) each, they would undoubtedly have exploded into fits of Gallic laughter. Perhaps there were some members of the group who were having last-minute doubts as the minutes raced towards three o'clock. One or two had given up safe jobs to make this trip. One or two *needed* to win big money for personal reasons. But were the 'experts' correct in saying that there never had been and never would be a perfect system for winning at roulette? Were we within smelling distance of a tax-free fortune – or prime candidates for all the ignominies heaped on those broken by the wheel?

As far as I was concerned I had no fears. In a London gambling club, we had already proved that my method could work, proved it so successfully that every dirty, intimidatory trick in the book had been used to frighten us off. No, my own apprehensions at that moment were of a more serious nature.

Finishing my black coffee, I looked round the twelve faces and smiled.

'Well, ladies and gentlemen, three o'clock looms closer. I won't wish you luck, because luck has no place in what we are about to do. Are there any final questions, no matter how trivial?'

'If any of them casino blokes speaks to me in French I'll be struggling to keep my end up, won't I?' said Keith Robinson, a small, wiry man with ginger hair, a Londoner from Shepherd's Bush.

'Perhaps Mrs Richardson would act as interpreter if I'm not in sight,' I said. Emma Richardson was in her middle thirties, on the small side, with ash-blonde hair and extremely alert blue eyes. I knew little about her background at that point. Although I had gone out of my way to find sober, reliable people for this team, there were several whose specific backgrounds were something of a mystery. Being English is supposed to preclude any vulgar tendency to nosiness but it was not good manners that had stopped me prying too deeply into their domestic circumstances. The simply fact was that I did not give a damn.

My only interest in these people lay in their ability to play roulette six hours a day, strictly to my instructions. The 'clerk', I had just discovered, was a professional criminal travelling on a false passport. But like the rest he had survived a long and diffi-

12

cult series of hurdles to be part of this final group of twelve, and that was all that mattered to me.

'I'll be quite happy to act as interpreter, but what exactly should we do if we're questioned by the staff?' asked Mrs Richardson.

'Have as many witnesses present as possible if the management try to question you,' I said. 'Then produce your notepad and pen and ask for the questions to be put in writing. That always makes petty officials think twice – and you have a permanent record of what was asked.'

'And what chips are we to buy at the outset, Mr Leigh?' Blake asked.

It's hard with his type of Englishman, with a public-school background, to tell whether the excessive formality is a form of self-mockery. Blake was not without wit, but not everybody recognized it, and his mannered personality was to cause strain in the group. I knew already, for instance, that Mrs Richardson detested him. He was a portly young man, only thirty-two but extremely stout, black hair brushed severely back from a pale, podgy face. He had very definite ideas of how an Englishman should decently comport himself – no matter what the temperature or the surroundings, none of us had ever seen him dressed in anything other than a heavy blue pinstripe suit and waistcoat. We shared some hairy moments, but never once did he address me as anything but Mr Leigh. I presumed that like myself he had more complicated reasons for joining a roulette syndicate than the mere winning of tax-free money.

'This time I want you to put all your ninety pounds' staking capital into chips before you start,' I said. 'You won't lose anything like that in one shift, but it's better to have too many chips than to have to break off to buy more in the event of something going wrong.'

'We can just carry them about with us like cash,' Robinson said.

'No! It's illegal to be in possession of chips outside the casino. You must cash them in at the end of each shift.' I explained that each person should put a third of his £90 in the red 2-franc chips, a third in the pink 5-franc chips and the rest in blue 10-franc chips. 'When your stakes shoot up in a progression,' I continued,

13

'the table will pay you in high-denomination plaques, rather than waste time shoving across vast piles of chips. The plaques here go from twenty-five francs to a thousand.'

It was 2.30 p.m. One or two of the group signalled to the waiters. Apart from Hopplewell, who ordered his habitual large brandy, the others stuck to coffee or ice-cream. Hopplewell was sixty, some kind of company promoter in London, a morose and taciturn man whose livid drinker's face frequently took on a bluish tinge. In principle I would have preferred total abstinence, but I was not running a Boy Scout troop and if brandy or rum was vital to his performance at the table he was welcome to guzzle all day.

'Don't you blokes feel the heat with them suits on?' asked Keith Robinson, fanning his face. Knowing that Blake hated personal conversations which might come dangerously near to intimacy, I steered Robinson's mockery onto myself.

'I always wear these same clothes,' I said. 'It's my uniform – dark suit, white shirt, polka-dot bow tie, black shoes. Would any of you have trusted me to take you to a foreign country to play for high stakes if I'd been wearing jeans and a sweater?'

'What difference does clothes make?' he retorted.

'It's amazing what confidence a good suit inspires in people – getting into a hotel, parking a car. In a capitalist society it's up to each individual what price he puts on himself.'

'This jacket cost twenty quid,' he said indignantly, fingering his light grey, mass-produced sports coat.

'That isn't quite what I meant,' I said tactfully.

'One thing you've never actually told us, Mr Leigh,' said Mrs Richardson. 'Why have you always insisted we come to this particular casino in this particular town?'

'It's as good as any other and I like Nice.'

'You've been here lots of times, have you?'

'Once or twice. Just a little quirk, I suppose.'

It was 2.45 p.m. We paid our *additions* and moved off slowly across the square towards the casino building. Falling in step beside me at the rear of the group, Blake remarked in a gloomy voice: 'God knows what's going to come of all this, Mr Leigh.'

With some hesitation we entered the outwardly shabby build-raised eyebrows among the other players but as the salon began to fill up, the activities of our first shift soon became submerged in the general flow of the casino. For the first two or three hours nothing much happened: that is, there were no spectacular gains or losses. Our six players merely placed their chips and worked out their next stakes on their notepads.

My role was that of nonplaying captain and permanent reserve. As I moved round the table behind them, watching for any signs of difficulty with the unaccustomed French chips and plaques, I noticed how little the place had changed down the years. Under the chandeliers, the patrons could almost have been taking part in a silent film, especially those elderly local residents who came there each day to reflect on the long-lost glories of more warm-blooded times. For me that afternoon, the huge salon with its marble pillars and faded plush seemed haunted by the ghosts of my own past. Any casino is purely and simply an efficient trap for parting customers from their money, but this particular trap had taken up a major part of my life.

'Not at all what I imagined,' observed Oliver Blake when I joined him briefly at the bar. He eyed me curiously. 'There are better places, aren't there?'

I had no desire to explain to him my obsession with roulette and with this casino in particular. I was sure a man of his standing would not understand, even if I understood myself. On the other hand I did not want him worrying that I might have something to hide – our sole business here was to play method roulette with as few distractions as possible.

I said casually: 'I came here once with my father a few years ago. We lost quite a bit, at least by our standards. I think that's why I've always thought it would be nice to have a success here if one was going to have a success at all.'

It was around 6 p.m. on that first day when Mrs Heppenstall, a rather timid little widow from the seaside town of Hastings, ran into a favourable progression on her particular chance, *pair* (the even numbers). The basis of my system, the Reverse Labouchère, was to maximize one's winnings during a favourable run and to end quickly a losing sequence, the cunning part being that when the stakes rise during a winning run the player risks the bank's money, that is, money he or she has already won. I will explain later in detail how I evolved the system and how it works.

Within half an hour of the start of her progression Mrs Heppenstall was in a sequence where *pair* (even) predominated over *impair* (odd) by roughly 3 to 1. Adhering faithfully to the staking pattern, she began to accumulate a loose pyramid of chips and plaques.

Blake and I stood behind her, ready to help with her paperwork if she showed signs of faltering. With approximately thirty spins to the hour on a French table she had on average only a minute to calculate her next stake and then select chips and plaques to the exact amount. She was too busy with her calculations to sort out her winnings so I moved beside her chair and put her plaques and chips into neat denominational piles so that she could easily see what to pick for each bet.

It was as well that I was within reach in my role of nonplaying captain. Throughout their training period I had warned the team against the three greatest dangers a method-roulette player faces – drink, women and conversation. The slightest interference can upset the concentration of a method player and produce a mental blockage. Obviously drink and women were not serious contenders for the attention of the fifty-four-year-old widow from Hastings, but sure enough, just as she was working out a stake in the order of 1,500 francs (roughly £110 at over 13 francs to the pound – about $300 at almost 5 francs to the dollar) another woman player leaned over intrusively.

'Do tell me, *please* – what system are you using?' she asked.

I had a drill to cover such situations. Whipping out my own notebook, I quickly wrote on a blank page: DO NOT ENTER INTO CONVERSATION WITH THAT WOMAN!

I tore the sheet out and placed it on the green baize in front of Mrs Heppenstall. Without the slightest sign of a fluff, she selected a handful of plaques and chips.

It was then that the team first experienced the weirdest phenomenon in gaming, one of the eeriest sounds I know.

The table staff began to clap their hands, a quietly insistent handclapping just loud enough to be audible throughout the enormous salon. They clapped to a slow, rhythmic code.

'What are they doing?' Blake whispered urgently.

'It's a language they have for passing messages,' I replied. 'I don't know the whole code, but at the moment they're spreading the word that someone is winning heavily.'

Within seconds, casino officials began to arrive at the table to watch Mrs Heppenstall as she went on winning and increasing her stakes. A few minutes later the Chef de Casino himself appeared.

'Look at them,' Blake said in astonishment. 'Their eyes are positively *willing* the ball to drop into an odd number!'

Mrs Heppenstall's progression was our very first, and by casino standards her gains were not significant – but there they were, from the director downwards, summoning up all the psychic powers at their disposal to govern the destination of that small ivory ball.

They did not succeed in altering the pattern being thrown up by the wheel. For another hour Mrs Heppenstall went on winning roughly three times to each time she lost. Under my method she would have stopped escalating her stakes and returned to a completely new sequence of bets starting with a mere 5 francs when she reached the 2,600-franc maximum. She never got that far. As she was selecting plaques and chips for a stake of around £170 ($475) the *Chef de Partie*, who supervises play at the table and adjudicates in case of dispute, announced that no more bets could be taken until fresh reserves of capital had been brought up from the bank. The table had run out of chips.

Mrs Heppenstall had broken it!

The casino officials stared at her with a mixture of curiosity and bewilderment. Other players craned and jostled to get a look at her notepad.

Seeing that Mrs Heppenstall was clearly embarrassed by all this attention, I leaned forward to congratulate her. One of these protracted winning progressions – 'mushrooms' as we called them – can be a terrifying ordeal for a shy person. There is no harsher spotlight than that directed on a roulette player who seems to have found the magic formula.

'I can't believe it,' she said, shaking her head at the heaps of plastic discs and rectangles spread before her on the green baize.

'I should put the large-denomination stuff into your handbag,' I told her. I saw the Chef de Casino coming round the table.

'*Vos amis jouent un système très formidable, n'est-ce pas, Monsieur Leigh?*' he said, producing one of his selection of smiles. The fact that he spoke in French was a sure sign that he was annoyed, a trait of his I'd noticed down the years. He left, giving a slight bow.

I turned to Blake. 'He says we're playing a formidable system.'

'It's a bit early for him to be getting shirty with us,' Blake said. 'All this panic over a few thousand francs? I should have thought they'd be big enough to take it in their stride.'

'Obviously if somebody starts winning with a system they want to know what the system is. That's their job. Don't worry. It's early days yet.'

Blake's uneasiness stemmed from his aversion to any form of public scandal or notoriety. My main concern, which I didn't communicate to him, was how many more such wins we could have before the casino authorities decided to eliminate the danger of our group breaking the bank in the grand manner, and in what way they would go about it. Suicides, deaths and mysterious disappearances are major themes in the shadowy history of French casinos, much of it rumour perhaps but nonetheless disquieting for that.

Naturally I kept these thoughts from the rest of the group, most of whom had known absolutely nothing about roulette until they had met me. Hints of how ruthless French casinos can be would only upset their concentration.

At 9 p.m., our second shift of six gathered at the table, each standing behind the chair of the player whose allocated chance he was taking over. As the first six rose from their seats, leaving their notepads and loose chips on the table, the second six quickly took their places. This was another key factor in my planning – a straight session of six hours' non-stop roulette is arduous enough, both mentally and physically, without having to do it on your feet. There are usually only nine or ten chairs at a French roulette table, with possibly forty people standing. We had learned in London to forget all considerations of etiquette: those seats *had* to be ours.

Having seen the second shift of six taking up the staking progressions of those they had replaced, I was preparing to go with Mrs Heppenstall to the cash desk to pay in her winnings when Emma Richardson asked if she might have a word with me. I asked Mr Milton to go with Mrs Heppenstall and then give the cash to Blake. Mrs Richardson and I went to the bar.

'I wanted to tell you this morning, but I didn't know where you were staying and I was pretty sure you wouldn't want the others to know,' she said, lighting a cigarette. 'Guess who was in my compartment in the train from Victoria.'

'Who?'

'No sooner was I in my compartment when a tall and quite distinguished-looking man took the seat opposite. He was reading *Le Figaro* but when the train started he asked me in good English if I would watch his luggage for a few minutes. When he came back we started chatting. He said he was returning to the south of France after a business trip to London. Mr Leigh' – she took hold of my arm, urgently – 'can you imagine my surprise when he told me he was a senior officer in the Police des Jeux, attached to their headquarters in this very town?'

'Are you sure he said Police des Jeux?' I asked, without undue excitement.

'Oh yes – he even showed me his warrant card. Quite a coincidence, I thought.' She sipped her martini, waiting for my reaction. The Police des Jeux is the section of the French legal system responsible for the municipal casinos.

'What else did he say?' I asked.

'Only that he had been to Scotland Yard for a conference. Oh yes – and he invited me to a cocktail party tonight. Should I go?'

Our group had caused a stir in one of London's better known casinos. Our own police were satisfied I was not using the roulette group as a front for smuggling or currency evasion (I knew this because the detective they had infiltrated had resigned from his job to come with this group and was playing at that very moment at our table!) Yet, legal or not, our intentions were obviously of interest to the French authorities, even though it appeared from my earlier conversation with the Chef de Casino that he had not been warned about us in advance.

'Yes, go to the party,' I said. 'No harm in that. Play it by ear. Don't say anything about the group – and don't tell anybody else. Perhaps you'll find out if they're aware of our existence.'

'Not even tell *Mister* Blake?'

'He'd only worry unnecessarily. You know what he's like.'

'Stuck-up pompous prig. I know bloody well what he's like. I –'

'Look, Emma, I don't care how much some of you may loathe and detest each other privately but I'd be very angry if silly personal animosities ruined this team's chances. We can only work this thing with multiples of six players – one drops out now and the whole thing collapses.'

'I'll keep it bottled up in future, don't worry.'

She went off to dinner with those of the first shift who were too hungry or tired to stay and watch how the second shift fared. At 10.30 p.m. the casino was at its busiest, the elderly relics having retired to bed to dream of grander days, making way for the greedy, curious and brainless of all nationalities, when Hopplewell hit a progression on black. Even with a predominance of only minimally above 2 to 1 in his favour, he quickly reached the table limit on his staking pattern, which by the rules of our system meant he must immediately revert to the smallest stakes.

Hopplewell had won 29,000 francs (£2100 – $5,900). Mrs Heppenstall's win had been much larger, 49,000 francs – she had had a much longer winning progression – which was why the table had found itself without enough capital.

When Blake, our treasurer, finished cashing up at 3 a.m. he invited those of our group still in the casino to come back to what he referred to as his 'pub' for a drink. We went by car and taxi and found that by *pub* he meant one of the town's better hotels. (The use of the word *pub* for any hotel, be it Claridge's in London or the George V in Paris, was his only concession to slang.) When we went upstairs we discovered that he was occupying a substantial suite, which at Riviera prices cannot have been cheap.

It was extremely hot, perhaps 95 degrees, even at four in the morning. Outside in the gardens cicadas were chirruping in the thousands. On the dining table Blake began to lay out thin wads of French currency. The cash desk had paid out mainly in large denominations, brownish 500-franc notes showing the head of Pascal, and multi-coloured 100-franc notes depicting Cardinal Richelieu in his skullcap.

There was, however, enough of the smaller stuff to make a substantial spread of money. For several moments nobody spoke.

'I make it seventy-eight thousand francs,' Blake said.

'What's that in real money?' asked Keith Robinson.

'At about thirteen point seven francs to the pound – five thousand seven hundred pounds, give or take a franc or two [$15,900].'

'Almost six grand, first day out? Must be encouraging,' Robinson commented, pretending to faint by collapsing backwards onto the large sofa. Nobody laughed.

'As agreed, we will share out our winnings every day,' Blake said. 'Arrangements have been made through my own bank in London with a bank here if anyone wishes to avail themselves of that facility.'

'Oh, I wouldn't trust no foreign banks,' Robinson said. 'Give us the cash, Oliver.'

And so Blake divided up those thin, crisp wads of French currency. He and I were each taking 10 per cent of the total winnings, which gave us 7,800 francs each (£570 – $1,590) and the other eleven divided the remainder equally, which gave them about 5,600 francs each (£410 – $1,150).

Blake had brought a supply of his favourite white envelopes from London and into these he put shares for those who had preferred to go to bed.

'I've got to let my wife have some of this straightaway,' said Terry Baker. 'What's the situation about getting money out of this country?'

'There's a government limit, but all you have to do is post it home by ordinary mail,' I said. 'Put each big note in a separate envelope so that if there is an interception you won't lose too much. Fold the note in a sheet of paper and use a different post-box for each envelope. Naturally you don't put your name or address here on it.'

'But that's illegal,' exclaimed the gloomy Mr Fredericks. 'You've always been most careful to warn us not to do *anything* illegal.'

'There's no way of tracing who sent the notes if they're intercepted,' I said patiently. 'What's more, we wouldn't be breaking our own laws. You do want to send your winnings home and have something to show for this, don't you?'

'Yes, of course.'

'Right then. We're not taking much of a risk.'

When the others had gone, and Blake and I were left alone, he said· 'One sometimes envies the ease with which other nationalities express their feelings. At a time like this, one almost feels like shouting "Whoopee" and throwing one's arms about.'

'Please do, I won't mind.'

'What a ludicrous thought. Come on, I'll drive you back.'

Driving through the dark, deserted streets, he finally allowed himself the indulgence of a verbal arm-fling. 'Mr Leigh, one sees the occasional drama as a stockbroker, but I'm *bloody* sure that never before has a scheme of this magnitude been launched by a single individual. It astounds me frankly. If somebody had told me a year ago this would be happening to me now I would have called him a liar to his face.'

'Let's see how things work out.'

He stopped the red Sunbeam Alpine outside my hotel. I was exhausted. As I made to open the car door he said: 'One hesitates to pry, of course, but it all seems too amazing. Where did you get the idea in the first place?'

'From an old book actually. I must show it to you sometime. Good night.'

Blake drove off back to his palatial apartments while I climbed the stairs of my second-class hotel to my modest, ten-pound-a-day room.

It was stiflingly hot, and the din of the insects together with my own overtiredness kept me awake. I got out of bed, poured myself a large whisky and drank it in the dark, sitting on the edge of the bed.

Before the sudden arrival of the Mediterranean dawn I had finished the bottle, fighting off a black mood of loneliness and doubt. How often in the past fifteen years had my obsession with beating the casino brought me this far, right to the brink of success, only to suffer defeat and humiliation? How could I explain to an upper-class Englishman like Blake the compulsion that had ruled most of my adult life, when even to me it remained an enigma.

24

Chapter Two

My obsession with roulette is easier to trace than to explain. I was born in 1928 in the City of London, where my father was a pub licensee. Subsequently he moved south of the Thames to Peckham Rye, where he had a pub called the Queen, and later to Hertford Heath, where he had the Townshend Arms. We were always fairly well off. At school I was naturally fluent at languages but extremely bad at maths. I had no liking for any organized sport, not because I was a weedy boy but simply because I rejected any idea that the individual should be made to succumb to the majority view.

Reading was my passion during the teen-age years, especially history. The barren, austere life of wartime Britain could be forgotten in the novels of Alexandre Dumas. I developed a strong fantasy identification with a type of hero best described as the *grand seigneur*. Sir Percy Blakeney, the Scarlet Pimpernel, was my idol when other boys were collecting photographs of football players and film stars.

In those days I read everything in sight including, at one desperate stage, an old *Chambers' Encyclopedia* published in 1896. I read it like a novel, from cover to cover. For some reason I found myself studying the entry under roulette until I had practically memorized it.

Basically roulette is a banking game – the individual bets his money against the bank's money. The equipment consists of a wheel and a cloth layout, usually green. Each compartment of this layout signifies a different form of bet.

Instead of cash it is normal throughout the world to use chips of different shapes and colours to represent various amounts of money. The odds vary. The bank will pay from 35 to 1 if you bet on one particular number, down to even money – the amount of your bet – if you bet on any of the six outside compartments:

red (*rouge*), or black (*noir*); odd (*impair*), or even (*pair*); high (*passe*), the numbers between nineteen and thirty-six, or low (*manque*), the numbers between one and eighteen.

The French wheel has thirty-seven compartments, one for each number up to thirty-six and one for zero. Half the numbered slots are red, the rest black. The game starts when the *tourneur*, the croupier who turns the wheel, calls, '*Faites vos jeux*' (Make your bets), and spins the wheel in one direction while throwing in the ball in the opposite direction. As the ball begins to slow down the tourneur calls, '*Rien ne va plus*' (The betting is closed). When the ball stops he announces the winning number and whether it is red or black, odd or even, high or low.

Another croupier drags in the losing chips with his stick (or rake) and pushes out the winnings. There are many ways of betting, on groups or lines of numbers, but the bank always has an advantage in that it wins all bets when the balls ends up in the zero compartment. (Not quite *all* bets, for you can stake on zero.)

One thing puzzled me, right from the start. 'Nobody has ever yet succeeded in making a profit out of the game of roulette,' said the encyclopedia, although the advantage to the bank from zero was only 1.4 per cent on even chances.

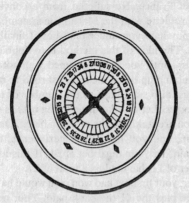

It is possible I had heard my father talking about roulette. Nevertheless, of all the dreary stuff one is exposed to in reading encyclopedias for relaxation why was it I stored that fact away?

When I left school my father assumed I would join him in the hotel business, but I associated that with a certain subservience. Having no real interest in any other career, I became a printing apprentice. Then, under the government's powers to direct labour, I was sent to be an apprentice aviation electrician at Broxbourne in Hertfordshire. I was, strangely enough, quite happy about this. I have always liked working under a duly constituted authority – provided its decisions are manifestly fair. To know exactly what the rules are and then to triumph *without breaking* authority's own code – that is my idea of a challenge.

I was then called up into the army, which decided to use my electrical qualifications by giving me clerical duties in prisoner-of-war camps, first at Wookey Hall in Somerset and then at Oxford, where I became a German interpreter after teaching myself that language from gramophone records.

On leaving the army, I worked for the Hertfordshire War Agricultural Committee as a branch petroleum manager, touring the district in my official car checking petrol station stocks with a dipstick to ensure that nobody was cheating. The war was over, but the restrictions remained, to the profit of the crooked.

It was at this time that my father took me on several trips to the casinos of France. He suffered from a conviction that he could win at roulette with the Martingale system. A look at the Martingale may help you understand how I finally devised my own method. The idea of this method is to double up your bet after each loss, until you have recouped your total losses. Unrestricted doubling up being the quickest road to ruin known to man, you must also set a limit to the number of times you will chase your losses. Let us take three losing bets as our limit.

Imagine you are staking units of £1 on black. On the first spin red comes up, and you lose. Your next bet is, therefore, £2. You lose again; so your third bet is £4. If this also loses, you revert to a bet of £1, having lost a total of £7.

If, however, your first bet had won, you would have taken back your £1 stake plus the £1 the bank paid. Your next bet would again have been £1 on black. You would have carried on with bets of £1 until the next time you lost. In theory the Martingale should show a profit of one unit for every spin of the wheel, and it is, of course, a remarkably simple system to operate.

In practice it put my father in a constant war of attrition with the wheel. The insidious attraction of the Martingale is that it produces small but consistent winnings and also seems such an easy way of recovering losses. In fact the wins are never big enough to compensate for the amounts you lose when the wheel turns against you. The table has almost unlimited capital and can stand long sequences when the player is winning on even-chance bets; the player cannot sustain equally long sequences when he is doubling up and losing. The law of averages says that red and black will even out eventually, but following the law of averages to infinity is not for mortals.

We went to casinos in Deauville, Trouville, Nice and other French towns and invariably we had to come home sooner than we planned because our money had run out. Fair enough. One goes into a gaming salon perfectly well aware that it is a jungle where welfare-state safety nets do not exist. That is the main attraction of gambling, the exposure to genuine drama. You win or you lose, and your character is put to the test in both eventualities. My father and I could never have won consistently, because we treated the whole thing too casually. This is typical of most players, even those who think they are working methodically. Still, our losses were hardly ruinous, a few hundred pounds at most.

An experience we had one summer in the late fifties was to have a lasting effect on me. It was in the same Casino Municipale in Nice to which I brought my party of twelve to play the Reverse Labouchère ten years later. Having played for three days, my father ran into an adverse sequence of some magnitude. Doubling up to recoup his losses, he came to the end of all our money, about three hundred pounds, not only our roulette capital but the rest of our subsistence allowance too.

'I'm getting up now,' he said to the table staff. The Chef de Casino was beside the table, as always taking a friendly interest in regular patrons who were losing.

'But why, monsieur?' he asked. He was younger then, with a few more strands of hair, but little else that would change over the years.

'I've run out of money,' my father said, matter-of-factly.

The Chef de Casino laughed. A short laugh, neither malicious nor particularly triumphant. A short laugh, that was all, in our faces.

We walked to the British Consulate to apply for financial assistance. There is no need to tell anyone who has had the misfortune to require help from a consulate how degrading it is to ask to borrow money after losing at roulette.

'Leigh, put out that cigarette,' snapped a snotty young underling to my father as we stood before his desk. I would have reacted, but my father frowned at me to keep quiet. This pipsqueak then demanded to know why we had no money.

'We lost it,' I said, knowing that any mention of the casino would be a mistake.

'How do you mean, *lost* it?' he asked contemptuously.

'We can't find it,' I replied. 'It may have been stolen or it may just have dropped out of our pockets.'

Grudgingly it was decided we were entitled to help. They took our passports as security and gave us temporary travel documents and distress warrants for the rail fare, a matter of fourteen pounds each. They also paid our hotel bill. These were loans, of course.

My father is an extremely conventional man, staid, deter-

29

minedly respectable, yet if this incident caused him any embarrassment or humiliation he did not show it. He never again referred to it.

That particular episode made me more interested in the actual mathematics of roulette. It seemed puzzling that nobody was supposed to be able to win at it when the odds in the bank's favour were only 1.4 per cent on even-chance bets, a slight advantage that comes from the zero slot on the wheel. If you bet on a single number or combination of numbers and the ball drops into zero, the bank wins. On the six even-chance bets, if the ball drops into zero, the table either takes half of your stake (*partager*) or you can leave your chips (*en prison* – imprisoned) until the next spin. If you win on the next spin, you get the whole stake back, but the bank does not pay you. If you lose on the next spin, you lose the lot. This option reduces the average amount the bank wins in the case of even-chance bets and didn't seem reason enough to me for the apparent fact that the bank always wins.

Whether I would have taken my interest in the theory of roulette any further than idle scribbling on bits of paper but for a coincidence is hard to say. At least it seemed like a coincidence at the time – now I see it as one more link in a pattern, for I have no doubt I was fated to spend much of my life trying to find a way to beat the wheel.

When my parents moved to the south coast to take over a New Forest hotel near the Hampshire village of New Milton I went with them and took a job as a clerk with a local firm of builders' merchants. Like so many people who have a vague idea they are destined for some special role in life, generally with little justification, I was content to drift from day to day in humdrum jobs, waiting for The Sign that would tell me where my life was destined to lead.

I met Walter Green one sunny day in his builder's yard in the village of Ashley. He was one of our customers, and there was a dispute over a load of cement. For some reason the subject of Grace Kelly's marriage to Prince Rainier of Monaco came up during our argument about the cement. That took us to gambling, via Monte Carlo, and then to his claim that he thought he had found a way of winning at roulette.

We spent the whole afternoon standing among those bags of cement in his yard, excitedly telling each other what we knew about Martingales, *paroles*, *montants* and *démontants*, all the elaborate numerical rituals roulette players have devised to achieve the impossible. He was the very first person with whom I had been able to discuss the theory of roulette, and when he asked me to his flat in Bournemouth that night to show me his system I jumped at the chance.

When I arrived at his place that evening it was not, however, to learn much about roulette but to fall immediately in love with the woman he was living with: Mary – elegant, forty years old, glorious auburn hair, sad brown eyes in a pale face. The contrast between her and the coarse-mannered builder was well-nigh incredible, and I quickly developed romantic visions of myself gallantly rescuing her.

'Well, now, old boy,' said Walter Green, rubbing his hands together, 'I suggest you and I get down to brass tacks – I've ordered a case of whisky from the off-licence.'

I had not misheard him. A case of whisky and soda siphons arrived shortly afterwards. Two hours later we were garrulous and glowing. In the time it took him to make a phone call from another room, Mary and I decided we had a truly great passion for each other.

Drink, women and conversation – these defeat more roulette players than the laws of chance.

For two months I went almost every evening to Walter's flat in Holdenhurst Road, Bournemouth, where he had a toy roulette wheel and limitless supplies of graph paper. I did not know for some time that he had never actually seen a real table, having picked everything up from a book. Nor did I learn until later that his building company was almost bankrupt and that in his desperation he had decided a major gaming coup was his only hope of financial salvation. I might have been more sceptical if I had given our practice sessions all my concentration – Mary and I had developed such passion for each other that we could hardly wait for his incessant intake of whisky to put him under.

Despite all this, however, he did manage to show me the Fitzroy system. Like all the others it is a method of controlling both the amount you stake and also your chances of hitting a favourable sequence. Walter's variation should ideally have been played by eight people. It involved staking on colour combinations and using three columns to control the amounts won or lost.

Of course, his system did not *guarantee* that you would win. No system does that. When the wheel runs against you it is implacable.

Despite Walter's fondness for whisky we completed tens of thousands of sequences on his toy wheel, and the results were impressive. We decided to find someone with five thousand pounds to invest in backing us. That was when Walter discovered that Mary and I were having an affair.

We broke up one beautiful August evening in the South Western Hotel, Bournemouth, where we were meeting to compose an advertisement that would intrigue potential backers.

As soon as Walter entered the lounge bar I sensed trouble. He was drunk and opened proceedings by shouting, 'You filthy bastard.'

In defence of my own irresponsible conduct I can only say that I had been shy with girls in adolescence and that early manhood had given me a powerful urge to make up for lost time. However, I learned something, the ease with which a great deal of hard work had been destroyed by mixing sex with roulette – and also that I must curb my own weakness for playing the *grand seigneur* role, that of the aristocrat who takes his pleasures where they come and does not give a damn for the consequences. The most important lesson I learnt from this – and was to go on learning – is the paradox that the people who are seriously attracted to the idea of casinos and gambling are the very last to be temperamentally capable of the single-minded dedication required to implement a system. Walter Green, like so many of the men I was subsequently forced to take on as partners, was not a real method player but a gambler. There is a fundamental difference. I think it was Dr Johnson, fount of most English common sense, who summed it up when he said that a gambler resigns to chance those things that are best left to reason alone.

A gambler is always looking for a big win, a magic thrill. A method player concerns himself with percentages and the ultimate results of prolonged sequences.

This is one of the hardest parts of organizing a gaming syndicate. Few newspapers are willing to take advertisements connected with gambling, always suspecting a confidence trick, but on the staff of the local evening paper, the Bournemouth *Daily Echo*, happened to be a distant cousin of mine. He was willing to slip a small ad into the paper without putting it through the usual channels. A few days later the following appeared in the personal column of the classified section:

FRENCH RIVIERA. ACTIVE PARTNERSHIP AVAILABLE
IN ENTERPRISE ON THE CÔTE D'AZUR. QUALIFICA-
TION – £250. BOX ...

I bought a toy wheel and waited for replies. There were a dozen or so. I made appointments to see them in the evening after work, fired not by any sense of destiny and not yet at the obsessional stage but merely hoping to make money.

At my first appointment, at a large house in Oxford Road, Bournemouth, I was shown into a sumptuous bedroom where reclined a petite but outstandingly beautiful blonde girl wearing only a short blue housecoat and nylon panties. Standing at the end of the bed was a tall good-looking man smoking through a cigarette holder. He was easily six feet four inches in height, with dark curly hair and an aquiline nose. He was wearing a velvet smoking jacket and, just in case the message wasn't clear enough, in one hand he held a silver-topped cane

'I am Mrs Mark Saunders,' said the young woman. 'Thank you very much for calling.'

'My name is Norman Leigh,' I replied. 'I am looking for someone to provide the capital for a roulette system and to go to the south of France to play in a casino.'

The tall man addressed me in a superior drawl.

'I am Mark Saunders. I deal in property here in Bournemouth and in Bristol. I merely answered your little advertisement from curiosity. Now you're here I suppose we might as well see if there's anything to it.'

Ignoring the dismissive tone of his voice, I laid out the small wheel and some notepads on the bed, firmly refusing to let my eyes linger on the naked limbs of the unabashed Mrs Saunders. For an hour she acted as tourneur while I demonstrated the

Fitzroy method. The results were impressive. The haughty Mr Saunders told me to leave my address. I was fairly certain I would never hear from him again.

My next call was to a substantial house in the wealthy Bournemouth suburb of Dean Park. There was a Bentley in the drive, and for a moment I thought of turning back. Mark Saunders had obviously dismissed me as a clerk with delusions of grandeur. Perhaps that's all I was. However, some kind of latent obstinacy made me go through with it. Feeling extremely embarrassed, I was shown into the lounge to meet Mr Albert Dimmock, a substantial local bookmaker, flashy in dress and speech.

As soon as I said that long study had convinced me I had a method of winning at roulette he exploded. 'What the bloody hell do you take me for – a steamer?' he snapped (*steamer* being underworld rhyming slang for a fool or sucker: steam-tug, mug).

'I'm sorry,' I replied stiffly. 'I was hoping you were an intelligent man and would give me a fair hearing.'

'Listen, son,' he growled, his face red with anger, 'if you're on the con game you'd better get yourself a cleverer pitch than that. Do you think I look like a bloody mark?'

'If I were a confidence trickster do you think I'd see an intended victim in his own home?' I said weakly. He looked me up and down, shaking his head, obviously realizing that I was too naïve to be a conman. I offered to demonstrate my method but he was not interested. He did, however, give me a fatherly lecture intended to frighten me off the idea of roulette systems for life.

'You don't know what dangerous waters you're dabbling in, son,' he said. 'Five years ago my nephew got some mad idea he'd found a winning system. *He* was going to clean up on the roulette tables at Monte Carlo. He wouldn't listen to anybody. He mortgaged and borrowed until he had a few thousand quid, then he raced down to Monte to make his pile. Poor bastard – lost the lot in a week. Came back here to Bournemouth too bloody ashamed even to go home. A few days later a hotel cleaner found him in his room with his brains spattered all over the bed. That's why I get so mad when I hear anybody talking about unbeatable systems. Do yourself a bit of good, son – forget it.'

Ignoring this ominous warning, I went ahead with my appointments. Most people were quite polite. 'Not quite our cup of tea' was the kind of phrase they used to brush me off. I don't think any of them regarded me as dishonest, for I always stressed the point that the £250 (about $700) I was asking them to invest on fares, expenses and staking money would always be in their possession, and that we would be working as genuine partners, myself standing to gain nothing unless my system worked, in which case I would take 50 per cent of the profits. But if they didn't think I was crooked, they certainly classed me as insane – everybody has these fantasies, but only a madman would try to make them reality. Night after night I would return to my parents' home, feeling utterly depressed and worthless. How could I, a young clerk in a cheap suit, convince anyone that I had found a way to beat the bank?

There was one name left on my list of replies to the advertisement. More out of politeness than with any hope of finding a partner, I set off to call on him. The name was Harper-Biggs. The address turned out to be a large house in Westbourne, another of Bournemouth's moneyed districts. I was shown into an enormous lounge by the daily help. Mrs Harper-Biggs, a tall, raw-boned woman, was sitting by the hearth of an open fireplace that lacked only an ox roasting on a spit. Knowing rejection was inevitable, I thought I might as well get it over with quickly and introduced myself without hesitation.

'My name is Norman Leigh. I'm looking for a partner in a gambling scheme.'

Her long and rather fearsome face showed no reaction.

'Please take a seat, Mr Leigh, and tell me what it's all about,' she said.

Putting the small roulette wheel on the coffee table, I said, 'I believe I have a system for winning at roulette and wish to find a partner who will put up the capital for us both to travel to the south of France and try my system on the tables at one of the municipal casinos. The sum required is two hundred and fifty pounds. Naturally I'm prepared to demonstrate the system on this toy wheel.'

Without hesitation she said, 'Very well, then, get on with the demonstration.'

Two hours later I stopped the wheel and waited for her to say something. She must have been in her middle forties then, an impassive yet strangely awkward-looking woman, not exactly thin but with such prominent bones that she looked positively gaunt; her clothes were expensively tailored yet there was always too much wrist showing and when she stood up the impression of awkwardness was even more pronounced, for she was easily six feet tall! Equally striking was her manner; nothing, it seemed, could ever surprise her or, indeed, move her into any display of emotion whatsoever.

Still with the same long, sad face she said, 'Well, Mr Leigh, when do we start?'

Concealing my own excitement, I said there was a Channel steamer leaving Southampton for Le Havre the following Thursday.

'Yes, I agree,' she said in her well-bred monotone. 'As Shakespeare said, "'twere better 'twere done quickly".' She stretched out a long arm and gave a couple of tugs on a cord hanging by the fireplace. A few seconds later a small man with horn-rimmed spectacles came deferentially into the room.

'Herbert, dear,' said the expressionless voice, 'this is Mr Leigh. He and I have decided to travel down to Nice next Thursday. You remember I said his advertisement probably referred to some gambling scheme or another. Well, I've decided to take the bull by the horns. The capital Mr Leigh needs is two hundred and fifty pounds.'

'Very well, my dear,' said Mr Harper-Biggs, politely leaving the room. Amazed as I was that the staid, middle-aged wife of a Bournemouth bank inspector was coolly prepared to leave for France at a moment's notice on what was by any conventional standards a harum-scarum scheme, one proposed moreover by a total stranger half her age, I was even more amazed at my own good luck.

'You have only three days to learn the system,' I said. 'I should tell you it is not gambling – what we will have to do is sit there hour after hour, day after day. It is very hard work. You'll have to have some pretty intensive coaching.'

'Come as early as you like tomorrow. By the way, are you interested in insects?'

'I beg your pardon?'

'It's my hobby, collecting moths and beetles and that sort of thing. I've got *cases* of them. Will there be time in France for me to look for specimens?'

'You'll be free in the mornings,' I said, tactfully declining an invitation to examine her scarab beetles.

Only five days later, in August, 1957, this unusual woman and I stepped out of the brilliant Riviera sunshine and climbed the gloomy stairs to the swing doors of the Casino Municipale. By that time I had realized that Mrs Harper-Biggs was one of those middle-aged, middle-class women who find that comparative affluence is no compensation for boredom, a tweedy English lady faced with that most poignant question: Is *this* the best life has to offer? I daresay that if I had suggested going up the Orinoco by canoe, she would have agreed just as readily. Escape was all that mattered.

We took our seats at one of the tables. The French were still using old francs and at one table the minimum stake was only 200 francs – about 4 shillings in those days (60 cents), 20 new pence today.

The low stakes puzzled Mrs Harper-Biggs. While we waited for the table staff to take up their positions she said: 'I always thought these places were for the rich.'

'Not at all. They don't care about the social tone of the clientele – even if you're not wearing a tie, they'll lend you one. You have to be a known criminal, a prostitute or on their blacklist to be refused admittance.'

'Yet it looks rather imposing.'

'Believe me, the decor isn't designed to attract the blue blood of Europe. The flunkeys, the chandeliers, the marble pillars – they're all part of a psychological gambit. If the atmosphere were that of a Wild West saloon, with drunkenness and revelry on all sides, you might begin to suspect that the gambling could be less than honest. But what possible harm could befall you in the pomp and circumstance of all this?'

'Are these people just devious or do they cheat as well?'

'They don't have to. All the odds are in their favour. Every mathematical and psychological advantage acquired over a hundred years is being turned against you at this very moment.'

We placed our first stakes of the day, both of us putting down 200-franc chips to start nine solid hours of gambling. Her very lack of emotion helped Mrs Harper-Biggs ignore the many distractions of the casino. In three days she had acquired a good grasp of the theory of the Fitzroy and had no difficulty with her three staking columns and her combinations of colour sequences. As always the Fitzroy provided small but seductively consistent wins. Towards the end of the day the croupiers began to take an interest in us, but after a while they shrugged and shifted their attention elsewhere. It takes a great deal to excite an experienced casino croupier. He has seen all the world can offer in the way of human ingenuity, greed and stupidity.

When Mrs Harper-Biggs and I left the table at midnight and cashed in our chips, we had won about £200 ($560). On an empty table we divided our bundle of franc notes and then walked across the square to the nearest café – the Massena – for a drink. She had a gin and tonic while I had a grenadine. We were an unlikely couple to be sitting tête-à-tête in the warm air of a Mediterranean night, myself aged twenty-seven, dressed as always in a dark suit, white shirt and bow tie, she in her middle forties, an inch taller than myself, dressed in a tweed suit that was not so much old-fashioned as timeless and a hat of Edwardian vintage.

'I must admit, Mr Leigh, I really am amazed,' she said, for all her amazement sounding just as unmoved as before. 'You said we would win about a hundred pounds each and that's exactly what's happened. I didn't believe you could predict our profits so accurately.'

'Ah, yes, but then I've gone into this subject rather deeply, you see,' I said expansively. 'Other people look at the roulette table and what do they see? A green baize layout with thirty-six numbered squares – like a bingo card.'

'I suppose it is when you think of it.'

'Yes, but a very deadly game. What I see is a machine for taking the money off mugs. Those people round the table looking so worldly and sophisticated – most of them are nutcases, Mrs Harper-Biggs, absolute idiots!'

'Doesn't that include us?'

'We're not stupid enough to be betting on single numbers at

38

thirty-five to one, are we? With our staking patterns and our colour combinations we're trying to make the percentages favour us. Percentages, Mrs Harper-Biggs, that's what it's all about.'

Even that phlegmatic lady was impressed.

'But how did *you* come to these theories, Mr Leigh? I mean, why don't all the other players follow your example?'

I raised a nonchalant hand. 'I'm obsessed with *winning*, not living out a gambler's fantasies. Everybody will tell you it's impossible to win consistently at roulette: but the bank's only advantage on even chances is one point four per cent – in theory. How could a tiny percentage like that account for the vast numbers who've been ruined at the roulette table? The simple answer is that they gambled while the bank played percentages – not just the pure mathematics of the wheel but all the other advantages in the bank's favour: sober croupiers against tipsy players, unlimited bank capital against the individual's limited reserves, and – most crucial of all – the inhuman patience of the bank against the emotional fallibility of the player. That's the whole point of our system – to remove intuition and hunches and all that nonsense from our minds. We do our thinking in advance and when we're at the table we are as logical and cold-blooded as the bank.'

Unfortunately there was a lot more to it than that, as I would later discover.

For several days the method worked exactly according to theory. Starting each day with a capital of £100 each, we played from 3 p.m. until midnight and would then come away from the cash desk with a profit of around £100 each. I began to believe it could go on forever. Each day became a carbon copy of the day before. Mrs Harper-Biggs spent her mornings on the hills behind the town looking for unusual insects, which she collected. She had scores of them in little bottles in her room and was always arriving at lunchtime with exciting tales of the hunt. I passed my mornings meandering about the town, having an occasional aperitif in the cafés, enjoying myself in the study of the teeming human life. We would meet at the Café Massena each day and take in the passing scene over lunch, a strangely

39

matched English couple sitting among the dice players and the sun worshippers. Apart from roulette we did not have much in common, and as she was liable to fill any gap in the conversation with dissertations on insect life I generally tried to confine it to casinos. She wasn't particularly interested in roulette theory, but she did like to hear about fraud and crime. Shocking her deep-seated sense of propriety became a sort of game with me.

'Oh, there have been weird and wonderful attempts to cheat the casinos,' I would say. 'One was rather clever. In the old days suicide was fairly common and the casinos became very sensitive to bad publicity. With all this cash floating about they have always been a magnet for conmen. The fake-suicide dodge needed two sharpies working in a team with a fair amount of capital, a starting pistol and a bottle of tomato sauce. They would both stake a thousand pounds, one on red, one on black, so that between them they never actually lost any money. The one who lost would break down in tears and rush out into the gardens, fire the starting pistol, pour ketchup over himself and play dead. The other one would tell the table staff he'd overheard him saying he was ruined. An ambulance would be called, but meanwhile the casino officials would rush out into the gardens and stuff sums of money into the dead man's pockets so that nobody could blame the casino for having destroyed him.'

'Are you sure you're not – '

'Mrs Harper-Biggs, there is no limit to human deviousness when one is this close to a veritable ocean of money.'

'I suppose they were foreigners,' she said firmly.

On our seventh day the Chef de Casino, the same swarthy, balding man who had laughed at my father, let me know our activities had been noted.

'Monsieur,' he said jokingly, 'your profits each day have been so consistent I think we should come to a simple arrangement whereby you merely report to the cash desk at midnight and collect the same amount without the inconvenience of playing.'

'Ah yes, wonderful idea,' I replied. We both laughed, though I was not particularly pleased that he had noticed us.

The very next day Mrs Harper-Biggs began to crack. 'I can't stand all those Italians,' she announced abruptly at lunch in the café.

40

'I don't understand,' I said, glancing round at the other tables.

'All those Italians who've started coming to the casino.'

'They're only day parties from the border towns. Why do they bother you?'

'They're noisy. They stink of garlic. I find them most distasteful.'

It was not, of course, the Italians who were bothering her, but the strain of method roulette over such long hours day after day, which requires a degree of will-power and stamina far beyond that needed for most occupations. However, we played as usual that day and won around £100 each ($280).

The following day at lunch she issued a strange ultimatum.

'I'm not prepared to go on playing with these Italians,' she said. 'There is an excellent casino at Leopoldville in the Belgian Congo. I want to go there.'

The whisky shook in my glass.

'The Belgian Congo?'

'Herbert and I lived there for some years. The casino is first-class, and there are no Italians, thank God.'

The years have taught me patience with people who do not share my obsession or my stamina, perhaps taught me they are fortunate to be better balanced psychologically than myself, but I was an impatient young man then. What right did she have to break up a trip which was vindicating my theories so profitably?

'I like this casino,' I said coldly. 'I have no intention of changing the venue, particularly for some sweaty equatorial hothouse.'

We argued for an hour and reached a compromise. From the next day we would switch to another casino in Nice, a privately run establishment much more opulent than the Municipale. In other words, no noisy day trippers from Italy.

Though the 100-franc admission charge was the same, this other place had higher social pretensions than the Municipale – certainly the drink prices were much grander. The staff was dressed in eighteenth-century attire, knee breeches, stockings, powdered wigs – just another psychological gimmick to lure players into a false sense of security. At 3 p.m. the following day we took our seats and began staking.

The wheel was spinning for only the second time when a large group of Italians made a conspicuous entrance. Mrs Harper-Biggs went paler than usual. Even then she might have survived, but within a few more spins she hit a 'run' on the four colour combinations she was handling. In the Fitzroy system, a run is and adverse sequence which causes the figures in the staking and imaginary 'loss' columns to assume large proportions as the player endeavours to recoup his losses. Mrs Harper-Biggs' stakes quickly went up to £30 and £40.

Then she faltered. With a complicated system, any break in concentration is enough to cause a mental blockage. The paper calculations become terrifyingly difficult, and panic paralyses the brain.

'I'm feeling faint,' she said, getting up from the table. I hurried after her. 'Let's have a drink,' I said, leading her to the bar. She said it was the heat making her feel giddy, then claimed it was the smell of garlic from those confounded Italians. Finally she looked at me and said aggressively: 'What you really need is not a partner but a human zombie.'

She went back to Bournemouth the next day. I went to Cannes with the £300 ($840) I had left of our winnings. I wanted to find another partner, for there was no way that I could handle the eight permutations of colour sequences on my own. The local paper refused to accept any advertisement. I returned to Bournemouth not so much dispirited as damnably annoyed at having been let down by the human element.

Chapter Three

Over the next two years my obsession became overwhelming. I spent patient hours training people to play the Fitzroy system and made several sallies to the south of France. Each time disaster struck in one form or another and I had to return. On one occasion after a promising start when we won £300 we encountered a terrible adverse sequence and lost both our winnings and our capital.

More often than not, however, it was the personalities of the individual members which prevented success. The ability to play, in Mrs Harper-Biggs' phrase, like 'a human zombie' over long hours in the south of France, when the attendant glamours of wine, women and song are constantly beckoning, is rare.

The closest I came to success was with a team of eight in Nice. On our first day's play we won over £1,300 ($3,600). As I sat having breakfast on the balcony of my hotel room the next morning, contemplating the orange groves bathed in sunlight and the fortune we were about to make, a member of the team came to the room and told me that he was, in fact, a police officer who had been ordered to investigate me and my team to make sure there was no fraud involved.

I was appalled. 'And you have been disabused of that idea?' I asked curtly.

'Yes, I have. I realize it's all quite genuine now. I'm returning to Bournemouth. I'm sorry for any embarrassment you may have been caused.

'Have you informed the other members of the team?'

'Yes. I had to explain why I was leaving. But I did tell them you were cleared of all suspicion.'

'But they didn't know I was under suspicion,' I said angrily. 'You know as well as I do that when a man is dragged through the courts and then told he is innocent his reputation is never really restored. Is it?'

'I can't comment on that.'

'No, I didn't expect you could. Well, perhaps you will allow me to comment that you don't emerge very creditably, Inspector. Now, perhaps the less we say to each other, the better. Goodbye.'

When I joined the team for lunch that day the atmosphere was notably tense. A conversation ensued in which four members of the team said they couldn't afford any hint of scandal and were returning forthwith.

With less than half the team remaining we had little choice but to pack our bags and do likewise.

Back in England while total depression set in, something happened which, though I did not know it at the time, was to change my life. One afternoon while browsing through a second-hand bookshop, my eye was caught by a small volume with faded brown bindings and an intriguing title, *How To Really Beat the Bank at Monte Carlo*. It had been published in 1926, the author Lord Beresford; obviously one of those self-indulgent memoirs published at the writer's expense. I bought it for sixpence and put it in my overcoat pocket. That night at a party I found myself talking to someone about roulette (I talked to *everybody* about roulette) and happened to show him Lord Beresford's book.

'I'd like to read that,' he said. 'If I promise to let you have it back in a week, will you lend it to me?'

I let him borrow the book and forgot about it for the time being. A fortnight or so later I ran into him again and asked him when I would get it back.

He looked at me oddly and said, 'But surely you remember – I gave it back to you the last time we met, in the bar of the Norfolk Hotel. You must remember.'

'I don't, actually.'

'Sure you're not hitting the bottle a bit hard, old boy?' were his parting words.

This entirely accurate remark sowed the seeds of a radical alteration in my thinking which was eventually to reach a successful climax when I led the twelve to victory in Nice. I was sure my system could work, yet all my efforts had been

44

ruined by the type of people I was forced to use as partners. Sober, reliable citizens were not interested in gaming forays to France, and even if I could find them there was no way I could train them properly in real conditions before putting them to the test. It was also obvious that system roulette could not be run by committee. Yet how could I assume dictatorial powers over people when they had all the capital? At the time I felt I was finished with roulette – finished every way as well. I resolved to cut my losses and move to London to try to knuckle down to some kind of career and cure myself of this insane obsession with making gambling history. I was unaware that The Sign had already manifested itself.

Lord Beresford's little memoir, bought for sixpence from a secondhand dealer, was The Sign. It turned up almost four years later, in circumstances that leave me in no doubt that Fate had chosen roulette as my destiny. Consider the evidence before you judge me a crank.

I had spent those four years in London trying to settle down in business careers of various kinds, some successful, like a dabble in the property market, some disastrous, like a car-hire scheme I floated. But even when I was doing well my heart was not in commerce. Those early roulette fiascos had toughened me considerably, however, and I was no longer given to introspective suffering, my philosophy being that as we are here for only a short time, we might as well have as smooth a passage as possible. I had dismissed my addiction to roulette as a fantasy of youth. Even when gaming was made legal in Britain and a casino seemed to sprout round every corner I was never once tempted to enter one. For me there was no pleasure in the rigmarole of betting, only in the challenge of outwitting the men who control the machine.

Then I fell in love. Her name was Pauline – petite, dark-haired, only twenty years old. I was thirty-six. We met at a party in South Kensington in May, 1965.

Her first words to me were: 'I've been watching you all evening – you drink far too much whisky.'

We talked for an hour. She telephoned me next morning, and we saw each other several times in the next few days. A

45

couple of weeks later we were strolling by the picturesque church in The Boltons off Old Brompton Road. I hadn't planned such a drastic step, but on the spur of the moment, the sun shining, a warm breeze on our faces, I asked her to marry me. I can only ascribe her acceptance to the romantic stimuli of the day's climate, for I was no great catch. Whatever my last business venture had been it was a flop. I had no job, no prospects, and was barely able to pay my part of the rent of a flat I was sharing with three other people. Not that any of this worried me in the slightest.

We borrowed a friend's car and drove to Ryde on the Isle of Wight to meet Pauline's parents.

Inevitably the moment came when her father, one of the stiff old school, enquired about my prospects.

'I have none at all,' I said, preparing for the storm.

'Well, tell me about yourself.'

'I can tell you about a wide variety of disasters if they are of any interest,' I said. I did. I may even have given him a few philosophical musings on work being spiritual death and the sheepishness of most people in allowing themselves to be submerged in jobs in which they found no chance to use their energies or imaginations.

To my surprise he burst out laughing. Then he told me about *his* more startling escapades. Far from the stuffy man he appeared, he had been one of those balk-at-nothing adventurers who were responsible for this country's former greatness. He had worked in the nitrate fields of Chile, fought a duel in Valparaiso, hunted tigers in Sumatra, pursued adventure round the world.

Pauline and I were married at Binstead Church, Isle of Wight, in a torrential downpour. We drove back to our flat in London. No sooner had we crossed the threshold than Pauline said sweetly, 'What are we going to do now?'

It was a devastating moment. The little money I had was rapidly dwindling, and I had given no thought to how to make more. The euphoria of irresponsibility cleared like a fog before a gale as I looked down into her trusting face, which radiated absolute confidence in her new husband's ability to give her the best of all possible worlds.

My new scheme was to rent a large Georgian house and,

unbeknown to the property company from which we leased it, sublet it before signing any contract.

Within two days of placing an advertisement we had three paying guests, a professional lady from Australia and two male bank executives. In another week we had rented five of the bedrooms. I was paying £30 a week in rent and collecting roughly £85, which gave us a substantial roof over our heads and £50 a week to live on. It was enough. And it was quite legal.

Then, one afternoon while she was sorting out the contents of an old chest of drawers we had had to store at her parents' home while house hunting, Pauline found The Sign: Lord Beresford's book on how to beat the bank at Monte Carlo.

'How the hell did it get there?' I asked myself. I hadn't seen the book for at least four years. I must have had it wrapped in a bundle of papers in that drawer ever since it had been returned to me by my friend in the bar of the Norfolk Hotel, the night I was so drunk I hadn't remembered meeting him.

Never having opened the book since the day I'd bought it in Boscombe Arcade, I sat down to read it there and then. I was still reading it at three the next morning. Lord Beresford, whoever he might have been, was no harebrained crackpot. He gave a cool and factual assessment of roulette and his explanation for the failure of all players to win at it consistently. By the time I had finished his monograph for the second or third time that night the old fever was raging in me. At last I saw how the wheel could be beaten!

Like myself, Lord Beresford had been puzzled by the universal failure of all roulette systems; he reasoned that there had to be another reason, apart from zero's percentage, for the table's apparent inability to lose. This tiny mathematical advantage could hardly be responsible for the vast number of people ruined by roulette. So he proceeded to analyse the 'career' of a typical method player using the popular system known as *montant et démontant*.

Let us say he stakes £1 on red. If he wins he has £2. He takes back £1 and stakes the pound he has just won on red again. If he loses the pound he then stakes £2. If he loses £2, he stakes £3, always increasing his stake by one unit. When he next wins he decreases his stake by one unit, so that if he has £3 on the table and he wins his next bet will be £2. It's a simple progression. He increases his stake by one unit after a loss and decreases it by one unit after a win.

Beresford imagined a method player starting with a capital of £1,000 and betting in units of £1. He plays for five hours each day, which on a French table gives him 150 spins to work on. Betting on any of the six even chances (red, black; odd, even; high, low), he will almost certainly win an average of £75 a day – in theory, the method being geared to win half a unit per spin.

On his first day the Beresford player makes his theoretical profit for the first three hours when he hits an adverse run, in which black predominates. Having to increase his stake by £1 after each loss, he is soon betting in high stakes. Before he recovers his previous losses he has to stake £300 of his capital. Nevertheless, after a further two hours' play he is able to finish with his £75 profit. However – and this is the crucial point – in the five hours he was at the table he needed to risk £300 of his own money, which meant that the bank had at that stage four times as much of his money as he now has of the bank's money when he leaves.

The second day, the Beresford player is immediately hit with an adverse sequence of black predominating. He has to stake £450 of his money to recover initial losses. However, at the end of the session, he has made his £75 profit.

On the third day his profits go according to plan for four and a half hours, then he runs into an adverse sequence of such magnitude (black predominating by 3 to 1) that he has to stake all of his £1,000 capital in an attempt to recover his losses. He fails. He loses the £1,000 plus his accumulated profits of £225.

Through all this the bank has merely been playing a waiting game, quite content to let him take £225 of its capital because it knows that sooner or later an adverse sequence will deprive him of his profits and his entire capital as well. Why wouldn't the player give up before that happens? Because he is a gambler, and the bank knows his psychology. It is always willing to speculate £225 to win £1,000, for there are very few *gamblers* temperamentally capable of applying common sense, especially if they are hooked on the quasilogic of a system. All systems fail, no matter how ingeniously designed, because the adverse sequences cause the player to risk sums out of all proportion to his modest wins.

All known systems, that is. Yet here in his book, with one of those devastatingly simple insights that always make one wonder why nobody thought of it before, Beresford put forward an idea that literally turned the tables on the bank. All known systems were devised to minimize losses in the first instance and then to produced small but consistent wins. As long as the wheel produced a pattern of results roughly in accordance with the laws of chance all went well. But the wheel has never heard of the laws of chance. Where that little ivory ball falls is purely arbitrary. Over infinity the incidence of red and black will be equal but over a whole day the laws of probability make it certain that one will predominate over longer or shorter periods. That is where the caution built into all systems becomes of no avail.

All right, said Lord Beresford, why not play the system in *reverse order*? Suppose the player with £1,000 should *decrease* his stakes after a loss and increase them after a *win*. At one stroke everything has been changed. Instead of setting out to win £75 a day the player sets out prepared to lose £75 a day. He makes no attempt to chase his losses – the basic philosophy behind most systems. If he bets £1 on red and it loses, he then places a smaller bet. If that loses, he reduces his stake once again, the amount being determined by whichever staking system it is he chooses to reverse.

In effect he is now playing the bank's role. And the bank, compelled to play the system against the player, becomes subject to all the disadvantages inherent in systems. Furthermore, whereas the player can lose only his capital of £1,000, the table is at risk for virtually all it carries, which is normally £5,000. The table cannot get up and walk away when it chooses.

The obvious snag, said Beresford, was having to resign yourself to a dreary succession of small losses over a period of a week or more before a favourable sequence occurred. However, when that sequence does appear only two things can happen. Either the table is broken, that is to say fresh reserves of capital have to be brought up, which means it would have lost some £5,000. Or alternatively – and this seemed more likely – the upper staking limit will be reached and the player prohibited from taking his staking progression any further. His probable winnings in this eventuality would be around £2,000.

I read this explanation again and again and failed to see any major flaw in Beresford's reasoning. He had taken an apparently immutable law, that systems must fail, and found the way to turn it to the player's advantage. All he was asking the player to do was come to the table with a different psychological approach to gambling, not to look for consistent wins but to adopt the inhuman patience of the bank.

By this time I was literally aching with a premonition – no, a *certainty* – that this tattered old sixpenny book was the answer. Not that I was so enthused that I could see myself going all the way with Lord Beresford, who must be given due credit for a truly aristocratic disdain for such petty ambitions as the mere winning of a few thousand pounds. In his last chapter he revealed, quite simply, that he had thought up this scheme with a view to becoming the *owner* of the casino at Monte Carlo. The way to do this, he claimed, was to find the most dangerous roulette system, dangerous from the player's point of view – any system that could be shown to have caused an outstanding number of financial disasters and suicides – to apply it in reverse, to select and train no fewer than three hundred players, pack the tables at Monte Carlo and compel the casino to play the wrong end of a dangerous system against three hundred opponents simultaneously.

This trained army would win so much that casino shares would drop to rock bottom on the Paris Bourse. Then Beresford and friends would buy up the shares and make themselves effective owners of the most famous casino in the world. He thought all this could be achieved in twenty-eight days!

I have never met anyone who could tell me anything about Lord Beresford. He sounded more like a financier than a true gambler – though perhaps not a financier to whom one might have entrusted one's life savings with any great confidence. Yet the roulette part of his theory made sense. It struck at the very flaw which had ruined all my previous attempts to beat the wheel.

All I had to do now was discover the most dangerous system ever devised.

For the next two or three days I took myself to the secondhand bookshops of Charing Cross Road in the West End. Most of the literature available concentrated on the social life of Monte Carlo between 1900 and 1925, the scandals, the financial disasters, the suicides. Only obliquely did any of the books I browsed through deal with the actual mechanics of roulette, but after a great deal of reading the name of one particular system came to the fore.

That name was Labouchère.

Named not after a Frenchman as the name might suggest but after one of Queen Victoria's ministers, the Labouchère was second to none in the suicide stakes. Like most methods it is based on the even chances, that is, the six bets (red or black, odd or even, high or low), which pay even money winnings of £1 for every £1 staked. It has an insidious ability to lull the player into a sense of euphoria by the constant winning of small sums. Simplicity makes it even more ruinously attractive. Pauline, a complete roulette novice, picked it up without much difficulty. I sat her in the lounge with a notepad and pencil and told her to write a line of figures, 1, 2, 3, 4, down the left-hand side of the page, which then looked this way:

1
2
3
4

'In this system you always stake the sum of the figures at either end of the line – so what would your first stake be?' I asked her.

'Um – one and four – five?'

'Correct. You're staking five units on the first spin.'

'What am I staking them on?'

'Any of the six even chances, it doesn't matter which. Let's say black. You've staked five units, let's call them pounds. You win. When you win you automatically delete the figures at either end of the line. What does that leave you with?'

Her notepad then looked like this:

~~1~~
~~2~~
3
~~4~~

'So your next stake is –'

She thought for a moment. 'There are only two figures so they must be the end figures. Two and three – I'm staking five again, am I?'

'Very good. Let's say black comes up again and you win. What do you do now?'

'I'm supposed to delete the figures at the end of the line but –'

'That's right, delete them.'

What she had now was this:

~~1~~
~~2~~
~~3~~
~~4~~

'I've nothing left,' she said.

'So that line is finished with. You've had a short winning sequence and you've won two bets of five pounds at even money – that gives you ten pounds. Now you start all over again.'

1
2
3
4

'This time you stake five pounds as before but red comes up and you lose. In that case you always add the amount of your last stake to the end of the line, which is now

1
2
3
4
5

So what do you stake?'

'One plus five – six?'

'That's it. When you win you cross off the figures at either end of the line. When you lose you add the stake to the end of the line. If you went on losing you can see how the line would lengthen and your stakes would increase, always betting a little more to get your losses back when a win comes along. Every time the line is crossed out completely you have won ten units. You have only to follow the two basic rules and the figures will tell you what to stake next.

'You see, the limit to the calculations most people can do in their heads is doubling up – '

'Surely that would be a lot simpler?'

I told her the old gambler's story about the grains of corn. An ancient philospher had done his king a great service and was offered any reward he named. He told the king he would like as many grains of corn as it took to double up on each square of the chessboard, one grain on the first square, two on the second, four on the third and so on up to the sixty-fourth square. The king saw this as a fairly modest request – until he started putting corn on the board. Then he discovered that to double up all the way round sixty-four squares would require something like ten trillion grains of corn, more than there was in all the barns in the kingdom.

'That's what happens when you double up,' I said. 'Ruination.'

Hiram Maxim, of machine-gun fame, said there was no way to win at roulette unless you actually stole from the table. You would need *unlimited* capital to go on doubling until the law of averages let you win. And there is also the crucial factor of the table limit. If you could eventually recoup your losses with one large bet doubling up might be possible – but most tables have a maximum stake, say £200 on the even chances. You would need a phenomenally long winning run at bets of £200 to get back all you had lost while your stakes were going up to the limit. Even Einstein could not see a way of winning at roulette.

'Well? Is this system any better?' Pauline asked.

'Not at all. It's damnably destructive. I've seen people working up their stakes to thousands of units – and to get that far they

53

must have been losing on the grand scale. Yet they were still trying to win a miserable ten units!'

With the perplexity of the innocent she asked, 'But why are people so insane as to use a system like that if they know it's going to ruin them?'

'Small wins on a steady basis. You're deceived into thinking the system is infallible and as a result you are trapped. When you hit a losing run you chase your losses far beyond what you can afford because you're convinced you cannot lose. Hence all the suicides.'

'I suppose people get carried away in all the excitement. I still don't see how your idea makes any difference – "reversing", you called it, didn't you?'

'Well, playing the system the orthodox way means playing for small but steady wins and taking big risks when a losing sequence comes up. Suppose you went to the table prepared for small steady *losses* and then seized on a favourable sequence to maximize your wins. All you have to do is change those two rules. Try it again – write the same line on your pad.' She wrote the figures on a clean page.

1
2
3
4

'You stake five on black and it wins. This time you *add* the amount of the winning stake to the line, which becomes . . .'

1
2
3
4
5

'Now – your stake will be what?'
'One plus five – six?'
'Correct. On the next spin you win again.'
'I add the amount of the winning stake again?'
'Yes.' The line became

54

1
2
3
4
5
6

'Now your stake will be –'
'One plus six – seven.'
'Right. But this time you lose.'
'And I score out the end figures?'
Her notepad then looked like this:
'Yes.' The line now read

1
2
3
4
5
6

'All right. Your next stake is two plus five – seven. Only you lose again.'
The line became

1
2
3
4
5
6

If she won with her next spin, the line would change to

1
2
3
4
5
6
7

Once a figure has been crossed off it is forgotten; 3, 4, 7 was the effective line. I told her that she had lost again. She scored off 3 and 7.

'But I've only got one figure left,' she said.

'That's right. Four. So that's your next stake. If you lose again you cross off the four and you have deleted the whole line. If you win, you write down another 4 and you stake 8. No matter how long it has become, once it's crossed off entirely you have lost only ten units. This would be the rule, hour after hour, starting new lines, winning a little, losing a little, finally crossing off the whole line and then starting again,

1
2
3
4

but having lost only ten units. What the orthodox method player doesn't realize is that the very caution of the normal system *is* its weakness. He can *never* win enough to compensate for what he loses in a major adverse sequence, because he is crossing his line out when he has *won* ten units. His bets only go up when he is losing. What we would do is turn the orthodox system upside-down, still having the figures to control the staking pattern but going for maximum winnings rather than minimum losses.'

'I think I see – but who do you mean by *we*?'

'One small ad in the papers and we'll have no shortage of volunteers, believe you me. Trouble is, half of them will be drunks or rascals.'

At dinner that night I was preoccupied with that same old problem – how to find reliable people. What I needed was a team exactly like Pauline – respectable, staid, sober, loyal – and preferably people who had never seen a roulette table. How on earth to find them, though? My Bournemouth advertisement had only hinted at gambling, yet it always attracted eccentrics. This time I would have to advertise in the national papers, where I had no convenient cousins. I wanted people to play roulette, but no newspaper would allow me to mention roulette. I wanted people who could leave England for an indefinite period but I didn't want idle playboys. I wanted people with some capital, but the newspapers would assume that any advertisement asking for money involved a confidence trick.

Then I had an idea. I would let the applicants eliminate themselves!

Of course! I could make a *virtue* out of the fact that I couldn't advertise directly. I would put them through such an obstacle course that all the fly-by-nights and chancers would drop out along the way. And I would save myself the drudgery of tramping the streets with a toy wheel in a carrier bag, being shown the door as soon as I mentioned gambling.

The wording of that ad was positively artistic.

> FRENCH RIVIERA. A LIMITED NUMBER OF VACANCIES OF A CLERICAL NATURE OCCUR IN A GROUP TO BE FORMED ON THE CÔTE D'AZUR. SOME SPEED AT FIGUREWORK ESSENTIAL. APPLICANTS WILL BE EXPECTED TO SUPPLY IMPECCABLE REFERENCES. BOX ...

Artistic? It was accepted without hesitation by the advertising departments of the *Daily Telegraph*, *The Times*, the *Sunday Times*, the *Sunday Telegraph* and the *Guardian*!

As I was phoning the newspaper offices the next morning Pauline looked more and more worried. A brain wave was one thing, but to put it into reality seemed to her extremely risky.

'Do you really think you'll get any answers?' she asked.

'By the score,' I said confidently.

If I had known of the deluge to come it's possible that even I might have felt a certain chill about the lower extremities. Experience had taught me there is no easy money to be made at roulette, but to call what happened when my advertisements appeared a nightmare would be to give bad dreams a good name.

Chapter Four

While waiting for the first replies I bought a proper sixteen-inch roulette wheel for 25 guineas ($75). With the wheel came a cloth layout and chips, as real a set-up as one could approximate without investing around £10,000 ($28,000) in genuine casino equipment.

For the next two days I ran a series of experiments to see how long it would take a single player working the Reverse Labouchère, as I decided to call my variant, either to break the table or reach the maximum staking limit. Assuming that a player worked twelve hours a day – that is, 360 spins of the wheel – I crammed a week's work into a morning, positively devouring notepads as I recorded sequence after sequence. The obsession became all-devouring. I could see that Pauline was going round the bend but I could only trust in her sense of loyalty to give her patience – at that stage I was grimly prepared to sacrifice *everything* to make this scheme work.

On average I found that the player would go on losing for five solid days, playing twelve hours a day, before he had a favourable sequence on the sixth day. There are six even-chance bets on the table: red (*rouge*) and black (*noir*); even numbers (*pair*) and odd numbers (*impair*); high (*passe* – the numbers from nineteen to thirty-six) and low (*manque* – the numbers from one to eighteen). Six people covering these simultaneously would give the group every likelihood of one winning progression per day's gaming. Four-hour shifts would be ideal – which meant that I needed three teams of six, eighteen players in all.

'Won't they be put off by the idea of having to supply character references?' Pauline asked doubtfully.

'I hope so – the ones who aren't willing to work at it, anyway. After all, darling, Everest wasn't climbed by civil servants with a fetish for tea breaks, was it?'

The advertisements appeared, and for the first few days the letters could be counted in dozens. By the end of the week they were coming by the sackload. The whole house seemed to be swamped. This could have been more daunting than a meagre response, the sheer weight of replies giving the operation an almost frightening dimension. However, I could only swallow hard and press on. I decided to hire two full-time typists from a local agency. I bought two desks for them to work at, two Olivetti typewriters and three filing cabinets. What's a little expense and inconvenience when you're planning to make gambling history?

Once the two girls had started replying to all the applicants, arranging a schedule of initial meetings at our house, my next job was to decide which of London's casinos would best serve as a training ground. It had to be reasonably easy to reach, large enough to accommodate the group and to sustain heavy losses without complaint, and it also had to be reputable, which was not always the case in those wide-open years when gaming was first legalized in Britain in January, 1961.

I bought a copy of *What's On*, a weekly guide to London night life, and ticked off the casinos that sounded most likely. I visited a dozen in all. Having been used to the high standards common to French casinos, this process was an eye-opener. Some of the casinos were too flashy and opulent, to the trained eye an obvious indication that they were out to fleece their patrons. Some were tatty and full of drunks, the Gaming Board not then in existence to ban alcohol, and some ruled themselves out by the predominance of scantily clad girls on the floor, naked flesh there not to delight the eye but to distract the players.

After visiting a dozen, I eventually picked on a gaming club I shall call the Regency. It seemed a sober enough establishment, impressively functional, most of the clientele being nouveau riche but with enough of what I would call the real McCoy type of gambler to indicate that the tables were honestly run.

Now I had the interviewing to do: twelve hundred people had replied to our box numbers, and my typists had replied to them all. With so many people interested, I could afford to be choosy, so I had made it far from easy to join the group. The applicants would have to undergo three separate interviews, which would mean three separate trips to my house in Twickenham, and would have to supply three character references, all of which my girls would write to. Then I would insist on a month's coaching and practice at my house before they could set foot in a casino. The interviews would weed out the lazy ones, the character references would eliminate the shady customers and the month's training would put off the easy-money brigade.

Over the next seven weeks I actually interviewed 951 men and women, a monumental task that all the money in all the casinos in the world would hardly induce me to repeat. The common misconception that professional gambling is an idler's escape from hard work always amuses me in a wry sort of way. Any person tempted to mastermind a gaming coup must be prepared for labours which, if suggested to the average trade unionist, would cause a general strike. My first appointment of each day was at 10 a.m., and with only half an hour for lunch I went on seeing people until nine at night. I usually went to bed in a state of collapse.

The necessarily oblique wording of my advertisements brought me many applicants who thought they were being offered a nice clerical job in the sun. Most of them took the news that I was recruiting for a gaming syndicate with the politeness one would like to think is still an English characteristic, though a few were a trifle irate.

'This is a bloody cheek, dragging me all the way to Twicken-ham for a fly-by-night gaming caper,' raved one particularly disappointed lotus-eater.

To those who neither ranted nor turned tail I made the same formal speech. (Complete formality, I had decided, was to be the keynote).

'I am looking for people to form a team which will attempt systematically and continuously to win money from casinos. You probably think that all roulette systems fail. My basic premise is that I have found a way of making the bank play the system and the player reap all the advantages the bank normally has. It will require from you a little capital and a lot of hard work, a month's training here and then practical experience of real conditions in a London casino – possibly three months of preparation in all before we are ready to travel to the south of France, probably late this year.'

60

Quite a number began to nod their heads enthusiastically at this stage, but I had learned my lesson the hard way.

'Don't make up your mind now,' I would continue. 'Here is my card. Go away and think it over and then ring me if you are still interested, and we can arrange a second interview. You will also be asked to supply the names and addresses of three people to whom I can write for a character reference.'

This was pure flannel, of course – on a venture like this they should have been asking *me* for written evidence of my good character. I presumed that unmitigated drunkards and scoundrels would be put off by the thought of having to produce independent testimony to their social worthiness. Those early abortive trips had taught me that nobody can tell from one formal interview if a man or woman is reliable and honest. (Once we had started narrowing down the numbers, my girls did write off for these references, though this was done largely to maintain the note of respectable formality.)

What sort of people turned up? Every kind. Young, old, successful, shabby, loud, meek – apart from any *obvious* ministers of religion, almost every other trade and profession was represented in that avalanche.

One rather timid, grey-haired lady in her early fifties listened deferentially to my formal declaration of intent and then said: 'Oh. I thought the advertisement was for a job in the south of France.'

'I'm sorry, madam,' I replied. 'I could not be specific in the ad but you will agree that it does not offer paid employment.'

'I don't understand – how can you take people to the Côte d'Azur if it isn't to work for a business?'

'We would hope to win money, Mrs – er – Heppenstall. As I've explained, I think I know how to make a profit playing roulette. I'm not guaranteeing anything, only that there is a strong likelihood that one would come out of the experience with more money than when one went in.'

'Oh. It isn't what I expected. You see, my husband died in February – it's so difficult at my age. I was a secretary, but that was twenty-four years ago. Most employers think I'm out of date.'

'I'm sorry. Have you come far?'

'From Hastings, actually.' Her face was so mournful I had a momentary impulse to refund her train fare. Only momentary. There were many sadder cases than hers if I had been tempted to do welfare work.

'I'm sorry you were inconvenienced,' I said, taking her to the front door.

'Oh, no, it was very good of you to see me.' She walked off down the drive, a small woman in a dark green coat, walking slowly with short steps.

Careful as I was not to make snap judgements about individuals in that human Niagara flowing through our house, one man did make an impression on me from the start. His name was Blake. He looked like a grown-up Billy Bunter, the schoolboy glutton of English comic-books, but was immaculately dressed in a pinstripe suit with a waistcoat, his black hair brushed flat. His manners were almost eccentrically formal for someone his age.

Having heard my preamble, he fixed me with a cold, patrician eye and said, in clipped tones: 'Mr Leigh, you are wasting my time. I thought this was a serious proposition.'

Something about him, a genuine steeliness behind the podgy features and stiff manners, made me instinctively feel that he merited special attention.

'Just hear me out,' I said. 'This method compels the bank to play the system against the player. If you know anything about roulette you will be aware that nobody has ever tried to implement a system in reverse before.'

'I know little about roulette except that all systems fail,' he said disdainfully. 'Good day to you.'

'You've come ten miles – why not hear a bit more about it?' I said. He nodded curtly, still poised to rise. 'I've spent the better part of my adult life trying to find a winning method for roulette,' I went on. 'I've taken all sorts of people to this casino in Nice. Sometimes we won, and then my associates cracked under the strain. Sometimes I discovered too late that they were dipsomaniacs or womanizers or straightforward lunatics. This time I'm going for reliability. I'm not promising easy money – far from it. But it would be a chance to do something unique in gaming history – to be the very first. The idea of reversing the system is – '

'All systems fail!'

'Agreed. But all known systems are based on increasing your stakes to recoup your losses. What we would do is stake more when we are *winning*, stake *less* when we are losing. Therefore, the bank is playing the normal system – and as we know, all normal systems fail. We also have a crucial advantage. When our stakes go up we will be playing with the bank's money –'

'How the hell can one play with the bank's money?'

'Naturally we require capital to start with – but not a great deal. Under the staking system we bet at the minimum stake when we are losing, because that is our own capital. It is theoretically possible we could go on losing over days, even weeks. In that case we would eventually lose our capital. Probability, however, says that *some* of us would be winning every day. And only when the player starts winning does he increase his stakes. But he never increases them beyond what he has just won. In other words, he is playing with the bank's money.'

He shook his head, although his manner seemed less dogmatic. 'Surely the zero wheel gives the bank a permanent advantage?'

'Yes, but only of one point four per cent on the even chances. Suppose you had a hundred pounds capital, Mr Blake, what is one point four per cent of that? You may lose your hundred pounds but *not* because of the zero percentage.'

'I have *seen* people play roulette, you know. They win, they lose – more frequently the latter in my experience. Surely it is only in trashy films that one sees long winning sequences with the chips piling up? I mean to say – '

'You are talking about *gamblers*, Mr Blake, hunch players and the like, people chasing dreams. My method involves a dedicated team playing percentages to a scientific staking method. We won't be trying our luck for a couple of hours, you know, we'll be applying ourselves to a rigid pattern for days on end. We will be playing as a team, pooling our capital, covering *all* the even chances, most important of all – pooling our winnings.'

'I must say I like the concept,' he said grudgingly. 'However, it seems too obvious – why has nobody thought of it before?'

'A certain Lord Beresford thought of it in 1926, in principle at least. I came across an old copy of a book he wrote. Others may have tried to put his idea of reversing a system into practice; I don't know. What I really think is that the world is full of die-hards calling themselves experts. Has any major scientific discovery not been howled down by established opinion? Yet years later people say, how blindingly obvious, why did nobody think of that before? I must stress that, Mr Blake. We are trying something *unique*.'

'Mmmm.' Blake gave himself a few moments to ponder. Then he looked up, almost smiling. 'I admit I'm attracted to this idea of forcing the bank to play the system against the player, Mr Leigh. Its impudence appeals to me. Very well – when do we start?'

'Here is my card. Think it over and then give me a ring. You do understand I'm not offering a Cook's tour? My other teams floundered through stupidity and wilfulness. This time the key-note will be hard work. There will be no democratic decisions, no discussions, simply a blind acceptance of my instructions. You will be trained so rigorously that by the time we go to France everybody in the group will be able to play the Reverse Labou-chère as instinctively as breathing. In my experience there is no more *shabby* feeling than that of leaving a casino in defeat. I have no intention of ever again enduring that sort of humiliation.'

'I'm not given to suffering defeat easily, Mr Leigh,' he said stiffly. 'If I decide –'

'If you do, give me a ring.' I rose to show him out. He seemed like an officer and a gentleman, but only time would tell.

Peculiarly enough, the people who lasted the obstacle course best were not those who showed immediate enthusiasm but the passive types who merely listened to what I had to say and then left without showing much reaction at all. Among these was a Mr Richardson, in his fifties, moustachioed, a bony face not so much sunburnt as turned to leather by a lifetime of colonial service in Afghanistan – or so a romantic imagination led me to conjecture. He came to the first interview with a lady he intro-duced as his wife, although I had my doubts. She was at least twenty years younger than he, blonde, not tall but elegant. She had on a jaunty yachting ensemble, little peaked cap, blue blazer, white trousers.

Richardson listened to me without visible reaction and then asked about the money side of the operation.

64

'First of all I should make it clear that I will at no stage take any money whatsoever from the group,' I said. 'There will be an initial training period in this house and then a dummy run in a London casino. For that, each member of the team will supply his own staking capital of ninety pounds. I will take ten per cent of all winnings – if there are no winnings, I get nothing. When we go to France each member will be required to bring another ninety pounds each – plus whatever he or she needs for fares and expenses. Again I will take ten per cent of the winnings. I hope to make a great deal of money out of this project, but it won't be from the people who go with me.'

'That's all I wished to know.'

Fewer than half the original interviewees returned for a second interview. To my surprise little Mrs Heppenstall, the shy widow from Hastings, was one of them. Thinking I had not made myself clear at our first meeting, I said to her tactfully, 'You do realize I'm not offering you a job in the south of France, Mrs Heppenstall?'

'Oh yes, I know that,' she replied. 'I've thought about it very seriously, and I would like to come along with you – that's if you think I could be useful.'

'We'll be in casinos all day, and there'll be a great deal of involved paperwork – it can be very tiring, you know. If I might ask – what makes you think you'd enjoy an experience of this kind?'

'I've always so much wanted to travel abroad,' she said apologetically, her eyes watching me hopefully.

It was a glorious evening in June when cars and taxis began to arrive at our home carrying the chosen thirty-seven for the initial training. Pauline and I had spent the whole day dragging chairs, and any item of furniture that could be used as a chair, into the lounge, a magnificent room, forty-two feet by twenty-one, with French windows, Restoration furniture and cream-coloured wallpaper in a cracked-ice motif.

Apart from one foreigner, Mr Lee Kuan, a young economics student from Hong Kong, the assembled group was a typical cross-section of middle-class England. At that stage only a few had made any impression on me as individuals – Mrs Heppenstall, of course, smiling shyly; a young man called Terry Baker about whom I had certain suspicions, his three references having returned identically worded letters; Oliver Blake, dressed as if he were attending a Palace investiture; and a rather prissy man called Bateson, who was a company book-keeper and seemed to think that made him an expert on the mathematics of staking. The glamorous Mrs Richardson was also present, but her husband didn't seem to be with her.

For the rest, there were male filing clerks, female secretaries, business executives, company directors, one or two of 'independent means', a pub-keeper and the manager of a cement firm.

They knew very little about me, and it was obvious that they were curious. I might have been more nervous but for three or four large Scotches consumed rapidly before the apprehensive eyes of my wife. There is a terrifying sense of responsibility involved in dragging other people into one's private obsession and I needed the stuff to insulate my nervous system.

'Ladies and gentlemen,' I began, when they were all seated in our sizeable lounge, 'before we go any further I'm afraid that at the risk of boring you I must give you a few words of advice concerning this venture. Once we enter a casino the success or failure of our efforts will depend entirely on how well you have assimilated the lessons I propose to teach you in this room. If we are to make any money, your cooperation and obedience is essential. I am *determined* that once we start we shall not fail. You will be up against this little gadget' – I tapped the spokes of the wheel – 'and to beat it you will have to become something not unlike machines yourselves. There must be no deviation from the system I'm going to teach you. All human reason has to be rigorously excluded. You may feel tired, you may at times think it is just not your day, your nerves may well reach breaking point – well, towards all these excuses you will find me unsympathetic. This is to be a team effort, and my responsibility is to ensure that no individual lets the rest of the team down. To this end you will be disciplined and trained until you can work the system without thinking. If you find the practice sessions here too arduous, you should drop out before we come to play with real money. Contrary to myth, the real stumbling block to success at roulette is neither in the law of averages nor in chance

66

– it is that people are happier losing. They would deny it vehemently, but I've seen it countless times – losing is more comfortable than winning. Winning demands ruthlessness and a willingness to forget all other considerations.

'From the moment you step inside a casino you will be faced with every temptation known to man – drink, sex, greed, egomania, even fear. While you are working you will have to become puritans. I have been careful to stress all along that I guarantee nothing. I'd like you all to think of this as an adventure which offers a reasonable chance of making money, but it will be an adventure we can look back on with satisfaction only if we all pull our weight.

'What I propose to do this evening is run through the basic rules of the system, the Reverse Labouchère. This will give you a taste of what playing method roulette is all about. Some of you may very well feel that such involved paperwork is not your cup of tea – if so, have no hesitation in telling me. Better to be honest with yourselves now than waste your time and mine. Well then, to business. I asked you all to bring notepads. In a straight line down the left-hand side of the page write the numbers one, two, three, four . . .'

I stopped spinning the wheel at about ten o'clock. Reactions were varied. Some seemed to think it was all too easy and wondered why I was making such a fuss. A few were still frowning at the effort required in taking their rusty adult minds back to the classroom. Bateson the book-keeper wanted to ask a number of technical questions.

'One step at a time if you don't mind, Mr Bateson,' I said firmly. 'You all have some idea of what the method entails. Is there anyone who would rather drop out now?'

'I'll tell you one thing,' said a young Londoner with ginger hair. 'It looks a whole lot easier when James Bond's doing it in the movies. I got a headache with them sums.'

'I found it easy enough,' said Blake.

'Funny, you don't look like James Bond,' retorted the ginger-haired man. Blake coloured but said nothing.

'Right,' I said. 'I'm glad the headaches haven't put anyone off. To save the group's time with the kind of questions you were asking, Mr Bateson, I've had run off some copies of a leaflet which outlines the fundamental principles of my system. You can each take a copy home and study it before your next get-together. I would ask you not to let anyone else read it.'

As they were leaving, Mrs Richardson came up to me.

'My husband decided it would be easier if I came along instead of him,' she said, her voice so hoarse I assumed she had a stiff cold. 'Will that be all right?'

'Of course – there's no sex discrimination here, I assure you.'

'Will it be all right to show him this?' She held up the stapled sheets of the leaflet I had distributed. 'I promise he won't talk about it.'

'I was half-joking, actually. It isn't likely that anyone would – '

'You don't want to be too trusting, Mr Leigh,' she said seriously. 'There are a lot of sharks about these days.'

As I watched the last of them going down the drive to their cars I found myself wondering – was it too much to hope that my obstacle course of interviews and character references had eliminated all the bad eggs? A team of thirty-seven? I could have *six* shifts, cover *two* tables, double the chances of winning progressions . . .

As I got into bed Pauline, obviously surprised, remarked that my wild project seemed to have attracted a very decent assortment of people.

'Well, you can't tell at this stage,' I said wearily.

'Don't be so cynical. They all seemed totally respectable.'

'So did all the other maniacs, at first.'

Chapter Five

The pamphlet I had given the group to take home explained everything one would need to know in order to beat the table, the master plan if you like. I reproduce it here in a slightly shortened form. It was headed:

PRIVATE AND CONFIDENTIAL

As a preliminary, it might be as well to dispose of one or two misconceptions concerning the game of roulette. In the first place, nobody ever 'beats the bank'. The bank has in its favour zero, which over a period of time appropriates 2.1 per cent of all monies staked on the table (2.8 per cent on numbers and combinations of numbers, and 1.4 per cent on even chances). Thus, in effect, the bank acts as broker, levying its brokerage of 2.1 per cent on winner and loser alike. When a player has a substantial win he does *not* take it from the bank but from the other players.

Let us imagine a player who has been playing on even chances and numbers and has won £1,000 in the process staking a total of £100. He will have lost to the bank by way of zero the sum of £2 2s (2.1 per cent). The sum he has won came initially from the other players so that it, too, was subject to zero.

As result of these transactions the bank has acquired exactly £23 2s. To the casual eye it might appear that the player has won £1,000 from the bank – yet as we see it is the bank which has actually gained, by taking its percentage of all monies passing across the table. Besides which, over a period of time the player would almost certainly lose his temporary profits and in the meantime all monies staked by him, either to increase these profits or to recover them, would still be subject to the remorseless toll of zero.

The second point is that *all* systems fail in the long run. Every system player knows this, but few realize why. Many, with only a superficial knowledge of the subject, would ascribe this failure to zero. A simple example will prove this false. A hypothetical player with £1,000 capital, playing on even chances and staking flat stakes of £1, would on average lose $3\frac{1}{2}$ pence to zero for every spin of the wheel. Apart from this, of course, his wins and losses will exactly cancel out, and at this rate he will need to stake continually for 72,000 spins before his entire capital is lost, which virtually amounts to an attendance of two hundred days, playing twelve hours a day! Obviously the incidence of zero by itself cannot be held responsible for dramatic changes of fortune.

In point of fact, the really dramatic losses at roulette, especially among system players, can normally be compressed into a very short time, often a matter of hours. Since zero is the only factor (apparently) in the bank's favour, and since its toll of 2.1 per cent is negligible as far as the average player is concerned, we are forced to seek elsewhere for the reasons behind 'system failure' . . .

[At this point I gave Lord Beresford's account of the 'career' of a typical system player using the orthodox Labouchère method of staking, with a capital of £1,000. It showed that he had to increase his stakes to recover previous losses until an adverse sequence of magnitude takes both his winnings and his capital, the process lasting six days.]

The bank had indeed reaped a rich harvest, for it only needed a capital of £100 (the amount the player won in his first five days), plus a wait of six days, to acquire £1,000. One fact emerges with startling clarity – if the bank itself could be forced to play the system in its *correct* order *against the player* then obviously the tables would be completely turned. This is not as difficult as it sounds. Suppose our hypothetical player, instead of increasing his stakes after a loss and decreasing them after a win, had decreased them after a loss and increased them after a win. The net result would be that instead of setting out to win £20 a day he would actually lose £20 a day and force the bank to take the brunt of the hitherto adverse sequences. It would now be the bank's turn to be content with a paltry £20 a day, coupled with the ever-present danger of an adverse sequence. It would have exactly the same chance (apart from zero) as our player had of continuing to win £20 per day, every day, ad infinitum. The bank would probably succeed in winning £100 over the first five days, only to lose that and its entire capital on the sixth day. It must be remembered that our player has only £1,000 to lose, whereas the bank stands the risk of actually being broken: unlike the player it cannot simply get up and walk away because it has lost £1,000.

The simile is complete except for one small detail. Let us suppose our player has decided to cease play after recovering from the bank his previous losses of £100, plus £1,000 of the bank's capital. In order to win a total of £1,000 on even chances he must actually have staked that amount, although £900 of it actually belonged to the bank, so that he would still have been subjected to zero – 1.4 per cent on £1,000. Our player would have won £1,000 less £14, or £986.

[I then outlined the idea of six players covering all the even chances in shifts, staking on the reversed Labouchère method.]

Now, however, *all* six even chances are being played upon simultaneously, so that instead of having to wait an average of six days before the bank is in difficulty any one of the players will on average place the bank in jeopardy at least *once every day*. Not only is the bank forced to play a dangerous system, it is forced to play it against six players at the same time. By way of contrast imagine the folly of a single player attempting to play the Labouchère in its *correct* order against six different tables at the same time (assuming this were physically possible). He would certainly lose his capital on the first day.

To return to our six players, however, we find that within a very short space of time one of them at least has placed the bank in grave difficulties. The other players will continue to lose at a rate of about 100 units per session of four hours. The one who hits a favourable progression will increase his stakes, and since he will be playing with the bank's capital (i.e. his winnings) the size of his stakes will not worry him. Unlike the player using the system in its orthodox order, he can sit there and wait. He does not have to wait very long, for quite suddenly one of two things has happened.

A) His stakes have reached such gigantic proportions that he is barred from staking upwards by reason of the table limit (generally the equivalent of £200 for a single bet on the even chances). At this stage his probably winnings are in the region of £2,000. Now he either terminates his staking on that progression and returns to the basic units, or he is relieved.

B) The size of his stakes has not reached the bank's limits, presumably because the progression is a longer and more gradual one; the alternatives here are either a collapse of the favourable sequence of breaking the bank. Should the latter be the case he will again either return to normal staking or be relieved. His win here is likely to be in the order of £5,000, which is roughly the capitalization of a roulette table.

Breaking the bank, of course, does not mean that the casino has lost all its available capital, merely that the table concerned has lost all its available chips and plaques and that reserves will have to be brought up from other tables.

The foregoing, it will be obvious, is beyond the scope of the individual operator. In many clubs and casinos the tables are open round the clock and the individual would require relief players – even then he would be covering only a single chance.

[I then described the staking system, Labouchère's starting line of 1, 2, 3, 4, explaining that in its orthodox form it is extremely dangerous because the stakes become so vast, to recoup losses, that they are out of all proportion to the comparatively small amounts won.]

Concerning capital requirements, the interesting thing is that as no player will be working for more than four hours a day (roughly 120 spins) and since the maximum possible loss is 80 per cent of the total number of spins (i.e. 96 units) the theoretical requirement for each day will be roughly £12. In practice, however, each player will be required to have available for his own use at least £90.

The player will often find a favourable sequence building up only to see it collapse – that is, indeed, the rule rather than the exception. This can be disheartening, but remember that the bank has exactly the same experience when the method is being used in its correct order against it – but the bank never becomes disheartened. Why should it? Like ourselves it has but to wait; its croupiers probably work for more than four hours a day so that from the standpoint of mental and physical stamina alone we will have the edge on them. The keynote to the whole operation is diligence and attention to detail.

Players should experience little difficulty in maintaining the simple calculations of the Reverse Labouchère and staking at the same time, since the average interval between spins is about one minute, although it can vary between thirty seconds and as much as three minutes.

Since zero is the only attribute to the bank that we cannot duplicate, its treatment deserves mention. When the ball lands in zero one of two things happens to monies staked on even chances; the player's stake is imprisoned and he may *partager*, that is remove one half of it, leaving the other half to the bank, or he can leave it on for its fate to be decided by the next spin. Thus if he bets on red and zero comes up, his stake would be imprisoned. If black comes up next he loses the whole stake. If red comes up he recovers it in its entirety (although he does not *win* any money). Either way the result over a long period is the same 1.4 per cent to the bank.

In practice players should leave the stake in 'prison', treat zero as if it had not occurred, and place their stakes on the selected chance a second time, taking care, however, to recover their previous stake in the event of its being released from prison.

Finally, the golden rule: never allow yourself to be flustered; never take part in other people's disputes – you are there to make money, they are probably only there for a flutter – and strive at all times to keep up with the wheel.

TO THE READER:

My group had the advantage of applying the lessons set out in my pamphlet in many hours of practice in my home at Twickenham, and even then some of them were slow to assimilate everything. Do not despair, therefore, if you fail to grasp all the subtleties of roulette after one reading. If, however, you feel you've grasped the principle there is one thing I must stress.

This is, indeed, a system for winning at roulette, but before anyone packs in his job and mortgages his house to rush to the nearest casino with his life savings I must state categorically – it is not easy money. It needs a carefully selected team, a great deal of practice, physical stamina and a fairly stern frame of mind. That still leaves you with the conditions of a casino to contend with. And as we were to discover, nobody is going to let you win big money without putting up a fight, dirty or otherwise.

Chapter Six

The roulette academy, as the group took to calling our practice sessions, lasted for five weeks from May to June, 1966, probably the first and last roulette school – for players, not croupiers – in this country. People came and went in streams. Every night of the week and all day on the weekends, I stood behind the table, spinning the wheel, throwing the ball, calling the stock phrases. As most were learning roulette from scratch they had to be taught the basic French vocabulary and the elementary rules before they could be drilled in the mathematics of the Reverse Labouchère. Occasionally we would break off for a drink to give their brains a rest from figure work, but even then I discouraged conversation on any topic but roulette.

A rather retiring man called Nathan asked at one break: 'How can you tell who is a mug in this game and who isn't? I mean, how do we know we won't be mugs as well?'

'By *mug* I mean someone who lets the casino take his money and doesn't care because he gets a kick out of playing the big shot,' I said. 'He's always well dressed, generally drinks a lot and almost invariably has a good-looking female in tow. He's very popular with the table staff – naturally, he always shows how important he is by chucking them a big tip.'

'Do we tip the croupier?' asked Mrs Richardson.

'I object to tipping in principle,' I said. 'However, from a practical point of view it's advisable to give them something or they'll start messing you about, pretending not to hear you when you want to change a high-denomination plaque for chips, that sort of thing. Give them no more than two or three pounds at the end of your session. By the way, the croupier is the one who has the stick and rakes in the chips – the one who spins the wheel is the tourneur. Then there's the Chef de Partie – he's there to supervise the table and he also acts as a sort of umpire if there are any disputes.'

'You mentioned drinking,' said a burly man called Milton. 'Do you object to us having the odd drink while we're playing?'

I smiled. 'Mr Milton, I am not running a temperance campaign. I object to nothing – provided it in no way impairs your ability to play the system. Some people can drink and remain sensible, a lot more only *think* they can. That's the danger, but basically it's up to the individual. If you're asking my advice, I'd say stick to coffee. A roulette salon is a peculiar environment, you know. It brings out strange elements in the personality. Shy people can become show-offs, cautious people can turn into maniacs. It's often hard to remember that you're actually dealing in hard cash – that's why chips were invented in the first place, to delude players into forgetting that they're betting in real money.'

'Surely casinos make money anyway, though, without having to rely on a lot of tricks and gimmicks?' somebody asked.

'No?' I said. 'The whole thing is a psychological gimmick. The first thing you'll notice is the atmosphere – it won't be like the poker school in Dodge City. It's deliberately contrived to be formal and sombre to overawe the player. They're implanting in the clientele the idea that here is the utmost respectability – what could you possible have to worry about? The truth is that casinos attract an undesirable element. The sophisticated and beautiful young lady giving you a charming smile is less likely to be a debutante than a harpy looking for a winner to fleece. Those ultrapolite croupiers, so helpful and cooperative? Yes, when you are losing. Start winning seriously and that tugging you feel at your feet is the red carpet being brutally pulled from under you. The great thing is to speak to nobody, to trust nobody. For instance, whenever possible keep your high-denomination chips and plaques out of sight in a handbag or pocket. Leave only the low-demonination chips on the table in front of you.'

'Why – would anybody seriously try to steal chips from under your nose?' asked Blake increduously.

'There are people who make a living by doing simply that,' I answered. 'Look, I'll show you.'

76

I put a pile of the plastic chips on the table and asked Blake to take the chair. I stood at his left shoulder.

'You are very busy,' I said, 'You're watching the wheel, you're doing your calculations and selecting chips and plaques for your next stake. I'm one of the thirty or forty people standing round the table behind the few who have seats. I go to place my own bet – so.' My arm stretched across him and as my wrist passed over his chips I let my shirt cuff cut the top two or three chips off his pile. They fell off the pile on to the cloth. 'Now, if I had the professional thief's razor-sharp cuffs, those chips would have disappeared up my sleeve,' I said. 'Would you have noticed? Twenty or thirty pounds of your capital has gone. It's quite common – in France they usually get seven or eight years' jail if they're caught.'

After that particular session I was seeing them off at the front door when I saw Mrs Richardson giving me a curious look.

'Well, Mrs Richardson,' I said, 'how does your husband feel about all this, you being out every night?'

'Oh, he gives me plenty of rope. He would have liked to come himself but he has his job.'

'Let me guess – army, I should say. Brigadier, perhaps?'

She frowned and laughed at the same time. 'Brigadier? That's very funny. I must tell him. Anyway, when we realized you were serious about going to France we decided I could best be spared from the domestic front – our three boys are all at boarding school and George – the Brigadier! – said I could have a little break. He's a better cook than I am in any case.'

'Three sons?' I said. 'If I may say so –'

'Oh, *don't*. Everyone does, it gets so boring to be always hearing tributes to one's fecundity,' she said in her perpetually hoarse voice. 'I say it to myself enough, I *am* too young to have three sons at boarding school. Between you and me, that's why the Brigadier gives me plenty of rope. I was a child bride!'

What could I say to that?

As she was stepping out into the porch one of the men, Peter Vincent, a languid, rather too handsome young man, came back up the drive.

'Care for a lift?' he asked Mrs Richardson.

She turned back to me, apparently giving him the cold shoulder.

'Just one point – I've always been good at maths, but some of them feel you're a bit impatient: you expect them to grasp everything at first telling.'

'I'll watch that. Good night.'

As she walked away, I heard her accept Vincent's offer of a lift: 'Only snag is that I doubt your boot is big enough to give my car a lift as well.'

Pauline could see I was impressed by Mrs Richardson, but she restrained herself from comment. Not once had she complained during these weeks when our house seemed like Waterloo Station, with streams of people taking over her lounge for non-stop roulette sessions. Her tolerance was all the more praiseworthy considering that she didn't have a great deal of faith in this grandiose scheme of mine; but not once did she nag at me to give it up. Far from it, she even volunteered to act as a permanent reserve when we began to play in the Regency. I'd been explaining to her that I was playing a trick on the team by drumming into them the absolute necessity of staking on every single spin of the wheel.

'But they'll need to go to the toilet, won't they?' she asked.

'I'll be there at all times.'

'What if two want to go at once?'

'Look, it doesn't rally matter a jot if they miss a spin or two, it's only a psychological gambit on my part – tell them every spin is vital and they stay keyed up. Creative tension. They've only got a minute or so between spins, they've got to calculate the next stake, select the chips and get the bet on. If I tell them it makes no difference to the system to miss the odd spin for a trip to the lavatory, they'll start taking little rests when they feel like it. The smallest break in concentration is enough to cause a mental blockage. I've got them believing that total continuity is a kind of magic spell: if it breaks the whole system collapses. They're going to discipline themselves, and that's the only discipline you can rely on.'

'All the more reason for having me there,' she said firmly.

I instigated phase two after three weeks of practice in my lounge.

'I want you all to have enrolled as members of the Regency

by next Wednesday,' I said. 'You can go there on your own or in twos or threes – but no more than that. The longer we disguise the group from the club's management the better. Just walk through the front door and tell the receptionist you want to join. You should be proposed for membership by an existing member, but they'll soon find somebody to sponsor you. Then you just pay your thirty shillings [$4.20] and collect your card. Once you've all been infiltrated we start playing in earnest.'

'Why all the secrecy?' demanded, as I might have guessed, the pedantic Mr Bateson.

'Don't worry, we're not breaking the law,' I told him. 'We want simply to avoid the sensation that a phalanx of thirty-seven roulette players would cause marching in as a body.'

The date set was 13 June. By 11 June all thirty-seven had their membership cards. On the evening of 12 June we had our final meeting at my home. I handed round sheets of paper with the shift allocations and which of the six even-chance bets each member of the group would be covering. Then I gave them the final briefing.

'We start work seriously tomorrow at three,' I said. 'I think I've managed to fit everybody into a shift that will suit him. The first group of twelve must be in the casino promptly at two forty-five to make sure they get seats. We will occupy two roulette tables, entering the club in small groups. We will not speak to each other except in an emergency, when I will be there to help you. As individuals you must not dress conspicuously or draw attention to yourselves in any way. You will each have your day's staking capital of ten pounds [$28]. If anything untoward happens, you will behave with the utmost formality. Remember – once we start winning the casino boys will be watching like hawks for some excuse to bar us from the club. You must not drink to excess nor allow yourself to be picked up by any of the good-time girls. The first shift will play from three until seven. You will not leave your seat until your replacement is actually standing at your shoulder; otherwise someone else could grab the chair. You will leave any loose chips or plaques in front of your place when you vacate your seat. The second shift should be in the casino by six forty-five and will take up the staking exactly where the first shift left off. The third shift will be present

79

in the casino at ten forty-five when the same procedure will be followed. At all times my wife or myself will be available to take over the chair of anyone who wishes to use the lavatory. If for any reason you can't make one of your allocated sessions you must phone me here as quickly as possible so that I can arrange a cover for you. I should hope this would happen only in a genuine emergency. You have all reached the stage where you can work the system with ease – let us now see if you can work it under real conditions. Remember the three main dangers – drink, women and conversation. Stick to the system, don't miss a single spin, ignore all distractions and you will not need luck. Are there any questions?'

'All we need is Jack Hawkins to tell us the target,' drawled the handsome Peter Vincent. The laughter was too loud for what the joke merited, a clear indication of the general tension.

Oliver Blake gave Vincent a severe glare. 'Mr Leigh,' he said stiffly, 'I think I speak for everyone here when I say how much we appreciate the hard work you've invested in this venture. I for one have no intention of letting you or the team down by treating it in a casual manner.'

This was met with murmurs of agreement. Vincent shrugged.

'Mr Vincent, that's a fine bit of cloth you're wearing,' I commented. 'What will your reaction be tomorrow if in the middle of a progression some half-drunk oaf standing behind you rams the lighted end of a cigar into your back?'

Vincent smiled about the eyes but kept a straight face.

'I'll carry on staking, of course. Have no fear, Mr Leigh, I'm learning something about the Eton code.'

The portly Blake pretended not to hear Vincent's jibe.

Chapter Seven

The fifteen graduates of the roulette academy who infiltrated the Regency that sunny June afternoon – the first shift of twelve plus three whose freedom from economic bondage enabled them to come along out of curiosity – were not a happy bunch of fun-loving friends. One or two had struck up mild liaisons, several of the men showing willingness to get on closer terms with Mrs Richardson, but basically they were strangers who had nothing in common but a strong desire to make money. Not that I held greed against anybody – I was *praying* I might at last have found people who were truly hungry for cash rather than less profitable pleasures. Yet I found myself thinking nostalgically of earlier episodes in France with aristocratic drunks and irrepressible eccentrics. This current bunch seemed stuffy and dull by comparison. Still, I had chosen them for these very qualities, and success meant more to me than personal amusement.

That first day nothing happened. Nothing. Nobody succeeded in reaching the table's limit or breaking the bank. Rogers had the first whiff of a progression on black but when his stakes had reached £30 or £40 (about $85 to $110), red began to predominate and soon he had crossed out all the figures on his line, meaning of course that he had lost his original investment of 10 shillings.

The combined losses for the day came to £110, each of the thirty-six who actually played having staked only a percentage of the £10 I had told them to bring for each session.

It was about ten minutes to four on the afternoon of our second day that we had our first smell of action. It happened to Sydney Hopplewell, a company director of around sixty, a white-haired man who during the weeks of training had always been reserved to the point of rudeness.

'What the hell does he think he's doing?' I muttered to Pauline as I saw Hopplewell getting up from his chair, his place being taken by a middle-aged woman. Moving quickly between the tables, I came up beside Hopplewell to issue my first rebuke. His last bet on *impair*, odd, had just won. I waited while he picked up his chips and wrote in his notebook. To my surprise I saw that he had started a progression. *Impair* was coming up in a predominance of 5 to 2. His stakes rose quickly.

Saying nothing that might divert his attention, I stood at his elbow, ready to give assistance. He was a portly figure with a complexion not so much highly coloured as congested. Jostled on all sides, having to hold his notepad in his hand, trying to keep track of the chips and plaques being shoved at him by the croupier, he started to sweat profusely. His stakes reached £14 and then £16. I held my breath; was this it, our first winning progression?

He cracked up without warning. Before I could stop him he drew a shaky pencil line through his row of three-digit figures, turned to a new page and wrote 1, 2, 3, 4.

His first stake of 5 shillings lost. So did the next. The favourable run of *impair* had petered out.

Nothing else happened that second day. After the casino closed in the early hours a dozen or so of the group came back to Twickenham for a chat. Hopplewell was so embarrassed he could not speak, though nobody but myself had noticed that he had had the start of a progression. I could have kept quiet, but the purpose of playing the Regency was to drill these people into a reliable team, not mollycoddle the sensitive. After I had offered everyone a drink I turned to him and said, 'Well, Mr Hopplewell?'

With a face like his it was impossible to detect a blush. Gruffly he said, in a louder voice than usual: 'I'm terribly sorry. I had a progression under way this afternoon and I fluffed it.'

'What do you mean *fluffed it*?' Rogers demanded aggressively.

'I was staking in hundreds of units and then I lost concentration – I just couldn't think. I went back to five shillings.'

'Jesus Christ!' snapped Rogers, expecting me to launch a tirade.

'It wasn't quite as simple as that, Mr Hopplewell,' I said,

82

neither aggressively nor sympathetically. 'Why did you stand up?'

'There was a lady standing behind me, an American. I heard her saying she felt a bit giddy, so I gave her my seat,' he explained.

'Of all the stupid bloody – '

'You were too much of a gentleman, Mr Hopplewell,' I said. 'I'm afraid good manners don't win money in a casino. I would hate to be responsible for advocating a further deterioration in public behaviour, but your sense of etiquette might very well have cost us two or three thousand pounds.'

'You were bloody told about getting hold of the seats and sticking to them,' Rogers ranted.

Then Blake stepped in. 'None of us is so perfect that we can criticize at this stage,' he said authoritatively.

'I just didn't think,' said Hopplewell. 'I am very sorry.'

'Don't feel too bad about it,' I said, prepared to be sympathetic now that I saw the lesson had gone home. Hopplewell did not seem the type to apologize easily. 'It was the first progression any of you has had to deal with, and it's precisely to obviate such mistakes that we're playing in real conditions before we go to France. That woman probably tricked you deliberately, Mr Hopplewell. She could not have been standing for very long, and it wasn't particularly hot in the salon that early in the afternoon.'

'Dear oh dear, you just can't trust nobody these days,' joked Robinson, the ginger-haired young clerk, a joke that was to have greater point at a later stage.

This incident helped the whole team – and certainly had a deep effect on Hopplewell. At his first interview he had told me bluntly he despised all forms of gambling as catering to adolescent minds. My explanation of the scheme had decided him that for the small amount of capital involved it might be worth a short dabble – purely as a business speculation, he said. He was one of the group most likely to drop out at any excuse I would have said but the tantalizing nearness of £2,000 ($5,600) on only our second day proved to be exactly the right psychological carrot. Mr Hopplewell had made his last mistake.

Pandemonium broke loose in the Regency at precisely 7.12 the following evening, our third day in the casino. I remember the time so precisely because the second shift had just taken over the seats and I had just come back upstairs from seeing Pauline off home in a taxi. I had a stroll round the two tables where our second shift of twelve was settling down for four hours' solid roulette. Seeing that Mrs Richardson's stakes were moving up slightly, I stood behind her. The casino was not particularly busy, the afternoon crowd having drifted off and the late-nighters not yet emerging from restaurants and theatres. There were possibly a dozen people standing round that table.

From her notepad I could see that Mrs Richardson had already played four spins. She was betting in units of 1 shilling (14 cents), on *pair*, the even numbers.

This is what happened, spin by spin, stake by stake. As always she had taken a clean page and written that familiar line, 1, 2, 3, 4.

Spin 1. She had staked 5 units (5 shillings – one 5-shilling chip). *Pair* came up, so she won 5 shillings and got her stake back. She added the amount of the win to her line, which then read 1, 2, 3, 4, 5. Her next stake was, therefore, $1 + 5 = 6$.

Spin 2. *Pair* came up again. Having won 6 units, she added that figure to the line, which now read 1, 2, 3, 4, 5, 6. Her next stake was, therefore, 7 units.

Spin 3. She lost. She scored off the figures at either end of the line, which now read 1̶, 2, 3, 4, 5, 6̶. She still had to add the figures at either end, so her next stake was $2 + 5 = 7$.

Spin 4. She lost again, making her line read 1̶, 2̶, 3, 4, 5̶, 6̶. There were only two figures left, so her next stake was $3 + 4 = 7$. If she had lost again, her whole line would have been deleted and she would have restarted with a 5-unit stake. However ...

Spin 5. *Pair* came up. Having won, she added the amount of the last stake to the line, which on her pad now looked like 1̶, 2̶, 3, 4, 5̶, 6̶, 7. As the end figures were now 3 and 7 her next stake was 10 units.

Spin 6. *Pair* came up again. She added 10 to the line, which became 1, 2, 3, 4, 5, 6, 7, 10. Her next stake was, therefore, $3 + 10 = 13$.

Spin 7. She lost. Scoring out the end numbers the line was now 1̶, 2̶, 3, 4, 5̶, 6̶, 7, 1̶0̶. This reduced her next stake to 11 units and also put her back in the position where another loss would
84

have ended the sequence, taking her back to a fresh start with 1, 2, 3, 4.

In this way her stake gradually increased from 5 units to 11 units, the brakes going on when she started losing. Scoring out the figures at either end of the line when losing ensures that in the event of a prolonged losing sequence, the line would have quickly been deleted altogether, preventing the player from losing a succession of large stakes while chasing previous losses. That is the whole point of reverting to 1, 2, 3, 4. It is not a numerical abracadabra but merely a dead-man's-handle to ensure that, in Mrs Richardson's case, even if she had gone on losing all day, she would never have been down more than 10 units (10 shillings – $1.40) on any sequence.

At this level of staking, Mrs Richardson's activities interested nobody else at the table. Waiters came and went with drinks and coffee. Other players were placing much larger bets on single numbers or combinations, some winning, more losing. The low murmur of voices, the clicking of plastic chips on the croupier's stick and the delicate rattling of the ball provided a constant background of noise that was almost reassuringly monotonous.

Spin 14. The stake was now 39 units, and she lost. Her line read 11, 18, 25, making her next stake $11 + 25 = 36$.

Spin 15. *Pair* came up. She had won 36 units and the line became 11, 18, 25, 36. Next stake – 47 units.

Spin 16. She lost. After the end numbers had been scored out the line became 18, 25. Next stake – 43 units.

Spin 17. She won. The line became 18, 25, 43. (Wins rapidly increase the stake once the smaller opening figures have been deleted.) Mrs Richardson's next stake was 61 units.

Spin 18. She won. The line was now 18, 25, 43, 61. Her next stake: 79 units.

Spin 19. She won again. The line became 18, 25, 43, 61, 79. Her next stake was 97 units.

Spin 20. *Pair* came up again. Mrs Richardson was well into the progression by now. Her line was 18, 25, 43, 61, 79, 97. Her next stake was $18 + 97 = 115$ units. (£5 15s – $16). By this stage the croupiers were beginning to show interest as they saw a staking pattern emerging, but her bets were not yet dramatic enough to alert the other people at the table.

Spin 30. She had been playing for roughly an hour. Her stake was 413 units. Having started with a 5-shilling stake, everything she was now betting had been won *from the bank*. This time she lost. The line was reduced to two figures, 146, 235. These had both been winning bets originally; added together they showed her current winnings less the 10 units represented by the starting line 1, 2, 3, 4.

Her next stake was 381. If she had lost, her winnings would have been wiped out and she would have lost her capital of 10 units for the sequence.

Spin 31. Pair came up. The line became 146, 235, 381. Her next stake was 527 units.

The difference in the atmosphere was marked now. Waiters could hardly take orders for drinks or coffee for trying to watch the woman who was piling up the chips and plaques. Youngish, attractive women are not generally expected to play roulette with professional skill. Mrs Richardson had had her blonde hair re-styled with those honey-coloured streaks. In deference to my instruction that the team should dress inconspicuously, she was wearing a black cocktail dress, but the simplicity of its lines only underlined her attractiveness.

Blake had turned up by then, although he was not due to play until the third shift took over at eleven. 'You've come just in time to see some action,' I said, nodding in the direction of Mrs Richardson. Blake surveyed the table for a few minutes, looking every inch a City gent who had wandered into something sleazy by mistake.

'She's certainly attracting a great deal of attention,' he said. 'You warned us against that.'

'There's no way you can hide a long winning streak, not when the player is relentlessly upping the stakes.'

'Certainly not when the player looks like Mrs Richardson.'

Spin 32. Pair came up, giving her a win of £26 7s ($73). Her line became 146, 235, 381, 527. Her next stake was 673 units.

Spin 33. She lost and had to score out the end numbers, which gave her a line of 235, 381. Adding these, she next staked 616 units.

Spin 34. Pair came up. The line became 235, 381, 616. She selected plaques and chips for 851 units from the piles in front of her. One or two players were trying to latch onto her luck by now, and as soon as she placed her handful of plaques and chips on the rectangle marked *pair* other hands shot out to place stakes beside hers. Of course, they thought it was luck – if they had been following her betting from the start they would have known that she never bet on anything but *pair*.

Spin 35. Pair came up! The croupier pushed plaques and chips worth £42 11s ($119) across the green baize. Mrs Richardson had time only to push them among the stuff piled loosely in front of her. She wrote the winning stake at the end of the line, which now read 235, 381, 616, 851. Her next stake was 1,086 units.

Spin 36. She won again. Other players tried to get a glimpse of her notepad, but all they could see was a neat mass of figures, many of them crossed out. Her line was now 235, 381, 616, 851, 1,086. Her next stake was 1,321 units –

Spin 37. Pair! She won 1,321 units and put that figure at the end of her line, which was now 235, 381, 616, 851, 1,086, 1,321. Smiling, she picked out plaques and chips for 1,556 units.

Spin 38. Pair again. Her line was now 235, 381, 616, 851, 1,086, 1,321, 1,556. Her next stake was 235 + 1,556 = 1,791 units.

Spin 39. She won again! Her line was now 235, 381, 616, 851, 1,086, 1,321, 1,556, 1,791. Her next stake: 235 + 1,791 = 2,026. She was over the £100 mark and currently winning 7,837 shillings ($1,100).

Spin 40. Another win. Her line became 235, 381, 616, 851, 1,086, 1,321, 1,556, 1,791, 2,026. Other players stared at her in disbelief. A roulette table is a place where small amounts of money change hands quickly in the normal way of things, the whole thing being so geared that no one bet can win more than approximately £200 ($560). This staking pattern, however, was giving her a whole run of bets at less than the table maximum – and her accumulated winnings were beginning to look extremely impressive. Her next stake was 235 + 2,026 = 2,261.

Spin 41. She won again! The atmosphere round the table was electric. Everybody present was watching every move she made. She selected chips to make up a stake of 2,496 units. She was so quick with her calculations she had time to look up and give Blake and myself a grimace of amusement. '*Rien ne va plus*,' called the tourneur. The clicking of the ball as it circled the rim of the wheel was the only sound I could hear.

Spin 42. She won again. Her line was now 235, 381, 616, 851, 1,086, 1,321, 1,556, 1,791, 2,026, 2,261, 2,496. Her next stake was 235 + 2,496 = 2,731.

Spin 43. Pair! 'By jove, she's done it again. She can't lose!' exclaimed Blake. It was the first time I had seen him so excited, but I said nothing. A fat man in a blue corduroy suit seemed on the point of asking Mrs Richardson what system she was using. Her line was now 235, 381, 616, 851, 1,086, 1,321, 1,556, 1,791, 2,026, 2,261, 2,496, 2,731. Her next stake was 235 + 2,731 = 2,966.

Spin 44. She lost. Other players watched her face but saw no sign of disappointment. Why should she have been upset? She had started with a stake of 5 shillings, after all, so the bank had merely won some of its money back. She crossed out the end figures on her line and put down her next stake: 381 + 2,496 = 2,877. The strain on her now was enormous and the slightest interference might have blown her up. The fat man chewed his cheek. I started to move in close to shield her. He said something before I could intervene. She ignored him completely! The fat man frowned but didn't persist. I took a deep breath.

'Good God, I had no idea it would be this nerve-wracking!' said Blake.

Spin 45. She won. Her line was now 381, 616, 851, 1,086, 1,321, 1,556, 1,791, 2,026, 2,261, 2,496, 2,877. Her next stake was therefore 381 + 2,877 = 3,258.

Spin 46. She won again and added her last stake to the end of the line. Her next stake would be 381 + 3,258 = 3,639. We were getting near the crucial test now. The maximum possible bet was £200 or 4,000 units ($560). How well would she remember all that I had taught her?

Spin 47. Pair. She had won – but did she know it was for the last time? I had already added the end figures of her line, and her stake would have been 4,020 units, above the staking limit. If she had tried to stake above the limit, the croupier would have politely refused the bet, his eye so well trained he could tell at a glance the value of a pile of plaques and chips. No great harm would have been done – unless she had decided to go on with stakes just below the maximum. That's what a gambler would do in the middle of a favourable progression like that. The whole success of the system depends on an upward *progression* of stakes when you are winning. To bet on at the ceiling without being able to increase the stakes gives the mathematical advantage straight back to the bank.

Blake was going to say something, but I pushed at his arm to keep him quiet. The tourneur made his call: '*Faites vos jeux.*'

Mrs Richardson glanced again at her pad and frowned. She looked up and caught my eye. I nodded. She smiled, scored out her whole line and ripped that page off her pad. On a new sheet she wrote 1, 2, 3, 4, the gold wedding ring on her left hand shining dully under the lights. With delicate, precise movements, she picked out a 5-shilling chip and almost disdainfully placed it on the space marked *pair*.

'Perfect,' I exclaimed to Blake.

'How much has she won?' he asked incredulously.

'That's easy to tell,' I said. I leaned over and picked up the last sheet she had torn off her notepad, at the same time murmuring to her, 'Not bad for a first attempt.'

I showed Blake her page. 'You see these figures she scored off at the end, the ones with the vertical line through them? Those are the ones she had left when she reached the limit. All you have to do is add them and that's what she's won.'

We needed a pen to work it out. The line was 381, 616, 851, 1,086, 1,321, 1,556, 1,791, 2,026, 2,261, 2,496, 2,877, 3,258, 3,639. It adds up to 24,159 units. The units are, of course, shillings. She had won £1,207 19s (about $3,400).

'Incredible,' said Blake. Mrs Richardson lit a cigarette and blew smoke up towards the lights. She smiled serenely at the croupiers. The ball was already running round the rim of the wheel. Our first winning progression, and she had handled it beautifully!

Later she told us: 'It all seemed to happen so quickly. After only a few spins I knew I was winning. I said to myself, "This is it!" The instant rush of activity literally drove everything else out of my head. I think *pair* (even numbers) was coming up about three times more often than *impair* (odd numbers). Within about twenty spins I was betting what seemed like an awful lot of chips, but I'd forgotten by then it was real money, totally forgotten! My stakes kept getting bigger and bigger – I couldn't keep track of what the man was shoving at me across the table. I remembered you telling us to put the large-denomination plaques out of sight in my handbag but I didn't have time. It just seemed to be running away with me. Then I realized I was getting near the limit. I kept thinking – you have to score out all these figures and start with one, two, three, four again. I was sure I was going to make a mistake and I couldn't remember what would happen if you tried to be above the limit. It was a fantastic experience.'

'I'm sorry I couldn't stop that man from speaking to you,' I said.

'What man? I didn't hear anybody speaking to me.'

It was then about half-past eight. Puzzled by her decision not to make the most of this phenomenally lucky streak, the other players gradually lost interest in Mrs Richardson. The atmosphere began to return to normal.

I was thinking of going to the bar for a whisky with Blake when Mrs Heppenstall, the apologetic little widow from Hastings, began to get a few wins on whatever chance she had been allocated, black if my memory is correct. It had seemed brave of her even to enter such an unlikely place as a gambling club (the nearest she had been to organized gaming before were church whist drives), but to see her small grey head bent over her notepad and her small, white hand shoving on the chips was unbelievably incongruous.

'I'd better stay and watch her,' I said to Blake. 'I'm sure she doesn't really grasp what this is all about.'

As Mrs Richardson had just proved – and remember, that had been my first experience of a Reverse Labouchère progression under real conditions as well – a prolonged winning streak puts the player under a very harsh spotlight. The sheer weight of attention can be quite terrifying. As I was standing at Mrs Heppenstall's shoulder Vincent appeared beside me. Looking at my watch, I saw that it was just after nine. He was not due to take over with the third shift until eleven. When he saw that she was staking something like £60 ($170), he turned to me and said quietly, 'Inspiring, isn't it, an old dear like her playing with the big boys?'

'I've seen so-called big boys crack up under less strain than she's going through,' I replied.

Vincent, who carried himself in such a lounging manner one was always surprised to realize just how big he was close up, gave me a little nod, the half-smile about his eyes seeming to indicate that he could see through me. 'You get your kicks this way, do you, corrupting innocent old ladies?'

'I'm under the impression I am running a serious gaming coup,' I said. 'How do you get your kicks?' He shook his head imperceptibly, his mocking eyes telling me I would have to do better than that to needle him.

Mrs Heppenstall's progression was a long one. It had started with a lot of winning bets, which meant that her line of figures remained on the small side, producing stakes that edged up much more slowly than Mrs Richardson's. It wasn't until about ten minutes to eleven that she reached four-digit figures. When Vincent came back from the bar, I told him to let her see the progression out. He shrugged, apparently finding the whole thing rather childish. The third shift took over at eleven, the switching of seats taking place without incident, happening with such quick precision none of the other players standing round the table had a chance to grab any of the chairs.

At fifteen minutes past eleven Mrs Heppenstall drew a neat line through her long list of uncrossed figures, wrote 1, 2, 3, 4 on a clean page and prepared to place a stake of 5 shillings.

'It's after eleven,' I whispered in her ear. 'Mr Vincent will take over now. Leave all that loose stuff on the table.'

I went with her to the cash desk to pay in the large-denomination plaques she had put in her handbag. Mrs Richardson was waiting for us. When the cashier had counted out the last 10-pound note I turned to them both with a smile.

'You won a great deal of money there, Mrs Heppenstall,' I said. 'Over two thousand pounds with what you left on the table. You won one thousand two hundred and seven pounds, Mrs Richardson. I think that calls for a drink, don't you?'

'Oh, no, I must hurry or I'll miss my train,' said Mrs Heppenstall. I went down with her to the front entrance. 'Will I get a bus to Victoria Station at this time of night?' she asked.

'Treat yourself to a taxi, Mrs Heppenstall. After all – two thousand pounds!'

'Perhaps I will, just this once.' We went out onto the pavement. As I watched for a cab she said, sounding worried, 'It's an awful lot of money, isn't it? Are you sure it's all right?'

Thinking she meant the cab fare, I said I would give her £10. 'We'll have a proper share-out when I've had time to work out the amounts. The taxi won't be more than a pound.'

'Actually I meant' – she looked nervously back into the club's brilliantly lit foyer–'I only started with ten pounds. Are you sure it's all right – taking all that much from them?'

'All right?' I looked at her small, country-fresh face to see if this were a joke. It was not. 'Of course it's all right – that's what it's all *for*. Didn't you realize we could win that much?'

'Well, not really – I'm terribly afraid what we're doing is illegal. Are you sure we – '

'My dear lady, don't worry. I wouldn't drag you into anything even remotely shady. That's what gambling means – you bet your money against theirs. If you win you take it all away with you. If you'd lost, they wouldn't be shedding any tears over you, believe me.'

I watched her go off in a taxi and went back upstairs, where Mrs Richardson was having a martini at the bar.

'Incredible – she didn't realize we kept the money! I think she was under the impression this is merely a ritual that goes on in here and that people do it just for the amusement!'

'That's probably why she sailed through her progression so calmly – just imagine what a state she would have been in if she'd thought she was staking hundreds of pounds for real!'

'That's the whole point of playing here, to get everybody acclimatized.'

'I'll tell you one thing,' she said, lighting a cigarette. 'The greasy boys are watching us like hawks now.'

'The greasy boys?'

'The croupiers and the rest of them.'

'Very apt. You certainly haven't taken long to acclimatize yourself to the cynical world of casinos.'

'Talking about cynics, that man Rogers hasn't turned up, has he?'

'I haven't seen him. Just as well we have one spare member. I wondered if he phoned my house.'

'I don't think you'll be seeing him again. I was naïve enough to lend him his staking money yesterday – he said he didn't have time to get to the bank. I suppose he decided to forget the whole idea after two days of winning nothing.'

'Yes, that was a bit silly of you. Still, better to make that kind of mistake now. Care for another drink?'

'Thank you but no. I must get home and tend to the Brigadier's needs.'

'Well, you did extremely well, Mrs Richardson. You handled our very first progression beautifully.'

'I've always been very good at figures. By the way, you could call me Emma – unless you follow your fat friend in such matters.'

'Blake? Don't you like him?'

'Since you ask – no.'

'Would you say he's honest?'

'Probably.'

'I notice that quite a lot of the group take note of what he says.'

'All the little snobs looking up to that Eton bullshit.'

'Perhaps. I think I might make him our treasurer. That would remove any final doubt that I'm running some complicated form of fraud.'

Grinding out the fifth or sixth cigarette she had smoked in those few minutes at the bar, she patted at her honey-streaked hair and said, 'That should suit him. His type is well used to handling money that somebody else made.'

She left to go home to Pimlico. I went back to the roulette salon. The fact that we had now won over £3,000 ($8,400) had left me feeling not so much elated as relieved. On a venture like this three consecutive days of non-stop losing, however small the sums, might have been enough to start the group breaking up.

Unbelievably I found myself watching our third progression of the day. It happened to Terry Baker, the sales representative whose three identically worded character references had made me suspect he was using a false name for some reason. Not that

93

he was necessarily a crook – quite a number of the people I had interviewed had said they couldn't afford to be associated with casinos and gambling because their families or their employers would not consider it respectable.

Midnight. The casino was full of the late-night crowd, visiting Americans, bands of Japanese corporation executives in identical suits, would-be sophisticates from the Swinging London scene, the inevitable Arabs and the equally inevitable sharks of both sexes. In the middle of all this superficial sophistication Terry Baker looked conspicuously average: blue blazer and flannels, hair shorter than was modish and in need of a wash, a shirt and tie suggesting better days. However, his general scruffiness was reassuring. No conman would have been happy with such an indifferent front.

I watched him carefully throughout his progression and found no fault with his paperwork or his behaviour. He never faltered in his calculations, always had time in hand to select his plaques and chips for his next stake and showed no sign of yielding to a temptation particularly common among younger men, that of showing off. It is a dramatic experience of what one might call 'theatre' to find yourself the object of all attention at a roulette table. Some find it embarrassing, even terrifying, but just as many begin to show off in the limelight. Terry Baker sailed through the whole progression on red with neither blush nor bravado. Just after midnight he reached the table limit, calmly reverted to 1, 2, 3, 4, put on a 5-shilling stake and started to put his winnings in neat denominational piles.

As soon as I had seen the progression come to a successful conclusion I went to the club's washroom, a long and narrow room with basins spaced along one wall. As I was washing my hands and reflecting that things had gone remarkably smoothly, one of the casino bigwigs came into the room followed by four or five men whose dinner jackets served to accentuate their heavy physiques. I was at the basin farthest from the door. The looks on their faces told me not to expect a pat on the back for a jolly day's sport.

They stopped a few feet short of my basin, more or less penning me at the end of the washroom.

'Right, you little ponce – who d'you think you are?' said the

94

stocky man whom I knew to be one of the club's senior officials and directors. Although we had been at pains not to look like an organized group it would not have taken any competent table-man long to realize that I was a link between the three people who had won so heavily that day, seeing me hovering at their sides, checking their notepads and occasionally murmuring advice.

Drying my hands and maintaining an outward calm, I decided there was no point in prevarication.

'I'm merely a club member with some friends who think they have a system to beat you. Have we broken any of the club rules?'

Whatever sangfroid I had acquired over the years seemed to be evaporating quickly before all those intensely unattractive faces.

'Don't give me any bloody fanny,' snarled the director. I could see there was going to be no elegant way out of this situation. I was just trying to convince myself that things like this didn't happen in England, even in gaming clubs, when the door opened and a man came in, one of the regular patrons as far as I could tell.

'Just the bloke I want to see,' he said to the casino director.

I shall never forget that man. He had on his head a dark brown wig, every artificial hair of it as conspicuous as a cloth cap on a blackbird. While the mob was looking at him I pushed past quickly and slammed the door behind me, safe again in the more crowded part of the casino.

Once the danger was over I had time to think and I realized that I had, in fact, had a very lucky escape. We had won over £5,000 ($14,000), in one day; most important from the casino's point of view we had won it systematically, which meant that we were potentially a major threat to its profits.

Realizing I had badly miscalculated the degree of tolerance the Regency's management would show to a winning group, I went back to the salon. A bit shaken, I had a quick whisky at the bar and only then returned to the tables. The first thing I noticed was that the team member who should have been handling black on the second table was missing.

'Where's Mr Lee Kuan?' I asked Fredericks, a civil-servant member of the group, who was sitting next to what had been Kuan's seat, now occupied by an ageing Greek.

'Two of the staff asked if he would go to the club offices,' said Fredericks, a rather dull man in his forties.

'Didn't you say anything?' I demanded. 'I told everybody not to – oh, forget it.'

I went immediately to the reception desk and asked for someone in authority. The sleek young Frenchman at the desk, one of Mrs Richardson's aptly named 'greasy boys', said officiously, 'What is the problem, monsieur?'

'I wish to know where my friend Mr Kuan is,' I said. 'Two of your officials asked him to leave the salon.'

He smirked and spread his hands expansively. 'I know nothing of this, monsieur.'

'In that case, I propose to search this establishment. If anyone tries to prevent me I shall call the police and inform them I have reason to believe Mr Kuan has been kidnapped.'

My brush with the management in the washroom had quickly made me aware of the fact that the Regency was not run by gentlemen. Hence my anxiety on Kuan's behalf. These people had obviously decided to pick on our weakest link.

I went up the stairs to the offices on the next floor. The first three rooms were empty. As I came to the door of the fourth I could hear voices. I did not hesitate.

Bursting into the room, I saw Kuan sitting in an armchair surrounded by the same men who had tried to corner me in the washroom. He was obviously being interrogated.

'What's the meaning of this?' I demanded.

'None of your business,' said the director, a stocky and impressive man.

'This man is a friend of mine. You're taking advantage of his bad English. Why don't you grill me instead?'

'Don't you come barging in here throwing your bloody weight about,' shouted one of the toughs.

'Release this man or you'll have thirty witnesses giving evidence against you on a kidnapping charge,' was my counter. I nodded at Kuan to get up. One of the heavies made a move towards us, but the casino director waved him away.

They made no move to stop us as we left the office and went downstairs. It was late, and in view of what had happened I

96

spread word round the two tables that we were ceasing operations for the day.

'Tell everybody I'm holding a meeting at my house – now,' I said to Blake.

By half-past one that morning sixteen or seventeen of the group were sitting in my lounge. I asked Kuan to tell us what had happened to him. He said an official had asked him up to the office over some question about his membership. Then they had started asking him about the group – how many members did it have, who was behind it, what system were we using? When he had tried to leave they had pushed him back into the chair. That was when I appeared.

'I had a slight brush with them as well, in the toilets,' I said. 'It seems we've given them a bit of a shock, but I shouldn't imagine they'll try anything more serious.'

Bateson, after a demonstration of sucking air through clenched teeth, complained petulantly: 'We didn't bargain for intimidation. If I'd thought for a moment this would lead to trouble I wouldn't have considered the idea. My firm would react strongly if I got involved in anything disreputable –'

'Any scheme worth its salt must have some disadvantages,' I said. 'The greater the prize the bigger the obstacles. After all' – I started bringing money out of my pockets, placing wads of tens and twenties on the table – 'we haven't done too badly, have we? Mrs Richardson won one thousand two hundred and seven pounds. Mrs Heppenstall won two thousand and seventy-three pounds' – I put down another sheaf of notes – 'and then Mr Baker won two thousand and twenty. I make that five thousand three hundred. . . .' I stood back and let them gaze at the spread of notes on the table. Five thousand pounds ($14,000) in cash is not an everyday sight for many people. 'Of course, divided among thirty-eight of us it isn't all that much,' I went on. 'But you won't have to pay tax on it.'

They all stared at the money. Bateson had stopped his disapproving air-intake.

'Well,' said Blake, looking round at the others, 'I wouldn't like to think we could be frightened off *that* easily.'

Heads nodded, though I noticed that Mr Kuan's was not among them.

'What do you think we should do, Mr Leigh?' asked Carter, the cement-yard manager.

'Carry on as we have started. We have the law on our side, not to mention moral right, so to hell with them!'

'Of course we'll go on,' said Terry Baker, apparently speaking for everyone, including Bateson.

Then Blake got to his feet. It seemed he had never heard of an *informal* meeting.

'I regret to say that Mr Sherlock broke one of your firmest rules today, Mr Leigh. He spent most of his shift in the company of a young woman who picked him up at the table and sat beside him. They consumed a considerable amount of brandy, and there was a good deal of laughing and talking. It looked very bad.'

He sat down. I had, in fact, noticed Sherlock chatting to the woman but had assumed she was another player, the kind who wants to make jokes and is very difficult to ignore.

'*Did* she pick you up, Mr Sherlock?' I asked. He was a clerk in his late twenties, unmarried, with mousy brown hair and a touch of acne.

'She did, I suppose,' he said shamefacedly. 'She just appeared at the next seat and started chatting. I got a bit carried away, I must admit.'

Quite a few of us looked at him curiously, wondering what on earth any good-looking casino tart could have seen in him – he had not been winning, and his general manner, quite apart from his spots, was hardly that of a boudoir champion.

'You must realize the dangers in situations like that, Mr Sherlock,' I said. 'You didn't know the woman. She could have been an informer planted by the management to find out what system we're using, or at best, a common tart out for your money, I cannot stress too highly the importance of not getting involved with other people while you are playing. This is work, not a spree. If we allow silly impulses to sidetrack us, we'll ruin the chances of profits altogether, not merely for ourselves but for the whole team.'

Sherlock mumbled abjectly: 'I can assure everyone it won't happen again.'

I thought it was unlikely, too, for several reasons, so I let the matter rest.

Terry Baker put up his hand, the prevailing atmosphere possibly reminding him of school.

'I never really thought we'd win as much as that,' he said. 'Only – if we're stopping our progressions at the two-hundred limit, we're throwing money away, aren't we? I mean, I was having a real lucky streak, I could have gone on winning all night.'

'Betting at the flat two hundred?' I said. 'Surely you know that isn't how the system works. You won two thousand. If you'd gone on betting at two hundred a time without being able to progress upward you'd merely have been in the position of a man with two thousand pounds' capital coming to the table and risking large amounts on even-chance bets, a sure way to lose the lot.'

'Aren't there any casinos without a limit?' he asked, unabashed.

'Yes, the Salle Privée, Monte Carlo. The minimum stake there is in the region of one pound. The Regency minimum is two shillings, although we are betting in shilling units. A losing sequence at the Salle Privée would mean an initial capital outlay of twenty times our present risk. It's an interesting thought, Mr Baker, but I think we should forget it – at least until the group has accumulated a working capital of around a hundred thousand pounds.'

'Oh.' Baker sat back, looking sheepish.

'I've something else to say to you all,' I continued. 'I would like Mr Blake to act as treasurer for the group. I have enough to do making sure the shifts are organized and watching you all at the table. There's the cashing up to do and then the division of our winnings. Would you do it, Mr Blake – if everyone is agreeable?'

I dare say that if I had asked anyone other than Blake, Bateson would have exploded. He was, after all, an accountant of some kind. His snobbery, however, made it possible for him to accept the superiority of an old Etonian.

'I should be happy to serve the group as treasurer,' said Blake.

By the time I went with him to the front door and watched his bulky silhouette going down the drive to his car, dawn was

99

breaking, and I had made him my 'Number Two' – my second-in-command. For his trouble, he would receive 10 per cent of our profits. He was one of the very few men whom I would have trusted at such short acquaintance to walk off into the night with five thousand pounds. My trust, however, owed less to any snobbery about his Eton tie than to the severely practical consideration that he had too much to lose to risk public scandal over £5,000. Family honour, and all that, in his case, wasn't a joke.

Chapter Eight

By 2 o'clock the next day – or rather, that afternoon – eleven of the first shift and myself were in the coffee-house near the Regency. The missing player was Peter Vincent – as Blake had labelled him, our playboy friend. I presumed he had lost interest, until, a few minutes later, he walked into the coffee shop with the exaggerated control of a man who knows he has had too much. He was trying hard to hide it. Only a stiffness of the tongue and the delayed reactions of his eyes indicated that he was loaded to the gills. As he sat down beside Mr Milton, the pub-keeper from Essex, he waved at one of the waitresses.

Blake gave me a nudge. Vincent asked the girl for a black coffee and beamed at us all.

'Nice weather, isn't it?' he said. 'Makes you feel more like a gambol than a gamble. Eh?' He gave Milton a dig in the ribs. 'Don't laugh then.'

'Are you fit?' I asked him.

'Yes,' he answered, his eyes holding mine just long enough to let me know he was in control.

'Woe betide you if you aren't,' I said. Some of the others looked curious, but no more was said. Vincent stirred four lumps into his black coffee and drank it like medicine, with a shudder.

As we came out onto the pavement Blake murmured angrily, 'The bloody man is plastered!'

'All we are interested in is whether he can play roulette or not,' I said. 'Let's see how he behaves at the table.'

Hostilities were declared within ten minutes of the first spin.

I was standing behind Blake when he signalled to one of the waiters and asked for a black coffee. The man turned his head away. Blake tried again, but there was no mistaking the cold shoulder. I caught up with the man.

'Will you kindly bring a cup of black coffee for that gentleman?'

He muttered something in French or Italian and walked off. Trivial as this may appear to the non-roulette player, it was more than just a pinprick. To the serious player, sitting at the table for hours at a stretch, the atmosphere heavy with smoke, a dry throat is serious enough a discomfort to upset his concentration. You'll hear people say that casinos offer wonderful food and drink at extremely low prices because their gambling profits enable them to be generous. In Las Vegas they do it with star-studded entertainment at nominal cost. It may be generosity – you will certainly pay well for it.

The waiter took twenty minutes to return with a jug of coffee on a tray.

As he edged close to Blake's shoulder he allowed the tray to tilt.

Hot black coffee poured down into the lap of Mrs Richardson's black dress. I froze. A scene was inevitable.

Incredibly, Mrs Richardson simply rubbed at her skirt with a handkerchief and went on with her calculations. I took the fellow to one side. He seemed cowed, her stoicism being the last reaction he could have expected.

'Now you will have to bring more coffee for that gentleman,' I said firmly. This time it took forty minutes. However, he poured it without spilling a drop. (Later Blake said, 'Of course he was cowed. English phlegm – it generally rattles the lesser breeds.' I am *almost* sure he was joking.)

Around 4.30 p.m. Vincent had the start of a progression on *manque*, or low (the even-chance bet that the ball will fall in any number between one and eighteen). After twenty minutes it petered out, four successive losses wiping out his line of figures. He had only reached a stake of £2 or £3, but even if he had been up to £180 and the wheel had turned against him to the extent that all his figures had to be deleted, he would have lost all his winnings and his original capital, for that sequence, of 10 shillings. To win anything under the Reverse Labouchère you have to reach the limit of your progression or break the table. Every time you cross out your line you know you have lost ten units. (Think of the 1, 2, 3, 4 line. Your first bet is $1 + 4 = 5$. Your second bet, if that one loses, is $2 + 3 = 5$. If your second loses, you cross out your line. At any given moment the uncrossed figures in your line add up to what you are winning, and no matter how long the line or how high the individual figures if you lose often enough to delete all the figures, you lose all accumulated winnings – plus your original 10 units.)

Half an hour later Vincent ran into another progression. Drunk as he had been at 2.30 p.m. he now seemed fully in control of himself. From the first stake of 5 shillings his stakes steadily increased to £80 and then £100 and then £150 ($420). As always happens in a casino the winning run quickly drew a crowd. This was why I had instructed the team to remain as inconspicuous as possible in dress and behaviour, for any degree of notoriety in a casino attracts so much attention one is surrounded by gaggles of curious spectators, many anxious to speak to you. People who are well mannered in normal life think nothing of butting in to ask questions about your system. You also become a magnet for every shark and parasite in the salon.

As we watched Vincent scribbling away at his figures I heard one elderly woman say she had come from Crockfords, the doyen of London's casinos, 'to enjoy the fun'. The news of a winning syndicate is never slow to spread in gaming circles. From a practical point of view publicity is the last thing one wants, but for a few moments I allowed myself to relax and enjoy the sight of Vincent applying all my lessons with apparently effortless precision, drunk as he had been a couple of hours before.

Sheer repetition finally brings an almost lyrical quality to the inevitable ritual of the roulette table, the tourneur giving the brass spokes of the wheel a twist, at the same time throwing the ball in the opposite direction, the skill of a French-trained operative ensuring that the little white ball completes exactly five circles of the wheel before it drops into a slot, the moment of silence as all eyes follow the numbers as the wheel slows, the swift precision of the croupier's stickwork as he drags in the losing stakes and shoves out the winning plaques and chips. There is the wheel and there is the ivory ball running round the track and here are we, putting ourselves for this brief moment at the mercy of the wheel's arbitrary whim.

Have we won? Yes! The gods have favoured us. It is not mere

money we have won, the money is only a token; no, we have been *recognized*.

Have we lost? We are sick in the stomach, we are fools and failures – but only for a moment. Next time the omens will be favourable, next time we will triumph, next time . . .

Vincent reached the table limit in under an hour. By then he was the star of the salon. All eyes were on him, the man who had mastered the unknowable. As he crossed out his line, wrote 1, 2, 3, 4 and placed a stake of 5 shillings the silence was such I could hear the faint roar of traffic from the street outside. As he started to arrange the pile of chips and plaques in neat piles he was watched by scores of people, some nakedly jealous, some childishly elated, a good many merely astonished.

Scarcely had Vincent started betting again at minimum stakes when Blake began a progression on red. By this time everybody in the salon seemed to be round that table, including the director and his muscular flunkeys. I wondered how easy it would be to succeed as a criminal if, like these fellows, one had an obviously criminal face.

Blake went on to reach the table limit. He had won £1,650 ($4,600). Vincent had won £2,150 ($6,000). The club's management was clearly on edge. When Mrs Richardson asked a waiter for coffee I saw the director speak to him. He came back to Mrs Richardson and said, 'We are taking no more orders for coffee.'

'Why not?' she said coolly. 'It's half-past six in the evening, not the morning – what is it those other people are drinking?'

The waiter shrugged and smirked. All refreshment was shut off as far as we were concerned. When Blake's throat was so dry he couldn't go on without something to drink my wife slipped into his chair to relieve him for a few minutes.

Immediately a young woman came round the table.

'Why did you take that chair?' she demanded shrilly. As nothing like this had happened before my wife was nonplussed.

'I beg your pardon,' was all she could say. I went to her assistance.

'Has my wife done something wrong in taking this seat?' I asked the young woman, maintaining total formality in the event of her being an *agent provocateur* under instructions to create the kind of incident that would justify them barring us.

'Yes, she has,' she replied. 'I've been waiting much longer than she has.'

This was true. Pauline had been wandering about the club, having the occasional soft drink or a rest. According to the etiquette of the table a vacant chair goes to the person who has been standing longest.

'The gentleman whose chair this is has only gone to the bar for a quick drink,' I said. 'He will be back in a few seconds.'

'I don't believe you,' snapped the young woman.

'It's immaterial whether you believe me or not,' I replied, controlling my temper. She was carrying a handful of plaques and may very well have been an ordinary member of the club – in which case her genuine anger would have suited the management even better. They could have simply chucked us out, but to bar people simply for winning too much would hardly have been good for business.

'My wife is giving up that seat to nobody but Mr Blake,' I said to the young woman. She pushed forward aggressively, obviously bent on forcing herself into the seat when Pauline rose to let Blake back in. I saw him coming from the bar and quickly intercepted him.

'That young woman in the red silk dress standing behind Pauline, she's going to grab the chair,' I explained. 'We don't want to be involved in any scuffling, so let Pauline sit out the rest of your shift.'

'Of all the damned cheek! Are you sure Mrs Leigh will be able to cope?'

'I'm sure of it.'

'That is a relief. By the way, what are we going to do about Vincent?'

'Congratulate him on handling his progression so well, I suppose.'

'But he turned up drunk. We shouldn't let that pass without comment.'

'If he makes a habit of it, we'll ditch him. But in a way, if it was just a lapse, I'm even more impressed.'

'I don't follow that.'

'A man who has a weakness and can superimpose his will on that weakness when the moment demands is a better bet for

105

us than somebody who's never known temptation – they're the kind who go to pieces at the wrong time.'

'It's your decision,' he said.

'Yes, it is.'

The rest of that day was without incident, though from the faces of the staff as we left it was clear that trouble was inevitable. While Blake went to drop our winnings into the bank's night safe a dozen or so of us headed for Twickenham. In the car Terry Baker asked me how many times we could expect to break the table or reach the limit in one week.

'Six people covering all the even chances through a whole day at one table could expect one progression per day – with twelve of us covering two tables it would be two progressions a day. On average, of course.'

'But the law of probability comes into it, doesn't it? Isn't it possible we could pull it off four or five times in one day?'

'We could also go four or five days on the trot without winning anything,' said the gloomy Mr Fredericks.

'You're both right,' I said. 'However, I'd rather have the occasional spell of a few days without a win than do it five times in a day. The losses would be catastrophic for the casino – we don't want to kill the golden goose.'

'Yes, but we would have won a big bundle, a really big bundle,' said Baker.

'I see that Mr Kuan has not made an appearance today,' I remarked, 'and as he didn't ring me I assume he's been frightened off. Mr Rogers has also bowed out. That leaves only thirty-five players, plus myself. This doesn't matter too much at the moment because the whole point of playing at the Regency is to give all of you a chance to accustom yourselves to real conditions and, ideally, for each of you to have coped with a progression. When we go to France, however, we will need thirty-six people to work the system profitably. It's possible I may be able to interest some of the people who came here originally.'

'Does it matter if we're one or two short?' asked Simpson. 'Surely that means more money for the rest of us?'

'It doesn't, in fact,' I said. 'The whole point is to cover the six even chances through every spin of the day. We've decided three shifts of four hours each are required to obviate undue physical strain. That means eighteen people per table. With thirty-six we can cover two tables. Suppose, however, we had only five people for one of the tables. We would have to leave one of the even bets uncovered – that might be the one which would have thrown up a progression. Therefore those five are working a lot less profitably than the six at the other table. They would still, however, come in for an equal share of the day's profits. Do you see now why we have to work in multiples of six?'

It's doubtful if they did, but at that stage I was not really worried. Better to have too many than too few – and if I wasn't going to have a team of thirty-six I could pick and choose among the remainder to select the best team of eighteen. We had been playing for only four days. It was on the cards a few more would drop out when the going became tougher.

'I'd like to know what the hell we're supposed to do if we have another scuffle over seats like today?' Mrs Richardson asked.

'Frankly, I'm at a loss to give you any firm guidance,' I said. 'Somebody who's been standing for a long time expects to get the first vacant seat. It's the unwritten law of any decent casino. However, we are not there for amusement – one might say we are there to make our living. Having a seat is very important to us. On the other hand the management would dearly love some incident to give them an excuse to bar us. I'm afraid you'll have to play it by ear.'

'Isn't it about time we set a date for going to France?' Baker asked impatiently.

'It's a little early for that,' I said, beginning to wonder if Baker's impatience might be due to something more than youthful enthusiasm. 'Only five or six of you have experienced a progression so far – until most of you have gone through the ordeal it would be unwise to transport the whole group to a strange casino a thousand miles away in a foreign country. We're making our mistakes on our own doorstep, so to speak. I think we'll give it another three or four weeks.'

Baker grimaced, but nobody else seemed inclined to support him.

As they were leaving it was almost dawn, and I was exhausted to the point of physical pain – yet *again* Baker bore down on me, waiting until the others were opening their cars before coming back up the drive.

'Could we have a quick word, just you and me?' he said.

We went back into the lounge, where the ashtrays were overflowing and the air was stale with smoke.

'Look, Norman,' he began, 'you know I said I was a salesman?'

'Yes?'

'Well, I'm not.'

'Oh?'

'I'm a copper. Temporary detective constable, actually, south London.'

'Not *again*, for God's sake,' I groaned, staring out through the French windows at the first pink traces of sunrise.

Chapter Nine

'What do you mean – *not again*?' Terry Baker asked.

'I must be slipping – they infiltrated a detective inspector last time. You were planted to catch me in the act of conning these people, I take it.'

'Yeah. Only –'

'Well, now you know it isn't a confidence trick, so good-bye. By the way, next time you play undercover man don't send three identically worded character references. I don't suppose there's any point in asking you to put in writing that I've been cleared of suspicion.'

'What I was going to say is that I'm thinking of chucking my job in – you know, resigning.'

'Why?'

'For the money, of course – when I put in my report that your scheme is kosher they'll take me off it, won't they?'

I was standing at the French windows, looking out at the garden and noticing how the early dawn light has a way of draining the colour from everything, as if one were watching black and white television. Tiredness was making me feel utterly detached. When I turned to look at him he was only a few feet away. His face was pale and tense with a stubble shadow that made him look almost dangerous.

'Are you telling me you want to resign from the police to join this scheme?'

'That's what I need to speak to you about – am I definitely going to be one of the lot you take to France?'

'What – you want to chuck in your job to play roulette for a living? Are you mad?' I laughed at him. He stared back. 'You haven't even had any money yet,' I said. 'How do you know it *isn't* a bloody con trick? Blake and I might be in it together, we might –'

'No, I've checked him. He isn't going to risk his reputation and all that crap for a few grand.'

'But you're going to risk your career and pension? When we divide that money it isn't going to add up to more than a couple of hundred each. You're mad. Go home and sleep on it and – '

'A couple of hundred for three or four days' work? You know the kind of money a detective constable makes? I got a wife and a baby and half the bloody time I can't afford a pint or a pack of fags.'

'How many times have I told you I guarantee nothing? We could lose everything, the team could fall apart – I've run syndicates that didn't last a week, I've even had to go begging to the British consul for the fare home – you think you've found the key to the Bank of England?'

'You know what I think?' he said firmly. 'I think we'll make a mint!'

'Perhaps we will. On the other hand we might be turned away from the Regency tomorrow, we might – '

'All I want to know is can you tell me if I'll be going to France?'

'Everything going to plan, I see no reason why you shouldn't. But that's not the point. What have you got ahead of you – twenty years at steady wages and then a healthy pension?'

He grimaced. 'There are complications. I'm in a bit of a dodgy situation financially. I do need to get some money somewhere –'

'Just remember – I advised you strongly against giving up your job. If you want to do it, then that's your business, of course. Personally, I don't give a damn how stupid you are.'

The first shift moved into the club at 2.55 p.m. the next day. They could not get the waiters to take their orders for coffee or soft drinks. I went to the bar and ordered three gin and tonics. As I picked up the glasses the bar manager said only waiters were permitted to carry drinks out of the bar.

'Why won't the waiters serve us then?' I demanded. He merely grinned. Saying nothing, I drank the three gins one after the other and walked back to the salon.

The first shift played to 6.45 p.m. without encountering a progression, and I was checking that the second shift had all

110

turned up when Mrs Heppenstall hit a progression on *pair* (even). At 7 p.m. the second shift managed to take over without any arguments about seating. Mrs Heppenstall remained at her place to see the progression to a conclusion. When her stakes reached £40 ($112) she looked up at me and said, with a distinct roguishness: 'Would you believe it, Mr Leigh, I've got another of those mushrooms?'

It was an entirely appropriate description for progressions, appearing suddenly and unexpectedly and then billowing out in an upwards explosion of wins.

'I think Mrs Heppenstall has just added a new term to the language of gaming,' I said to Blake. He raised his eyebrows and indicated that I should look behind me. The club's director was standing at the other side of the table with a group of his less Neanderthal employees, those who could read and write presumably – they started to record Mrs Heppenstall's staking pattern in notebooks. As her stakes went on rising the inevitable crowd flocked to the table. The club director looked ready to suffer a stroke, his fleshy face becoming diffused with blood. It was one of those eerie moments when one has the curious feeling that it is not real life one is participating in but a stage play. Craziness seemed to be in the air. Anything could happen, and when it did it was a large foreign woman, possibly Dutch, who elbowed her way vigorously to the table. She was in her sixties, rather grandly dressed. She rummaged into a large square handbag and produced a handful of high-denomination plaques and an ear trumpet.

Yes, an ear trumpet. London was then supposed to be the 'Swinging' capital of the world but youth and beauty don't rate so highly in a casino as cash, a commodity that is usually and regrettably in the hands of the old and ugly. Muttering to herself in guttural undertones, this silver-haired matron finally turned to me: 'Can you tell me what is last number that comes up?'

'Seven,' I said.

Cocking an imperial head to one side, she put the ear trumpet in place. 'What you say, please?'

'Seven,' I said into the trumpet.

She shook her head.

'Seven,' I said again in a louder voice.

She frowned. Taking out my notepad, I wrote a large 7 on a blank page. She peered at it and shook her head again.

'Can you make it more large please – I cannot see well.'

I wrote a 7 that was at least six inches high. She screwed up her eyes, failed to comprehend – and dived once more into the big handbag to produce a *magnifying glass*.

'Ah – *seven*,' she exclaimed. Nodding wisely, she leaned past Mrs Heppenstall and put a £5 plaque on seven. It is quite a common hunch among gamblers to back the same number to come up twice running. However, in the time taken to give her the information there had been another spin, twenty-eight having come up. She lost – £5, no doubt just a blur before her eyes.

This incident, not untypical of the underlying madness in a casino, may explain the hostility shown towards us by the management. We knew what we were doing, and for that reason we were a genuine threat. That half-deaf, myopic but wealthy Dutchwoman might occasionally win at odds of 35 to 1, giving her £175 if by any chance her vision allowed her to get the bet on a number, but her regular losses would more than make up for it. Most casino patrons are mentally comparable to the dull-faced queues one sees waiting in draughty streets for bingo halls to open – the stakes are higher, and the clothes are better, but basically they share the same lack of scientific knowledge and for the thrill of an occasional win are happy to go through a childish rigmarole time and time again.

When Mrs Heppenstall's progression reached the stage where her next bet would have been £222 she calmly scored out all her figures, wrote 1, 2, 3, 4 on a clean page and put down a 5-shilling chip. She had won 40,000 units – an even £2,000 ($5,600). This was just too much for the management of the Regency. After a short confab with the director, the Chef de Partie, who supervises play at the tables, announced in a loud voice that *all* roulette tables were being closed for the rest of the day, although the other games, *trente et quarante*, blackjack and so on, were continuing as usual.

'We're beginning to hurt them,' said Blake as we cashed Mrs Heppenstall's chips and plaques. He went off to pay the £2,000 into the night safe while the rest of us went back to Twickenham. Inside, I took the floor, forestalling any inclination the group might have to talk itself into a panic.

'Ladies and gentlemen,' I said, 'they closed down the roulette tables because they didn't want us to win any more money. We are not mindreaders, so it is idle to speculate what they will do next. The only way to find out is to be at the Regency at three o'clock tomorrow afternoon, take up our usual positions and wait and see. It should be interesting.'

'They'll ban us, won't they?' said Milton, the pub-keeper from Essex.

'They could have done that today,' I said. 'I have the feeling they'll try something else.'

'Suppose we are banned, what will we do then?' asked Fredericks. 'You said a month's training in real conditions was essential.'

'I consider that it would be suicidal to begin operations in France until every one of us is absolutely *au fait* with the method and with every contingency that can arise at a roulette table. If we were to be barred, I think we should all have to buy a small wheel and practice with something like five hundred spins a day.'

The Regency's management made its move before the first spin of the wheel the following afternoon. Our first shift was preparing to place the opening stakes of 5 shillings when the Chef de Partie made an announcement.

'Ladies and gentlemen, the casino directors wish to inform you of a change in the club rules. Henceforth the minimum bet for the roulette tables will be ten shillings, not two shillings as before. Thank you.'

Blake looked at me.

'We'll pack it in for today,' I said. 'I'll stay here and wait for the second and third shifts and warn them not to come.'

'Want me to stay with you?' Blake asked.

'No point in both of us wasting a day. No, I'll see you at seven tomorrow.'

The following evening most of the group was at my home, looking depressed. Knowing that my chance of taking a properly

113

trained group to France was in the balance, I used a bit of practical psychology.

'Ladies and gentlemen,' I began, 'as you all know, the Regency has raised the minimum bet from two shillings to ten shillings ($1.40) and I have no doubt this was solely to throw us out of gear. Our staking method requires bets of five, six, seven, eight and nine shillings at the outset of a progression. These are now ruled out. Before I give you the simple answer to this manoeuvre I'll ask Mr Blake to give his report.'

Blake had a briefcase (new, black, brass fitments) and a cash book (new, black, gilt lettering embossed on the cover). Sounding like the church garden-fête treasurer, he intoned his report.

'On day one,' he began, 'we had no winnings. Day two we had no winnings. On day three we won five thousand three hundred pounds from three progressions. On day four we won three thousand eight hundred pounds from two progressions. On day five we won two thousand pounds from one progression. Our total winnings so far are, therefore, eleven thousand one hundred pounds ($31,000). I have a print-out of the bank statement to verify these figures.'

He looked round, but nobody was inclined to challenge his accuracy. Maurice Nathan leaned forward to congratulate Mrs Heppenstall on being the only one who had experienced two progressions. She blushed girlishly.

'The money is allocated as follows,' Blake went on. 'Under the agreed arrangements Mr Leigh and I each take ten per cent. By the way, there are odd shillings to all these amounts, but I am leaving these in the bank to keep the account open, if no one has any objection. Twenty per cent comes to two thousand two hundred and twenty pounds between Mr Leigh and myself. That leaves eight thousand eight hundred and eighty pounds. As Mr Rogers and Mr Kuan have dropped out, and as I do not propose to pay myself twice – '

'Hear, hear,' said a deep male voice.

' – that means thirty-four equal shares, two hundred and sixty-one pounds each ($730), with a balance of a few pounds which I also propose to leave in the bank. I have here an envelope for each of you. . . .'

Reading out names from the list in his cash book, he began

handing out the envelopes. I waited until they were counting bank notes.

'It's not exactly a fortune,' I began.

'How do I put it down on my tax form?' Keith Robinson asked innocently.

'You don't breath a word of this to the Inland Revenue, you fool,' Bateson snapped.

'I think Mr Robinson was joking,' I said.

'Course I was,' Robinson exclaimed, pretending to be aggrieved. 'I've never seen a tax form in my life, have I?'

'It's not a fortune, but it's encouraging considering that we are supposed merely to be learning the method,' I went on. 'Now, as to what happens next – my solution to their increase in the table minimum is merely to maintain your paperwork up to ten shillings without physically staking any money. Once your calculations take you over ten shillings, you can start putting down stakes. Similarly, when a progression comes down below ten shillings you will revert to paperwork alone. On average the results will be the same as if the limit had not been altered. In fact there will be a slight percentage advantage to us in that zero will be taking nothing from us while we're working below ten shillings. Is that clear to everybody?'

'It seems absurdly simple,' said Blake.

'Perhaps,' I said, drily. 'It won't make the management any happier to have a lot of people occupying seats when they are betting merely on paper. They will probably try to provoke scenes, so from now on be doubly careful.'

Day Seven. Our first shift gave the croupiers at both tables something to think about. Twelve people seated at the tables and doing involved paperwork without placing any chips on the green baize? The casino boss was summoned in short order. I watched his plump face carefully as he went into muttered discussion with the Chef de Partie.

Before they could come to any decision Mr Hopplewell ran into a progression which lasted for fifty minutes. Everybody watched with fascination – disgust in the case of the director – as shilling stakes turned into pounds, then tens of pounds and scores of pounds. And then hundreds.

A curious change came over Hopplewell. Aged sixty, florid, overweight, gruff and withdrawn, the man who had professed contempt for all forms of gambling, he began to change with each winning bet. Bravado is the only word for it. Each new pile of plaques and chips went down with a flamboyant flourish. He grinned at various women hanging round the table, smacked his hands noisily after each win, even threw a £5 plaque to the croupier as a tip.

Then I drew in my breath. I could see the four-digit figures on his notepad, and before he had added the two at either end of the line I knew his next stake would be £225 ($630).

Instead, however, of crossing out his figures and reverting to 1, 2, 3, 4 he began to assemble a handful of plaques, apparently ready to place a bet above the table maximum.

Remembering that he had fluffed our first chance of a winning progression, even I, witness to every form of casino madness, was surprised at how quickly he had succumbed to a temptation which besets many roulette players, the latent desire to achieve notoriety as an arrogant devil who rides roughshod over petty rules and regulations. Taking money is only the most obvious way the table has of destroying people, perhaps even the *least* dangerous.

Hopplewell – unimaginative, surly, hostile, probably bored by life but frightened at how quickly it was passing – had made himself wealthy by stolid application to commerce. Suddenly he had become a daredevil, a pirate, a dashing hero, liberated by a brass wheel, a little ivory ball and a few plastic discs. Other men envied him. Attractive women admired him. In a few moments he had rediscovered the sweet bravado of youth.

At the time I was too angry to indulge in such fanciful philosophizing. I got to his elbow just as he was assembling a handful of plaques. He looked round to make sure he had the attention of all the people jammed at the table. Then he caught my eye.

He gave me a slow wink and put the plaques back on the green baize in front of him. Smiling slyly, he scored out his line of figures and wrote 1, 2, 3, 4. Excited faces waited to see what he would do next. He scribbled the figure 5 on his pad and then sat back, arms crossed, lips tightening in a little smile of triumph.

116

His face was wet with perspiration. The club's director went into agitated conversation with his associates, all of them keeping us under hostile surveillance. Blake came back from the restaurant.

'Hopplewell has just won two thousand or thereabouts,' I said. 'You know what he did? He made as though he was going to put down a stake far above the limit! He was only joking, but –'

'They were talking about it in the restaurant. I hurried through my meal so that I wouldn't miss it. Those chaps don't look too happy now, do they? By the way, what would they have done if he'd tried to stake over the limit?'

'The croupier would have spotted it before the ball was thrown, and he'd have been told quietly to remove his bet. At least that's what normally happens – I don't know what this lot would have done.'

'I imagine they're making feverish plans to deal with us now.'

At about five o'clock Mrs Richardson hit a progression on black. As soon as her stakes began to rise the director and two or three of his henchmen crowded round her chair.

They began to talk at her from all sides.

'Would you like a cigarette, madam?' said one, shoving a packet in front of her face. She shook her head and went on with her calculations.

'Can I get madam some coffee?' said another. She shook her head again. I eased in close behind her and leaned down.

'Say nothing to them. Ignore them completely,' I murmured.

She nodded calmly and put on a stake of £50, her right eye slightly screwed up against smoke rising from the cigarette she was forced to keep between her lips while her hands were occupied.

It was an incredible spectacle, three or four aggressive men doing everything short of physical assault to distract a handsome young woman, who resolutely refused to be distracted. When she reached the table limit of £200 and reverted to 1, 2, 3, 4 she had won just over £3,000. The faces of the director and his staff were a picture of vicious frustration.

'I think I'll have a bite in the restaurant,' I said to Blake. 'You keep an eye on things here.'

'I dare say the worst they can do is chuck us out,' he said.

'You wouldn't find that – embarrassing?'

He huffed at the very idea.

In the restaurant while I was waiting to be served, two waiters began to discuss our group. Perhaps they knew who I was.

'They've just won another whack,' said one with noticeable relish, apparently unsympathetic to his employers' suffering.

'You wait. They won't be here much longer,' said the other.

'How come?'

'You'll see,' said the second one, tapping his nose

I paid my bill and went back to the tables. We did not have another progression that night. None of the staff said a word to us when we left at 3 a.m. Keith Robinson and I went with Blake and deposited the cash in the bank.

The Regency management dropped their bombshell before the first spin of the wheel the following afternoon. Our first shift was seated at the two tables, lines of 1, 2, 3, 4 on clean pages of their notebooks, chips piled neatly on the table, when the Chef de Partie made an announcement.

'Ladies and gentlemen, the management wishes to initiate a change in the rules for roulette. The minimum stake on even chances will remain ten shillings – and henceforth only multiples of ten shillings [$1.40] will be accepted as stakes on the even chances. Thank you.'

The others looked at me. To those nearest I said, 'Cash your chips at the desk and we will go to my house for a meeting. Spread the word around, would you?'

'Why aren't we playing?' Terry Baker demanded, catching up with me as I made for the exit.

'They found a way to stop us, of course.'

'What do you mean? All we got to do is bet in units of ten bob.'

'Is that all? Are you prepared to lose a hundred pounds a day instead of ten?'

'I don't see – '

'I'll explain it later at my place.'

The entire management seemed to be present, most of them smirking, as our party reached the exit. Knowing there was no possibility of our playing there again, I went across to the director.

118

'I'm surprised it took you so long to find the answer,' I said cheerfully.

He shrugged. 'No hard feelings?' he said. 'Only we couldn't have your lot hogging the seats and sitting there all day betting peanuts, could we?'

'Peanuts? Sixteen thousand pounds, give or take a hundred or two? I think we gave you a good run for your money.'

'We don't mind our members winning a bit.'

We both smiled. 'As we shall not be returning I wonder if I could ask you to do me a favour,' I said.

'What is it?'

'Quite a number of my associates will be turning up throughout the rest of the day. Could your staff pass on the word that they should go straight to Norman Leigh's house? I would wait for them myself but I hate the atmosphere of casinos.'

'Delighted,' he said. 'Come back soon, won't you – in about two hundred years!'

'We should go straight to the police,' Blake protested when we were on the pavement. Our withdrawal had been witnessed by a lot of people, and he was mortified.

'They outmanouevred us. It's as simple as that,' I said. 'They found a way to make the system ruinously expensive, and there's nothing we can do about it. Do you have yesterday's winnings with you?'

'Yes.'

'What does it come to?'

'You and I split one thousand and forty-five pounds [$2,920], and the others share four thousand one hundred and eighty between them – about a hundred and twenty-three pounds each [$344]. Why?'

'It might be enough.'

'Enough for what?'

'To make it a fair wind for France, of course.'

By dint of phoning we managed to contact most of the other members of the group before they left work or home for the second and third shifts, and by eight o'clock that night they were all present in my lounge. Eventually even the least mathematically minded grasped what the Regency's management had achieved

119

by making ten shillings the basic unit for betting on the even chances.

'Your line wouldn't be one, two, three, four,' I explained. 'It would be ten, twenty, thirty, forty. Our capital risk would be multiplied exactly ten times. Instead of each of you bringing ten or fifteen pounds a day you would have to bring a hundred or more.'

'But the system would still work just the same,' said Simpson. 'In fact, we'd be winning a lot more, wouldn't we?'

'We're not all rich enough to invest a hundred a day, Mr Simpson,' I said. 'The whole point of the Reverse Labouchère is that it enables us to deal in shillings while we are losing, and that is most of the time. If your line is ten, twenty, thirty, forty, you would be losing fifty units each time you crossed it out – that's two pounds ten shillings. And when we *did* get a winning progression we wouldn't win any more. They haven't increased the maximum bet, have they?'

'So where do we go now?' asked Milton, the burly pub landlord.

'There are plenty of casinos in London,' said Terry Baker. 'Even if we only last a few days in each of them, we can still pick up thousands. Next time we can be a bit cleverer about disguising ourselves as a group.'

'News travels with the speed of light in those circles,' I said. 'As soon as we appeared at another casino they would know who we were and what we were up to. They would simply change their staking requirements as the Regency did today. No, I think the time has come.'

'To go to France?' said Fredericks, making it sound like a trip in the tumbril. 'But you said we needed a full month's training in a real casino, and I haven't even been through a mushroom yet.'

'We have no choice,' I said. 'All the London casinos now know how to drive us away. At least in France the staking limits are fixed by government regulation. Nothing short of legislation can alter them. It's France now or nothing.'

Blake had suggested that we postpone a decision, but I had explained to him that to delay now would probably kill the whole thing. A few weeks before none of these people had ever played

120

roulette seriously – many had never been inside a casino. I had led them gently into what they regarded as an adventure, and so far they had all done well enough out of it. Most of them had missed the various threatening ploys used by the Regency management to intimidate a few individuals. They still regarded the whole thing as a novelty, but give them a few weeks of inactivity and they might begin to realize how deep these waters could be. The time to strike was now.

'We've had enough practice sessions, I think,' I said. 'They're boring and they take up a lot of time. I propose that we set a date for France. While Mr Blake is handing out his envelopes will you all think seriously of how soon you can make arrangements to go? How does a fortnight from now sound?'

Blake stood up with his cash book. As he sonorously ploughed through the figures I watched faces. I needed eighteen people to give us three shifts of six covering one table twelve hours a day. Any more than eighteen would cost the group money. If all thirty-four decided to come I was going to be in an embarrassing situation.

Waiting until the white envelopes were being torn open, I said, 'Well, ladies and gentlemen, I realize it's shorter notice than we anticipated, but how do you feel about leaving for the Riviera in two weeks?'

Not one hand went up!

I allowed myself no sign of disappointment.

'If you had a month to get ready, how many could make it then?'

Six hands went up.

'Suppose we set it for late September, that would give you seven weeks. How many could make it then?'

Five more hands went up.

For a moment I had an urge to scream at the rest of them. They had done all those weeks of practice, they could see the system was all I claimed for it, they had each made £400 ($1,120), from what was supposed to be only a dress rehearsal. What more did I have to do, damn it?

Bateson got to his feet.

'I don't see why we should rush into it,' he said. 'I could probably get a week or two off in the spring.'

121

'Look, we're psychologically ready for it right *now*,' I exclaimed.

'It's all very well for some people,' he went on, glancing round the lounge ceiling, clearly intimating that I was one of the idle rich, 'but those of us with families and jobs can't just be dashing off abroad when the mood takes us.'

'Seven weeks' notice is hardly dashing off, Mr Bateson,' I said patiently. 'You did know from the start that my intention was to take the group to France in the late autumn.'

'Yes, but of course none of us had any idea then whether your scheme would work.'

'Well? You've each won four hundred pounds already – '

'Could be we've pushed our luck as far as it'll go,' he said quickly. I eyed him coldly.

'How does one win a lot of money except by pushing one's luck?'

Bateson sensed that he had strong support. There was a new note of amusement in his voice as he looked at me across the lounge. 'I think you've got some romantic notion about France, Mr Leigh,' he said patronizingly. 'The rest of us can't be expected to share your private dreams, can we?'

I swallowed hard. 'Whatever my original reasons for wanting to take the group to France, the fact is that we've had it as far as any London casino is concerned. Therefore, to carry out the scheme France is now a practical necessity – unless you'd rather make it Las Vegas.'

Bateson smiled. 'I don't think I can be accused of being a stick in the mud. I wouldn't be here if I was. However, let's be sensible about this. We haven't done too badly, but we have no guarantee – '

'Guarantee?' I snapped. 'Has the government seen fit to put roulette on the National Health Service? Until gambling becomes part of the welfare state I'm damned if – '

Sensing the ultimate horror – raised voices – Blake rose to his feet, wielding his sense of propriety like a bull-fighter's cape.

'This is Mr Leigh's show,' he said. 'We all knew what he planned when we joined the group. If seven weeks is too soon for most of you, why don't those who can get away leave for France at the end of September? We can start playing immediately and the rest of you can join us as soon as it is convenient.'

'Going to stay in the south of France for the winter, are you?' said Bateson.

'As long as we can milk casinos I'll stay in France for the rest of my life,' said Keith Robinson.

'Me too,' said another, glaring ferociously at Bateson.

Several said they would try hard to bring forward holiday entitlements and the like but I could see they were itching to get away. Some credit was due to them for having come this far, however, and I thanked each for the hard work he or she had put in, saying that if anyone changed his mind not to hesitate to call me up. They filed out.

I smiled at the ten who remained and were prepared to take the plunge. For a few minutes I had been depressed and angry at what seemed like mass betrayal, but that soon passed. Counting Blake, I had eleven, not necessarily the best roulette players nor even the most attractive personalities – but the best for my purposes. They wanted to do it almost as badly as I did and to me that made them ideal.

As might have been expected, all those who had enjoyed the spicy thrill of a winning progression were ready to take the scheme to its next phase, but there were also a few surprises. The eleven left in my lounge that night were:

Oliver Blake, *thirty-two, single, stockbroker.*
Emma Richardson, *thirty-five, married, housewife (formerly a commercial designer).*
Lettice Heppenstall, *fifty-four, widow, housewife.*
Keith Robinson, *twenty-six, single, 'clerk'.*
Terry Baker, *twenty-seven, married, one child, policeman.*
Alec Sherlock, *twenty-nine, single, office manager.*
Maurice Nathan, *thirty-seven, single, textile industry executive.*
Sydney Hopplewell, *sixty, divorced, company director.*
George Milton, *forty-seven, married, pub-keeper.*
Thomas Fredericks, *forty-one, single, civil servant.*
Peter Vincent, *thirty, married (separated), company director.*

'There's nothing to worry about,' I said to Blake. 'We've got the makings of a very good team here. We'll have to rethink the situation, that's all.'

'But you told us eighteen was the absolute minimum.'

Looking at Mrs Richardson, I kept a straight face and said, 'One couldn't expect a gaming coup to go as smoothly as a convocation of suffragan bishops, Mr Blake. We'll all just have to work harder at it. But there will be fewer of us to share the profits.'

'That little bastard Bateson spoiled everything,' said Mrs Richardson. 'Perhaps if we could talk to the others without him –'

'No, the whole scheme depends on total enthusiasm,' I said. 'If they can be put off so easily at this stage, how could we rely on them if things turned rough, especially in a foreign country?'

'Advertise again?' Vincent suggested, with untypical practicality.

'Never! Six or seven weeks ago I started out by interviewing nine hundred and fifty-one people – and produced eleven of you!'

'We could do it in two shifts working six hours each,' suggested Sherlock.

'Could you cope with that?' I asked, wondering why it was I had ever disliked the man. The self-indulgence of emotion was over. Those who had dropped out twenty minutes before might as well have been dead. Certainly they were already fading from *my* memory. As well as Sherlock, I had never really cared much for Vincent, Fredericks, Hopplewell and Milton, who was very much the old-soldier type, full of mother-in-law jokes and embarrassingly vocal about his allegedly monstrous wife. Yet now that they had selected themselves, they seemed like the salt of the earth.

'I'll tell you, I graft eighteen bloody hours a day in my pub and I don't get four hundred quid a week tax-free for it,' Milton said, adding ruefully, 'I don't even get any thanks for it. Six hours is nothing.'

Blake pointed out that there were only eleven players. 'Out of all those who've just left, isn't there *one* person we could persuade to join us?'

'No,' I replied. 'That's very bad pyschology. We must go into this together on the same basis, not because I've talked you into it but because you are a hundred per cent behind it. Anybody we persuaded to come against his better judgement would always

124

have a good excuse for carping and grumbling. I suggest we give it a day or two before we allow depression to set in. Some of the others might change their minds – as long as their decision is spontaneous.'

I waited for several days. Occasionally I was tempted to phone Blake and say to hell with it, let's have a bash with what we've got, but if the years hadn't taught me wisdom exactly, they had provided enough painful lessons about going off half-cocked. We might be able to permutate eleven into two daily shifts of six, but the strain would be enormous and if only one of the team cracked up, the whole thing would collapse.

'This time it's got to go like clockwork, or I don't do it at all,' I told Pauline a few days later, having heard nothing from any of those who had dropped out.

'That *would* be a pity after all the work you've put into it,' she said loyally.

Then suddenly I had the answer: 'Mrs Harper-Biggs!'

'*Who?*'

'She was the one who cracked up and wanted us to hare off to the Belgian Congo – she'd be ideal for our twelfth player. I bet you she'd come.'

'She doesn't sound very ideal if she cracked up.'

'It was only because she had to work very long hours. I'll go down to Bournemouth and see her.'

'That was a long time ago – she might have moved – she might even be dead.'

'Her kind don't die. Anyway, I'm only risking a few gallons of petrol.'

I rang Blake. 'Look, I think I know the very person to make up the team,' I said when he came on the phone. 'Can you drive us down to Bournemouth tomorrow?'

'Tomorrow? That's a bit short notice, I don't really know if – '

'Good. It will be better with you there. Don't want her to think it's another of my one-man wild-goose chases. Pick me up about ten, eh? By the way, whatever you do – don't mention Italians.'

Chapter Ten

The surly young maid who showed us into the lounge with the huge fireplace was a new girl, but nothing else seemed to have changed in the ten or eleven years since I had come to this house as a young clerk in a ten-pound suit. Certainly Mrs Harper-Biggs had changed so little we might have parted only the day before.

'Mr Leigh!' she exclaimed. 'When the girl announced the name I couldn't believe it was you. I'm so glad to see you. I've so often wanted to tell you how sorry I was for letting you down.'

I introduced Blake and we all shook hands. For a blessed moment I thought Blake was going to shake *my* hand, so extended were the social niceties. We sat down and exchanged the usual pleasantries. I was impatient to tell her the reason for our unexpected visit, but Blake seemed to have forgotten why we were there in his enthusiasm for complimenting her on her paintings and furnishings. Mrs Harper-Biggs asked me if I would pull the bellrope. On this occasion it was not her small, dutiful husband who appeared but the aggressively silent maid. Mrs Harper-Biggs asked her to bring a tray of coffee. Blake said a few admiring words about yet another of her paintings, to my eyes just a dark rectangle with the barely discernible outlines of a face with ferrety eyes.

'Family heirloom, I suppose,' he said.

'No. Herbert bought it at a sale.'

Coffee was served in exquisite china cups so small one sip was sufficient to require a refill. Before she got round to giving Blake a guided tour I decided to interrupt.

'Mrs Harper-Biggs,' I began. 'I've come down with Mr Blake from London to ask you a question. You remember the last time I came to see you in this room?'

'I do indeed. By the way, poor Herbert passed away four years ago, dear man. More coffee, Mr Blake?'

126

'Excellent,' said Blake.

'And what is this question?' she asked me.

'I have formed a group to go to that same casino where we tried out the Fitzroy system all those years ago. We're leaving at the end of September. The method we're using is much simpler than the Fitzroy, and with twelve players we'll be able to work in shifts of only six hours. Would you like to join the group? I realize you may not have altogether happy memories of our last venture – '

'The number of times I could have kicked myself for being so silly,' she said to Blake. 'Mr Leigh had a wonderful method for winning money, and I let him down badly. End of September, you said? I'd be delighted to come.'

'Naturally I don't ask you to commit yourself without hearing more about it – '

'Mr Leigh, I am a fifty-six-year-old widow, with no relatives and a few boring friends who probably find me even more boring than I find them. Nothing would give me greater pleasure than to go with you. Besides, going away for a spell will give me a good excuse to get rid of that awful girl. She drives me mad with her continual sniffing.'

'Sniffing?' said Blake. 'Can't she use a handkerchief?'

'No, *disapproval*. She comes from a background of religious dementia. It's very common in rural Dorset. I think she suspects me of entertaining strange men late at night when she goes home. Mr Blake, I haven't offered to show you my collection.'

'You would have to come up to my place in Twickenham for a bit of practice in the system,' I said.

'Wonderful. I can go to the Natural History Museum in Kensington. Do you know anything about beetles and such things, Mr Blake?'

'Fascinating,' he said.

The more I saw of the group during the next seven weeks the more confident I became. Here was no collection of dilettantes' and drunken eccentrics but sober, reliable people from diverse walks of life united by an enthusiasm which owed more to common sense than fantasy. Terry Baker was the only one I had doubts about – simply because his enthusiasm ran away with him. At one meeting in the middle of September he told me he he had resigned from the police.

'Well, on your head be it,' I said. 'I would have thought that with a wife and a young child you would have been better advised to stick to a good career with prospects and a pension. But you're a grown man, and I'm not your guardian.'

He smiled. 'You're too bloody cautious, Norman. Look, I want to show you something.'

He brought out a notebook and showed me page after page of figures. 'I've been putting in the hours on my toy wheel at home,' he said. 'That's a real progression, just the way the wheel threw it up. I was working without a table limit. Know what the winnings are? Only four hundred thousand pounds, that's all.'

I checked his figures and could find no flaw with them – except, of course, that they were only on paper. Baker showed them to the others later. Milton was ecstatic. 'One of them and we'd be set for life! No more crates of bloody ale to hump up and down. First thing I'd book myself on a world cruise and throw away the return ticket!'

'Yes, but it depends on playing without a table limit,' I said.

'The Salle Privy!' exclaimed Baker, who had remembered the name of the Monte Carlo establishment I had once talked about where no table limit operates.

'The Salle Privée indeed! For a start we'd need capital of a thousand each. Our lines would be composed of six-digit figures – all very feasible in the comfort of your own home, but could you maintain an astronomical line like that in a crowded casino?'

'We could buy larger notepads,' drawled Vincent.

'Or hire a portable computer,' said Mrs Richardson.

Baker said he still thought we should try it. The Regency management had taken only eight days to beat us; in France they might be quicker, he reasoned. Why not go for the big one straight off? To end this discussion without giving him cause for resentment I said that if we did extraordinarily well in the Casino Municipale I, for one, might be willing to use my winnings to have a crack at the Salle Privée in Monte Carlo. Baker seemed satisfied with that.

'How long do you expect us to be staying down there on the Riviera?' asked Sherlock.

'If the shekels are rolling in I won't be breaking a leg to dash back to the arms of my old woman, believe me,' said Milton.

'You can count on me to stay as long as we're showing a profit,' said Maurice Nathan. 'My last firm went kaput, and the doctor says my nerves are bad. A change of scenery and a chance to make myself some capital, just what I need.'

Blake said his father was willing to give him indefinite leave of absence from the family firm. Keith Robinson said he was between jobs anyway. One by one each person indicated that he would postpone any commitments. That left only Fredericks.

'Bit tricky I'd imagine, switching holidays about in the Civil Service,' I said to that sombre gentleman.

He fidgeted and looked at his large, pale hands. 'No, I'm all right,' he said. Then he looked at me sheepishly and said, 'I handed in my resignation on Friday.'

'You didn't, did you?'

'Yes, I'd used up all my holiday entitlement. My mother was ill in May and I had to look after her.'

I asked him to stay behind when the others left. For the head-strong Baker to chuck in his job was one thing; he had hinted that he was already in some kind of trouble and in any case he didn't strike me as the type who would have lasted thirty years at any job let alone the police. But Fredericks was forty-one and extremely passive, and I did not want him ruining his life – to be honest, I did not want the run any risk of being blamed, however inaccurately, for feeding him false illusions.

'It's not too late to withdraw your resignation, is it?' I asked, pouring him a stiff whisky.

'Look, Norman – you don't mind me calling you Norman, do you?'

'Not in the slightest.'

'It's just that Mr Blake always – '

'Blake has been to Eton; we have to make allowances.'

'I said my mother was ill in May – actually she'd been ill for twenty years. I had to look after her. She's dead now – '

'I'm sorry to hear that.'

'Oh, don't be sorry. She was a selfish old woman and she stopped me from having much of a life. When I saw your advertisement in the *Telegraph* – this will sound stupid, but I don't have many friends really and being with all of you and coming to this house – well, it's almost like having a family, do you know what I mean? I don't think I've ever enjoyed anything so much in my whole life. When you wanted to fix a date for going to France I knew I'd have to bow out because I'd already used up my holidays for this year. Then I just thought – why should I give up the only interesting thing that's happened to me for years? I'm not chucking away a fancy career by any means. I'm only a low-grade clerk really. You keep warning us not to expect too much – I don't care if we don't make a penny. It will be the most exciting experience of my whole life. My mother – well, tell you the truth I've never even had a girlfriend, not seriously.' He looked at his watch, painfully embarrassed by this confession. I brought over the bottle of Scotch.

'It's getting late,' he said apologetically. 'The last tube goes from Richmond in twenty minutes, I – '

'For a man who's chucked in a safe governmental career to go gambling on the Riviera it's a bit late to be worrying about the last bloody tube train, Thomas,' I said. 'Have another whisky and let's finish the bottle.'

The following week we set out for France. The three younger men, Robinson, Baker and Sherlock, went by plane; the others by car; I by train, alone.

At 8.30 on the morning of Tuesday, 27 September, I kissed Pauline good-bye on the steps in front of our rented house, without which the Mushroom Mob (as Robinson had called us) could not have been.

'Give me a ring when you get there. I should be down by the end of the week,' Pauline said. 'And take care of yourself.'

'Are you really sure you want to come?'

'Of course. I want to make sure you're managing without me. Good-bye, darling. Take care of yourself.'

On the night train south to the Côte d'Azur a day later I shared a compartment with a Frenchwoman nursing a baby that yelled all night. I was too preoccupied to mind.

When I arrived in Nice I went to my hotel and rang Blake, arranging to meet him at our agreed rendezvous spot, the Café

Massena. It was lunchtime when we met, and within half an hour six or seven or the others joined us. Blake was a bit upset that I had not driven down with him.

'I had to visit a friend in Paris,' I told him. 'It might save time if we go across to the casino now and pick up our admission cards for tomorrow. Give you all a look at the place.'

As we were climbing the stairs inside the casino building I explained that passports would have to be shown. Keith Robinson said he had left his at the hotel. I said he could bring it tomorrow when he started playing. He pulled me back, letting the others go on up.

'What do they want passports for?'

'Just a formality – they check the names against the banned list.'

'You sure it's just a formality?'

'Yes. Why?'

He smiled and gave me a wink. 'Just wondered, that's all. Never gone much on bureaucracy and red tape and that.'

I knew there was more to it than that but said nothing until we had looked round the huge salon of the casino and gone back across the square to the café. When the others went back to their hotels to get ready for dinner I got him on his own.

'I want to know what's wrong with your passport,' I said.

'What do you mean, Norman?'

'I want a straight answer.'

He thought about it for a few moments, then became his usual droll self again.

'I can trust you, Norman, can't I? Of course I can. Only I never bothered to get a kosher passport, did I?'

'You mean you're travelling on a false passport?' I snapped.

'Yeah – here it is – not a bad bit of work, is it?'

I didn't bother looking at it.

'What the devil do you need a false passport for? Good God, man, something like this could ruin the whole scheme.'

'Don't panic so, Norman. It got me past the immigration and all that crap, didn't it?'

'Just tell me *why*.'

'All right. The fact of it is, Norman, I told you I'm a clerk but actually I'm a burglar.'

'You're not serious!'

'Never more. You think burglars look different from normal people?'

'But why the false passport?'

'It's a long story, Norman, I don't think you really want to hear it – I mean, like my name isn't Keith Robinson and so forth? Don't look so sick; I'm not up to anything dodgy. I'll tell you. I saw your ad and thought well, go along, my son, have a bit of a giggle. Maybe give the man's house the once over. Then I got really interested in the scheme. Don't worry. I wouldn't pull any strokes on you. We're all mates in this team, aren't we?'

I took a deep breath.

'It's no business of mine what you say you are. I'm interested only in how you perform at the table. I won't tell anyone else and I presume you don't intend to. Just one thing – keep your hands off the team's money.'

'I'm a burglar, remember, not a pickpocket,' he said cheerfully.

I had a good few whiskies that night, both with Blake and afterwards on my own. In the end I decided it was too late to worry about Robinson. I needed him and he was reliable, and with only a few hours before our first day's play I was in no position to develop strong moral attitudes. As long as his passport could stand inspection I didn't care if he was the Boston Strangler.

As you will remember from the opening of this account our first day at the Casino Municipale in Nice went extremely well, to the tune of 78,000 francs. Almost six thousand pounds ($15,900). Blake said, as he dropped me back at my hotel after the share-out in his apartments, that it felt too good to be true.

I didn't bother to tell him that the first day was always the easiest.

Chapter Eleven

When I awoke on 1 October, the second day of our assault on the Casino Municipale, the temperature was in the nineties and the sky blue enough to put an ache in the heart of any sun-starved Briton. After a hearty English-style breakfast I put the shirt and socks I'd worn the day before into the wash basin for a soak, checked that I still had my 7,800 francs from the share-out, and set out through the scorching streets to call on Mrs Richardson, anxious to hear what had transpired at her cocktail party with the Police des Jeux officer. She had managed to rent a furnished apartment near the casino. Mrs Harper-Biggs and Mrs Heppenstall had apartments in another residential building nearby. Apart from Blake with his suite of rooms the rest of us were in pensions and small hotels scattered about the town.

When I arrived it was eleven o'clock and Mrs Richardson was in her little kitchenette washing clothes. Because of the heat she was wearing only a brassiere and nylon slip. To give her a chance to put some clothes on I said I would have a look round the other room. She didn't feel like bothering. Her streaked blonde hair was tied severely back in a pony-tail. Standing with her bare arms deep in the suds, her eyes slightly screwed up against smoke from the cigarette stuck in her mouth, she presented a strangely attractive picture. It was hard to believe she had three sons at boarding school.

'You like this place?' she asked, draining the sink and spreading out a pair of panties on the window ledge.

'Very pleasant. What –'

'I had to fork out a month's rent in advance – a hundred and forty pounds. Still, it means I can save money cooking for myself and I can have a bath whenever I feel like it.'

'That will be convenient for you,' I said, smiling at the idea

133

of her and the Brigadier having to worry about saving a few pounds. 'What happened at the cocktail party?'

'It was interesting,' she said, putting on a kettle. 'Philippe either fancies me or he's on to us – he stuck by me all night.'

'What did he actually say?'

'The usual sort of things. What was I doing here on my own, how long was I staying, was I married? I said my husband and I always took separate holidays – to keep the magic in our marriage. They're so old-fashioned, Frenchmen – he found the very idea shocking. He asked me if I'd come here to gamble. I said I didn't know much about gambling and casinos but had always rather fancied myself raking in piles of chips. I thought I'd pump him for a bit. I said I'd read in the papers that a gang of Australian conmen were working in casinos along the Riviera – did people like that make much money? He said his people were already on to the Australians. He said it's impossible to put one over on the casinos. He started showing off a bit. You know how silly men can be. I couldn't imagine *you* being silly like that – you're always so precise and formal.'

'I find it helps to inspire confidence.'

'What are you really like, then?'

'I can't remember.'

'Smile more. It will give people a clue when you're joking.'

'I've had this obsession with roulette most of my adult life and in the process I've probably become – well, almost mechanical. Making this system work in this casino is more important to me than anything else, even my wife. I'm sorry, but please don't expect me to be the life and soul of the party. What else did your friend tell you?'

'He was showing off, so I did my empty-headed-blonde act and pumped him like mad. Do you know they have a special group of expert croupiers they can call in when anybody is doing too well? Seemingly these chaps can make the ball finish up wherever they want on the wheel. Not in any particular number – he says that's impossible – but they can put it in whatever section they want. Do you think that's likely?'

'I must think about that. Anyway, I'll wander round to Blake's hotel now.'

'He's gone swimming. Peter Vincent is driving to Cap Ferrat,

134

and Maurice Nathan is inspecting the delights of the maritime museum.'

'You're very well informed.'

'I've never had so many invitations in one morning. The concierge was a bit miffed with all the running up and down to the phone.'

'Blake as well? Vincent, yes, even Nathan I suppose – but *Blake*? I thought he was engaged to some well-bred filly from the county stable. Well, well.'

'It was only for a swim. Good God, I'm an old married woman with three sons.'

As she said this she was standing in the doorway of her bedroom, still wearing the white bra and flimsy slip, the sun behind her in the bedroom window. She had the silhouette of a ripe seventeen-year-old.

'You might carry snapshots of your boys to show around,' I said. 'Help to remind everybody that you're an old married woman.'

When we met at the pavement tables of the Café Massena at two, I told the others what Mrs Richardson had learned from her police admirer.

'It took the Regency staff eight days to fathom out what method we were using,' I said. 'You can take it the staff here is much more professional. Once we have been identified and they have discovered our method there are many ways they can put pressure on us, so let's try to keep one jump ahead. Don't let anyone see what you're writing in your notepad. I'm inclined to believe your police friend was telling the truth, Emma. In a gaming industry of this size nothing would be left to chance. I want you to watch for any new faces among the croupiers. From now on you must place your stakes on the table only *after* the tourneur has thrown the ball. I'm not saying the game will be rigged, but the longer we keep them in the dark the better. You'll all be covering the same chance as yesterday. By the way, where's Mr Sherlock?'

'He's asked me to take his turn this afternoon and he'll do mine tonight,' said Keith Robinson, who was wearing new and expensive sunglasses.

'Something wrong with him?'

'He's got a bit of a headache, hasn't he?'

'Well?' said Blake coldly. 'Has he or hasn't he?'

Robinson turned his dark glasses in Blake's direction. 'I just told you he had, didn't I?'

'We had a drop of champagne last night at the hotel,' Terry Baker said.

Robinson groaned theatrically, 'More'n a drop. We didn't get to bed till eight this morning, did we?'

'What you mean is that Sherlock is too drunk to get out of bed,' Blake snapped. Robinson turned the dark glasses on him once more.

'You could say that, Olly old boy,' he said slowly and with more than a hint of menace, 'if it was any of your business.'

I intervened before Blake could react to what was clearly a challenge. 'I don't care in the least what you all do in your spare time but I must insist on being consulted before anyone changes shifts.'

'I could go back and roust him out of his pit,' Robinson said.

'No, if he's under the weather he'd go through hell this afternoon in there,' I said. 'The heat will be fantastic.'

'May I put in a word, Mr Leigh?' said Blake, dressed despite the temperature in his usual rig-out of heavy blue pinstripe suit, with waistcoat, stiff white collar and tightly knotted Old Etonian tie. I wondered if he had enjoyed the rampant informality of the beach. 'From our experiences in the Regency I'd say that casinos prefer to harass a winning team and provoke incidents that give them the excuse of bad behaviour for banning people. I'd suggest we make doubly sure we are on our best behaviour and avoid *any* kind of incident.'

'I agree. And under no circumstances allow yourselves to be questioned by the staff without either Mr Blake or myself being present. Well now, two forty-five. Shall we go across?'

Walking across the square in blinding sunshine, I caught up with Robinson.

'You seem a bit tetchy with Blake,' I said quietly. 'I hope you're not letting his little mannerisms rub you up the wrong way.'

'Every time he opens his bloody mouth he gives me a pain.'

'He can't help the way he speaks.'

136

'Go on, nobody talks like that for real.'

'For Christ's sake, if you're going to be foolish enough to develop a phobia about Blake and the way he talks, you're going to ruin this team's chances of success and lose us all a lot of money. Pull yourself together!'

'Yes, you're right. I'll feel better once this hangover's gone. Expensive down here, innit? I think we were paying ten quid a bottle for the bubbly.'

'It's one of the most expensive places in the world.'

'Sure is: even if you win you still lose.'

As we stepped out of the blinding sunshine into the shade of the casino stairway I said to Mrs Harper-Biggs and Mrs Heppenstall that if they found the heat too much I would arrange to have them relieved for a rest.

'*Heat?*' said Mrs Harper-Biggs, who was wearing her usual tweeds and carrying a string bag big enough to hold a large dog. 'I don't call this heat. Herbert and I spent some years in the Belgian Congo; *that's* what I call heat, Mr Leigh.'

'I bought myself a new summer dress this morning,' said Mrs Heppenstall with a guilty little giggle.

'Yes, Lettice and I went on a *most* extravagant shopping spree,' said Mrs Harper-Biggs.

'I daresay we'll be hearing next that you've both been on champagne binges,' I remarked.

The little widow from Hastings looked shocked. 'Oh, Mr Leigh! As if we would!'

The salon was fairly busy, the usual mixture, aged relics of bygone days stalking among the genuinely affluent of many nationalities, here and there groups of curious tourists nervously building up courage for a flutter. The first shift came to the table in twos and threes, trying to create as little attention as possible among the other players. Once they were seated I had a quiet word with Blake.

'Be careful not to let any tension build up between you and Robinson,' I said. 'It's up to you and me to handle everybody with tact. We're operating at the bare minimum and we can't afford the risk of losing anyone through heavy-handedness.'

'If we let slackness creep in we may lose the whole lot,' he replied stiffly. 'What are you going to do about Sherlock?'

'I'll have a word with him. He did make sure he had a replacement.'

'You don't think some sort of fine would be in order?'

'If I thought he was going to let me down, I'd suggest a good flogging, but this isn't the Foreign Legion.'

It took a couple of hours before anything happened that second afternoon. Keith Robinson had the beginnings of a progression on black, but it petered out before his line produced stakes in the hundreds. (The exchange rate at that time was approximately 13.7 new francs to the pound [4.94 francs to the dollar]; the table minimum was 5 francs and the maximum, on even chances, 2,600 francs [£190 – $525].)

Half an hour later black again began to predominate over red by slightly more than 2 to 1. As his staking calculations began to involve him in four-digit additions he kept licking his lips and frowning. Time and time again his scribbled calculations gave him the amount he had to stake with just enough time to grab the right selection of plaques and chips. He had not been playing long enough in the Casino Municipale to know automatically which colours of plaques and chips represented different values. Adding sums like 179 and 1,554 is not difficult in normal circumstances, but at the table the seconds are racing towards the next play and those figures represent real money to be won or lost depending on how accurate you are.

Besides watching over Robinson's shoulder I also had to keep an eye on Mrs Harper-Biggs, who was showing signs of being in trouble. Normally a roulette table has nine or ten players seated and perhaps another twenty standing. As the news of Keith's winning progression spread through the salon more people began to congregate at our table. As Keith started piling up the plaques and chips the crowd grew thicker, pressing closer to see what he was betting on. Some even tried to count the exact number of chips he was staking so that they, too, could stake the same amount and thereby, they hoped, be brushed by the magic of success.

By the time Keith's progression had taken him to stakes of above 1,000 francs there must have been a hundred people jammed round the table. Once again we heard the slow rhythm of the coded handclaps as the croupiers alerted officials in other parts of the large salon. Black came up three times in succession. His stakes rose, nearing the table limit of 2,600 francs. People pushed and craned from the back to get a glimpse of the action.

'The temperature must be into the hundreds in here,' Blake said, perspiration forming on his forehead and his pale, fleshy cheeks.

'I think Mrs Harper-Biggs is looking a bit shaky too,' I said.

'If she faints, I'll take over her chair,' said Blake. I realized with some slight sense of surprise that I had been worrying more about Mrs Harper-Biggs herself than about missing a few spins.

She did not faint, however, and at 5.45 p.m. the Chef de Partie, the table supervisor, had to announce that play was stopping temporarily at this table.

'He's broken the table,' Blake said excitedly. 'I take back all I said about him.'

Keith sat there calmly sorting out his winnings while the crowd stared at him. Those nearest asked him what system he had been using. He gave them cheery little winks, lifting the 1,000- and 500-franc plaques into his jacket pockets.

With an interval of around twenty minutes before fresh reserves of chips and plaques could be brought to the table the crowd began to dissipate, and I picked up Keith's notepad to see what he had won. There were too many uncrossed figures to add up in my head.

'It looks like something around sixty thousand francs,' I said to him.

He nodded, giving Blake a knowing smile. 'Should be enough for a few magnums there, eh, *Oliver*?'

Blake managed a smile.

One person who did not drift away from the table during the lull was my old friend the Chef de Casino, the director of the establishment. He stood behind the tourneur eyeing Keith thoughtfully.

When play started again the crowd returned to see more fireworks. But what was there now to see? Keith had pocketed his winnings and had written 1, 2, 3, 4 in the top left-hand corner of a fresh page in his pad. What excitement was there in watching someone bet 5 miserable francs?

The second shift began arriving between eight and nine.

Moving far enough from the table to avoid being overheard, I beckoned Alec Sherlock over. He looked uneasy.

'Look,' I said, 'I don't care how drunk you get at night but I must remind you of the group's rules. If you think you'd prefer to be on the second shift, I'll switch you over and you can sleep all afternoon.'

'That would be better actually,' he said. 'I'm sorry about –'

'These things can happen to anyone. You're due to cover black – better get in position behind Keith now. With a crowd like that we'll lose the seats if we aren't spot on.'

'Yes, okay. There's just one thing – could you lend me some money?'

'I shouldn't leave it lying about your hotel room. Or have you posted it home already? I should keep –'

'No, I haven't done that.'

'You mean you – but you had four hundred pounds from the share-out last night!'

'I was a fool,' he said, shuddering.

'What happened?'

'Well, Keith and Terry and I had a few drinks in the hotel and these girls appeared and – oh God. I was as drunk as a lord. When I woke up this morning she was gone and so was the money.'

'*All* of it?' He nodded. 'Well, who was she? The hotel staff must know her. Ordinarily I'd tell you to write it off as experience, but four hundred pounds is too expensive a lesson. The police –'

'She didn't steal it. I gave it to her.'

'You did *what*?'

Blake came up and tapped my elbow. 'I think Mrs Richardson is on to something,' he said.

'I'll be with you in a moment.' I waited until he was out of range. 'I'll lend you two hundred francs. You'd better cure yourself of these generous impulses.'

'Don't worry. I've learned my lesson, Norman,' he said fervently.

I went back to the table. Mrs Richardson was into a sequence where red predominated over black by roughly 5 to 2. It was one of those progressions which showed little initial promise, always threatening to peter out and then coming to life again when she

140

had only two uncrossed figures on her line and one more loss would have sent her back to 1, 2, 3, 4.

No longer the half-clad girlish figure of our morning tête-a-tête but wearing the black cocktail dress she kept for casino work, she looked incredibly attractive. Possibly the best arithmetician in the group, she could do all her calculations without writing them down and always had time to spare for her selection of chips. The more she won the more relaxed she became.

She had been sitting at the table for six hours and forty minutes when she came near the limit of 2,600 francs. Peter Vincent should have taken over her chair at 9 p.m., but I had told him not to break into her progression.

Again we had the complete paraphernalia, the agitated curiosity of the chattering crowd, the softly insistent hand-clapping of the croupiers, the arrival of the senior staff, the unemotional calls of the tourneur – and then, the moment which always floored staff and spectators alike, the moment that was so crucial to our success and which so mystified everyone else, when she crossed out the line of figures she had been working on, turned to a new page, wrote 1, 2, 3, 4, selected a pink 5-franc chip and placed it on the section of the green baize marked red.

She had reached the limit and won, at the subsequent count, 39,375 francs – £2,800 ($8,000)!

'In you go,' I said to Vincent. Mrs Richardson rose, and he eased into her place before any of those crowded behind realized a switch was taking place.

I went with her to the cash desk, Blake being at the table by then with the second shift. She was as fresh as the dew, but I had been on my feet since 3 p.m. When she suggested I go with her and the other two ladies, Lettice and Cynthia (Mrs Harper-Biggs' other name, it appeared), to her apartment for coffee, I was tempted to call it a day.

It was as well I did decide to stick it out until close of play at 3 a.m. Hopplewell had been having one of those frustrating sessions which rarely got beyond stakes of 20 francs. As quickly as he wrote down a fresh line of 1, 2, 3, 4 the wheel went against him and he had to cross the line out and start again.

At 1.30 a.m., when only the obsessed and the insomniac remained at the tables besides the eternally bland and tireless

141

staff, the wheel began to run for him. He was betting on *pair*, the even numbers. The ball began to fall in even numbers three times to every once it landed in an odd number.

His mushroom went fairly quickly. This time, however, with fewer people in the casino, there was not such a crowd round the table and when the inevitable ritual of the coded handclaps drew what seemed like the entire management to his table there seemed to be more staff present than patrons.

'I have a distinct feeling they're ready to take steps against us,' Blake said to me without looking round. I looked at my watch.

'They'll have to look sharp about it,' I said. 'There's only half an hour to go.' I saw Hopplewell saying something quickly to a waiter between spins. In a few minutes the waiter reappeared and set a brandy glass down beside his pile of winning plaques and chips. 'Likes a brandy, does our Mr Hopplewell,' Blake muttered. 'You know that's his seventh since we sat down?'

'Hardly more than one an hour, is it? Doesn't seem to be affecting him much.'

Blake placed a stake of 76 francs on red. It lost, and he deleted the last two figures of that sequence. Hopplewell had won, however. Brandy glass in his left hand, he did his paperwork with his right hand and then frowned. He was too tired on this occasion to think of showing off. I saw him drag the pen through his page of figures. He had reached the limit.

He and the other five played out the last few spins and then it was all over for another day. We went to the cash desk. Hopplewell had won 33,125 francs.

'My God, I feel as if I've been down the mines for a fortnight,' Milton groaned. 'The only thing that could revive me right now is a large Scotch.'

'The sight of the loot's my tonic,' said Keith Robinson, who had come back to the casino after eating. 'How much did we take the frogs for today, Oliver?'

Onto Blake's Georgian dining table dropped the wads of French currency. 'It seems to come to one hundred and thirty thousand four hundred and fifty francs,' Blake said.

Robinson squinted at the notes. 'Very colourful,' he said. 'Who's the geezers they've got here instead of the Queen?'

'That's Pascal,' I said, pointing to a 500-franc note. 'Ironically enough, some historians believe he started roulette. He was a philosopher investigating the laws of chance with a cartwheel in his yard, spinning it to see where it stopped. He had to stop work when it rained so he had a miniature wheel made for indoor work. The other one is Cardinal Richelieu.'

Keith looked at me and nodded approvingly. 'Pascal the rascal, eh? Did us a good turn, didn't he, brainy old bastard.'

Blake began to write in his cash book. Like everything else about him his numerals were almost painfully neat and correct.

Vincent yawned and said, 'About ten thousand pounds, isn't it?'

Blake pointedly ignored this statement. Eventually he looked up and said, 'It's nine thousand five hundred and twenty-one pounds with about eight francs left over [$26,600].'

'I never was any good at maths,' Vincent drawled. Blake again ignored him determinedly. Reading from his cash book, he said that he and I were due 13,045 francs each and that the balance of 104,360 francs split eleven ways produced a share of 9,487 francs each, or £690 ($1,930).

Vincent, Hopplewell, Sherlock, Milton, Robinson, Fredericks, and I each took a wad of francs from Blake, who then filled a white envelope for each of those who had preferred to turn in. It was now 4 a.m.

'I thought we might all have a snort or two to mark our success,' Blake said stiffly. Whether he liked Vincent or not, good form decreed that the invitation should include everybody.

'I've never been one for stag parties much, ducks,' said Vincent, drooping a queenly wrist and then mincing across the room to the door.

'Did you say something about a brandy?' Hopplewell asked gruffly, when he had gone.

'Yes, of course.' Blake produced a bottle of five-star and some glasses from the cocktail cabinet. As he was pouring Hopplewell remarked: 'Damned hot in there today.' Blake handed him his glass. He drank it all and held the glass out. 'Bad for the throat, smoky atmosphere like that,' he grunted, leaving Blake little option but to pour him a refill.

'Couldn't one of us tactfully suggest to Mrs Harper-Biggs that

143

she might wear something a little more suited to this climate,' Fredericks said. 'Poor old thing was near to fainting this afternoon.'

'I'll mention it to Emma,' I said.

'It's the damned smoke, gets in your chest,' said Hopplewell coughing and tapping his throat.

'There's one thing strikes me,' said Milton. 'It was the same in the Regency – what really gets their goats, those casino wallahs, is not so much that we win a lot of money. It's the way we immediately go back to one, two, three, four. That really sickens them.'

'I quite enjoy watching their faces when we have a mushroom,' said Fredericks, beaming gleefully, clearly just beginning to realize he did not have to apologize for his existence.

'Yes, it is a bit strong,' said Robinson. 'I mean, one minute we're taking them for thousands of francs, next we're putting on a measly five. We ought to put on a few silly bets just to give them some of the loot back.'

'No, seriously,' said Milton, 'it does ram it down their throats a bit.'

Hopplewell made a few coughing noises. 'Must do something to clear this up,' he said, reaching for the brandy bottle. 'Don't mind, do you, Blake?'

He was already pouring when Blake said no, of course not, by all means, at the same time glancing at me meaningfully. Hopplewell sat down. His face looked slightly bluish, but that could have been the light. He didn't seem drunk.

'Is there any way we could make the drop in stakes less obvious?' said Sherlock.

'I'm afraid not,' I said, 'apart from deliberately throwing away money as Keith suggested. Stopping as soon as the progression reaches the limit is the linchpin of the whole scheme. We only bet when the percentages suit us and we don't give them a chance to win the money back.'

'Forgive my stupidity, but could you tell me again why it is exactly we have to go back to a five-franc bet as soon as we reach the limit or break the table?' Fredericks asked. I was astonished that he had come this far without grasping the point.

'The method depends on the ability to increase your bets while you're winning,' I said as patiently as possible. 'If we carried on betting at the limit, the table would have an even chance of winning the money back without our being able to compensate with higher bets. Suppose you have two thousand pounds in front of you after a long upwards progression. If you go on betting at two thousand pounds, you immediately cease to be a system player – you're exactly in the position of a man who comes to the table with two thousand pounds and starts betting on an even chance at the maximum. Would you do that with two thousand of your own money?'

'Yes, but we're not risking our own money. All that two thousand has just come from the table.'

'Exactly. And we want to keep it, don't we? The seeds of our own destruction lie within all of us. The system safeguards us against our own human weaknesses. Study the case history of any compulsive gambler and you will see the pattern – he starts with a big win and spends or ruins the rest of his life trying to recapture that magic moment. Left to ourselves without a rigid frame of rules we would all succumb to temptation. Win two thousand and we want to make it four. Lose two thousand and we would try to win it back, and lose another two thousand in the process. The system *forces* us to be clever, to give up while we are ahead. Do you think you've grasped it now?'

'Yes,' said Fredericks, no doubt wishing he had never opened his mouth. Hopplewell made some chesty noises and reached for the brandy bottle. Blake wasted no time with subtle hints but stood up and said it was time he drove me to my hotel. Hopplewell pretended that he had only picked up the bottle to read the label. 'Good stuff that,' he said. 'Must get some for my cough.'

We all left Blake's hotel and said our farewells on the pavement in the comparatively cool air of pre-dawn.

As soon as Blake and I were alone in his Sunbeam Alpine he said, 'I have no doubt we shall be banned within the next forty-eight hours.'

'Why do you say that?'

'Did you see their faces when we left tonight? They were positively malevolent.'

'They'll think hard before they ban us merely for winning,

145

especially a government-run municipal casino. Wouldn't be good for business.'

'Do you think they'll worry about their public relations if they go on losing ten thousand pounds a day? I think not.'

'If they ban us, they ban us, and that will be that. As long as we have committed no crime –'

'We have committed the unpardonable crime of being successful. By the way, Hopplewell was punishing the brandy in no uncertain fashion.'

'Doesn't seem to have much effect on him.'

'That might be a bad sign. Know much about the man?'

'Not a great deal. He owns several companies. I don't know what line he's in.'

'Looks prosperous enough. Wonder why he joined a scheme like this.'

'He told me it was purely a business speculation – he hates gambling, he said. Come to that, why did you join?'

He hesitated, sensing the dangerous currents of personal intimacy. I was too tired to care. It wasn't until we were outside my hotel that he turned towards me with some deliberation.

'Back there in my digs – I think that was the single most satisfying moment of my life. Would you really like to know why I came on this trip?'

Groaning inwardly at my own stupidity, I closed the door again and prepared for the stiff upper lip to pour out repressed emotions.

'I suppose it sounds rather vulgar but obviously I do not need this money.' After a short but awkward silence he went on: 'Perhaps that's wrong. I don't need money as such, but I do need *this* money. Does that make sense?'

'Not exactly.'

'I've had money all my life. Born into the stuff; never been without it. Nothing but Eton was good enough for *my* father's son. Eton, Oxford – I even had a year at Harvard. Straight into the family firm. Easy progress to the day when I would take over – hard work of course but many, many compensations. People like to say money has its own problems – generally people with no money. I've never found any problems. Quite the reverse. It's too easy, life, if you have money. Look, you may not believe this,

146

but that money we shared out – it's given me more satisfaction than anything else in my whole life. I mean it. It didn't come through my father or my accent or my Eton connections. No, I made it in a venture where none of that counted, something my father had no hand in. Not that I dislike the –'

'I understand,' I said, wondering if his invitation to swim with Mrs Richardson indicated another area in which he wished to prove his independence.

2 October, our third day; temperature 90 degrees Fahrenheit. I spent the morning sitting outside a café near my hotel, having a dry martini before buying a packet of envelopes and stamps for sending home some of the 21,000 francs (approximately £1,500 – $4,200) I had won in these first two days. Life seemed very good, sitting in the sun. Pauline was coming down as soon as she could get on a flight, probably tomorrow. At last she would see that I was making the wild dream work.

I had seen the corpulent man in the pink shirt and dark glasses walk past the café but had taken no great interest in him at the time. Then I saw him stop, turn round and come back through the tables towards me.

'Monsieur, may I introduce myself?' he said. 'My name is Charles Berteille. I have seen you and your friends at the casino.'

'Have you?' I said, pleasantly enough.

'May I sit with you? Forgive my intrusion.' He snapped finger and thumb to attract a waiter. 'Would Monsieur like –'

'No, thank you.'

He ordered cognac. 'I am from Perpignan. I own a small factory,' he said. I nodded. Leaning across the table, he said in a much lower voice, 'I have been gambling in the casino for three months and you and your friends are the first people I have seen winning with such regularity. Amazing.'

'Yes, we've been rather lucky.'

'Lucky?' He leaned even closer. 'Are you moving from casino to casino or is your intention to concentrate on the Casino Municipale here?'

'Why do you ask?'

'Have you ever thought of what happens to people who win large sums from a casino with consistency?'

'They get rich, I suppose.'

'Perhaps. There is a book you should read, by a German baron. He has evidence that over the years numbers of people have disappeared both here on the Côte d'Azur and in Monte Carlo. The common denominator in their disappearance was that they had been winning large sums of money over a long period.'

'Perhaps they were tired of their wives.'

'You always joke, you English. I was in London through the war. I have many good English friends. That is why I wanted to speak to you when I saw you sitting here. You are already well known in this town, monsieur, you and your friends, especially the young men who hold the wild parties.'

'Must be some other people you're thinking of,' I said. 'My friends are very respectable, no wild parties.'

'No?' He examined my face, then shrugged. Drinking his cognac in the precise French way, he put down the glass and looked at me again.

'Wonderful weather for October,' I said.

'You may laugh at me, monsieur, but because I like the English so much I want to warn you. You should listen.'

'I must say, you speak English quite well,' I said pleasantly. He went off abruptly, apparently insulted. I paid my *addition* and went back to the hotel.

It took me half an hour to address eight or nine envelopes. Each contained three or four 100-franc notes or one 500-franc note, folded into sheets of blank notepaper. I posted these in different boxes and had lunch on my own. It was 2.40 p.m. when I arrived at the Café Massena. The first shift was preparing to cross the square to the casino. They all seemed in good spirits. Fredericks said he had noticed that the players here tipped the croupiers a good deal more than in the Regency.

'I object to tipping them in principle,' I said, 'but it probably makes them more congenial. No more than forty francs, though, and only at the end of your shift.'

'They do seem very friendly and helpful,' said Mrs Heppenstall.

148

'They must be very clever: all those people putting down chips on different numbers yet they never make mistakes, do they? I could never remember which players put on all those different stakes.'

'They're highly trained – they have to be. But don't make the mistake of regarding them as your friends.'

'Are they – you know – gigolos?' Mrs Heppenstall asked timidly.

'Don't fall for one of them if that's what you mean,' I said sternly. 'You may well find yourself involved with the fringes of criminal life.'

'Oh, Mr Leigh! As if I ever would!'

I patted her on the shoulder and said we would keep an eye on her nevertheless.

We had to wait only thirty minutes for the first progression to appear. Hopplewell had asked for a switch to the first shift because, he alleged, he preferred to get to bed before dawn. He had taken over black from Sherlock, who had moved to the second shift.

(The first shift in full consisted of Mrs Richardson, on red; Hopplewell, black; Mrs Heppenstall, *pair* (even); Mrs Harper-Biggs, *impair* (odd); Maurice Nathan, *manque* (low); George Milton, *passe* (high). Covering these chances in the same order for the second shift were Blake, Fredericks, Sherlock, Robinson, Vincent and Baker.)

In something like sixty-two spins Hopplewell was getting very near the table limit of 2,600 francs. He had been chasing this progression for two hours (the longest time span of the progressions we had had so far had been about three hours, the shortest an hour). His progress had been accompanied by the usual handclapping, the gathering of an excited crowd and the stern attentions of the senior staff, though not, on this occasion, those of the tireless Chef de Casino.

Hopplewell's line read 285, 360, 435, 526, 633, 740, 847, 978, 1,109, 1,240, 1,399, 1,554, 1,709, 1,864, 2,043, 2,222. His next bet would have been $285 + 2,222 = 2,507$, which was a bare 93 francs below the maximum stake. This line of figures of course represented winning bets, which meant that he had plaques and chips worth about 18,000 francs piled up in front of him on the green baize.

One more win would have taken him over the limit – and produced total winnings for the progression of over 20,000 francs, approximately £1,500 ($4,000).

The wheel, however, decided to tantalize him and his next bet did not win. He scored out the figures at either end of the line. His next stake was $360 + 2,043 = 2,403$ francs. It lost as well. Again he had to score out the end figures. With stakes of that size it does not take too many losing bets for the accumulated winnings to start shrinking. Having favoured black for two hours, the wheel developed a strong preference for red. While this looked as though it might wipe out Hopplewell's profits it naturally gave Mrs Richardson the beginnings of a mushroom, which was, of course, the great strength of playing as a team covering all the even chances simultaneously. The wheel does not often throw up a sequence long enough to take a player to the table limit (once every six days, I had worked out), but when it does a team of six acting as a collective unit must reap the profits.

On the other hand, every scientific law states quite categorically that each spin is a random event entirely disconnected from all previous and all future spins. Hopplewell had gone a long way on a sequence which favoured his chance, black, but just as the finishing tape was in sight it looked as if all his winnings were to be taken back. Why did he not stop betting as soon as he felt that his luck had run out and save some of the winnings? Because we were playing to a strictly ordained method; allow each player to exert individual choice based on a feeling or a hunch and the whole thing would have collapsed.

Hopplewell's next stake was $435 + 1,864 = 2,299$. As he was putting it on I listened to a conversation between an elderly Frenchman and two younger men whom I took to be his sons. He was explaining what Hopplewell was doing, and I was surprised to realize that despite all precautionary measures – hiding what was on the notepads and placing stakes at the last moment – this man had grasped completely the staking principle of the Reverse Labouchère.

150

Hopplewell lost again. His line now read 526, 633, 740, 847, 978, 1,109, 1,240, 1,399, 1,554, 1,709. His next stake was, therefore, 526 + 1,709 = 2,235.

This time he won. His next stake would have been 526 + 2,235 = 2,761, over the limit. That little adverse sequence at the end had more or less halved his winnings, which were, if you care to add up that last list of figures, 10,735 francs.

As soon as he had scored out that page and written 1, 2, 3, 4 in the corner of the next sheet of his pad, Hopplewell began to look round in an anxious fashion.

'Is there something wrong?' I asked him.

'Oh yes,' he said, patting his chest and giving a few rasping coughs. 'Can you see a bloody waiter, my throat's terrible.'

Looking round for a waiter, I caught sight of Blake. He came as near as the crowd permitted, and I asked him to order a large brandy for Hopplewell. When I turned back to the table I saw that the spotlight had fallen on George Milton. He was getting a predominance on *passe* (the numbers nineteen to thirty-six on the wheel) of 3 to 1. Paradoxically, too many wins at the early stage of a progression are something of a handicap; if you start with 1, 2, 3, 4 and keep winning three times to every once that you lose it takes a long time for the stake to get into three figures. If you start with 1, 2 ,3, 4 and win your first twenty consecutive bets, these low figures are never deleted, and each stake increases by only one unit. Ideally what you want are just enough wins to keep the line from being deleted altogether at the early stages, a predominance of 5 to 2 or 7 to 3 in your favour. By spin 22 you may have a line that reads 16, 24, 34, 50. That means forty-five minutes in which you have won 124 units. However, you have got rid of the smallest numbers, and if you go on enjoying a 5 to 2 predominance, the stakes will begin to mushroom quite quickly. Then, ideally, you want the last lap of the progression to coincide with a greater predominance in your favour – 3 to 1 being ideal. This means you finish with a fair number of winning bets at high stakes.

It was about half-past five when Milton's staking progression brought him to the limit. He had won 21,680 francs. Back he went to 1, 2, 3, 4. From what I could see over the heads of those crowded round the table the rest of the salon was pretty well deserted. I looked for the Chef de Casino and saw him standing beside the Chef de Partie, his face impassive.

Around 6.45 p.m. Mrs Richardson went into a progression on red. This one lasted well over two hours. Although she was on the other side of the table from where I was standing, with her left hand shielding her notepad from prying eyes, I could follow her staking pattern well enough to know that it was one of those mushrooms which continually look like petering out. That meant her line was often reduced to only two figures before another sequence of wins brought it back to life. These slow ones often won most in the end, if they lasted.

This one did. Shortly before the shifts were due to change over the Chef de Partie announced that the table was closing temporarily. Mrs Richardson had broken it. A complete hush fell on the mob round the table. As she began to put the large plaques into her handbag Mrs Richardson might have been on a stage in front of a silently engrossed theatre audience. Nobody moved. I kept my eyes on the Chef de Casino.

For a few long seconds he stood there motionless. Then he said something to the tourneur. The message was passed to the croupier. No announcement was made, but the table staff left their posts.

'Are they going to bring more chips?' Mrs Richardson asked me when I moved round the table.

'It doesn't look like it. You did very well there.'

'Funny, you hardly notice the crowd and the hand-clapping after a while. Where has all the glamour gone? I feel that I'm just doing a job.'

'That's good. Let's have a look at your figures and we'll see how much you've won.'

'I've added them already. It's thirty-three thousand, seven hundred and fifty francs. By the way, I heard one of those bigwigs saying something about tabulating our results – it was time they started tabulating our results. What would that mean?'

'They want to know exactly how we're working. It's an obvious move.'

An announcement was then made that our table had been closed for the day. Everybody had to move to another table. In the general confusion only Mrs Harper-Biggs and Mrs Heppenstall were lucky enough to get seats. Mrs Richardson told us later how it felt to stand.

'That was really like hard work. I honestly hoped I wouldn't get a progression because it would have been so difficult to concentrate with all those people jostling around – my handbag with my chips in one hand, trying to do my paperwork with my pad balanced on my arm. I won't be wearing such high heels when I'm playing in future, that's a certainty.'

The fact was that she had shown more guts than most men I had known. Like the rest of the group she had very little previous experience at roulette and therefore had no idea just how arduous a task they were being asked to perform. I have known scores of alleged devotees of the game who regard a couple of hours at the table as hard work. Even then they are liable to become bored and start playing single numbers on hunches to break what they call the 'monotony'. What I required of my twelve players was that they become professional roulette players in the strict sense of the word – instantly. If they had spent more time in casinos, they would have realized how much I was asking of them. I did not feel any purpose would be served by bringing this to their attention – it isn't the narrowness of the tightrope that upsets the balance but the drop below. My little band was walking the tightrope blindfold and nobody had told them that it was impossible.

Blake was coming from the bar when he noticed a group of smartly dressed men having words with the Chef de Casino. He pointed them out to me. It was obvious they were discussing us.

'Who do you think they are?' he asked.

'Officials of some description. They can stand there and discuss us all night for all I care.'

'I met Vincent down at the seafront this afternoon,' said Blake. 'He had some girl in tow. It's difficult to get much out of him, but he did tell me that Robinson and Baker and Sherlock are becoming a bit of a public scandal in this town. Did you know that they're throwing *orgies?*'

'Baker – throwing orgies?' I said. 'I can hardly believe that. He's been posting his winnings home – he told me that, anyway.'

'I should press him harder on that score. Hasn't he got a wife and young child?'

'Yes, they're due to join him down here in a day or two. My wife is arriving tomorrow. I think we should have a serious chat after play finishes tonight.'

We had no more progressions that day. While Blake was cashing up at the desk I got hold of Terry Baker and suggested we walk to Blake's hotel so that we could have a little chat.

It was a ten-minute walk. At first he stuck to his story that he had been sending most of his winnings home. I said I wondered who then was paying for the champagne parties I had been hearing about. He said that he and Alec Sherlock and Keith Robinson had been having a bottle or two of champagne once the casino had closed, that was all.

'And when is your wife arriving?'

'I'm phoning her in the morning. The baby had a bit of a temperature when I last called her, but if it clears up she's flying down the day after tomorrow.'

'Just as well, possibly.'

'What do you mean?'

'It won't cost me any sleep one way or the other, but if you don't come out of this with a reasonable amount of money, it will all have been a dreadful mistake, won't it?'

'I don't know what you're on about,' he said heatedly. 'I've spent a few quid, but we're making plenty, aren't we? No point in pulling a stroke like this if we've got to live like monks, is there?'

'It's your life.'

At the meeting I said that the casino management obviously knew now that they had a problem on their hands and that we should stay alert for any form of provocation designed to foment incidents.

'I should also bear in mind that these casinos come under the auspices of the French government. Indirectly we are challenging the state. I want to remind you all that we are in a foreign country and one whose civilized approach to life goes hand in hand with a certain brutal logic as far as threats to its interests are concerned. If they can't find an excuse to bar us from the casino they might try to find evidence for classifying us as undesirable aliens. I should be extremely careful of the company you keep.'

'Yeah, there's lots of thieves and villains about,' said Keith Robinson, giving me a wink. 'So, how's about divvying up the lolly, Olly – sorry, Oliver.'

Blake gave his daily treasurer's report. The total winnings from three progressions were 66,165 francs. He and I had 6,616 francs each (£482 – $1,350), leaving 52,933 francs to be split eleven ways, a share each of 4,812 francs (£350 – $982).

As soon as they had the money in their hands Robinson, Sherlock and Baker were off. Blake asked the rest of us to stay for a coffee or a brandy. I preferred some exercise.

'I think I'll get some fresh air into my lungs. Fancy a walk, Emma?'

Walking through the quiet streets in the soft Mediterranean night Mrs Richardson and I decided to have a glass of wine at a bistro. We sat at a table by the open door. She lit a Disque Bleu.

'Changed your brand, I see,' I said.

The waiter brought us two glasses and a bottle of Châteauneuf du Pape.

'Can't get mine down here,' she said. 'Still, these are cheap enough.'

'I'm glad the money isn't going to your head. I wish I could say the same about some of the others.'

'You mean the three musketeers?' She blew smoke at the ceiling.

'If they want to make fools of themselves, they are perfectly welcome. My only concern is that they ruin the whole thing for everybody else, by getting in trouble.'

'I think Terry's feeling guilty, but he doesn't want the other two to think he's a goody-goody. They had another swing-ding last night. Keith was boasting that he spent three hundred pounds on champagne alone. And Alec Sherlock – women? You'd think he'd just found out women existed.'

'I don't care what they do as long as they turn up on time and stay sober enough to play the system.'

'Alec Sherlock is a real surprise. Would you have guessed he would turn out to be – well, what do *you* call it?'

'Sex mad? Perhaps he wasn't until we came down here. Inter-

155

esting the way various people react when money starts flowing in.'

'It makes me quite angry. If I wasn't a respectable old married woman, I might try to get them to squander some of it on me.'

'Ah, yes, the old married woman. More wine? Lovely night, isn't it? Strange thing about money. Those who've never had it and need it most spent it fastest, while those who're used to it like Blake and yourself and – '

'I hope you're not classing me with Blake!'

'You know what I mean, people who have money – '

'Norman, you've got it all wrong. All this Brigadier nonsense – it is just a joke. You do know that, don't you? Would you like me to tell you what George's last job was?'

'If you want to.'

'He was a butler! As a matter of fact he is now an out-of-work butler.'

'Really?'

'He wasn't always a butler. He used to run a coffee plantation in Kenya, but after independence there was a big campaign to give Africans the good jobs. Poor George had to come back to an England he hardly knew and didn't like. He was too old to get another job at the same level. He's tried lots of things, but you know how it is. After a lifetime giving orders he finds it hard to take them, especially from jumped-up nobodies who've never been anywhere. Of course I make good money as a commercial designer, but he doesn't like living off me. He even tried to be a film extra! Somebody told him there was a part for a distinguished-looking man to play a butler. He didn't get it, but he said he might as well go the whole hog and *be* a butler – make a joke of out of it. Said it was the only way he could at least still *see* the standard of living he'd been used to. He didn't last long, of course.'

'What about your job?'

'I'm a free-lancer. This is my holiday for the year. I can always get plenty of work. You see, what we'd really like to do is buy a small hotel somewhere on the south coast, Chichester maybe. That's why your scheme appealed to us so much, the chance to make some money tax-free. I've been posting it home like mad!'

'Wouldn't it have been more sensible for your husband to play roulette and you to carry on working?'

She shrugged. 'He knows himself too well. He wouldn't have been any good in a group effort unless he was the boss. Well, I've given you my secrets. What are yours?'

'I have no secrets.'

'Go on, you're one of the cagiest men I've ever known. All this organizing and dedication to take money from this casino? You don't think I haven't noticed that every time somebody asks you what's so special about this casino you change the subject?'

'It's very simple. I played here a long time ago with my father and watched him lose every penny we had.' I paused, then continued: 'And I can still remember the face of the Chef de Casino convulsing himself with laughter.'

'I see, revenge.'

'Nothing so dramatic. Just remember that I want you and the rest, and *myself*, to be convinced of one thing. I am not an unusually emotional or obsessive man. I have brought us together for rational, cordial, commercial motives and nothing else. Understand?'

She looked at me curiously. 'We've only been here a few days, and already I have the distinct impression that nobody is what I thought they were back in London.'

The bottle was finished. 'I'll walk you back to your hotel,' I said.

When I reached my hotel day had dawned and I was meeting people who had just risen from a decent night's sleep. I felt grey and weary. Two messages had been shoved under my door, one to say that Pauline had phoned and would phone back, the second to say that she had phoned back and would be arriving on the midday flight from London. I got my head down at half-past seven.

Despite the heat I slept soundly until about eleven when Blake arrived downstairs in a state of some agitation.

Chapter Twelve

'I decided to go out for breakfast,' Blake said. 'I was tucking into a plate of bacon and eggs in one of those small places near the Quai. The bill came to about forty francs. I gave the waiter a five-hundred-franc note – we've been seeing so many of them I'd almost forgotten they were anything out of the ordinary. He still hadn't brought my change after ten minutes, so I went to the cash desk. Suddenly two men appeared and asked me to go with them to the manager's office. Police! They made me sit down and asked me a lot of questions about where I had obtained the five-hundred-franc note. I asked if it were forged, and they said no, but these large notes were being passed all over the town and they wanted to know the source.'

'What did you tell them?' I asked, pouring more black coffee.

'What else but the truth? I said I was playing roulette in the Casino Municipale and had been fortunate enough to win substantially. Do you know, one of them more or less called me a liar to my face! That did it as far as I was concerned. I asked if they were charging me with anything. They said no, so I went to the cash desk and demanded my change – then simply walked out. Do you think it's significant?'

'Five-hundred-franc notes *are* on the conspicuous side. We want to draw as little attention to ourselves as possible. I'll have a word with the others when we meet at two o'clock. I'm going to the airport now to meet my wife off the lunchtime flight.'

'I'll drive you, shall I?'

When Pauline came off the plane, she looked ravishing.

Blake drove us back to the hotel, and over lunch I told her how much money we had won. When she didn't seem particularly impressed I said, 'You're not surprised we've done so well?'

158

'I'm only surprised you're still playing. I thought you would have been banned by now.'

'Between you and me, I'm about as surprised as you are.'

At the Massena I gave the group a general warning about the inadvisability of using 500-franc notes in restaurants and cafés. As the three musketeers were presumably still sleeping off the champagne they had consumed the night before I decided to save my warning against other forms of notoriety until later.

We arrived in the casino at the usual time of 2.45 p.m. As soon as play started three officials came to the table and tried to look over the shoulders of our six players. Mrs Richardson immediately turned her notepad upside down. The others followed her example.

At 4.30 p.m. Maurice Nathan commenced a progression on *manque* (low). It went in fits and starts, not a steady predominance but protracted winning runs and then almost equally long adverse sequences when his line several times came down to two figures. It took him about an hour and a half to reach a stake above 2,000 francs. A hush fell on the crowd round the table, broken only by the clicking of the ivory ball and the calls of the croupiers. The Chef de Casino came to the table. He had not smiled for several days.

At 5.45 p.m. Maurice Nathan looked up from his notepad and smiled. From the toppling piles of plaques and chips in front of him he carefully picked one pink 5-franc chip and placed it on *manque*. He had reached the table limit.

No casino official could be expected to see something like this without becoming hostile. We were making it all too obvious that not only could we win large sums (Nathan's mushroom brought him 40,300 francs – £2,900; $8,150), but that we would then deny them the chance to recover the money. This was a complete reversal of what is expected to happen between the player and the table (expected by the casino staff, of course – most players have the illusion they will win). Hunch gamblers will lose their fluky wins sooner or later and system players, if they are using an orthodox method, reach the table limit only when they are trying to recover previous losses, that is, when the table has been winning heavily.

159

On this occasion the quiet, almost mousy Maurice Nathan made it even more noticeable by the triumphant way he began to smile at everybody standing round the table, including the Chef de Casino. He had found in winning dramatically before a wide-eyed audience the chance to reveal the latent daredevil. Instead of shoving the larger denomination stuff into his pockets he left all his plaques and chips lying there in front of him.

For the first time in my obsessional affair with roulette I found myself praying that we would not have any more wins that day. The expressions of the Chef de Casino and his associates were alarming.

The inevitable happened. Of course. Almost as a punishment for my loss of nerve George Milton hit a progression on *passe*.

A man giving away gold bars in Trafalgar Square could not have drawn such a feverish audience. Eyes strained through tobacco smoke to see what he was writing in his notepad. Members of the staff appeared with notebooks of their own, each busily writing down every stake and result of Milton's progression.

As soon as Milton reached the table limit, crazy piles of rectangular plaques and round chips rising before him like the turrets of a gothic castle, I retreated to the bar.

No sooner was the whisky in my hand than two men approached me. Speaking in excellent English, one of them said, 'Mr Leigh?'

'Yes?'

'We understand you informed the Chef de Casino that you and your friends are a group formed to play roulette to a system.'

'That is correct.'

'We wonder, would you care to tell us something more about the system you are playing?'

'By all means.' I pulled out my notebook and handed it to the one who was doing the talking. 'If you'd like to write down your questions and sign the page at the bottom, I will be happy to answer anything you ask.'

They frowned at each other, talked rapidly in French, shrugged and walked away.

Blake hurried towards me. 'What did they want?' he asked.

'They wanted to interrogate me on our system. Strange, isn't it, how eager officials always are to ask questions and how reluctant to commit themselves on paper? I shouldn't panic.'

'I'm worried,' he said gravely.

The second shift played until 3 a.m. without another mushroom. All six players and myself were kept under strict surveillance by the staff. When we left Blake was carrying 67,000 francs from the day's two progressions. Although we were well into October the temperature was still in the eighties and the combined effect of the heat and my customary twelve hours in the casino had made me too tired to find any great thrill in the sight of the money. Blake and I had 6,700 francs each (£490 – $1,365) while the others had £355 ($994) apiece.

As soon as Blake had handed out the cash I stood up.

'It's very hot and we're all tired, so I'll be brief. The fact is that we are at the dangerous stage of this operation. You are finding that the novelty is wearing off – perhaps even the money is losing its thrill. We've had four successful days at the casino, and the management is clearly worried. Some of you may even think we've proved our point. Well, I haven't proved *my* point. To me this money is only the beginning. If we falter now, we'll be written off as a bunch of lucky amateurs who folded up before the real test. We can make gambling history, instead of just slipping off home with a few hundred pounds' profit. Of course we're getting heavy looks from the staff. Did you expect bouquets?'

'I don't know who could have been suggesting that we give up,' Blake said sternly. 'I'm certainly in no doubt that we should go on to the bitter end.'

'Bitter end?' said Keith Robinson. 'Seems pretty sweet to me.' He held up his wad of francs. 'I don't know what all the fuss is about. I've never had it so good. They can stare themselves blind at me for all I care. When they start whacking us over the skull with lead pipes that'll be the time to start moving.'

'Of course we're going on,' said Terry Baker quietly. 'I'll work double shifts if anybody's thinking of walking out on us.'

'Does everybody feel that way?' I asked. The eight or nine present all nodded. 'And do you agree that the team has a right to

161

expect a hundred per cent from each member? Yes, I'm glad of that because it makes the next thing I have to say easier. Quite apart from our winnings in the casino this whole town seems to be seething with gossip about wild parties – I've even heard them described as orgies. At the very least this is advertising our presence in the worst possible way. Now I'm not here to supervise morals. What I *am* concerned about is the risk of any one of us becoming known to the local police as an undesirable visitor. It's just the excuse they're looking for to throw us out of the country.'

Careful as I had been not to look at anyone in particular, Alec Sherlock immediately assumed, rightly, that I was referring to him.

'There's no harm in a few bottles of champagne,' he said.

'No harm at all if that's as far as it goes.'

'Come along and see for yourself.'

'I'm older than you. I need all the sleep I can get. I'm not mentioning anybody by name. What I am saying boils down to two points. One, the casino bars people who are suspected of association with criminals. Two, the group might have two or three days when it doesn't win anything. As we are all painfully aware, the Riviera is not the cheapest place in the world. I hope you are all putting enough to one side to see you through a lean spell.'

'We haven't been spending all that much,' said Sherlock. Terry Baker stared at his feet.

'A good deal more than you ever spent at home on champagne, I'd imagine,' I said sharply. 'Three hundred pounds in one night?'

'Yeah, well, you're only young twice I always say,' said Keith Robinson. 'Don't worry – we've got a few bob tucked away under the mattress, haven't we?' He looked at Sherlock and Terry Baker. They both nodded. 'Rely on us, Norman,' he said, getting up. 'We'll be with you to the death. You two ready to blow?'

He said this to Baker and Sherlock. For a moment it looked as though Terry had decided to stay with the rest of us, but what chance did common sense have against the pull of a wild

162

night with the boys, especially when his wife and child were due to arrive the next day?

As we were leaving his suite, Blake asked me to stay behind for a minute.

'I'm worried,' he said.

'Oh, I was laying it on a bit thick. Baker's got a wife and child. The others can throw their money into the Mediterranean for all I care – '

'No, it's something else that's bothering me. Have you noticed that there's a pattern to the incidence of these progressions? I first spotted it in London. They generally seem to occur shortly after the same player has had one which petered out.'

'I have noticed that. Almost like a warning, isn't it?'

'We've been having more than our fair share of these false starts in the last two days. I have the distinct feeling we're building up to a colossal bunching of limit reachers and table breakers.'

'What's worrying about that?'

'The management is hostile enough as it is. I imagine they'd go berserk if we started having more progressions in a day.'

'It's a risk we have to take,' I said. 'I'll walk home. Good night, Blake.'

It was almost five when I got back to our room. Pauline woke up while I was undressing. 'Emma said I was to tell you she spoke to her friend Philippe in the restaurant tonight,' she said. 'He came across to our table. She said I wasn't to tell you in front of the others. He told her he knows all about her now. He said the whole town knows there's a successful team working in the municipal casino. She asked him if there was anything wrong in what you were doing and he said he could guarantee we wouldn't be doing it for much longer, but wouldn't say why.'

'No, because he doesn't know himself. We won't be frightened off that easily.'

As I climbed into bed she asked me, unable to control the worried note in her voice: 'When does this stop, Norman?'

'It stops when we are stopped,' I said firmly. Pauline accepted this and not once again in the fraught days that followed did she ever hint that she wanted me to give up.

*

The following day dawned hotter than ever – I say 'dawned', but it was midday when I awoke. Pauline was already up. After breakfast we decided to take a stroll, ending up at Blake's hotel just after twelve. Blake's morning swim had cooled him off only temporarily. Incredibly he was back into his heavy blue suit. The heat was beginning to tell on his sixteen or seventeen stones. As we went out on the terrace of his hotel for a coffee he seemed to be moving with some effort, constantly touching his face with a large white handkerchief.

'I was followed this morning,' he told us.

'I'm not unduly surprised,' I said casually. 'Round about now they're just beginning to think of ways to frighten us off. But we're not criminals and we're not robbing the casino: that's their problem. Nonetheless we're making serious inroads into the safe.'

'I'm sure the same man has been watching me for a day or two,' said Mrs Harper-Biggs when I asked the first shift if they had noticed anything. 'I didn't like to say anything. Old women like me have a reputation for panicking unnecessarily.'

'Why would they want to follow us?' asked Maurice Nathan.

'We are an unusual phenomenon, therefore we invite investigation,' I said. 'Don't worry about it. In fact, if you catch sight of the same man again, why not write down your name and address on a bit of paper and simply hand it to the man? Tell him it will save a lot of time and effort on his part if he simply comes along to see you at your hotel.'

'That's a good idea,' Mrs Heppenstall commented calmly.

'Yes, I'd love to see the look on his face,' said Mrs Harper-Biggs.

It was on this day that Fredericks began to emerge from his shell. Although he was on the second shift he turned up that lunchtime at the Café Massena, so changed in appearance we didn't recognize him at first. He had been very busy that morning. He was wearing windscreen-shaped dark glasses, his mousy hair had been shampooed and restyled in a forwards direction to cover his thin patch – most startling of all, he had on a dove-grey silk suit that must have cost at least a couple of hundred pounds. He took our exclamations of surprise with undoubted pleasure. 'I got a bit tired of looking like a dowdy office worker,' he said.

'It looks very nice, Thomas,' said Mrs Richardson.

To go with his new image Fredericks went so far that particular lunchtime as to order not his usual ice-cream but a vermouth.

'Give him a couple of days and he'll be dashing off with the three musketeers for champagne orgies,' said Milton.

'Has anybody seen a place that mends clothes in this town?' Maurice Nathan asked. He showed us a small tear in the pocket of his sports jacket. 'Silly, really. I was in such a hurry to get here on time I barged against the door and caught the pocket on the handle.'

'Round here they'll charge you the earth to mend it,' said Mrs Richardson. 'Why don't you bring it round to my apartment when we finish this shift and I'll sew it up?'

'Oh no, this is your holiday. I wouldn't want to land you with housework –'

'If I don't have anything to do tonight I'll only end up watching another dreary French film in the fleapit.'

'There is a cinema that shows English and American films,' I said.

'Ah yes – we all went there the other night. What was that film called, Lettice?'

'*Guns Across the Rio Grande*,' Mrs Heppenstall said authoritatively, adding with a trace of her old shy self, 'I like cowboy films because it doesn't really matter who gets shot, does it?'

'I couldn't enjoy it for thinking how much it cost,' said Mrs Richardson. 'Two pounds to see a bunch of cowboys? No thank you. No, Maurice, I insist. I can have that sewn up in three minutes.'

This exchange, trivial in itself, may serve to illustrate how sensibly some of the party, especially the three ladies, took to the life of professional gambling. In fact, as I told Pauline that afternoon while we were watching play, I often thought I would have done better to recruit a team of women from the start. These three certainly showed more common sense than some of the men. Mrs Harper-Biggs occasionally went up into the hills behind the town to look for bugs and beetles. Mrs Richardson's one indulgence was to have her hair done *every* morning. 'It costs the *earth*,' she told Pauline, 'but I don't suppose I'll ever again have five pounds to throw away on one hairdo.' Mrs

Heppenstall guiltily revealed that she was having regular manicures. They saved a few francs by going to a backstreet cinema which showed French films for the purely local audience; they organized such exotic escapades as supermarket explorations; Nathan hired a car and drove them to Monte Carlo for an early morning sightseeing trip. For two days or more we heard nothing else but descriptions of Prince Rainier's wonderful palace and of how they had actually seen Princess Grace, or someone remarkably like her.

'If I had twelve like them I think I would chance it and go for broke in the Salle Privée in Monte Carlo,' I told Pauline one day. 'I had a few words with Sherlock last night – but you can't tell a fool he's a fool can you?'

One strange development was that Sherlock's complexion had cleared up remarkably in the few days we had been on the Riviera; a dull, respectable life in a London office is no match, it seems, for six hours gambling and champagne orgies till well after dawn when it comes to curing acne. The Riviera sun had nothing to do with it – I doubt if he saw the beach once during our whole stay.

The improvement in his skin, however, was not matched by a corresponding improvement in his character. He became much more confident but in an aggressive way. On one occasion when I was with him in the casino bar waiting for the shifts to change, I dropped him a hint about the advisability of saving some of the money he was making.

'You said we'd make a fortune and we're making it, so why the hell shouldn't we enjoy ourselves?' he said, annoyed.

'I never said we'd make a fortune,' I corrected him. 'But as we are doing well I'd like to see us all coming out of this with more money than when we started.'

'Don't worry about me.'

'I don't worry in the slightest about you. I don't care personally if you end up penniless. My only concern is to keep the team working smoothly.'

'That's all right then,' he said.

To Pauline I said, 'We're on thin ice. You can't drink and fornicate every night without cracking up sooner or later.'

166

'Maybe some of them need to go wild or they would explode,' she suggested. 'Look at poor Mr Hopplewell.'

'Poor? I should think he's one of the richest of the lot.'

'I didn't mean that way. Do you know he drinks two bottles of brandy a day? He told me the other night when we went to eat in that bistro by the Quai.'

'I knew he liked his brandy – but two bottles a day!'

'He's an alcoholic. He told me all about it. He can't do without it, so apparently he goes through sheer torture playing for six hours with only one or two. That's why he wanted to go on the early shift – to avoid the temptation of going back to Blake's suite for the share-outs. He thinks you're all watching him. So he just goes to his own room with a bottle and quietly drinks the lot. He doesn't drink to get drunk, but just so that he can feel normal. He's a very nice man, actually, if you can get him talking. His children won't have anything to do with him because of his drinking. Do you know he has five grandchildren he's never been allowed to see? Isn't that cruel?'

'I've had dealings with alcoholics, darling, He probably put his family through unmitigated hell. Pity we're not working twelve-hour shifts; in time he might be cured altogether.'

'They're not machines, you know. Honestly, Norman, your attitude is very brutal.'

'I don't have time to be a father confessor. If the money brings out the hidden truth about their real characters, I'm not to blame, am I?'

'No, but you could be more sympathetic.'

'Making people rich is sympathetic enough as far as I'm concerned.'

This conversation did make me think. As we crossed the sunscorched square towards the casino on our fifth day, Mrs Harper-Biggs and Mrs Heppenstall on either side of Emma Richardson, Maurice Nathan discussing French cars with Milton, Hopplewell and myself in the rear, they all seemed like different people. Yet, at the same time, I had a strange feeling that I had known them all my life. I realized it mattered to me that *they* came out of this with – well, with money, certainly, but something more besides.

In my obsession with proving that I could beat the casino I had had to ignore them as individuals, to relegate them to the role of puppets whose purpose was to make my plan succeed. I suppose I was actually finding a belated sense of humanity. At the time I told myself I was merely grateful to them for not having let me down.

Day five. The casino made another move against us. When we got to our table all the seats had already been taken, though it was only 2.50 p.m. The people occupying the chairs looked like ordinary players. Obviously I couldn't ask them if they had been prompted to grab the seats by the management. It seemed too much of a coincidence, however.

'Just stand as close to the chairs as possible and grab them as they become vacant,' I instructed the first shift. 'If you get into any difficulty let me know. I'll take over and give you a rest.'

Having seen them place their first pink 5-franc chips, I said to Pauline that we should lose ourselves in the throngs of the large salon.

'They know the system backwards now,' I said, 'and standing is sheer torture. Keep an eye on Mrs Harper-Biggs in case she looks like fainting.'

Standing within viewing distance of our table some ten minutes later, I saw Milton signalling to me. I went across.

'They seem to have stopped the waiters from serving us,' he said, leaning forward to place the chips for his next bet on *passe* (high). 'I asked that old bugger for a coffee ten minutes ago. He's been back with drinks for other people but not for me.'

'I'll have a word with him.'

I went across to the oldest of the waiters, a man whose face told of unspeakable anguish and suffering. ('It's their feet, poor devils,' Blake said.)

'I'd like a coffee for my friend,' I said politely, pointing to Milton. The old idiot shrugged and walked away.

'Only a cup of coffee, but in these circles a sure sign that war has been officially declared,' I said to Pauline.

It didn't take long for hostilities to be stepped up.

Chapter Thirteen

The casino's next move was more subtle.

The first shift had been playing for an hour and a half when Mrs Harper-Biggs simultaneously got a seat and started a progression on her chance, *impair* (the odd numbers). After nine spins her line read something like 3, 4, 7, 10, 13, 16 and her next stake was 19 francs, nothing to excite any casual observer. However, four or five women standing at her corner of the table began to ask her questions, the usual things people ask at a roulette table: What number came up last? What colour is predominating? What system are you using?

These women were of differing ages, fairly well dressed but nothing out of the ordinary. Until then there had been nothing to suggest that they were together.

As I moved nearer, Mrs Harper-Biggs was on spin 14, and her line read 7, 10, 13, 17. She won 24 francs and added that figure to the end of her line, giving her a stake for spin 15 of 7 + 24 = 31. This lost. On spin 16 her stake was 10 + 17 = 27. This won. Only 27 francs, but the women round her increased the intensity of their questions, speaking rapidly in French. I knew then they were no ordinary players but an organized group deliberately setting out to upset her concentration.

Mrs Harper-Biggs did not need me to tell her to ignore them. They began to ask the same questions in English. Mrs Harper-Biggs went on ignoring them, only a tightening of her mouth indicating that she was conscious of their presence. By spin 23 her line read 17, 27, 37, 54 giving her a stake of 71 francs. She lost, bringing her line down to two figures, 27, 37. Then she had four wins in a row. By spin 27 her line was 27, 37, 64, 91, 118, giving her a stake of 145 francs. The women tried to put her off by pushing even closer, firing questions from all sides, even going so far as to nudge her elbow. At this she looked up and gave the offending female a glare of the kind that had no doubt kept the late Mr Harper-Biggs in line.

I eased myself between the woman on her left hand and the chair to lend her moral support.

By spin 33 her line read 37, 64, 91, 118, 155, 192, 229, 266. This looked very promising, with enough of the lower figures left to give her a chance of progressing slowly to the limit and thereby having more winning bets on the way than would have been the case if wins and losses had alternated in such a way as to delete the smaller figures early in the sequence.

During all this these determined she-wolves kept yapping at her from all sides. A hardened professional gambler would have found it hard to maintain concentration, but for her, a rather grand lady of uncertain temperament, to keep on with her calculations and find the exact plaques and chips for each stake was a tremendous feat of concentration. I was proud of her.

It was a long and profitable ordeal. It took her over two hours to reach the table limit. By that time, however, the team of women had decided she could not be upset and had turned their attentions on Mrs Richardson, who had started a small progression on her chance, red. I had no doubt then that they were working under instructions to concentrate on flustering whichever of our players was having a winning sequence.

They started asking Mrs Richardson the same questions. Mrs Richardson ignored them. Meanwhile the croupiers were sending out the usual alert by handclap, and a fair crowd was assembling at the table.

One of the women leaned over and started fiddling with Mrs Richardson's chips.

'I'll help you put them in order,' she said in French. Mrs Richardson calmly pushed her arm away. I eased over and stood by her.

'It's all right,' said Mrs Richardson grimly.

'Don't give them the satisfaction of upsetting you,' I said, arranging her chips and plaques in some semblance of order. Red was predominating in fits and starts, and at several stages her line was down to two figures, but always it took life again.

Mrs Harper-Biggs reached the limit at about twenty minutes to seven. Her progression had lasted over two hours. Mrs Richardson reached the limit about half an hour later, although hers had lasted less than two hours. (This may sound like an account of unbroken triumph, but during this time the other four members of the shift were losing steadily on short sequences.) There were two winning progressions on that shift of six hours at thirty spins to the hour. As a collective unit our six players made over a thousand separate bets in that shift. To get the two winning progressions Mrs Harper-Biggs and Mrs Richardson possibly had fewer than two hundred winning bets between them.

As Mrs Richardson pulled the scattered piles of plaques and chips together the Chef de Casino came close to the table and glowered at her.

Mrs Richardson gave him a sweet smile and started betting again – one miserable 5-franc chip. The Chef muttered something and stalked off.

The rest of that day passed without incident, excepting the blanket refusal to serve any of us with coffee or drinks, a small argument over seats when the shifts changed and a noticeable slowness on the part of the croupiers when any of our team asked them to change a high-denomination plaque into smaller chips.

There were no more progressions. The first shift went off to eat, but several of them returned later in the evening. Only Mrs Heppenstall, Mrs Harper-Biggs and Hopplewell were missing when we met in Blake's hotel for the share-out. Everybody was complaining about the strain of having to stand and go without refreshment.

'I don't mind telling you I was near to screaming when those women kept pestering me,' said Mrs Richardson.

'They gave up in the end,' I said. 'I thought you and Mrs H-B did extraordinarily well. If that's the best they can do we've got them beaten.'

'Was I seeing things, or did anybody else notice lights flashing?' Fredericks asked.

'I saw something flashing, too,' said Maurice Nathan. 'I thought it was bulbs burning out in the chandeliers.'

'No, it was a flash camera,' said Sherlock. 'I saw the bloke taking pictures.'

Nobody else had seen a photographer, it seemed.

'Who knows, in a few weeks you may see photographs of yourselves as part of the international jet-set elite,' I said. 'How did we do, anyway, Mr Blake?'

'Not bad, considering the difficulties we were under. Two progressions – a healthy figure of fifty-five thousand three hundred and eighty-five francs.'

'Can't be bad,' said Keith Robinson, rubbing his hands together. Terry Baker thought otherwise.

'I don't think it's all that brilliant,' he complained. 'We're getting a lot of abortive runs petering out halfway. I still think we would save a lot of time by going for the high stakes in the Monte Carlo casino rather than carrying on here day after day for dribs and drabs.'

'I dare say three or four hundred pounds a day hardly meets your bar bill,' Blake said icily.

There was an embarrassed pause. Baker blushed and for a few seconds it seemed that he might bluster. Then, calmly, he said, 'All right. No point in denying it. I've been chucking money away like a drunken sailor. Still, my wife's arriving tomorrow, so the party's over. From now on I'll behave.'

Blake did the sharing out. He and I had 5,538 francs each, about £400 ($1,120). The other eleven shared 44,309 francs, giving them about 4,028 francs each, about £294 ($822). Everyone departed.

Baker brought his wife and baby from the airport in time for the usual rendezvous at the Café Massena the next day, our sixth day at the Casino Municipale. Lyn Baker was a quiet little girl with a pale face, hardly into her twenties. It looked as though they had already been arguing in the taxi, for he was looking very grim. I had been hoping for an extrovert wife with a temperament robust enough to put the reins on Terry, but the more I watched her listening nervously to what must have been our incomprehensible discussion about casino tactics the more I felt certain her presence might even make the situation worse.

On our way across the square to the casino I held Pauline back. Terry and his wife were still sitting outside the café.

'If you get a chance to speak to her alone, do you think you

172

could persuade her to go straight back home?' I said. 'I'll suggest it to Terry, but you know how obstinate he can be.'

'It might calm him down a bit having her here with the baby.'

'More likely it will be too much for his emotional capacity to cope with. They're all complaining already about the strain we're under – how's he going to react with her and the baby hanging about all the time?'

'But you said having her here would stop him throwing his money away! You don't mind if he's broke as long as he keeps playing, is that it?'

It was a question I couldn't answer.

When we entered the salon at 2.50 p.m. only two of the chairs at our table were occupied. Milton and Nathan elected to stand. I saw no signs of the women who had tried to harass Mrs Richardson and Mrs Harper-Biggs the day before. The table staff were, as always, bland and polite.

At 3.30 p.m. Nathan hit a progression on *manque* (low – numbers one to eighteen). Within twenty spins he was staking 100 francs (about £7, or $20). The handclapping started. Senior members of the staff arrived at the table to have huddled conversations with each other. Another ten spins took Nathan to a stake of 500 francs. The Chef de Casino came to the table. Nathan had a phenomenal run of consecutive wins, the ball dropping in low numbers eight successive times. His lowest number on the line was 135, which meant that his stakes increased by only 135 units at each spin, giving him a satisfyingly long line of winning bets. When he reached the table limit he had won 27,475 francs (approximately £2,000 – $5,600). In total silence he put the large plaques into his pockets.

He smiled graciously as bystanders tried to question him about his system. The Chef de Casino kept remarkable control of himself. Only the fists clenched at the seams of his trousers showed the extent of his anger. When one of the spectators made a joke to him about the Englishman bankrupting the casino he even managed a tight-lipped smile.

Blake arrived in the salon a few minutes later. He listened impassively as I told him about Nathan's progression.

'Our good friend Monsieur le Chef looked fit to go out of his mind,' I said. 'I think we can expect fresh counter measures.'

'To hell with him,' Blake said grimly. 'They're so damn used to fleecing tourists they can't tolerate anybody who gives them a run for their money. If they want to cause trouble we'll give them a fight.'

From a man whose punctilious avoidance of any form of unpleasantness marked him out from the rest, this new attitude was surprising.

Around 6.30 p.m. George Milton started on a progression of the very best kind, from our point of view. The predominance of *passe* (high – numbers nineteen to thirty-six) made itself felt when his line still comprised low numbers, something like 42, 56, 73. Normally a predominance averages 5 to 2 or even 3 to 1 over its opposite, but this doesn't mean that the player has five wins followed by two losses and so on. More likely the arbitrary patterns thrown up by the wheel (detectable only as patterns in retrospect) would give freak runs of seven, eight or nine consecutive wins followed by one loss and then another five wins.

Milton's progression went on so long that soon every senior member of the casino staff was watching him.

They had the galling experience of witnessing a table breaker. As our pub-keeper stalwart was about to place a stake well below the table maximum, around 2,000 francs, the Chef de Partie announced that play was temporarily suspended at that table. It had run out of plaques!

'It's their own fault. They've been hoist by their own damned cleverness,' I said to Blake.

'How is that?' He seemed preoccupied.

'They were paying Milton in high-denomination stuff, five-hundred-franc plaques, even a thousand-franc plaque, then they were taking their time about giving him change, hoping he couldn't get the proper stake together before "*Rien ne va plus*". Now they've run out of the big stuff.'

Milton sat there wiping his forehead while the crowd stood silently watching him.

'I think I'll have a drink,' I muttered to Blake. 'It's getting a bit hot in here.'

I had hardly finished my whisky when Blake came hurrying

into the bar. 'I think you should come back to the table,' he said urgently. 'Mrs Heppenstall is on to something.'

This was probably the moment that made up the minds of the casino bigwigs to take conclusive action against us. Milton had just won 32,000 francs on a progression where high had predominated for almost two hours. No sooner had play recommenced at our table than the wheel began to throw up a predominance of *pair* (even) over *impair* (odd).

No matter which way the wheel went, it was now startlingly obvious, it was bound to favour us. Milton was back to bets of a few meaningless francs, while Mrs Heppenstall was busily reaping the profits from the wheel's change of mood.

Whether the crowds who gathered round the table to watch the little Englishwoman in the plain summer dress scooping in the chips understood any of this is hard to say; they certainly sensed that something unnatural was happening. So many people crowded forward to watch that the waiters had to ask them to move away so that they could serve the other players – not of course, our players. The heat and the smoke became unbearable.

'How she's coping I'm damned if I know,' said Blake. 'I could quite easily faint just standing here watching.'

'There's nothing we can do. Let's go and have a drink.'

The barman took ten minutes to serve us, although he was by no means busy. We looked through the open doorway to the roulette tables. Our table was surrounded by at least a hundred people all pushing forward, none too decorously, to get a view of this famous syndicate in action.

'I wonder how many of them are desperately rushing to get bets on *pair* just because Lettice is betting on it,' I said to Blake.

'They were doing that when Hopplewell had a tiny little progression – they certainly seem to know every one of us by sight now.'

'Might be better if Lettice doesn't reach the limit then. If even half a dozen people follow her all the way, the casino will be cleaned out.'

'Wasn't that part of your idea?'

'What, to break the bank altogether? Not at all.'

'I had the distinct impression you wanted to bring this place to its knees.'

'It would certainly be a coup, but let's be practical: killing the golden goose and all that . . .'

'To hell with them, I say. If we break this place we can always go to another.' He spoke with a bitterness I had not heard in his voice before. Pauline came out of the crowd and hurried towards us. She was just telling us that Mrs Heppenstall had reached the limit (she had won 11,768 francs) when Peter Vincent ambled into the bar.

'Hello, you chaps,' he drawled. 'How are things at the cash and carry?'

Blake looked at his watch. 'Ten to nine,' he snapped. 'Time we were getting in position for the seats.' He left abruptly.

'Glass of wine I fancy,' said Vincent, in near-perfect imitation of Blake's voice. He caught my eye and smiled. 'Pity you're stuck in here all day, Mr Leigh. Wonderful swimming down here.'

The bar staff were continuing to ignore us, and he was unable to get service. I went with him to the table to see the shifts change. Three failed to get seats, one of them being Blake, whose weight must have heightened his general discomfort as the crowds – and the heat – increased.

Paradoxically, the team's fame began to help us here. Having become celebrities, every bet made by the team was watched and copied by dozens of other players. This meant that Blake was given ample elbow room to place his stakes, though he still had to do his calculations with the notepad balanced on his forearm and his hand full of plaques.

Fredericks, who was also standing, hit a progression on black just before midnight. It turned out to be one of the most protracted mushrooms we had experienced. After eighteen spins the lowest number on his line was still 6. After an hour the poor man was almost in a state of collapse. I stood beside him and eventually took over his paperwork. The progression lasted for two and a quarter hours. By the time the line was producing stakes of 2,000 francs Fredericks was only going through the motions. I was doing the paperwork, telling him what plaques and chips he needed for his next stake, finally even placing the stakes for him, leaving him the minor task of picking up our winnings. His brilliant new suit began to bulge with the chips we were winning.

We reached the limit around 2.30 a.m.

Never was 1, 2, 3, 4 written on a clean page with such relief. It was a colossal mushroom considering that it had not broken the table – no less than 51,760 francs.

There wasn't much of a turnout at Blake's place that morning. Fredericks went to his hotel, saying that if he had only one drink his legs would fall off. The novelty of seeing bundles of francs being counted out had worn off. None of the first shift had bothered to return to the casino after dinner.

'Not a bad day,' said Blake when he looked up from his cash book. 'From four progressions we made exactly one hundred and twenty-three thousand and three francs. Satisfactory, Mr Leigh?'

'How do we share out the three spare francs?' asked Keith Robinson. Nobody else found this funny at the time, but it made me laugh uncontrollably. Maybe it was a delayed reaction to the tension of the evening. The rest of them waited until I was able to regain my composure.

'I'm sorry,' I said. 'Let's leave the three francs as a floating cash reserve.'

That started Keith off. Watching him heave with laughter, I seemed to see another man altogether, a much stronger and resourceful character than the quasi-cockney joker. He has had the right attitude towards all this, I thought: win, spend it, keep a smile on your face. He would survive, no matter what.

Blake announced the results of his arithmetic. He and I had 12,300 francs each, not far short of £900 ($2,490). The other eleven shared 98,400, a share each of 8,945 francs, £652 ($1,825). He handed out the cash to those present: Sherlock, Robinson, Baker, Vincent and myself.

'I think I should drive you home, Mr Leigh,' suggested Blake.

Outside, Keith Robinson made some remark about the town's night life only starting at dawn. Terry Baker hesitated.

'Come on,' said Keith. 'The morning's only young yet.'

'Aren't you going back to your wife and child?' Blake said.

'Why the hell should I?' asked Baker. 'I've got the rest of my life to go home early, haven't I?'

He went off with Robinson and Sherlock. Vincent stretched his arms and yawned. 'Nice night for a swim, eh?' he said. Incredibly he started into a little tap dance, singing, 'I like

177

swimmin' with wimmin, and wimmin like swimmin' with me.'
Blake stared at him. Vincent gave us a deep bow, ambled off to
his car and had soon roared off in it.

'The man's unbalanced,' Blake said as we got into his car.

'I think he knows what he's doing,' I said. 'Baker's the one who
is genuinely unbalanced. Would you like to guess how much of
that money sees daylight?'

'I dare say the strain is beginning to tell.'

'If they drank less and got more sleep, they wouldn't find it
such a strain.'

'On their own heads be it.'

'I think it's *pitiful*. Hundreds of tax-free pounds a day – and
they decide to chuck it away as fast as they get their hands on it.
Do they think we'll be allowed to go on winning forever? Bloody
fools. And Baker with that child-wife of his! I'd like to shake
him until – '

'As you said, this isn't a Boy Scout troop. You've shown them
how to make money. You can't be expected to wet-nurse them
through life as well.'

'I must be going soft.'

As he dropped me at my hotel he suggested we should pray
for cooler weather. It was not until I was in bed that I realized
why our conversation had felt so strange. He had been saying
the things I should have been saying. I lay there in the dark, too
tired to sleep, listening to the endless chirruping of the accursed
cicadas.

Day seven. Another scorcher. Baker's wife turned up at the
Café Massena with their child but without Baker. She said he was
still in bed. Pauline had told me that morning that Lyn Baker
was more mature than one might have guessed: 'She's had a lot
of trouble with Terry,' she said. 'She didn't tell us in so many
words, but I think he didn't leave the police solely to come on this
trip. More likely he jumped before he was pushed. She can't get
him to save any of the money!'

'Married too young I suppose – same old story.'

'She says she's hoping he'll get rid of all his bad blood on this
trip and then be prepared to settle down.'

'I should say she's being wildly optimistic.'

We crossed the square at 2.45 p.m. As we went in out of the sunshine I realized that I was almost wishing the whole thing was over. Six hours' sleep had not been enough. The six members of the first shift, Emma, Lettice Heppenstall, Mrs Harper-Biggs, Sydney Hopplewell, Maurice Nathan and George Milton, all looked fresh and unworried – but they had finished at 9 p.m. the previous night and gone off to dinner and an early bed. I had eaten breakfast and lunch within a hour of each other, had a bath, put on clean clothes and come straight to the Massena with Pauline.

As soon as we left the relentless glare of the street for the shabby gloom of the casino entrance, we were once again in the timeless, unreal world of the gaming salon, our existences governed by a segmented wheel, an ivory ball, a numbered grid of green baize. Even the six people I knew had the remoteness of strangers, as if they might be half-remembered faces from a dream. Had *I* brought that imposing woman in the green tweed suit to a foreign country to take part in this monotonous ritual?

Past and future do not exist in the casino. We had all become part of an endless charade. Practical motives had long been forgotten – we were here simply because we were here. It had been ordained.

But six days in the Casino Municipale had made considerable inroads on my reserves of stamina and will-power. I was near delirium.

Chapter Fourteen

At 3.35 p.m. on that scorching afternoon Mrs Harper-Biggs ran into a progression on *impair* (odd numbers). Within twenty minutes the table was surrounded. The usual handclapping, which we were all beginning to find less ominous than boring, brought the distraught Chef de Casino to our table. In something like forty spins Mrs Harper-Biggs' stakes were hovering under the limit of 2,600 francs.

Then she ran into an adverse sequence where the ball favoured the even numbers. Just as quickly as the chips had accumulated they began to dwindle, each even number demolishing more and more of her line. Eventually she had only three figures left. Two more losses would have wiped her out on that sequence. The Chef de Casino looked pleased: perhaps our system was going to fail like all the others.

Then Mrs Harper-Biggs found that the wheel was favouring her again. To everybody's amazement she reached the limit at 5.30, winning 15,645 francs. I made a point of not catching the eye of my old friend M. le Chef.

To take some of the work off her hands I arranged her plaques and chips in some kind of order while she reverted to 1, 2, 3, 4 and placed a pink chip on *impair*. The silence of the crowd round the table was eerie, broken only by the buzzing of wasps or flies.

Mrs Harper-Biggs won her first bet on the new sequence. She staked 6 francs. *Impair* paid off again.

Within twenty minutes she had hit *another* progression!

The faces of the Chef de Casino, the Chef de Partie and their minions were varied in reaction from astonishment to downright chagrin. This was impossible – but it was happening, here and now, every assumption of their professional lives being proved wrong. No longer could the English team's system be written off as a fluke. For six days we had laboured profitably and now on the seventh we were reaping a golden harvest. The rules which governed the closed world of the casino had been completely reversed. Even the croupiers, who until then had maintained a neutral attitude to our successes, were visibly impressed.

At 6.45 p.m. Mrs Harper-Biggs reached the table limit for the second time and once again wrote 1, 2, 3, 4 on a clean page. I do not believe there was a single player at any of the other tables.

'Would you like me to take your place for a while?' I said, controlling an urge to pat her on her tweedy back.

'I would,' she said flatly. I slipped into her chair before anyone knew she was getting up.

Nothing much happened to the six of us until around 8 p.m. when I commenced a small progression on *impair*. It looked like petering out on several occasions but then picked up in no uncertain fashion. Soon I was staking 1,000 francs and more.

For the first time I began to experience the incredible tension of being the centre of attraction. As I struggled with the flow of chips and the unwieldy figures I was having to add I felt inadequate. I was as nervous as a beginner. The handclapping began to sound threatening. Whenever I looked up from my notepad to place a stake I could see only those eyes staring at me, scores of them, women's eyes, old men's eyes, hostile eyes, jealous eyes, lascivious eyes, all of them on me.

The progression lasted until just before 9 p.m. Almost breathless from the heat and lack of oxygen, I did a quick calculation, assembled a handful of high-denomination plaques and some chips, pushed them forward to the rectangle marked *impair* – and saw a hand restraining my wrist.

Looking up, I found the croupier shaking his head at me.

The stake I had tried to put was 2,750 francs – 150 francs above the limit.

I sat back, blinking stupidly at the vast spew of plastic in front of me. The eyes. Silence.

One face stood out from the rows around and above me, that of the Chef de Casino.

As I wrote 1, 2, 3, 4 on the fresh page I could not help sneaking looks at him. His solid, shiny face was like stone.

I leaned forward with my first pink 5-franc chip. Suddenly it all seemed too much. I had won all this and I was betting a pathetic 5 francs?

I laughed out loud.

The Chef de Casino's face contorted with fury. Pointing to me, he shook one of his assistants by the arm. ' *C'est le chef* [He's the boss],' he barked, and strode off.

Some of the people nearest me patted my back, loudly congratulating me on this achievement. I said nothing, bitterly regretting the momentary loss of control that had made me laugh out loud. To the Chef de Casino it must have been an unforgivable insult.

The second shift took over at 9 p.m. Blake offered no explanation as to why he had turned up only in time to take his place at the table. I went with George Milton and Emma to the bar. We were all shaken.

'Three progressions on one shift – all on the same chance?' said Milton, his solid ex-sergeant's face aghast.

'I don't know why we're so nervy,' said Emma, giggling. 'This is what we came for. We're going to be rich. Come on, Norman, relax – '

'We're killing the goose,' I said. 'Two progressions a day and they might have tolerated us for a while longer, but three – besides, I tried to stake above the limit. I could kick myself.'

'Yes, well, you haven't had the practice we've had,' George said sympathetically. The three of us found this very funny. Pauline couldn't understand what we were laughing at when she came to pick up Emma for dinner. I had a quick snack in the casino restaurant and went back to the table.

Madness continued to reign that day.

Peter Vincent got a progression on *manque* (low), within forty minutes of sitting down. It was a monster! It took him until 11 p.m. to reach the limit, one of the largest mushrooms of all (48,640 francs at the count), an amazing amount to have won without breaking the table.

While he was handling this monstrous sequence Fredericks got a progression on black. He went very quickly to the limit, finishing long before Peter and winning a mere 12,895 francs – £940 ($2,610).

It dawned on me as Vincent came to the end of his mushroom

that something was missing. There had been no handclapping. And the Chef de Casino had not appeared.

'Even he's got to sleep sometime,' Emma said when she and Pauline, Maurice and George came back to the casino at midnight.

Coming back from the bar, I noticed something else. Standing in a group at one end of the table were a group of odd-looking men – odd in the sense that they were dressed more appropriately for a merchant bank than a casino on the Côte d'Azur, formal lounge suits and stiff collars. They looked at me in a manner which suggested they knew all about me and wanted only to check my appearance.

At 2 a.m. Fredericks got another progression on black, one we could well have done without.

Two of these men in the lounge suits moved round the table to stand behind his chair. Without any attempt at concealment they peered over his shoulder to see what he was writing in his notepad.

I signalled to him from the other side of the table and he immediately cradled the pad with his left arm.

When he reached the limit it was five minutes to three. The casino was nearly empty apart from the curious hard core at our table.

'Don't bother starting again,' I said to Fredericks, signalling to the other five to leave the table. He had won 26,500 francs on his second progression. We had to help Blake cash up at the desk. Never before had I seen so many plaques and chips being exchanged for cash.

It took Blake half an hour to count out the piles of francs on his Georgian dining table. Most of us just sat there and stared, too tired or too astounded to shout for joy. 'One hundred and fifty-nine thousand, six hundred and sixty francs,' Blake said eventually, with a note of awe in his voice.

The money was shared out. Blake and I had about £1,150 each (about $3,220). The eleven others got a fraction less than £850 ($2,380) each.

'You know, I think we've only just started,' Blake said. 'Can't you feel it in your bones? Didn't I tell you this would happen, Mr Leigh?'

Keith Robinson and Sherlock were already on their feet.

'I shouldn't allow yourselves to be carried away by today's events,' I said coldly. 'This bunching of progressions can do us nothing but harm. Six mushrooms in one day will be intolerable as far as the casino is concerned. There were some strange faces watching us tonight. We will have to be even more careful about everything we do in the casino. Mrs Harper-Biggs was near to fainting today. If you think you're going to faint, let me know immediately. If I'm not available and you're going to pass out, make a note on your pad of what your next stake would have been and leave the table. Start where you left off when you next take up play.'

'You don't think maybe we should move to another casino?' Sherlock said. 'Give this place a chance to cool off?'

'Why move?' George Milton retorted. 'They haven't thrown us out yet, have they? I'm buggered if I'm going to start trekking up and down the south of bloody France like a gypsy – I like it here.'

'We wouldn't gain anything by moving,' I said. 'Every municipal casino will have heard of us by now. Anything planned for us here would happen just as quickly anywhere else. We'll carry on as we're doing and let the casino make the first move. Now if you'll excuse me I must get some sleep.'

7 October dawned just as hot as before, but when we opened the windows there was a slight breeze blowing off the Mediterranean.

'Thank God for that,' I said to Pauline. 'Let's pray it whips up a gale through the casino.'

Over breakfast I told her about the money we had won the day before. 'Almost twelve hundred pounds for us, in one day – not such a hare-brained scheme after all, was it?'

'What will the casino do now?'

'That's the interesting part.'

'Funnily enough, I don't think you would really be sorry if they stopped you.'

'Whatever gave you that idea?'

When we met at the Massena at 2 p.m. most of the group were looking apprehensive.

184

'I'm surprised at you all,' I said briskly. 'I thought you'd be enthusing just a little over the money we won yesterday.'

'It doesn't seem like real money actually,' said Mrs Harper-Biggs. 'It comes too easily, I suppose.'

'It's funny,' said George Milton. 'If you'd told me a few months ago I could be knocking down five or six hundred quid a day for a few hours' roulette I'd have been like a cat on hot bricks, but after a while it gets monotonous, doesn't it?'

'It's what most people fail to understand about being wealthy,' Blake drawled. 'Why doesn't the millionaire stop working, sort of thing. As Mr Leigh told us months ago, most people are much happier losing – they wouldn't admit it, of course.'

'As a matter of fact I think Norman was wrong there,' George said quietly but with enough authority to let Blake know he was not to be patronized. 'Most people only put up with losing because nobody's ever told them how to win.'

'Most people are pretty lazy,' said Mrs Harper-Biggs. Lettice Heppenstall shook her head.

'I couldn't disagree more, Cynthia,' she said. 'I think most people are much better than everyone gives them credit for.'

Although they had seemingly become close friends it was not the first time in the last two or three days I had noticed Mrs Heppenstall turning quite sharply on Mrs Harper-Biggs. The flustered, self-effacing little widow had acquired a lot of new confidence in herself, perhaps in the knowledge that she was just as important to the team as anyone else. They were all changing in some way or another. George Milton had such a tan he was beginning to look positively Italian. Maurice Nathan, who had been almost primly reserved when I first met him, now stared openly at the legs of any woman who passed in front of the café and was becoming quite sharp with the waiters.

We crossed the square at 2.45 p.m. In the salon there was no sign of the men in regulation suits.

'Seems a lot cooler,' said Pauline.

'You're the only one who's never complained about the heat, love,' George Milton said to Mrs Heppenstall, patting her on the back. 'You'd do well in a pub, actually. You should think of that with all this gelt you're tucking away.'

'Lettice in a *pub*?' said Mrs Harper-Biggs severely. 'Ridiculous.'

'I haven't been in a pub since the end of the war,' Mrs Heppenstall said calmly. 'I must come and visit yours, George.'

'Drinks on the house, Lettice,' he said, giving her a thumbs-up. Mrs Harper-Biggs grimaced.

At 3.30 the fun started. Two progressions occurred simultaneously, Maurice Nathan on *manque* (low), Sydney Hopplewell on black.

'The fat's in the fire now,' I said to Pauline. The handclaps started while both of them were still staking under the 100-franc mark. The Chef de Casino came to the table for his customary inspection of the people who were eating into his profits. When our eyes met I was struck by the change in his manner. The man seemed positively serene!

Maurice and Sydney both had short progressions which jointly netted a mere 37,000 francs.

They had barely restarted with 1, 2, 3, 4 when six men wearing suits of a cut and quality rarely seen in France came into the salon.

'That's officialdom of a very high order or I'm much mistaken,' Blake said.

The six men broke up as they came to our table, and each took up position directly behind one of our first shift. They brought out notebooks and started to copy what our players were writing in their notepads. I signalled to the six to hide their figures, but the six officials merely waited until the stakes were placed before entering the amounts in their books.

'They're going to write down every stake and every result for this session,' Blake said. 'That should more or less give them everything they need to know about our system, damn them.'

'But they must know by now what system you're using,' Pauline said.

'The Chef de Casino knows, but these chaps are from higher up,' I told her. 'Ministry of the Interior probably. Flattering, isn't it?'

'I don't like the sound of that,' said Blake.

Mrs Harper-Biggs – or rather the wheel – could not have chosen a worse time to commence a progression on *impair* (odd).

186

'They'll get the whole picture now,' I said, watching the spy behind Mrs Harper-Biggs carefully noting everything she did.

'Why don't we call everybody off for the day, Mr Leigh?' Blake suggested. 'That would spike their guns.'

'No, they'll come back tomorrow and the day after if needs be. We might as well push the damn thing to the limit now.'

Mrs Harper-Biggs' progression petered out. For half an hour our six players did nothing more dramatic than lose a series of 10 francs.

At 7.30 p.m. the six mystery men put away their notebooks and left the table.

'They've tumbled the system or else they've got writer's cramp,' I said.

'Don't sound so cheerful about it,' said Blake.

'I like a bit of drama – proves we're hitting them hard, doesn't it?'

'I don't want drama. I want to go on winning money.'

During the next twenty minutes Sydney Hopplewell got a start on black. It took him until well after nine to reach the limit, having won 18,390 francs. When Thomas Fredericks took over his chair at the end of the progression he said, as he passed us: 'If I don't get a drink, I'll fall apart.'

'Well, well,' I said to Pauline, 'you realize he just went six and a half hours without one single brandy?'

'I don't think the temperance movement would be too keen on gambling as a cure for drinking.'

Midnight. Keith Robinson started on a two-hour progression. The Chef de Casino arrived at the table in response to the handclapping. Keith was on a beauty, his stakes going up by only around 50 francs or so at a time, this slow progress to the limit giving him what seemed like a yard of uncrossed figures on his line, all of them representing winning bets.

While he was raking in the chips in veritable piles Alec Sherlock got a progression on *pair* (even). Keith reached the limit after something like sixty-six spins. He had won no less than 47,665 francs. Sherlock's stakes went up to the 1,000-franc mark.

A waiter came across the salon and handed a note to the Chef de Casino. He read it and then walked quickly to the exit. It was 2.15 a.m. Sherlock reached the limit at 2.25 a.m. He had won a lot less than Keith, 16,540 francs. I told the team to pack it in for the day.

As we cashed in our masses of plaques and chips the Chef de Casino stood a few feet away, watching us impassively.

Back in Blake's suite we shared out 119,595 francs. Blake and I split 23,919 francs and the remaining 95,676 divided eleven ways gave each of the team about 8,700 francs each, about £630 ($1,775). As Vincent said, picking up his bundle of 100- and 500-franc notes, 'All this paper is beginning to clutter up my pockets.'

'Come and spend some of it with us,' said Keith Robinson. Vincent shook his head.

'Where do you go when you're not playing?' Sherlock demanded. Vincent turned on him and said, in his most insulting drawl, 'I got over the thrill of having *two* prostitutes at a time some time ago.'

'What the hell do you mean by that?' Sherlock snapped.

'Let's not have any unpleasantness,' Blake said firmly. 'We're all very tired and may say stupid things we'll regret in the clear light of day. I suggest we all plod off to our respective digs.'

'I don't want to sound defeatist,' Fredericks said,' but I don't think Mrs Harper-Biggs is going to last out much longer. The atmosphere in there is unbearable.'

'Mrs Harper-Biggs will last as long as any of us,' I said. 'I would hope that none of you was so naïve as to believe it would be a cakewalk to take this amount of money from a casino. Of course they have been trying to intimidate us and of course it would be very cosy if we just packed it in now and went home. But I didn't come all this way to give up as soon as things became a little rough.'

'Calm down, Norman my old son. Nobody's packing it in,' said Keith Robinson. 'We've found the pot of gold, haven't we? Never had such a good time, personally.'

He alone, it seemed, had not been turned into a zombie, so tired were we all when we broke up. I noticed that he was the only one of the 'musketeers' who seemed impatient to get to whatever venue they had chosen for that morning's wild night.

I did not sleep well, and when eventually my brain stopped

racing with scenes from the casino the noises from the early morning traffic kept me awake. Pauline brought me breakfast in bed at ten before she went shopping. I was taking my first weary bite of bacon when the phone rang. It was Blake.

'I must see you urgently,' he said.

'What's wrong?'

'I can't discuss it on the phone. Could you come round here?'

'I suppose so. I'll be there at eleven.'

Pauline came back a few minutes later. She looked agitated.

'There were two men following me!'

'Are you sure? What kind of men?'

'They were French, well dressed, in their thirties. I'm frightened, Norman.'

'I think Blake's had a fright as well by the sound of it. I'm going round to his place. I think you should stay here today. I'll ring you every so often to make sure that you're all right.'

I started out for Blake's hotel by a back street.

Passing a pharmacy, I remembered that Pauline had asked me to buy some soap. As I stood at the counter I looked in the mirror and saw two men staring at me. They fitted Pauline's description. I bought the soap and then went to the telephone to call a taxi.

I waited in there until the Citroën cab pulled up outside. I walked fairly quickly out of the shop, got in and gave the driver a fictitious address in a street near Blake's hotel. By the time this had happened, it was too late for the two men to follow in their own car, presumably parked in the vicinity of my hotel.

I paid off the taxi and walked to Blake's hotel. He was alone in his suite.

'Mr Leigh,' he said, 'sorry to bother you, but I thought you'd want to know. Strange thing – this phone rang twenty or thirty times between six and nine this morning. Each time I picked it up there was a weird clicking noise at the other end, but nobody spoke.'

'Fault in the line probably.'

'That isn't all. Ever since about half-past eight this place has been watched. I saw them from the window, three or four of them standing at the corner down there. They kept walking up and down, maybe waiting for somebody to come out.'

'Pauline was followed when she went out this morning. I didn't fully believe her until the same couple came after me. I gave them the slip.'

'But why on earth do they want to follow us?'

'If they're going to make any moves against us, they'll want to make sure they know where we all are.'

'You think then they are planning something?'

'I would say it's a distinct possibility. Could you ring for a taxi? I'll meet you at the café as usual.'

'Where are you going?'

'Nowhere in particular. Maybe give them a run for their money.'

'You sound as if you're enjoying all this. I'm bloody sure I'm not.'

'This is what it was all for – didn't I tell you?'

'I don't understand. We came here to see if your system could work.'

'The system? I never had the slightest doubt it would work. I wanted to see what happened when it did. Taking them for a lot of money wouldn't be satisfying unless we caused a bit of a furore, would it?'

'I don't believe it! You wanted to provoke them all the time?'

'Not necessarily. I wanted to take this thing to the limit and see what they would do when they knew we had them beaten.'

Startled, Blake nevertheless phoned for a taxi. It came five minutes later.

As we pulled away from the kerb two black Simcas came out from a line of parked cars and started to follow us. I had given the driver the name of our hotel but changed my mind and told him instead to take me to the municipal gardens. The incessant phone calls Blake had been getting sounded like psychological warfare; now I'd give them a taste of their own medicine, and wipe the smiles off their faces.

Chapter Fifteen

As I was paying my taxi driver I saw the two black Simcas pull into the side some twenty yards further along the pavement. We were outside the municipal gardens. I strolled back along the pavement, reaching into my breast pocket for one of my business cards.

The driver of the first Simca was sitting with the window open, heavily intent on not looking at me. I scribbled the address of our hotel on the back of the card.

Coming up to the car, I threw the card into his lap and said casually: 'Why don't you contact me at that address? All this cops-and-robbers stuff is a waste of the taxpayers' money.'

My French may not be perfect, but he understood well enough. The expression on his face was a joy to behold.

It was then midday. I strolled over to a café and ordered a dry martini. Within a couple of minutes two men strolled past on the other side of the street, eyeing me intently. They walked on a few yards, turned, came back and then stood against the railings of the municipal gardens. As sleuths they were either rank amateurs or, more likely, they wanted me to see them. I found myself laughing.

I finished my drink and waved at a passing cab, telling the driver to take me to the local museum. Sure enough, the two black Simcas pulled away from the kerb.

Alighting at the museum, I walked slowly up a flight of stairs to where a fair was being held on a high piece of ground. This was thirsty work. I had a lager at one of the stalls. There was no sight of my tail.

At 12.30 p.m. I went back down the hill, caught another cab and told the driver to take me to the promenade. Failing to see anyone following me, I walked into a small public garden and sat on a bench under a palm tree. The faint buzzing of insects and the murmur of the traffic had a relaxing effect. I began to drowse. Then I heard footsteps on the gravel path.

This time it was the two youngish men who had picked me up at the pharmacy. I saw them coming round the angle of the path before they saw me. I sat exactly where I was and stared at them openly.

As soon as they saw me they hesitated, then turned off along a side path. This seemed to indicate that they were, in fact, incompetent rather than deliberately menacing. I found myself laughing again.

At one, I decided to walk slowly to the Café Massena. It was extremely hot, and the glare of sunlight reflected off predominantly white buildings was giving me a headache, so much so I had to sit down on another bench. For a moment I thought I was going to faint.

Knowing I had to get out of the sun, I more or less staggered as far as a small café in the nearest side-street. I ordered a grenadine. My pursuers were not in evidence. I recovered enough to set out walking again. I reached the Massena at 1.25 p.m. and went inside to have another grenadine in the shade.

At 1.30 Mrs Harper-Biggs and Mrs Heppenstall arrived. I waved for them to come inside. I called Pauline at the hotel, but she had nothing dramatic to report. A few minutes later I saw Sherlock and Hopplewell taking seats at one of the outside tables.

'Let's take our drinks outside,' said Lettice. 'It's a pity to waste the sunshine.'

We went outside. Hopplewell ordered a coffee! When Sherlock made some sarcastic remark he replied, apparently by way of explanation, 'This place has done wonders for the old chest. I'm thinking of moving here permanently.' Blake arrived, followed shortly afterwards by Emma Richardson, Terry Baker and his wife, and Keith Robinson. For ten minutes or so we talked about the weather. Maurice Nathan and George Milton arrived, followed a few minutes later by Peter Vincent and then Fredericks. By two o'clock all twelve of the team were there. I said nothing about my morning chase. Suddenly Lyn Baker blurted out that she and Terry thought they had been followed when they went out to buy baby food that morning.

'We're all getting a little edgy,' Blake said sympathetically.

'I say we ought to go home before something happens,' Lyn Baker exclaimed, sounding genuinely frightened.

'We're seeing this through no matter what,' Terry said sharply.

'I think we should go home!'

Baker raised his voice, 'You aren't a member of the team so don't interfere!'

'I've got as much right as anyone else to give my opinion.'

'Why don't you shut up?' Baker shouted.

'Shut up yourself!'

By this time we were the centre of attraction for everyone else in the café. 'Come, come now,' said Blake. 'Let's not give them the satisfaction of seeing us squabbling among ourselves.'

The Bakers glared at each other.

'Why don't we go to the cocktail lounge of the hotel round the corner?' I said. 'We can get a bit more privacy there.'

We entered the cocktail bar in a group and ordered a variety of drinks. Nobody had much to say. Even Vincent was looking fairly serious. Terry Baker came back from seeing his wife into a taxi. He smiled at me. I called Pauline at the hotel. She seemed quite relaxed. Back at the bar Keith Robinson was telling jokes. 'What do you think will happen?' Terry Baker asked me. I shrugged. 'As soon as we've finished these drinks we go across to the casino and find out.'

'I've told Lyn she's got to go back home. The heat's too much for the baby.'

'I think that's sensible.'

'Yeah well, we all learn in time, I suppose. Tell you something, I've done all the roistering I need for one lifetime, from now on I save every bloody franc I get my hands on. God, I feel terrible.'

'Good. Right then, ladies and gentlemen, time to go to work.'

At 2.40 p.m. we crossed the square towards the dull ochre building. Blake walked beside me. He murmured something about having put the cash book in a safe place. 'If the authorities got their hands on it they would know exactly how much we had won; it could lead to awkward questions about where the money went.'

'You're right, of course. Actually all we have to say is that we spent it. Champagne and wild women.'

'In Baker's case all too true, probably. Not to mention Sherlock and Robinson.'

'At least they'll have had an experience to talk about when they are old men.'

'All you and I have had is hard work.'

'I wouldn't say that.'

'No?'

'We have proved it can be done – that's something, isn't it? We've made history of a sort, no matter what happens now.'

'Not the kind of history one would write to *The Times* about.'

'You're not ashamed of all this, are you?'

He made no reply.

The casino doors were still locked at 2.45 when we reached the first-floor landing. We stood there waiting for the commissariat desk to give the order to open them. Most of the faces were apprehensive. 'Remember what Mr Blake said on our first day?' I said cheerfully. 'One doesn't make history biting one's nails?'

'I don't have any nails left to bite,' said Maurice Nathan.

Three p.m. The doors opened. As we entered the salon M. le Chef de Casino was standing a few feet from the doorway, flanked by some of his minions, smiling sardonically at us.

The first shift took up their positions at our usual table. At 3.03 by the salon clock the tourneur made the first spin of the day. 'Thank God they all got seats,' said Blake.

'What's wrong with Hopplewell?' I asked.

'He wants to speak to you, I think.'

I moved round the table. Hopplewell had a small accumulation of chips in front of him. After some twenty spins his line was 27, 44, 71, bringing his next stake to 98 francs. 'What's wrong?' I asked him.

'I'm going to faint,' he groaned. 'I need a drink.'

'I'll take your place.' By this time the salon was filling up. We waited until everybody round the table was watching to see where the ball would land. I tapped him on the shoulder. He moved quickly off the chair to his right and I slipped into it from the left. Black came up on that spin and the croupier shoved chips worth 98 francs against his stake. I put on a stake of 125 francs: a 100-franc plaque and a 25-franc plaque. This won. My line

194

became 27, 44, 71, 98, 125. My next stake was 152 francs. This won. My line became 27, 44, 71, 98, 125, 152. I lost my next two stakes and my line was down to two figures, 71 and 98, giving me a stake of 169 francs.

Then black came into predominance with a vengeance. It came up seven times in a row (ten consecutive wins was the most we saw in all our time at the Casino Municipale). My stakes reached the 600-franc mark.

It looked like being one of the fastest progressions we had experienced.

Then I looked up to see the Chef de Casino staring at me. I smiled gaily at him.

His face tightened.

Then he stepped back from the table and shouted, '*Cessez les jeux!*'

A great silence fell on the salon.

Everybody in the salon waited to hear what the big boss would say next. He said nothing. Then a number of men appeared at our table. Ignoring the other players, they asked the six of us for our admission cards.

We brought them out of our pockets. Maurice Nathan had his snatched from his hand when the two men standing over him thought he was prevaricating. The Chef de Casino approached the table and made a short speech in French.

'Ladies and gentlemen, for reasons I cannot enter into at the moment this casino will now be closed until further notice. As for you, Mesdames Harper-Biggs, Richardson and Heppenstall, and Messieurs Nathan, Milton and Leigh' – his eyes met mine briefly – 'you will all consider yourselves under restraint. You will remain here until the gendarmerie are called.'

Any light-headedness I might have been suffering from quickly disappeared. I rose from my chair.

'Monsieur le Chef,' I said calmly, 'you will recall the undertaking you gave us only a few days ago, that we would suffer no obstacle to playing a system against the table? What has happened to change your mind?'

'Shut up!' he barked. I was amazed. All round me faces were registering shock at this scandalous outbreak.

'I will not shut up,' I said. 'Am I to understand that we are not to leave this casino?'

'Yes!'

'Then I demand that I be allowed to contact the British Consulate.'

'You may use the telephone at the desk – and remember to pay for the call!'

None of the desk staff would give me the number of the British Consulate. I thumbed through the Nice directory until I found the entry, *Conseil Britannique*.

When I got through, an arrogant voice told me the consul was too busy to speak to me.

'My name is Leigh,' I said. 'I am with some friends in the Casino Municipale. We are all British citizens and we are being held here under unlawful restraint. They refuse to let us leave the salon. Does that sound less important than whatever else the consul is doing?'

There was a good deal of humming and hawing. I was told that somebody would come over to the casino as soon as circumstances permitted.

'In that case will you kindly give me the number of the British Embassy in Paris?'

'There is no need to make such a fuss –'

I put the receiver down on him and dialled enquiries. I got through to the Embassy in Paris after about ten minutes and explained the situation to the official who took my call. He promised to take immediate action.

I went back into the main part of the salon. Our group was being questioned by the men who had demanded their admission cards. 'Say nothing to these people until the consul gets here,' I told everybody.

By the time the man from the Consulate turned up the salon was empty save for the thirteen of us and the staff of the casino. Her Majesty's delegate was a weedy man in his fifties, apparently out of his depth in this situation.

However, he was the best we were going to get, so I gave him a brief résumé of what had happened. 'You can see we are being physically restrained from leaving this casino. We have committed no crime – indeed, these people have not even made any allegations against us.'

'I'm sure it's all a misunderstanding,' he burbled. His ineffectuality exasperated me. 'If the gendarmerie is not here within a couple of minutes,' I announced, 'we will walk out. Let them try to stop us by force if they like. We'll see then what kind of scandal you have on your hands, Monsieur le Chef.'

'Come come, let's be reasonable,' said the man from the Consulate.

I snarled: 'Be reasonable? Why don't you give *them* that advice? We have done nothing except play roulette. And win, of course.'

A smallish man detached himself from the group who had taken our admission cards. 'We would like to know what you and your friends have done with the money you won from this casino – you realize there are restrictions on the amount of French currency that can be sent out of France?'

I handed him my notepad. 'Will you put your questions in writing and sign the page? Here is my pen if you don't have one.'

He grimaced and then turned his back on me. I burst out laughing. The Consulate official frowned at me to keep quiet.

'Keep quiet yourself, sir,' I snapped at him, ready now to explode. 'What the hell have you done to help us anyway? If the police are not here forthwith we go out through that door – fighting if necessary.'

The idea of Cynthia Harper-Biggs and Lettice Heppenstall battling against the phalanx of men surrounding us made me laugh out loud as soon as I had finished this tirade. No doubt I was a little out of control.

That was when five or six uniformed gendarmes came into the casino. One of them brought out a notebook.

'When I call your name please answer,' he said. He started reading from his list. We all answered correctly.

'I wish you to come with us if you please,' said the senior policeman.

'Where to?' Blake demanded.

'The headquarters of the Police des Jeux.'

'Do we go?' Blake asked me.

'We must – don't give them any excuse for accusing us of failing to cooperate with the law.'

The Chef de Casino and his minions impassively watched us go through the swing doors with the gendarmes. Nothing was said.

We came out into the blinding sunshine. It was 5.30 p.m. We started off walking through the town behind the gendarmes.

'Funny way of arresting us,' said Keith Robinson. 'Follow-my-leader to jail?'

I looked back. There was not a single policeman behind us.

'I don't think these chaps consider we've broken the law,' Blake said.

'We could just run for it then,' Keith said.

'Then we *would* be in trouble,' I told him. 'Let's just wait and see what they have planned for us.'

After ten minutes' meandering through the back streets we came to a dilapidated blue building with white louver shutters.

We were led in through the main entrance. Our police escort, who had hardly bothered to look back once during our progress through the town, went down a passageway, stopping at the door of a large, sparsely furnished room with a long table under a window high in the wall.

Seated behind the table were five high-ranking police officers. The heat in the room was terrific.

One of them started to read out a list of our names. Each of us answered in turn. We were then told to sit down, a strange invitation as there were thirteen of us and only two shaky cane chairs. Mrs Harper-Biggs and Mrs Heppenstall lowered themselves into them gingerly. The officer who had read out our names sat down and another stood up.

'Ladies and gentlemen,' he said in passable English, 'I wish to assure you that you have done nothing criminal and you have not broken the casino regulations – as far as we of the Police des Jeux are concerned you are honourable men and ladies. However, and without assigning any reason, we have to inform you that you are hereby banned for life from playing roulette in the Casino Municipale.'

I started to say something, but he waved me down. 'I cannot enter into discussions with you; it is pointless to put any questions to me. I would warn all of you that if you should make any

198

attempt to regain admission to the Casino Municipale that will constitute a criminal offence. That is all I have to say to you. You may go now. Good day.'

The great coup was over. We were shown out into the sunshine. Dazed and bewildered, our little party hesitated on the pavement. 'What do we do now then?' asked Keith Robinson.

'I think we should all go back to my place for a drink,' said Blake. 'It looks as if our little venture has come to an end.'

'I don't see why,' Terry Baker said aggressively. 'Plenty more casinos, aren't there?'

'I should imagine we're banned from all of them,' said Blake. 'I can make enquiries, if you like.'

'Of course we *could* go to the Salle Privée, Monte Carlo,' I said, looking at Baker. 'How are you off for capital?'

'Need you bloody well ask?' Baker retorted.

We decided to wait while Blake attempted to discover whether we had been banned from all the municipal casinos and meet the following day as usual at the Café Massena. When we did so, Blake said he had been on the phone all morning. 'We've been banned by the French Ministry of the Interior. These municipal casinos are administered centrally from Enghien-les-Bains, and if you are banned from one of them, you are automatically banned in all the others.'

'There are other casinos, private ones,' said Sherlock.

'Go through all that again?' said Maurice Nathan.

We were having an inconclusive discussion, only Baker and Sherlock apparently having the stomach for starting the whole process again, when I noticed three or four men watching us from the other side of the square. I nudged George Milton. The others turned to see what we were looking at. One of the group, a tall thin man in a dark suit, came across the square towards us, walking deliberately, without haste.

He came up to the three tables we had pushed together and looked at us all in turn.

'When are you leaving for England?' he said finally, in good English.

'What concern is it of yours?' I asked. 'Are you from the police? If so, may I see your credentials?'

He gave me a long look, shaking his head. 'I think it will be better for all of you to leave here quickly,' he said. Then he walked back across the square. His associates stood there listening to him and watching us.

That did it.

We had a dinner party that night in Mrs Harper-Biggs' hotel. After a few drinks Blake let himself go as far as to recite by heart Kipling's poem 'If'. Released from the tension of the past few days, we all became fairly jolly. I contented myself with a short speech of thanks to all of them for the magnificent way they had worked together.

'We've all come a long way from my roulette academy in Twickenham,' I said. 'We don't need any histrionics, we know what we've proved. We made the system work, we won a lot of money, we were so successful we made a government nervous – above all I think I can truthfully say we have all shared an experience we won't easily forget. I don't know if we'll ever meet again, but before we break up I should very much like to thank each and every one of you for having faith enough in me to take part. I give you a toast: to our gallant band of thirteen.'

Postscript

What did it all prove?

At the time I was satisfied merely to think that all those years, all those disasters and farces, finally produced an undeniable triumph. The thirteen of us made gaming history in proving that a determined group of people working to a scientific system can beat the casino on its own terms. In our eight days at the Casino Municipale our winnings came to about 800,000 francs – £58,000 ($163,000).

I kept up contact with some of the twelve over the next few years, although our general mood was against annual reunions and the like – we had done it together and there was no need to surround our memories with ritual celebrations. Mrs Harper-Biggs and Mrs Heppenstall had become close friends on the trip and remained so. Blake married the girl he'd been engaged to before we went to France. Sydney Hopplewell, who told Pauline at that last night's dinner party that he had never known such good friends, eased up on his drinking. Each of the team made about £4,230 (approximately $11,844) in the eight days we actually played in the Casino Municipale, but even tax-free it was hardly enough to change the whole course of their lives.

It is very likely that Terry Baker's life was changed for the worse. It seemed probable that he and his wife would split up. How much of the money he and Sherlock and Robinson managed to salvage from their headlong adoption of riotous living I prefer not to conjecture. I know that Maurice Nathan kept most of his winnings and set himself up in business again. What happened to Thomas Fredericks I don't know, although I'm fairly sure he was not going back to polish a humble office chair, not wearing the kind of suits he took home from the Riviera.

Peter Vincent got fairly drunk on that last night and made

some sort of pass at Emma Richardson, who turned him down, needless to say.

As for myself – Pauline and I separated and were finally divorced. I would not blame it entirely on my obsession with roulette.

One thing I can say with some certainty, however. I proved my point and I had the supreme satisfaction of doing it before the eyes of the man who had found my father's bankruptcy so amusing all those years before. Yet by the time we had become so successful that we had to be marched out of the casino and banned for life by the French government I had lost any lurking desire to flaunt my triumph in his face. Winning is the cure for a gambling obsession. I remember something Peter Vincent said one night in the casino. The usual mocking smile about his eyes, he surveyed the crowded tables and remarked, 'Amazing to what lengths we higher primates will go for a bit of amusement, isn't it?'

That seemed to put roulette in perspective. Having achieved the goal which had ruled most of my adult years, I found life strangely empty. A cured addiction leaves a very large void. One would like to think that the years bring maturity – looking back, I can only conclude that there are no half-measures with an obsessive personality. I have always had a bee in my bonnet about the way Authority loads the dice in its own favour and I dare say my life would have been more fruitful if I had been content to knuckle down to the preordained order of things.

However – I did make a little bit of history.

Do you wonder *now* why a man who discovered the 'perfect system' for beating the wheel could regard roulette as something of which he had, finally, been *cured*?

And yet . . . is an addict ever really cured?

When news of this book began to spread I was approached by an American who wanted to know if my system would work in Las Vegas.

I explained the difference between the French and the American wheel. The latter has thirty-eight compartments and two zeros. The double zero gives the bank an advantage of 5.26 per cent – an additional feature being that on the double-zero wheel the bet *cannot* be halved (*partager*) if zero appears, neither can it be left on the table 'imprisoned' (*en prison*), to have its fate decided by the next spin. On the American wheel all bets are lost when zero comes up.

How would this affect the Reverse Labouchère? The additional advantage would probably make the difference between winning say $2,500 (single-zero wheel) and $2,350 (double-zero wheel) in a day. This would hardly worry the serious player – but there is another complication.

The spin of the American wheel in a Las Vegas casino is governed purely by time. The croupiers do not wait for players to place their stakes. On a French wheel you will have approximately thirty spins to the hour – the American wheel will be spun sixty to sixty-five times in the same period.

This is a minor disadvantage – the player has less time for calculations between spins. Yet once the brain can cope, this faster rate becomes a positive advantage. The team would require twice as much capital but it should show slightly more than *double the profits*, simply because there are more spins to work on.

'Well, what's stopping us forming a syndicate to have a crack at one of the casinos in Vegas?' this American asked.

'No!' was my immediate reaction. 'I'm finished with roulette.'

'All that money waiting to be won, but you're not interested? Are you sure?'

I tried to make a joke about it. 'After all, does one wish to climb Everest *twice*?'

'Really?' he said sarcastically. 'Sure you aren't frightened your win in Nice wasn't just a fluke?'

I was so annoyed I could hardly speak. I had *proved* that my theory worked. I did not have to go on and on proving it, did I? We had made *history*, damn the man.

And yet, the more I think about it, the more I hear myself asking:

Why not?

More about Penguins and Pelicans

Penguinews, which appears every month, contains details of all the new books issued by Penguins as they are published. From time to time it is supplemented by *Penguins in Print*, which is our complete list of almost 5,000 titles.

A specimen copy of *Penguinews* will be sent to you free on request. Please write to Dept EP, Penguin Books Ltd, Harmondsworth, Middlesex, for your copy.

In the U.S.A.: For a complete list of books available from Penguins in the United States write to Dept CS, Penguin Books, 625 Madison Avenue, New York New York 10022.

In Canada: For a complete list of books available from Penguins in Canada write to Penguin Books Canada Ltd, 2801 John Street, Markham, Ontario L3R 1B4.

Derek Marlowe

NIGHTSHADE

A trip to the Caribbean takes Edward and Amy to Haiti, a place of unaccountable fear and peculiar coincidence.

Paradise turns to hell, the hell of Baron Samedi, the voodoo lord of death.

SOMEBODY'S SISTER

'Excellent specimen of Neo-Chandlerism' – Maurice Richardson in the *Observer*

'An excellent mystery right to its ironic finale. As a valentine to a romantic legend it is even better' – Matthew Coady in the *Guardian*

DO YOU REMEMBER ENGLAND

Who is Dowson?

'When he left on the Sunday – the others had gone to visit Aunt Beth's rose garden (plus *bosquet*) and returned to find his room empty – there were no regrets . . . he had stayed thirty-six hours, had glimpsed Hallam's wife only for a second . . . and I knew that nothing could ever be the same again'

A DANDY IN ASPIC

A Dandy in Aspic is the story of a man ordered to Berlin to track down and kill a ruthless Russian assassin and double agent, Krasnevin. A difficult assignment, since he himself is Krasnevin.

THE DISAPPEARANCE

Search for Celandine. Carry out the assignment. Think. Worry.

For Jay, a professional killer, time is running out.

Paul Theroux

THE GREAT RAILWAY BAZAAR

Fired by a fascination with trains that stemmed from childhood, Paul Theroux set out one day with the intention of boarding every train that chugged into view from Victoria Station in London to Tokyo Central, and to come back again via the Trans-Siberian Express.

And so began a strange, unique and hugely entertaining railway odyssey.

THE FAMILY ARSENAL

A novel of urban terror and violence set in the grimy decay of South-East London.

'One of the most brilliantly evocative novels of London that has appeared for years . . . very disturbing indeed' – Michael Ratcliffe in *The Times*

'An uncomplicated pleasure . . . with this writer the thrills are never cheap and obvious' – Robert Nye in the *Guardian*

'This is a thriller, tightly plotted, terribly evocative' – Elizabeth Berridge in the *Daily Telegraph*

Also published in Penguins:

SAINT JACK

Michelle Celmer is a bestselling author of more than thirty books. When she's not writing, she likes to spend time with her family and their menagerie of animals.

Michelle loves to hear from readers. Like her on Facebook or write her at PO Box 300, Clawson, MI 48017, USA.

Kat Cantrell read her first Mills & Boon novel in third grade and has been scribbling in notebooks since she learned to spell. What else would she write but romance?

Kat, her husband and their two boys live in north Texas. When she's not writing about characters on the journey to happily-ever-after, she can be found at a football game, watching the TV show *Friends* or listening to eighties music.

Kat was the 2011 Mills & Boon So You Think You Can Write contest winner and a 2012 RWA Golden Heart® Award finalist for best unpublished series contemporary manuscript.

Sarah M. Anderson may live east of the Mississippi River, but her heart lies out West on the Great Plains. Sarah's book *A Man of Privilege* won an RT Reviewers' Choice Best Book Award in 2012.

Sarah spends her days having conversations with imaginary cowboys and American Indians. Find out more about Sarah's love of cowboys and Indians at www.sarahmanderson.com and sign up for the new-release newsletter at eepurl.com/nv39b.

Dreams & Desires

MICHELLE CELMER
KAT CANTRELL
SARAH M. ANDERSON

MILLS & BOON

First Published in Great Britain 2019
by Mills & Boon, an imprint of HarperCollins*Publishers*
1 London Bridge Street, London, SE1 9GF

DREAMS & DESIRES © 2019 Harlequin Books S. A.

The Doctor's Baby Dare © 2016 Harlequin Books S.A.
The Seal's Secret Heirs © 2016 Harlequin Books S.A.
A Surprise For The Sheikh © 2016 Harlequin Books S.A.

Special thanks and acknowledgement are given to Michelle Celmer, Kat Cantrell and Sarah M. Anderson for their contribution to the *Texas Cattleman's Club: Lies and Lullabies* series.

ISBN: 978-0-263-27481-3

0319

MIX
Paper from
responsible sources
FSC™ C007454

THE DOCTOR'S
BABY DARE

MICHELLE CELMER

One

Dr. Parker Reese considered himself an all-around great guy.

He was affable and easygoing and had a great sense of humor. He was also honest and respectful and always willing to lend a hand. He was a rock in a crisis and a natural born leader. And despite the fact that he'd lived in Texas for only three months and knew nothing about cows, he had just been accepted into the prestigious Texas Cattleman's Club. And they didn't let just anybody in.

Parker was one of those rare individuals who got along with everyone. Everyone who knew him liked and respected him.

Well, almost everyone.

Parker glanced across the hospital cafeteria to the table where the object of his recent fascination sat eating her lunch, phone in hand, earbuds in place to deflect any unwanted attention. Head nurse of the new pediatric ward at Royal Memorial Hospital, Clare Connelly was smart and competent, by far one of the best nurses he'd ever worked with. She ran a tight ship on her ward, and was highly regarded by her coworkers.

And for reasons that escaped Parker, she refused to like him.

Lucas Wakefield, chief of surgery and fellow Texas Cattleman's Club member, set his tray down on the table and dropped into the seat across from Parker. "Mind if I join you?"

Parker grinned. "I think you just did."

If it wasn't for Luc, Parker wouldn't even be in Texas. The two had met at a conference when they were both medical students. At the time, Parker had been working toward a career in cosmetic plastic surgery for the rich and famous, the only medical field his father considered lucrative enough for a tycoon's son, and one that Parker knew would never elicit any real sense of pride. As was often the case, his father's own selfish demands and archaic values trumped Parker's happiness.

Luc had told him to screw the old man and convinced Parker to follow his true passion. Pediatrics. And for the first time in his life Parker stood up to his father. There had been a fair amount of shouting, and threats to cut Parker off financially. His father had even threatened to disown him, but Parker told him that was a chance he was willing to take. His father finally, though reluctantly, conceded. That put an end to the threats and manipulations his father had always used to control him, and for the first time in his life, Parker felt truly independent. But the event had caused a fissure in their relationship, one that took many years to heal. Even so, by the time his father had passed away last year, they'd managed to resolve most of their differences.

After a lifetime of coveting his father's approval, he'd earned it. And now, with his inheritance, Parker had the means to do anything he wanted, wherever he wanted. He knew that he needed a change, that the only reason he'd stayed in New York was to be near his ailing father. Aside from his practice, and a few good friends, there was nothing tying him there. He knew it was time to move on. But where?

Enter Luc. He'd called out of the blue to offer Parker a job in the town of Royal, Texas. Dr. Mann, Royal Hospital's neonatal specialist, was retiring and they were looking for a replacement. The salary wasn't all that impressive, but Parker's inheritance left him set for life. So he sold his practice and relocated to Texas.

Best move he ever made.

"So, did you ever call that girl you met in the gift shop?" Luc asked, dumping a packet of sugar in his coffee.

"We had dinner," Parker told him.

"And..."

"Then I took her home."

"Your home or hers?"

"Hers."

"Did she invite you in?"

They always did. And he didn't doubt that the next stop would have been her bedroom, and a couple of months ago he wouldn't have hesitated. But something about it, about all of his romantic relationships lately, felt hollow. "She invited, I declined."

Luc made a noise like he'd been punched in the gut.

"Dude, you're killing me. I'm married and I'm having more sex than you are."

At thirty-eight, the ever-widening age span between Parker and the twentysomethings he'd been dating was losing its luster. What he was looking for now was an equal. Someone to challenge him. He glanced over at Clare again. Someone capable of stimulating his intelligence as well as his libido.

Luc followed Parker's line of sight and rolled his eyes. "Dude, let it go already. How many times have you asked her out?"

Parker shrugged. He'd honestly lost track. A couple dozen at least. At first her rejection was firm, but polite—for the most part. Not so much anymore. Lately he could feel the tension when they were forced to work together. Which was often. But that was okay. It would just be that much more satisfying when she gave into him. And she would. They always did.

"What do you think it is about me that she finds so offensive?" he asked Luc.

"Could it be your inability to accept *no* as an answer?"

Parker shot him a look. "She wants me. I guarantee it."

He glanced over at her again. Her eyes were lowered, but she knew he was looking. He wasn't sure how he knew, he just did. He could feel her from across the cafeteria. In her early thirties, she was nearly a decade older than the women he typically dated, but he liked that.

"You really can't stand it can you?" Luc said and Parker turned to him.

"Can't stand what?"

"That she won't bend to your will."

It would irritate him a lot more if he didn't know that it was temporary. But yes, he was used to women falling at his feet. And honestly, it wasn't as great as it sounded. "Clare will change her mind. I just have to catch her at the right time."

"When the chloroform kicks in?"

Parker laughed in spite of himself and said, "Let me tell you a story. When I was a kid, there was a girl at my school named Ruth Flanigan. And for reasons unknown to me, Ruth relentlessly picked on me."

"You were bullied by a girl?" Luc laughed. "Is that some sort of ass-backward karma?"

"It's funny now, but at the time it was traumatic. She would shove me in the lunch line or kick my shins on the playground. She pulled my hair and knocked me off the swings. For years I was afraid of girls."

"Clearly you got over that."

Had he? Sometimes he wondered. When it came to relationships, he was always the one calling the shots, the one in control. He only dated women who were substantially younger and intellectually inferior. That had to mean something.

"So, what happened?" Luc asked him.

"At some point in the second grade she either moved or switched to a different school. I don't remember exactly. I just remember coming back to school in the fall, and being relieved that she was no longer there. I didn't have any contact with her again until college. I was home for the holidays and I ran into her at the party of a mutual friend."

"Did she kick your shins?"

"No. She confessed that she'd had a huge crush on me, and torturing me was just her way of showing it."

"Don't tell me you're going to kick Clare in the shins and pull her hair."

"Of course not." Though he was sure the hair-pulling part would come later, if she was into that sort of thing. "My point is, just because someone acts as if they don't like you, it doesn't mean it's true."

"Are you seriously suggesting that Clare is only *pretending* not to like you?"

Parker shrugged. "It's not impossible."

"You clearly have your pick of female companions. Why this infatuation with Clare?"

Because she fascinated him, and not just because she was the only woman he'd ever met who was seemingly immune to his charms. Weird as it sounded, he just felt drawn to her. He wanted to crack her open, peek inside and see what made her tick. Metaphorically speaking of course.

Clare had been on the hospital staff for almost a decade, but Parker had yet to find a single person who knew her on a deeply personal level. Which he thought was weird. He spent far more time with his coworkers than anyone. He liked to think of them as extended family. But then, he had always been a very social person. Clare was not. She always sat alone in the cafeteria, and kept to herself on the ward. He'd heard that she had never been married or had kids, and had lived with her old-maid aunt since college. But like the librarian who wore sexy lingerie under a conservative and drab suit, Clare had layers, and boy would he love to be the one to peel them back. He was sure he would find sexy underthings in there somewhere. He was betting that if she wanted to, Clare could teach him a thing or two about having fun.

"I'd just like to get to know her."

"I've never known you to fixate on a woman this

way," Luc said. "I have to say it's a little disconcerting. It's like you're obsessed."

He had no explanation for why he felt such a deep connection to Clare. In the past he'd avoided deep connections like the plague. Why this time did it feel so...natural?

He knew her work routine like the back of his hand. Knew exactly when she started her rounds, when she ate her lunch, when she worked on charts. He knew her smile, and the melody of her voice, though when she used it to address him it was always filled with irritation. But he was getting close, he could feel it.

Okay, maybe he was a *little* obsessed.

"Even if you're right," Luc said, "and she doesn't hate you as much as she lets on, everyone knows that Clare doesn't date coworkers."

"There's a first time for everything," Parker told him. "And I never say never."

"I think that's your biggest problem."

Luc could poke fun all he wanted—Parker was confident he would wear her down. "I give it a month, probably less."

With a sly grin that said he was up to something, Luc asked, "Are you willing to bet on that?"

"You'll lose," Parker told him.

"If you're so sure, put your money where your mouth is."

It wouldn't be the first time they had entered into a friendly wager. "The usual amount?"

"You've got a deal," Luc said and they fist-bumped on it.

Parker's phone rumbled and he pulled it from the pocket of his lab coat. It was Vanessa, a nursing assistant from the NICU.

"I'm sorry to bother you, Doctor, but we need you up here. Janey's vitals are erratic again."

He cursed under his breath. Born premature and abandoned on the floor of a truck stop, Baby Janey Doe had been brought into Emergency last month and had instantly captured the heart of everyone on the ward. And though she was getting the best medical care available, her little body just wasn't ready to heal.

"Be right there," he told her, then rose, telling Luc, "Gotta go."

"Janey?" Luc asked, and when Parker nodded Luc shook his head grimly. "No improvement?"

"It doesn't make sense," he said, gathering up what was left of his lunch. "I've run every test I could think of, scoured the internet and medical journals for similar cases, but nothing fits. I'm at a loss. In the meantime her little body is shutting down. I'm worried we might lose her."

"It sucks, but you can't save them all."

He knew that, and he'd lost patients before. "Maybe I can't save them all," he told Luc, "but I'll never stop trying."

Clare Connelly sat in the hospital cafeteria, headphones in, wishing this day would hurry up and be over. This morning when she'd gotten into her car, it had stalled several times before she finally got it running. Then it had stalled again at a red light when she was halfway there, and she'd wound up with a line of angry drivers behind her. As she'd pulled into the hospital lot the skies had opened up and dumped a deluge of rain on her as she walked to the building.

Yesterday had been their monthly family dinner at

her parents' horse farm an hour away, and though she had warned them that she might have to work, apparently Clare's absence had caused a stir again. Her phone had been blowing up all morning with calls from her seven siblings. When her brothers or sisters missed dinner no one freaked out. Of course, they all saw each other on a regular basis.

Her three brothers and two of her sisters worked on the farm, and her other two sisters were stay-at-home mothers with four children each. In total Clare had twenty-two nieces and nephews ranging in age from newborn to twenty-six. It seemed as if every time she turned around one of her siblings was expecting another child, and her oldest niece and nephew were both newly married with first children on the way. An entirely new generation to remind Clare how much of a black sheep she really was.

Being single and childless in such a traditional family made her a target for well-meaning and sometimes not-so-well-meaning relatives. No one could grasp the concept that she actually enjoyed being single, and that she wasn't deliberately going against the grain. She was just trying to be happy on her own terms. Refusing to join the family business after high school had sent relations into a tizzy; they'd tagged her as the rebel. If they had bothered to pay attention they would have known she had always dreamed of being a nurse. But from the day she graduated from nursing school they had teased her relentlessly, saying that she'd only entered the profession to snag a rich doctor and live in a mansion.

Her gaze automatically sought out her new boss.

An attractive, smooth-talking multimillionaire well-known for his philanthropy, Parker was every woman's dream. With his *GQ* model physique, rich brown hair always in need of a trim and eyes that looked green one minute and brown the next, he was way above average on the looks scale. Way, *way* above. At the sight of him on his first day at the hospital, her female staff had been reduced to giggling, blushing, hormonally driven adolescent girls.

He was hands down one of the finest physicians she'd ever worked for. He was trustworthy, honest, reliable, and she had never once seen him in a foul mood. He was as charming as he was funny, and his often rumpled, shabby-chic appearance only added to his appeal. And despite being an East Coaster, he had exceptionally good manners. But most important, his rapport with children made him an outstanding pediatrician.

He was also a shameless, womanizing serial dater. Or so she had heard. One who had apparently set his sights on her.

As if.

She'd learned the hard way that emotional entanglements with a coworker, especially one in a position of power, were a prescription for disaster. It was how her no-dating-coworkers rule had come to be. And though she'd made every effort possible to ignore him, he made that nearly impossible with his relentless teasing and barely veiled innuendo. All of that unwanted attention had resulted in a mild crush.

Mild crush? She nearly laughed out loud at the understatement. She could fool her family and her coworkers, but she couldn't fool her own heart. And though she would die before admitting it to another human being, she wanted him. Badly.

Getting that first guilty glimpse of him every morning, with his slightly rumpled hair and lopsided tie, was by far the highlight of her day. She would imagine brushing back that single soft curl that fell across his forehead and straightening that tie and then she would push herself up on her toes…

And that was where it always ended because if she let herself go any further, she would forget all of the reasons she needed to keep him at arm's length. But even if he wasn't her boss, he was off-limits. If her family got wind that she was dating a doctor, especially a rich one, they would never let her live it down.

She just wished he would stop *watching* her. He had her so tied in knots she could barely eat her lunch. She supposed that was one of the advantages of a crush, or lust, or whatever this thing was. Inevitable weight loss. Since Dr. Reese had moved there, Clare had dropped a total of eighteen pounds. She hadn't been this skinny since her first year of college. She felt so good without the extra weight that she'd begun jogging again. Though she did realize she would have never put on those eighteen pounds in the first place if she hadn't gotten lax with her exercise regimen. Then again, she'd had no one to look good naked for. Nor the time or even the desire to go out and find someone.

In her peripheral vision she saw Dr. Reese rise from the table where he'd been sitting with Dr. Wakefield, and her stomach did a flip-flop. He would have to walk past her to leave the cafeteria. Keeping her eyes on her phone, she watched in her peripheral vision as Parker neared her table, and when he walked past she could feel the air shift.

Would he stop and give her a hard time? He was always making excuses to talk to her about things that weren't work related. Probably because he knew it annoyed her. That's what she wanted him to think anyway.

Parker must have been in a hurry because he didn't stop this time. She should have been relieved, so why the feeling of disappointment? She couldn't go on this way, harboring an irrational lust for a man who was completely wrong for her, walking around in a state of constant confusion.

Her phone rang and she answered, instantly back in work mode when Vanessa, one of her nurses, told her Janey's vitals were no longer stable and getting worse by the minute.

Clare jumped up, leaving her tray on the table and shoving her phone in her cardigan pocket as she headed for the closest elevator. Since she'd been discovered in the truck stop, just minutes after her birth and barely clinging to life, Janey's condition had been touch and go. Being in the medical field, Clare had been trained to put her personal feelings aside and remain objective, but Janey was like no other patient she'd ever had. She had no one, and despite efforts to find her family, or anyone who may have known who her family was, the police had come up empty, so Janey had become a ward of the state. Clare couldn't imagine being so helpless and alone, nor could she understand how a woman could abandon her child that way. Though she had no children of her own, or plans to have a baby anytime soon, Clare could see how fiercely protective her sisters were of their children. What could have happened to Janey's mom to make her think that her baby would be better off without her? Or maybe she hadn't been given a choice.

The idea gave Clare a cold chill.

She rounded the corner to see the elevator doors
sliding closed and broke into a run, calling, "Hold the
elevator!"

A hand emerged to stop the door, a hand that she realized, as she slipped inside, was attached to the very
person she was trying to avoid. And now she was the
last place she wanted to be.

Stuck alone with him.

He hit the button for the fourth floor, wearing a look
that made her knees weak, and as the doors slid shut
said, "Hey there, sunshine."

Two

Clare shot Parker one of those looks. This one seemed to say, *Seriously, did you really just call me that?*

But a month ago she would have completely ignored him, so that was progress. Right?

"They called you about Janey?" he asked her.

"Erratic vitals," Clare said, her concern for the infant clear on her face. Janey had made an emotional impact on everyone in the NICU, but Clare seemed more attached to her than anyone. He couldn't deny that Janey's case had tested his objectivity from the minute she was admitted to the hospital, barely clinging to life. And now, with treatment options diminishing, he was feeling the pressure.

There had to be something he was missing...

"She's not getting better," Clare said as if she were reading his mind.

"No," he agreed. "She isn't."

A code blue was called over the PA for the fourth floor. Parker looked at Clare, and she looked at him, and they cursed in unison. Their fragile patient had gone from unstable to arrest.

Knowing it wouldn't do a bit of good, he stabbed the button for the fourth floor again. Janey could be dying and the two people responsible for her care were stuck on a damned elevator.

"If this thing moves any slower I'll have to get out and push," he told Clare.

It felt like an eternity before the elevator dinged for their floor. They stood side by side, like sprinters at the starting line. The instant the doors slid open they broke into a run. By the time he reached her, Janey was in full cardiac arrest. Nurses stood around watching anxiously as a pediatrics resident performed manual CPR on her pale and limp little body. The sight of it was so heartbreaking Parker had to dig down extra deep for the focus to perform his duties.

"Let me through," he barked, and a group of startled staff instantly cleared the way. He never raised his voice to his team, or anyone for that matter, but this was bad.

"She's not responding," the resident said as Parker took over the heart compressions.

"Call her cardiologist," he barked to no one in particular, knowing someone would do it.

He tried to find a pulse, and couldn't. "Come on, little one. Fight for me."

He continued the compressions to no avail.

Damn it, he had hoped it wouldn't come to this. "Paddles," he said, turning to his left where Clare always stood, surprised to find a different nurse there.

He glanced around and found Clare standing *way* over by the door. Her face looked pale and her eyes wide, and for an instant he was sure she was about to either be sick or lose consciousness. Unfortunately he had a sick infant who took priority.

Even using the paddles it took almost thirty minutes to get Janey stable, and afterward everyone breathed a huge sigh of relief, including him. She was okay for now, but that had been a really close call. He turned to find Clare, who he had assumed wouldn't leave Janey's side for the reminder of her shift, but she was gone.

He texted her, checking the hallway as he waited for an answer, but after several minutes the message was still tagged as unread. Clare always read and answered her messages.

He frowned. Something was definitely up.

Assuming she'd gone back to the nurses' station, he headed that way. "Have you seen Nurse Connelly?" he asked Rebecca, the nursing assistant sitting there.

"She walked by a second ago." She looked up at him through a veil of what he was sure were fake lashes. "So, I was thinking we could get together again this weekend."

Oh, no, that was not a good idea. He liked Rebecca, but she was a party girl and these days he could barely stay awake past eleven thirty. His father used to tell him, *You're only as old as you feel*. After a night of partying with Rebecca and her friends, he felt about eighty. She was fun and sexy, but the inevitable hangover wasn't worth it. He could no longer stay out till 3:00 a.m. then make it to work by seven and still function. He was pushing forty. His party days were over.

He checked his phone but still no text.

"Did you see where Nurse Connelly went?" he asked Rebecca, ignoring her suggestion completely, which she didn't seem to like very much.

"Sorry, no," she said tartly.

He doubted he would be getting any more help from her. Ironically, this very situation was probably why Clare didn't date people from work. A lesson he clearly hadn't learned yet.

So, where the hell had she disappeared to? Did she go back down to the cafeteria? Had she slipped past Rebecca and gone to the elevator? No, he thought with a shake of his head. Knowing Clare, she wouldn't want anyone to see her lose her cool, so where would she go for guaranteed privacy? At the end of this hall there was a family waiting room—the last place she would go—and the door to the stairs…

Of course! That had to be it. He'd taken a breather or two in the stairwell himself. Or used it to sneak a kiss with a pretty young nurse. She had to be there.

He found Clare sitting on a step halfway between the fourth and fifth floor, arms roped around her legs, head on her knees so her face was hidden.

"Here to harass me in my moment of weakness?" she asked without looking up.

"How did you know it was me?"

"Because that's the kind of day I've been having." She lifted her head, sniffling and wiping tears from her cheeks with the heel of her palms.

Tears?

Clare was *crying*?

Just when he thought she couldn't be more interesting, or perplexing, she threw him a curveball.

"And I know how your shoes sound," she added. "From hearing you walk up and down the halls."

He would be flattered that she paid attention, but she paid attention to everything on the ward.

"Are you all right?" He offered her one of the tissues he kept in his lab coat pocket. He dealt with parents of sick children on a daily basis. Tissues were a part of the uniform.

She took it and wiped her nose. "I'm okay. Just really embarrassed. I don't know what happened in there."

"You choked," he said, knowing Clare would want an honest answer. "It happens to the best of us."

She lifted her chin stubbornly. "Not to me it doesn't."

If she had been standing, and was a foot taller, he was sure she would be looking down her nose at him. "At the risk of sounding like a tool, all evidence is to the contrary, cupcake."

Outraged, she opened her mouth, probably to say something mean, or respond to the *cupcake* remark, then something inside her seemed to give. Her face went slack and her body sort of sank in on itself. She dropped her head to her knees again, groaning, "You're right."

He was? She really *must* have been out of sorts because she never thought he was right about anything.

"Are you okay?" he asked.

"You know those days when you feel like you could take on the world? When everything goes exactly the way you want it to?"

"Sure."

She looked up at him with red-rimmed, bloodshot eyes. "This is not one of those days."

He cringed. "That bad, huh?"

She dropped her head back down to her knees. "Choking on the job is just the icing on the cake."

Clearly. "So you really never choked?"

She shook her head, making her messy bun flop from side to side, and said, "Not even in nursing school."

He took a chance and sat down beside her. She didn't snarl or hiss, or unsheathe her talons, so that was good. "Is there anything I can do?"

"Shoot me and put me out of my misery."

"I think you're being a little hard on yourself," he told her. He had heard of surgeons who choked during surgery and never got their confidence back, but this was different. This wasn't a matter of confidence, this was pure human emotion.

"What if it happens again, when she *needs* me?" Clare said, looking up at him. She had the prettiest eyes, and she smelled amazing. It would barely take anything to lean in and kiss her. Her lips looked plump and delicious. It might even be worth the concussion afterward, when Clare clocked him.

"If there hadn't been fifteen other people in the room to compensate, if it had been just you and me, or even just you, I have no doubt that you would have performed admirably," he said.

"It's getting more difficult to be objective with her," Clare said, looking genuinely distraught. "When they called the code I thought for sure that this was it, that this time she wouldn't snap back. It made me sick inside, like she was my own flesh and blood."

"Your compassion is what makes you such a good nurse."

"Yeah, I'm awesome," she said. "I was so limp with fear I barely made it out of the elevator. I was sweating and my heart was pounding and I felt like I couldn't breathe, and all the way down the hall it was like I was walking through quicksand."

It sounded like a panic attack, but to suggest it would probably only make her feel worse. "These are special circumstances."

"How do you figure?"

"Until they find Janey's mother, or get her into foster care, you and I are the only 'parents' she has. She may be a ward of the state, but it's up to us to see that she gets the best care. That's a huge responsibility."

"You're right," she said, sounding cautiously optimistic. "Maybe that's why I have this deep need to protect her."

"Right now, she needs protecting."

She looked up at him and there were those lips again. Plump and juicy and pink. She had pale, flawless skin and the brightest, clearest green eyes that he had ever seen.

He would never forget the day he'd met her, when she'd walked into the staff meeting and the administrator had introduced them. He had been totally blown away. He'd probably held her hand a little too long when he shook it, and all through the meeting he hadn't been able to stop staring at her. Which, in retrospect, might have seemed a little creepy. Maybe they'd just gotten off on the wrong foot.

"I'm not sure if I've ever said it, but you're a really good doctor," she said.

He wiggled his brows and said, "Flattery will get you everywhere."

"Now if we could just do something about your personality," she grumbled with an exasperated shake of her head, but there was the hint of a smile, and a twinkle of something sly and impish in her eyes. She was teasing him.

"Admit it," he said, teasing her right back. "I'm starting to grow on you."

"I admit nothing," she said, nose in the air, trying not to smile, but he could see that she was having as much fun as he was. "Though I will say that after this, it might be a little more difficult to dislike you."

He grinned and wiggled his brows. "Then my evil plan is working."

Clare laughed. She couldn't help it. Because it was just so *Parker*. And boy did it irritate her that she knew him well enough to say that. Five minutes ago she'd felt lower than low; now he had her laughing. How did he do that?

Try as she might to push him away, he always pushed back a little harder. Was this campaign to keep him at arm's length a futile waste of time? Was falling for him an inevitability?

She refused to believe that. She would just dig extra deep for the will to resist him.

No meant no, not maybe.

"You know that I don't date people from work," she said. "Especially doctors."

He grinned. "Who said anything about dating?"

The way he was looking at her mouth… If only he knew how tempting that really was.

On second thought, it was probably good that he didn't know. "I don't sleep with people at work either," she said.

"We definitely won't be sleeping. And we won't be

doing it at work." His grin was teasing, but there was a fire in his eyes, and it was one hell of a blaze. He was so damned sexy and he smelled so good. He'd missed a small strip of stubble on the underside of his chin. Any other man would look sloppy or unkempt. On Parker it looked sexy and charming. And she wanted to kiss him there. And pretty much anywhere else.

Okay, *why* was she saying no? He had a body to die for; he was beyond gorgeous. Not to mention nice, with a really good sense of humor, and she had the feeling that he would not disappoint in the bedroom. Maybe, if they could keep it a secret…

No, no, no!

What was wrong with her? She was a strong, independent woman. When she made up her mind about something, there was no changing it. So why this sudden ambivalence? What was it about being around this man that made her go all gooey?

The dynamics were fairly simple: rich doctor, bad.

Parker was watching her, looking amused. "Penny for your thoughts."

Considering the semismug grin he wore, her inner struggle must have been pretty obvious.

Swell.

"Tell you what," he said. "Since you seem to be having a rough time with this, I'm going to give you an easy out."

Why would he do that?

Suspicious, she asked, "What's the catch?"

"No catch. If you can *honestly* tell me that you aren't attracted to me, and that you want me to leave you alone, I promise I'll back off."

Really? After all this time he would really just give up? "I'm not attracted to you," she said.

His smile was smug. "That was great. Now tell it to *me*, cupcake, not your shoes."

Darn, she was hoping he wouldn't notice the lack of eye contact. The truth was, she was a terrible liar. As a child she could never get away with anything.

There was no avoiding it—she had to look at him, and the instant their eyes met, she was totally tongue-tied. He seemed to know every button to push and he pushed them liberally. But that was what womanizers did, right?

"You *are* evil," she said.

"Nah, just irresistible." He stood and held his hand out to give her a boost. "We'd better get back on the floor before someone misses us."

Without thinking, she took his hand, realizing as he pulled her up how insanely stupid it had been. Though they bumped elbows and shoulders occasionally, other than a handshake when she met him, they had never deliberately touched each other. And while she didn't actually see any sparks arcing between them as his hand wrapped around hers, boy did she feel them. And so did he.

"Interesting," he said, with a slight arch of his brow. "*Very* interesting."

That single word spoke volumes. But mostly it just told her that she was in *big* trouble.

Three

HER arms loaded with bags of donated clothes, Clare trudged through the brisk February wind to her car in the staff lot. It had gotten so cold the puddles of rain from earlier that day had turned to patches of ice. All she wanted now was to go home, take a long hot shower, crawl into bed and forget today ever happened. Although mostly she just wanted to forget the part with Parker.

Janey had begun to show very slight signs of improvement over the course of the day, but she was nowhere close to being out of the woods. Fragile as she was, her condition could turn on a dime. Until they could figure out what was wrong, they were treating the symptoms, not the cause.

Clare left the night staff very strict instructions to contact her if Janey went into distress again. She wasn't obligated to come in on her off hours, but this wasn't about obligation. And hopefully it wouldn't come to that.

Shivering, Clare popped the trunk, dropped the bags inside and then unlocked her car with the key fob and slid onto the icy-cold seat. Shivering, she stuck the key into the ignition and turned…

Nothing happened.

"Are you kidding me?" she grumbled.

She tried again, and again, but the engine was dead.

She got out, pulling her collar up to shield her face from the icy wind. She popped the hood and looked at the engine for anything obvious, like a loose battery wire. She'd watched her brothers work on cars her entire childhood and she had learned a thing or two. Her car was almost fifteen years old and malfunctioned from regular wear and tear. She had been planning to look for a new one next month when the weather was better, but it looked as if she might have to do it sooner.

With her aunt away for a week she really had no one to pick her up. She would just have to call a tow truck and wait around. Hopefully it wouldn't take long.

She dialed the garage and was informed that they would be there ASAP. Which meant no more than an hour.

"I'm supposed to wait in the freezing cold for an hour?"

"Just leave your keys in the glove box."

Grumbling to herself, she hung up. Now she would have to call a cab to get home. But she would do it inside the hospital where it was warm.

She put her keys in the glove box and shut the door. She was getting ready to close the hood when she heard a vehicle pull up behind her car. She knew before she even heard him call out to her who it was. Because that was the kind of day she was having.

"Looks like you could use some help, angel face."

There he was, in his sporty import, grinning at her. She wanted to be exasperated but she couldn't work up the will.

"Car's dead. I called for a tow."

"Need a lift?"

It sure beat waiting for a cab, though she knew she was asking for trouble. But she was exhausted and frustrated and she just wanted to get home. "If it's no trouble."

Oh, that smile. "Hop in."

"Can I put something in your trunk?"

"Is it a dead body?"

She opened her trunk. "Well, not the whole thing."

He grinned and popped his trunk. "In that case, absolutely."

She tossed the bags inside, closed the trunk and climbed in the passenger's side. The interior was soft black leather and her seat was toasty warm.

She took off her gloves and held her hands in front of the heat vent.

"Where to?"

She told him her address, and how to get there, but as he pulled out of the lot he went in the opposite direction. "Hey, genius, my house is the other way."

"I know. But dinner is this way."

She blinked. "Who said anything about dinner?"

"I just did. If I don't eat something soon I'll go into hypoglycemic shock."

"You really think I'm going to fall for that?"

His grin said that she didn't have a whole lot of choice.

Damn it. She should have known better than to get in his car. But she was too exhausted to argue. She let her head fall back against the seat rest.

"You can't tell me that you're not hungry. I know for a fact that you didn't get to eat your lunch."

Of course she was hungry. She was starving, but he was the last person she wanted to be seen with in a social setting. The way gossip traveled in the town of Royal, people would have them engaged by the end of the week.

"No offense, but I really prefer that we not be seen together outside of work."

"So, not only do you not date coworkers, but you don't dine with them either? Is that why you always eat lunch alone?"

"That's not why I eat alone, and no, I have nothing against dining with coworkers. It's just something I don't do often."

"So then having a meal with me shouldn't be a big deal, right?"

She was pretty sure he already knew the answer to that question. And as he pulled into the parking lot of the Royal Diner, the number one worst place to go when trying to avoid the prying eyes of the town gossips, she found herself wishing that she'd called a cab instead.

"I can't risk someone seeing us and getting the wrong idea."

"We're just two colleagues sharing a meal while you wait for a tow. Not to mention that I'd like to talk about Janey. Bounce a few ideas off of you. Think of it as an offsite work meeting."

Well, if it was a work meeting…

"Just this one time," she said. "And I mean that."

He grinned, shut the engine off and said, "Let's go."

Since he was the type of guy who would insist on opening a car door for a woman, she hopped out before he could get the chance. And when he reached past her to open the diner door, she grabbed it first. She didn't want anyone getting even the slightest impression that this was a date.

The hostess showed them to a booth near the back. It was after eight so most of the dinner rush had already cleared out. Which could only be a good thing. "What would you two like to drink?"

"Decaf coffee," Clare said.

"Make that two," Parker told her.

"Enjoy your meal," the hostess said, laying their menus on the table.

As they sat down Parker said, "See, it's not so bad. There's hardly anyone here."

He was right. The subfreezing temperatures must have kept people inside tonight. But it would take only one nosy person to see them together and draw the wrong conclusion.

Their waitress, Emily, was someone Clare knew well. She often brought her autistic daughter to the free clinic on the weekends when Clare was volunteering, and her husband worked at the auto-repair shop. She set their coffees down and Clare didn't miss the curious look as she said, "Hey, Clare, Dr. Reese. Looks cold out there."

"So cold Clare's car wouldn't start," Parker told her.

"Are you still driving that old thing?" Emily asked her.

"I know I need to get a new one," she said, warming her hands with her coffee cup. "I just haven't had time."

"Do you know what you'd like to order or would you need a minute to look at the menu?"

"I know what I want," Parker said, eyes on Clare. From his mischievous grin, Clare knew he wasn't talking about the food.

"Caesar salad with the dressing on the side," she told Emily.

"Would you like chicken on that?"

Would she ever, but she was only five pounds away from her high school weight and she wanted to hit that number by swimsuit season. "No chicken."

"My usual," Parker told Emily.

"One Caesar, one bacon cheeseburger and fries, comin' right up."

When she was gone Parker said, "She knows what car you drive?"

"Everyone around here knows what everyone drives."

His brows knit together. "That's weird."

Not for Royal it wasn't. "You've never lived in a small town, have you?"

"Nope. I've always lived in the city, but I like the slower pace. Though it has taken some getting used to."

"You must eat here often if you have a usual," Clare said.

"Several times a week at least, and sometimes I come in for breakfast."

"You eat a burger and fries several times a *week*?"

"I'm a carnivore. I eat meat."

"There's this thing called vegetables…"

He shrugged, sipping his coffee. "Sometimes I order a side salad."

He was a doctor, for God's sake. He should have known better. "What do you have the other four days?"

"That depends on who I'm with," he said, and his cheeky smile said that once again they were no longer talking about food. But she'd sort of walked into that one, hadn't she?

Why did he have to be so damned adorable, with his stubbled chin and dark, rumpled hair? The soft waves begged to be combed back by her willing fingers and his hazel eyes smoldered, though they looked more whiskey-colored in this light. He'd loosened his lop-sided tie and opened the top button on his dress shirt…

"Have you lived in Royal your whole life?" he asked her.

Jarred by the sudden change of subject, she realized she was staring at his chest and lifted her gaze to his handsome face instead. Which was just as bad, if not worse. Sometimes when she was sitting at the nurses' station and he was nearby she would watch him in her peripheral vision. He had such a nice face to look at.

"I moved here to live with my aunt about a year after nursing school," she told him.

"Where are you from originally?"

"My parents own a horse farm about an hour from here. Five of my siblings work there."

He blinked. "*Five?* How many siblings do you have?"

"Seven. All older. Three boys, four girls."

"Wow." He shook his head in disbelief. "That's a lot of kids."

"Tell me about it."

"Catholic?"

"No, just very traditional. My mom has six siblings and my dad has four. They both grew up on farms."

"What about your siblings. Do they have kids?"

"As of last month I have twenty-two nieces and nephews, and two great-nieces on the way."

"Wow. That is a *big* family. And you're the baby?"

There was nothing more annoying than being referred to as *the baby* by her family. It was their way of pushing her down and keeping her in her place. But when Parker said it, with that teasing smile, it wasn't demeaning at all.

"I'm the youngest, yes."

"Were you spoiled?"

As if. "My parents were pretty burned out by the time I came along. As long as I did my chores and kept my grades up they pretty much left me alone. I would rather be invisible than get sucked into all the family drama."

"I used to wish that I had a big family."

"Do you have siblings?" she asked him.

"Only child."

"I had a friend in school who was an only child and I was always so envious."

Emily returned to the table with their food and Clare's stomach howled. Though getting a salad had been the responsible thing to do, Parker's juicy burger and greasy fries beckoned her.

"Well, it's not all it's cracked up to be," he said, popping a fry in his mouth, and when he offered her one, she couldn't resist. Her mouth watered as the greasy, salty goodness sent her taste buds into overload.

She looked at her plate, then his, and thought, *Man, I should have ordered a burger.*

"Growing up I always wanted siblings," Parker said, pushing his plate toward her, gesturing to her to take more.

"I had to share a room with three of my sisters. I had no privacy whatsoever." There hadn't even been anyone who'd keep things in confidence. If one sibling knew, they all knew. Because of that it had always been difficult for her to trust people to keep her secrets. Her aunt was the only person in her life she could be totally honest with.

"For what it's worth, I didn't either," he said, and she watched his lips move. She loved looking at his lips. It was always the first place her eyes landed.

"My father was very strict throughout my entire childhood," Parker said. "He controlled pretty much every aspect of my life, like which friends I was allowed to have, what books I was allowed to read. He even chose the classes I took in high school. He was grooming me to take over his business. I always thought that if he had another child he might not be so focused on my every move."

"What does he do?"

"He was a financial tycoon. He passed away last year."

"I'm so sorry."

"We had a very tenuous relationship. I had no interest in finance, and he considered practicing medicine beneath me. He agreed to pay for medical school, but only if I studied to be a cosmetic surgeon. He even set up a job for me with his own cosmetic surgeon when I graduated."

As amazing as he was with children, that would have been a terrible waste. "Clearly you changed his mind."

"It was Luc Wakefield who talked me into standing up to my father."

"How did that go over?"

"There was a lot of shouting and threats. He said

he would disown and disinherit me. I said go for it. At that point I was so sick of being controlled I honestly didn't care."

Her family may have been a ginormous pain, but his father sounded a million times worse. "What did your mom have to say about it?"

"Not much," he said, and his casual reply belied the flash of something dark and sad in his eyes. But as soon as it was there, it was gone again. "She wasn't around."

For whatever reason, she had just assumed that someone as successful as Parker would come from a well-adjusted and happy home. She imagined him as the golden child, probably captain of the football team, valedictorian and loved by all.

It would appear that she was wrong. Again. That's what she got for drawing conclusions without facts.

"Have I got something between my teeth?" Parker asked suddenly.

She blinked. "No. Why?"

"Are you sure? Because you haven't stopped staring at my mouth."

Her cheeks went hot with embarrassment. Was she really doing that?

"It's either that, or you're thinking about kissing me."

She was almost always thinking about kissing him. She really had to be more careful in the future where she let her eyes wander. And her thoughts.

"I don't suppose you played football in high school?" Clare asked, and Parker laughed.

"No, I didn't. But if I had, boy, my father would have loved that." The only thing that would have pleased his dad more than Parker taking over the family business

was if he'd become a professional athlete. But it had
been obvious from a very early age that Parker had no
interest, and more important, no natural talent.

He was barely out of diapers when his father began
pushing him into various sports. First soccer, then
T-ball, but he'd sucked at them both. He'd been more
interested in sitting on the sidelines, searching the
grass for bugs and snakes.

His dad had enrolled him in tag football when Parker
was six, and had forced him to stay for the entire season.
Luckily Parker had had a sympathetic coach who'd let
him spend most of his time on the bench. Because as
fanatical as his father had been about his son's physical abilities, he'd never once made it to a practice or
even a game.

Swimming lessons had come next, but Parker got
so many ear infections as a result that the doctor told
his father the lessons had to stop. Parker's equestrian
training was probably the least horrible thing he'd been
forced into, and though being so high up on the horse's
back had always made him nervous, he loved animals.
Until his horse was spooked and threw him, and nearly
trampled him to death. That was the last time he'd ever
gone near a horse.

"My father played ball in college," Parker told her.
"I guess he just assumed that I would want to play, too.
He was real big on me following in his footsteps. He
wanted a mini me, and I seriously didn't fit the bill. I
was skinny and scrawny and kind of a geek."

"You were not," she said, taking another fry, eyeing his burger with a look of longing. She had barely
touched her salad, but she'd already eaten half his fries.

"I'm serious. I was a total nerd. Remind me and

I'll dig out some old pictures." He slid his plate closer. "Take a bite."

She blinked. "Of what?"

"My burger. You haven't taken your eyes off of it, and I think I see a little drool in the corner of your mouth."

She hesitated, looking a little embarrassed, but her stomach won the battle. "Well, maybe a little bite…"

There was nothing little about the bite she took.

"I didn't start to really fill out until my third year of college," he said. "When I started weight training."

"So you were what, like, twenty-one?"

"Eighteen. I graduated high school when I was fifteen."

"Wow, you really were a geek. But your dad must have been happy about that."

"My dad was never happy about anything. He was a tyrant. Thankfully I saw more of the nanny and the house staff than him."

"I went through sort of the same thing when I was a kid. Although not the tyrant part. Everyone assumed I would work on the ranch after high school, but I wanted to be a nurse. I knew from the time I got my first play doctor kit as a kid that I wanted to work in medicine. I wanted to help people."

"Did you ever tell your family that?"

"Probably a million times, but I was more or less invisible. No one ever listened to what I had to say. Hell, they still don't. If it isn't ranch business, or my various nieces' and nephews' academic accomplishments, they don't discuss it. So I worked my butt off in school and got a scholarship to a college far away from home and haven't looked back since. My parents were not very happy with me."

In what universe did that make even a lick of sense? "Aren't most parents proud when their kids go to college?"

"Like I said, they're very traditional. Nothing was more important to them than their children 'paying their debt to the family,'" she said, making air quotes with her fingers. "Whatever the hell that meant. I didn't ask to be born. I never felt as if I owed my family anything."

It amazed him that despite their very different upbringings, their childhoods weren't really all that different. "I felt the same way about my father. He had my entire life planned out before I was out of diapers. With no regard whatsoever to what I might want. But that was just who he was. People were terrified of him and he used that to manipulate. No one dared deny him anything."

"Stubborn as I am, my parents' archaic thinking probably only pushed me further from the fold. The thought of staying on the farm and working with my family for the rest of my life gives me hives. And they have no respect for what I do. To this day I still hear snide remarks about going into medicine just to snag—" She stopped abruptly, but it was already too late. He knew exactly what she'd been about to say.

"A wealthy doctor?" he said.

Her cheeks flushed a deep red and she lowered her eyes to her salad, her juicy bottom lip wedged adorably between her perfect teeth. He'd never seen her blush, but damn, she sure was pretty when she did. But then, she always looked good to him. And suddenly her attitude toward him made a whole lot more sense.

"I didn't mean to tell you that," she said, looking mortified.

"At least now I know why you spend so much time pretending you don't like me."

She lifted her chin, getting all indignant on him. "Who says I was pretending?"

He laughed. "Sweetheart, I've dated a lot of women. I know the signals."

She opened her mouth to argue—because she always argued when he was trying to make a point—then must have had a change of heart and closed it again. "Okay, yes, that is *part* of the reason I can't see you. But there are other factors, as well, things I'm not comfortable getting into right now."

"So you do like me," he said.

"I respect you as a physician and peer, and you seem like a good person. I could even see us eventually becoming friends, but it can never be more than that."

Four

"Do you want to be friends?" Parker asked her.

She wanted that and so much more, and it wasn't fair that she couldn't have it. But she of all people knew that life was not often fair. She also realized that neither of them had said a word about Janey. Not that it surprised her. It was all just a ruse to get her alone. And she'd fallen for it. Willingly. She looked at her phone to check the time. "It's late. I should go home. I want to get up early tomorrow and go jogging."

Her very obvious brush-off didn't seem to faze him. "You don't strike me as the jogging type."

"I like it. There's a cute little park behind my house."

"Are you one of those die-hard joggers who's on the road before the sun's up?"

"God, no. If I'm on the track at seven thirty it's a good day."

He just grinned and said, "Could you be more intriguing?"

She didn't even know how to respond to that. She led a pretty unexciting life. What did he see that was so special? So interesting? If he was just looking to get laid, he was seriously overplaying his hand.

Parker motioned Emily for the check, and refused to let Clare pay her portion.

"You can buy next time," he said, but she didn't think there was going to be a next time. It was stupid to think that she could ever be friends with Parker without wanting more. *So. Much. More.* So she figured, why tempt herself? Out of sight, out of mind. Wasn't that the way it was supposed to work?

"Where to?" he asked when they got into the car. He blasted the heat and switched the seat warmers on.

"We're just outside of town. Turn left." Thankfully this time he followed her directions.

"Didn't that area get hit pretty hard by the tornado?" he asked as he pulled out of the parking lot.

"Our house was leveled," she said, realizing that she could look at his mouth all she wanted now; he was focused on the road.

"Tell me you and your aunt weren't in the house," he said.

"My aunt was away on a trip and I was at the hospital."

"Were you able to salvage anything?"

"We lost everything. Clothes, furniture, keepsakes. My aunt travels extensively and she had things from all over the world. Things she'd been collecting for decades. By the time it was over, they were scattered all over the city. Wet and broken. My aunt's file cabinet, with the papers still in it, was found over a mile away. The tornado picked her car up and launched it through the house across the street. It was utter devastation."

"I can't even imagine," he said. "I've seen some major hurricane damage on the East Coast, but nothing that bad. And you saw it? The tornado, I mean."

She nodded. "It was surreal at first. I kept thinking that it couldn't happen to Royal, that at the last second it would change course or blow itself out, then the debris started to hit things. Windows started breaking and cars in the hospital lot were getting pummeled with softball-sized hail and we knew we were going to be right in the middle of it. You feel like a sitting duck. All you can do is take shelter, hang on tight and hope for the best."

"The hospital has a shelter, right?"

"Yes, but I wasn't in it. It happened so fast, there was no time to move the patients, so, along with the rest of the staff I stayed on the ward."

"That was very brave."

"No." She shook her head. "I was terrified. It was the longest five minutes of my life."

"You were terrified but you did it anyway. You put the lives of those kids before your own. That's the definition of bravery."

The compliment, coming from him, made her heart go pitter-pat. Why did he have to be so nice? And so ridiculously handsome? Did the man have a single negative attribute? Other than being extremely stubborn. But to be fair she was guilty of that, too. He turned into her subdivision and took a right onto her street.

"It's the third house on the left."

"You know, I've learned more about you tonight than in the past three months," Parker said.

"There isn't much to know. The tornado aside, I don't lead a very exciting life."

"Excitement is highly overrated. And believe me, I'm speaking from experience. I love the slower pace here. The people are so different, so much more laid-back. For the most part. It's exactly what I needed."

It was all about perception, she supposed, because for her this was just normal. But she was sure that moving from Royal to somewhere like Dallas, or even New York City, would be a jarring change of pace. But she never would. She was a country girl at heart and that would never change.

He pulled into the driveway and the automatic outdoor lights switched on, illuminating the exterior of her aunt's sprawling colonial. "This is nice."

"Thanks. It's pretty much identical to the old one, just a little more modern."

"It's a lot of house for two people."

"My aunt has out-of-town guests frequently, so she likes the extra space." She gathered her purse and gloves and said, "Thanks for the ride. And dinner."

"I'll help you with your body," he said, shutting off the car.

She blinked. Oh, man, if he only knew the things she wanted him to do to her body. Sexy, tantalizing things...

Uh-oh, was she drooling a little again...?

She must have looked confused, because he said, "In the trunk. The body bags."

Oh, right, she would have completely forgotten and left them there. "I can get them," she said.

"Nonsense, I'll help." He popped the trunk open and got out of the car. She met him around back.

"Did you really just say *nonsense*?"

"Isn't that how people talk in Texas?"

"If you're eighty. And a woman."

"My bad," he said, but he was grinning. Did the man ever stop smiling? No one should be that happy that much of the time.

She reached for the bags but he snatched them up first. Darn it, the last thing she wanted was to let him into her house. She had the feeling that once she did, it would be near impossible to get him back out the door.

"I've got it," she said, but he was already heading up the walk. Her exasperated breath crystalized in the air as she jogged to catch up. She had no choice but to go along with it. And of course there was a small part of her that wanted him in her house. Or maybe not so small.

"I think you have a hearing problem," she told him as they walked up the porch steps.

"No, I hear you just fine," he said, waiting for her to unlock the front door. "I think what you mean is that I have a *listening* problem."

She laughed; she couldn't help it. "If I say I've got it from here, and it's been a long day and I'm tired, is there *any* way I'm going to stop you from coming in?"

He considered that for several seconds then shook his head. "Probably not. I'll just make up some lame excuse like needing to use the bathroom and we both know that you're too polite to say no."

He was right. Damn those pesky Southern manners her parents had drilled into her. She couldn't decide if it was more disturbing or pathetic that she had little to no ability to deny him anything. Like the tornado, he'd blown into her life and had the potential to make a huge mess of things.

"You could have the decency to look a little less smug," she said, pushing the door open and letting him inside.

"Kidding aside, I really would like to discuss Janey's case," he said, stepping into the foyer, which led into the open-concept great room and kitchen. "We didn't get a chance at dinner."

As if she would say no to that. Besides, this time he sounded sincere, and less like he was trying to get into her pants.

She wondered what he would do if she invited him up to her bedroom. There was no point pondering the possibility, as it would never happen. Not in this lifetime anyway. But it was the kind of thing that she liked to think about. When she was alone. Usually in bed. If he was as good as her fantasies…

No man was as good as the fantasy. She had pretty high standards when it came to casual sex. Her philosophy was simple. Why did she need a man around when she could do it better herself?

"I have to make an early start in the morning, so you've got thirty minutes," she said, shrugging out of her coat and hanging it on the coat tree by the door. He did the same, looking even more rumpled than he had at dinner. Since it would be rude not to offer him a beverage—there were those pesky manners again—she said, "I'm going to make myself a cup of tea. Would you like one?"

"I'd love one," he said.

She gestured to the couch, probably the safest place to confine him. "Make yourself comfortable."

She stepped into the kitchen and filled the kettle, then set the burner on high. The stove, like the rest of the kitchen, was a chef's dream. Major overkill considering neither she nor her aunt liked to cook, but her aunt only bought top-of-the line appliances. She bought top-of-the-line everything.

Clare grabbed two cups from the cupboard and set them by the stove, then pulled out a box of chamomile tea. "Do you take sugar or honey?" she asked him, bracing herself for some sort of suggestive innuendo, but he didn't say a word. She turned to him, and realized that he hadn't answered because he was *gone*.

"Where the heck did you go?" she called, and heard him answer from the second floor.

"Up here."

She was fairly sure that his voice was coming from her bedroom. So much for having to actually invite him to her bedroom. He'd found it all on his own.

Did the man have no boundaries? No shame?

She should have known. She never should have turned her back on him. Hell, she never should have let him into her house.

She charged up the stairs to her bedroom. She found him *sitting* at the foot of her bed, looking around the room. It had been a really long time since she'd had a man under, or even on top of, her covers and he looked damn good there.

"What the hell, Parker?" she said, realizing, as his name rolled off her tongue, that as long as she had known him she had referred to him as Dr. Reese. This was her first time addressing him by his first name. It felt a little odd, but also kind of natural.

He flashed her a toothy smile. "Hey there, short stuff."

At five-five she was hardly short, but she let it slide. "What do you think you're doing?"

"You said to make myself comfortable."

"I meant on the couch."

"But you didn't *say* the couch."

"I pointed to it!"

"Clearly I don't take direction well. You're going to have to be a little more specific next time."

Next time? After this did he seriously think she would let him back in?

Who was she kidding? Of course she would.

She folded her arms. "Get off my bed."

He grinned. "You didn't say please."

"*Please* get off my bed," she said, feeling a little desperate. The urge to jump in there with him was almost too strong to fight. She felt a little winded and tingly all over, as if her libido had just awakened from a long hibernation.

"No need to shout," he said, pulling himself to his feet and walking to the door.

"I don't like having people in my bedroom. I like my privacy." She straightened the covers where he'd been sitting. They were still warm from his body heat, and the slightest hint of his aftershave lingered in the air.

She turned to him to say that it was time for him to go, but he wasn't there!

"Are you kidding me?" she mumbled. "Parker!"

She found him in her craft room next door. He'd switched the light on and was examining the quilt samplers she had sewn and tacked to the wall. "Oh, my God, are you for real? Did I not just say that I like my privacy. You have the attention span of a *three-year-old*!"

"You said you don't like having people in your bedroom. This isn't your bedroom, is it?"

She didn't justify that one with a response. And her thin-lipped glare only seemed to amuse him further. "The truth is, I just wanted to hear you say my name again. Or shriek it, as the case may be."

She ignored the warm shiver that whispered across the surface of her skin and raised the fine hairs on her arms. Or tried to at least. He wasn't making it easy. "I'll say it a thousand times if it will make you go downstairs."

"These are fantastic," he said, gesturing to the wall. She wasn't buying it. He was the kind of guy who knew quality when he saw it and this was definitely not quality sewing.

"Compliments won't get you anywhere," she told him.

"I'm actually serious," he said, leaning in closer. "Where did you get them?"

"I made them, and for the record, they suck. The fabric is puckered and the rows are crooked. My stitching is totally uneven. Which is why I keep them in here. Where no one will see them."

"But the colors are striking," he said, and she realized that he really wasn't bullshitting her. He was genuinely impressed.

Weird.

"You have a gift," he said.

"It's just a hobby. It relaxes me."

"Did you do these drawings, too?"

He was looking at the pages she'd laid out on her craft table.

"I couldn't draw my way out of a paper bag. I just

colored them in. It's the new big thing in stress relief for adults."

"Coloring?"

"Absolutely. There are like a million adult coloring books to choose from."

"No kidding. It seems a little…pointless."

"That's the whole point." She gestured to a pile of coloring books on the shelf beside her craft table. "I've finished all of those. I did a lot of coloring in the park last summer. And look how calm I am."

"Yeah," he said with a wry smile. "You looked pretty calm in the stairwell today."

Of course he would point that out. But it was hard to get angry when he was flashing her that adorable grin.

"May I?" he asked, nodding to the pile.

No one had looked at her coloring books before. It had never even occurred to her to show them to anyone. "Go ahead, but they're nothing special."

He took the top book, a panoramic foldout of a magical fairyland. "Wow, you sure do have a way with color."

The compliment made her feel all warm and squishy inside. "I just pick what looks right."

"That's the weird thing. Normally these colors don't even go together, but you make it seem like they do."

She shrugged, thinking he was making a way bigger deal about this than he should be. "Maybe I wasn't clear. You can rave all you want and I'm still not going to sleep with you."

"You should frame some of these," he said, looking through a book of flowers, ignoring her completely. Or, knowing him, he was only pretending to. She had the feeling that he didn't miss much.

"Why?" she asked him. "They're not art."

"No, this is definitely art."

"Okay, but it's someone *else's* art."

"Yes, the shapes are already there, but the color adds dimension. It brings it to life. That's the hardest part."

Maybe, maybe not. Either way, his enthusiasm was giving her warm fuzzies all over the place. Her inability to resist his charms bordered on the absurd.

"How many finished books do you have?" he asked her, flipping through a collection of mandalas.

She didn't even want to go there. "Too many. I don't get out much."

"Me neither," he said, and she gave him a dubious look. "I'm serious."

"That's not how I hear it."

"Keeping tabs on me?"

She was making it sound that way, wasn't she? "Word gets around. You're reputed to have a very busy social calendar."

"When I first got here I was going out pretty frequently. But I was in a new place and meeting lots of new people."

"New women, you mean."

He shot her a sideways glance through the curtain of his unfairly thick lashes, then winked. He actually *winked*. "Be careful, Clare, you almost sound jealous."

Probably because she was. A little.

He moved closer, looking like a tiger on the prowl, his eyes shining with male heat. If this were the wild, he would take her in an instant. And because it was the wild she would be helpless to stop him. He looked as if he was going to kiss her, and she wanted him to.

His eyes locked on hers, he started to lean in, slowly,

cautiously, as if he was expecting her to hit him over the head with something.

Up until today he had been subtle but consistent. He had never pushed, exactly, but he'd made sure that she knew he was around. Something told her now that all bets were off.

Five

Downstairs in the kitchen the kettle whistled but Clare didn't move. She stood totally still, her eyes locked on Parker's, the energy whirling between them electrically charged. Parker knew that he could have her right now if he wanted to. This was the moment he'd been waiting for, but half the fun of a relationship was the chase. No matter who was doing the running. And call him a megalomaniac, but it would be much more fun if she made the first move. If she came to him.

Just for fun, he dropped his gaze to her mouth. Her chin lifted a fraction and her tongue darted out to wet her lips.

Oh, yeah, she wanted it bad.

"Your water is boiling," he said.

Clare blinked several times, as if waking from a daydream. "Huh?"

"The kettle, it's boiling."

"Oh. I should probably get that," she said, but she didn't move. She was waiting for him to kiss her. He could feel the anticipation, see the throb of her pulse at the base of her throat.

A wisp of dark blond hair had escaped the messy bun she wore, so he reached up and tucked the silky-soft strand back in. Clare's breath caught and her pupils dilated, and as the tips of his fingers brushed the shell of her ear, she leaned into his palm. He realized, with spine-tingling awareness, that this was the first time he'd touched her. They had bumped shoulders or elbows a time or two while treating a patient, and he'd held her hand to pull her up on the steps today. Touching her felt exciting, and a little naughty.

Her skin was just as smooth and soft as he thought it would be, and damn, she smelled good. He knew that if he kept touching her this way the chase would end right here, right now.

He dropped his hand to his side. "You need a push?"

She blinked with confusion. "A push?"

"To get the kettle. I don't think it's going to turn itself off."

"Right, the kettle," she said, peeling her eyes from his, taking a slightly unsteady step back. The truth was, he was feeling a little unsteady himself.

He gestured her through the office doorway, and she shook her head. "Uh-uh. There's no way I'm taking my eyes off you for even a second," she said. "Next thing I know you'll be going through my closet or something. You're too sneaky."

And she was way too much fun.

He went down first, with Clare watching him like a

hawk. When they got to the kitchen, Clare shut off the burner, never once turning her back on him. Not that he blamed her.

"I'm going to head out," he told her.

Her look of disappointment made him smile. "I thought you were staying for tea."

"Watch yourself, Clare, or I might have to assume you like having me around."

"We wouldn't want that," she said, but it was too late. It was written all over her face. "Thanks for the ride home. And dinner."

"My pleasure." And boy, did he mean that. He walked to the door and pulled his wool coat on. Clare met him in the foyer.

"Do you need a ride to work tomorrow?" he asked her.

"I can use my aunt's car until she gets back next week. I don't like relying on other people."

"And you're afraid that someone will see us together and get the wrong idea." Or the right one.

She folded her arms across what he was sure were a perfect pair of breasts. And he would know soon enough. "We never did discuss Janey."

"Good night, Parker."

He winked. "Good night, hot stuff."

Her eye roll was the last thing he saw as she closed the door. Oh, yeah, she was definitely into him. As if there had ever been a question.

Clare lay awake half the night, and the other half she spent dreaming about Parker. It was as if she couldn't escape him, no matter how hard she tried. Not even when she was sleeping. He was starting to get under her skin. And that was a very bad thing.

The absence of any physical contact between them had been her secret weapon, but he'd taken care of that, hadn't he? The warm weight of his palm against her cheek had been unexpected and startling and so erotic that the resulting surge of estrogen had short-circuited the logic pathways in her brain. It was a wonder smoke hadn't billowed out of her ears. She had been positive that he was going to kiss her, then he didn't and she didn't quite understand why.

She got out of bed late, pulling her hair back into a ponytail and dressing in her warmest jogging outfit. According to the weather report she had seen online last night, the daytime high would barely break thirty degrees. She was so ready for spring and warmer weather.

Her breath crystalized and the icy air burned her lungs as she stepped out the back door onto the multilevel deck. She crossed the yard to a gate, which led right to the jogging path.

She was getting warmed up, stretching her hamstrings, when she heard a familiar voice, using a really bad fake Southern accent.

"Fancy meeting you here, ma'am."

Oh, no, not this morning. She turned to see Parker leaning casually against a barren tree in what looked like a brand-new jogging getup.

"God, give me strength," she mumbled, and told Parker, "You *really* need to stop trying to sound Southern. You're not any good at it."

He just grinned that adorable grin, making her a tiny bit weak in the knees.

"What are you doing here?"

"It just so happens that I jog, too, and I'm always looking for a change of scenery. A different path to take. Your description of the park intrigued me so I thought I would check it out."

"I said it was a cute little park. Which word got you? *Cute?* Or *little*?"

Despite her snippy tone he smiled.

"If I asked you to go away, would you?"

Looking apologetic, he shook his head.

Of course not. She sighed and said, "Let's get this over with."

They started down the path toward the pond, Parker huffing along beside her. But gradually he started to fall behind. They were no more than five minutes in, and Parker was gasping for air. She hadn't even broken a sweat.

Then he stopped altogether, and she had to backtrack. He stood hunched over and out of breath, holding his side. "Damn, this is harder than it looks."

Clearly he was not a jogger. And of course she planned to use that to teach him a lesson. "I'll race you to the pond," she said.

"Are you trying to kill me?"

"I'll make you a deal. If you can beat me there, I'll sleep with you."

His stunned expression was the last thing she saw as she took off running, leaving Parker in the dust.

She got to the pond and was using a bench to stretch when Parker finally wheezed his way over. He dropped like a lead weight onto the grass at her feet, red-faced and sucking cold air into his lungs.

She shook her head sadly. "I know eighty-year-olds in better shape than you."

"You really *are* trying to kill me," he gasped.

"You did lie about being a jogger. You sort of asked for it."

"Technically I didn't lie, because starting this morning I plan to be a regular jogger. If I don't die from exhaustion first. Or a heart attack. I don't suppose you have water."

She took the bottle from her jacket pocket and handed it to him.

"Thanks." He sat up, chugging half the bottle.

"Maybe you should head back to the house while I do my laps. When I'm finished I'll make you breakfast. I guess I owe you that much, since I did almost kill you. Not that I was trying or anything."

"Sure you weren't." He pushed himself to his feet. "Can I wait in the house?"

Did he honestly think she would fall for that one again? "Sure. If you can figure out the alarm code."

She took off running again and he shouted after her, "You're really going to make me sit out in the cold? I could freeze to death!"

She waved without turning around, feeling not an ounce of guilt. More than likely he had a still-warm luxury vehicle parked somewhere nearby. There would be no freezing to death for him.

She jogged her usual laps around the park, then just for fun added a few more, pushing herself harder. Maybe if she was gone a really long time, he would get bored and leave.

As if. If it had been possible to shake him off that easily, he would have been long gone by now.

When she stepped through the gate into the backyard,

Parker was sitting on the steps of the upper deck, tapping away on his cell phone. So much for him leaving.

Parker heard the back gate open and looked up from his phone. Clare was cute when she was all sweaty, her hair a mess. "Good run?"

She nodded, only slightly out of breath. "It got better when I ditched you. You were dragging me down."

"Do I still get my breakfast?"

"Yes," she said grudgingly. She opened the back door and disarmed the alarm. "But don't expect anything fancy."

He tugged off his jacket and took a seat at the kitchen island. "Do I at least get coffee?"

She reached over to the coffeemaker and pressed the start button.

She used the term *making breakfast* loosely. What she should have said was that she would warm up breakfast for him. She "made" him one of those individually wrapped breakfast sandwiches out of the freezer.

"Make yourself useful and get the juice out of the fridge," she said, putting the sandwich in the microwave.

He opened the refrigerator. Aside from the juice and various condiments, there were mostly just carryout containers.

He had the distinct feeling that Clare didn't cook, which was fine, as it was one of his favorite things to do. It was a little spooky the way they seemed so perfectly matched. It was like destiny, or fate or some other crap like that.

Serendipity maybe.

She took two glasses down from the cupboard for

him to fill. Then the microwave dinged and she handed him the sandwich. "Bon appétit."

He bit in to find the middle still partially frozen, but the look she was giving him said not to push it. He forced a smile and said, "Delicious."

"As soon as you're finished eating you have to leave," she said.

"Actually, it's my day off. I can stay as long as I want."

She gave him one of those *looks*, and he grinned. Damn, did he love teasing her.

"You look like a grown man," she said. "You even sound like a grown man…"

He grinned. "If it walks like a duck and talks like a duck."

"You're going to make me late for work," she said.

"As your boss, I give you the day off."

"I don't want to take the day off. I actually like going to work."

"That's probably why you're so good at it."

She shrugged. "Well…"

"I'm serious, Clare. I've never seen a more efficiently run children's ward. Your employees respect you. They look up to you. Sometimes they even fear you a little."

She blinked with surprise. "Really?"

"You can be a little intense at times, and intimidating."

She frowned. "I don't want them to be afraid of me."

"They fear your authority, not you personally. You hold everyone to a super high standard. You demand the best performance at all times. They don't like to let you down."

She actually blushed. "I couldn't ask for a better staff."

"They're as good as they are because of you."

"I'm sure you had something to do with it, too. You're incredibly easy to work for. I liked Dr. Mann, but he was incredibly arrogant. He was always right, and God help you if you disagreed with him. Especially in front of a patient. I've seen some really good nurses get fired for challenging his authority. And even if it turned out they were right, he would never admit it."

"Sounds like he had a God complex."

"Don't get me wrong, he was a good doctor. Just not a very good person. I think he got into medicine for all the wrong reasons."

"We all have our reasons," he said.

"What were yours?"

"Mostly to get laid," he said, wiggling his brows. "Chicks love doctors."

"Chicks?"

"That's right, baby. They dig me."

She was trying really hard not to grin. "The 1960s called. They want their slang back."

He laughed and she cracked a smile.

"Your time is up, daddy-o. Make like a tree and leave."

She was funny, too. And really snarky.

Could she be more enchanting?

Figuring he'd hassled her enough for one morning, he slugged back the last of his coffee, and then left.

Parker spent the remainder of the day catching up on his reading. Medical journals mostly. Then he did some online research regarding Janey's case. Once again, he found nothing that fit her symptoms. He finished around nine that evening, more frustrated than ever. Feeling restless and edgy, he headed over to the Texas Cattleman's Club for a drink. Only a few tables in the lounge were occupied; Logan Wade sat at the bar, hunched over a beer. A hockey game played on the television, but he didn't seem to be watching it. He just stared into the beer mug, mesmerized as he swirled the dark lager around and around. Barely a month ago, Logan had taken custody of his twin brother Seth's baby daughter after Margaret, the child's mother, died in a car crash giving birth. Paramedics were able to deliver the baby, who was surprisingly unharmed, but Margaret never regained consciousness. Margaret's mother, in her grief over losing her daughter and believing that Logan was the baby's father, left the child in his care. Logan swore he'd never met Margaret, and a blood test confirmed that he was related to the baby, but not the parent. So it had to be Seth.

Parker took a seat next to him, and Logan greeted him with a very unenthusiastic, "Hey."

The bartender, without prompting, brought Parker his regular, a scotch and soda. "Who's winning?" he asked Logan, but his friend stared at him blankly.

Parker gestured to the television. "The game?"

"Oh, right," Logan said, and then shrugged. "I guess I have no idea. To be honest, I don't even know how long I've been sitting here. Is it possible to sleep with one's eyes open?"

Parker chuckled. "Baby Maggie not letting you get much rest?"

"She's so fussy. Hadley keeps telling me it's normal, but damn…" He shook his head in exasperation. "Don't get me wrong, she's my niece, and I love her, but I really wasn't prepared for this."

"No luck reaching your brother?"

He shook his head. "The navy took the message, but Seth is on a mission. Who knows when he'll get it. If and when he does, there's still no guarantee he'll come back to claim her. I honestly don't know what I would do without Hadley."

Hadley, Logan's new bride, had come to work for him as a nanny, and the two had fallen hard for each other. It seemed as if everyone around Parker was finding their perfect match and settling down. A year ago that would have given him the heebie-jeebies. Now he wanted what they had.

"She's a keeper," Parker said.

The game went to commercial and the station broke in with a special news report. Both men looked up at the wide-screen behind the bar. Janey's picture flashed across the screen with the caption "Abandoned Baby, Mother Found?" Parker sat up straighter, asking the bartender, "Can you turn that up?"

According to the anchor, a truck driver who had been in the lot of the truck stop the night Janey had been found had come forward with a video. While videotaping his rig, he'd caught a glimpse of a woman, now presumed to be Janey's mother, entering the building. They played the clip, which was grainy and difficult to make out clearly.

"Holy shit!" Logan jumped up so fast the bar stool flipped over backward and everyone in the room turned toward the commotion.

"You recognize her?" Parker asked him.

Logan rubbed his tired eyes and squinted at the television. "That looks like Margaret!"

"Margaret? You mean Maggie's mother?"

"Margaret's mother showed me a picture. I'm pretty sure that's her," he said, and asked the bartender for the remote to rewind the clip. He rewound it twice. "Yeah," he told Parker, "I'm positive. That's Margaret."

And just like that Parker knew exactly how to treat his fragile little patient. He laughed and shook his head. Could it really be that simple?

"Call the police," Parker told Logan, pulling on his coat. "I have to get to the hospital."

Stunned, Logan said, "If Margaret is Janey's mother, that means…"

"It means you have *two* nieces."

A look of shock crossed his face. *"Twins?"*

"A simple DNA test will prove it definitively." Honestly, it was a wonder they hadn't put it together before now. "But if I were you I would go home and get some sleep. If they are twins, your life is about to get a bit more complicated."

Six

Clare woke the next morning to her phone ringing.

She sat up and looked at her phone. Of course it was Parker. Who else would call her at *7:00 a.m.*? On her day off?

"Hello," she grumbled.

"You awake?" he asked.

Duh. "I am now!"

"Good. Come down and let me in."

"You're *here*?"

"I have some very good news."

"Fine," she grumbled, tossing the covers off and rolling out of bed. She tugged on her beat-up terry-cloth robe, and still half asleep, trudged down the stairs to the front door.

"Good morning," he said with a smile when she flung open the door.

"It's 7:00 a.m.," she told him.

"I know."

"On my day off."

"I know." He walked right past her without invitation and took his coat off, dropping it over the back of the sofa on the way to the kitchen, acting as if he owned the place.

It took a good minute to notice that he was unshaven and his clothes were a wrinkled mess.

"You look like hell," she said.

He took in her messy ponytail, puffy eyes and ragged old robe. "Look who's talking."

At least she had a good reason. What was *his* excuse? And what man in his right mind would tell the woman he was trying to sleep with that she looked like hell?

She supposed that was what made him so…*Parker*. When he poured on the charm he was tough to resist. But didn't he know that honesty was not always the best policy?

"Did you not go home last night?" she asked, regretting the words the instant she spoke them. She didn't want to know where he'd been. Or whom he had been with.

Grinning from ear to ear he said, "I did not. I spent the night with a beautiful girl."

Because you're not man enough for a real woman? she wanted to say. "And you woke me at 7:00 a.m. on my day off to tell me this? Are you on drugs?"

He shook his head.

"Mentally challenged?"

He just smiled, then he looked toward the coffeepot and sniffed. "What, no coffee?"

Was he kidding? He really *was* mentally challenged.

"*Seven a.m. Day off. Sleeping.* Is any of this ringing a bell?"

"I'll make a pot," he said.

Ooookay. She flopped down on the sofa. "Knock yourself out."

This was her own fault. She never should have let him get in her head. Or her house. But it was too late now. Now that he was here there was no getting rid of him. And she hated that somewhere deep down she didn't *want* to get rid of him.

She let her head fall back, closed her tired eyes and pinched back the migraine building at the bridge of her nose with her thumb and forefinger. She must have dozed off for a minute or two, or maybe ten, because the next thing she knew Parker was waking her, holding a steaming cup of coffee.

"Time to get up," he said, holding it out to her. "Black, one sugar."

She took the cup, grumbling under her breath as she did. It irritated her to no end that after just one shared meal at the diner he already knew exactly how she fixed her coffee.

"Not a morning person?" he asked, sitting down beside her with his own cup.

"Not on my *day off.*" Especially when she'd spent the previous night tossing and turning, and all because of the man sitting next to her.

"So, about that girl…"

"Ugh! Do I really need to hear this?" she said, resisting the urge to stick her fingers in her ears and sing, *Lalalalala.*

"There you go again, thinking the worst of me," he said.

She had to. It was the only way to keep him at arm's length.

"I spent the night at the hospital," he said. "With Janey."

Clare's heart dropped so fast and hard that she felt woozy. She set her coffee on the table for fear of dropping it from her shaking hands. And though she needed to know what happened, she was terrified to ask.

"She's okay," he assured her with a smile, laying a hand on her arm. "She's been improving all night."

Oh, thank God.

The sudden gush of relief had her shaking even harder. "How? What happened?"

"I finally figured out what's wrong. From watching the news, no less."

"So what is it?"

"It's called twin-to-twin transfusion."

She blinked. "But…she's not a twin. And if she is, where is the other baby?"

"Healthy and happy, and living with her uncle Logan."

She gasped. "Baby Maggie? But…"

"Some truck driver filming his rig got a video of Janey's mother at the Lucky Seven truck stop. She was identified as Margaret Garner by several people. Which means that Maggie and Janey are twins—we confirmed it with a blood test. Although she isn't Janey anymore."

"They gave her a new name?"

"Madeline. But they're calling her Maddie."

"Maddie and Maggie. That's cute. But how did we not make the connection?"

"I beat myself up over that all night. They were brought in separately, worked on by two different teams. She was healthy. There was really nothing to connect.

We're thinking that Margaret didn't know she was having twins. I think she had Maddie at the rest stop. She was probably in shock, and losing blood. I'm sure she had no idea she was still in labor when she got back in her car."

Meaning she probably got little to no prenatal care. "If she'd seen an OB-GYN she would have known it was twins and they could have treated their condition in utero."

"But we both know that it doesn't always work that way. And all things considered, Maddie is lucky to be alive. She'll always have issues with her heart, but for the most part she'll lead a normal life."

"Now what? She's still too sick to go home, even if she has one."

"There's a children's center in Plano that specializes in the disorder. She'll be moved there until she's well enough to go home. And even then she'll need special care. She's still a very sick little girl, but at least now there's a light at the end of the tunnel. We have effective treatment options."

It was usually a happy occasion when a patient left the hospital, and while Clare was relieved that Maddie—that name would take some getting used to—was improving, she would miss the baby terribly.

"When are they moving her? I'd like to see her before she goes."

"She's being taken over by ambulance tomorrow morning," he said.

Clare fought the irrational urge to cry. "I want to get over there and spend some time with her."

"Of course. And I know this is difficult because we're all very attached to her. But it's for the best."

Logically, yes.

"Would you mind if I just lie here on the couch and take a catnap?"

"It will have to be a short one," Clare told Parker. "I won't be long."

"Take your time," he said with a huge yawn, putting his head back and closing his eyes. "I'm beat."

He looked beat, and kind of harmless. But she was still a little unsure…

"You're staying right here?" she said.

He looked up at her with bloodshot, sleepy eyes. "I'm not going to move, I promise. And this time I really do promise."

"I'll only be five minutes," she said.

His eyes slipped closed again and he mumbled something incoherent.

Feeling a little on edge, but also fairly certain he was telling the truth, she jogged upstairs to her bedroom. If she gave him too much time alone he might get bored and into trouble.

She picked her clothes out and laid them on the bed then went into the bathroom to brush her teeth and hair. She'd slept like hell last night. Not even a date with the water jets in her spa tub had been enough to soothe the restless, itchy feeling in her soul. She knew of only one person who could throw her into such turmoil, and he was napping on her couch.

She brushed the knots from her waist-length hair, reminding herself that it was time for a trim. She reached for a hair band, still thinking about Parker, wondering what he could be getting into down there. Her hand stopped in midair halfway to the drawer, then fell to her side, and she asked her reflection, "What *could* he be getting into?"

That was a really good question, because knowing Parker the way she did, he was definitely getting into some sort of trouble. He couldn't seem to help himself.

She frowned at her reflection. What the hell was she doing? Instead of making him promise not to snoop, she should have sent him on his way instead. Politely but firmly. It wasn't as if she needed him to drive her to the hospital. She had her aunt's car for that. He literally had no reason to be there. Other than to frustrate and annoy her.

Still in her robe she headed back down the stairs, calling out to her uninvited guest. "Hey, Parker, I was thinking—"

Parker didn't hear her. He was stretched out on her couch, hands tucked behind his head, sound asleep and snoring softly. He was taking a catnap, just as he'd said he would. But that wasn't what had her tripping over her own feet, or whimpering like a wounded animal.

Parker still had his pants on, which was a really good thing. Unfortunately that was *all* he had on. His shirt, undershirt, shoes and socks were on the floor beside the sofa. And oh, did he look good. Better than she had ever imagined he would.

Damn him!

Hard as she'd tried to deny it, there was definitely some sort of connection there. An irrational and scary kind of connection. It didn't make any sense. But lately it seemed that very few things in her life made much sense anymore. So if she just crawled up there with him…

You cannot let that happen, Clare.

No, she could not.

She closed her eyes and shook her head, wishing away the mental picture of him lying there looking all sexy and perfect. Wishing *him* away. But when she peeked through the small slit between her mostly closed lids he was still lying there, still looking amazing with his muscular chest and wide shoulders. And his abs? They were freaking perfect. She could do a million crunches a day and never look that good.

On the bright side, this was without a doubt the least obnoxious she had ever seen him. But now more than ever he really needed to go. And she really needed to stop staring at his chest.

"Parker," she said, keeping a safe distance between them. When he didn't respond she said it louder. "Parker!"

Still nothing.

She clapped her hands hard and loud, thinking it would startle him awake. He didn't even flinch.

This was not working.

She stepped just close enough to the couch so that she could reach him with her foot. She gave him a firm jab in the leg with her toes then stepped back. Parker kept on snoring.

Wow, he was out.

She stepped a little closer and nudged him again, then once more.

Nothing.

This was getting ridiculous.

She laid her foot on his stomach, intending to give him a good hard shake, right up until the second the sensitive bottom of her bare foot touched his warm, smooth skin.

Oh, that was dumb.

He didn't budge, and she realized, as she dropped her leg, that if he had woken he would have opened his eyes to an X-rated, full view of her goods from the waist down.

And why was she more disappointed than relieved that he remained asleep?

Okay, it was time to get serious. He really had to go. She wasn't thinking straight at all.

Using her opposite foot, in case he actually did wake up at some point, she hauled off and kicked his leg.

He mumbled something and shifted onto his side, facing her, and when he did his phone slipped out of his pocket, hit the hardwood floor with a thud and slid under the couch.

Crap.

She would have just left it there, but Parker was on call. If his phone rang he needed to be able to hear it.

Realizing that the odds of him waking at this point were slim to none, she got down on her knees and fished his phone out from under the couch, finding a couple of dust bunnies under there, as well.

Sitting back on her haunches she laid the phone on the arm of the couch next to his ear, then changed her mind and set it down on the cushion next to him. As she did, the backs of her fingers "accidentally" brushed against his stomach. She felt the contact with the intensity of an electric shock and it left her feeling limp and shaky.

This was getting out of hand fast, and she knew she should stop. Problem was, she really, *really* wanted to touch his abs. Not for long. She just wanted to know how it would feel. A few seconds tops. He would never have to know.

The idea of touching him was terrifying. And intoxicating. Her hands shook in anticipation. But did she have the guts to do it?

Her aunt was always telling Clare that she needed more excitement. That she was in the prime of her life, and she needed to take chances every now and then. Kay's life had been one long adventure, and despite what the family may have believed, she had no regrets.

Clare gnawed on her lip, fists balled tight. Should she or shouldn't she? He was sleeping like the dead. So what was the harm? It would quench her curiosity, and he would never have to know about it.

Just do it, Clare.

Her hand trembled as she reached out. She let it hover over his stomach for a second, so close she could feel the heat of his skin, working up the courage to take it one step further.

She was really going to do this. She was going to *touch* him.

Nervous, and excited, she lowered her hand, and the charge she felt as her skin touched his would have buckled her knees if she hadn't already been on the floor. The contrast of her pale skin against his much darker olive complexion was a crazy kind of erotic, and she sat there like that, watching his face for any sign that he was waking. She was playing with fire and it was more exhilarating than she could have ever imagined. It had been so long since she allowed herself to let go and follow her heart, she had forgotten how good it could feel to want someone. And now that she had a small taste of what it felt like to touch him, to be so close to him, she didn't want to stop.

Once she rang that bell, it was impossible to un-ring it.

She let her hand drift upward, toward his pecs, which were as impressive, or even more impressive, than his abs.

She looked back up at his face and froze. His eyes were open.

Damn, caught in the act. She muttered a very unla-dylike word.

"Am I dreaming?" he asked, his voice gravelly, eyes glossy from sleep, or lack thereof.

This had to be a dream. Real life never felt this good.

"You're dreaming," she told him, sliding her hand up-ward, through the sprinkling of silky hair on his chest.

He groaned and closed his eyes again. "If this is a dream I don't ever want to wake up."

"It is," she said, gently dragging her nails down his pecs, over his small dark nipples. The scent of his skin was inebriating, and so delicious she wanted to eat him up. "This isn't really happening."

A sleepy smile curled his lips. "So I can do this?"

He covered her hand with his own and lifted it to his lips, brushing a kiss against her wrist.

She whimpered and cupped his face in her hand, his beard rough against her palm. She brushed her thumb over his full bottom lip and his tongue darted out for a taste. It just about did her in.

"Come here," he said. He hooked his hands behind her neck and pulled her against the hard wall of his chest for a kiss. He tasted like coffee and sleep and some-thing wild and exciting. Her heart pounded its way up into her throat and her skin felt electric. She was no longer thinking of the consequences. Screw the consequences. She wanted him, and she was going to take what she wanted.

His hand slid down her throat and slipped inside the opening of her robe, and when he cupped her breast, she stopped thinking altogether.

Seven

Her lips still pressed to Parker's, Clare climbed on the couch with him, straddling his thighs, her eyes dark with desire. He'd been fantasizing about this for so long, it was almost hard to believe it was really happening. When he first woke up to find her touching him, he thought it really *was* a dream. But if she wanted to pretend this wasn't happening who was he to shatter her illusion? If that was what it took to ease her conscience, to keep her in his arms, that was fine by him.

Then she was out of his arms, but only so she would be free to attack the zipper on his pants. She did it with the enthusiasm of someone on a time clock. Or someone trying not to change her mind. If she backed out now, the pain of what he would be missing out on would be excruciating. But it was a risk he was willing to take.

"No one can know about this," she said breathlessly

as she stripped him from the waist down. "And I mean no one."

Even if he wanted to disagree, there was no way in hell he would risk blowing this. Not now. He'd slept with a fair amount of women over the years. Sometimes the sex was fantastic, sometimes not, but they had all been missing something. The emotional connection he felt with Clare, maybe. He had never been one to chase women. The truth was he'd never had to. They always seemed to come to him. Maybe having to work for it made him appreciate the end result that much more. Because, damn, did he appreciate her right now.

"I promise I won't say a word to anyone." He tugged at the tie on her robe until it fell open. Clare whimpered softly. Either she believed him or she didn't care anymore.

"You're not worried about your aunt coming home?" he asked her.

"She's away for the week. She's always out of town."

"Good to know." Sliding his hands inside her robe, he pushed it off her slender shoulders, running his hands down her toned arms, over her soft stomach. She was all pale skin and soft curves, and everything in his being sighed with pleasure. She was perfect. Her dark blond hair hung like spun silk over her shoulders, giving him a peekaboo view of her perfectly shaped, supple breasts.

"You're amazing," he said. "I've never seen you with your hair down."

"Was it everything you hoped it would be?" She smiled at him with heavy-lidded eyes. "Because flattery will get you *everywhere*."

That was what he liked to hear.

"Will it get me here?" he asked her, cupping her firm

breasts, testing their weight against his palms, rolling the small pink tips between his fingers.

"Oh, yeah," she said, covering his hands with her own, showing him what she liked.

"How about here?" He ran his hands up her thighs, using his thumbs to tease the crevice where her legs met. She gasped as he touched her most sensitive spot. She was hot and wet and ready for him, but he wasn't about to rush this.

Clare had different ideas. She came up on her knees, and with one quick downward thrust he was inside of her. It was so erotic, and so unexpected, he nearly lost it right then. He moaned and his body arched upward to meet her, driving himself as deep as he could go.

Clare hissed with pleasure and threw her head back, her long hair brushing across his knees like the tickle of a feather. He gripped her hips, tried to slow her down as she rode him, but she was so deep in the zone, she didn't even seem to realize he was there.

Mild-mannered Nurse Clare had a naughty side after all.

She used his body, putting a friction shine on the leather sofa cushion, and he let her. When he was sure he couldn't take any more he wrapped his hands around her waist and tried to think about baseball, but she took him by the wrists and held them on either side of his head, using her weight to pin them there.

He could have easily gotten free, but why the hell would he want to? She seemed to get off on being in control, and he preferred a shameless and aggressive woman who knew what she liked. She could dominate him whenever and wherever she wanted.

Clare started to moan and ride him faster, and the

last shred of his control took a vacation. He never let himself be the first to orgasm, but he beat her to the punch by about thirty seconds. Clare didn't even seem to notice. She rode out her own release, then collapsed on his chest, breathing hard, her heart pounding in time with his own, and said, "I *really* needed that."

"Me, too," he said, folding his arms around her. Damn, she felt good. Holding her close this way was almost as good as the actual sex.

Almost.

He'd been anticipating this since the moment he'd first seen her, and she didn't disappoint.

She tucked her face into the crook of his neck, her silky hair catching on his chin stubble. "If I had known it would be this amazing I would have jumped you months ago."

"If I had any energy left, I would pin you down on the floor and do it again." He was so relaxed and so completely satisfied that he could barely keep his eyes open. Besides that catnap, which he was guessing by his intense fatigue couldn't have been more than a few minutes, he hadn't slept in more than twenty-four hours. As a resident he could function on one or two hours of sleep a night for a week or more, but he was getting too damned old now.

"Sure you won't change your mind?" she said, nibbling his earlobe.

Oh, man, did he want to. Maybe if he were ten years younger… "I wouldn't be much good to you like this."

She frowned, looking disappointed.

"I don't mean to sound ungrateful, because believe me, I'm not, but I have to know, why now?"

She shrugged. "I thought I would give the water jets in my tub a break."

Oh, damn. "Seriously?"

She grinned. "I shudder to imagine my next water bill."

The mental picture had his neurons firing and his blood boiling, but exhaustion won out. So he shelved the image for future reference. Not that he believed her. Or maybe he did.

"So," she said, disentangling herself from his arms to sit up, "I want to make sure we're on the same page."

Oh, boy, here we go. The Talk. "What? No afterglow?"

"I don't do afterglow. This isn't a relationship. This was just sex."

He'd used that same line on dozens of women and the irony of the situation wasn't lost on him. Because this time, he didn't want "just sex." He wanted her, in every way there was to want someone. It felt almost as if the force of the universe was propelling them toward one another. He knew that she felt it, too. She just wasn't ready to let herself accept it. But she would in her own time, and thankfully he was a very patient man.

"Whatever you want," he told her, and she looked as if maybe she didn't believe him.

"No one can know about us. And I mean *no one*."

"Be careful, you're going to bruise my tender ego."

She laughed and climbed off his lap, grabbing her robe from the floor. "Somehow I doubt that."

"Where are you going?"

"I have to get dressed and get out of here. I'd like to spend some time with Janey before they take her."

"Maddie," he reminded her.

"Right. It's going to be weird calling her by a different name. I also promised I would work a few hours at the free clinic this afternoon."

"Can I see you later?"

She hesitated, then said, "That's probably not a good idea."

"Why?"

She shot him a look as she tugged the robe back on. "You know why."

"I knew it," he said, throwing his arm dramatically over his eyes. "You're ashamed of me."

She grabbed his shirt off the floor and tossed it to him. "I need you dressed and ready to go by the time I come back down."

"Sure thing," he said, but the second she was gone he tossed his shirt on the floor and dropped his head back against the arm of the sofa. He must have drifted off, only to be roused by a loud thud.

He peered out through the slits of his eyes, trying to get his bearings, then saw his clothes in a pile on the floor beside the couch and grinned. Clare must have decided to let him stay, or maybe she had tried to wake him and he hadn't responded. The house was quiet and the angle of the sunshine filtering through the closed blinds meant it had to be late afternoon. Clare had covered him with one of her quilts before she left, and it smelled like her. He knew he should get dressed and get home for a few more hours of shut-eye, but he was so comfortable…

He looked back over at his clothes and a few feet away sat an unfamiliar pair of shoes. Women's shoes. He didn't recall them being there that morning. Clare hadn't been wearing them. Then one of the shoes started tapping, and he realized that there was an actual person inside of them.

And he had the sinking feeling that it wasn't Clare.

Parker bolted up on the couch, catching the blanket just before it fell to the floor.

The shoes were on an older, attractive woman, and the noise that roused him must have been the front door closing after she'd come in.

He was assuming she was Clare's aunt. So much for her being out of town.

Having heard her referred to as an old maid, Parker had formed a specific impression in his head of how Kay probably looked, but reality bore no resemblance to his imagination. Her clothes were casual but neat, fashionable and very expensive. She had long dark blond hair like Clare's, but hers was peppered with shades of silver and gray, and while Clare's hair had a sort of wild and free quality to it, this woman's was smooth and sleek.

Thankfully, she wasn't holding a gun on him. Because people in Texas loved their guns. And he was guessing she had one or two herself.

"It's not every day a woman comes home to find a naked man on her couch," she said with a heavy Texas twang. "This must be my lucky day." Then she looked him up and down, smiled and added, "Or maybe it's yours."

Boy did he hope she was joking. "You must be Aunt Kay."

"I must be."

He could only imagine what she was probably thinking, and damn would he like to put some clothes on. The blanket was feeling awfully thin and a little small.

"And who might you be?" she asked.

"Parker," he said. "Parker Reese. I work with Clare."

One brow rose slightly. "Among other things?"

No, this wasn't awkward at all. "Uh…yeah."

"You're better looking than I imagined. But that might just be the absence of clothes."

So she knew who he was? That was interesting. "Has Clare mentioned me?"

She gave him one of those *bless your heart* looks. "I'm afraid that I'm not at liberty to say."

Ooookay.

"She was right about one thing," Kay said. "They would have a field day with you."

Huh? "They who? And why would they have a field day?"

She flashed him another placating smile. "I'm not at liberty to say."

Of course she wasn't. This was too weird. He was the naked stranger in her house, yet he was the one asking all of the questions. Though she seemed to have a pretty good idea of who he was. "Maybe I should call Clare," he said.

"Maybe you should put your clothes on first."

Yeah, that would probably be a good idea. He just hoped she wasn't expecting to watch him.

"Go on up to Clare's room, and for the love of all that is holy, take the blanket with you. My heart isn't what it used to be."

Somehow he doubted that. Despite her age, she looked strong as an ox. Sturdy, yet refined. And as much as he appreciated the offer of privacy—and oh, did he appreciate it—he wasn't so sure Clare would appreciate him using her bedroom. He'd gone up there the other night to tease her, but this was different. It felt like an invasion of privacy to be in there when she wasn't around. If he was going to make this relationship work, he had to respect Clare's boundaries. "Would it be all right if I just use a bathroom down here? I don't want to invade Clare's space."

His request seemed to surprise Kay, and he was betting it earned him a few brownie points, too.

"That's awfully thoughtful of you. There's a half bath just off the kitchen."

"Thanks." He grabbed his clothes and his phone and with the blanket tucked firmly around his midsection, he hightailed it to the bathroom. Once he was in there, there was no hurry, but he threw his clothes on as quickly as possible. So fast he was pretty sure he put his boxers and socks on inside out.

When he was dressed he checked his phone, surprised to find that it was almost four o'clock. He'd slept for nearly *eight* hours. Far more than his typical five or six. And it was a deep restful kind of sleep that usually evaded him.

Must have been the sex.

He dialed Clare, and she answered her phone saying, "You had better not be snooping."

He smiled and shook his head. "Houston, we have a problem."

"What's wrong?"

"You know how you thought your aunt was still out of town?"

"Uh-oh."

Uh-oh was right. "Yeah, well, she's not. She's here."

He could feel her cringe over the phone line. "Tell me you weren't still on the couch."

"I wish I could."

"Naked?"

"As the day I was born."

She made a noise and it took a second for him to realize what he was hearing. "Oh, my God, are you *laughing*?"

"No, of course not," she said, clearing her throat. "She's not holding you at gunpoint, is she?"

He knew she had guns! "Not yet, and frankly, she's scary enough without one."

"Yeah, she can be," Clare said, and he could hear the mirth in her voice. Was she enjoying this?

"This isn't funny. Stop laughing."

"I'm sorry, but the mental picture…"

Okay, maybe it was a little funny. "I take it my name has come up before."

There was a slight pause, as if she were choosing her words carefully. "A time or two, yes."

"You don't seem too upset that our *secret* is out."

"Aunt Kay won't tell anyone. I trust her absolutely."

"She said that you were right, they would have a field day. What's that supposed to mean?"

"Long story," she said. "And I'm sorry she walked in on you like that. I really had no idea she would be home early."

"Are you coming back?"

"Not for another hour or so. I'm volunteering at the free clinic."

"So basically I'm on my own?"

"Yeah, sorry."

"You promise she's not going to hurt me?"

"If it makes you feel better, she's never actually shot anyone."

Oh, yeah, that made him feel so much better.

"However…" she said.

"*What?*"

"She might give you a hard time."

"*Might?* She already did!"

"Well, it's probably not over yet. Aunt Kay is very protective of me."

Swell.

"Did you see Ja—I mean Maddie?" he asked her. "I didn't get a page so I'm assuming things are good."

"I did see her, and she's doing really well. Logan and Hadley were there with Maggie. She's so much bigger and healthier, it's hard to imagine that they're the same age."

"Maddie will catch up."

"I'm going to miss her, but I know this is for the best. And I'm so glad to know that she has family."

"Did Logan say if he was able to contact his brother?"

"They left messages for him but so far they haven't heard back. Won't he be surprised to find out that not only is he a father, but to twins no less."

"And one with special needs. He'll have his hands full."

"Hold on a sec," Clare said, and he heard her talking to someone, then she was back. "Parker, I have to go. Can I call you later?"

He was hoping she would. "Of course."

"Okay, I'll talk to you then. And, Parker?"

"Yeah?"

"Good luck."

She seemed to be enjoying this a little too much.

He hung up and stuck his phone in his pocket, then folded the blanket he'd been wearing and opened the door. Clare's aunt was standing in the kitchen, sipping on a bottle of beer. She gestured to an open bottle in front of a bar stool at the kitchen island and said, "Have a seat, Parker."

"I should really get going," he said.

One brow rose slightly, and she gave him a look that said compliance was not optional.

Wow. She was tough. And a little scary.

No, she was *a lot* scary.

He handed her the blanket and did as he was told, feeling like a teenager meeting his girlfriend's parents for the first time. "I guess I can spare a few minutes."

"What are your intentions with my niece?"

Talk about getting right to the point. But who knew, maybe he would glean some insight on what made Clare tick. "I find her utterly fascinating," he said. "From the minute we were introduced I was drawn to her, and though she won't admit it, I think the feeling is mutual."

Kay neither confirmed nor denied it. "Clare is not as tough as she likes people to think."

"I know."

"She's a little broken."

"Who isn't?"

His answer seemed to satisfy her. "You're a smart man, but I'll be keeping my eye on you."

No surprise there, and he couldn't help but respect her for it. "Aunt Kay," he said, "I would expect no less."

Eight

It was just starting to get dark when Clare pulled in the driveway. Parker's car was gone, and she realized that deep down she had been hoping he was still there. Which was completely ridiculous. He had better things to do than hang around all day waiting for her.

But it would have been a little cool if he had. And a little terrifying.

She parked her aunt's car in the garage and stepped inside the house. "I'm home!"

"In here!" her aunt called from the living room.

Aunt Kay sat in her recliner, a book in her lap. She loved murder mysteries and psychological thrillers. The darker and gorier the better.

"So," Clare said, setting her purse down on the coffee table. "Is he buried in the backyard in a shallow grave?"

"Oh, please," her aunt scoffed. "There are much more effective ways to get rid of a body. And a car."

Clare gave her a look.

"I'm kidding. I like him."

Huh? Aunt Kay never "liked" anyone without getting to know them first, and that process could take weeks, and sometimes even months. "Just like that? You like him."

She shrugged. "Sometimes you just know. I would think you of all people would realize that."

"What's that supposed to mean?"

"You know *exactly* what I mean, Clare. You've got it bad for the man."

Yeah, she did. "He doesn't know that."

"He sure thinks he does."

Of course he did. He was a man. He thought he knew everything. It just so happened that in this case he was right.

Lucky guess.

"He is a little stubborn. I almost ran him to death on the jogging path the other day. Then I served him a half-frozen breakfast sandwich, which he actually ate. I should have known he would be too damned polite to complain."

"Sounds as if you've been having fun with him," Kay said.

"At his expense."

"Nothing wrong with that. Is he good in bed?"

Clare collapsed onto the sofa. "We never made it to the bed, but he's good on a couch."

"I'm just happy to hear that you're letting your hair down and having fun for a change. You need a man in your life."

"Don't get ahead of yourself." It had *bad idea* written all over it. She couldn't think straight when she was around him. All she could feel was an edgy sort of excitement, and she had been displaying a dangerously blasé attitude. She'd left him alone in her house, for God's sake. She *never* did that.

Although to be fair, removing him would have required dragging him sound asleep out the front door and leaving him on the porch. She'd tried to wake him when she was ready to go, but the man slept like the dead. "I haven't even decided if I'm going to sleep with him again," she told her aunt.

"Well, that just breaks my heart," Aunt Kay said. "A body that perfect should be put to good use."

Though she and Kay looked a little bit alike, and they both shared a deep aversion to farm life, Clare and her aunt couldn't have been more different. Kay grabbed life by the horns and didn't let go, while Clare wouldn't even venture on the other side of the fence.

"Here's something you might find interesting," Kay said. "I told him he could go up to your room to change."

Clare's jaw fell. "Why? You know I hate that."

"He apparently knows, too, because he asked to change in the bathroom down here instead. Said he didn't want to invade your space."

She blinked. "Oh."

"Sounds like he knows you pretty well already."

Yeah, it sort of did.

"And he respects your space."

Finally.

"And he's so hot."

Yes, he was.

"Maybe you should cut the guy a break and give him a chance. Not all men are liars and cheats. Something tells me that he's one of the good guys. Go out on a date or two. Have some fun, see where it goes."

"Why would I date someone that I can't even take home to my family? You said it yourself. They would have a field day with him."

"Maybe you should stop worrying about what they think."

She wished it were that easy. "How badly did you scare him?"

She shrugged. "If he scared easily you would have been rid of him months ago."

That still didn't make a relationship a good idea. It just meant that he was stubborn.

"I wish you could have seen the look on his face when he woke up and saw me standing there," Kay said with a smile. "If only I'd had my camera."

Clare would have paid big money to see that. "I hope you don't mind but I had to use your car. Mine committed suicide last night. It will cost almost as much as a new one to fix it."

"Of course I don't mind. Do we need to go car shopping?"

"I'm thinking it's time." Her aunt was a ruthless haggler. Be it a car or a refrigerator, when the salesman gave his rock-bottom price, she always managed to talk him down just a little lower. When they were rebuilding the house after the tornado she'd haggled the builder into paying out of pocket for the upgrades the insurance refused to cover. People just had a hard time telling her no.

"What brought you home so early?" Clare asked her.

"Claud and I had a fight. He asked me to marry him again."

"I take it you said no?"

She sighed, shaking her head. "Some men never learn."

She could have been talking about Parker, but Clare didn't bother to point that out.

"Are you hungry?" Kay asked. "Let's order dinner."

"I could go for sushi."

"Hmm, sounds good," she said, pulling out her phone. Neither of them cooked, so her aunt had the number of every restaurant in Royal that delivered on speed dial. "You want the usual?"

"Yes, please. While I'm waiting I'm going to go upstairs and get out of these scrubs." She was exhausted, thanks to a certain someone waking her at the crack of dawn that morning. But in all fairness it had been worth it.

"I'll let you know when it gets here," her aunt told her.

With sore, tired feet Clare climbed the stairs. A soak in the tub sounded good, but with the food on the way she took a hot shower instead. And though they were barely stubbly, she shaved her legs and cleaned up the bikini line, as well.

Just in case.

After her shower, as she was drying off, she took note of her new svelte figure. She looked damn good. Not that she'd been overweight, per se, but she hadn't exactly been healthy before.

She was still standing at the mirror naked, brushing the knots from her wet hair when her aunt knocked on the bedroom door. "Come on in! Just leave it on the bed."

She heard the door open, then close again, and a second later saw movement in the bathroom doorway. She turned and her breath caught in her lungs.

It was Parker standing there.

He grinned, his eyes raking over her from the top of her head all the way down to her pink-tipped toes, and every inch of her skin came alive all at once. He looked sexy as hell in faded jeans and a black T-shirt with the hospital logo. She had never seen him dressed so casually. She took in the way those biceps stretched the armholes of his shirt, and the way the jeans hugged his lean hips. But as good as he looked in his clothes, she knew he looked even better out of them.

He held up the sushi bag and said with a frustratingly sexy smile, "Special delivery."

Clare would have grabbed her robe to cover herself, but by the look in his eyes, and the fact that he had put the bag down and begun to peel off his clothes, she had the feeling the damage was already done.

"Your aunt sent me up," he said, taking off his shirt and dropping it on the floor. "Remind me to thank her profusely."

Aunt Kay would hear about it later, all right. Because she was meddling. Unfortunately she was really good at it.

The jeans went next, and Clare just stood there like a dummy watching, when she should have been kicking him to the curb for being so presumptuous. But then the boxers dropped and that was all she wrote. She couldn't tell him no now if her life depended on it.

"Come here," he said, taking her hand and leading her to the bed, walking backward so he didn't have to take his eyes off her. "You are so sexy."

Before she could censor herself, she said, "Look who's talking."

With a grin, he pulled her in and kissed her. And

kissed her. Oh, did she love kissing him. He smelled freshly showered and his chin was smooth. And as he hauled her up against the length of that ripped physique she was no more sturdy than her trembling hands. Lucky for her he wasted no time getting her off her feet and into bed.

He laid her on her back. Typically she didn't like being on her back, but as he climbed in beside her, she decided to let it slide. Then he started to kiss her again and she ignored that irrational need to be in control. She liked the feel of his weight pressing her into the mattress, his hands skimming her body, igniting a trail of fire across her skin. Then he began to kiss his way downward. It felt so good, and she wanted to relax and enjoy it, but as he reached the lowest part of her stomach, she automatically tensed.

Parker froze and lifted his head to look at her. "What's wrong?"

"Nothing."

He frowned and pushed himself up on his elbows. "Don't lie to me."

Damn it. Why did he have to be so intuitive? So concerned about her needs and her weird hang-ups. He needed to stop being so wonderfully thoughtful. "It's nothing."

"The hell it is. Talk to me, Clare."

The tone in his voice when he said her name sent shivers across her skin. After months of listening to the annoying nicknames he came up with for her, he had to choose *now* to start using her real name? When she was feeling most vulnerable? And did he have to say it with so much…*feeling*?

"What you're doing, what you're getting ready to do, it makes me feel very…"

"Vulnerable?"

"*Yes.* Very vulnerable."

"Do you want me to stop?"

"Yes. And no. I don't know, it's weird. I'm weird."

To his credit he didn't ask why she felt that way, because that was one big ole can of worms she would rather not spill just yet. Or maybe ever. He was just so darned open and honest, it was difficult not to give him some sort of explanation.

"You're not weird." He kissed her stomach once more, then made his way back upward. "And I don't want to do anything that makes you uncomfortable. This is supposed to be fun."

"I don't want you to think that I don't trust you."

"Clare, you barely know me. Trust is earned." He kissed her so sweetly she could have cried, or punched him, then he rolled onto his back and pulled her on top of him, grinning that devilish smile. "Better?"

"You don't mind?"

"I get to lie here while a gorgeous woman rides me like I'm a rodeo bull. What do you think?"

She leaned down to kiss him, for fear that if she didn't do something, she really would cry. Why did he have to be so wonderful? So understanding?

So damn *hot.*

He clearly had no reservations about being dominated, because she did ride him like a rodeo bull. He let her take the lead and set the pace, and even though he was on his back he didn't just lie there. He kept his hands and his mouth and his hips plenty busy making her crazy, and when he cradled her face in his hands and gasped her name as he shattered, that sent her sailing. Her own release came on like a tsunami that set her soaring headlong into ecstasy.

And he wasn't even through with her. He rolled her over and started from the top again. Her senses blurred and her body quaked and she forgot all about being in control, being nervous, and let him do his thing. And boy, did he do his thing. When she couldn't take it any longer, he was still champing at the bit to pleasure her again.

She'd rediscovered muscles tonight that she hadn't used in a long time, and it was way past time to take them out, dust them off and put them to good use. But she was going to pay for it tomorrow.

"I need to rest," she told him, flopping down on her back.

"I've heard that more than once tonight," he said with a grin, his hand teasing its way downward.

She intercepted it just above her navel. "I really mean it this time. I'm exhausted."

Looking disappointed, he rolled onto his back beside her. She didn't usually do the afterglow part, but as he took her hand, weaving their fingers together, she was too tired to move. Besides, it felt good to be near to him, their bodies close, their fingers intertwined. She liked it way too much.

"So what did my aunt say to you when you got here?" she asked him.

"She handed me the bag and said, 'Clare is in her bedroom, go on up.'"

She and Aunt Kay were going to have to have a talk about boundaries. About how it was not okay to send sexy men up to her bedroom. Although in this particular case Clare was willing to overlook the transgression.

"Your aunt is tough," he said. "But I think she likes me."

She wouldn't have sent him up here otherwise. "She has to be tough. She's been on her own most of her life. At a time when women didn't stay single and have careers instead of families."

He pushed himself up on his elbow. "She's never been married?"

"She was once, a really long time ago. But only for a few months."

"What happened? If you don't mind my asking."

"As a kid Kay hated farm life. Probably more than I do. She always dreamed of being a 'sophisticated city slicker,' as she put it. When she was seventeen she met a wealthy businessman from Tulsa. He was fifteen years older and worldly and she fell hard for him. Everyone loved him. He was charming and personable, and he showered her and her family with gifts. He took her to fancy restaurants and bought her nice clothes.

"I guess times were pretty hard and her parents were so happy to have a rich son-in-law, they didn't bat an eyelash when she turned up pregnant. So they had a shotgun wedding, then he took her to his house in Tulsa. Everyone thought he was perfect, and that Kay was such a lucky girl."

"No one is perfect."

"Yeah. They were married about a week when he started beating her."

Parker winced. "He was a predator."

"A predator with a volatile temper. She said he was like Jekyll and Hyde. The first time he hit her it was over the grocery money. He got angry because she bought a magazine. She called him stingy, and he back-handed her."

Parker cringed. "She didn't leave?"

"She had nowhere to go. Her parents were too poor to take her and her baby in, and back then a pregnant woman couldn't just go out and get a job, or even get a credit card without her husband's signature. Plus, he'd been subsidizing her family's farm. She knew that if she tried to leave, he would cut them off. Without that money, they would have fallen into poverty and lost everything. There would be no place for her parents and her five siblings to go. She was, as she puts it, in one hell of a pickle."

"Did her parents know what was going on?"

"No, of course not. If they had they would have driven to Tulsa and taken her back home, even if it meant losing everything. But she said the guilt would have hurt far worse than his fists ever could."

"That's one hell of a sacrifice. But she obviously got away."

"Yes, when he almost killed her. He came home from work angry and she said the wrong thing, so he used her as a punching bag. It was dumb luck that a neighbor had her window open and just happened to hear him screaming at her. When he stormed off the neighbor came by to see if she was okay. She found her bleeding and battered on the kitchen floor and called for help. Kay had internal injuries and would have bled to death if not for her. They got her to the hospital in time to save her life, but she lost the baby. And her uterus."

He closed his eyes and shook his head. Jesus.

"But she made sure it would never happen again. To her or anyone else."

"How?"

"Long story short, the day she got out of the hospital he said he was going to teach her a lesson, so she ran him over with his car."

His eyes went wide and his jaw fell. "Did she kill him?"

"Almost. He never walked right again. Or beat anyone else, I'm sure."

"Did she get in trouble?"

"She claimed it was self-defense, and after the way he beat her before that, people believed her. And Kay being Kay, she pulled herself up by her bootstraps and started over. When she was healed she wound up getting a job as a stewardess. She worked the international flights, so she's traveled pretty much everywhere, and has friends all over the world. When she was labeled 'too old' to do the job, she started a travel agency in Dallas. When the industry was at an all-time high she retired and sold the business for a small fortune. Now she spends most of her time traveling and volunteering for domestic-abuse organizations. She counsels young people trapped in abusive relationships."

"Wow, that's one hell of a life."

"I keep telling her that she needs to write a memoir. Her story could help a lot of people."

Parker's stomach rumbled loudly and Clare laughed. "Hungry?"

"I guess I skipped dinner," he said, rubbing a hand across his belly.

"I've got sushi and I'd be willing to share. And I could probably find a couple of beers in the fridge."

For several seconds he just looked at her, a funny little half smile on his face.

"What?"

"You surprise me, Clare."

"Why is that?"

"I thought for sure you would kick me out of your bed the second we were finished."

So did she. And normally she would have. "If I wasn't so tired I probably would," she lied, when the truth was she didn't want him to go anywhere.

She was playing a dangerous game, letting him get so close. If she wasn't careful she might do something stupid like fall head over heels in love with him.

Nine

Though she'd had only one day off work, when Clare pulled into the hospital lot the next morning it felt as if weeks had passed. So much had happened in such a short span of time.

She and Parker had had a picnic on her bed last night—sushi and beer—then had sex again. She couldn't imagine where he found the energy. He had impressive stamina, and loads of patience. She must have fallen asleep immediately afterward, and when she woke at midnight he was gone. He could have easily taken advantage of her unconscious state and hung around, but he really seemed to respect her space now. As hard as he'd pushed the past three months, suddenly he seemed to know just when to back off. It was a little disconcerting—no, make that terrifying—the way he was so attuned to her needs. Most men didn't have a clue.

Parker was in meetings all morning so she didn't see him right away, and as a result spent the first half of her day fighting the nervous excitement building in her belly. It wasn't as if she didn't see him almost every day at work. What a difference a few days could make. It felt as if her entire life had been flipped on its head. And somewhere in the back of her mind there was a nagging little voice asking her, what if it was all a game to him? What if he said something to make people believe they were an item. What if he hauled her up out of her chair behind the nurses' station and kissed her senseless?

As quickly as she had the thought, she dismissed it. Now that she knew him a little better, she didn't think he would be capable of anything so underhanded. Her aunt was right: he was one of the good guys. And Clare needed to get her priorities straight.

In her experience, the hotter the sex, the faster the relationship burned, until there was nothing left but ash. At the rate they were going, they wouldn't make it a week.

But he had been so sweet and so understanding about her reservations. Because of her hang-ups, a first intimate encounter with a man could be a bit awkward, and usually was. Men always thought they would be the one to "cure" her. As if she was broken or something. Which she was a little, she supposed. But they inevitably pushed her too far, or sometimes not far enough. It just always seemed to end in disaster for everyone. Eventually, she'd just stopped trying.

But this thing with Parker had her reevaluating that decision.

She was at the nurses' station looking up a chart on the computer when she heard his familiar footsteps, and as he neared, her heart sailed right up into her already tight throat and lodged there, pounding relentlessly.

Oh, man, this was *bad*.

She heard him talking to Rebecca. Clare knew for a fact that he'd dated the young nurse a time or two, and Clare felt her hackles rise. Though from the look on Rebecca's face when Clare glanced up, there was no love lost there. Her eyes settled on Parker for no more than a second, but the damage was done. Her heart did a nose-dive with a triple twist to the pit of her belly, knocking her insides all out of whack.

She heard him send Rebecca to check on a patient, then his footsteps as he came closer. Her heart sailed back up into her throat again and the crown of her scalp felt tingly and warm.

"Hey there, sweet cheeks," he said, which was exactly the way he would have greeted her before they slept together. And it would have annoyed the hell out of her. Now the sound of his voice strummed across her nerve endings, the friction warming her from the inside out.

"Dr. Reese," she said, not looking up from the screen. She was afraid that if she looked at him again, her true feelings would wind up on display for everyone to see. Including him. She was so beside herself her hands were trembling.

What was *wrong* with her?

He leaned down and looked over her shoulder at the computer screen, as if they were discussing a patient, and said quietly, "Have I mentioned that you're amazing?"

It was difficult not to swoon, or throw her arms

around his neck and kiss him. Hoping her voice wasn't as shaky as the rest of her, she said, "Once or twice."

"Sleep well?"

She nodded. Oh, had she ever. He had completely worn her out. "I was a little surprised that you left."

"You sound disappointed."

Yeah, she sort of did, didn't she?

"I would have stayed." He pointed at nothing in particular on the screen. "But I left because I knew that would be what you wanted."

And he was right. Or was he? If she had woken up beside him this morning, they could have had a little fun before work.

Which just goes to show how much this is clouding your judgment, you big dummy.

He really needed to get a handle on this habit he had of being so wonderful. Couldn't he say something sexist or rude? Or even better, condescending.

"Busy tonight?" he asked.

"What were you thinking?"

His breath was warm against her ear when he said, "You know exactly what I'm thinking, cupcake."

Back to the nicknames, were they? She was sort of getting used to hearing him use her name. But this time the teasing didn't bother her so much. "I promised my friend Violet that I would go to a stained-glass class with her tonight at Priceless, the antiques store just outside of town."

"Sounds like fun. Violet is Mac McCallum's sister, right? He owns the Double M Ranch."

"That's the one."

"Okay," he said. "How about afterward?"

She wanted to, she really did. It was all just moving

so fast. "I think I need some time to think. You know, about us."

"At least you're willing to admit there is an *us*."

At least.

As he straightened, his hand brushed her bare arm and her senses went into extreme overload. "Call me if you change your mind, princess."

Clare really, *really* wanted to see him tonight, and wrestled all day with what she should do. Should she be smart and reasonable, and take the time she needed to sort her feelings out, or be wildly irresponsible, say what the hell and jump him again? When Violet called later that afternoon to confirm their plans, Clare felt torn.

After small talk about the ranch she and her brother Mac owned, Violet asked, "Are we still on for tonight?"

An excuse was on the tip of her tongue, and Clare would have canceled, but the idea of seeing Parker socially four days in a row scared her a little.

"I can't wait," she told Violet with more enthusiasm than she was feeling. But she also knew she was doing the right thing. She was sure when she got to Priceless she would have a good time. She'd always had an interest in making stained glass and she'd heard that Raina Patterson's studio was impressive. In addition to teaching crafts, Raina sold antiques out of the space. Clare had shopped in Priceless, but never taken a class there.

She remembered her car situation and asked Violet, "I know it's a little out of your way, but could you give me a lift? I'm carless right now."

"Is that how you wound up at the Royal Diner with

Dr. Reese the other night?" Violet asked, a teasing lilt in her tone.

Ugh. Clare hated small towns sometimes. Violet was well aware of Parker's shenanigans and how much they irritated Clare. She and everyone else Clare knew.

She made a sound of disgust and said, "He basically kidnapped me. He offered to drive me home then took me to the diner instead. Short of walking, or calling a cab, I was stuck. But I was hungry and he paid the check, so it could have been worse, I guess."

"Why don't you just go out with him?"

"Because he's a womanizing, insufferable, mega-lomaniac."

"Yeah, but he's *so* hot."

"Then why don't you go out with him?"

There was a slight pause, then she said, "It's not me he wants."

Touché.

She heard footsteps behind her and turned to see Grace Haines, Janey's caseworker, approaching. *Madeline*, she reminded herself. For a second she thought the worst, that something was wrong, but Grace was smiling.

"I have to let you go, Violet. I'll see you tonight."

They hung up and Clare greeted Grace with a smile and a hug. "What brings you here?"

"I came to pick up some paperwork for Madeline's transfer and I thought I would stop and say hello."

"How is she doing?"

"She's great. She may get to go home in a couple of weeks. She'll have monitors, of course, but Hadley and Logan are taking a class at the center so they'll know what to do in an emergency."

"No word on the father?" Clare asked.

Grace shook her head somberly. "Either he can't be reached, or doesn't want to be. Logan doesn't speak too highly of his brother. Thankfully if Seth doesn't claim the twins, Logan and Hadley have already committed to adopting them. Honestly, I'm thinking that it would be for the best. I'm all for keeping children with their biological parents, but Seth is anything but reliable."

"After such a rotten start in life, those girls deserve a happy, stable family."

"They sure do," Grace said. "I dated Seth in high school. Even then there was nothing *stable* about him."

"Grace!"

Clare and Grace both turned to see Parker coming toward them, all smiles. "How's my favorite caseworker?"

Grace smiled. "Great, and how is my favorite pediatrician?"

"Couldn't be better," he said, not even acknowledging that Clare was standing there. Then they hugged and though it was totally platonic Clare felt the slightest twinge of jealousy. Grace was tall and curvy with chestnut hair that tumbled down in soft natural curls. She was also beautiful, and so very nice, and Clare had never met a caseworker more dedicated to the kids in her care. Standing together she and Parker made an extremely attractive couple.

"How's our girl doing?" Parker asked her.

"Still improving. I was just telling Clare that she might be able to go home in a couple of weeks."

"That makes my day," he said.

Grace looked at her watch. "I'd love to stay and chat but I have a home visit to get to. But I'm sure I'll see you guys again soon."

"It was great to see you," Parker said, then he turned to Clare and his smile disappeared. "When you get a minute I need to see you in my office."

Her heart plummeted and landed with a messy splat. He looked genuinely upset with her and she had no clue what she had done wrong.

"Um, yeah, sure," she said. "Now is good."

He nodded sternly, turned and all but marched down the hall. The two women watched him walk away in stunned silence.

"What was that about?" Grace asked, looking as taken aback by his demeanor as Clare was.

"I have no idea. I guess I'm about to find out."

"Well, good luck."

They headed in opposite directions down the hall. When Clare got to Parker's office the door was partially closed so she knocked gingerly.

"Enter."

She stepped inside expecting to see him at his desk. Then the door shut behind her and she spun around. Parker stood there grinning. "Hey there, sweet cheeks."

"Hey," Clare said, looking hopelessly confused.

Parker took her hand and pulled her against him, then proceeded to kiss her socks off. When he finally let her go she gave him a playful shove. "You creep! I really thought you were mad at me."

"Pretty good, huh?" Parker said with a grin. He probably could have made his point without sounding angry, but the crushed look on Clare's face had been worth it. If he'd snapped at her a week ago, she would have stood there stony faced and emotionless, as if she only had to listen because he was the boss. Not that he snapped at his staff all that often, but it did happen occasionally. But her reaction said something that up until now he could only hypothesize.

She cared. A lot.

She slid her arms up around his neck, pressed her body to his and pulled him down for an enthusiastic kiss. He got an instant hard-on. She was sexy as hell, and so completely unaware of it.

"Did you really need to talk to me or did you just want to make out?" she asked him. "Because the longer I'm in here the more suspicious it will look."

"I saw the way you looked at us when I hugged Grace. I thought we should talk about it."

"How did I look?" she asked, even though she knew that he knew exactly what was going on.

"A little green, actually."

She backed out of his arms, nose in the air. "That's ridiculous."

"Is it?"

She folded her arms stubbornly. "Yes, it is."

"Admit it, you were jealous."

"Why would I be jealous? We're not in an exclusive relationship."

"Well then, maybe we should be."

Her eyes went wide and up went the wall. "That's crazy. I haven't even decided if I'm going to sleep with you again."

Yeah, right. "Then what was that kiss you just laid on me all about? Are you a tease, Clare?"

She didn't seem to have a comeback for that, but her inner struggle was written all over her face.

"You do what you need to do," he told her. "But as

long as we're *involved*, I'm not going to date, or have any sort of physical relationship with anyone else."

She looked as if she might cry, or barf. As if she didn't know *how* to feel. And all she managed was a shaky, "O-okay."

He tugged her back into his arms with no resistance and tipped her chin up so he could look into her eyes. "That's a promise, sweetheart."

Something dark flashed in her eyes. "In my experience men have a very limited grasp on the concept of a promise."

"Sounds like you've been hanging around the wrong kind of men."

Clearly he'd hit a sore spot. She untangled herself from his arms and said, "This is not the time or the place to get into this. I have to get back to work. If anyone asks, we're discussing Janey—I mean, Madeline's case. Finishing up paperwork or something."

He nodded. "As you wish."

After she left, he took a seat at his desk. Boy, had he hit a nerve.

Luc popped his head in a second later. "Hey, have you got a minute?"

"Sure, what's up?"

He flopped down in the chair opposite Parker and propped his feet up on the desk. "I haven't seen you in a few days so I wasn't able to congratulate you on solving the mystery."

Mystery? Had he somehow figured out that Parker and Clare were intimate?

He decided to play dumb. "I'm not sure what you mean."

Luc looked at him as if he was an idiot. "Madeline. I hear that she's getting better."

Oh, *that mystery.* "Twin-to-twin transfusion," he said with a shrug. "Who knew?"

"Was that Clare I just saw leaving your office?"

"We were discussing a patient," he said.

"I also heard you were at the diner with her the other night. Sounds as if you're wearing her down."

It took a second for Parker to realize that Luc was referring to their bet. Parker had completely forgotten about it. What seemed like an innocent joke then could have real repercussions for his relationship with Clare if she ever caught wind of it.

"Actually I haven't made any progress at all. And I'm thinking I'm just wasting my time."

"You might want to rethink that," Luc said. "I mentioned our bet to Bruce Marsh in Radiology and he wanted in. He must have told someone, and they must have told someone else. Last night I heard a member mention it at the club."

Suddenly Parker was the one who felt like barfing. And he couldn't even get angry because it wasn't unusual for their little bets to make the rounds of their fellow doctors. To have this one running rampant through the hospital was bad enough. Now that it was out in public, God only knew who would get wind of it.

What the hell had he done?

"I'm clearly not getting anywhere with her, so let's just call you the winner and be done with it," he told Luc.

Luc frowned. "It's not like you to give up so easily. Is there something you're not telling me?"

He wrestled with his options. If he told Luc the truth

he would be breaking a promise to Clare, but if he didn't he could find himself in the hot seat.

Breaking a promise to Clare to save himself? Really? That sounded like something his father would do. There had to be a better way.

"The truth is, I've started seeing someone," he told Luc, sticking as close to the truth as possible. "She works here at the hospital and wants to keep the relationship quiet while we see where this goes."

His curiosity piqued, Luc asked, "Is it someone I know?"

"Maybe. Maybe not. But I have strong feelings for this woman, and if she hears about the bet she might take it the wrong way."

"I see what you mean," Luc said. "I'm sorry, Parker. I'll see what I can do to make this discreetly go away, but it seems to have taken on a life of its own."

Parker felt sick to his stomach. How the hell had he gotten himself in this mess? What had he been thinking? Innocent bet or not it had been sexist and chauvinistic. That was exactly the person he'd been struggling *not* to be. There was a time when he saw women as playthings…as an interesting and pleasurable way to pass the time. And while he'd never been openly or deliberately disrespectful to any member of the opposite sex, his actions spoke for themselves.

If Luc couldn't get a handle on this, Parker would have no choice but to fess up to Clare and take his lumps. Even if that meant losing her.

Ten

As promised Violet picked Clare up on the way to Priceless.

It was currently housed in a giant renovated red barn in the Courtyard, the growing artist's community on the outskirts of town. Clare used to be a regular shopper in the antiques store when it was located downtown, but it had been devastated by the tornado. Since Raina had changed locations, Clare never seemed to get out that way often enough. Seeing all of the amazing stock up front in the shop as Raina led them back to the workshop was motivating Clare to come back very soon.

Violet had been quiet for most of the drive there, which was very unusual for her. She was one of the spunkiest women Clare knew. And weirdly enough, Clare, who was usually the quiet type, couldn't seem to stop talking. She felt all bubbly and excited inside, while at the same time questioning her own sanity.

Exclusive, my ass. How could the hospital playboy make such an outrageous claim? She was betting that he'd never even been in a committed relationship. Now he wanted one with *her*? They didn't even...*match*. He should be with someone like Grace. Someone as beautiful as he was.

Once they were inside the building under the bright studio lights, Clare realized that Violet didn't look so good. Her skin looked especially pale against her thick auburn hair, and Clare could swear she was a little thinner than the last time she saw her.

When the class was under way, she leaned close to Violet. "Are you feeling okay? You look a little green."

The minute the words were out she realized that Parker had said nearly the exact same thing to her earlier today. Oh, great, he was beginning to rub off on her.

"I don't know what's wrong," Violet said, sipping gingerly on the water bottle she'd brought to class. "I'll be fine for a while, then get this weird overwhelming nausea. It must be some sort of virus."

It didn't sound like a virus to Clare. "When do you seem to feel sick the most?"

"I wake up feeling pretty lousy every day, and though I'm starving all the time, if I eat I can barely hold it down. I've been really tired, too."

Clare made her voice even lower and asked, "Is there any possibility that you're pregnant?"

Violet sucked in a breath and a myriad of emotions flashed across her face. Shock, fear, confusion. Then she shook her head and said, "No, that can't be it. I'm not even seeing anyone."

"Are you sure, because early prenatal care—"

"That's not it," she insisted. "It's just a virus or a parasite or something. I'll be fine."

Clare let it go, but a few minutes later, as she snapped a piece of glass in the wrong place, Violet nudged her with her elbow and whispered, "Oh, my God! Is that a hickey?"

Clare glanced at the people sitting around them. "Where?"

"On your neck, genius."

Clare gasped and slapped a hand across the side of her neck, felt herself starting to flush. "No, of course not."

Violet wasn't buying it. "You haven't stopped smiling since I picked you up and you practically talked my head off on the way here. No wonder you've been in such a good mood."

She was going to deny it. Say that it was… Well, that was the problem. She didn't know what to say. Besides, the inferno burning in her cheeks was a dead giveaway.

Violet leaned in close and whispered, "Did you do what I think you did? And if so, with whom?"

Clare opened her mouth but nothing came out.

"Was it Dr. Reese?"

Still speechless, Clare just looked at her, and Violet's eyes went wide. "Oh, my God, it *was* him!"

"Shhhh," Clare scolded, as people turned to look at them. "Keep your voice down."

"I knew it," Violet whispered. "I knew you had a thing for him. And who can blame you?"

"You can't tell anyone," Clare said, tugging the band from her hair so it would tumble down and cover the evidence. "And I mean *no one*."

"Why? You guys make an adorable couple."

No, he made her look good. He and Grace? *They* made an adorable couple.

"I'm not even sure if I'm going to see him again," she told Violet. "If people knew it would just be awkward. You have to promise me you won't say anything to anyone."

"Of course I promise," Violet said, laying a reassuring hand on her arm. "But you can't keep it a secret forever."

If she tried hard enough she could. The alternative was unacceptable. If her staff were to learn how flighty and irresponsible she'd been behaving, they would lose all respect for her.

Parker still on her mind, Clare could hardly concentrate on the class. And no matter how hard she tried she couldn't get the damned glass pieces cut without mangling them horribly.

First stained-glass class. Major fail.

She looked up and saw Raina's little boy Justin, dressed in a cowboy get-up, clomping around the perimeter of the room as if he was riding a horse.

Their eyes met and Clare waved. Justin changed direction and trotted over to her table.

"Hey there, partner," Clare teased, then realized almost immediately that she sounded just like Parker and his silly nicknames. He really was starting rub off on her.

But Justin giggled and stopped at her table, all smiles. "Hi, Clare."

"I like the threads," she told him, tugging on his fringed faux-suede vest.

"Santa brought it," he said, very matter-of-factly. *"And* he brought me a *daddy.*"

Clare gasped. *"No way!"* Everyone knew that Raina and Nolan Dane were engaged, but Clare played along, telling Justin, "You must have been super good all year."

"Super, *super* good," he said proudly.

"Hey, mister," Raina said to her son, stopping at the table to check Clare and Violet's progress. "Do we bother the customers during classes?"

His little bottom lip rolled into a pout and he shook his head.

"Skedaddle."

He sighed and said, *"Okay."*

Raina chucked him on the chin and he trotted off on his invisible steed. Then she looked down at the mess on Clare's table and tried to smile.

"I guess stained glass just isn't my thing," Clare told her.

"It takes practice," Raina said.

Not to mention concentration and a steady hand. Neither of which Clare possessed at the moment. She still couldn't believe Parker had given her a hickey, when he knew how important it was to keep their relationship secret. If people in town got wind that she was seeing someone—*anyone*—she would be under the microscope. Because that's the way it was in Royal. Everyone was all up in each other's private business.

The longer she thought about what he'd done, the angrier she became, and by the time Violet dropped her at home she was so hot under the collar it was a wonder steam wasn't shooting out her ears. She knew she had to settle this or she would be up all night fuming.

Thankfully her aunt was home. She sat in her recliner reading one of her murder mysteries.

"Would it be okay if I use your car?" Clare asked her.

"Sure, hon, help yourself." Her head tipped a little to the left. "Are you okay? You look upset."

Upset didn't begin to say it. "You have no idea."

"Uh-oh. Parker?"

"I'll explain when I get back." She dialed Parker's number on her way to the garage.

"Hello," he answered.

"I need your address."

There was a slight pause. "You do?"

She started the car and initialized the navigation. "Yes, I do."

He recited the address and she punched it in. He was only fifteen minutes away. "Thanks."

"You don't sound happy."

"I'm not."

"So why did you want my address?"

"So I can come over there and kill you."

Parker wasn't sure what was going on, or why Clare would be unhappy, but it didn't take long to find out. She got there in ten minutes flat and started pounding on his front door. He opened it and there she stood on his porch looking *incredibly* unhappy. After they'd hung up he'd wondered if this was some sort of revenge for pretending to be mad at her earlier that day.

Apparently not.

"Whatever you're unhappy about, I'm certain it's not the door's fault."

She glared at him. "You gave me a *hickey*?"

Was that what had gotten her panties in such a twist? He stepped back and gestured her inside. "Come on in. Let's talk."

She charged past him. "Violet saw it, and she made me admit I'm seeing someone. And she knows it's *you*."

"Clare, I didn't give you a hickey."

She made a rude noise. "Well, I didn't give it to *my-self*."

"Let me see," he said.

She took her coat off and dropped it over the back of the couch, baring her neck to him. "See? How do you explain that?"

He examined her neck. "Explain what?"

"What do you mean, what? Don't tell me you don't know what a hickey looks like."

"Clare, there's nothing here."

Her lips pressed into a tight line. "That's not funny."

"I'm not trying to be funny. Is it maybe on the other side?" Frowning, she turned so he could look. "Sorry, nothing there either."

"How can that be? Violet said—" She blinked, then blinked again. "Oh, my gosh, that little sneak."

"I don't get it," he said.

She collapsed onto the couch, dropping her head in her hands. "She suspected that I was seeing someone so she lied about the hickey to make me spill my guts. And I fell for it, hook, line and sinker."

Was that all?

"I'm sorry," she said.

"It's okay." He sat down beside her, took her hand, which she promptly retracted.

"No, it's not. I'm an intelligent person. You'd think that I would have the good sense to at least confirm it in a mirror before I started flinging accusations."

"I could think of a few ways you could make it up to

me," he said, but he didn't get the smile he'd been hoping for. He wasn't sure if she'd even heard him.

"This is ridiculous," she said, and was up on her feet again, pacing the rug. "I'm acting like a crazy person."

He took her hand to hold her still. "Don't you think you might be overreacting a little? I'm assuming you told Violet the truth because you trust her." Or because deep down, she actually wanted the truth to come out. It was too soon to say.

She looked up at him. "Did you mean what you said today? About being exclusive? It wasn't just a line to get me back into bed?"

They were back to that? He should have known that this wouldn't be easy, that she would question his every move. What had made her so afraid to follow her heart?

"Come here," he said, pulling her down into his lap, surprised when she didn't resist. He looked her dead in the eyes, so she would know he was telling the truth, and said, "It was not a line. I meant every word I said."

She looked as though she really wanted to believe him but wasn't quite there yet. Which was a little frustrating, but not a deal breaker. She would get there.

"Have you ever even been in a committed relationship?" she asked him.

He shook his head. "Nope."

"Then how can you promise to be exclusive to me? Do you even know how?" She paused then said, "Don't answer that."

Oooookay.

She looked around his living room, as if actually seeing it for the first time since she got there. "Nice condo. Although I would have imagined you in something a lot bigger. I like the decor, though."

"It's an executive rental—it came this way."

"Oh."

"I'll buy something eventually. I just thought I should settle into the job first, before I tied myself here."

"So you're not sure you're staying?"

Definitely not what he'd said. "I wasn't sure *then*." He picked up her hand and kissed the inside of her wrist. "But I am now."

"If you tell me you're staying because of me, I'll probably have a panic attack. Just sayin'."

He grinned. "No panic attacks tonight."

"I'm sorry."

"Would you *stop* apologizing?" He rearranged her on his lap so she was straddling his thighs. "I have a great idea. Why don't you kiss me."

"You're just trying to shut me up."

He grinned. "Pretty much."

She tried to look offended, but laughed instead. "There is such a thing as *too* honest, you know. But this time, I guess I'll let it slide."

"I think it's time for a tour of the house," he told her. "Specifically my bedroom, though I do have a fairly sturdy desk in my office. Just sayin'. Or there's the trundle bed in the spare room—"

She folded a hand over his mouth, a saucy grin on her glossy lips. "We can do it wherever you want. Now, shut up and kiss me."

Despite all the options Parker had mentioned, they went to the bedroom first, then never left. Every time she told herself that the sex couldn't possibly get better, he pulled out the stops, making her even crazier than he had the time before. It was as if someone had written a handbook on her emotional and sexual needs, and he'd read it from cover to cover. Twice.

Afterward he pulled on a pair of flannel pajama bottoms and headed to the kitchen for a snack. Which wound up being leftover reheated spinach and bacon quiche—coincidentally, her favorite kind—and a huge bowl of grapes. And it was delicious. They sat side by side on his bed, eating the quiche and feeding each other grapes.

"This is so good," she said, and always on the lookout for palatable frozen fare, asked, "What brand is it?"

"It's not," he said.

"Oh. Did you get it from a restaurant?"

He looked at her a little funny. "No."

"Does someone cook for you?"

He shook his head. "Guess again."

"Elves?"

He laughed. "Is it really so hard to believe that a man can cook?"

In her family it was. "The men in my family don't cook."

"How about you?"

"I was banned from the kitchen a long time ago. Forget to turn off the burner under the frying pan and almost burn down the kitchen *one time*, and you're branded for life." Which was fine because she had always hated cooking. And still did. "You really made this?" she asked.

"I really did." He popped a green grape in her mouth. She bit down and the sweet juice exploded onto her tongue. Lately food seemed to taste so much better than before. In fact, everything about her life felt pretty darn good.

If only she could let go and just trust it. Trust him.

"Can you cook anything else?" she asked him.

"Anything you want, as long as I have the ingredients. And a recipe."

"Did you take classes?"

"I dated a chef. We saw each other on and off for about six months, I guess. She would cook for me and I would watch. Then I started experimenting on my own. I realized I was pretty good at it, and I found it incredibly relaxing. And I'm not gonna lie, the chicks dig it."

"Hit me again," she said, nodding to the grapes.

"For someone so trim you sure can put the food away." He fed her another grape, the pad of his thumb grazing her lower lip.

"I've lost almost twenty pounds since December."

He looked genuinely surprised. "Seriously?"

"Seriously."

"That's a lot."

"Did you not notice that I was a bit on the chubby side?"

He shrugged. "You looked good to me. Besides, chubby is okay."

Was this guy for real? "Aside from your weird fascination with me, I was under the impression that you were more attracted to the Barbie-doll type."

"So was I."

What the hell was that supposed to mean? Was he deliberately trying to confuse her?

"So what changed?" she asked him.

"I saw you."

If it was a lie, it was the sweetest lie anyone had ever told her. And the idea that it might be true scared her half to death. "Haul out the boots and shovels," she said. "The BS is getting deep."

He laughed. "Why is it so unbelievable?"

"Because everyone knows the kind of man you are. You're a womanizer and a serial dater. That sort of guy doesn't settle down. He conquers. And when he gets bored he moves on. And even if he does eventually settle, it never lasts."

"Yep, that pretty much sounds like me."

She blinked, taken aback by his honesty. He sure wasn't helping his case. "So I'm right?"

"I didn't say that."

"What *are* you saying?"

"People change. Priorities change. I'm not the man I used to be."

In her experience, people could change, but not that much. "So you're telling me that you're ready to settle down?"

"I don't know. Maybe. There was a time when I never would have considered a wife and kids. Now it doesn't seem so far-fetched."

He would make an excellent husband and father, and she envied the woman who snagged him. And she wished that it could be her. Even though she knew it was impossible.

"As much as you love kids, I'm surprised you don't have any," he told her. "Just haven't found the right man?"

She hadn't even been looking. "My patients are my children," she said. "Besides, I'm only thirty-three. I still have a few good childbearing years ahead of me. Or maybe I'll follow in my aunt Kay's footsteps and never have any. God knows there are enough of us already. Another baby in the family would be like white noise. Especially a child of mine."

Eleven

"Why is that?" Parker asked Clare.

"Forget it," she said with a shake of her head, as if she were clearing away an unpleasant memory. "It's a long story."

Something told him not to push the issue of her family, but eventually they were going to talk about it, and he was going to get to the root of the problem. Even if he had to take drastic measures. The key to her heart was in there somewhere under all the baggage, and he was going to find it.

But for now he would let it slide.

"By the way, I noticed last night that the toilet in your bathroom was running like crazy," he said.

"I know. I have to call a plumber."

"You want me to take a look at it?"

"You know how to fix a toilet?"

"Yup."

"What kind of millionaire are you?"

He laughed. "Not a very good one, I guess."

"You sure don't act like a rich guy."

"Are you forgetting? I drive a luxury import."

"That you put a Santa hat and antlers on for Christmas."

He grinned. "I like Christmas."

"And you are the least pretentious person I know. There's a rumor going around that you give a lot of your money to charity."

"My *dad's* money," he said. "And my reasons are not as philanthropic as you might think. I give his money away to charity because I know that's the last thing he would want me to do with it."

"Not the charitable type?"

"For him it was all about making more money. It was never enough. He died a very wealthy man, but his money never did anyone much good. Not even him."

"And now it does."

"Exactly. I may have to live with the millionaire label, but that doesn't mean I have to like it."

"So, when did you learn to fix a toilet?"

"My father believed I should know everything about running his business, from the ground up. Including building maintenance. So instead of letting me volunteer for Greenpeace during summer break—which is what I really wanted to do—I was forced to follow George the maintenance guy around for three months. I thought it was all a total waste of time. As a doctor I wouldn't need to know how to fix a toilet or unclog a drain."

"Unless your home toilet breaks and the plumber can't make it over for a week."

"Exactly. Looking back, I'm thankful for everything I learned. I really have used a lot of that knowledge in my adult life. Not everything he taught me was a total waste of time. His tyrannical way of running his business taught me the best way not to talk to my staff. He thought that he was better than anyone who had less money than him. I was supposed to take over his business. Instead, I sold it all off before the body was cold."

Her brows rose.

"I know that sounds crass, and probably a little selfish, but the offer was made and I took it. I never wanted his business. From the time I was small I was into nature and conservation. There was a time when I seriously considered becoming a veterinarian."

"No way."

"I loved animals, and it got me into trouble sometimes."

"How so?"

"When I was a kid, maybe thirteen or fourteen, I got wind of a project my dad and his company would be working on. They were trying to buy land and develop on a nature preserve. I went on a campaign to stop them."

"You must have been a really confident kid to take on not only a huge company but also your own father."

"I'm not sure if it was confidence, stupidity or just a glaring lack of common sense, but when he figured out what I was up to he grounded me for a month."

"And you said that your mother wasn't around?"

"It was a pretty strange situation actually. My father

hired my mother as a surrogate. He wanted an heir, a mini me, if you will. Long story short, they fell in love."

"Wow, it sounds like the plot of a romance novel or movie. What could be more romantic?"

"Shortly after my birth she left us both for the limo driver."

Clare cringed. "Okay, so not that romantic," she said. "How sad that must have been for your father, especially with a newborn baby."

"I think he was more angry than sad. For pretty much my entire childhood he drilled into me that women were all liars and cheaters and were not to be trusted. He considered them playthings."

"And you believed him?"

"You hear something enough times, you can't help but believe it. He more or less had me brainwashed."

One bad experience and Parker's father felt the need to judge all women? "What a horrible thing to do to you," she said.

"I had money to burn, a career I loved and women champing at the bit, willing to do pretty much anything to land me. And I let them, knowing damn well I would never settle down. In my eyes, life should have been perfect. In reality I felt empty, and disgusted with myself. At that point I knew things had to change. I can't really blame my mother for leaving," Parker said. "If you knew my father you would understand why. To put it in simple terms, he was a bully. It was his way or the highway."

"So you've never even met her?"

He shook his head. "I haven't even seen a picture. I thought I might find some when he died, but he probably burned them."

"If she thought your father was that terrible, why did she leave you there with him?"

"I've asked myself that same thing a million times."

"I just… I don't understand. I'll *never* understand how a woman could leave her own child."

"I'll probably never know why she did it, but I'd like to think she left out of her love for me. That I was somehow better off without her. I guess I'll never know for sure."

"You've never tried to find her? It probably wouldn't be that difficult."

"I'm not difficult to find either."

There was so much buried pain and bitterness in those words it hurt her heart.

"Why don't we talk about something else?" he said, stretching out across the bed and pulling her down with him. "Or better yet, let's not talk at all."

Tempting, but there was something she had to say to him, something he deserved to hear, hard as it would be. She untangled herself from his arms and sat up. "No, we do need to talk."

He sat up, too. "What?"

"I need to explain to you why I'm the way I am. You know, my need to be in control of myself at all times. Especially in bed."

"Clare, you don't have to explain."

"No, I do. I want you to understand." She took his hand between her two and squeezed it. "I trust you."

The smile he flashed her made her feel all warm inside. She was starting to believe that he genuinely cared about her. Which was awful, of course, and wonderful. And she didn't have a clue what to do about it.

One step at a time, Clare.

"This happened a long time ago, at my first job out of nursing school. Before I started working at the hospital I worked very briefly at an OB-GYN practice. It was my first real job besides working on my parents' farm and I was incredibly naive. One of the doctors sort of took me under his wing. Then into his bed."

Parker looked pained, but stayed quiet.

"He was older, and way more sophisticated. I felt so honored that he picked me. For a month he was my entire world. We had to keep it a secret, of course. For my sake, he said. So it wouldn't look like favoritism. I thought we were falling in love, then his pregnant wife showed up at the office."

Parker mumbled a curse. "I take it you didn't know he was married?"

She shook her head. "He never talked about her, or even had a picture in his office. I didn't have a clue. Needless to say I ended it the second she was gone. I never would have gone near him if I knew. He came on strong and was so persistent."

"And I did the same damn thing, didn't I?" His laugh was a wry one. "All the time I thought I was being charming, you thought I was a total creep."

She cracked a smile. "Well, not a *total* creep."

"I'm really sorry, Clare."

"There's no way you could have known. Besides, I'm not the person now that I was back then. I'd been so sheltered up to that point. My family is really big and very traditional. My parents wouldn't even talk about letting me date until I was seventeen, and by then I was cramming to get on the honor list so I could get a scholarship and get the hell out of there. Nursing school was brutal, so I spent most of my time studying. I didn't have much experience with boys, and I had virtually no experience with men. It never even occurred to me that a married man would initiate an intimate relationship. Where I was from men didn't do that sort of thing. Or if they did, no one talked about it."

"So what happened? Did the pregnant wife find out?"

"She found an old text that he'd saved. A very personal and explicit text."

"You were sexting."

She nodded. "She was not happy about it. It was a huge blowout. He said that *I* seduced *him*. Needless to say I lost my job. And my dignity. No one believed me when I said I didn't know he was married."

"It wasn't your fault."

"Most people didn't see it that way, my family included. I was devastated and I needed someone to talk to. My aunt was away on business and I couldn't get ahold of her. I called my sister Sue instead. Growing up, she was the one I was closest to. I made her swear that she would take it to the grave. Two minutes after we hung up my mother called in hysterics. She said that I should have known better and I should come right back to the ranch where I belonged. I was a simple country girl and people would always try to take advantage of me. And it was high time I realized that I would never make it on my own, and I needed my family. She wouldn't even let me try to explain. She ended the conversation by saying how disappointed she was in me."

"That's a tough one," he said.

"It gets worse. My dad called me later that day to say that the family had had a meeting and everyone agreed that I had to come home."

His eyes went wide. "Your mom told the whole family?"

Clare nodded. "Of course I told my dad no, I wouldn't be coming home. I was too ashamed and mortified to show my face. No one even bothered to ask if I was okay. Then my siblings started calling me, trying to shame me into coming back home, saying how much everyone missed me. It's horrible when everyone you love and care about turns their back on you. I was devastated."

"You had every right to be. They betrayed your trust."

"They would tell you that I betrayed theirs."

"They're dead wrong. And shame on your brothers and sisters for not being there for you."

"Aunt Kay was the only one who believed me. Who cared. She invited me to come stay with her until I was back on my feet. I spent most of the first month in bed. But Kay was friends with the hospital administrator at Royal Memorial and she got me an interview. I didn't want to go, but she insisted. It was probably the best thing she could have done for me. With work to focus on I was able to put what happened behind me. Originally I had planned to get my own place, but we realized that it didn't make sense. Kay only uses the house as a home base when she isn't traveling, which isn't very often. She likes having someone here to keep an eye on things. It ended up being a perfect situation for both of us."

He shook his head, looking baffled. "I don't even know what to say."

"You don't have to say anything. Besides, I'm not finished."

"It gets worse?"

"I've only ever told Aunt Kay, because I knew she of all people would understand. It's very difficult to talk about the things that he did to me. But I have to tell you."

He looked pained. "You don't have to tell me."

She took a deep breath and blew it out, trembling from head to toe. "No, I want to. I *need* to."

He put his hand on her shoulder. "Only if you're ready."

"He was my first. And I know that sounds crazy considering my age, but I wanted to save myself for someone special. It's how I was raised. I honestly thought he was the one. That's why I let him do what he wanted to do."

"Which was?"

She swallowed hard. *You can do this.* "He liked it… rough."

Parker winced. "But not your first time. Right?"

Though she wanted to bow her head in shame, she held it high instead. "He didn't force me, and I could have said no, but I was so head over heels for him, I would have done anything he asked. Even though it terrified me. He got off on my fear."

Looking confused, Parker asked, "So, am I to understand that every time you had sex with him, you were scared? Or am I way off base?"

She took a deep breath and blew it out. "*Every* time. Some more than others. It depended on his mood. Near the end of the relationship he had begun to get very aggressive. And again, I could have walked away. I chose to stay."

"This doctor have a name?" Parker asked, jaw

clenched. "In honor of your dignity and self-respect, I'd like to kick his teeth in."

"He wouldn't be worth the effort. He was a sleazebag. He'll probably always be one. It was just poor judgment on my part."

"Listen to me," Parker said, gently cradling her face in his hands. "It's not your fault."

She folded her hands over his. "I know that now, but it still stings after all this time. I'm still humiliated. Without fail, every time I'm visiting the farm someone makes a snide remark about the relationship. They'll never let me live it down."

"You're giving them way too much power," he said.

"Probably. And I hope that someday I can let it go. I'm just not ready yet."

"What can I do?" he said.

"Just be patient with me. "

"I can do that," he said with a smile. After everything she'd just revealed, all the pain she had spilled out, she could smile, too. It felt good to talk about it. To let off some of the pressure.

"After it was over, it took years before I wanted to have sex again," she told him, "and a long time after that before I could let myself enjoy it. I've come a long way since then, but I'm still not one hundred percent there. Maybe I'll never be."

"No, you will be."

Twelve

Parker sounded so sure, Clare wanted to believe him. If anyone could pull her back from the dark recesses of her mind, it would probably be him. For whatever reason, he seemed to "get" her. And she was nowhere close to ready to admit that to him.

"I'm thirsty. You want something to drink?" she asked him. She needed a minute to regroup, and could see the understanding in his eyes.

"I could go for a beer," he said.

"I'll be right back." She hopped up from the bed and headed downstairs to the kitchen. It was a very nice condo, but as she got a better look around, it seemed a little barren and impersonal. Definitely temporary. She wondered what sort of place he would be looking for...

Nope, she didn't even want to know, because what if it was exactly the same thing she wanted? That would just be awkward.

The refrigerator was well stocked with a variety of foods. Lots of fruits and vegetables and cheeses. She grabbed two beers off the door and headed back up. After this beer she had to go home. She'd never done well sleeping in strange places. She was a creature of habit. If she stayed here, in an unfamiliar bed, she would probably toss and turn all night long.

Yeah, Clare, just keep telling yourself that.

The truth was that she was scared, plain and simple.

And wasn't she being a little presumptuous? He hadn't even asked if she wanted to stay. It was possible that he didn't even want her to.

As if. He would probably love it. It would make him very happy.

A cold chill raised the hair on her arms. Wasn't that exactly what had gotten her into trouble before?

Don't you want me to be happy? her ex would ask when something he did made her uncomfortable. *You know I would never do anything to hurt you.*

It was a lie. He wasn't happy *unless* he was hurting her.

But this was different. Parker went out of his way to make *her* happy. She thought that telling him the truth about her past would make her feel vulnerable and weak, but in reality she felt empowered. And it was a *good* feeling. She felt good when she was with him. So why was she still fighting this? Everything about their relationship felt right. He seemed like someone she could really learn to trust. She was already partway there. Didn't she owe it to herself to at least *try*?

When Clare stepped back into the bedroom Parker was sound asleep and snoring softly. And here she thought he'd worn her out, when it looked as if it was the other way around. She considered waking him, but he looked so adorable when he slept.

She set the beers down on the night table and slid into bed beside him. He was facing her, so she could lie there and watch his beautiful face all night if she wanted to.

She thought about his mother abandoning him and her heart broke. It was so sad she wanted to cry. No wonder he didn't let himself get close to women. The most important woman in his life had walked away without looking back. And his horrible father had only exacerbated the problem by filling his head with lies.

It made her wish things could be different for him, that she could be the one to make him see that mother or no mother, he was an amazing human being. Truly one of the good ones.

She must have dozed off, because when she opened her eyes again the lights were out and she was in the exact same position on the bed. Parker was gone.

She rubbed her eyes and rolled over to grab her phone, which was almost dead. Six o'clock.

She'd done it. She'd spent the night and the world hadn't come to an end. And she hadn't slept lousy either.

She leaned over and switched on the lamp, temporarily blinding herself. As her pupils adjusted, Parker walked into the room wearing his flannel pajama bottoms, holding two steaming cups of coffee.

"Good morning, sleepyhead," he said, his usual chipper, cheerful self. He may have been the most positive, upbeat person she had ever known.

She pushed herself up into a sitting position. "Good morning."

He handed her one of the cups, sat on the edge of the mattress beside her and kissed her forehead. There

was something so sweet about it, so deeply affection-
ate. "Sleep well?"

Amazingly well. "I must have been in a coma," she
said. "I didn't move once. I don't even think I dreamed."

"I did," he said, wiggling his brows, "but we'll save
that for later."

Hmm, something to look forward to.

"Did you mean to stay, or did you fall asleep before
you could leave?"

"A little of both."

"Are you sorry that you stayed?"

She smiled and shook her head. "But I can't stay
long. I have to go home and get ready for work. And
return my aunt's car."

"How are you planning to get to the hospital?"

"Kay can drive me."

"Or you can shower here. I'll follow you home, wait
while you change, then take you to work."

And risk being seen together? That would most certainly get the rumor mill spinning.

She was getting sick of living afraid, always worried
about what people would think of her. Maybe it was
time she got her priorities straight. Maybe it should be
about what she wanted for a change.

"Okay."

He looked a little taken aback, but he smiled. "Really?"

"Really. It's on your way. Why not."

"If you want I can drop you around the block, so no
one sees us together."

She did and she didn't. And what did that say about
her? She was acting as though he was some dark, dirty
secret when really, their relationship was far from con-

troversial. They were two consenting adults and what they did outside the hospital was no one else's business. As long as they didn't let the physical relationship bleed into their work relationship. She already lost one job that way.

"I have to stop worrying what other people think. Like you said, I give people too much power."

"True story," he said with a smile. "So, you want me to shower first? Or we could even shower together."

"One step at a time," she said. Though most people wouldn't consider something as innocuous as sharing a shower a "step," they probably hadn't been brutally shoved face-first into a shower stall and pinned against the cold, hard tile.

Parker accepted her decline with a smile, because that's who Parker was. "I'll go first."

Her eyes glued to his tight behind as he walked to the closet to pick out clothes, she felt around the bedside table for her phone so she could check the weather. The low battery warning flashed, then the screen went black.

Damn.

"Do you know what the temperature is supposed to be today?" she asked as Parker laid his clothes out on the bed. "My phone just died."

"Look it up on my phone," he said. He leaned over to grab it off the bedside table and held it out to her.

She hesitated.

"I promise it won't bite."

She took it. "You really don't mind me looking at your phone?"

"Why would I? The code is 0613, my birthday."

"You were born on the thirteenth of June?"

"And yes, it was a Friday. I looked it up."

Well, that explained a lot.

"To me a phone is a very personal thing," she said. "I would never give out my code. Practically my whole life is on this phone."

"Me, too. If you did feel the need to snoop, you would probably find something interesting. You might even see something you wished you hadn't. Or you could just not snoop. Your choice."

She looked at the phone, then back at him. "You have my word, I definitely won't snoop."

He laughed. "I'll be out in ten minutes."

The following week Clare got a surprise call from her sister Jen. "I'm going to be in the area this afternoon picking up a mare, and I want to come see you," she told Clare.

Clare cringed, thankful Jen couldn't see her through the phone. Every visit with a family member seemed to end in disaster, and things had been going so well lately, she hated to push her luck. The past week and a half had been weird but wonderful. Clare *felt* wonderful. All her family ever did was bring her down. "I'm working today," Clare told her sister.

"I know, but you can take a quick break, right?"

"I have patients to care for. I can't just leave them." It was a lie. She could have asked someone to cover for her.

"But we haven't seen you in months. I miss you."

Don't have anyone else to embarrass and shame? she wanted to ask. "I'm sorry. Maybe if you would have given me a little advance notice."

"I only found out this morning that I had to go."

"Oh."

"You can't spare five minutes to see your own sister?"

Clare could feel herself caving. It was the guilt that always got her. "Tell you what. Call me when you get to Kay's house and I'll let you know if I can get away."

"I'll call you in about an hour."

And Clare wouldn't answer the phone. Problem solved.

She stuck her phone in her pocket. Maybe she was being selfish, but she wanted to be happy just a little while longer before she opened that wound again. She was learning that it was okay to be selfish every once in a while.

She got a text and looked at her phone again. It was from Parker, asking to see her in his office. They were extremely careful to keep their relationship platonic and professional at the hospital, but every so often they would meet in his office to steal a kiss or two. Sometimes more. Once when they were both working late he summoned her to his office and she found him sitting behind his desk wearing nothing but his lab coat and stethoscope.

His door was closed when she got there, so she knocked.

"Come in."

He was fully dressed—darn it—and sitting at his desk, his laptop in front of him. "Come in and close the door."

"What's up?"

"I need your opinion on something." He turned the laptop around so she could see the screen. "I've been on this site. It's called Family Finder. They help people connect with their biological family."

"Are you thinking of contacting your mom?"

He took a breath and blew it out, brow furrowed. "Since we talked about her it's been on my mind. I was thinking about Maddie and Maggie. They'll never get the opportunity to meet their real mom. But I can meet mine, and I can't deny that I'm curious."

"I think it would be a great idea."

"All I need to do is fill out a form with the information I have, which thankfully is extensive. If she's already posted on the site looking for me, I'll be notified."

"So, if she's already on the site, you'll know it right away."

He nodded. "I'm not sure how I feel about that. On the one hand I feel as if it's time to deal with this, and on the other I can't help but worry that I'll be disappointed. The forms are all filled out and ready to go. I'm just having a little trouble hitting Submit."

She loved that he wasn't too macho to let her see his vulnerabilities. He was very honest about his feelings. Sometimes too honest, so much so that it made her squirm a little. He knew the *L* word was currently off the table, but that didn't stop him from creatively hinting around. But he did it with so much charm it was difficult to be annoyed.

"I don't know what to say."

He snapped his laptop shut. "I have to think about this."

"There's no rush."

He pushed himself up from his chair. "Sorry to drag you in here for nothing."

She rose up on her toes and kissed him. "No problem."

They both walked out to the nurses' station. She sat

down, ready to get back to work, and Parker asked, "Are you expecting company?"

How could he possibly know that? "Did you bug my phone or something?"

"No, but there's a woman who just stepped off the elevator and she looks like she could be your twin."

Oh, crap! Clare shot up in her chair, and sure as anything there stood her sister by the elevator. How had she gotten there so fast?

Jen saw Clare and waved.

Parker was looking at her, waiting for an explanation.

"It's my sister Jen," she said. "I asked her not to come, but that's my family. Constantly ignoring what I say."

"Hey, sweetie," Jen said, and Clare walked around the station to hug her.

"An hour away?"

"Okay, I lied. I was already in Royal when I called you. And I didn't come for a horse. I came to see you."

Thirteen

"Dr. Reese," Clare said, hoping he would play along. "This is my sister Jen."

"Pleasure," Parker said, shaking her hand.

"Dr. Reese is my boss," she told her sister, hoping she would be less likely to say something embarrassing or inappropriate. Of all her siblings, Jen, six years her senior, was the most vocal, and the most blunt.

"You must be proud of your sister," he said, "being chief nurse of one of the highest-rated children's wards in the state."

"We all are," Jen said, shooting Clare a look.

Somehow Clare found that very hard to believe. They had never supported her in her career.

"We would be lost without her." Parker laid a hand on Clare's shoulder, giving it a reassuring squeeze. Then he flashed one of those charming smiles. "If you'll excuse me, ladies, I have a patient to check on."

"That man is like a cool glass of lemonade on a hot day," Jen said.

My *cool glass of lemonade, thank-you-very-much.* "Last I checked you were a married woman."

Jen grinned. "It doesn't hurt to look, honey. As long as I bring my appetite home."

Clare grimaced. "Ew."

Her sister laughed. "Can we go somewhere private and talk?"

Alarm made her heart skip a beat. Was Jen here because something bad had happened? "Sure, we can use the break room."

"Sounds good."

She showed her sister down the hall to the break room, which thankfully was empty, and said, "Have a seat."

Jen made herself comfortable in a chair. "So, are you and the doctor…?"

Oh, boy, here we go. "What makes you think that?"

"He was a little defensive, and you didn't seem to like me lookin' at him. And he squeezed your shoulder. That was a little personal."

"You noticed all that?"

"Honey, I have four boys. I don't miss a thing."

Clare raised her chin a notch, ready to take her lumps. "As a matter of fact, we're dating."

Jen nodded approvingly. "He's cute."

Clare waited for more. For a rich-doctor crack. Or some other disparaging remark.

"Is it serious?" Jen asked.

"We've only been dating for two weeks."

"Beau proposed to me on our second date. Fifteen

years later and we're still going strong. I think if you know, you just know. You know?"

Clare laughed, remembering why, of all her siblings, Jen was by far the most honest and outgoing. "You're weird."

She smiled. "That's what my boys tell me."

Times like now, Clare missed being a part of her family, wished she wasn't such an outsider. "So, you said you needed to talk to me. About what?"

"The seven of us had a family meeting."

"Seven?"

"Just the siblings."

"About what?"

"You mostly, and the fact that you never come around. And when you do you're so defensive."

Confused, she asked, "What about Mom and Dad? Were they at this meeting?"

"They weren't included."

As far as Clare knew, the family never made a group decision without first getting their parents' blessing. "You had a family meeting without Mom and Dad?"

"It's been known to happen. It wouldn't surprise you if you came around, or called."

"I'm busy."

"You want to talk about busy, try being the mom of four rambunctious boys, and I still make it to dinner at Mom and Dad's once a month. If we at least knew why you're so distant…"

"*Why?* Are you kidding me?"

"I know that something happened between you and Mom and Dad. I know what a pain they can be, but you have a very large family who misses you."

A kernel of anger popped in Clare's belly, causing

a chain reaction, until she felt like exploding. She'd always hated confrontation, but right now she was too furious to think straight. To be afraid. The new Clare stood up for herself, and didn't take any crap from anyone, damn it. "You miss me? Well, where the hell were you all when I needed you? When my entire world fell apart. You didn't miss me so much then."

"Clare—"

"I'm not stupid, you know. I know what you all think of me. What Mom and Dad think of me. You've made it obvious that I'm a huge disappointment."

"Clare—"

"People make mistakes, you know, but they shouldn't have to pay for it forever! It wasn't even my fault!" she shrieked, and for the first time actually believed it. "I was young and stupid and he took advantage of me. He lied to me. End of story."

"Clare, shut up!" Jen shouted.

Startled, Clare closed her mouth.

"What the *hell* are you talking about?"

She was going to play dumb? Seriously? "I know Mom and Dad told everyone. They said there was a family meeting. She said that everyone agreed I should come home. I was a simple country girl who could never make it on her own."

"We all knew something was wrong," Jen said. "But there was no family meeting. If Mom and Dad said there was, they were lying. They told everyone that you were in trouble, but they refused to say how or why. They just wanted us all to call and try to get you to come home. We were all worried sick about you. We still are. We want you back in the family."

"If Sue had kept her mouth shut, no one would have

known anything. She promised me she would take it to her grave, then she turned around and told Mom."

Jen frowned. "No, she didn't."

"*Yes*, she did."

"No, Clare, she did not. She heard Mom on the phone with you and assumed you had called her."

"If she didn't tell her, how did Mom find out?"

"If I had to guess, I would say she was listening on the extension. She used to do it all the time."

Taken aback, Clare blinked and said, "Since when?"

"Since my entire childhood. That's how she kept tabs on all of us."

Clare had no idea. But she hadn't spent much time on the phone as a kid either. And if she did it was to discuss homework, or equally innocuous things. She hadn't had much of a social life.

"She did it to everyone?"

"Yup. She was always listening to our calls and going through our stuff. There was no privacy in that house."

And Clare had thought it was just she who had no privacy. Had it not occurred to her that her brothers and sisters felt the same way?

"Sue seriously didn't tell them?"

"No, Clare. She wouldn't tell *anyone*, and we badgered her, believe me. We wanted to know what was wrong. Anytime we tried to bring it up, you went on the defensive. Then you stopped coming around. We were all very hurt."

Clare could barely wrap her head around it. All these years she had stayed away, thinking everyone was judging her, and they didn't even know what had happened? "She really didn't tell anyone?"

"No, hon," Jen said patiently. "She didn't."

Tears stung Clare's eyes. Was it possible that what she had conceived as wisecracks and ribbing from her family had in reality only been their way of trying to figure out what was wrong? Were they just trying to *talk* to her?

How could her mom go all this time letting her believe Sue had ratted her out? Was it possible she didn't even know that Clare blamed Sue?

Clare shook her head, still having trouble grasping this. How could she have been so wrong about her family? She could only imagine all the things that she had missed out on over the years. How much fuller and richer her life would be.

She felt sick inside. She'd lost out on so much, just because she had been afraid to speak her mind.

"I thought everyone abandoned me," she told Jen. "That no one cared."

"Oh, honey." Jen rose from the chair, wrapped her arms around Clare and hugged her hard, and Clare hugged her back just as firmly. "Everyone cared. We always have. You know what this is?"

Clare sniffled and shook her head.

"This is one big cluster eff," she said, patting Clare's back. She was such a *mom*.

Clare smiled in spite of herself. "Cluster eff?"

Jen held her at arm's length and said, "I'm the mother of four boys. I have to set a good example."

"I miss the boys," Clare said. "I've missed out on so much…"

"So things will be different now."

"It might take some time to forgive Mom and Dad for lying to me." It had begun a chain reaction that left

Clare feeling isolated and alone. Like an outcast. How did you forgive someone for that?

"For what it's worth, I truly believe that they thought they were doing the right thing. They didn't want to hurt anyone. They just didn't think about the consequences of their actions."

"That doesn't make it okay."

"No, but you should talk to them about it and tell them how you feel. They won't be around forever."

Jen was right of course. Clare did need to talk to them. And her siblings needed to know what really happened. She didn't even know why she wanted to tell them. She just felt as if she needed to get it off her chest. Or maybe, after all this time, she just needed their acceptance.

"I want to tell you what happened," Clare said.

"Are you sure?"

"Very sure."

"I swear I won't tell a soul."

"No, this time I actually want you to."

Parker stood at the nurses station pretending to work on a chart, keeping his eye on the door of the break room. Clare and her sister had been in there for a while now and he was beginning to worry. Clare hadn't looked happy to see her. Things had been going so well, he hated to see something like this set them back.

"I'm sure she's fine," Rebecca said from behind the desk.

Parker turned to her. "Who?"

"Clare. You've been on edge since she went in there."

He didn't realize that he was being that obvious, or that careless. "It's complicated."

"You seem to be spending a lot more time together lately."

That was none of her business and he didn't justify it with a response.

"I'm sorry I got snippy with you," she said. "I was jealous, I guess. It's been pretty obvious that you have a thing for Clare."

"Since when?"

"Pretty much since you started at the hospital."

Had it really been that noticeable?

"I knew you and I didn't have a chance. And the truth is, you're a little old for me."

"And feeling older every day," he said, but that was okay. He felt more settled, and more content than he ever had in his life. There was no way that was a bad thing.

Convincing Clare would be another matter altogether. She was so terrified to trust this. To trust *herself.* Who knew how long it would be before she felt okay with taking their relationship to the next level. Maybe never. She was so worried about what other people would think, how they would judge her. When would she learn that it didn't matter what anyone else thought? He was in love with her. There was no other explanation for this inexorable need to protect her. He wanted to spend the rest of his life with her. He knew somewhere deep down in his soul she was the one for him. His perfect match. And he couldn't even tell her. He was paying the price for all the other people who had hurt and betrayed her.

It was frustrating as hell. And it wasn't fair. Not to her and not to him.

When Clare introduced him to her sister, his first

reaction had been to go on the defensive, and he was afraid he'd been a little rude. He was hoping to apologize to the both of them.

The break room door finally opened and Clare and her sister walked out. He could tell from where he stood that they had both been crying. But he couldn't tell if that was a good or bad thing.

Clare and her sister embraced, holding each other tight. After a moment they parted and started to walk toward him and he met them halfway. He must have looked confused, or concerned, because Clare told him immediately, "Everything is okay."

"So you'll definitely be there for dinner?" Jen asked her.

Clare smiled and nodded. "I promise."

"And you'll bring this guy along?" she asked, gesturing to Parker.

"It's a distinct possibility. If he wants to go."

"Of course he wants to go," Jen said, giving his arm a playful nudge with her elbow. "Don't you."

"Go where?" he asked.

"To meet Clare's family. There are so many of us, it can be a bit intimidating."

She wanted him to meet her family? Since when? Was it something she'd said just to placate her sister? Knowing the way they treated Clare, he wasn't sure if he wanted to meet them. It would be difficult to keep his feelings hidden.

She and her sister said goodbye, then she turned to him and smiled. "You are not going to believe what just happened to me."

Fourteen

The Texas Cattleman's Club meeting wasn't due to start for another hour, but Clare was working late and Parker was bored so he showed up early. He sat at the bar at the clubhouse, sipping his usual drink, the Family Finder app open on his phone, his profile taunting him. As it had for nearly two weeks now. It would take one tap on the screen to submit his request, but he still couldn't seem to make himself do it. Which wasn't at all like him. When he wanted something, he went after it. This time something was stopping him. The question was what.

The idea of family, and possibly one of his own, weighed heavily on his mind since the impromptu family gathering he and Clare had attended at her parents' farm this past weekend. At first she'd hemmed and hawed about bringing him, which he had tried not to take personally. He'd learned that in that sort of situation it was best to step back and let her work it out alone. If she asked for input he gave it, but trying to convince her to do something usually had her digging her heels in to do the exact opposite. But her siblings, whom she'd had a very open and honest dialogue with lately, nagged and cajoled her for a week until she finally agreed to bring him.

On the morning of the party she'd called him with the idea to bring overnight bags in case they were too tired, or more likely too hammered, to drive the hour back to Royal.

His second surprise, when they'd arrived at her parents' farm, was the sheer size of her family. He'd met countless nieces and nephews, aunts and uncles, and more cousins than should be allowed in one family. He'd tried to keep up with all the new names and faces, but somewhere around his fourth beer he'd given up. From that point on he'd addressed everyone as *sir* or *ma'am*. Even the children, who'd seemed to get a big kick out of that.

The food had been incredible, and there'd been so much of it. Roasted pig and smoked ribs and of course authentic Texas chili. Clare had told him that it was customary to bring either a side dish or dessert to share, which explained the rows and rows of platters and casserole dishes on the serving tables. There was literally enough food for a small army.

Parker had eaten himself into a food coma, and drank way more than he should have. From around dusk on, his memory had been a little spotty. He remembered a huge bonfire out in the field, and Clare's brothers joking around that they were going to throw Parker into it.

He remembered live music, and square dancing badly. Really, *really* badly. But what he remembered most was the constant smile on Clare's face, and her laugh, and how happy she'd seemed. And how sexy she'd looked when she jumped him later that night in the tent she'd borrowed from her parents. And she hadn't been exaggerating when she said her family was traditional. The fact that she and Parker were sharing a tent out of wedlock had raised a few eyebrows from the older set.

Despite his vow to never ride any breed of four-legged animal again, Clare had talked him into going horseback riding the next morning and given him a proper tour of the land. They'd stayed for a lunch of leftovers, and her mom had sent bags and bags of food home with them.

Though much of the party was a blur, he distinctly recalled thinking about his biological mother. And though meeting Clare's entire gargantuan family all at once had had him feeling a little intimidated at first, it made him realize what he had missed out on all these years. Was it possible that he had siblings somewhere, too? Would they be interested in meeting him? Did they have gatherings like Clare's family?

To find out, he would have to hit Submit. Just one tap of the mouse.

Cursing under his breath, he shut the app again.

Maybe he just wasn't ready. With everything else in his life going so well, would he only be tempting fate?

It still astounded him a little that after a lifetime of having no desire to settle down, much less have a family, he could be so sure in less than a month's time that Clare was the *one*. She was smart and sexy and fun. She challenged him emotionally and intellectually. And in the bedroom, as well. She had a sharp wit and snarky sense of humor.

She was still hesitant about their relationship going public, but they had been spending almost all of their free time together, and he knew that people were beginning to notice.

Parker heard his name called and turned to see Luc gesturing him over to a table in the back of the bar. Parker had been so lost in thought he hadn't even seen him come in. He stuck his phone in his pocket and walked over. Though Parker was far from knowing all the members of the club, he recognized the men sitting at the table with Luc. Case Baxter, who was the recently elected president of the club, and beside him Nathan Battle, the sheriff of Royal.

The men shook hands and Parker sat down, asking Luc, "How was Mexico?"

He and his wife, Julie, had just returned from a long-overdue vacation. Which had Parker thinking that maybe he and Clare should take a few days away, just the two of them.

"Hot," Luc said. "But relaxing. We got back this afternoon."

"Do anything fun?"

"We slept a lot. And caught up on our reading. Our last day there we chartered a boat."

"Sounds like the perfect vacation."

"I'd go back tomorrow if I could."

"Parker," Case said, "we were discussing the Samson Oil land grab. We still have no idea why any oil company would buy up land with no oil. Any thoughts?"

Parker shook his head. "I'm afraid I don't know

enough about the town to be much help. But I agree that it's suspicious."

"Listen and learn," Nathan said, spreading a map out across the table that marked the property the company had purchased so far, and all the land it was still trying to obtain. Parker tried to pay attention so he would appear at least slightly informed during the meeting, but his mind kept wandering.

When Case and Nathan left the bar to get ready for the meeting, Luc asked him, "Everything okay? You seem awfully distracted tonight."

"I have a lot on my mind," he said, and told Luc about his desire to meet his biological mother.

"Why now?" Luc asked.

"Let's just say that lately I've been reevaluating my priorities."

"This wouldn't have anything to do with Clare, would it?"

There was really no point in denying it. "Almost exclusively. Who told you?"

"I can tell you who didn't tell me. It's a much shorter list. If you haven't noticed by now, secrets are tough to keep in a town this small and tight-knit."

"I know." And he was okay with that. The question was how Clare would feel about it.

"I had a feeling, when you mentioned the new woman you were seeing, that it was probably Clare," Luc said. "Once you set your mind to something you don't just give up."

"I'm in love with her."

"Wow. That's the first time I've ever heard you say that."

"That's because I've never said it before. Until I met

Clare I didn't think I would ever settle down. Now I want it all. A wife and a child, or even two. I want to be everything to my kids that my father never was for me."

"Have you told her how you feel?"

"Not yet."

"What are you waiting for?"

"The right time. I'll know it when I see it."

"On the subject of marriage and family, Julie and I have a little news of our own to share. We've been throwing around the idea of starting a family for a while now, so she quit taking her birth control. We were assuming it would take at least a couple of months for her system to regulate."

"How long did it actually take?"

He grinned. "Closer to two weeks. We found out just before we left for Mexico."

Parker laughed. "Congratulations. That's great news."

He was happy for Luc, and at the same time he was a little jealous. Maybe it was time he stopped tiptoeing around the issue and told Clare how he felt. It had taken him a long time to get to this place, and he didn't want to waste a minute of it.

When Clare made it to Parker's house after work he wasn't home yet. She parked her new car in the driveway and, using the key he'd given her last week, let herself into his condo. It still felt a little strange being there alone, but he would hopefully be home soon. It had been a hellish day at work. The kind that had her questioning humanity. An unresponsive eight-month-old infant with severe brain swelling had been brought in to emergency. Though they'd done everything they could, the child had died shortly after. The worst part was that it was a textbook case of shaken-baby syndrome. The parents had been arrested, and their two other children taken by protective services. Clare had called Grace only to learn that both kids, ages two and four, had signs of abuse, as well. It was so heartbreaking that she gave herself permission to sit in the stairwell and sob, but even that didn't help much.

Clare shed her coat and dropped her purse on the cluttered coffee table, feeling depressed, her heart breaking for that poor little baby. At least she was at peace. Even if she'd survived she would have been severely mentally disabled. She probably would have spent her life in a group home, since her own parents clearly had no business raising children.

At least little Maddie's story had a happy ending. She was getting stronger every day, and would hopefully get to join her twin sister at home.

What Clare really needed was one of Parker's hugs. Feeling his arms around her somehow always managed to make the bad stuff go away for a while. Besides, she had an awful lot to be happy about these days.

She grabbed herself a beer from the fridge and flopped down on the sofa to wait for Parker.

Her relationship with her family was the best it had ever been, though things with her parents were still a little strained. It would just take her time to forgive them for lying to her. She believed that they had been truly afraid for her, and had had her best interests in mind, even though their actions had seemed to say the opposite. They had hurt her deeply, even if they hadn't meant to, and it would take a while to sort those feelings out. On the bright side, Parker had been extremely well received by her entire family, and though she'd been a bit hesitant to bring him at first, she was glad she had. For all her fears about "rich doctor" cracks, no one had said a disparaging word. And though Parker had looked thoroughly overwhelmed by the number of relatives there when they first arrived, he'd fit right in.

Only after seeing everyone all together like that had she realized how much she missed being part of a family. Before they'd left the next day her siblings had made her promise to regularly attend the monthly family dinners. She'd promised, and this time she meant it. So much had changed.

She had changed.

She'd been insistent that she and Parker continue to keep their relationship a secret, but people were beginning to put two and two together. Though no one had the guts to come right out and ask her about it, it was only a matter of time. Besides, all of her reasons for keeping it quiet seemed a little silly now. She had tried to convince herself that it would put her job in jeopardy, sleeping with the boss. But that was just a lame excuse to not let him close.

She tried putting herself in Parker's place, tried to imagine how she would feel if the tables were turned, if he wanted to keep it a secret. The truth was, it kinda sucked.

Maybe deep down she felt as if she didn't deserve someone like him, that people would see them as mismatched, and her as pathetic. She realized today, with complete certainty, that she didn't give a damn what anyone thought. She was so happy these past few weeks that sometimes she wanted to shout it from the rooftops. So tonight she planned to tell him that she wanted to take things public. She was tired of hiding, tired of watching what she said, and whom she said it in front of.

There was something else she wanted to say to him, something that she had never said to anyone but her family. The *L* word. Up to now, in her mind, love had always meant obligation, and sacrifice, and often heartbreak. It meant giving without getting anything in return.

With Parker it was different. He gave as much as he took. More even. And he must have been a saint to put up with all of her weird hang-ups and personality quirks. But without fail he accepted her for exactly who she was, no question.

Until now the only place she'd ever felt truly in her element was at work. For the first time in forever, with her family and with Parker, she felt as if she truly belonged. As if she fit in.

She heard the garage door open and her heart leaped up into her throat. Despite being with one another nearly every day, the excitement of seeing him walk through the door was a thrill that never went away. She met him at the door, greeting him with a kiss, and as his arms went around her she felt the stress of the day slipping away. She held him as tight as she could.

"If you let go for a second and let me take my coat off I could hug you properly," he teased, and she held him even tighter. "Hey, is everything okay?"

She looked up at him, into his beautiful eyes, and though she meant to tell him about her crummy day, and say how happy she was that he was home, something altogether different came out.

"I love you, Parker."

He blinked. Then blinked again. Then he grinned and said, "I love you, too, Clare."

That wasn't all that hard. And she liked that he didn't make a big deal out of it.

"How was your meeting?" she asked, loosening his tie.

"Good. Luc and Julie are expecting."

"No kidding."

"Yeah, he seems pretty excited. They want me to be the baby's doctor."

"Of course they do. You're the best."

He grinned and kissed her. "Thanks. You're not so bad yourself. How was work?"

"Not so good."

"Let me grab a beer and you can tell me about it."

They snuggled on the sofa, her head resting on his shoulder as she told him about her rotten afternoon. "It was a very stressful day."

"Do I need to pull out the coloring books?" he teased. She did in fact have a few there, as well as a set of colored pencils. But right now she just wanted to be with him.

"Are you staying over tonight?" he asked.

She should probably head home, but she didn't feel like going back out into the cold. "If you don't mind."

He gave her a *yeah right* look. "Do I ever mind when you spend the night?"

"I'm warning you, I'm too tired to do anything but sleep."

He laughed. "Okay."

"I'm serious. I'm exhausted."

"Yet somehow you always manage to find the energy."

After they finished their beers they went up to his bedroom and he switched on the news while they undressed. Then she remembered her purse was still downstairs with her phone in it.

"I left my phone downstairs," she told him. "I'm going to grab it."

He patted the pockets of his pants. "I think I left mine in the kitchen. I'm pretty sure I set it down when I was taking my coat off."

"I'll get yours, too." Her feet ached as she trudged down the stairs. She hooked her purse over her shoulder, then grabbed his phone, which was sitting on the kitchen counter. She was almost to the stairs when his phone buzzed. She glanced at the screen and saw that it was an incoming text message from Luc Wakefield.

The two-word preview on his locked screen said, About Clare...

She stopped at the bottom of the stairs. *About Clare* what? Had Parker told Luc about his relationship with Clare? Even though he *swore* he wouldn't? Or had Luc just heard about them through the hospital grapevine.

She itched to read the rest of the text, then thought about their conversation regarding his phone, and the dangers of snooping. But it probably wasn't a big deal. He wouldn't have given her his code if he had something to hide.

She tapped in the code and the text flashed on the screen.

She read it once, then read it again, then read it a third time.

Well, he'd been right about one thing. She definitely wished she'd never seen it.

Fifteen

Parker was sitting on the edge of the mattress watching CNN when something hit him hard in the back. "Ow! What the…"

He turned to see his phone lying on the blanket behind him, then he looked up to see Clare standing in the bedroom doorway. That had really hurt, not to mention that if she'd missed she might have broken his phone. "Thanks, I think."

At first he thought she was teasing him, and had just underestimated her own strength. Then he saw her face. She was wearing a look like he'd never seen before. As if someone had died. Or worse.

His heart skipped a beat. "What's wrong?"

"You got a text from Dr. Wakefield."

Uh-oh. What the hell had Luc said?

She didn't move from the doorway. "Aren't you going to read it?"

"Um, sure." He punched in his code and the text flashed on the screen.

About Clare... I know we ended the bet, but since you slept with her before that, you technically win. I'll stop by the bank on my way to work. You want that in small bills?

He cursed under his breath. Then cursed again.

"It was a bet?" she asked, her voice trembling. "You bet Luc that you would sleep with me?"

He wanted to deny it, but he couldn't.

The outrage and devastation were written all over her face, making him feel like the giant ass that he was. He tried to think of something to say, anything to make her stop looking at him like that.

"I know it sounds awful," he said. "But if you let me explain—"

"Did you or did you not bet Luc that you would sleep with me?"

Shit.

"I did. But it's not... It isn't..." He didn't even know what to say. He had no excuse, no logical explanation. He wanted to kill Luc, but this was his own fault. He'd done a bad, stupid thing and now he had to own up to it and take his lumps.

"I was going to tell you, it just never seemed like the right time."

"No, you're just a coward."

"Clare, I'm sorry."

"So am I, Parker." She turned around and he jumped up to follow her.

"Clare, wait!"

He caught up with her at the bottom of the stairs. He grabbed her arm and she violently jerked it away. "*Do not* touch me. You don't get to touch me *ever again*."

She was so furious, her face was bright red and her hands were trembling as she shoved her arms into her coat sleeves. "I am so stupid. I can't believe I let myself trust you."

"No, I'm the stupid one, Clare. And I cannot begin to tell you how sorry I am. I wasn't thinking. I didn't know—"

She raised a hand to stop him midsentence. "Save your breath, I'm not buying it. Not anymore."

She walked out the door and he let her go. She was too angry to listen to reason, even if he did have some sort of reasonable excuse. Which he didn't. He'd worked so hard to earn her trust, and in a matter of seconds he'd lost it.

Maybe she just needed time to think it through. Maybe after a day or two she would give him a chance to explain. Maybe, if he was totally honest from now on, she could learn to trust him again.

Or maybe it was just over.

Yeah, it was over.

In this day and age, with all the communications technology available, it was still possible to go radio silent and drop completely off the map. He knew because that's what Clare had done. She'd taken a week's vacation then disappeared.

Every time he let himself remember the way her face had looked when she'd walked out the door—the bitterness and hurt—his gut tied itself into knots. Which was probably why he hadn't been able to eat in two days. Nothing would go down.

Having never had a broken heart, he'd had no idea just how dreadful it could feel. He wished he could go back and apologize profusely to all of the women he'd seduced then discarded over the years. If any of them felt even a fraction of what he was feeling now…

In a word, it *sucked*.

His days of using and manipulating women to get what he wanted were officially over.

He'd left a few things at Clare's house, things he would really like to have back, like his tennis shoes, but knowing Kay had guns, he wouldn't dare. He knew how it worked in that family. He hurt Clare, so Kay would hurt him. She had brothers, too. Big ones, who could snap him like a twig, or throw him off a cliff. With all that land they had, no one would ever find the body…

But killing him would mean putting him out of his misery, and he deserved every bit of misery he was feeling. And he was sure they knew that.

He took Wednesday off and lay around the house in his pajamas flipping through the TV channels. He didn't even have anyone to talk to. Luc was the one he called with a problem. But if Parker told him it was his text that had blown everything wide-open, Luc would never forgive himself.

There was nothing on TV so he grabbed his laptop. Out of habit he clicked on the Family Finder link in his browser and the page popped up. It was times like this when having a family would come in handy.

He read through the letter section of his profile. He'd written a few short passages about himself, describing his career and his various degrees. It sounded…wrong.

Awkward or forced or something. He highlighted all the text and hit Delete. He sat for a second, looking at the blank page, wondering what it was he really wanted to impart to the woman who'd abandoned him.

He typed five words, but they pretty much said it all.

I want to meet you.

And before he could change his mind he hit Submit.

It was finally done. He'd sent it. Now all he could do was sit back and wait. He wasn't sure if he felt excited or nervous.

He wondered how long it would take—

The computer beeped as a message window popped up on his screen. I want to meet you, too.

Apparently not that long.

After exchanging phone numbers and one very short and awkward conversation, Rachel Simpson, his biological mother, had immediately purchased a plane ticket for her trip to Texas from her home in Nebraska.

Heavy traffic made him a little late picking her up, and when he walked into the baggage-claim area where they planned to meet, she was already there. Though he had never even seen a picture of her, he knew her the moment he saw her. They looked alike. And the second her eyes landed on him, it was obvious that she could see it, too.

She looked younger than he expected. But she had been only eighteen when he was born, putting her at fifty-six now.

She was very attractive—tall and slender, with long dark hair streaked with gray.

Suddenly his feet felt glued to the floor, but she came to him. And for some strange reason her uncertainty was a comfort. At least he wasn't the only one flying blind.

Then she was standing in front of him, saying, "Parker."

She held a hand out and he automatically took it, but instead of shaking it, she held it tight. "I've been looking forward to this for a very long time," she said. "It's so good to see you."

He wished he could say the same, but right now he wasn't sure how he felt. He was feeling so many things he couldn't sort them all out. All he could manage was, "How was your flight?"

"It was good. My return flight leaves in three hours. I'd have stayed longer but I couldn't get the time off work. Is there somewhere that we can go and talk?"

They chose a coffee shop close to the airport, and she asked him question after question about himself. He waited to feel some sort of connection, or affection.

"You must have questions about me," she said finally.

He did, but all he could think to say was, "You answered my request so fast."

"I've been registered on the site since it was created. I figured that if you wanted to see me, this would be one of the first places you looked."

"You could have just contacted me."

"I didn't think it would be fair to disrupt your life. I knew that you had the resources to find me if you wanted to."

"Why didn't you want me?"

His blunt question seemed to surprise her, and he surprised himself. But he had never been one to dance around an issue. He'd met with her to get answers, and he was going to get them.

"I did want you, I swear, but I was only eighteen when you were born and I had signed a contract. He told you that I was a surrogate?"

Parker nodded.

"I only agreed to do it to make money for college, but your father was so charming and sweet to me. I was very young and naive, and it was the late seventies so that sort of thing wasn't common, and not looked upon too favorably. My family would have been horrified to learn what I did. Your grandparents were very old-fashioned."

His grandparents? The ones that he hadn't even known existed? "Were?"

"They were over forty when they had my brother and me. They passed years ago."

He hoped she wasn't expecting any sympathy from him.

"So you just disappeared for nine months? Didn't your parents wonder where you were?"

"I told them that I got a job as a nanny to save money for school."

He picked up his coffee cup to take a sip, but put it back down untouched. The truth was, he felt a little sick to his stomach. "Did you love him?"

"I thought I did. I wanted to, and not just because he was rich. Though that was what everyone believed. It was wonderful at first. You know how charming he could be. He could also be cold and cruel. But by that time I wanted you so much, I was willing to stay with him."

"Yet you left."

"Parker, he didn't give me a choice. He *made* me leave."

"Was it true what he told me about the limo driver?"

"Darren was the only friend I had."

"I heard it was more than that. He said you ran off with him."

"Your father and I had a terrible fight. He was never around, and when he was, though he claimed to love me, he treated me like a subordinate."

Parker could certainly relate to that.

"Darren was just consoling me, but your father got the wrong idea. He accused me of cheating on him. He kicked me out, said I broke the terms of our agreement, and sent me away without a penny to my name. I hadn't earned the money. You were only two weeks old. I was devastated."

"What did you do?"

"The only thing I could do. I went home to Nebraska and tried to convince everyone that my heart wasn't breaking. I tried to forget."

"It would seem you did a pretty good job."

There was regret and pain in her voice when she said, "No, Parker, I haven't. In thirty-eight years a day hasn't passed that I didn't think of you, and wonder what you were doing."

"But you didn't try to see me."

"I signed a contract saying I wouldn't. And at the time I thought I was doing the right thing. I thought that he could give you a better life than I ever could. But once I got to know him, when I realized how wrong I was about him, it was too late."

"I'm no attorney, but I'm fairly certain that any contract would become null and void the day I turned eighteen. Yet here we are *twenty* years later."

She winced, as if his words actually stung, and he felt a stab of guilt. "As I said, I didn't want to disrupt your life. I felt as if I had no right."

"Because thinking that you abandoned me for the limo driver was so much better."

"You have every reason to be angry. And I will never forgive myself for robbing you of the opportunity to be a part of our family."

"Family?"

"You have two brother and two sisters. You also have seven nieces and nephews. Your brother David is thirty-five. He's a country vet. He has three boys. Jeanie is thirty-two. She's a schoolteacher, and she has four children. Two of each. Now, the twins, Aaron and Ashley, came along later. They graduate high school next year."

It was hard to imagine that he could have a brother and sister still in high school. The whole situation was making him feel weirdly left out. And resentful. "Do they know about me?"

"They do. And they would have all flown here with me if I let them. They can't wait to meet you. If that's something you want."

He didn't know what he wanted. He just felt angry and annoyed. "Did your husband know about me?"

She nodded. "It took me years to work up the courage to tell him. But he was one hundred percent supportive. He was a good man, Parker. A good father. I wish you could have known him."

"He's not…?"

"He passed away last year. Lung cancer."

It was so much to take in all at once. There were years' and years' worth of things he'd missed.

"There's something else that you need to know," she said, her tone ominous. "Something you probably don't know about your father. He was sterile. He couldn't have children of his own."

"So how am I here?"

"I was already pregnant when I met him."

Sixteen

The coffee shop spun around him. Of all scenarios he had imagined over the years regarding his mother, this had never even crossed his mind. But it sure did explain a lot. Why he and the man he thought was his father were so completely different. Somewhere deep down Parker had always felt an odd detachment from his father. Now he knew why.

"So who is my real father?"

She wrapped her hands around her coffee cup looking so sad. "I didn't know him very well. I had just graduated high school and we were on vacation. Every summer my parents would rent a cabin at the lake and we would spend a month there. Your father's name was Michael Johnson. He was eighteen, and on vacation with his grandparents. He had joined the army and was leaving for boot camp as soon as their vacation was over. It was love at first sight for both of us. We were inseparable for two weeks. We spent every second we could together. I was back in Nebraska when I discovered I was pregnant."

"Did you try to contact him?"

"He was in basic training by then. I didn't have a clue *how* to get in touch with him, and by the time I found him, it was too late. He was dead."

So his biological father was dead.

He wanted to feel remorse, or regret, or pride, but he just felt numb. "How did he die?"

"I don't know much, only that he was on a rescue mission and the helicopter he was in was shot down. Everyone on board was killed. He died a hero."

That meant more to him than she could possibly understand. Since his father—the man who raised him— had never done a decent thing in his life.

"I've used the internet to follow your career over the years," she told him. "I know this probably doesn't mean much, but I'm so proud of the man you've become."

His laugh was a bitter one. "Don't believe everything you read. The truth is, I'm a screw-up."

The sympathy in her eyes nearly did him in. She really cared. "Do you want to talk about it?"

Though he hadn't planned to bring up his relationship with Clare, or anything else about his life, he heard himself spilling his guts. And once he got started, he couldn't seem to stop. He told her the entire sordid story.

"She sounds very special," his mother said when he was all talked out. "What are you planning to do to get her back?"

"There's nothing I can do," he said. "I betrayed her trust. It's over."

"But you love her, don't you? And she loves you?"

He nodded. "Or she used to."

"Then you have to at least try." She laid a hand over his and squeezed gently, and in that instant he felt a connection. A sense of familiarity. It was…nice. So he left his hand there. "Trust me when I say people don't fall out of love overnight. She probably just needs time to sort things out."

"You have no idea how stubborn she is."

"It sounds to me as if you're a little stubborn, too. Or you're just afraid of being rejected again."

Maybe she was right. He'd never been rejected before, so he had no idea how to handle it, or what to do to get her back. He was stumbling around in the dark, and his instincts were failing him.

"Okay," he said, "tell me what I should do. How I can fix this."

"Parker, only you know the answer to that question."

But that was the problem. He didn't. "I don't even know where she is."

"Don't you?"

Of course he did. She was at her parents' ranch. But talking to her meant going there and facing her entire family.

Jesus. Clare was right. He really was a coward.

He and Rachel talked up until the minute it was time to take her back to the airport, and all the way to the terminal, where he dropped her outside the doors. They parted with a promise that they would keep in touch, and he gave her permission to give his contact information to his brothers and sisters.

He drove home, weighing his options, and he realized Rachel was right. Clare was worth fighting for.

And if he failed, he would live the rest of his life regretting it. But at least he could say that he'd tried. He would stop home and pick up a few things, then drive to her parents' farm. If she refused to talk to him, he would camp out with the horses until she changed her mind. He would even take on her brothers if he had to. He was willing to go to any lengths to get her back.

But when he pulled down his street, her car was in his driveway and he felt a rush of hope that made his scalp tingle.

He hit the brake and stopped in the road. He had planned to use the hour's drive to the farm to figure out what he was going to say to her. It looked as if he would have to wing it.

He pulled in beside her car. She wasn't in it. Then he remembered that she still had his key. He shuddered to think what she might be doing in there. Setting his house on fire maybe?

He parked in the garage, then let himself inside, nerves roiling in his belly. He hadn't been this nervous, or this determined, in his life. She may have been stubborn, but so was he, and he refused to let her leave until he'd had the chance to explain.

She was sitting on the sofa, and the deep love and respect that he felt for her propelled him forward when what he really wanted to do was turn around and run. Never in his adult life had he been intimidated by a woman, but Clare scared the hell out of him right now.

As he walked into the room she stood. She didn't say a word; she just looked at him, her expression blank. And he couldn't think of a damned thing to say. He stood there, trying to make his brain work.

She walked over, until she was standing in front of

him. She had her hair up in one of those messy buns, and he itched to pull the band out so it would tumble out over her shoulders.

For several excruciating seconds she just looked at him. Searching his face. He waited for her to punch him, or scratch his eyes out. Instead, she threw her arms around him.

He was so stunned that for a second he just stood there, speechless.

"I'm so sorry," she said, laying her cheek against his chest, holding him so tight.

Wait a minute. Had she really just apologized to *him*?

"Clare, you have nothing to be sorry for. I betrayed your trust. I'm the bad guy here."

She looked up at him. "And I betrayed yours."

He blinked. What the hell was she talking about? "I don't understand."

"I said I loved you, and at the first sign of trouble I exploded. I didn't even give you a chance to explain. I was so wrapped up in my own feelings I didn't even stop to think about yours."

"Clare, this was my fault."

"Not completely. I should have been more understanding. I was just scared, and feeling vulnerable."

"You had every right to be. I screwed up."

"And I forgive you."

He blinked. "Just like that?"

"You made a mistake."

"It was a stupid move. I don't even know what I was thinking. I guess I wasn't."

"After all the soul-searching you've done, and the changes you've made, you were bound to have a setback and do something the old Parker would have done.

But I'm not in love with that guy. I'm in love with you, right now, just the way you are."

"I never meant to hurt you. And I was a coward for not telling you about the bet. It was stupid and childish."

"And I'm sorry that I overreacted so badly. And I don't want to fight. I want to fix this. Fix me."

"There's nothing to fix," he said, pulling her close and holding her tight, hardly able to conceive that she was giving him a second chance. "You're perfect."

"Far from it." She rose up on her toes and kissed him gently. "All I know is that I love you, and the past few days I've been miserable without you. The idea that I might never kiss you again, or feel your arms around me…" Her voice wavered and tears swam in her eyes. "We can figure this out."

"Yes," he said, "I want that, too."

She cupped his face in her hands, smiled up at him. "I really love you, Parker. So much."

"I love you, too. And I have so much to tell you. I met my mother today."

Clare gasped and her eyes lit. "You did?"

"You're not the only one with a big family. Turns out I have two half brothers and two half sisters. But we can talk about that later. Right now I just want to hold you."

After another long and wonderful embrace, she looked up at him and said, "I was thinking that since you won the bet because of me, it would only be fair to give me half of the prize."

"You can have it all," he said, letting go of her so he could take out his wallet. He pulled out a ten-dollar bill and handed it to her.

She looked at the bill, then back to him. "Ten bucks?"

"Yup."

"That's it?"

"'Fraid so. They're not serious bets. We always goof around."

She laughed, and shook her head, and it was the most beautiful thing he'd ever heard. They were okay. And he was never letting her go again.

"You know, this is all Maddie's fault," he said.

Clare looked at him funny. "Why do you say that?"

"Sharing in her care brought us together in a way no other patient has before. It's because of her that we connected."

"That's true," she said. "Remind me to thank her someday."

"I know things moved pretty fast with us, and to ask you to marry me right this minute would be pushing it."

"A little," she agreed.

"I just want you to know that I have every intention of spending the rest of my life with you. Whether you like it or not."

She grinned. "I think I like it."

"I don't care if we wait ten years to get married, as long as I know I have your heart." He cradled her face in his hands, kissed her gently. "Because, cupcake, you definitely have mine."

* * * * *

THE SEAL'S
SECRET HEIRS

KAT CANTRELL

To Cat Schield. Thanks for all the collaboration
and for being my guide into the TCC world!

One

Royal, Texas was the perfect place to go to die.

Kyle Wade aimed to do exactly that. After an honorable discharge from the navy, what else lay ahead of him but a slow and painful death? Might as well do it in Royal, the town that had welcomed every Wade since the dawn of time—except him.

He nearly drove through the center of town without stopping. Because he hadn't realized he was *in* Royal until he was nearly *out* of Royal.

Yeah, it had been ten years, and when he'd stopped for gas in Odessa, he'd heard about the tornado that had ripped through the town. But still. Was nothing on the main strip still the same? These new buildings hadn't been there when he'd left. Of course, he'd hightailed it out of Royal for Coronado, California, in a hurry and hadn't looked back once in all his years as a Navy SEAL. Had he really expected Royal to be suspended in time, like a photograph?

He kind of had.

Kyle slowed as he passed the spot where he'd first kissed Grace Haines in the parking lot of the Dairy Queen. Or what used to be the spot where he'd taken his high school girlfriend on their first date. The Dairy Queen had moved down the road and in its place stood a little pink building housing something called Mimi's Nail Salon. Really?

Fitting that his relationship with Grace had nothing to mark it. Nothing in Royal proper anyway. The scars on his heart would always be there.

Shaking his head, Kyle punched the gas. He had plenty of time to gawk at the town later and no time to think about the woman who had driven him into the military. His shattered leg hurt something fierce and he'd been traveling for the better part of three days. It was time to go home.

And now he had a feeling things had probably changed at Wade Ranch—also known as home—more than he'd have anticipated. Never the optimist, he suspected that meant they'd gotten worse. Which was saying something, since he'd left in the first place because of the rift with his twin brother, Liam. No time like the present to get the cold welcome over with.

Wade Ranch's land unrolled at exactly the ten-mile marker from Royal. At least *that* was still the same. Acres and acres of rocky, hilly countryside spread as far as Kyle could see. Huh. Reminded him of Afghanistan. Wouldn't have thought there'd be any comparison, but there you go. A man could travel ten thousand miles and still wind up where he started. In more ways than one.

The gate wasn't barred. His brother, Liam, was running a loose ship apparently. Their grandfather had died a while back and left the ranch to both brothers, but Kyle had never intended to claim his share. Yeah, it was a significant inheritance. But he didn't want it. He wanted his team back and his life as a SEAL. An insurgent's spray of bullets had guaranteed that would never happen. Even if

Kyle hadn't gotten shot, Cortez was gone and no amount of wishing or screaming at God could bring his friend and comrade-in-arms back to life.

Hadn't stopped Kyle from trying.

Kyle drove up the winding lane to the main house, which had a new coat of paint. The white Victorian house had been lording over Wade land for a hundred years, but looked like Liam had done some renovation. The tire swing that had hung from the giant oak in the front yard was gone and a new porch rocker with room for two had been added.

Perfect. Kyle could sit there in that rocker and complain about how the coming rain was paining his joints. Maybe later he could get up a game of dominos at the VA with all of the other retired military men. *Retired.* They might as well call it dead.

When Kyle jumped from the cab of the truck he'd bought in California after the navy decided they were done with him, he hit the dusty ground at the wrong angle. Pain shot up his leg and it stole his breath for a moment. When a man couldn't even get out of his own truck without harm, it was not a good day.

Yeah, he should be more careful. But then he'd have to admit something was wrong with this leg.

He sucked it up. *The only easy day was yesterday.* That mantra had gotten him through four tours of duty in the Middle East. Surely it could get him to the door of Wade Ranch.

It did. Barely. He knocked, but someone was already answering before the sound faded.

The moment the door swung open, Kyle stepped over the threshold and did a double take. *Liam.* His brother stood in the middle of the renovated foyer, glowering. He'd grown up and out in ten years. Kyle had, too, of course, but it was still a shock to see that his brother had changed from the picture he'd carried in his mind's eye, even though their faces mostly matched.

Crack!

Agony exploded across Kyle's jaw as his head snapped backward.

What in the... Had Liam just *punched* him?

Every nerve in Kyle's body went on full alert, vibrating with tension as he reoriented and automatically began scanning both the threat of Liam and the perimeter simultaneously. The foyer was empty, save the two Wade brothers. And Liam wasn't getting the drop on him twice.

"That's for not calling," Liam said succinctly and balled his fists as if he planned to go back for seconds.

"Nice to see you, too."

Dang. Talking hurt. Kyle spit out a curse along with a trickle of blood that hit the hardwood floor an inch from Liam's broken-in boot.

"Deadbeat. You have a lot of nerve showing up now. Get gone or there's more where that came from."

Liam clearly had no idea who he was tangling with.

"I don't cater much to sucker punches," Kyle drawled, and touched his lower lip, right above where the throb in his jaw hurt the worst. Blood came away with his finger. "Why don't you try that again now that I'm paying attention?"

Liam shook his head wearily, his fists going slack. "Your face is as hard as your head. Why now? After all this time, why did you finally drag your sorry butt home?"

"Aww. Careful there, brother, or people might start thinking you missed me something fierce when you talk like that."

Liam had another thirty seconds to explain why Kyle's welcome home had included a fist. Liam had a crappy right hook, but it still hurt. If anything, Kyle was the one who should be throwing punches. After all, he was the one with the ax to grind. He was the one who had left Royal because of what Liam had done.

Or rather *whom* he'd done. Grace Haines. Liam had broken the most sacred of all brotherly bonds when he messed around with the woman Kyle loved. Afghanistan wasn't far enough away to forget, but it was the farthest a newly minted SEAL could go after being deployed.

So he hadn't forgotten. Or forgiven.

"I called your cell phone," Liam said. "I called every navy outpost I could for two months straight. I left messages. I called about the messages. Figured that silence was enough of an answer." Arms crossed, Liam looked down his nose at Kyle, which was a feat, given that they were the same height. "So I took steps to work through this mess you've left in my lap."

Wait, he'd gotten punched over leaving the ranch in his brother's capable hands? That was precious. Liam had loved Wade Ranch from the first, maybe even as early as the day their mother had dropped them off with Grandpa and never came back.

"You were always destined to run Wade Ranch," Kyle said, and almost didn't choke on it. "I didn't dump it on you."

Liam snorted. "Are you really that dense? I'm not talking about the ranch, moron. I'm talking about your kids."

Kyle flinched involuntarily. "My...what?"

Kids? As in children?

"Yes, kids," Liam enunciated, drawing out the *i* sound as if Kyle might catch his meaning better if the word had eighteen syllables. "Daughters. Twins. I don't get why you waited to come home. You should have been here the moment you found out."

"I'm finding out *this* moment," Kyle muttered as his pulse kicked up, beating in his throat like a May hailstorm on a tin roof. "How...wha..."

His throat closed.

Twin daughters. And Liam thought they were *his*? Someone had made a huge mistake. Kyle didn't have any children. Kyle didn't *want* any children.

Liam was staring at him strangely. "You didn't get my messages?"

"Geez, Liam. What was your first clue? I wasn't sitting at a desk dodging your calls. I spent six months in…a bad place and then ended up in a worse place."

From the city of Kunduz to Landstuhl Regional, the US-run military hospital in Germany. He didn't remember a lot of it, but the incredible pain as the doctors worked to restore the bone a bullet had shattered in his leg—that he would never forget.

But he was one of the lucky ones who'd survived his wounds. Cortez hadn't. Kyle still had nightmares about leaving his teammate behind in that foxhole where they'd been trapped by insurgents. Seemed wrong. Cortez should have had a proper send-off for his sacrifice.

"Still not a chatterbox, I see." Liam scrubbed at his face with one hand, and when he dropped it, weariness had replaced the glower. "Keep your secrets about your fabulous life overseas as a badass. I really don't care. I have more important things to get straight."

The weariness was new. Kyle remembered his brother as being a lot of things—a betrayer, first and foremost—but not tired. It looked wrong on his face. As wrong as the constant pain etched into Kyle's own face when he looked in the mirror. Which was why he'd quit looking in the mirror.

"Why don't you start at the beginning." Kyle jerked his head toward what he hoped was still the kitchen. "Maybe we can hash it out over tea?"

It was too early in the morning for Jack Daniel's, though he might make an exception, pending the outcome of the conversation.

Liam nodded and spun to stride off toward the back of the house. Following him, Kyle was immediately blinded by all the off-white cabinets in the kitchen. His brother hadn't left a stone unturned when he'd gotten busy redoing the house. Modern appliances in stainless steel had replaced the old harvest gold ones and new double islands dominated the center. A wall of glass overlooked the back acreage that stretched for miles until it hit Old Man Drucker's property. Or what had been Drucker's property ten years ago. Obviously Kyle wasn't up-to-date about what had been going on since he'd left.

Without ceremony, Liam splashed some tea into a cup from a pitcher on the counter and shoved the cup into his hand. "Tea. Now talk to me about Margaret Garner."

Hot. Blonde. Nice legs. Kyle visualized the woman instantly. But that was a name he hadn't thought about in— wow, like almost a year.

"Margaret Garner? What does she have to do with any—"

The question died in his throat. *Almost a year.* Like long enough to grow a baby or two? Didn't mean it was true. Didn't mean they were his babies.

It felt like a really good time to sit down, and he thought maybe he could do it without tipping off Liam how badly his leg ached 24-7.

He fell heavily onto a bar stool at the closest island, tea forgotten and shoulders ten pounds heavier. "San Antonio. She was with a group of friends at Cantina Juarez. A place where military groupies hang out."

"So you did sleep with her?"

"Not that it's any of your business," Kyle said noncommitally. They were long past the kiss-and-tell stage of their relationship, if they'd ever been that close. When Liam took up with Grace ten years ago, it had killed any fragment of warmth between them, warmth that was unlikely to return.

"You made it my business when you didn't come home to take care of your daughters," Liam countered, as his fists balled up again.

"Take another swing at me and you'll get real cozy with the floor in short order." Kyle contemplated his brother. Who was furious. "So Margaret came around with some babies looking for handouts? I hope you asked for a paternity test before you wrote a check."

This was bizarre. Of all the conversations he'd thought he'd be having with Liam, this was not it. *Babies. Margaret. Paternity test.* None of these things made sense, together or separately.

Why hadn't any of Liam's messages been relayed? Probably because he hadn't called the right office—by design. Kyle hadn't exactly made it clear how Liam could reach him. Maybe it was a blessing that Kyle hadn't known. He couldn't have hopped on a plane anyway.

Kyle couldn't be a father. He barely knew how to be a civilian and had worked long and hard at accepting that he wasn't part of a SEAL team any longer.

It was twice as hard to accept that after being discharged, he had nowhere to go but back to the ranch where he'd never fit in, never belonged. His injury wasn't supposed to be a factor as he figured out what to do with the rest of his life, since God hadn't seen fit to let him die alongside Cortez. But being a father—to twins, no less—meant he had to think about what a busted leg meant for a man's everyday life. And he did not like thinking about how difficult it was some days to simply stand.

Liam threw up a hand, a scowl crawling onto his expression. "Shut up a minute. No one wrote any checks. You're the father of the babies, no question."

Well, Kyle had a few questions. Like why Margaret hadn't contacted him when she found out she was pregnant. While Liam had little information on his whereabouts,

Margaret sure knew how to get in touch. Her girlfriend had been dating Cortez and called him all the time. She'd known exactly where he was stationed.

It was nothing short of unforgivable. "Where's Margaret?"

"She died," Liam bit out shortly. "While giving birth. It's a long story. Do I need to give you a minute?"

Kyle processed that much more slowly than he would have liked. Margaret was dead? It seemed like just yesterday that he'd spent a long weekend with her in a hotel room. She'd been a wildcat, determined to send him back to Afghanistan with enough memories to keep him warm at night, as she'd put it.

He was sad to learn Margaret had passed, sure. He'd liked thinking about her on the other side of the world, living a normal life that he was helping to secure by going after bad guys. But they'd spent less than forty-eight hours together and had barely known each other, by design. He wasn't devastated—it wasn't as if he'd lost the love of his life or anything. Not like when he'd lost Grace.

"We used protection," he muttered. As if that was the most important thing to get straight at this point. "I don't understand. How did she get pregnant?"

"The normal way, I imagine. Moron." Liam rolled his eyes the way he'd always done when they were younger. "Do you have any interest whatsoever in meeting your daughters?"

Kyle blinked. "Well…yeah. Of course. What happened to them after Margaret died? Who's taking care of them?"

"I am. Me and Hadley. Who's the most amazing woman. She's the nanny I hired when you didn't respond to any of my calls."

Reeling, Kyle tried to gather some of his wits, but they seemed as scattered and filmy as clouds on a mild spring day. "Thanks. That's... You didn't have to. That's above the call of duty."

Liam crossed his arms, biceps rippling under the sleeve of his T-shirt. "They're great babies. Beautiful. And I didn't do it for you. I did it because I love them. Hadley and I, we're planning to keep on taking care of them, too."

"That's not going to happen. You've spent the last ten minutes whaling on me about not coming home to take responsibility for this. I'm here. I'm man enough to step up." He set his jaw, which still throbbed. "I want to see them."

The atmosphere fairly vibrated with animosity as they stared each other down, neither blinking, neither backing down. Something flickered through Liam's gaze and he gave one curt nod.

"Fine." Liam called up the stairs off the kitchen that led to the upper stories.

After the longest three minutes of Kyle's life, he heard footsteps and a pretty, blonde woman who must be the nanny came down the stairs. But Kyle only had eyes for the pink bundles, one each in the crook of her arms.

Sucker punch number two.

Those were real, live, honest-to-God babies. What the hell was he thinking, saying that he wanted to see them? What was that supposed to prove? That he didn't know squat about babies?

They were so small. Nearly identical. Twins, like Kyle and Liam. He'd always heard that identical twins skipped generations, but apparently not.

"What are their names?" he whispered.

"Madeline and Margaret Wade," the woman responded, and the babies lifted their heads toward the sound of her voice. Clearly she'd spent a lot of time with them. "We call them Maddie and Maggie for short."

Somehow that seemed perfect for their little wrinkled faces. "Can I hold them?"

"Sure. This is Maggie." She handed over the first one and cheerfully helped Kyle get the baby situated without being asked, which he appreciated more than he could possibly say because his stupid hands suddenly seemed too clumsy to handle something so breakable.

Hey, little girl. He couldn't talk over the lump in his throat, and no one seemed inclined to make him, so he just looked at her. His heart thumped as it expanded, growing larger the longer he held his daughter. That was a kick in the pants. Who would have thought you could instantly love someone like that? It should have taken time. But there it was.

Now what? What if she cried? What if *he* cried?

He'd hoped a flood of knowledge would magically appear if he could just get his hands on the challenge. You didn't learn to hack through vegetation with a machete until you put it in your palm and started hacking.

"You can take her back," he said gruffly, overwhelmed with all the emotion he had no idea what to do with. But there was still another one. Another daughter. He found new appreciation for the term *double trouble*.

"This one is Maddie," the woman said.

Somehow, the other pink bundle ended up in his arms. Instantly, he could tell she was smaller, weighing less than her sister. Strange. She felt even more fragile than her sister, as if Kyle should be careful how heavily he breathed or he might blow her to the ground with an extra big huff.

Equal parts love and fierce devotion surged through the heart he'd already thought was full, splitting it open. She'd need someone to look out for her. To protect her.

That's on me. My job.

And then being a father made all the sense in the world. These were his girls. The reason he wasn't dead in a foxhole flopped out next to Cortez right now. The Almighty got it perfectly right some days.

"And this is Hadley Wade, my wife," Liam broke in with

the scowl that seemed to be a permanent part of his face nowadays. "We still introduce ourselves in these parts."

"It's okay," Hadley said with a hand on Liam's elbow. Her palm settled into the crook comfortably, as if they were intimate often. "Give him a break. It's a lot to take in."

"I'm done." Kyle rubbed his free hand across his military-issue buzz cut, but it didn't stimulate his brain much. He contemplated Hadley, the woman Liam had casually mentioned that he'd married, as if that was some small thing. "I don't think there's much more I can take in. I appreciate what you've done in my stead, but these are my girls. I want to be their father, in all the ways that count. I'm here and I'm sticking around Royal."

That hadn't been set in his mind until this moment. But it would take a bulldozer to shove him onto a different path now.

"Well, it's not as simple as all that," Liam corrected. "Their mama is gone and you weren't around. So even though I have temporary custody, these girls became wards of the state and had a social worker assigned. You're gonna have to deal with the red tape before you start joining the PTA and picking out matching Easter dresses."

Wearily, Kyle nodded. "I get that. What do I have to do?"

Hadley and Liam exchanged glances and a sense of foreboding rose up in Kyle's stomach.

With a sigh, Liam pulled out his cell phone. "I'll call their social worker. But before she gets here, you should know that it's Grace Haines."

Grace. The name hit him in the solar plexus and all the air rushed from his lungs.

Sucker punch number three.

Grace Haines had avoided looking at the date all day, but it sneaked up on her after lunch. She stared at the letters and numbers she'd just typed on a case file.

March 12. The third anniversary of the day she'd become a Professional Single Girl. She should get cake. Or a card. Something to mark the occasion of when she'd given up the ghost and decided to be happy with her career as a social worker. Instead of continually dating men who were nice enough, but could never live up to her standards, she'd learn to be by herself.

Was it so wrong to want a man who doted on her as her father did with her mother? She wasn't asking for much. Flowers occasionally. A text message here and there with a heart emoticon and a simple thinking of you. Something that showed Grace was a priority. That the guy noticed when she wasn't there.

Yeah, that was dang difficult, apparently. The decision to stop actively looking for Mr. Right and start going to museums and plays as a party of one hadn't been all that hard. As a bonus, she never had to compromise on date night by seeing a science fiction movie where special effects drowned out the dialogue. She could do whatever she wanted with her Saturday nights.

It was great. Or at least that was what she told herself. Loudly. It drowned out the voice in her heart that kept insisting she would never get the family she desperately wanted if she didn't date.

In lieu of a Happy Professional Single Girl cake, Grace settled for a Reese's Peanut Butter Cup from the vending machine and got back to work. The children's cases the county had entrusted to her were not going to handle themselves, and there were some heartbreakers in her caseload. She loved her job and thanked God every day she got to make a difference in the lives of the children she helped.

If she couldn't have children of her own, she'd make do with loving other people's.

Her desk phone rang and she picked up the receiver, accidentally knocking over the framed picture of her mom and dad celebrating their thirtieth wedding anniversary at a luau in Hawaii. One day she'd go there, she vowed as she righted the frame. Even if she had to travel to Hawaii solo, it was still Hawaii.

"Grace Haines. How can I help you today?"

"It's Liam," the voice on the other end announced, and the gravity in his tone tripped her radar.

"Are the girls all right?" Panicked, Grace threw a couple of manila folders into her tote in preparation to fly to her car. She could be at Wade Ranch in less than twenty minutes if she ignored the speed limit and prayed to Jesus that Sheriff Battle wasn't sitting in his squad car at the Royal city limits the way he usually did. "What's happened to the babies? It's Maddie, isn't it? I knew that she wasn't—"

"The girls are fine," he interrupted. "They're with Hadley. It's Kyle. He came home."

Grace froze, mid-file transfer. The manila folder fell to the floor in slow motion from her nerveless fingers, opened at the spine and spilled papers across the linoleum.

"What?" she whispered.

Kyle.

Her first kiss. Her first love. Her first taste of the agonizing pain a man could cause.

He wasn't supposed to be here. The twin daughters Kyle Wade had fathered were parentless, or so she'd convinced herself. That was the only reason she'd taken the case, once Liam assured her he'd called the USO, the California base Kyle had shipped out of and the President of the United States. No response, he'd said.

No response meant no conflict of interest.

If Kyle was back, her interest was so conflicted, she couldn't even see through it.

"He's here. At Wade Ranch," Liam confirmed. "You need to come by as soon as possible and help us sort this out."

Translation: Liam and Hadley wanted to adopt Mad-

die and Maggie and with Kyle in the picture, that wasn't
as easy as they'd all assumed. Grace would have to convince him to waive his parental rights. If he didn't want
to, then she'd have to assess Kyle's fitness as a parent and
potentially even give him custody, despite knowing in her
heart that he'd be a horrible father. It was a huge tangle.

The best scenario would be to transfer the case to someone else. But on short notice? Probably wasn't going to
happen.

"I'll be there as soon as I can. Thanks, Liam. It'll work
out."

Grace hung up and dropped her head down into the
crook of her elbow.

Somehow, she was supposed to go to Wade Ranch and
do her job, while ignoring the fact that Kyle Wade had
broken her heart into tiny little pieces, and then promptly
joined the military, as if she hadn't mattered at all. And
somehow, she had to ignore the fact that she still wasn't
over it. Or him.

Two

Grace knocked on the door of Wade House and steeled herself for whatever was about to happen. Which was what she'd been doing in the car on the way over. And at her desk before that.

No one else in the county office could take on another case, so Grace had agreed to keep Maddie and Maggie under the premise that she'd run all her recommendations through her supervisor before she told the parties involved about her decisions. Which meant she couldn't just decide ahead of time that Kyle wasn't fit. She had to prove it.

It would be a stringent process, with no room for error. She'd have to justify her report with far more data and impartial observations than she'd ever had to before. It meant twice as many visits and twice as much documentation. Of course. Because who didn't want to spend a bunch of time with a high-school boyfriend who'd ruined you for dating any other man?

Hopefully, he'd just give up his rights without a fight and they could all go on.

The door swung open and Grace forgot to breathe. Kyle Wade was indeed home.

Hungrily, her gaze skittered over his grown-up face. *Oh, my.* Still gorgeous, but sun worn, with new lines around his eyes that said he'd seen some things in the past ten years and they weren't all pleasant. His hair was shorn shorter than short, but it fit this new version of Kyle.

His green eyes were diamond hard. That was new, too. He'd never been open and friendly, but she'd burrowed under that reserve back in high school and when he really looked at her with his signature blend of love and devotion—it had been magic.

She instantly wanted to burrow under that hardness once again. Because she knew she was the only one who could, the only one he'd let in. The only one who could soothe his loneliness, the way she'd done back then.

Gah, what was she *thinking*?

She couldn't focus on that. Couldn't remember what it had been like when it was good, because when it was bad, it was really bad. This man had destroyed her, nearly derailing her entire first year at college as she picked up the broken pieces he'd left behind.

"Hey, Grace."

Kyle's voice washed over her and the steeling she'd done to prepare for this moment? Useless.

"Kyle," she returned a bit brusquely, but if she started blubbering, she'd never forgive herself. "I'm happy to see that you've finally decided to acknowledge your children."

Chances were good that wouldn't last. He'd ship out again at a moment's notice, running off to indulge his selfish thirst for adventure, leaving behind a mess. As he'd done the first time. But Grace was here to make sure he didn't hurt anyone in the process, least of all those precious babies.

"Yep," he agreed easily. "I took a slow boat from China all right. But I'm here now. Do whatever you have to do to make it okay with the county for me to be a father to my daughters."

Ha. Fathers were loving, caring, selfless. They didn't become distant and uncommunicative on a regular basis and then forget they had plans with you. And then forget to apologize for leaving you high and dry. Nor did they have the option to quit when the going got tough.

"Well, that's not going to happen today," she said firmly. "I'll do several site visits to make sure that you're providing the right environment for the girls. They need to feel safe and loved and it's my job to put them into the home that will give them that. You might not be the best answer."

The hardness in his expression intensified. "They're mine. I'll take care of them."

His quiet fierceness set her back. Guess that answered the question about whether he'd put up a token fight and then sign whatever she put in front of him that would terminate his parental rights. The fact that he wasn't—it was throwing her for a loop. "Actually, they're mine. They became wards of the state when you didn't respond to the attempts we all made to find you. That's what happens to abandoned babies."

That might have come out harshly. So what. It was the truth, even if the sentiment had some leftover emotion from when Kyle had done that to her. She had to protect the babies, no matter what.

"There were…circumstances. I didn't get any of Liam's messages or I would have come as soon as I could." His mouth firmed into an inflexible line. "That's not important now. Come in and visit. Tell me what I have to do."

"Fine."

She followed him into the formal parlor that had been restored to what she imagined was Wade House's former glory. The Victorian furniture was beautiful and luxurious, and a man like Kyle looked ridiculous sitting on the elegantly appointed chair. Good grief, the spindly legs didn't seem strong enough to support such a solid body. Kyle had gained weight, and the way he moved indicated it was 100 percent finely honed muscle under his clothes. He'd adopted a lazy, slow walk that seemed at odds with all that, but certainly fit a laid-back cowboy at home on his ranch.

Not that she'd noticed or anything.

She took her own seat and perched on the edge, too keyed up to relax. "We'll need to fill out some paperwork. What do you plan to do for employment now that you're home?"

Kyle quirked an eyebrow. "Being a Wade isn't enough?"

Frowning, she held her manila folder in front of her like a shield, though what she thought it was going to protect her from, she had no idea. Kyle's diamond-bit green eyes drilled through her very flesh and bone, deep into the soft places she'd thought were well protected against men. Especially this one.

"No, it's not enough. Inheriting money isn't an indicator of your worth as a parent. I need to see a demonstration of commitment. A permanency that will show you can provide a stable environment for Maddie and Maggie."

"So being able to buy them whatever they want and being able to put food on the table no matter what isn't good enough."

It was not a question but a challenge. She tried not to roll her eyes, she really did. But if you looked up "clueless" in the dictionary, you'd see a picture of Kyle Wade. "That's right. Liam and Hadley can do those things and have been for over two months. Are you prepared for all the special treatments and doctor's visits Maddie will require? I have to know."

Kyle went stiff all at once, freezing so quickly that she got a little concerned. She should really stop caring so much but it was impossible to shut off her desire to help people. This whole conversation was difficult. She and Kyle used to be comfortable with each other. She missed that easiness between them, but there was no room for anything other than a professional and necessary distance.

"Doctor's visits?" Kyle repeated softly. "Is there something wrong with Maddie?"

"Maddie suffers from twin-to-twin transfusion syndrome. She has some heart problems that are pretty serious."

"I...didn't know."

The bleakness in his expression reached out and twisted her heart. She wanted to lash out at him. Blame him. Those girls had been fighting for their lives after Margaret died, and where was Kyle? "Just out of curiosity, why did you come home now? Why not two months ago when Margaret first came looking for you? Or for that matter, why not when she first found out she was pregnant?"

She cut off the tirade there. Oh, there was plenty more she wanted to say, but it would veer into personal barbs that wouldn't help anything. She had a job to do and the information-gathering stage should—and would—stay on a professional level.

Besides, she knew he'd been stationed overseas. He probably hadn't had the luxury of jetting off whenever he felt like it. But he could have at least called.

Crossing his arms, he leaned back against the gold velvet cushions of the too-small chair, biceps bulging. He'd grown some interesting additions to what had already been a nicely built body. Automatically, her gaze wandered south, taking in all the parts that made up that great physique. Wow, had it gotten hot in here, or what? She fanned her face with the manila folder.

But then he eyed her, his face a careful mask that dared her to break through it. Which totally unnerved her. This darker, harder, fiercer Kyle Wade was dangerous. Because she wanted to understand why he was dark, hard and fierce. Why he'd broken her heart and then left.

"You got me all figured out, seems like," he drawled. "Why don't you tell me why I didn't hop on a plane and stick by Margaret's side during her pregnancy?"

Couldn't the man just answer a simple question? He'd always been like this—uncommunicative and prone to leaving instead of dealing with problems head-on. His attitude was so infuriating, she said the first thing that popped into her head.

"Guilt, probably. You didn't want to be involved and hoped the problem would go away on its own." And that was totally unfair. Wasn't it? She had no idea why he hadn't contacted anyone. This new version of Kyle was unsettling *because* she didn't know him that well anymore.

Really, she wasn't that good at reading people in the first place. It was a professional weakness that she hated, but couldn't seem to fix. Once upon a time, she'd thought this man was her forever after, her Prince Charming, Clark Gable and Dr. McDreamy all rolled into one. Which was totally false. She'd bought heavily into that lie, so how could she trust her own judgment? She couldn't. That's why she had to be so methodical in her approach to casework, because she couldn't afford to let emotion rule her decisions. Or afford to make a mistake, not when the future of a child was at stake.

And she wouldn't do either here. Maddie and Maggie deserved a loving home with a family who paid attention to their every need. Kyle Wade was not the right man for that, no matter what he said he wanted.

"Well, then," he said easily. "Guess that answers your question."

It so did not. She still didn't know why he'd come home now, why he'd suddenly shown an interest in his daughters. Whether he could possibly convince her he planned to stick around—if he was even serious about that. Kyle had a habit of running away from his problems, after all.

First and foremost, how could she assess whether the time-hardened man before her could ever provide the loving, nurturing environment two fragile little girls needed?

But she'd let it slide for now. There was plenty of time to work through all of that, since Maddie and Maggie were still legally in the care of Liam and Hadley.

"I think I have enough for now. I'll file my first report and send you a copy when it's approved." She had to get out of here. Before she broke down under the emotional onslaught of everything.

"That's it, huh? What's the report going to say?"

"It's going to say that you've expressed an interest in retaining your parental rights and that I've advised you that I can't approve that until I do several more site visits."

He cocked his head, evaluating her coolly. "How long is that going to take?"

"Until I'm satisfied with your fitness as a parent. Or until I decide you're unfit. At which point I'll make recommmendations as to what I believe is the best home for those precious girls. I will likely recommend they stay with Liam and Hadley."

Without warning, Kyle was on his feet, an intense vibe rippling down his powerful body. She'd have sworn he hadn't moved, and then all of a sudden, there he was, staring down at her with a sharpness about him, as if he'd homed in on her and her alone. She couldn't move, couldn't breathe.

It was precisely the kind of focus she'd craved once. But not now. Not like this.

"Why would you give my kids to my brother?" he asked, his voice dangerously low.

"Well, the most obvious reason is because he and Hadley want them. They've already looked into adoption. But also because they know the babies' needs and have already been providing the best place for the girls."

"You are not taking away my daughters," he said succinctly. "Why does this feel personal?"

She blinked. "This is the opposite of personal, Kyle. My job is to be the picture of impartiality. Our history has nothing to do with this."

"I was starting to wonder if you recalled that we had a history," he drawled slowly, loading the words with meaning.

The intensity rolling from him heightened a notch, and she shivered as he perused her as if he'd found the last morsel of chocolate in the pantry—and he was starving. All at once, she had a feeling they were both remembering the sweet fire of first love. They might have been young, but what they'd lacked in experience, they made up for in enthusiasm. Their relationship had hit some high notes that she'd prefer not to be remembering right this minute. Not with the man who'd made her body sing a scant few feet away.

"I haven't forgotten one day of our relationship." Why did her voice sound so breathless?

"Even the last one?" he murmured, and his voice skittered down her spine with teeth she wasn't expecting.

"I'm not sure what you mean." Confused as to why warning sirens were going off in her head, she stared at the spot where the inverted tray ceiling seams came together. "We broke up. You didn't notice. Then you joined the military and eventually came home. Here we are."

"Oh, I noticed, Grace." The honeyed quality of his tone drew her gaze to his and the green fire there blazed with heat she didn't know what to do with. "I think we can both agree that what happened between us ten years ago was a mistake. Never to be repeated. We'll let bygones be bygones and you'll figure out a way to make this pesky custody issue go away. Deal?"

A mistake. Bygones. Her heart stung as it absorbed the words that confirmed she hadn't meant that much to him. Breaking up with him hadn't fazed him the way she'd hoped. The daring ploy she'd staged to get his attention—by letting him catch her with Liam, a notorious womanizer—hadn't worked, either, because he hadn't really cared whether she messed around with his brother. The whole ruse had been for naught.

Stricken, she stared at him, unable to look away, unable to quell the turmoil inside at Kyle being close enough to touch and yet so very far away. They'd broken up ten years ago because he'd never seemed all that into their relationship. Hadn't enough time passed for her to get over it already?

"Sure. Bygones," she repeated, because that was all she could get out.

She escaped with the hasty promise that she'd send him a set schedule of home visits and drove away from Wade Ranch as fast as she dared. But she feared it would never be fast enough to catch up with her impartiality—it had scampered down the road far too quickly and she had a feeling she wasn't going to recover it. Her emotions were fully engaged in this case and she'd have to work extra hard to shut them down. So she could do the best thing for everyone. Including herself.

Kyle watched Grace drive away through the window and uncurled his fists before he punched a wall. Maybe he'd punch Liam instead.

He owed his brother one, after all, and it sure looked as though Liam was determined to be yet another roadblock in a series of roadblocks standing between Kyle and fatherhood. Most of the problems couldn't be resolved easily. But Liam wanting Kyle's kids? That was one thing that Kyle could do something about.

So he went looking for him.

Wade land surrounded the main house to the tune of about ten thousand acres. There was a time when a scouting mission like this one would have been no sweat, but with a messed-up leg, the trek winded Kyle about fifteen minutes in. Which sucked. It was tough to be sidelined, tough to reconcile no longer being in top physical condition. Tough to keep it all inside.

Kyle found Liam in the horse barn, which was situated a good half mile away from the main house. *Barn* was too simplistic a term to describe the grandiose building with a flagstone pathway to the entrance, fussy landscaping and a show arena on the far end. The ranch offices and a fancy lounge were tucked inside, but he didn't bother to gawk. His leg hurt and the walk wasn't far enough to burn off the mad Kyle had generated while talking to Grace.

Who was somehow even more beautiful than he recalled. How was that possible when he'd already put her on a pedestal in his mind as the ideal? How would any other woman ever compare? None could. And the lady herself still got him way too hot and bothered with a coy glance. It was enough to drive a man insane. She'd screwed him up so bad, he couldn't do anything other than weekend flings, like the one he'd had with Margaret. Look where that had gotten him.

Grace was a great big problem in a whole heap of problems. But not one he could deal with this minute. Liam? That was something he could handle.

He watched Liam back out of a stall housing one of the

quarter horses Wade Ranch bred commercially, waiting until his brother was clear of the door to speak. He had enough respect for the damage a spooked eleven-hundred-pound animal could do to a man to stay clear.

"What's this crap about you wanting to adopt my kids?" he said when Liam noticed him.

Liam snorted. "Grace must have come by. She tell you to sign the papers?"

No one ordered Kyle around, least of all Grace.

"She told me you've got your sights set on my family." He crossed his arms before he made good on the impulse to smash his brother in the mouth for even uttering Grace's name. She'd meant everything to Kyle, but to Liam, she was yet another in a long line of his women. "Back off. I'm taking responsibility for them whether you like it or not."

Sticking a piece of clean straw between his back teeth, Liam cocked a hip and leaned against the closed stall door as if he hadn't a care in the world. Lazily, he rearranged his battered hat. "Tell me something. What's the annual revenue Wade Ranch brings in for stud fees?"

"How should I know?" Kyle ground out. "You run the ranch."

"Yeah." Liam raised his brows sardonically. "Half of which belongs to you. Grandpa died almost two years ago, yet you've never lifted a finger to even find out what I do here. Money pours into your bank account on a monthly basis. Know how that happens? Because I make sure of it. I made sure of a lot of things while you ran around the Middle East blowing stuff up and ignoring your responsibilities at home. One of those things I do is take care of Maddie and Maggie. Because you weren't here. Just like you weren't here to take on any responsibility for the ranch. I will not let you be an absentee father like you've been an absentee ranch owner."

"That's a low blow," Kyle said softly. Liam had always

viewed Kyle's stint as a SEAL with a bit of disdain, making it clear he saw it as a cop-out. "You wanted the ranch. I didn't. But I want my girls, and I'm going to be here for them."

Wade Ranch had never meant anything to him other than a place to live because it was the only one he had. Then and now. Mama had cut and run faster than you could spit, once she'd dumped him and Liam here with her father, then taken the Dallas real estate market by storm. Lillian Wade had quickly become the Barbara Corcoran of the South and forgot all about the two little boys she'd abandoned.

Funny how Liam had been so similarly affected by dear old Mama. Enough to want to guarantee his blood wouldn't ever have to know the sting of desertion. Kyle respected the thought if not the action. But Kyle was one up on Liam, because those girls were his daughters. He wasn't about to take lessons from Mama on how to be a runaway parent.

"Too little, too late," his brother mouthed around the straw. "Hadley and I want to adopt them. I hope you have a good lawyer in your back pocket because you're not getting those girls without a hell of a fight."

God Almighty. The hits kept coming. He'd barely had time to get his feet under him from being sucker punched a minute after crossing the threshold of his childhood home, only to have Liam drop twin daughters, Grace Haines and a custody battle in his lap.

They stared at each other, neither blinking. Neither backing down. They were both stubborn enough to stand there until the cows came home, and probably would, too.

Nothing was going to get fixed this way, and with Grace's admonition to prove he was serious about providing a stable environment for Maddie and Maggie ringing in his ears, he contemplated his mule-headed brother. He wanted help with the ranch? By God, he'd get it. And

Kyle would have employment to put on his Fatherhood Résumé, which would hopefully get Grace off his back at the same time.

"Give me a job if it means so much to you that I take ranch ownership seriously. I'll do something with the horses."

Liam nearly busted a gut laughing, which did not improve Kyle's grip on his temper. "You can feed them. But that's about it. You have no training."

And Kyle wasn't at 100 percent physically, but no one had to know about that. His injuries mostly didn't count anyway. It just meant he had to work that much harder, which he'd do. Those babies were worth a little agony.

"I can learn. You can't have it both ways. Either you give me a shot at being half owner of Wade Ranch or shut up about it."

"All right, smart-ass." Liam tipped back his hat and jerked his chin at Kyle. "We got a whole cattle division here at Wade Ranch that's ripe for improvement. I've been concentrating on the horses and letting Danny and Emma Jane handle that side. You take over."

"Done."

Kyle knew even less about cows than he did babies. But he hadn't known anything about guns or explosives before joining the navy, either. BUD/S training had nearly broken him, but he'd learned how to survive impossible physical conditions, learned how to stretch his body to the point of exhaustion and still come out swinging when the next challenge reared its ugly head.

You had to start out with the mind-set that quitting wasn't an option. Even the smallest mental slip would finish a man. So he wouldn't slip.

Liam eyed him and shook his head. "You're serious?"

"As a heart attack. I'll take my best shot at the cattle side of the ranch. Just one question. What am I aiming at?"

"We have a Black Angus breeding program. Emma Jane—she's the sales manager I hired last year—is great. She sold about two hundred head. If you want me to call you successful, double that in under six months."

That didn't sound too bad, especially if there was a sales manager already doing the heavy lifting. "No problem. Now drop the whole adoption idea and we'll call it even."

"Let me see you in action, and then we'll talk. I have yet to see anything that tells me you're planning to stick around. If you take off again, the babies will be mine anyway. Might as well make it legal sooner rather than later." Liam shrugged. "You made your bed by leaving. So lie in it for a while."

Yeah, except he'd left for very specific reasons. He and Liam had never been close, and Kyle hadn't felt as if he was part of anything until he'd found his brothers of the heart on a SEAL team. That's where he'd finally felt secure. He could actually care about someone again without fear of being either abandoned or betrayed.

He'd like to say he could find a way to stay at the ranch this time. But what had changed from the first time? Not much.

Just that he was a father now. And he owed his daughters a stable home life. They were amazing little creatures that he wanted to see grow up. With the additional complications of Maddie's health problems, he couldn't relocate them at the drop of a hat, either.

"I'm not going anywhere," Kyle repeated for what felt like the four hundredth time.

Maybe if he kept saying it, people would believe him. Maybe he'd believe it, too.

Three

Kyle drove into town later that night on an errand for Hadley, who had announced at dinner that the babies were almost out of both diapers and formula. She'd seemed surprised when he said he'd go instead.

Of course he'd volunteered for the job. They were his kids. But he'd made Hadley write down exactly what he needed to buy, because the only formula he'd had exposure to was the one for making homemade explosives. List in his pocket, he'd swung into his truck, intending to grab the baby items and be back in jiffy.

But as he pulled into the lot at Royal's one-and-only grocery store, Grace had just exited through the automatic sliding doors. Well, well, well. There was no way he was passing up this opportunity. He still had a boatload of questions for the girl he'd once given his heart to, only to have it handed back, shredded worse than Black Angus at a slaughterhouse.

Kyle waited until she was almost to her car, and then

gingerly climbed from his truck to corner her between her Toyota and the Dooley in the next spot.

"Lovely night, isn't it, Ms. Haines?"

She jumped and spun around, bobbling her plastic sack full of her grocery store purchases. "You scared me."

"Guilty conscience maybe," he offered silkily. No time like the present to give her a chance to own up to the crimes she'd committed so long ago. He might even forgive her if she just said she was sorry.

"No, more like I'm a woman in a dark parking lot and I hear a man speaking to me unexpectedly."

It was a perfectly legitimate thing to say except the streetlight spilled over her face, illuminating her scowl and negating her point about a dark parking lot. She was that bent up about him saying *hey* outside of a well-lit grocery store?

He raised a brow. "This is Royal. The most danger you'd find in the parking lot of the HEB is a runaway shopping cart."

"You've been gone a long time, Kyle. Things have changed."

Yeah, more than he'd have liked. Grace's voice had deepened. It was far sexier than he'd recalled, and he'd thought about her a lot. Her curves were lusher, as if she'd gained a few pounds in all the right places, and he had an unexpected urge to pull her against him so he could explore every last change, hands on.

Okay, the way he constantly wanted her? *That* was still the same. He'd always been crazy over her. She'd been an exercise in patience, making him wait until they'd been dating a year *and* she'd turned eighteen before she'd sleep with him the first time. And that had been so mind-blowing, he'd immediately started working on the second encounter, then the third. And so on.

The fact that he'd fallen in love with her along the way

was the craziest thing. He didn't make it a habit to let people in. She'd been an exception, one he hadn't been able to help.

"You haven't changed," he said without thinking. "You're still the prettiest girl in the whole town."

Now why had he gone and said something like that? Just because it was true didn't mean he should run off at the mouth. Last thing he needed was to give her the slightest opening. She'd slide right under his skin again, just as she'd done the first time, as if his barriers against people who might hurt him didn't exist.

"Flattery?" She rolled her eyes. "That was a lame line. Plus, I already told you I'd handle your case impartially. There's no point in trying to butter me up."

Oh, so she thought she was immune to his charm, did she? He grinned and shifted his weight off his bad leg, cocking his right hip out casually as if he'd meant to strike that stance all along. "I wouldn't dream of it. That was the God-honest truth. I've been around the world, and I know a thing or two about attractive women. No law against telling one so."

"Well, I don't like it. Are you really that clueless, Kyle?"

The scowl crawled back onto her face and it tripped his Spidey-sense. Or at least that's what he'd always called it. He'd discovered in SEAL training that he had no small amount of skill in reading a situation or a person. Before then, he'd spent a lot of time by himself—purposefully—and never paid much attention to people's tells. Honing that ability had served him well in hostile territory.

So he could easily see Grace was mad. At *him*.

What was that all about? She was the one who'd dumped him cold with no explanation other than she wanted to concentrate on school, which was bull. She'd been a straight-A student before they'd started dating and maintained her grade point average until the day she graduated a year after he had. Best he could figure, she'd wanted Liam instead and hadn't wasted any time getting with his brother once she was free and clear.

"You got something to say, Grace?" He crossed his arms and leaned against her four-door sedan. "Seems like you got a bee in your bonnet."

Maybe Liam had thrown her over too quickly and she'd lumped her hurt feelings into a big Wade bucket. And now he was giving her a second shot to spill it. He just wanted her to admit she'd hurt him and then say she was sorry. That she'd picked the wrong brother when she'd hooked up with Liam. Then maybe he could go on and meet someone new and exciting who didn't constantly remind him that Kyle, women and relationships didn't mix well. Maybe he'd even find a way to trust a woman again. He could finally move on from Grace Haines.

She licked her lips and stared at the sky over his shoulder. "I'm sorry. I'm not handling this well. The babies are important to me. All my cases are, but because we used to date, I want to ensure there's no hint of impropriety. All the decisions I make should be based on facts and your ability to provide a good home. So please don't say things like you think I'm pretty."

Something that felt a lot like disappointment whacked him between the eyes. She had yet to mention the episode with Liam. Maybe she didn't even know that Kyle had seen them together, or didn't care. No, he'd never said anything to her about it, either, because some things should be obvious. You didn't fool around with a guy's brother. It was a universal law and if he had to spell that out, Grace wasn't as great a girl as he'd always thought.

"Well, then," Kyle said easily. "Maybe you should transfer my case to someone else in the county, so you don't have to deal with my brand of truth."

She probably didn't even remember what she'd done

with Liam and most likely thought Kyle had moved on. He *should* have moved on. It was way past time.

She shook her head. "Can't. We're overloaded. So we're stuck with each other."

Which meant she'd checked into it. That was somehow more disappointing than her skipping over the apology he was owed.

No matter.

Grace was just a woman he used to date. That's all. There was nothing between them any longer. He'd spent years shutting down everything inside and he'd keep on doing it. Nothing new here.

And she had his babies and their future in the palm of her hand. This was the one person he needed on his side. They could both stand to act like adults about this situation and focus on what was good for the children. It would be a good idea to do exactly as he suggested to her and let bygones be bygones. Even though he hadn't meant a word of it at the time.

"You're right. I'm sorry, too. Let's start over, friendly-like." He held out his hand for her to shake.

She hesitated for an eternity and then reached out to take it.

The contact sang through his palm, setting off all kinds of fireworks in places that had been cold and dark for a really long time. Gripping his hand tight, she met his gaze and held it.

The depths of her brown eyes heated, melting a little of the ice in his heart.

Her mouth would be sweet under his, and her skin would be soft and fragrant. The moon had risen, spilling silver light over the parking lot, and the gentle breeze played with her hair. The atmosphere couldn't be more romantic if he'd ordered it up. He barely resisted yanking her into his arms.

Yeah, he was in a lot of trouble if he was supposed to keep this friendly and impartial. She was his babies' case-worker. But the fact of the matter was that he had never gotten over Grace Haines. He could no sooner shut down his feelings about her than he could pick up her Toyota with one hand. And being around her again was pure torture.

The next morning, Kyle woke at dawn the way he always did. He'd weaned himself off an alarm clock about two weeks into BUD/S training and hadn't ever gone back.

He lay there staring at the ceiling of his old room at Wade House. Reorientation time. *Not a SEAL. Not in Afghanistan. Not in the hospital*—which had been its own kind of nightmare. This was the hardest part of the day. Every morning, he took stock, so he'd know who and where he was. Then he thanked God for the opportunity to serve his country and cursed the evil that had required it.

This was also the time of day when he made the decision to leave the pain pills in the bottle, where they belonged.

Some days, that decision was tougher than others. There was a deep, dark place inside that craved the oblivion the drugs would surely bring. That's why he'd never cracked open the seal on the bottle. Too easy to have a mental slip and think *just this once*. That was cheating, and Kyle had never taken that route.

Today would not mark the start of it, either.

Today did mark the start of something, though. A new kind of taking stock about the things he was instead of the things he wasn't. *A father. A cattle rancher.* He liked the sound of that. It was nice to have some positives to call out. He needed positives after six months of hell.

Of course, Grace would be watching over his shoulder, and Liam was going to be smack in the middle of Kyle's steps toward fatherhood *and* ranching. The two people he distrusted the most and both held the keys to his future.

He rolled from bed and pulled on a new long-sleeved shirt, jeans and boots. Eventually, his wardrobe would be work-worn like Liam's, but for now, he'd have to settle for looking like a rhinestone cowboy instead of a real one. Coffee beckoned, so he took the back stairway from the third floor to the ground floor kitchen, albeit a bit more slowly than he'd have liked.

Hadley had beaten him to the coffeepot and turned with a smile when he entered. "Good morning. Sleep well?"

"Fine," he lied. He'd lain awake far too long thinking about how this woman and his brother wanted to take his kids away. "And you?"

"Great. The babies only woke up once and thankfully at the same time. It's not always like that. Sometimes they wake up all night long at intervals." She laughed good-naturedly and lowered her voice. "I think they plan it out ahead of time just to make me nuts."

Guilt crushed Kyle's lungs and he struggled to breathe. Some father he was. They'd agreed the night before that Hadley would continue in her role as Maddie and Maggie's caretaker until Kyle got his feet under him, but it didn't feel any more right this morning than it had then. His sister-in-law was getting up in the middle of the night with his kids, scant hours after he gave Liam and Grace a big speech about how he was all prepared to step up and provide a loving environment.

No more.

"I appreciate what you're doing for my daughters," he rasped, and cleared his throat. "But I want to take care of them from now on. I'll get up with them at night."

Hadley stared at him. "You have no idea what you're talking about, do you?"

"Uh, well…" Should he brazen it out or admit defeat?

God Almighty, he hated admitting any kind of weakness. But chances were good she'd already figured out he wasn't the brightest bulb on the board when it came to babies. "I'm going to learn. Trial by fire is how I operate best."

"They're not going to pull out AK-47s, Kyle." Hadley hid a smile but not very well and handed him a cup of steaming coffee. "Sugar and creamer are on the table."

"I like it black, thanks." He sipped and added *good coffee* to his list of things he was thankful for. "Tell me the things I need to know about my kids."

"Okay." She nodded and went over a list of basics, which Kyle committed to memory. Eating. Bathing. Sleeping. Check, check, check. Stuff all humans needed, but his little humans couldn't do these things for themselves. He just had to help them, the way he would a wounded teammate.

"Can I see them?" he asked. Felt weird to be asking permission, but he didn't want to mess up anything.

"You can. They're sleeping, but we can sneak in. You can be quiet, right?"

"Quiet enough to take out a barracks full of enemy soldiers without getting caught," he said without a trace of irony. Hadley just smiled as though he was kidding.

He followed Hadley to the nursery, a mysterious place full of pink and tiny beds with bars. The girls were asleep in their cribs, and he watched them for a moment, his throat tight. Their little faces—how could anything be that tiny and survive? A better question was, how did your heart stay stitched together when it felt as if it would burst from all the stuff swelling up inside it?

"I was their nanny first, you know," she whispered. "Before I married Liam."

What did a nanny even do? Was she like a babysitter and a substitute mom all rolled up into one? If so, that seemed like a bonus, and he'd be cutting off his nose to spite his face to relieve her of her duties. She could keep on being the nanny as far as he was concerned, as long as Grace was okay with it. She must be. Liam had hired Hadley, after all, and Grace seemed pretty impressed with them as a team.

"I'm not trying to take away your job," he mumbled.

Did she see it as a job? If she and Liam wanted to adopt the girls, she'd obviously grown very attached to them. Was it better to cut off their contact with the babies instead? Get them used to the idea?

If so, he couldn't do it. It seemed unnecessarily cruel and besides, he needed the help.

"I didn't think you were. It's admirable that you want to care for them, but there's a huge learning curve and they won't do well with a big disruption. Let's take it one step at a time."

He could do that. You didn't drop a green recruit into the middle of a Taliban hotbed and expect him to wipe out the insurgents as his first assignment. You started him out with something simple, like surveillance. "Can I watch you feed them?"

"Sure, when they wake up."

They tiptoed from the room and Kyle considered that a pretty successful start to Operation: Fatherhood.

Next up, Operation: Do Something About Grace. Because he'd lain awake last night thinking about her more than he'd wanted to, as well. Somehow, he had to shut down the spark between them. Or hose it off with a big, wet kiss.

Grace sat in her car outside of Wade House and pretended that she was going over some notes in her case file. In truth, her stomach was doing a cancan at the prospect of seeing Kyle again, and she couldn't get it to settle.

She'd gone a long time without seeing him. What was so different now?

Nothing. She was a professional and she would do her job. *Get out of the car*, she admonished herself. *Get in there and do your assessment.* The faster she gathered the facts needed to remove the babies from Kyle's presence and provide a recommendation for their permanent home, the better.

Hadley let her into the house and directed her to the second floor, where Kyle was hanging out with the babies. Perfect. She could watch him interact with them and record some impartial observations in her files.

But when Grace poked her head into the nursery with a bright smile, it died on her face. Kyle dozed in the rocking chair, Maddie against one shoulder, Maggie the other. Both babies were asleep, swaddled in soft pink blankets, an odd contrast to Kyle's masculine attire.

But that wasn't the arresting part. It was Kyle. Unguarded, vulnerable. Sweet even, with his large hands cradled protectively around each of his daughters. He should look ridiculous in the middle of a nursery decorated to the nth degree with girlie colors and baby items. But he looked anything but. His powerful body scarcely fit into the rocking chair, biceps and broad shoulders spilling past the edges of the back. He'd always been incredibly handsome, but on the wiry side.

No more. He was built like a tank, and she could easily imagine this man taking out any threat in a mile-wide radius.

It was a lot more affecting than she would ever admit.

And then his eyelids blinked open. He didn't move a muscle otherwise, but his keen gaze zeroed in on her. Fully alert. Those hard green eyes cut through her, leaving her feeling exposed and much more aware of Kyle than she'd been a minute ago. Which was saying something, given her thoughts had already been pretty graphic.

It was heady to be in his sights like that. He'd always

looked at her as if they shared something special that no one else could or would be involved in. But he'd honed his focus over the years into something new and razor sharp. Flustered, she wiggled her fingers in a half wave, and that's when he smiled.

It hit her in the soft part of her heart and spread a warmth she did not want to feel. But oh, my, it was delicious. Like when he'd taken her hand in the parking lot last night. That feeling—she'd missed it.

She'd lain awake last night imagining that he'd kissed her the way she'd have sworn he wanted to as they stood under that streetlight. It was all wrong between them. Kissing wasn't allowed, wasn't part of the agenda, wasn't what should happen. But it didn't stop her from thinking about it.

She was in a lot of trouble.

"Hi," she murmured, because she felt that she had to say something instead of standing there ogling a gorgeous man as he rocked his infant daughters against an explosion of pink.

"Hi," he mouthed back. "Is it time for our visit already?"

She nodded. "I can come back."

She didn't move as he gave a slight shake of his head. Carefully, he peeled his body from the chair, not jostling even one hair on the head of his precious bundles. As if he'd done it a million times, he laid first one, then the other in their cribs. Neither one woke.

It was a sight to see.

He turned and tiptoed toward the door, but she hadn't moved from her frozen stance in the doorway yet. She should move.

But he stopped right there in front of her, a half smile lingering on his lips as he laid a hand on her arm, presumably to usher her from the room ahead of him. His palm was warm and her skin tingled under it. The feeling threat-

ened to engulf her whole body in a way that she hadn't
been *engulfed* in a long time.

Not since Kyle.

Goodness, it seemed so ridiculous, but the real reason it
hadn't been hard to stop dating was because no one compared. She was almost thirty and had only had one lover in
her life—this man before her with the sparkling green eyes
and beautiful face. And she'd take that secret to the grave.

Her cheeks heated as she imagined admitting such a
thing to a guy who had likely cut a wide swath through
the eligible women beating a path to his door. He hadn't
let the grass grow under his feet, now, had he? Father-
ing twins with a woman he'd written off soon after spoke
loudly enough to that question.

If she told him, he'd mistakenly assume she still had
feelings for him, and that wasn't exactly true. She just
couldn't find a man who fit her stringent criteria for intimacy. Call it old-fashioned, but she wanted to be in love
before making love. And most men weren't willing to be
that patient.

Except Kyle. He'd never uttered one single complaint
when he found out she wasn't hopping into his bed after
a few weeks of dating. And oh, my, had it been worth the
wait.

The heat in her cheeks spread, and the tingles weren't
just under his palm. No, they were a good bit more in a region where she shouldn't be getting so hot, especially not
over Kyle and his brand-new warrior's body, laser-sharp
focus and gentle hands.

Mercy, she should stop thinking about all that. Except
he was looking at her the way he had last night, gaze on
her lips, and she wondered if he'd actually do it this time—
kiss her as he had so many times before.

One of the babies yowled and the moment broke into
pieces.

Kyle's expression instantly morphed into one of concern as he spun toward the crib of the crying infant. Maddie. It was easy to tell them apart if you knew she was the smaller of the two girls. She'd worn a heart monitor for a long time but Grace didn't see the telltale wires poking out of the baby's tiny outfit. Hopefully that meant the multiple surgeries had been successful.

"Hey, now. What's all this fuss?" he murmured, and scooped up the bundle of pink, holding her to his shoulder with rocking motions.

The baby cried harder. Lines of frustration popped up around Kyle's mouth as he kept trying different positions against his shoulder, rocking harder, then slower.

"You liked this earlier," he said. "I'm following procedure here, little lady. Give me a break."

Grace hid a smile. "Maybe her diaper is wet."

Kyle nodded and strode to the changing table. "One diaper change, coming up."

He pulled a diaper from the drawer under the table, laid the baby on the foam pad, then tied the holding straps designed to keep Maddie from rolling to the ground with intricate knots. Next, he lined up the baby powder and diaper rash cream, determination rolling from him in thick waves. When the man put his mind to something, it was dizzying to watch.

With precision, he stripped the baby out of her onesie and took a swift kick to the wrist with good humor as he changed her diaper. It didn't help. The baby wailed a little louder.

"No problem," he said. "Babies usually cry for three reasons. They want to be held. Diaper. And…" A line appeared between Kyle's brows.

Then Maggie woke up and cried in harmony with her sister.

"Want me to pick her up?" Grace asked.

"No. I can handle this. Don't count me out yet." He nestled the other baby into his arms, rocking both with little murmurs. "Bottle. That was the other one Hadley said. We'll try eating."

Bless his heart. He'd gone to Hadley for baby lessons. He was trying so hard, much harder than she'd expected. It warmed her in a whole different way than the sizzle a moment ago. And the swell in her heart was much more dangerous.

The bottle did the trick. After Kyle got both girls fed, they quieted down and fell back asleep in their cribs. This time, he and Grace made it out of the room, but when they reached the living area off the kitchen, *flustered* was too kind a word for the state of her nerves.

Kyle collapsed on the couch with a groan.

"So," she croaked after taking a seat as far away from him as possible. "That was pretty stressful."

"Nah." He scrubbed his face with his hand and peeked out through his fingers. "Stressful is dismantling a home-made pipe bomb before it kills someone."

They'd never talked about his life in the military—largely because he was so closemouthed about it—and judging from the shadows she glimpsed in his expression sometimes, the experience hadn't softened him up any, that was for sure. "Is that what you did overseas? Handle explosives?"

Slowly, he nodded. "That was my specialty, yeah."

He could have died. Easily. A hundred times over, and she'd probably never have known until they paraded his flag-draped coffin through the streets of Royal. The thought was upsetting in a way she really didn't understand, which only served to heighten her already-precarious emotional state.

He'd been serving his country, not using the military as an excuse to stay away. The realization swept through her, blowing away some of her anger and leaving in its place a bit of guilt over never acknowledging his sacrifices in the name of liberty.

"And now you're ready to buckle down and be a father."

It seemed ludicrous. This powerful, strapping man wanted to trade bombs for babies. But when she recalled the finesse he used when handling the babies, she couldn't deny that he had a delicate touch.

"I do what needs to be done," he said quietly, and his green eyes radiated sincerity that she couldn't quite look away from.

When had Kyle become so responsible? Such an *adult*? He was different in such baffling, subtle ways that she kept stumbling in her quest to objectively assess his fitness as a parent.

"Did you give any thought to our discussion yesterday?" she asked.

"The job? I signed on to head up Wade Ranch's cattle division. How's that for serious?"

Kyle leaned back against the couch cushions, looking much more at home in this less formal area than he'd been in the Victorian parlor yesterday, and crossed one booted foot over his knee. Cowboy boots, not the military-issue black boots he'd been wearing yesterday. It was a small detail, but a telling one.

He'd quietly transitioned roles when she wasn't looking. Could it mean he'd been telling the truth when he'd said he planned to stay this time?

"It's a start," she said simply, but that didn't begin to describe what was actually starting.

She'd have to adjust every last thing she'd ever thought about Kyle Wade and his ability to be a father. And if she did, she might also have to think about him differently in a lot of other respects as well, such as whether or not he'd grown up enough to become her everything once again. But this time forever.

Four

Kyle reported to the Wade Ranch cattle barn for duty at zero dark thirty. At least he'd remembered to refer to the beasts as cattle instead of cows. Slowly but surely, snippets of his youth had started coming back to him as he'd driven to the barn. He'd watched his grandfather, Calvin Wade, manage the ranch for years. Kyle remembered perching on the top rail of the cattle pen while Calvin branded the calves or helped Doc Glade with injured cows.

Things had changed significantly since then. The cattle barn had been rebuilt and relocated a half mile from the main house. It was completely separate from the horse business, and Liam's lack of interest in the cattle side couldn't have been clearer. His brother had even hired a ranch manager.

Kyle could practically hear the rattle of Grandpa rolling over in his grave.

He'd always insisted that a man had to manage his own business and Calvin hadn't had much respect for "gentleman" ranchers who spent their money on women and whiskey and hired other men to do the work of running the ranch. Clearly Liam hadn't agreed.

The red barn dominated the clearing ahead. A long empty pen ran along the side of the building. The cattle must be roaming. Kyle parked his truck in a lot near a handful of other vehicles with the Wade Ranch logo on the doors. Easing from the cab, he hit the ground with bated breath. So far, so good. The cowboy boots were a little stiff and the heel put his leg at a weird angle, but he was going to ignore all that as long as possible.

He strolled to the barn, which had an office similar to the one in the horse barn. But that's where the similarities ended. This was a working barn, complete with the smell of manure and hay. Kyle had smelled a lot worse. It reminded him of Grandpa, and there was something nice about following in Calvin's footsteps. They'd never been close, but then Kyle had never been close with anyone. Except Grace.

The ranch manager, Danny Spencer, watched Kyle approach and spat on the ground as he contemplated his new boss.

"You pick out a horse yet, son?"

Kyle's hackles rose. He was no one's son, least of all this man who was maybe fifteen years his senior. It was a deliberate choice of phrasing designed to put Kyle in his place. Wasn't going to work. "First day on the job."

"We ride here. You skedaddle on over to the other barn and come back on a horse. Then we'll talk."

It felt like a test and Kyle intended to pass. So he climbed back into his truck and drove to the horse barn. He felt like a mama's boy driving. But he was in a hurry to get started and walking wasn't one of his skills right now.

Maybe one day.

Liam was already at the barn, favoring an early start

as well, apparently. He helped Kyle find a suitable mount without one smart-alecky comment, which did not go unnoticed. Kyle just chose not to say anything about it.

A few ranch hands gathered to watch, probably hoping Kyle would bust his ass a couple of times and they could video it with their cell phones. He wondered what they'd been told about Kyle's return. Did everyone know about the babies and Margaret's death?

Sucker's bet. Of course they did. Wade Ranch was its own kind of small town. Didn't matter. Kyle was the boss, whether they liked it or not. Whether he had the slightest clue what he was doing. Or not.

The horse didn't like him any better than Danny Spencer did. When he stuck a boot in the stirrup, the animal tried to dance sideways and would have bucked him off if Kyle hadn't kept a tight grip on the pommel. "Hey, now. Settle down."

Liam had called the horse Lightning Rod. Dumb name. But it was all Kyle had.

"That's a good boy, Lightning Rod." It seemed to calm the dark brown quarter horse somewhat, so Kyle tried to stick his boot in the stirrup again. This time, he ended up in the saddle, which felt just as foreign as everything else on the ranch did.

The ranch hands applauded sarcastically, mumbling to each other. He almost apologized for ruining their fun— also sarcastically—but he let it go.

Somehow, Kyle managed to get up to a trot as he rode out onto the trail back to the cattle barn. It had been a lifetime since he'd ridden a horse and longer than that since he'd wanted to.

God, everything hurt. The trot was more of a trounce, and he longed for the bite of rock under his belly as he dismantled a homemade cherry bomb placed carefully under a mosque where three hundred people worshipped. That he understood at least. How he'd landed in the middle of a job managing cattle, he didn't.

Oh, right. He was doing this to prove to everyone they were wrong about him. That he wasn't a slacker who'd ignored messages about his flesh and blood. That Liam and Grace and Danny Spencer and everyone else who had a bone to pick with him weren't going to make him quit.

When he got back to the cattle barn, Danny and the cattle hands were hanging around waiting. One of the disappointed guys from the horse barn had probably texted ahead, hoping someone else could get video of the boss falling off his mount. They could all keep being disappointed.

"One cattle rancher on a horse, as ordered," Kyle called mildly, keeping his ire under wraps. Someone wanted to know what he really thought about things? Too bad. No one was privy to what went on inside Kyle's head except Kyle. As always.

"That'll do," Danny said with a nod, but his scowl didn't loosen up any. "We got a few hundred head in the north pasture that need to be rounded up. You take Slim and Johnny and ya'll bring 'em back, hear?"

"Nothing wrong with my ears," Kyle drawled lazily. "What's wrong is that I'm the one calling the shots now. What do you say we chat about that for a bit?"

Danny spat on the ground near Lighting Rod's left front hoof and the horse flicked his head back in response. Kyle choked up on the reins before his mount got the brilliant idea to bolt.

"I'd say you started drinking early this a.m. if you think you're calling the shots, jarhead."

Kyle let loose a wry chuckle, friendly like, so no one got the wrong idea. "You might want to brush up on your insults. Jarheads are marines, not SEALs."

"Same thing."

Neither of them blinked as Kyle grinned. "Nah. The marines let anyone in, even old cowhands with bad attitudes. Want me to pass your number on to a recruiter? I'll let you go a couple of rounds with a drill sergeant, and when you come back, you can talk to me about the difference between marines and SEALs all you want. Until then, my last name is Wade and the only thing you're permitted to call me is 'boss.'"

Spencer didn't flinch but neither did he nod and play along. He spun on his heel and disappeared into the barn with a backhanded wave. Kyle considered it a win that the man hadn't flipped him a one-fingered salute as a bonus.

Now that the unpleasantness was out of the way, Kyle nodded at the two hands the ranch manager had singled out as his lieutenants, one of whom had fifty pounds on him. That one must be Slim. It was the kind of joke cowboys seemed to like. Kyle would probably be *jarhead* until the day he died after a recounting of his showdown with Danny Spencer made the gossip rounds.

"You boys have a problem working for me?" he asked them both.

Slim's expression was nothing short of hostile, but he and Johnny both shook their heads and swung up on their horses, trotting obediently after Kyle as he headed north toward the pasture where the cattle he was supposed to herd were grazing.

Then he just needed to figure out how to do it. Without alienating anyone else. Oh, and without falling off his horse. And without letting on to anyone that his leg was on fire already after less than thirty minutes in the saddle.

The north pasture came into view. Finally. It was still exactly where it had been ten years ago, but it felt as though it had taken a million years to get there, especially given the tense silence between Kyle and the two hands. Cattle dotted the wide swath of Wade land like black shadows against the green grass, spread as far as the eye could see, even wandering aimlessly into a copse of trees in the distance.

That was not good. He'd envisioned the cattle being easy to round up because they were all more or less in the same place. Instead, he and the hands had a very long task ahead of them to gather up the beasts, who may or may not have wanted to be gathered.

"How many?" he called over his shoulder to Johnny.

"A few hundred." Johnny repeated verbatim the vague number Danny Spencer had rattled off earlier.

He'd mellowed out some and had actually spoken to Kyle without growling. Slim, not so much. The man held a serious grudge that wouldn't be easily remedied. No big thing. They didn't have to like each other. Just work together.

"How many exactly?" Kyle asked again as patiently as possible. "We have to know if we have them all before we head back."

Johnny looked at him cockeyed as if Kyle had started speaking in tongues and thrown around a couple of snakes in the baptismal on a Sunday morning. "We just round 'em up and aim toward the barn. Nothing more to it than that."

"Maybe not before. But today, we're going to make sure we have full inventory before we make the trek." Kyle couldn't do it more than once. There was no way. "Liam didn't happen to invest in GPS, did he?"

Slim and Johnny exchanged glances. "Uh…what?"

"Satellite. RFID chips. You embed the chips in the cow's brand, for example, and use a GPS program to triangulate the chips. Technology to locate and count cattle." At the blank looks he received in response, Kyle gave up. "I'll take that as a no."

That would be Kyle's first investment as head of the cattle division at Wade Ranch. RFID chips would go a long way toward inventorying livestock that ran tame across hundreds of acres. That was how the military kept track of soldiers and supplies, after all. Seemed like a no-brainer to do the same with valuable livestock. He wondered why Liam hadn't done it already.

"All right, then." Kyle sighed. "Let's do this."

The three men rode hard for a couple of hours, driving the cattle toward the gate, eventually feeling confident that they had them all. Kyle had to accept the eyeball guesstimate from Slim and Johnny, who had "done this a couple of times." Both thought the number of bodies seemed about right. Since Kyle wasn't experienced enough to argue, he nodded and let the experts guide them home.

It was exhausting and invigorating at the same time. This was his land. His cattle. His men, despite the lack of welcome.

But when he got back to the cattle barn, Liam was waiting for him, arms crossed and a livid expression on his face.

"What now?" Kyle slid from his horse, keeping a tight grip on the pommel until he was sure his leg would support him.

"Danny Spencer quit." Liam fairly spat. "And walked out without even an hour's notice. Said he'd rather eat manure than work for you. Nice going."

"That's the best news I've heard all day." God's honest truth. The relief was huge. "He doesn't want to work for me? Fine. Better that he's gone."

Liam pulled Kyle away from the multitude of hands swarming the area by the barn, probably all with perked-up ears, hoping to catch more details about the unfolding drama.

"It's not better," Liam muttered darkly. "Are you out of your mind? You can't come in here and throw your weight around. Danny's been handling the cattle side. I told you that. This is his territory and you came in and upset the status quo in less than five minutes."

Kyle shook his head. "Not his territory anymore. It's mine."

"Seriously?" Liam's snort was half laugh and half frustration. "You don't get it. These men respect Danny. Follow him. They don't like you. What are you going to do if they all quit? You can't run a cattle division by yourself."

Yeah, but he'd rather try than put up with dissension in the ranks. Catering to the troops was the fastest way to give the enemy an advantage. There could only be one guy in charge, and it was Kyle. "They can all quit then. There are plenty of ranch hands in this area. I need men who will work, not drama queens all bent out of shape because a bigger fish swam into their pond."

"Fine." Liam threw up his hands. "You have at it. Don't say I didn't warn you. Just keep in mind that we have a deal."

His brother stomped to his truck and peeled out of the clearing with a spray of rock. Kyle resisted the urge to wave, mostly because Liam was probably too pissed to look in his rearview mirror and also because the hands were eyeing him with scowls. No point in being cocky on top of clueless.

His girls were worth whatever he had to do to figure this out.

Johnny approached him then. Kyle had just about had enough of cattle, his aching leg, difficult ranch managers and a hardheaded brother.

"What?" he snapped.

"Uh, I just wanted to tell you thanks." Johnny cleared his throat. "For your service to the country."

The genuine sentiment pierced Kyle through the stomach. And nearly put him on the ground where a day of hard riding hadn't. It was the first time anyone in Royal had positively acknowledged his time in the military. Not that he'd been expecting a three-piece band and a parade. He'd rather stay out of the spotlight—that kind of welcome was for true heroes, not a guy who'd gotten on the wrong end of a bullet.

Nonetheless, Kyle's bad day didn't seem so bad anymore.

"Yeah," he said gruffly. "You're welcome. You know someone who served?"

Usually, the only people who thought about thanking veterans were those with family or friends in the armed forces. It was just a fact. Regular people enjoyed their freedom well enough but rarely thought about the people behind the sacrifices required to secure it.

Johnny nodded, his eyes wide and full of grief. "My dad. He was killed in the first Gulf War. I was still a baby. I never got to know him."

Ouch. That was the kicker. No matter what else, Kyle and this kid had a bond that could never be broken.

Kyle simply held out his hand and waited until Johnny grasped it. "That's a shame. I'm sorry for your loss. I stood in for great fallen men like your dad and helped continue the job he started. I'm proud I got to follow in his footsteps."

The younger man shook his hand solemnly, and then there was nothing more to say. Some things didn't need words.

Kyle hit the shower when he got back to the house. When he emerged, Liam and Hadley asked if they could take the babies for a walk in their double stroller before dinner, and would he like to come?

A walk. They might as well have asked if he'd like to fly. He'd have a hard time with a crawl at this point. After the fishhooks Johnny had sunk into his heart, he'd rather be alone anyway, though it killed him to be unable to do something as simple as push his daughters in a stroller. He waved Liam and his new wife off with a smile, hoped it came across as sincere and limped into the family room to watch something inane on TV.

There was a halfway decent World War II documentary on the History Channel that caught his interest. He watched it for a few minutes until the doorbell rang.

"That was fast," he said as he yanked open the door with a grin he'd dare anyone to guess was fake, expecting to see Liam and Hadley with chagrined expressions because they'd forgotten their key.

But it was Grace. Beautiful, fresh-faced Grace, who stood on the porch with clasped hands, long brown hair down her back, wearing a long-sleeved sweater with form-fitting jeans. It was a hard to peel his eyes from her. But he did. Somehow.

"Hey, Kyle," she said simply.

His smile became real instantly. Why, he couldn't say. Grace was still a bundle of trouble tied up with a big old impossible knot. But where was the fun in leaving a tangle alone?

They'd agreed to forget about the past and start over. But they hadn't fully established what they were starting, at least not to his satisfaction. Maybe now would be a good time to get that straight.

"Hey, Grace." He crossed his arms and leaned on the door frame, cocking his busted leg to take the weight off. "What can I do for you?"

The sun shone behind her, close to setting for the day, spilling fiery reds and yellows into the deep crevices of the sky. As backdrops went, it wasn't half-bad. But it wasn't nearly as spectacular as the woman.

"We had an appointment. Earlier."

Kyle swore. He'd totally forgotten. Wasn't that just

dandy? Made him look like a stellar father to blow off his daughters' caseworker.

Fix it. He needed Grace's good favor.

"But you were off doing cowboy things," she continued. Her voice had grown a little breathy as if she'd run to the door from her car. But the scant distance between here and there sure didn't account for the pink spreading through her cheeks.

"Yep. Someone advised me I might want to find permanent employment if I hoped to be a daddy to my girls. Sorry I missed you." He raised a brow. "But it's mighty accommodating of you to reschedule, considering. 'Preciate it."

Good thing she hadn't wandered down to the barn so she could witness firsthand his impressive debut as the boss.

"No problem," she allowed. "I have to do the requisite number of site visits before I make my recommendations and I do want to be thorough."

Maybe there was room to get her mind off her recommendations and on to something a little more pleasant. *Before* she made any snap judgments about his ability to recall a small thing like an appointment with the person who had the most power to screw up his life. Well, actually, Grace was probably second, behind Kyle—if there was anyone who got the honor of being an A1 screwup thus far in this custody issue, it was him.

"Why don't we sit for a minute?" He gestured to the porch rocker to the left of the front door, which had a great view of the sunset. Might as well put Liam's revamp of the house to good use, and do some reconnaissance at the same time. Grace had to provide a report with her recommendations. He got that. But he wanted to know more about the woman providing the report than anything else at this moment.

"Oh." She glanced at the rocker and then over his shoulder into the interior of the house. "It would probably be best if I watched you interact with the girls again. Like yesterday. That's the quickest way for me to see what kind of environment you'll provide."

"That would be great. Except they aren't here. Liam and Hadley took them for a walk before dinner." Quickly, before she could ask why he hadn't joined them, he held up a finger as if a brilliant idea had just occurred to him. "Why don't you stay and eat with us? You can see how the Wade family handles meals. Meanwhile, we can hang out on the porch and wait for them to get back."

"Um…"

He closed the front door and hustled her over to the bench seat with a palm to the small of her back. To be fair, she didn't resist too much and willingly sank into the rocker, but as soon as he sat next to her, it became clear that *he* should have been the one resisting.

The essence of Grace spilled over him as they got cozy in the two-seater. It was too small for someone his size and their hips snugged up against each other. The contact burned through his jeans, sensitizing his skin, and as he tried to ease off a bit, his foot hit the porch board and set the rocker in motion. Which only knocked her against him more firmly so that her amazing breasts grazed his arm.

Actually, the rocker was exactly the right size for Kyle and Grace. Sitting in it with her might have been the best idea he'd ever had in his life.

Her fresh, spring-like scent wound through his head. They'd sat like this at her mama's house, but in the living room while pretending to watch TV on a Saturday night. It passed for a date in a place like Royal, where teenagers could either get in trouble sneaking around the football stadium with filched beer or hang out under the watchful eye of the folks. Usually Kyle and Grace had opted for the latter, at least until her parents went to bed. Then they got down to some serious making out.

He'd never been as affected by a woman as he'd been by this one. Even just a kiss could knock him for a loop. The memories of how good it had been washed through him, blasting away some of the darkness that had taken over inside. She'd always been so eager. So pliant under his mouth.

All at once, he wondered if she still tasted the same, like innocence laced with a warm breeze.

"Grace," he murmured. Somehow his arm had snaked across the back of the rocker, closing the small gap between them.

Grace's brown eyes peeked out underneath her lashes as she watched him for a moment. Maybe she was wondering the same. If that spark would still be there after all this time.

"How long will it be until Liam and Hadley are back with the girls?" she asked, her voice low.

"Later. Don't worry. We won't miss them."

"I, uh…wasn't worried."

She licked her lips, drawing his attention to her mouth, and suddenly that was all he could see. All he could think about. Her lips had filled out, along with the rest of her face. She'd grown into a woman while he'd been away, with some interesting new experiences shining in her eyes.

All at once, he wanted to know what they were.

"I've been wondering," he said. "Why did you become a social worker? I seem to recall you wanted to be a school-teacher way back."

That was not what he'd meant to ask. But she lit up at the question. And the sunset? Not even a blip in his consciousness. Her face had all the warmth a man would ever need.

"I did. Want to," she clarified. "That's what I majored in. But I went to do my student teaching and something just didn't work right. The students weren't the problem. Oh, they were a bit unruly but they were fourth graders. You gotta expect some ants in the pants. It was me. There was no…click. You know what I mean?"

"Yeah." He nodded immediately. Like when he hit his stride in BUD/S training on the second day and knew he'd found his place in the world. "Then what happened?"

"I volunteered some places for a while. Tried to get my feet under me, looking for that click. Then my mom calls me and says a friend of hers needs a receptionist because the girl in the job is going out on maternity leave. Would I do her a huge favor for three months?"

As she talked, she waved her hands, dipping and shaping the air, and he found himself smiling along with her as she recounted the story. Smiling and calculating exactly what it would take to get one of those hands on his body somewhere. He wasn't picky—not yet.

"Turns out Sheila, my mom's friend, runs an adoption agency. She's been a huge mentor to me and really helped me figure out what I wanted to do with my life. See, I love children, but I don't like teaching them. I do like helping them, though. I ended up staying at the agency for four years in various roles while I got my master's degree at night."

"You have a master's degree?" That revelation managed to get his attention off her mouth for a brief second. Not that he was shocked—she'd always been a great student. It was just one more layer to this woman that he didn't know nearly well enough.

"Yep." She nodded slowly. "The county requires it."

"That's great."

"What about you? I know you went into the military but that's about it. You went into the navy, Liam said."

"I did." He shifted uncomfortably, as he did any time his years in Afghanistan came up among civilians. The top secret nature of virtually every blessed op he'd completed was so ingrained, it was hard to have a regular conversation with anyone outside of his team. "Special operations. It's not as glamorous as the media makes it out to be. I sweated a lot, got really dirty and learned how to survive in just about any conditions. Meanwhile, I followed orders and occasionally gave a few. And now I'm home."

Something flashed deep in her eyes and she reached out. Her palm landed on his bare forearm, just below the rolled-up sleeve of his work shirt. "It doesn't sound glamorous. It sounds lonely."

"It was," he mumbled before he'd realized it. Shouldn't have admitted that. It smacked of weakness.

"I'm sorry." Her sympathy swept along his nerve endings, burying itself under his skin. The place she'd always been.

The place he'd always let her be. Because she soothed him and eased his loneliness. Always had. Looked as if for all the things that had changed, that was one constant, and he latched on to it greedily.

"It's over now."

His arm still stretched across the back of the seat. The slightest shift nestled her deeper against him and a strand of her glossy hair fell against her cheek. He wasted no time capturing it between his fingers, brushing it aside, and then letting his fingers linger.

Their gazes met and held for an eternity. A wealth of emotions swirled in her eyes.

Her skin was smooth and warm under his touch. She tilted her face toward his fingers, just a fraction of a movement. Just enough to tell him she wasn't about to push him away.

He slid his fingers more firmly under her chin and lifted it. And then those amazing lips of hers were within claiming distance. So he claimed them.

Grace opened beneath his mouth with a gasp, sucking him under instantly. Their mouths aligned, fitting together so perfectly, as if she'd been fashioned by the Almighty specifically for Kyle Wade. He'd always thought that. How was that still true?

The kiss deepened without any help on his part. He couldn't have said his own name as something raw and elemental exploded in his chest. *Grace*. The feel of her—like home and everything that was good in the world, blended together and infused into the essence of this woman.

He wanted more. And he couldn't have stopped himself from taking it.

Threading both hands through her hair, he cupped her head and changed the angle, plunging into the sensation. Taking her along with him. She moaned in her chest, and answering vibrations rocked his.

She clung to him, her hands gripping his shoulders as if she never wanted to let go. Which was great, because he didn't want her to.

Her sweet taste flowed across his tongue as he twined it with hers, greedily soaking up everything she was offering. It had been so long since he'd *felt*. Since he'd allowed himself to be so open. Hell, he hadn't *allowed* anything. She'd burrowed into his very core with nothing more than a kiss, and he'd had little to say about it.

And then she was gone. Ripped away.

She bolted from the rocker, her chest rising and falling as she hugged the split-pine railing surrounding the porch with her back. "I'm sorry. I shouldn't have done that."

"But you did." Ruthlessly, he shut down all the things she'd stirred up inside, since it appeared as if she wasn't up for seconds.

"I got caught up. That can't happen again."

Her expression glittered with undisguised longing, and no, he hadn't imagined that she'd welcomed his kiss. That she'd leaned into his touch and begged for more. So why was she stopping?

"I heartily disagree." He smiled, but it almost hurt to paint it on when his entire body was on fire. And this woman was the only one who could quench the flames. "It's practically a requirement for it to happen again."

"Are you that clueless, Kyle?"

Clueless. Yeah, he needed to catch a couple of clues apparently, like the big screaming back-off vibes Grace was shooting in his direction.

"I'm your daughters' caseworker," she reminded him with raised eyebrows. "We can't get involved."

His body cooled faster than if she'd dumped a bucket of ice water on his head. "You're right."

Of course she was right. When had he lost sight of that? This wasn't about whether she was interested or not; it was about his daughters. What had started out as a half-formed plan to distract her from work had actually distracted *him* far more effectively.

And he wanted to do it again. That was dangerous. She could take his girls away at the drop of a hat, and he couldn't afford to antagonize her. Hell, she'd even told him she had to treat the case as objectively as possible, and here he was, ignoring all of that.

Because she'd gotten to him. She'd dug under his skin without saying a word. Talk about dangerous. He couldn't let her know she had that much power over him, or she might use it to her advantage. How could he have forgotten how much better it was to keep his heart—and his mouth—shut? That's why he stuck to weekend hookups, like the one he'd had with Margaret. No one expected him to spill his guts, and then he was free to leave before anyone got a different idea about how things were going to go.

That was the best he could do. The best he *wanted* to do. But he couldn't ditch Royal this time around when things got too heated. He'd have to figure out how to get past one more tangle in the big fat knot in his chest that had Grace's name all over it.

She thought he was clueless? Just a big dumb guy who couldn't find his way around a woman without a map? Fine. It served his purpose to let her keep on thinking that, while he flipped this problem on its head.

"Sorry about that, then." He held up his hands and let a slow grin spread across his face. "Hands off from now on."

Or at least until he figured out which way the wind blew in Grace's mind about the custody issue. He couldn't afford to antagonize her, but neither could he afford to let her out of his sight. Once he had curried her good favor and secured his claim on his children, all bets were off.

And when she mumbled an excuse about having other dinner plans, he let her leave, already contemplating what kind of excuse he could find to get her into his arms again, but this time, without any of the emotional tangle she seemed to effortlessly cause.

Five

The kiss had been a mistake.

Grace knew that. She'd known *while* she was kissing Kyle. The whole time. Why, for the love of God, couldn't she stop thinking about it?

She'd kissed Kyle lots of times. None of those kisses was seared into her brain, ready to pop up in her consciousness like a jack-in-the-box gone really wrong. Of course, all her previous Kyle kisses had happened with the boy.

He was all man now.

Darker, harder, fiercer. And oh, how he had driven that fact home with nothing more than his mouth on hers. The feel of his lips had winnowed through her, sliding through her blood, waking it deliciously. Reminding her that she was all woman.

Telling her that she'd yet to fully explore what that meant.

Oh, sure, she'd kissed a few of the men she'd dated before she'd become a Professional Single Girl. But those chaste, dry pecks hadn't compared with being kissed by someone like Kyle.

She couldn't do it again. No matter how much she wanted to. No matter how little sleep she got that night and how little work she got done the next day because she couldn't erase the goose bumps from her skin that had sprung up the instant Kyle had touched her.

When Clare Connelly called with a dinner invitation, Grace jumped on it, nearly crying with relief at the thought of a distraction. Clare was a pediatric nurse who'd cared for the twin babies in the harrowing days after their premature birth, and she and Grace had become good friends.

Grace arrived at the Waters Café just off Royal's main street before Clare, so she took a seat at a four top and ordered a glass of wine while she waited. The café had been rebuilt as part of the revitalization of the downtown strip after the tornado had tried to wipe Royal off the map. The owners, Jim and Pam Waters, had nearly lost everything, but thanks to a good insurance policy and some neighborly folks, the café was going strong. Grace made it a point to eat there as often as possible, just to give good people her business.

Clare bustled through the door, her long blond hair still twisted up in her characteristic bun, likely because she'd just come from work at Royal Memorial. Grace waved, and then realized she wasn't alone—Clare had her arm looped through another woman's. Violet McCallum, who co-owned the Double M Ranch with her brother, Mac.

Wow, Grace hardly recognized her. Violet looked beautiful and was even wearing a dress instead of her usual boots and jeans. It had been a while since they'd seen each other. Not since they'd all met at Priceless, the antiques and craft store owned by Raina Patterson, to indulge in a girls' night of stained glass making, which had been so much fun that Grace had picked it up as a new hobby.

"I had to drag her out of the house," Clare said by way of greeting, laughing and pointing at Violet. It was a bit of a joke among the three ladies as Violet and Grace had done something similar for Clare when she'd been going through man troubles. "I hope you don't mind."

"Of course I don't. Hi, Violet!" Grace jumped up and embraced the auburn-haired woman. Violet gave her a one-armed hug in return and scuttled to a seat.

Grace and Clare settled into their own seats. Grace signaled the waitress, then leaned forward on her forearms to speak to Violet across the table. "What are you using on your skin? Because I'm investing in a truckload. You look positively luminous!"

Violet flinched and gave Grace a pained smile, which highlighted dark shadows in her friend's eyes. "Thanks. It's, um…my new apricot scrub. I'll text you the name of it when I get home."

"Sure," Grace said enthusiastically, but it felt a little forced. Something was off with Violet but she didn't want to pry. They'd been friends a long time. If Violet wanted to share what was up, she would. "Give me your hand, Clare. Dinner can't officially start until we ooh and aah over your ring!"

A smile split Clare's face, and she stuck her hand out, fingers spread in the classic pose of an engaged woman. "Stand back, ladies. This baby will blind you if you don't give it the proper distance."

Clare had recently gotten engaged to Dr. Parker Reese, a brilliant neonatal specialist at Royal Memorial, where they both worked. Their romance had been touch and go, framed by the desperate search for Maddie's mother after the infant had been abandoned at a truck stop shortly after her birth. Margaret Garner had then gotten into her car and given birth to Maggie a little farther down the road, ultimately dying from the traumatic childbirth. So the twins had ended up separated. When Maggie ultimately went home with Liam and Hadley, they were unaware she had a sister. Thankfully, they'd eventually realized Maddie and Maggie were twins and thus both belonged with the Wades.

Of course, that had all been before Kyle had come home.

And that was a dumb thing to start thinking about. Grace pinched herself under the table, but it didn't do any good. The kiss popped right back into her mind, exactly the thing she was trying to avoid thinking about.

Kyle was a difficult man to forget. She should know. She'd spent ten years trying to forget him and had failed spectacularly.

"Tell us about the wedding," Grace insisted brightly. Anything to take her attention off Kyle.

Clare gushed for a minute or two until the harried waitress finally made her way over to the three ladies. The ponytailed woman in her early twenties pulled a pen from behind her ear and held it expectantly over her order pad.

"Sorry for the wait, ladies," she apologized. "We're short-staffed today."

"No problem," Grace tossed out with a smile. "This Chardonnay is fabulous. Can you bring two more glasses?"

"No!" Violet burst out, and then her eyes widened as all three of the other women stared at her. "I, uh, didn't bring my driver's license, and I know you have to see my identification, so no drinking for me. Water is fine anyway. Thanks."

"It's okay, Ms. McCallum," the waitress said cheerfully. "I know you're over twenty-one. You were two years ahead of my sister in high school and she's twenty-four. I'd be happy to make an exception."

Violet turned absolutely green. "That's kind of you. But water is fine. Excuse me."

All at once, Violet rushed from the table, snatching her

purse from the back of the chair as she ran for the rear of the restaurant toward the bathrooms. In her haste, she knocked the straight-backed chair to the floor with a crash that reverberated in the half-full café. Conversations broke off instantly as the other customers swiveled to seek out the source of the noise.

Violet didn't pause until she'd disappeared from the room. *What in the world?*

"I practically had to force her to come tonight," Clare confessed, her voice lowered as she leaned close to Grace and waved off the beleaguered waitress, who promised to come back later. "I guess I shouldn't have. But she's been holed up for a few weeks now, and Mac called me, worried. He mentioned that she'd been under the weather, but he thought she was feeling better."

That was just like Violet's brother, Mac McCallum. He was the kind of guy Grace had always wished she'd had for a big brother, one who looked out for his sister even into their adulthood. Back in high school, he'd busted Tommy Masterson in the mouth for saying something off-color about Violet, and the boys in Royal had learned fast that they didn't cross Mac when it came to Violet.

"We should go check on her," Grace said firmly. Poor thing. She probably had a stomach flu or something like that, and they'd let her run off to the bathroom. Alone. "Friends hold each other's hair."

When Grace and Clare got to the restroom, Violet was standing at the sink, both hands clamped on the porcelain as she stared in the mirror, hollow eyed, supporting her full weight on her palms as if she might collapse if the vanity wasn't there to hold her up.

"You didn't have to disrupt your dinner on my account." Violet didn't glance at the other two women as she spoke into the mirror.

"Of course we did." Grace put her arm around Violet

and held her tight as she stood by her friend's side, offering the only kind of support she knew to give: physical contact. "Whatever it is, I'm sure you'll feel better soon. Sometimes it takes a while for the virus to work through your system. Do you want some crackers? Cold medicine? I'll run to the pharmacy if need be."

A brief lift of Violet's lips passed as a smile. "You're so nice to offer, but I don't think what I've got can be fixed with cold medicine."

She trembled under Grace's arm. This was no garden-variety stomach bug or spring cold, and Grace was just about to demand that Violet go see a doctor in the morning, or she'd drag her there herself, when Clare met Violet's eyes in the mirror as she came up on the other side of their friend.

"You're pregnant," Clare said decisively with a knowing smile. "I knew it. That night at Priceless... I could see then that you had that glowy look about you."

Oh. Now Grace felt like a dummy. Of course that explained Violet's strange behavior and refusal to drink the wine.

Shock flashed through Violet's expression but she banked it and then hesitated for only a moment. "No. That's impossible."

"Impossible, like you're in denial? Or impossible, like you haven't slept with anyone who could have gotten you pregnant?"

"Like, impossible, period, end of story, and now you need to drop it." Violet scowled at Clare in the mirror, who just stuck her tongue out. "It's just an upset stomach. Let's go back to the table."

With a nod that said she was dropping it but didn't like it, Clare hustled Violet to the table and ordered her hot tea with lemon, then ensured that everyone selected something to eat in her best mother-hen style.

The atmosphere grew lighter and lighter until their food came. They were just three friends having dinner, as advertised. Until Clare zeroed in on Grace and asked point-blank, "What's going on with you and Kyle Wade?"

Grace nearly choked. "What? Nothing."

Heat swept across her cheeks as she recalled in living color exactly how big a lie that was.

"Funny," Clare remarked to Grace. "I'd swear I heard mention of a highly charged *encounter* with Kyle in the parking lot of the HEB the other night. Care to fill us in?"

Violet perked up. "What's this? You're picking up with Kyle again?"

"Over my dead body!" That might have come out a little more vehement than she'd intended. "I mean…"

"I haven't seen him yet," Violet said to Clare as if Grace hadn't spoken. "But when I went to the bank yesterday, Cindy May said he's filled out and pretty much the stuff of centerfold fantasies. 'Smoking hot' was the phrase she used. Liberally."

Clare waggled her brows at Grace. "Spill the beans, dear."

Heat climbed up her cheeks. "I don't have any beans to spill. His daughters are on my case docket, and we ran into each other at the grocery store. This is Royal. It would be weird if I *hadn't* run into him."

"I haven't run into him." Violet sipped her tea. "Clare?"

The traitor shook her head. "Nope."

"Well, the Kyle train has left the station and I was not on board. I don't plan to be on board." Grace drained her glass of wine and motioned for another one the moment the waitress glanced her way. Wow, was it hot in here, and she was so thirsty. "Kyle Wade is the strong, silent type, and I need a man who can open his mouth occasionally to tell me what I mean to him. If that's not happening, I'm not happening. But it doesn't matter because nothing is going on with us. He's trying to be a father and I'm working to figure out how to let him. That's it."

All at once, she realized she'd already made up her mind about his fitness as a parent. Kyle was trying. She'd seen it over and over. What could she possibly object to in his bid for custody? Nothing. Any objections would be strictly due to hurt feelings over something that happened a decade ago. It was time to embrace the concept of bygones and move on.

"Men are nothing but trouble," Violet muttered darkly.

"That's not true," Clare corrected. "The right man is priceless."

"Parker is one in a million and he's taken. Unless you're willing to share?" Grace teased, and tried really hard to shut down the uncomfortable squeeze of jealousy surrounding her heart.

Clare had met her Dr. McDreamy. Grace had nothing. A great big void where Kyle used to be, and nothing had come along in ten years that could fill it. Well, except for the one man whom she suspected would fill that hole perfectly. She just had no desire to let him try, no matter how much she wanted a husband and family of her own.

Eyebrows raised, Clare cocked her head at Grace. "So you're sticking by your single-girl status, huh?"

She didn't sound so convinced, as if maybe Grace had been kidding when she'd vowed to be a Professional Single Girl from now on.

"I've been telling you so for months," Grace insisted. "There's nothing wrong with high standards and until I find someone who can spell *standards*, it's better to be on my own."

Actually, her standards weren't all that high—a run-of-the-mill swept-off-her-feet romance would do just fine. If she was pregnant and in love with a man who desperately loved her in return, she'd consider her life complete.

"Hear, hear." Violet raised her mug of hot tea to click it against Grace's wineglass. "I'll join your single girl club."

"Everyone is welcome. Except Clare." Grace grinned to cover the heaviness that had settled over her heart all at once. There wasn't anything on her horizon that looked like a fairy-tale romance. Just another meeting with a man who was driving her crazy.

Grace drove to Wade Ranch the next day without calling and without an appointment.

She didn't want to give Kyle any sort of heads-up that she was coming or that she'd made a decision. Hopefully, that meant she could get and keep the upper hand.

No more sunset conversations that ended with her wrapped up in Kyle's very strong, very capable arms.

No matter what. No matter how much she'd been arguing with herself that maybe Kyle had changed. Maybe *she* had changed. Maybe another kiss, exactly like that first one, would be what the doctor ordered, and then she would find out he'd morphed into her Prince Charming.

Yeah, none of that mattered.

Kyle and his daughters—that was what mattered. That morning she'd spent two hours in a room with her supervisor, Megan, going over her recommendation that Kyle be awarded full and uncontested custody of his children. With Megan's stamp of approval on the report, Grace's role in this long, drawn-out issue had come to a close.

Hadley answered the door at Wade House and asked after Grace's parents, then let Grace hold the babies without Grace having to beg too much. She inhaled their fresh powder scent—it was the best smell in the world. Out of nowhere, the prick of tears at her eyes warned her that she hadn't fully shut down the emotions from her conversation with Clare and Violet last night.

If this meeting went as intended, this might be her last

interaction with Kyle. And the babies. They were so precious and the thought of only seeing them again in passing shot through her heart.

"I'm here to see Kyle," she told Hadley as she passed the babies back reluctantly. She had a job to do, and it wasn't anyone's fault except hers that she didn't have a baby of her own.

"He's at the barn. Expect that will be the case from now on." Hadley shook her head in wonder. "I have to say, Kyle is nothing like I remember. He had no interest in the ranch before. Right? You remember that, too, don't you?"

Greedily, Grace latched on to the subject change and told herself it was strictly because she wanted additional validation that she was doing the right thing in trusting Kyle with his daughters. "I do recall that. But he's taking over the cattle side, or so I understand."

"That's right. Liam's about to come out of his skin, he's so excited about the prospect of focusing solely on his quarter horses. He didn't think Kyle was going to step up. But Liam has admitted to me, privately of course, that he might have been wrong about his brother."

Liam saw it, too. Kyle had changed.

That was very interesting food for thought.

"Do you think Kyle would mind if I visited him down at the barn? I need to talk to him about the report I'm filing."

Grace was already on her feet before she'd finished speaking, but Hadley just nodded with a smile. "Sure. Bring Kyle back with you and stay for lunch."

"Oh. Um…" Grace stared at Hadley gently rocking both babies in her arms and realized that her recommendations were going to affect Hadley and Liam, too. And not in a good way. She hated the fact that she was going to upset them after they'd spent so much love and effort in caring for Kyle's babies in his stead. There was a long conversation full of disappointment in Liam and Hadley's future.

All at once, she didn't want this job any longer. She should have figured out a way to pass the case off the moment she'd heard Kyle's name over the phone when Liam called. But she hadn't been able to, and people's lives were at stake here. She'd have to figure out how to handle it.

"Thanks for the lunch invite, but I have to be getting back to the office. Maybe next time," she said brightly, and escaped before Hadley could insist.

The cattle barn was a half mile down a chipped rock path to the west of Wade House, and faster than she would have liked, Grace pulled into the small clearing where a couple of other big trucks sat parked. She wandered into the barn, hoping Kyle would be inside.

He was.

The full force of his masculine beauty swept through her as she caught sight of him through the glass wall that partitioned the cattle office from the rest of the large barn. He was leaning against the frame of an open door, presumably talking to someone inside, hip cocked out in a way that should seem arrogant, but was just a testament to his incredible confidence.

Working man's jeans hugged his lean hips and yeah, he still had a prime butt that she didn't mind checking out in the slightest. There might be drool in her future.

And then Kyle backed out of the doorway and turned, catching her in the act of checking out his butt. *Shoot.* Too late, she spun around but not before witnessing the slow smile spreading across his face. How in the world was she going to brazen this out? Heat swirled through her cheeks.

Kyle exited the office area with a clatter. His eyes burned into her back and she had the distinct impression his gaze had dipped below her belt in a turnabout-is-fair-play-kind of checkout.

"Hey, Grace," he said pleasantly.

She couldn't very well ignore his greeting, so she sighed and faced him, smug smile and all. "Hi."

"See anything you like?"

How was she supposed to answer that? *Men.* They all had egos the size of Texas and she certainly wasn't going to cater to inflating his further. He was lucky she didn't smack him in his cocky mouth. "Nothing I haven't seen before."

Except she really shouldn't have been all high-and-mighty, when she was the one who'd been ogling his butt. It was her own darn fault she'd gotten caught.

"Really?" His eyebrows shot up and amusement played at his mouth. Not that she was staring at it or anything, or remembering how dark, hard and fierce that kiss had been. "You've been shopping for cattle before?"

"Cattle?" She made the mistake of meeting his glittery green eyes, vibrant even in the low light of the barn, and he sucked her in, mesmerizing her for a moment. "I...don't think... I'm not here to buy cattle."

Her fingers tingled all at once as they flexed in memory of clutching his shoulders the other night during their kiss. And then the rest of her body got in on that action, putting her somewhere in the vicinity of hot and bothered. A long liquid pull at her core distracted her entirely from whatever it was they were talking about.

"Are you sure? That's what we do here at Wade Ranch. Sell cattle. Figured you were in the market since you came all this way."

"Oh. No. No cattle." Geez, was there something wrong with her brain? Simple concepts like English and speaking didn't seem to be happening.

Kittens. Daffodils. She had to get her mind off that kiss with something that wasn't the slightest bit manly. But then Kyle shifted closer and she caught a whiff of something so wholly masculine and earthy and the slightest bit piney, it nearly made her weep with want.

"Well, then," he murmured. "Why are you here if it's not to peruse the goods?"

Oh, she was *so* here to peruse the goods. Except she wasn't and she couldn't keep falling down on the job. "I wanted to talk to you."

"Amazing coincidence. I wanted to talk to you, too."

"So I'm not bothering you?"

"Oh, yeah. Make no mistake, Grace. You bother me." His low, sexy voice skittered across her nerves, standing them on end. "At night, when I'm thinking about kissing you again. In the shower, when I'm *really* thinking about kissing you again. In the saddle, when I think kissing you again is the only thing that's going to make that particular position bearable."

A stupid rush of heat sprang up in her face as she pictured him riding a horse and caught his meaning.

It was uncomfortable for Kyle to sit in a saddle. Because he was turned on. By her.

It was embarrassing. And somehow empowering. The thrill of it sang through her veins. Being in love with Kyle she remembered. Being a source of discomfort, she didn't. Sex had been so new, so huge and so special the first time around. They hadn't really explored their physical relationship very thoroughly before everything had fallen apart due to Kyle's strange moods and inability to express his feelings for her.

She suddenly wondered what physical parts they'd left unexplored. And whether the superhot kiss—which had been vastly more affecting than the ones ten years ago—meant that he'd learned a few new tricks over the years.

"You've been thinking about our kiss, too?" she asked before she thought better of it.

"Too?" He picked up on that slip way too fast, his expression turning molten instantly as he zeroed in on her. "As in *also*? You've been thinking about it?"

He was aiming so much heat in her direction she thought she might melt from it.

"Um…" Well, it was too late to back out now. "Maybe once or twice. It was a nice kiss."

His slow smile set off warning bells. "*Nice.* I must be rusty if that's the best word you can come up with to describe it. Let me try again and I can guarantee *nice* won't be anywhere in your vocabulary afterward."

Before he could get started on that promise, she slapped a hand on his chest, and Lord have mercy, it was like concrete under her fingers, begging to be explored just to see if all of him was that hard.

"Not so fast," she muttered before she lost her mind completely. "I'm here in an official capacity."

"Well, why didn't you say so?"

"You were too busy trying to sell me a side of beef, if I recall," she responded primly, and his rich laugh nearly finished the job of melting her into a big puddle. She shouldn't let him affect her like that. Quickly, she snatched her hand back.

"Touché, Ms. Haines." He crossed his arms over his powerful chest and contemplated her, sobering slightly. "Is this about my girls?"

She nodded. "I've provided my recommendations in a report to my supervisor. But essentially, I have no objections to you having sole custody of your daughters."

Kyle let out a whoop and swept her up in his arms, spinning her around effortlessly. Laughing at his enthusiasm, she whacked him on the arm with token protests sputtering from her lips. This was not the appropriate way to thank his caseworker.

And then he let her slide to the floor again, much more

slowly than he should have, especially when it became clear that there was very little of him that wasn't hard.

She cleared her throat and stepped away.

"Thanks, Grace. This means a lot to me." Sincerity shone in his gaze and she couldn't look away. "So it's over? No more site visits?"

"Well…" She couldn't say it all at once. Her excuse to continue seeing him would evaporate if she said yes. "Maybe a few more. I still plan to keep an eye on you."

The vibe between them heated up again in a hurry as he leaned into her space. "But if you're not my daughters' caseworker any longer, then there's no reason I can't kiss you again."

True. But she couldn't have it both ways. Either she needed an excuse to keep coming by, even though that excuse would prevent anything from happening between them, or she could flat out admit she was still enormously attracted to him and let the chips fall where they may.

One option put butterflies in her stomach. And the other put caterpillars in it. The only problem was she couldn't figure out which was which.

"I'm not closing the case yet," she heard herself say before she'd fully planned to say it. "So I'll come by a couple more times, just to file additional support for the recommendation. It could still go the other way if anything changes."

"All right." He cocked his head. "But if you've already filed the report, there's no issue with your objectivity. Right?"

And maybe she should just call a spade a spade and settle things once and for all.

"Right. But—" she threw up a hand as a smile split his face "—that's not the only thing going on here, Kyle, and you know it. We haven't been a couple for a long time, and

I'm not sure picking up where we left off is the best idea. Not saying never. Just give me space for now."

So she could think. So she could figure out if she was willing to trust him again. So she could understand why everything between them felt so different this time, so much more dangerous and thrilling.

He nodded once, but the smile still plastered across his face said he wasn't convinced by her speech. Maybe because she hadn't convinced herself of it, either.

"You know where to find me. If you'll excuse me, I have some cattle to tend to."

She watched him walk off because she couldn't help herself apparently. And she had a feeling that was going to become a theme very shortly when interacting with Kyle Wade.

Six

Kyle didn't see Grace for a full week, and by the seventh day, he was starting to go a little bonkers. He couldn't stop thinking about her, about picking up that kiss again. Especially now that the conflict of interest had vanished.

But then she'd thrown up another wall—the dreaded *give me space*. He hated space. Unless he was the one creating it.

So instead of calling up Grace and asking her on a date the way he wanted to, he filled his days with things such as learning how to worm cattle alongside Doc Glade and his nights learning which of his daughters liked to be held a certain way.

It was fulfilling in a way he'd have never guessed.

And exhausting. Far more than going for days at a stretch with no sleep as he and his boys cleared a bayside warehouse of nasty snipers so American supply ships could dock without fear of being shot at.

Kyle would have sworn up and down that being a SEAL

had prepared him for any challenge, but he'd been able to perform that job with a sense of detachment. Oh, he'd cared, or he would never have put himself in the line of fire. But you had to march into a war knowing you might not come out. Knowing that you might cause someone else to not come out. There was no room for emotion in the middle of that.

Being a father? It was 100 percent raw emotion, 24-7. Fear that he was doing it wrong. Joy in simply holding another human being that was a part of him, who shared his DNA. Worry that he'd screw up his kids as his parents had done to him. A slight tickle in the back of his throat that it could all change tomorrow if Grace suddenly decided that she'd made a mistake in awarding him custody.

But above all else was the sense that he shouldn't be doing it by himself. Kids needed a mother. Hadley was nurturing and clearly cared about the babies, but she was Liam's wife, not Kyle's. Now that the news had come out about Grace's recommendations, it didn't seem fair to keep asking Hadley to be the nanny, not when she'd hoped to adopt the babies herself.

It was another tangle he didn't know how to unsnarl, so he left it alone until he could figure it out. Besides, no one was chomping at the bit to change the current living situation and for now, Kyle, Liam and Hadley shared Wade House with Maggie and Maddie. Which meant that it would be ridiculous to tell Hadley not to pick up one of his daughters when she cried. So he didn't.

Plus, he was deep in the middle of growing the cattle business. Calving season was upon them, which meant days and days of backbreaking work to make sure the babies survived, or the ranch lost money instantly. He couldn't spend ten or twelve hours a day at the cattle barn *and* take care of babies. That was his rationale anyway, and he repeated it to himself often. Some days it rang more true than others.

A week after Grace had told him he'd earned custody of his daughters, Kyle spent thirty horrific minutes in his office going through email and other stuff Ivy, Wade Ranch's bookkeeper and office manager, had dumped on his desk with way too cheery a smile. The woman was sadistic. Death by paper cuts might as well be Ivy's mantra.

God, he hated paperwork. He'd rather be hip-deep in manure than scanning vet reports and sales figures and bills and who knew what all.

A knock at his door saved him. He glanced up to see a smiling Emma Jane and he nearly wept in relief. Emma Jane had the best title in the whole world—sales manager—which meant he didn't have to talk to people who wanted to buy Wade Angus. She handled everything and he blessed her for it daily.

"Hey, boss," she drawled. "Got a minute?"

She always called him "boss" with a throaty undertone that made him vaguely uncomfortable, as if any second now, she might declare a preference for being dominated and fall at his feet, prostrate.

"For you, always." He kicked back from the desk and crossed his arms as the sales manager came into his office. "What's up?"

With a toss of her long blond hair, Emma Jane sashayed over to his desk and perched one hip on the edge, careful to arrange her short skirt so it revealed plenty of leg. Kyle hid a grin, mostly because he didn't want to encourage her. God love her, but Emma Jane had the subtlety of a Black Hawk helicopter coming in for landing.

"I was thinking," she murmured with a coy smile. "We've mostly been selling cattle here locally, but we should look to expand. There's a big market in Fort Worth."

Obviously she was going somewhere with this, so Kyle

just nodded and made a noncommittal sound as he waited for the punch line.

"Wade Ranch needs to make some contacts there," she continued, and rearranged her hair with a practiced twirl. "We should go together. Like a business trip, but stay overnight and take in the sights. Maybe hit a bar in Sundance Square?"

First half of that? Great plan. Spot-on. Second half was so not a good idea, Kyle couldn't even begin to count the ways it wasn't a good idea. But he had to tread carefully. Wade Ranch couldn't afford for Kyle to antagonize another employee into quitting. Liam still hadn't replaced Danny Spencer, and Kyle was starting to worry his brother was going to announce that he'd decided *Kyle* should be the ranch manager.

"I like the way you think," he allowed. "You're clearly the brains of this operation."

She batted her lashes with a practiced laugh, leaning forward to increase the gap at her cleavage. "You're such a flatterer. Go on."

Since it didn't feel appropriate for the boss to be staring down the front of his employee's blouse, no matter how obvious she was making it that she expected him to, Kyle glanced over Emma Jane's shoulder to the window. And spied the exact person he'd been hoping to see. *Grace.* Finally.

He'd been starting to wonder if she was planning to avoid him for the next ten years. From the corner of his eye, he watched her park her green Toyota in the small clearing outside the barn and walk the short path to the door. His peripheral vision was sharp enough to see a sniper in a bell tower at the edge of a village—or one social worker with hair the color of summer wheat at sunset, who had recently asked Kyle to give her space.

"No, really," he insisted as he focused on Emma Jane

again. Grace had just entered the barn, judging by the sound of the footsteps coming toward his office, which he easily recognized as hers. "You've been handling cattle sales for what, almost a year now? Your numbers are impressive. Clearly you know your stuff."

Or she knew how to stick her breasts in a prospective buyer's face. Honestly, there was no law against it, and he didn't care how she sold cattle as long as she did her job. Just as there was no law against letting Grace think there was more going on here in his office than there actually was.

She wanted space, didn't she? Couldn't give a woman any more space than to pretend he'd moved on to another one. If he timed it right, Grace would get an eyeful of exactly how much *space* he was giving her. He treated Emma Jane to a wide smile and put an elbow on the desk, right by her knee.

Emma Jane lit up, just as Grace appeared in the open doorway of his office.

"Thanks, sweetie." Emma Jane smiled and ran one hand up his arm provocatively. He didn't remove it. "That's the nicest compliment anyone's ever given me."

Grace halted as if she'd been slapped. That's when he turned his head to meet her gaze, acknowledging her presence, just in case she'd gotten it into her head to flee. She was right where he wanted her.

"Am I interrupting?" Grace asked drily, and Emma Jane jerked back guiltily as she figured out they weren't alone anymore.

Yes, thank God. He'd have to deal with Emma Jane at some point, but he couldn't lie—he'd much rather have Grace sitting on his desk and leaning over strategically any day of the week and twice on Sunday.

"Not at all." Kyle stood with a dismissive nod at Emma Jane, whose usefulness had just come to an end. "We were just talking about how to increase our contact list in the Fort Worth area. We can pick it up later."

"We sure can," Emma Jane purred, and then shot Grace a dirty look as she flounced from the room.

"That was cozy," Grace commented once the sales manager was out of earshot. Her face was blank, but her tone had an undercurrent in it that he found very interesting.

"You think so?" Kyle crossed his arms and cocked a hip, pretending to contemplate. "We were just talking. I'm not sure what you mean."

Grace rolled her eyes. "Really, Kyle? She was practically draped over your desk like a bearskin throw rug, begging you to wrap her around you."

Yeah. She pretty much had been. He bit back a grin at Grace's colorful description. "I didn't notice."

"Of course you didn't." Her eyebrows snapped together over brown eyes that—dare he hope—had a hint of jealousy glittering in them. "You were too busy being blinded by her cleavage."

That got a laugh out of him, which didn't sit well with Grace, judging by the fierce scowl on her face. But he couldn't help it. This was too much fun. "She is a nice-looking woman, I do agree."

"I didn't say that. She's far too obvious to be considered 'nice-looking.'" Grace accompanied this with little squiggly motions of her forefingers. "She might as well write her phone number on her forehead with eyeliner. She clearly buys it in bulk and layers it on even at ten o'clock in the morning, so what's a little more?"

The more Grace talked, the more agitated she became, drawing in the air with her whole hand instead of just her fingers.

"So she's a little heavy-handed with her makeup." He waved it off. "She's a great girl who sells cattle for Wade Ranch. I have no complaints with her."

Grace made a little noise of disgust. "Except for the way she was shamelessly flirting with you, you mean? I can't believe you let her talk to you like that."

"Like what?" He shrugged, well aware he was pouring gasoline on Grace's fire, but so very curious what would happen when she exploded. "We were just talking."

"Yeah, you're still just as clueless as you always were."

There was that word again. *Clueless*. She'd thrown it at him one too many times to let it go. There was something more here to understand. He could sense it.

Before he could demand an explanation, Johnny blew into the office, his chest heaving and mud caked on his jeans and boots from the knee down. "Kyle. We got a problem. One of the pregnant cows is stuck in the ravine at the creek and she went into labor."

Instantly, Kyle shouldered past a wide-eyed Grace with an apologetic glance. He hated to leave her behind but this was his job.

"Take me there."

Liam had put Kyle in charge of the cattle side of Wade Ranch. This was his first real test and the gravity of it settled across his shoulders with weight he wasn't expecting.

He followed Johnny to the paddock where they kept their horses and mounted up, ignoring the twinge deep in his leg bone, or what was left of it. He could sit in his office like a wimp and complain about paperwork or ride. There was no room for a busted leg in ranching.

Kyle heeled Lightning Rod into a gallop and tore after Johnny as the ranch hand led him across the pasture where the pregnant herd had been quartered—to prevent the very problem Johnny had described. The expectant cows shouldn't have been anywhere near the creek that ran along the north side of Wade Ranch.

Kyle hadn't been there in years but he remembered it. He and Liam had played there as boys, splashing through the shallow water and gigging for frogs at dusk as the fat reptiles croaked out their location to the two bloodthirsty boys. Calvin had made them clean and dress the frogs when he found out, and they had frog legs for dinner that night. It was a lesson Kyle never forgot—eat what you kill.

They arrived at the edge of the pasture in a couple of minutes. A fence was down. That explained it.

"What happened?" Kyle asked as he swung out of the saddle to inspect the downed barbed wire and wooden stake.

"Not sure. Slim and I were running the fence and found this. Then he went to the creek to check it out. Sure 'nuff, one of the cows had wandered off. Still don't know how she got down there. Slim stayed with her while I came and got you."

"Good man. Hustle back to the barn and grab some of the guys to get this repaired," Kyle instructed, his mind already blurring with a plan. He just had to check out the situation to make sure the extraction process currently mapping itself out in his head was viable.

Johnny nodded and galloped off.

Kyle let Lightning Rod pick his way along the line of the creek until he saw Slim down in the ravine, hovering over the cow. She was still standing, which was good. As soon as a cow lay down, that meant they had less than an hour until she'd start delivering. They'd have to work fast or she'd be having her baby on that thin strip of ground between the steeply sloped walls and the creek. If the calf was in the wrong position, it would be too hard to assist with the birth, and besides, all the equipment was back at the barn.

Somehow, he had to figure out how to get her out. Immediately. Clearly, Slim had no idea how to do it or he wouldn't have sent Johnny after the boss. This was Kyle's battle to lose. So he wouldn't lose.

Kyle galloped another hundred feet to check out the slope of the creek bed walls, but they were just as steep all the way down the culvert as they were at the site where the cow had gone down. As steep as they'd been when he was a boy. He and Liam had slid down the slope on their butts, ruining more than one pair of pants in the process because it was too steep to walk down. But that had been in August when it was dry. In March, after a cold winter and wet spring, the slope was nothing but mud. Which probably explained how the cow had ended up at the bottom—she'd slipped.

Kyle planned to use that slick consistency to his advantage.

"Slim," he called down. "You okay for another few minutes? I have to run back to the barn to get a couple of things, and then we're gonna haul her out."

Slim eyed Kyle and then the cow. "*Haul* her out? That's a dumb idea. And not what Danny Spencer would have done."

Too bad. Wade Ranch was stuck with Kyle, not the former ranch manager. "Yep."

Not much else to say. It wasn't as if he planned to blubber all over Slim and ask for a chance to prove he could be as good as Spencer. He firmed his mouth and kept the rest inside. Like always.

The ranch hand nodded, but his expression had that I'll-believe-it-when-I-see-it vibe.

Kyle galloped back to the barn and found exactly what he was looking for—the pair of hundred-foot fire hoses Calvin had always kept on hand in case of emergency. They'd been retrofitted with a mechanism that screwed into the water reservoir standing next to the barn. The stock was too valuable to wait on the city fire brigade in the event of a barn fire, so a smart rancher developed his own firefighting strategy.

Today, the hoses were going to lift a cow out of a creek bed.

Kyle jumped into the Wade Ranch Chevy parked near the barn and drove across the pasture, dodging cows and the stretches of grass that served as their grazing ground as best he could. Fortunately, Johnny and the other hands hadn't fixed the fence yet, so Kyle drove right through the break to the edge of the creek.

By the time he skidded to a halt, the hands had gathered around to watch the show. There was no time to have a conversation about this idea, nor did Kyle need anyone else's approval, so if they didn't like it, they could keep it to themselves. Grimly, Kyle pulled the hoses from the truck bed and motioned to Johnny.

"I'm going to tie these to the trailer hitch and then throw them down to Slim. I'll rappel down and back up again once we have the hoses secured around the cow. You drive while I watch the operation. We'll haul her out with good old-fashioned brute strength."

Johnny and the other hands looked dubious but Kyle ignored them and got to work on tying the hoses, looping one end around the trailer hitch into a figure-eight follow-through knot. It was the best knot to avoid slipping and his go-to, but he'd never used it on a fire hose. Hopefully it would hold, especially given that he was the one who would be doing the rappelling without a safety harness.

When the hoses were as secure as a former SEAL could get them, Kyle tossed the ends down to Slim and repeated the plan. Slim, thankfully, just nodded and didn't bother to express his opinion about the chances of success, likely because he figured it was obvious.

Kyle waited for Slim to drop the hoses, and then grabbed on to one. His work gloves gripped better than he was expecting, a plus, given the width of the line. Definitely not the kind of rappelling he was used to, but he probably had more experience at this kind of rescue than anyone there.

He'd lost count of the number of times he'd led an extraction in hostile conditions with few materials at his disposal. And usually he was doing it with a loaded pack and weapons strapped to his back. Going down into a ravine after a cow was a piece of cake in comparison.

Until his boot slipped.

His bad leg slammed into the ground and he bit back a curse as a white-hot blade of pain arced through his leg. *Idiot.* He should have counterbalanced differently to compensate for his cowboy boots, which were great for riding, but not so much for slick mud.

Sweat streamed down his back and beaded up on his forehead, instantly draining down into his eyes, blinding him. Now his hell was complete. And he was only halfway down.

Muttering the lyrics to a Taylor Swift song that had always been his battle cry, he focused on the words instead of the pain. The happy tune reminded him there was still good in the world, reminded him of the innocent teenagers sitting at home in their bright, colorful rooms listening to the same song. They depended on men like Kyle to keep them safe. He'd vowed with his very life that he would. And he'd carried that promise into the darkest places on the planet while singing that song.

Finally, he reached the bottom and took a quarter of a second to catch his breath as he surveyed the area. Cow still standing. Hoses still holding. He nodded to Slim and they got to work leading the cow as close to the slope as possible, which wasn't easy, considering she was in labor, scared and had the brain of a—well, a cow.

The next few minutes blurred as Kyle worked alongside Slim, but eventually they got the makeshift harness in place. Kyle hefted the heavy hoses over his shoulder and climbed back up the way he'd come. The men had shuffled to the edge of the ravine to watch, backing up the closer Kyle got to the top. He hit the dirt at the edge and rolled onto the hoses to keep them from sliding back to the bottom.

He was not making that climb again.

Johnny grabbed hold of the hoses so Kyle could stand, and then made short work of tying them to the trailer hitch next to the other ends. He waved at Johnny to get in the truck. It was do-or-die time.

Johnny gunned the engine.

"Slow," Kyle barked.

The truck inched forward, pulling up all the slack in the hoses. And then the tires bit into the ground as the truck strained against the load. The cow balked but the hoses held her in place. So far so good.

The hoses gradually pulled the cow onto her side and inched her up the slope as the truck revved forward a bit more. It was working. The mud helped her slide, though she mooed something fierce the whole time.

Miraculously, after ten nail-biting minutes, the cow stood on solid ground at the top of the ravine. Kyle's arms ached and his gloves had rubbed raw places on his fingers, but it was done.

Johnny jumped from the truck and rushed over to clap him on the back, breaking the invisible barrier around Kyle. The other ranch hands swarmed around as well, smiling and giving their own version of a verbal high-five. Even Slim offered a somewhat solemn, "Good job."

Kyle took it all with good humor and few words because what was he supposed to say? *Told you so? That's okay, boys. I'm the boss for a reason?*

The ranch hands wandered off, presumably to finish the job of fixing the fence. Eventually, Kyle stood there, alone. Which was par for the course.

Was it so bad to have hoped this would become his new team?

No. The bad part was that if a successful bovine extraction couldn't solidify his place, he suspected nothing would. Because everyone was still waiting around for him to either fail or leave. Except Kyle.

Even Grace didn't fully believe in him yet, or she wouldn't have qualified her recommendations with a "We'll see," and the threat that she wasn't closing the case.

What more did he have to do to prove that honor, integrity and loyalty were in his very fiber?

Grace stood at the wide double door of the barn and watched horses spill into the yard as the hands returned from the cow emergency. They dismounted and loudly recounted the rescue with their own versions of the story. Seems as if Kyle had used fire hoses to drag the animal out of the ravine, which the hands alternately thought was ingenious or crazy depending on who was doing the talking.

Apparently it had worked, since one of the ranch hands had the cow in question on a short lead.

She should have left. She'd told Kyle what she'd come to say, witnessed an exchange between Kyle and another woman that she hadn't been meant to see, and now she was done. But you could have cut the tension in the barn with a chain saw, and she'd been a little bit worried about Kyle. Sure, he'd grown up on the ranch, but that didn't automatically make him accident-proof.

No one mentioned anything about Kyle, so he must be okay. But she wanted to see him for herself. Once she'd assured herself of it—strictly in her capacity as his daughters' caseworker, of course, no other reason—then she'd leave.

Finally, the truck he'd taken off in rolled into the yard and he swung out of the cab, muddy and looking so worn, she almost flew to his side. Except the little blonde bearskin rug beat her to it. Emma Jane. Or as Grace privately liked to call her—The Tart.

Like a hummingbird auditioning for the part of the town harlot, Emma Jane fluttered over to Kyle, expertly sashaying across the uneven ground in her high-heeled boots, which drew the attention of nearly every male still milling around the yard, except the one she was after.

Kyle pulled long lines of flat, muddy hoses out of the bed of the truck, dragged them to the spigot on the water tower beside the barn and attached one, using it to hose off the other.

Which was also pretty ingenious in her opinion.

Emma Jane crowded Kyle at the water tower, smiling and gesturing. Grace was too far away to hear what she was saying, but she probably didn't need to hear it to know it was along the lines of *Oh, Kyle, you're a hero* or the even more inane *Oh, Kyle, you're so strong and brave!*

Please. Well, yes, he was all of those things, no question, but Grace didn't see the point in shoving half-exposed breasts in a man's face when you said them.

The strong and brave hero in question glanced up at Emma Jane as he performed his task. And smiled. It was his slow, slightly naughty smile that he'd flashed Grace right after kissing her senseless, the one that had nearly enticed her back into his arms because it was so sexy.

It was a smile that told a woman he liked what he saw, that he had a few thoughts about what he planned to do with her. And there he was, aiming it at another woman!

That...*dog.*

Breathe, Grace. He was just smiling.

She crossed her arms, leaning forward involuntarily though there was no way she would be able to pick up the conversation from this distance, not with the clatter going on in the yard, all the hands still chattering and watering their horses at the trough running between the water tower and the barn.

Then Emma Jane placed her talons on Kyle's arm and he leaned into it. Something hot bloomed in Grace's chest as she imagined him kissing Emma Jane the way he'd kissed her. He said something to Emma Jane over his shoulder and she laughed. Grace didn't have to hear what was being said. He was enjoying Emma Jane's attention, obviously.

Or he was just washing a hose and having a conversation with his employee, which was none of her business, she reminded herself. She didn't own Kyle, and he'd certainly had female companions over the years who weren't Grace, or he wouldn't currently have two daughters.

She'd just never had that shoved in her face so blatantly before.

Now would be a great time to leave. Except as she started back to her car, Kyle stood and walked straight toward her, calling to one of the hands to lay the hoses out to dry before putting them away. Emma Jane trailed him, still chattering.

He was coming to talk to Grace. With Emma Jane in tow.

Or Kyle could be walking toward the barn. Grace *was* standing in the doorway.

But then his gaze met hers and the rest of the activity in the yard fell away as something wholly encompassing washed through her.

Seven

"Ms. Haines." Kyle nodded.

And then walked right past her!

Had she just been dismissed? Grace scowled and pivoted to view the interior of the barn. Kyle squeezed Emma Jane's shoulder at the door of the office and The Tart disappeared beyond the glass, presumably to go sharpen her claws.

Then he strolled across the wide center of the barn and disappeared around a corner.

Without a single ounce of forethought, Grace charged after him. She'd waited around, half-crazy with worry to assure herself he was okay, and he couldn't bother to stop and talk to her? How dare he? Emma Jane had certainly gotten more than a perfunctory nod and a platitude.

She skidded around the corner, an admonishment already forming in her mouth.

It vanished as she rounded the corner into a small, enclosed area. Kyle stood at a long washbasin. *Wet. Shirtless. Oh, my.*

Obviously she should have thought this through a little better.

Speechless, she stared unashamedly at his bare, rippling torso as he dumped another cupful of water down it. Water streamed along the cut muscles, running in rivulets through the channels to disappear into the fabric of his jeans.

Some of it splashed on her. She was too close. And way too far.

Every ounce of saliva fled from her mouth, and she couldn't have torn her gaze from his gorgeous body for a million dollars. She'd have *paid* a million dollars, if she'd had it, to stand in this spot for an eternity.

"Something else you wanted, Ms. Haines?"

She blinked and glanced up into his diamond-hard green eyes, which were currently fastened on her as he glanced over his shoulder. Busted. Again. There was no way to spin this into anything other than it was. "I didn't know you were washing up. Sorry."

Casually, he turned and leaned back against the long sink, arms at his side, which left that delicious panorama of naked chest right there on display. "That really didn't answer my question, now, did it?"

He was turning her brain mushy again, because she surely would have remembered if there had been talking. "Did you ask me a question?"

His soft laugh crawled under her skin. "Well, I'm trying to figure out what it is that you're after, Grace. Maybe I should ask a different way. Are you here to watch, or join in? Because either is fine with me."

Her ire rushed back all at once, melding uncomfortably with the heat curling through her midsection at the suggestion. "That's a fine way to talk after flirting with Ms. Cattle Queen."

Kyle just raised an eyebrow. "Careful, or a man might start to think you cared whether he flirted with another woman. That's not the case. Right?"

She crossed her arms, but those diamond-hard eyes drilled through her anyway. "Oh, you're right. I don't care." Loftily, she waved off his question. "It just seems disingenuous to make time with one woman mere minutes before inviting another one to *wash up*."

All at once, she had a very clear image of him dumping a cup of water over her chest and licking it off. The heat in her core snaked outward, engulfing her whole body. And that just made her even madder. Kyle was a big flirt who could get Grace hot with merely a glance. It wasn't fair.

She didn't remember him affecting her that way before. And she would have. This was all new and exciting and frustrating and scary.

"Maybe." That slow smile spilled onto his face. "But you're the one standing here. I'm not offering to *wash up* with Emma Jane."

"Yeah. Only because she didn't have the foresight to follow you."

"You did." He watched her without blinking and spread his arms. "Here I am. Whatever are you going to do with me?"

That tripped off a whole chain reaction inside as she thought long and hard about the answer to that question. But she hadn't followed him for *that*. Not that she knew for sure he even meant *that*. But regardless, he had a lot of nerve.

Hands firmly on her hips—just in case they developed a mind of their own and started wandering along the ridges and valleys of that twelve-pack of abs, which she was ashamed to admit she'd counted four times—she glared at him. "This is not you, Kyle. Liam? Yeah. He's a playboy and a half, but you've never been like that, just looking for the next notch in your bedpost."

There. That was the point she was trying to make.

He laughed with genuine mirth. "Is that what you think this is? Kyle Wade, playboy in training. It has a nice ring. But that ain't what's going on."

"Then by all means. Tell me what's going on," she allowed primly.

"Emma Jane is my employee. That's it." He sliced the air with his hand. "You, on the other hand, are something else."

"Oh, yeah? What?"

He swept her with a once-over that should not have been so affecting, but goodness, even the bottoms of her feet heated up. "A woman I'd like to kiss. A lot."

As in he wanted to kiss her several times or he just wanted to really badly?

She shook her head. Didn't matter.

"Well, be that as it may." She tossed her head, scrambling to come up with a response, and poked him in the chest for emphasis. He glanced down at her finger and back up at her, his eyelids shuttered slightly. "You wanted to kiss Emma Jane a minute ago. Pardon me for not getting in line."

"Grace." Her name came out so garbled, she hardly recognized it. "I do not want to kiss Emma Jane."

"Could have fooled me. And her. She definitely had the impression you were into her. Maybe because you were telling her jokes and letting her put her hands all over you."

"And maybe I let her because I knew you were watching."

"I— What?" All the air vanished from her lungs instantly. And then she found it again. "It was on purpose? Flirting with Emma Jane. You did that on *purpose*?" She was screeching. Dang near high enough to call dogs from another county. "Oh, that's…"

She couldn't think of a filthy enough word to describe it. *He'd been playing her.* Kyle Wade had picked her up and played her like a violin. Of course he had. She might as well have Bad Judge of Character tattooed on her forehead so people could get busy right away with pulling one over on her. And she'd waltzed to his tune with nary a peep.

And speaking of no peeps, Kyle was standing there watching her without saying a word, the big jerk.

"It was all a lie?" she asked rhetorically, because he'd just said it was, though why he'd done it, she couldn't fathom. "What were you trying to accomplish, anyway?"

His grin slipped as he pinned her in place with nothing more than his gaze. He swayed forward, just a bit, but his heat reached out and slid along her skin as if he'd actually brushed her torso with his.

She couldn't move. Didn't want to move. The play of expression across his face fascinated her. The heat called to her.

"No lies. See this," he murmured and wagged a finger between them, drawing her eye as he nearly touched her but didn't. "Just what you ordered. Space. Anytime you feel inclined to make it disappear, I'll be the one over here minding my own business."

Oh! Of all the sneaky, underhanded, completely accurate things to say.

Mute, she stared at him and he stared right back. He'd been giving her exactly what she asked for. Never mind that she'd rather drink paint thinner than admit he might have a point. And the solution was rather well spelled out, too.

She didn't want him to flirt with other women? Then close the gap.

There was no more running, no more hiding. This was it, right here. He wanted her. But he wasn't going to act on it.

They shared a fierce attraction and the past was in the past. She'd held him at bay in order to get her feet under her, to make sure he wasn't going to hurt her again. It was the same tactic she employed with her cases. If she wanted to be sure she wasn't letting her emotions get the best of her, wanted to be sure she was making an unbiased decision, she stepped back. Assessed from afar with impersonal attention.

This wasn't one of her cases. This was Kyle. As personal as it got. And the only way she could fully assess what they could have now was to dive into that pool. Wading in an inch at a time wasn't working.

Rock solid, not moving a muscle, he watched her. This was her show and he was subtly telling her he'd let her run it. Except he was also saying she couldn't keep talking out of both sides of her mouth.

Either she could act like a full-grown woman and do something about the man she wanted or keep letting their interaction devolve into an amateurish high school game.

She picked doing something.

Going on instinct alone, she reached out with both hands and pressed them to Kyle's bare chest, her gaze on his as she did it, gauging his reaction. His eyes darkened as her fingers spread and she flattened both palms across his pectoral muscles. Damp. Hot. Hard.

One muscle flexed under her touch and she almost yanked her hands back. But she didn't. He hadn't felt like this before. He was all man and it was a serious turn-on, especially because it was still Kyle underneath. When he was looking at her the way he was right then, as if the center of the universe had been deposited in his palm, it was easy to remember why she'd fallen for him. All the emotion of being in love with this man rushed back.

"There you go," she said breathlessly. "No more space."

"Grace," he growled, and she felt the vibrations under her fingers. "You better mean it. I'm only human."

Her touch was affecting him. *She* was affecting *him*. It was something she hadn't fully contemplated, but she did get that it wasn't fair to lead him on and keep dancing back and forth between yes and no.

"I mean it. If you want to kiss me, it's fine."

"*Fine*." There came that slow smile. "That's almost as bad a word as *nice*. I think it's time to fix your vocabulary."

All at once, Kyle's arms snaked around her, yanking her tight against his hard body. But before she could fully register the contact, his mouth claimed hers.

The crash of lips startled her. And then she couldn't think at all as his hands slid down her back, touching her, trailing heat along her spine, sliding oh, so slowly against her bottom to finally grip her hips and hold them firmly, pulling her taut against his body.

His very aroused body. The length of him pressed into her soft flesh as he kissed her. It was a whole-body experience, and nothing like the front porch kiss that she'd thought was so memorable that she couldn't shake it. That kiss had been wonderful, but tame.

This was a grown-up kiss.

The difference was unfathomable.

This kiss was hungry, questing, begging for more even as he took it.

Kyle changed the angle, diving deeper into her mouth, thrilling her with the intensity. His tongue swirled out, and instinctively, she met him with her own. He groaned and she felt it to her toes.

Kyle. She'd missed the feel of him in her arms. Missed the scent of him in her nose.

Except this Kyle wasn't like the warm coat she'd envisioned sliding into, wholly familiar and so comforting.

No, this Kyle was like opening a book expecting a nice story with an interesting plot and instead falling into an immersive world full of dark secrets and darker passions.

His hands were everywhere, along her sides, thumbs circling and sliding higher until he found her breasts beneath her clothes. The contact shot through her as he touched her, and then he shoved a leg between hers, tilting his hips to rub against her intimately.

This was not a kiss—it was a seduction.

And she had just enough functioning brain cells to be aware that they were not only in a barn, but she hadn't fully figured out what was supposed to come next. She didn't know what had changed that might mean things would work between them this time. She didn't fully trust that he was here for good, and even if he was, that he was going to meet her standards any better today than he had ten years ago.

Oh, he was certainly earning a ten in the Sweeping Her Off Her Feet category. But Happily Ever After carried just as much weight as Expressing His Feelings. And neither of those were on the board yet.

Breaking off the kiss—and nearly kicking herself at the same time—she pushed back and mumbled, "Wait."

His torso shuddered as he dragged in a ragged breath. "Because?"

"You know why." Her Professional Single Girl status was in jeopardy and she had to make sure he was worth the price of relinquishing it. Sure, he was hot and a really great kisser, but she didn't sleep around. An interlude in the barn didn't change that.

"I did not develop ESP at any point in the last ten years," he rasped, his expression going blank as he stared at her.

"Because of what happened before, Kyle." Exasperated, she stared at the wall over his head so his delicious chest wasn't right in her field of vision. "There's a lot of leftover emotion and scrambled-up stuff to sort out. I have to take it slow this time."

"Then you should leave," he said curtly. "Because I'm definitely not in the mood for slow right now."

She took his advice and fled. It wasn't until she'd reached her car and slid into the driver's seat that she realized leaving was the one surefire way to *never* figure out what they could have together.

Maybe slow wasn't any better an idea than space.

And at this moment, the only *s* word she seemed capable of thinking about ended in *ex*, which was the crux of the problem. She and Kyle had a former relationship and it muddied everything, especially her feelings.

Kyle stabbed his hands through his shirt, nearly ripping the sleeve off in the process.

Grace wanted to take it *slow* because of what had happened before.

Furiously, he fingered the buttons through the holes haphazardly, none too happy about having to spend the rest of the workday with a hard-on he couldn't get rid of, no matter what he thought of to kill his arousal—slugs, the Cowboys losing the Super Bowl, his mother. Nothing worked because the feel of Grace in his arms was way too fresh, and had been cut way too short.

Because of what had happened *before*. She meant when she'd fallen for Liam and he'd thrown her over. While Kyle appreciated that she wanted to figure out her own mind before taking things further with him, he wasn't about to stand by and let what happened in the past with his brother ruin the present.

Liam was married now and Grace should be completely over all of that. Bygones included forgetting about *everything* that happened in the past.

He didn't have any choice but to let it go for the time being. He had a job to do and men to manage.

By the time the sun set, the entire Wade Ranch staff was giving Kyle a wide berth. So the cow extraction hadn't earned him any points. Figured. His surly mood didn't help and he finally just called it a day.

When he got back to the main house, Liam met him in the mudroom off the back.

"Hey," Liam called as Kyle sat on the long bench seat to remove his boots, which were a far sight cleaner than they'd been earlier, but still weren't fit to walk the floors inside.

Kyle jerked his chin, not trusting himself to actually speak to anyone civilly. Though if anyone deserved the brunt of his temper, it was Liam.

"Hadley and I are flying to Vail this weekend. Just wanted to give you a heads-up." Liam's mouth tightened. "You'll be okay handling the babies for a couple of days by yourself, right?"

"Yep."

Liam hesitated, clearly expecting more of a conversation or maybe even an argument about it, but what else was there to say? Kyle couldn't force the couple to stay, and Maddie and Maggie were his kids. He'd figure it out. Somehow. The little pang in his stomach must be left over from Grace. Probably.

"Okay. We're leaving in an hour or so."

Kyle let the first boot hit the floor with a resounding *thunk* and nodded. Liam kept talking.

"I'm flying my Cessna, so it's no problem to delay for a bit if you need to talk to Hadley about anything."

The other boot hit the floor. Hadley had already imparted as much baby knowledge as she possibly could. Another hour of blathering wasn't going to make a difference. "Not necessary."

Liam still didn't leave. "You have my cell phone number. It's okay if you want to call and ask questions."

"Yep."

Geez. Was his brother really that much of an ass? Liam had taken care of the babies before Kyle had gotten there without anyone standing over him waiting for his first mistake. Did Liam really think babysitting was something only he could do and that Kyle was hopelessly inept? Seemed so. Which only set Kyle's resolve.

He wouldn't call. Obviously Liam and Hadley had plans that didn't include taking care of Kyle's children. Who was he to stand in the way of that? Never mind that Kyle had never even stayed alone in the house with the babies. Hadley had always just been there, ready to pick up the slack.

This was the part where Kyle wished he had someone like Hadley. His kids needed a mother. Problem was, he could only picture Grace's face when thinking of a likely candidate. And she was too skittish about *everything*. Mentioning motherhood would likely send her over the edge.

Finally, Liam shuffled off to finish packing or whatever, leaving Kyle to his morose thoughts. It was fine, really. So he'd envisioned asking Grace if she'd like to drive into Odessa for dinner and a movie. Get out of Royal, where there were no prying eyes. Maybe he would have even talked her into spending the night in a swanky motel. He had scads of money he never spent and he couldn't think of anyone he'd rather spend it on than Grace.

Guess that wasn't happening. A grown-up field trip didn't sound too much like Grace's definition of *slow* anyway, so it hardly mattered that his half-formed plan wasn't going to work out.

No matter. He'd spend the weekend with his daughters and it would be great. They'd bond and his love for them would grow. Maybe this was actually a good step toward relieving Hadley permanently of her baby duties. He could keep telling himself that she loved them and didn't mind taking care of his daughters all he wanted, but at the end of the day, it was just an excuse.

He'd decided to stay in Royal, taking a job managing the cattle side of Wade Ranch, and it was time for him to man up and start building the family life his daughters needed.

Liam and Hadley left in a flurry of instructions and worried backward glances until finally Kyle was alone with Maddie and Maggie. That little pang in his stomach was back and he pushed on it with his thumb. The feeling didn't go away and started resembling panic more than anything else.

God Almighty. Maddie and Maggie were babies, for crying out loud. Kyle had faced down a high-ranking, card-carrying member of the Taliban with less sweat.

He wandered into the nursery and thought about covering his eyes to shield them from all the pink. But there his girls were. Two of 'em. Staring up at him with the slightly unfocused, slightly bemused expression his daughters seemed to favor. The babies were kind of sweet when they weren't crying.

They couldn't lie around in their room all night.

"Let's hang out," he announced to his kids. It had a nice ring.

He gathered up Maggie from her crib and carried her downstairs to the family room, where a conglomeration of baby paraphernalia sat in the corner. He dragged one of the baby seats away from the wall with one bare foot and placed Maggie in it the way Hadley always did. There were some straps, similar to a parachute harness, and he grabbed one of Maggie's waving fists to thread it through the arm hole.

She promptly clocked him with the other one, which earned a laugh even as his cheek started smarting. "That's what I get for taking my eye off the ball, right?"

The noise she made didn't sound too much like agreement, but he nodded anyway, as if they were having a conversation. That was one of the things Hadley said all the time. The babies were people, not aliens. He could talk to them normally and it helped increase their vocabulary later on if everyone got out of the habit of using baby talk around them.

Which was fine by Kyle. Baby talk was dumb anyway.

Once Maggie was secured, he fetched Maddie and repeated the process. That was the thing about twins. You were never done. One of them always needed something, and then the other one needed the same thing or something different or both.

But here they were, having family time. In the family room. Couldn't get more domestic than that. He sat on the couch and looked at his daughters squirming in their bouncy seats. Now what?

"You ladies want to watch some TV?"

Since neither one of them started wailing at the suggestion, he took it as a yes.

The flat-screen television mounted to the wall blinked on with a flick of the remote. Kyle tuned to one of the kids' channels, where a group of grown men in bright colors were singing a song about a dog named Wags. The song was almost horrifying in its simplicity and in the dancing that would probably lace his nightmares later that night, assuming he actually slept while continually reliving that aborted kiss with Grace from earlier.

The babies both turned their little faces to the TV and for all intents and purposes looked as though they were watching it. Hadley had said they couldn't really make out stuff really well yet, because their eyes weren't developed enough to know what they were looking at, but they could still enjoy the colors and lights.

And that's when Maddie started fussing. Loudly.

Kyle pulled her out of her baby seat, cursing his burning hands, which were still raw from his climb out of the ravine. Liam's timing sucked. "Shh, little one. That's no way to talk to your daddy."

She cried harder. It was only a matter of time before Maggie got jealous of the attention and set about getting some of her own with a few well-placed sobs. Hadley could usually ignore it but Kyle didn't have her stamina.

Plan A wasn't working. Kyle rocked his daughter faster but she only cried harder. And there was no one to help analyze the symptoms in order to arrive at a potential solution. This was a solo operation. So he'd run it to completion.

Bottle. That was always Plan B, after rocking. It was close to dinnertime. Kyle secured Maddie in the chair again, forced to let her wail while he fixed her bottle. It seemed cruel, but he needed both hands.

He'd seen some guys wear a baby sling. But he couldn't quite bring himself to go that far, and he'd never seen Liam do it, either, so there was justification for holding on to his dude card, albeit slight.

Maddie sucked the bottle dry quicker than a baby calf who'd lost its mama. Kyle burped her and resettled her in her bouncy seat, intending to move on to Maggie, who was likely wondering where her bottle was.

Maddie was having none of that and let loose with another round of wails.

In desperation, he sang his go-to Taylor Swift song, which surprisingly worked well enough to ease his pounding headache. He sang the verse over again and slid into the chorus with gusto. The moment he stopped, she set off again, louder. He sang. She quieted. He stopped. She cried.

"Maddie," he groaned. "Tim McGraw should have been your daddy if this is how you're going to be. I can't sing 24-7."

More crying. With more mercy than he probably deserved, Maggie had been sitting quietly in her seat the whole time, but things surely wouldn't stay so peaceful on her end.

Feeling like the world's biggest idiot, he sneaked off to the kitchen to call Hadley. There was no way on God's green earth he'd call Liam, but Hadley was another story.

She answered on the first ring. "Is everything okay?"

"Fine, fine," he assured her, visualizing Liam throwing their overnight bags into the cockpit of the Cessna and flying off toward home without even pausing to shut the door. "Well, except Maddie won't stop crying. I've tried everything, bottle, rocking, and it's a bust. Any ideas?"

"Did you burp her?"

"Of course." He hadn't changed her diaper, but his sense of smell was pretty good and he didn't think that was the problem.

"Temperature?"

He dashed back into the family room, cringing at the decibel level of Maddie's cries, and put a hand on her forehead. Which was moronic when he'd been holding her for thirty minutes. "She doesn't feel hot."

"Is that Maddie crying like that?" Now Hadley sounded worried, which was not what Kyle had intended. "Take her temperature anyway, just to be sure. Then try the gas drops. Call me back in an hour and let me know how it's going."

"Won't I be interrupting?" He so did not want to know the answer to that, but it was pretty crappy of him to call once, let alone twice.

"Yes," Liam growled in the background. "Stop coddling him, Hadley."

Kyle muttered an expletive aimed at Liam, but his wife was the one who heard it. "Excuse my French, Hadley.

Never mind. I got this. You and Liam go back to whatever you were doing, which I do *not* need details about."

"We should come home," Hadley interjected. This was accompanied by a very vehement "No!" from Liam, and some muffled conversation. "Okay, we're not coming home. You'll be fine," Hadley said into the phone in her soothing voice that she normally reserved for the girls, but whether it was directed at Liam or Kyle, he couldn't say. "Call Clare if you need to. She won't mind."

"Clare?" Liam's incredulity came through loud and clear despite his mouth being nowhere near the phone. "She's already got plenty of babies that Royal Memorial pays her to take care of. Call Grace if you're going to call anyone."

Grace. He could get Grace over here under the guise of helping with the twins and get to see her tonight after all. Now that was a stellar idea if Kyle had ever heard one. Not that he was about to let Liam get all cocky about it. "Sorry I bothered you. Good night."

Kyle eyed the still-screaming baby. Fatherhood wasn't a job for the fainthearted, that was for sure. Nor was it a job for the clueless, and thankfully, Ms. Haines already had him cast in her head as such. She thought he was clueless? Great.

Time to use that to his advantage.

Eight

When the phone rang, Grace almost didn't answer it.

The oven had freaked out. Worse than last time. It turned on and heated up fine, but halfway through the cooking cycle, the element shut off. Cold. Which described the state of her dinner, too. The roast was still raw inside and she could have used the potatoes to pound nails.

But there was no saving it now. The oven wouldn't start again no matter how much she cursed at it. She'd checked the power cord but it was plugged in with no visible frays or anything. Last time, she'd been able to turn it off and turn it back on, but that didn't work this time.

So why not answer the phone?

Except it was Kyle. His name flashed at her from the screen and she stared at it for a moment as the *wow* from earlier flooded all her full-grown woman parts. So this was taking it slow? Calling her mere hours after she'd broken off a kiss with more willpower than it should have taken—for the second time?

"This better be important," she said instead of hello, and then winced. Her mama had raised her better than that.

"It is." Something that sounded like a tornado siren wailed in the distance. "Something's wrong with Maddie."

That was *Maddie* doing the siren impression? *Relapse.* Her heart rate sped up. Those harrowing hours when they didn't know what was wrong with Maddie came back in a rush. Heart problems were no joke, and Maddie'd had several surgeries to correct the abnormalities.

"What's wrong? Where's Hadley?" She might be hyperventilating. Was that what it was called when you couldn't breathe?

"She and Liam went to Vail. I didn't want to bother them."

Vail? Suspicion ruffled the edges of Grace's consciousness. The couple had just gone to Vail a couple of months ago. Was this some kind of covert attempt to get Kyle to take his fatherhood responsibilities more seriously? Or an elaborate setup from the mind of Kyle Wade to get his way with Grace?

"Okay," she said slowly, feeling her way through the land mines. "Did you try—"

"Yep. I tried everything. She's been crying like this for an hour and it's upsetting Maggie. I wouldn't have called you otherwise." He was trying hard to keep the panic from his voice, but she could tell he was at the end of his rope. Her heart melted a little, sweeping aside all her suspicion.

It didn't matter why Liam and Hadley had gone to Vail. Maddie—and Kyle—needed help, and she couldn't ignore that for anything.

"Do you need me to come by?" She shouldn't, for all the reasons she hadn't stayed with him in the barn earlier that day.

Plus, and this was the kicker, he hadn't asked her to come over. Maybe it was supposed to be implied, but this was typical with Kyle. He had a huge problem just coming out and saying what he thought. That might be the number one reason she hadn't stayed in his arms, both back in high school and today.

Nothing had changed.

"That's a great idea," he said enthusiastically, and she didn't miss that he was acting as though it was all hers, and not what he'd been after the whole time. "I'll cook you dinner as a thank-you. Unless you've got other plans?"

Ha. If she couldn't hear Maddie's cries for herself, she'd think he'd set all this up. Grace glanced at her oven and half-cooked dinner, then at the lonely dining room table where she'd eaten a lot of meals by herself, especially in the past three years upon becoming a Professional Single Girl.

The timing was oh, so convenient. But even Kyle couldn't magically make her oven stop working at precisely the moment he'd asked her to come over for dinner. Thus far she'd avoided having any meals with him and his family because that would be too hard. Too much of a reminder that a husband and children was what she wanted more than anything—and that there was nothing on the horizon to indicate she'd ever get either one.

But this was an emergency. Or at least that was what she was going to keep telling herself.

"I'll be right there," she promised, and dumped the roast in the trash. If she freshened up her makeup and put on a different dress, no one had to know.

She drove to Wade Ranch at four miles per hour over the speed limit.

Kyle opened the door before she knocked. "Hey, Grace. Thanks."

His pure physical beauty swept out and slapped her. Mute, she stared at his face, memorizing it, which was silly when she already had a handy image of him, shirtless, emblazoned across her brain. She'd just seen him a few hours ago. Why did she have to have a reaction by simply standing near him?

"Where's Maddie?" she asked brusquely to cover the catch in her throat.

"Right this way, Ms. Haines."

Grace followed Kyle through the formal parlor and across the hardwood floor into the hall connecting to the back of the house. Why did it feel like the blind leading the blind? She didn't have any special baby knowledge. Most kids in the system were older by the time their cases landed on her desk, which brought back her earlier reservations about the real reason he'd called her. It wouldn't be the first time today that he'd manufactured a scenario to get a reaction from her.

In the family room, two babies sat in low seats, wide-eyed as they stared at the TV, both silent as the grave.

Grace pointed out the obvious. "Um. Maddie's not crying."

"I gave her Tylenol while you were on your way over here." He shrugged. "Must have worked."

"Why didn't you call me?"

"She didn't stop crying until a few minutes before you got here," he replied defensively, which was only fair. She'd heard Maddie crying over the phone. It wasn't as if he'd shoved Liam and Hadley out the door, and then faked an emergency to get her into his clutches.

She sighed. "I'm sorry. I'm being rude. It's just… I was convinced this was all just an elaborate plot to get me to have dinner with you."

Kyle blinked. "Why on earth would I do that?"

"Well, you know." Discomfort prickled the back of her neck as he stared at her in pure confusion. "Because you faked all that stuff with Emma Jane earlier today. Seemed like it might be a trend."

He cocked his head and gave her a small smile. "I called

you because it was the best of both worlds. I needed help with Maddie and I wanted to see you, too. Is that so terrible?"

Not when he put it that way. Chagrined, she shook her head. "No. But it just seems like I'm a little extraneous at this point. I should probably go. Maddie's fine."

"Don't be silly." His smile faltered just a touch. "She might go off again at any moment and Maggie could decide to join in. What will I do then? Please stay. Besides, I promised you dinner. Let me do something nice for you for coming all this way."

The panicky undercurrent had climbed back into his voice, bless his heart. She couldn't help but smile in hopes of bolstering his confidence. "It wasn't that far. But okay. I'll stay."

"Great. It's settled then." He held out his hand as if he wanted to shake on it but when she placed her hand in his, he yanked on it, pulling her toward the bouncy seats. "Come on, grab a baby and you can watch me cook."

Laughing, she did as commanded, though he insisted on taking Maddie himself. She gathered up Maggie, bouncy seat and all, and followed him to the kitchen, mirroring his moves as he situated the seat near one of the two islands in the center of the room, presumably so the girls didn't feel left out.

She kissed Maggie on the head, unable to resist her sweet face. This baby was special for lots of reasons, but mostly because of who her daddy was.

Wow. Where had that come from? She needed to reel it back, pronto.

"We'll let them hang out for a little while," Kyle said conversationally. "And then we'll put them to bed. Hadley has them on a strict schedule."

"Sure. I'd be glad to help."

It sounded great, actually. The children she helped always either had families already, or were waiting on her to find them the best one. Grace never got to keep any of the children on whose behalf she worked, which was a little heartbreaking in a way.

But here she was, right in the middle of Maddie and Maggie's permanent home, spending time with them and their father outside of work. The smell of baby powder clung to her hands where she'd picked up Maggie, and all at once, soft jazz music floated through the kitchen as Kyle clicked up an internet radio station at the kitchen's entertainment center. It was a bit magical and her throat tightened.

This was not her life. She didn't trust Kyle enough to consider where this could lead. But all at once, she couldn't remember why that was so important. All she had to do right this minute was enjoy this.

"Can I do something to help with dinner?" she asked, since the babies were occupied with staring at their fists.

Kyle grinned and pulled a stool from behind the island, pointing to it. "Sit. Your job is to keep me company."

Charmed, she watched as instructed. It wasn't a hardship. He moved fluidly, as comfortable sliding a bottle from the built-in wine refrigerator as he was handling the reins of his mount earlier that day.

The cork gave way with a *pop* and he poured her a glass of pale yellow wine, handing it to her with one finger in the universal "one minute" gesture. He grabbed his own glass and clinked it against hers. "To bygones."

She raised a brow. That was an interesting thing to toast to. But appropriate. She was determined not to let the past interfere with her family moment, and the future was too murky. "To bygones."

They both drank from their glasses, staring at each other over the rims, and she had the distinct impression he was evaluating her just as much as she was him.

The fruity tang of the wine raced across her tongue, cool and delicious. And unexpected. "I wouldn't have pegged you as a Chardonnay kind of guy," she commented.

"I'm full of surprises." With that cryptic comment, he set his wineglass on the counter and began pulling items from the double-doored stainless steel refrigerator. "I'm making something simple. Chicken salad. I hope that's okay. The ladies didn't give me a lot of time to prep."

She hid a smile at his description of the babies. "Sounds great."

Kyle bustled around the kitchen chopping lettuce and a cooked chicken breast, leaving her to alternate watching him and the twins. Though he drew her eye far more than she would have expected, given that she was here to help with the babies.

"I don't remember you being much of a connoisseur in the kitchen," she said as he began mixing the ingredients for homemade dressing.

They'd been so young the first time, though. Not even out of their teens, yet their twenties were practically in the rearview mirror now. Of course they'd grown and changed. It would be more shocking if they hadn't.

"In a place like Afghanistan, if you don't learn to cook, you starve," he returned.

It was rare for him to mention his military stint, and it occurred to her that she typically shied away from the subject because it held so many negative associations. For her, at least. He might feel differently about the thing that had taken him away from her, and she was suddenly curious about it.

"Did you enjoy being in the military?"

He glanced up, his expression shuttered all at once. "It was a part of me. And now it's not."

Okay, message received. He didn't want to talk about that. Which was fine. Neither did she.

"I'm at a stopping point," he said, his tone a little lighter. "Let's put the girls to bed."

Though she suspected it was merely a diversion, she nodded and followed him through the mysterious ritual of bedtime. It was over before she'd fully immersed herself in the moment. They changed the girls' diapers, changed their outfits, put them down on their backs and left the room.

"That was it?" she whispered as she and Kyle took the back stairs to the kitchen.

"Yep. Sometimes Hadley rocks them if they don't go to sleep right away, but she says not to do that too much, or they'll get used to it, and we'll be doing it until they go to college." He waved the mobile video monitor in his hand. "I watch and listen using this and if they fuss, I come running. Not much more to it."

They emerged into the kitchen, where the tangy scent of the salad dressing greeted them. Kyle set the monitor on the counter on his way to the area where he'd been preparing dinner.

He'd clearly been asking Hadley questions and soaking up her baby knowledge. Much more so than Grace would have given him credit for. "You're taking fatherhood very seriously."

He halted and whirled so fast that she smacked into his chest. But he didn't step back. "What's it going to take to convince you that I'm in this for the long haul?"

Blinking, she stared up into his green eyes as they cut through her. Condemning her. Uncertain all of a sudden, she tried to take a step back, but he didn't let her. His hands shot out to grip her elbows, hauling her back into place. Into his space. A hairbreadth from the cut torso she'd felt under her fingers earlier today.

"What will it take, Grace?" he murmured. "You say something like that and it makes me think you're surprised that I'm ready, willing and able to take care of my daughters. *Still* surprised, after all I've done and learned. After I've become gainfully employed. After I've shown you my commitment in site visits like you asked. This isn't about me anymore. It's about you. Why is this all so hard for you to believe?"

"Because, Kyle!" she burst out. "You've been gone. You didn't come home when Liam called you about the babies. Is it so difficult to fathom that I might have questions about your intentions? You just said the military was a part of you. What if you wake up one day and want to join up again? Those girls will suffer."

I'd suffer.

Where had that come from? She tried to shake it off, but as they stood there in the kitchen of Wade House with his masculinity pouring over her like a hot wind from the south, the emotions welled up again and she cursed herself. Cursed the truth.

Sometime between his coming home and now, she'd opened her heart again. Just a little. She'd tried to stop, tried asking for space, but the honest truth was that she'd never gotten over him because she still had feelings for him. And it had only taken one kiss to awaken them again, no matter how much she'd tried to lie to herself about it. Otherwise, that scene with Emma Jane would have rolled right off like water from a duck's back.

And she didn't trust him not to hurt her again. It was a terrible place to be stuck.

"Grace," he murmured. "I'm here. For good. I didn't get Liam's messages, or I would have been back earlier. You've got me cast in your head as someone with my sights set on the horizon, but that's not true. I want to live my life in Royal, at least until my daughters are grown."

He wasn't aiming to leave the moment he changed his mind. He was telling the truth; she could see it in his eyes.

Maybe she wasn't such a bad judge of character after all. Maybe she could let her guard down. Just a little.

The tightness in her throat relaxed and she took the first easy breath since smacking into him. "Okay. I'll shut up about it."

"Just to make sure, let me help you shut up."

He hauled her up and kissed her. His mouth took hers at a hard, desperate angle that she instantly responded to. Maybe she didn't have to resist if he wasn't going to leave again. Maybe she didn't have to pretend she didn't want more. Because he was right here, giving it to her. All she had to do was take it.

His hands were still on her elbows, raising her up on her tiptoes as he devoured her with his unique whole-body kiss. Need unfolded inside, seeking relief, seeking Kyle.

Yes. The darkness she sometimes sensed in him lifted as he dropped her elbows to encompass her in his arms, holding her tight. He backed her up against the counter to press his hard body to hers, thrusting his hips to increase the contact.

A moan bloomed in her chest, and her tongue vibrated against his as he took the kiss deeper, sliding a hand down her back, to her waist, to her bottom, molding it to fit in his palm. His touch thrilled her even as she pressed into it, willing him to spread the wealth. And then he did.

His hand went lower, gripping the back of her thigh, lifting it so that her knee came up flush with his thigh, which hiked her dress up, and *oh, my.* She was open to him under her skirt, flimsy panties the only barrier between her damp center and his very hard body.

He thrust his hips again, igniting her instantly as the rough fabric of his jeans pleasured her through the scrap of fabric at her core. Strung tight, she let the dense heat wash through her, mindless with it as she sought more. His mouth lifted from hers for a moment and she nearly wept, following him involuntarily with her lips in hopes of reclaiming the drugging kiss.

"Grace," he murmured, and dragged his lips across her throat to the hollow near her ear, which was so nice, she forgot about kissing and let her head tip back to give him better access.

He spent a long moment exploring the area, and finally nipped her ear lightly, whispering, "You know, when I said I wanted to live my life in Royal, I didn't picture myself alone."

"I hope not," she murmured. "You have two daughters."

He laughed softly, as she'd intended, and hefted her a little deeper into his arms as he lifted his head to meet her gaze. "You know that's not what I meant."

Of course she did. But was it so difficult to spell out what was going on his head? So difficult to say how he felt about her? She wanted to hear the words. This time, she wasn't settling for less than everything. "Tell me what you're picturing, Kyle."

"Me. You." He slid light fingertips down the sweetheart neckline of her dress until he reached the spot right between her breasts and hooked the fabric. "This dress on the floor."

Shuddering in spite of herself at the heated desire in his expression, she smiled. "Let's pretend for argument's sake I'm in favor of this dress on the floor. What would you say to me while you're peeling it off?"

The glint in his eye set off another shower of sparks in her midsection. "Well, my darling. Why don't we just find out?"

Slowly, he pulled down the shoulders of the dress, baring her bra straps, which he promptly gathered up, as well. She heartily blessed the impulse that had caused her to pick this semibackless dress that didn't require unzipping to get out of. Which might not have been an accident.

"Beautiful." He kissed a shoulder, suckling on it lightly, then following her neckline with the little nibbling kisses until she thought she'd come apart from the torture.

When she'd asked him to talk about what was on his mind, she'd been expecting a declaration of his feelings. This was so much better. For now.

All at once, the dress and bra popped down to her waist in a big bunch of fabric, baring her breasts to his hot-eyed viewing pleasure. And look he did, shamelessly, as if he'd uncovered a diamond he couldn't quite believe was real.

"Grace," he rasped. "Exactly like I remembered in my dreams. But so much more."

That pleased her enormously for some reason. It was much more romantic than what she recalled him saying when they were together ten years ago. He'd seen her naked before, but always in semidarkness, and usually in his truck. Bench seats were not the height of romance.

With a reverent curse, he brushed one nipple with his thumb, and her breath whooshed from her lungs as everything went tight inside. And outside.

"Kyle," she said, and nearly strangled on the word as he lifted her up onto the counter, spreading her legs and stepping between them. Then his mouth closed over a breast and she forgot how to speak as he sucked, flicking her nipple with his tongue simultaneously.

She forgot everything except the exquisite feel of this man's mouth on her body.

Her head fell back as he pushed a hand against the small of her back to arch her toward his mouth, drawing her breast deeper into it. She moaned, writhing with pleasure as the heat swept over her entire body, swirling at her core. Where she needed him most.

As if he'd read her mind, his other hand toyed with her panties until she felt his fingers touching her intimately. It was cataclysmic, perfect. Until he placed his thumb on her nub, expertly rubbing as he pleasured her, and that was even more perfect. Heat at her core, suction at her breast, and it all coalesced in one bright, hot pinnacle. With a cry, she crested in a long orgasm of epic proportions.

She'd just had an *orgasm* on the *kitchen counter*. She should probably be more embarrassed about that...

Before she'd fully recovered, Kyle picked her up from the counter and let her slide to the floor, then hustled her up the stairs to a bedroom. Heavy, masculine furnishings dominated the room, marking it as his, but a few leftover items from his youth still decorated the walls. He dimmed the light and advanced on her with his slow, lazy walk.

"Oh, there's more?" she teased.

"So much more," he growled. "It's been far too long since I've felt you under me. I want you naked. Now."

That sounded like a plan. The warm-up in the kitchen had only gotten her good and primed for what came next.

Breathless, she stood still as he peeled her dress the rest of the way from her body and let it fall to the carpet. She promptly forgot to worry about the extra pounds she'd gained in her hips and thighs since the last time he'd seen her.

He stripped off his shirt, exposing that beautiful torso she'd barely had time to explore earlier.

When his jeans hit the floor, she realized his chest was only part of the package, and the rest—*oh, my*. He turned slightly, holding one leg behind him at an odd angle, almost as if he was posing for her. Well, okay then. Greedily, she looked her fill, returning the favor from earlier when he'd gorged on the sight of her bare breasts.

In the low light, he was quite simply gorgeous, with muscles bulging in his thighs and a jutting erection that spoke of his passion more effectively than anything he could have said. The power of it coursed through her. She was a woman in the company of a finely built man who was here with the sole intent of pleasuring her with that cut, solid body. And she got to do the same to him.

Why had she waited so long for this?

"Grace."

She glanced up into his eyes, which were so hot, she felt the burn across her uncovered skin, heightening her desire to *get started* already. He was going to feel amazing.

"You have to stop looking at me like that," he rasped.

"Because why?"

He chuckled weakly. "Because this is going to be all over in about two seconds if you don't. I want to take my time with you. Savor you."

"Maybe you can do that the second time," she suggested, a little shocked at her boldness, but not sorry. "I'm okay with you going fast the first time if I get to look at you however much I want. Oh, and there's going to be touching, too."

To prove the point, she reached out to trace the line of his pectoral muscles, because how could she not? He groaned under her fingertips and that was so nice, she flattened her palms against his chest. "More," she commanded.

He raised his eyebrows. "When did you get so bossy?"

"Five minutes ago." When she'd realized she was a woman with desires. And she wanted this man. Why shouldn't she get to call a few shots?

With a small push at his torso, she shoved him toward the bed. And to his credit, he let her, because there was no way she'd have moved him otherwise. He fell backward onto the bed and she climbed on to kneel next to him, a little uncertain where to start. But determined to figure it out.

"Just be still," she told him as he stared up at her with question marks in his gaze. Then she got busy exploring.

What would he taste like? There was only one way to find out. She leaned down and ran her tongue across his nipple, and it was as delicious as she'd expected. He hissed as the underlying muscle jerked.

"Staying still is easier said than done when you're doing that," he muttered, his voice cracking as she ran her tongue lower, down his abs and to his thigh.

She eyed his erection and, curious, reached out to touch it. Hard and soft at the same time, it pulsed against her palm.

He cursed. "Playtime's over."

Instantly, he rolled her under him in one fierce move, taking her mouth in a searing kiss that rendered her boneless. She melted into the comforter as he shoved a leg between hers, rubbing at her core until she was in flames.

He paused only for a moment to sheathe himself with a condom, and then nudged her legs open to ease into her slowly.

Gasping as he filled her, she clung to his shoulders, reveling in the feel of him. This was so different than she remembered. The experience was so much stronger and bigger. The leftover emotion that she'd carried with her for the past ten years exploded into something she barely recognized. Before, Kyle had been in a compartment in her mind, in her heart. Something she could take out and remember, then put back when she got sad.

There was no putting this back in a box.

The essence of Kyle swept through her, filling every nook and cranny of her body and soul. No, he hadn't bubbled over with lots of pretty words about being in love with her. But that would come, in time. She had to believe that.

And then he buried himself completely with a groan. They were so intimately joined, Grace could feel his heartbeat throughout her whole body. They moved in tandem, mutually seeking to increase the pleasure, spiraling higher toward the heavens, and she lost all track of time and place as they lost themselves in each other.

The rhythms were familiar, like dancing to the same song so often you memorized the moves. But the familiarity only heightened the experience because she didn't have to wonder what would happen next.

Just as he'd done when they'd been together before, he stared into her eyes as he loved her, refusing to let her look away. Opening his soul to her as they joined again and again. The romance of it swept through her and she held him close.

This was why she'd fallen in love with him. Why she'd never had even the slightest desire to do this with any other man. He made her feel that she completed him without saying a word. Sure, she wanted the words. But times like this made them unnecessary.

Before she was fully ready for it to end, his urgency increased, sending her into an oblivion of sensation until she climaxed, and then he followed her into the light, holding her tight against him as they soared.

She lay there engulfed in his arms, wishing she never had to move from this spot.

Kyle must have been reading her mind, because he murmured in her ear, "Stay. All weekend."

"I don't have any of my stuff," she said lamely as reality nosed its way into the perfect moment.

"Go get a bag and come back."

It was a reasonable suggestion. But then what? Were they jumping back into their relationship as if nothing had happened and ten years hadn't passed? As if they'd dealt with the hurt and separation?

That was too much reality. She sat up and his arms fell away to rest on the comforter.

"I see the wheels turning," he commented mildly as he pulled a sheet over his lower half in a strange bout of modesty. "This is a beginning, Grace. Let's see where it takes us. Don't throw up any more walls."

She shut her eyes. Romance was great, but there was so much more that she wanted in a relationship. There'd been no declarations of undying love. No marriage proposal. Why did he get a pass that no other man got? She was caught between her inescapable feelings for Kyle and her standards.

And the intense hope that things might be different this time.

How would she ever find out if she left?

"Okay." She nodded and ignored the hammering of her pulse. "Let's see where it goes."

Nine

Kyle waited on Grace to come back by pretending to watch TV.

His body had cooled—on the outside—but the inside was still pretty keyed up. He wasn't really interested in much of anything other than getting Grace back in his bed, but this time for the whole night.

When the crunch of gravel sounded outside, breath he hadn't realized he'd been holding whooshed out. She'd come back.

He met Grace at the door, opening it wide as she climbed the front porch steps, her hair still mussed from their thorough lovemaking of less than an hour ago. Her face shone in the porch light, so beautiful and fresh, and his chest hitched as he soaked in the sight of her.

"Hey, Grace," he said, pretty dang happy his voice still worked.

He'd wondered if she might back out, call and say she'd changed her mind. She was still so skittish. She might have let him into her body but he didn't fool himself for a second that she'd let him into her head, or her heart. It wasn't the way it had been, when he'd been her hero, her everything. There was distance now that hadn't been there before and he didn't like it.

Of course, some of that was his fault. Not much. But a little. He didn't fully trust her, and while he'd sworn in theory to forget about the past, it was proving more difficult to do in practice than he'd thought it would be, so he didn't press the issue of the yawning chasm between them.

"Hey." She had a bag slung over her shoulder and a shy smile on her face.

Shy? After the temptress she'd been? It caught him up short. Maybe some of the distance was due to sheer unfamiliarity between them. As comfortable as *he* felt around Grace, that didn't mean she was totally in the groove yet. Plus, they didn't know each other as well as they used to. Ten years didn't vanish just because two people slept together.

"We never had dinner," he commented. "Come sit with me and we'll eat. For real this time."

She nodded and let him take her bag, following him to the table where he laid out silverware and refilled their wineglasses. They ate the chicken salad and polished off the bottle of wine, chatting long after clearing their plates. Grace told cute stories about the children on her case docket, and Kyle reciprocated with some carefully selected anecdotes about the guys he'd trained with in Coronado during BUD/S. Carefully selected because that period had been among the toughest of his life as his training honed him into an elite warrior—*while* he was fighting his own internal battle against the hurt this woman had caused. But he'd survived and wasn't dwelling on that.

Couldn't dwell on it. Liam wasn't a factor and he wanted

to do things with Grace differently this time. And by the time Kyle was done with her, she'd be asking, "Liam who?"

A wail over the monitor drew their attention away from their conversation and Grace gladly helped him get the girls settled again. It was nearing midnight; hopefully it would be the only time the babies woke up for the night.

Kyle didn't mind rolling out of bed at any hour to take care of his daughters, but he selfishly wanted to spend the rest of the night with Grace, and Grace alone. He got his wish. They fell asleep wrapped in each other's arms, and Kyle slept like the dead until dawn.

His eyes snapped open and he took a half second to orient. Not a SEAL. Not in Afghanistan. But with *Grace*. A blessing to count, among many.

Until he tried to snuggle her closer. White-hot pokers of pain shot through his busted leg as he rolled. He bit back the curse and breathed through it.

The pain hadn't been so bad last night, but of course, he'd been pretty distracted. Plus, he normally soaked his leg before going to bed but hadn't had a chance last night. Apparently, he was going to pay for it today.

All the commotion woke Grace.

"Good morning," she murmured sleepily, and slid a leg along his, which was simultaneously arousing and excruciating.

"Wait," he said hoarsely.

"Don't wanna." She stretched provocatively, rubbing her bare breasts against his chest, which distracted him enough that he didn't realize she'd hooked her knee around his leg. She fairly purred with sexy little sounds that meant she was turned on. And probably about to do something about it.

"Grace." He grabbed her shoulders and squared them so he could be sure he had her attention. "Stop."

Her expression went from hot and sleepy to confused

and guarded. Her whole body stiffened, pulling away from his. "Okay. Sorry."

"No, don't be sorry." Kyle swore. *Moron.* He was mucking this up and all he wanted to do was pull her back against him. Dive in, distract himself. But he couldn't. "Listen."

He took a deep breath, fighting the pain, fighting his instinct to clam up again.

He hadn't told anyone about what had happened to him in Afghanistan and didn't want to start with the woman who still had the power to declare him an unfit parent if he admitted to having a busted leg. But as he stared into her troubled brown eyes, his heart lurched and he had to come clean. This was part of closing that distance between them. Part of learning to trust her again.

She'd said she was going to let him keep his girls. He had to believe her. Believe *in* her, or this was never going to work, not now, not in a hundred years.

"I didn't tell you to stop because I wanted you to."

Her gaze softened along with her body. "Then what's going on, Kyle?"

"I got wounded," he muttered. Which made him sound as much like a wuss as he felt. "Overseas."

"Oh, I didn't know!" She gasped and drew back to glance down the length of his body, her expression darkening gorgeously as she took in his semiaroused state. "You don't *look* wounded. Everything I see is quite nice."

And now it was a fully aroused state. Fantastic. This was so not a conversation he wanted to have in the first place, let alone with a hard-on. "My leg. The bone was shattered. I had a lot of surgeries and they put most of it back together. But it still hurts, especially in the morning when I haven't stretched it."

Sympathy poured from her gaze as she sat up and pulled the sheet back, gathering it up in her hand as she sought the scar. When she found it along the far side of his calf, she touched the skin just above it lightly with her fingers. "You hid this last night. With the low light and striking that weird pose. Why didn't you tell me?"

"It's…"

How to explain the horror of being wounded in the line of duty? It wasn't just the pain and the fact that he wasn't ever going to be the same again, but he'd been unable to protect the rest of his team. He'd been unable to *do his job* because his leg didn't work all at once. A SEAL got back up when he was knocked down. *Every time.* Only Kyle hadn't.

Maybe he'd fail at being a parent, too, because of it. That was his worst fear.

"I don't like being weak," he finally said, which was true, if not the whole truth. "I don't like giving you ammunition to take away Maddie and Maggie. Like I might not be a good daddy because my leg doesn't work right."

"Oh, Kyle." She laid her lips on the scar for a moment, and the light touch seared his heart. "I would never take away your daughters because of an injury. That's ridiculous."

He shrugged, unable to meet her gaze. "You were going to take them away because I didn't come home for two months. But I was in the hospital."

"Well, you could have said that!" Exasperation spurted out with the phrase and she shook her head. "For crying out loud. Am I supposed to be a mind reader?"

Yes. Then he wouldn't have to figure out how to say things that were too hard.

"Now you know," he mumbled instead. "That's why I had to stop earlier. Not because I wasn't on board. I just needed a minute."

"Okay." But then she smiled and ran a hand up his thigh,

dangerously close to his erection. "It's been a minute. How about we try this instead, now that I know?"

The protest got caught in his throat as she rolled him onto his back and crawled over him, careful not to touch his leg, but deliberately letting her breasts and long curls brush his skin from thigh to chest. She captured his wrists and encircled them with her fingers, drawing his arms above his head, holding them in place as her hips undulated.

"What are you doing?" His voice scraped the lower register as she ignited his flesh with her sexy movements.

She arched a brow. "Really? I should hope it would be fairly obvious. Since it's not, shut up and I'll make it clearer for you."

He did as advised because his tongue was stuck to the roof of his mouth anyway. And then she leaned forward, still holding his wrists hostage, and kissed him. Hot. Open-mouthed. The kind of kiss laden with dark promise and he eagerly lapped it up. He could break free of her finger shackles easily, but why the hell would he do that?

She had him right where she wanted him, apparently, and since he could find no complaint with it, he let her have the floor. She experimented with different angles of her head as she kissed him, looking for something unknown and he went along for the ride, groaning with the effort it took to hold back.

Then she trailed her mouth down his throat, nipped at his earlobe and writhed against his erection all at once, slicing a long, hot knife of need through his groin. His hips strained toward hers, rocking involuntarily as he sought relief, and he started to pull his arms loose so he could roll her under him to get this show on the road. But she shook her head and tightened her grip on his wrists.

"No, sir," she admonished with a wicked smile. "You're not permitted to do anything but lie there."

This was going to kill him. Flat out stop his heart.

He got what she was doing. She wanted him to keep his leg still, while she did all the dirty work. Something tender hooked his heart as he stared up at her, poised over him with an all-business look on her face that was somehow endearing.

But he wasn't an invalid.

"I hate to break it to you, darling, but that's not happening." He flexed his hips again, sliding his erection against her bare, damp sex, watching as her eyes unfocused with pleasure. "I suggest you think about how you're going to get a condom on me with your hands occupied because I'm going to be inside you in about point two seconds."

"Don't ruin this for me." She mock-pouted and promptly crossed his wrists, one over the other, and held on with one hand as she wiggled the fingers of her free hand in a cheery wave. "I always dreamed of being a rodeo star. This is my chance."

He had to laugh, which downright ached. All over. "That's what's on your mind right now? Rodeo?"

"Oh, yeah." She leaned against his abs, holding on with her thighs as she fished around in the nightstand drawer and pulled out a condom, which she held up triumphantly. "I'm going for a ten in the bucking bronco event."

"I'll be the judge of that," he quipped, and then raised a brow at the condom. "Go ahead. I'm waiting."

In the end, she had to let go of his arms to rip open the foil package. But he obediently held his wrists above his head as she had so sweetly asked. Then there was no more talking as she eased over him, taking him gently in her hands to pleasure him as she rolled on the condom.

He groaned as need broke over him in a wave, and then she slowly guided him into her damp heat. He slid all the way in as she pushed downward and it was unbelievable. They joined and it was better than it had been last night.

Deeper. More amazing, because there were no more secrets between them.

She knew about his injury and hadn't run screaming for her report to revise it. She hadn't been repulsed by his weaknesses. Instead, she'd somehow twisted it around so they could make love without hurting his leg. It was sweet and wonderful.

And then she got busy on her promise to turn him into a bucking bronco, sliding up and down, rolling her hips and generally driving him mad with want. He obliged her by letting his body go with the sensation, meeting her thrusts and driving them both higher until she came with a little cry and he followed her.

Clutching her to his chest, he breathed in tandem with her, still joined and not anxious to change that. He held her hot body to his because he didn't think he could let go.

"You're amazing," he murmured into her hair, and she turned her head to lay her cheek on his shoulder, a pleased smile on her face.

"I wouldn't say no to thank-you flowers."

He made a mental note to send her a hundred roses the moment his bones returned and he could actually move. "Where'd you get that sexy little hip roll from?"

She shrugged. "I don't know. I've never done it before. It just felt right."

All at once, his good mood vanished as he wondered what moves she *had* done before with other men that she hadn't opted to try out on him. Like Liam. Was he better in bed than his brother? Worse? About the same? And yeah, he recognized that the burn in his gut was pure jealousy.

Totally unable to help himself, he smiled without humor and rolled her off him casually, as if it were no big deal, but he didn't really want her close to him right then. "It was great. Perfect. Like you'd practiced it a lot."

What an ass he was being. But the thought of Grace

with another man, some guy's mitts on her, touching her, put him over the edge. Especially since one of those Neanderthals had been his brother.

She quirked a brow. "Really? You're not just humoring me?"

The pleased note in her voice didn't improve his mood. What, it was a compliment to be well-practiced in bed?

"Oh, no," he said silkily. "You've got the moves, sweetheart. The men must line up into the next county to get in on that."

Not only was he jealous, he was acting as if he'd been a choirboy for the past ten years when there was nothing further from the truth. He'd been the king of one-night stands because that was all he could do. It wasn't what he'd wanted or what he'd envisioned for himself, but the reason he wasn't able to move on and find someone to settle down with was sitting in his bed smiling at him as if this was all a big joke.

But as always, he wasn't going to say what was really on his mind. That was how you got hurt, by exposing your unguarded soft places.

And then she laughed. "Oh, yeah. They line up, all right. As long as we're having confession time, I have one of my own."

He needed a drink first. A row of shots would be preferable. But it was—he scowled at the clock—barely 6:00 a.m., and the babies were going to wake up any second, demanding their breakfast. "We don't have to do this, Grace."

"No, I want to," she insisted. "You told me about your leg, which was clearly hard for you. I think this is just as important for you to know. I'm not practiced. At all. It's kind of funny you'd say that actually, since you're the last man I slept with."

Shyly, she peeked at him from under lowered lashes as she let that register.

He sat up so fast, his head cracked against the headboard. "You...what?"

She hadn't been with anyone since *him*? Since ten years ago? *At all?*

Grace nodded. "I guess you could say you ruined me for other men. But that's not the only reason. I just never found one I thought measured up."

To him. She'd never found another man she'd thought was good enough. Had he been working himself up for no reason?

Grace had never been with another man. She'd been a virgin when they met. Kyle Wade was Grace's only lover. The thought choked him up in a wholly unexpected way.

And then his brain latched on to the idea of Grace refusing suitors over the years and shoved it under the lens of what he knew to be the truth. His mood turned dangerously sharp and ugly again. "Well, now. That's a high compliment. If it's true."

Confusion crept across her expression. "Why would I lie?"

"Good question. One I'd like the answer to, as well." He crossed his arms over his thundering heart. "Maybe you could explain how it's possible that you've never been with another man, yet I practically caught you in the act with one. Liam."

Just spitting his name out cost Kyle. His throat tightened and threatened to close off entirely, which would be great because then he couldn't throw up.

"Oh, Kyle." She actually *smiled* as she tenderly cupped his face. "You've certainly taken your time circling around back to that. Nothing happened with Liam. I didn't think you'd even noticed."

"You didn't..." He couldn't even finish that sentence and jerked away from her touch. "His hands were all over you. Don't tell me nothing happened."

"First of all, we were broken up at the time," she reminded him. "Secondly, it was a setup, honey. I wanted to get your attention, and honestly, I was pretty devastated it didn't work. Liam was a good sport about it, though. I've always appreciated that he was willing to help."

Kyle's vision went black and then red, and he squeezed his eyes shut as he came perilously close to passing out for the first time in his life. *Breathe. And again.* Ruthlessly, he got himself back under control.

"A setup," he repeated softly.

She nodded. "We set it up for you to catch us. It was dumb, I realize. Blame it on the fact that I was young and naive. I was expecting you to confront me. For us to have it out so I could explain how much you meant to me. How upset I was that we weren't together anymore. It was supposed to end differently. But you left and I figured out that I wasn't all that important to you."

A setup. To force a confrontation. And instead, she'd decided his silence meant she wasn't important to him, when in fact, the opposite was true.

"Why?" He nearly choked on the question. "Why would you do something like that? With *Liam* of all people?"

His brother. There was a sacred line between brothers that you didn't cross, and she'd not only crossed it, she'd been the instigator. Liam had put his hands on the woman Kyle loved as a *favor*. Somehow, and he wouldn't have thought this possible, that was worse than when Kyle had thought his brother was just adding another name to his growing list of conquests. The betrayal was actually twice as deep because it had all been a *setup*.

The reckoning was going to be brutal.

"Because, Kyle." She caught his gaze and tears brimmed in her eyes. "I loved you. So much and so intensely. But you were so distant. Already seeking that horizon, even then. We'd stopped connecting. Breaking up with you didn't faze you. I figured it would take something bold to shake you up."

Yeah, it had shaken him up all right. "But *that*?"

He couldn't wrap his head around what she was telling him. He'd enlisted because of a lie. Because he'd felt as though he couldn't breathe in Royal ever again. Because he'd sought a place where people stood by their word and their honor, would take a bullet for you. Where he could be part of a team alongside people who valued him. And *found* that place.

Which wasn't here.

"Yeah. Like you used Emma Jane to make me jealous." She shrugged. "Same idea. Funny how similar our tactics are."

The roaring sound in his head drowned out her words. Similar. She thought the idea of Kyle flirting with a woman out in the open in broad daylight was the same as walking by Liam's bedroom and hearing Grace's laugh. The same as peeking through the crack at the door to see the woman he'd given his soul to entwined with his brother *on his brother's bed*.

"Go." He shoved out of the bed, ignored his aching leg and dressed as fast as he could. "I can't be around you right now."

"Are you upset, Kyle?" She still sounded confused, as though it wasn't abundantly clear that none of this was okay. And then her face crumpled as understanding slowly leached into her posture.

He couldn't respond. There was nothing to say anyway. *It wasn't the same.* He'd started to trust her again—no, he'd *forced* himself to forget the past despite the amount of pain he still carried around—only to find that her capacity for lies was far broader than he'd ever have imagined.

He slammed out of the room and went to make the babies' bottles because he couldn't leave as he wanted to. As he should. Grace would twist that around, too, and somehow find a way to rip his heart out again by taking his daughters away.

But he wouldn't give Grace Haines any more power in his life.

Since he couldn't leave, Kyle stewed. When Liam and Hadley returned from Vail the next afternoon, Kyle wasn't fit company.

Which made it the perfect time for a confrontation.

"Liam," Kyle fairly growled as he cornered his brother in the kitchen after Hadley went to the nursery to see the babies.

"What's up?" Liam chugged some water from the bottle in his hand.

"Grace fessed up." Crossing his arms so he wouldn't get started on the beating portion of the reckoning too soon, he shifted the weight off his bad leg and glared at the betrayer who dared stand there scowling as though he didn't know what Kyle was talking about. "Back before I went into the navy. You and Grace. It was a lie."

"Oh, that." Liam shook his head. "Yeah, you're a little slow on the uptake. That's ancient history."

"It's recent to me because I just found out about it."

With a smirk, Liam punched him on the arm. "Maybe if you'd stuck around instead of flying off to the navy, you'd have known then. That was the whole purpose of it, according to Grace, to get you to confront her. I was just window dressing."

"I went into the navy because of window dressing," Kyle said through clenched teeth, though how his brain was still functioning enough to spit out thoughts was beyond him. "Glad to know this is all a big game to everyone. I've been missing out. Where's Hadley? I'm looking forward to getting in on some of this fun. Would you like to watch while I feel up your wife or would you rather walk in on us?"

"Shut your filthy mouth."

Kyle was ready for his brother this time and blocked Liam's crappy right hook easily, pushing back on his twin's torso before the man charged him. "Not so fun when you're on the other side of it, huh?"

Chest heaving and eyes wild with fury, Liam strained against Kyle's immovable blockade. "What do you care? You ignored Grace to the point where she cried so much over your sorry hide, I thought she was going to dry up like an old withered flower."

"Aren't you the poet?" He sneered to cover the catch in his heart to hear that Grace had cried over him. And how did Liam know that anyway? It probably wasn't even true. This was all an elaborate bunch of hooey designed to throw Kyle off the scent of who was really to blame here. "I cared, you idiot. You're the one who didn't care about the big fat line you crossed when you put your hands on my woman."

"*Your* woman? I got a feeling Grace would disagree." Liam snorted and stepped back, mercifully, allowing Kyle to drop his hand from his brother's chest. Another few minutes of holding him back would have strained his leg something fierce. "What line did I cross? You broke up. You weren't even together when that happened, remember?"

"*She* broke up. I didn't," Kyle countered viciously. "I was trying to figure out how to get her back. Not so easy when a woman tells you she's through and then makes out with another guy. Who happens to be my brother. Which never would have happened if you'd told her no. *That's* the line, Liam. I would never have done that to you."

Something dawned in Liam's gaze. "Holy cow. You were in love with her."

"What the hell do you think I've been talking about?"

Disgusted with the circles and lies and betrayals, Kyle slumped against the counter, seriously thinking about starting on a bottle of Irish whiskey. It was five o'clock 24-7 when you found out your twin brother was a complete moron.

"You were in love with her," Liam repeated with surprise, as if saying it again was going to make it more real. "Still are."

Well, *duh*. Of course he was! Why did Liam think Kyle was so pissed?

Wait. No, that wasn't— Kyle shut his eyes for a beat, but the truth didn't magically become something else. Of course he was still in love with Grace. That's why her betrayal hurt so much.

"That's not the point." Nor was that up for discussion. It didn't matter anyway. He and Grace were through, for real this time.

"No, the point is that this is all news to me. Probably news to Grace as well, assuming you actually got around to telling her." More comprehension dawned in Liam's expression. "You haven't. You're still just as much of a jackass now as you were then."

Kyle was getting really tired of being so transparent. "Some things shouldn't have to be said."

Liam laughed so hard, Kyle thought he was going to bust something, and the longer it went on, the more Kyle wanted to be the one doing the busting. Like a couple of teeth in his brother's mouth.

Finally, Liam wiped his eyes. "Get your checkbook because you need to buy a clue, my brother. No woman is going to let you get away with being such a clam, so keep on being the strong, silent type and sleep alone. See if I care."

"Yeah, you're the fount of wisdom when it comes to women, Mr. Revolving Door. Do you even know how many women you've slept with over the years?" Cheap shot. And Kyle knew it the moment it left his mouth, but Liam had him good and riled. He started to apologize but Liam waved it off.

"That doesn't matter when you find the right one." Liam glanced up the back stairs fondly, his mind clearly on his wife, who was still upstairs with the babies. "But guess what? You don't get a woman like Hadley without knowing a few things about how to treat a woman. And keeping your thoughts to yourself ain't it. Look what it's cost you so far. You willing to spend the next ten years without the woman you love because of your man-of-few-words shtick?"

Yeah, he didn't blather on about the stuff that was inside. So what? It was personal and he didn't like to share it.

Keeping quiet was a defense mechanism he'd adopted when he was little to shelter him from constantly being in a place he didn't fit into, lest anyone figure out his real feelings. Some wounds weren't obvious but they went deep.

The old-fashioned clock on the wall ticked out the seconds as it had done since Kyle was old enough to know how to tell time. Back then, he'd marked each one on his heart, counting the ticks in hopes that when he reached a thousand, his mother would come back. When he reached ten thousand, she'd *surely* walk through the door. A hundred thousand. And then he'd lose count and start over.

She had never come back to rescue him from the ranch he didn't like, didn't comprehend. Nothing had ever fit right until Grace. She was still the only woman who ever had.

And maybe he'd messed up a little by not telling her what she meant to him. Okay, maybe he'd messed up a lot. If he'd told her, she probably wouldn't have cooked up that scheme with Liam. Too little, too late.

"We good?" Liam asked, his gaze a lot more understanding than it should have been.

"Yeah." Kyle sighed. "It was a long time ago."

"For what it's worth, I'm sorry."

Liam stuck his hand out and Kyle didn't hesitate. They shook on it and did an awkward one-armed brotherly hug that probably looked more like two squirrels fighting over a walnut than anything. But it was enough to bury the hatchet, and not in Liam's back, the way Kyle had planned when he'd stormed into the kitchen earlier.

"Listen." Liam cleared his throat. "If we're all done crying about your girlfriend, I've got something to tell you that's been rubbing me the wrong way."

"You need me to go underwear shopping with you so we can get you the right size?" When Liam elbowed him, Kyle knew they were on the way back to being brothers again instead of strangers. "Because you have a wife for that now."

"Shut up. This is for serious. There's an outfit called Samson Oil making noises around Royal and I don't like it. They're buying up properties. Even offered me a pretty penny for Wade Ranch. Wanted to make sure you're on the same—"

"You said no, right?" Kyle shot back instantly. This was his home now. The place he planned to raise his daughters. No amount of money could compensate for a stable home life for his family.

"Well, I wanted to talk to you first. But yeah. The right answer is no."

Relief squeezed his chest. And wasn't that something? Kyle had never thought he'd consider the ranch home. But there you go. The threat of losing it—well, he didn't have to worry about that, obviously.

"So it's a no. What's the big deal then?"

Liam shrugged. "I dunno. It just doesn't sit well. The

guy from Sampson, he didn't even look around. Just handed me some paperwork with an offer that was fifteen million above fair market value. How's that for a big deal?"

It ruffled the back of Kyle's neck, too. "There's no oil around here. What little there is has a pump on it already."

"Yeah, so now you're where I'm at. It's weird, right?"

Kyle nodded because his throat was tight again. It was nice to be consulted. As if he really was half owner of the ranch, and he and Liam were going to do this thing called family. He hadn't left this time and it might have made a huge difference.

It gave Kyle hope he might actually become the father his girls deserved. Grace, however, was a whole other story with an ending he couldn't quite figure out.

Ten

Grace kicked the oven. It didn't magically turn on. It hadn't the first time she'd hauled off and whacked it a minute ago, either.

But kicking something felt good. Her foot throbbed, which was better than the numbness she'd felt since climbing from Kyle's bed, well loved and then brokenhearted in the space of an hour. The physical pain was a far sight better than the mental pain.

Because she didn't understand what had happened. She'd opened her heart to Kyle again, only to be destroyed more thoroughly the second time than she had been the first time. This was a grown woman's pain. And the difference was breathtaking. Literally, as in she couldn't make her lungs expand enough to get a good, solid full breath.

Determined to fix something, Grace spent twenty minutes unscrewing every bolt she could budge on the oven, hoping something would jump out at her as the culprit. Which failed miserably because she didn't know what it was supposed to look like—how would she know if something was out of place? The oven was just broken. No matter. She wasn't hungry anyway.

She wandered around her small house two blocks off the main street of Royal. She'd bought the house three years ago when she'd claimed her Professional Single Girl status, and set about finding a way to be happy with the idea of building a life with herself and herself only in it. She had, to a degree. No one argued with her if she wanted to change the drapes four times a year, and she never had to share the bathroom.

The empty rooms hadn't seemed so empty until now. Spending the weekend with Kyle had stomped her fantasy of being single and happy to pieces. She wanted a husband to fill the space in her bed, in her heart. Children who laughed around the kitchen table. A dog the kids named something silly, like Princess Spaghetti.

A fierce knock sounded at the door, echoing through the whole house. She almost didn't answer it because who else would knock like that except a man who had a lot of built-up anger? At her, apparently. After ten years of turning over every aspect of her relationship with Kyle, analyzing it to death while looking for the slightest nuance of where it had all gone wrong, never once had she turned that inspection back on herself.

But she'd made mistakes, that much was apparent. Then and now. Somehow.

Only she didn't quite buy that what happened ten years ago was all her fault.

And all at once, she wanted that reckoning. Wanted to ask a few pointed questions of Kyle Wade that she hadn't gotten to ask before being thrown out of his bed two long and miserable days ago.

She yanked open the door and the mad she'd worked up faltered.

Kyle stood there on her doorstep in crisp jeans, boots and a work shirt, dressed like every other man in Royal and probably a hundred other towns dotting the Texas prairie. But he wasn't anything close to any other man the world over, because he was Kyle. Her stupid heart would probably never get the message that they were doomed as a couple.

He was holding a bouquet of beautiful flowers, so full it spilled over his hand in a riot of colors and shapes. Her vision blurred as she focused on the flowers and the solemn expression on Kyle's face.

"Hey, Grace."

No. He wasn't allowed to be here all apologetic and carrying conciliatory flowers. It wasn't fair. She couldn't let him into her head again, and she certainly wasn't offering up her heart again to be flattened. He didn't have to know she'd given up on getting over him.

"What do you want, Kyle?" She didn't even wince at her own rudeness. She got a pass after being shown the door while still undressed and warm from the man's arms.

"I brought you these," he said simply without blinking at her harsh tone. He held out the bouquet. "Thank-you flowers. Because I owed you."

Wasn't *that* romantic? She didn't take the bouquet. "You *owed* me? You definitely owe me, but not flowers. An explanation would be better."

Kyle dropped the bouquet, his expression hardening. "May I come in then? Your next-door neighbor is out on the porch with popcorn, watching the show."

"Mrs. Putter is seventy-two." Grace crossed her arms and propped a hip against the doorjamb. "This is all the fun she gets for the year."

"Fine." Kyle sighed. "I came to apologize. I shot first and asked questions later. It's the way I do things, mostly because people are usually shooting at me, too."

Not an auspicious start, other than the apology part. "And yet I still haven't heard any questions."

"Grace." Kyle caught her gaze, and something warm spilled from his green eyes that she couldn't look away from. "You meant something to me. Back then. You have to understand that I had a lot of stuff going on in my head that I didn't want to deal with, so I didn't. I shut down instead. That wasn't fair to you. But you were the best thing in my life, and then you were gone. I was a wreck. Seeing you with Liam was the last straw, so I left Royal because I couldn't stand it, assuming that you'd found the Wade brother you preferred. There was never a point when I would have confronted you about it."

Openmouthed, she stared at him. That was the longest speech she'd ever heard him give and it loosened her tongue in kind. "I get that I messed up with Liam. I was young and stupid. I should have been more up-front about my feelings, too."

Kyle nodded. "Goes for both of us. But I still owe you a thank-you. I joined the military because I wanted to be gone. I figured, what better way to forget Royal and the girl there than to go to the other side of the world in defense of my country? But instead of just a place to nurse my shattered ego, I found something I didn't expect. Something great. Being a SEAL changed me."

Yes, she'd seen that. He'd grown up, into a responsible, solid man who cared about his daughters. "You seem to have flourished."

"I did," he agreed enthusiastically. "It was the team I'd been looking for. I never fit in at the ranch. That's part of what was weighing me down back then. The stuff inside. I was contemplating my future and not seeing a clear picture of what I should do going forward. If you hadn't staged that ploy with Liam, I might never have found my unit. Those guys were my family."

The sheer emotion on his face as he talked about his fellow team members—it was overwhelming. He'd clearly loved being in the military. It had shaped him, and he'd soaked it up.

Her heart twisted anew. If he didn't fit in at the ranch, why had he taken over the cattle side? During one of her site visits, he'd told her that was his job now—he hoped to create a stable home for his daughters. He planned to stick around this time. Was that all a lie? Or was he just doing it because she'd forced him into it, despite hating that life?

"I don't understand," she whispered. "If you liked being in the military so much, why did you come home?"

"My leg." His expression caved in on itself, and it might have been the most vulnerable she'd ever seen him. She almost reached out to comfort him, was almost physically unable to prevent her heart from crying in sympathy at what he'd lost. He was hurting, and that was so hard for her to take.

But she didn't reach out. "You came home because you were injured," she recounted flatly.

That was the only reason. Not because he missed Grace and regretted splitting up. Not because he wanted his daughters, or the simple life on a ranch with his family. He'd been forced to.

And what would he do when he got tired of an ill-fitting career? What would happen when the allure of the great wide open called to him again?

He'd leave. Just as he'd done the first time, only he'd take his babies with him—there was no law that said he had to stay in Royal to retain custody. He'd go and crush her anew, once she'd fallen in love with three people instead of just one.

He hadn't confronted her about Liam ten years ago because he hadn't wanted to stay in the first place. Not for her, not for anything. If he had, he'd have fought for their love; she had no doubt.

Kyle could pretend all he wanted that he'd enlisted because he'd caught her with Liam, but that had been—by his own admission—the last straw. Not the first.

"Yeah." He jerked his head in acknowledgment. "I was honorably discharged due to my busted leg. I didn't have anyplace else to go. But when I saw Maddie and Maggie for the first time…and then you came back into my life… Well, things are different now. I want to do things different. Starting with you."

"No." Her heart nearly split in two as she shook her head. "We've already had one too many do-overs. You shot first and asked questions too late."

She'd begun to trust him again, only to have the carpet ripped out from under her feet. She couldn't do that again. She could be single and happy. It was a choice; she just had to make it.

"Don't say that, Grace." Kyle threw the bouquet on the wicker chair closest to the door and captured her hand, squeezing it tight so she couldn't pull away. His green eyes beseeched her to reconsider, hollowing her out inside. "I lie awake at night and think about how great it would be if you were there. I think about what it's going to be like for the girls growing up without a mom. It's not a picture I like. We need someone to keep us sane."

This was delivered with a lopsided smile that she ached to return. If only he'd mentioned the condition of his heart in that speech and how it was breaking to be away from her. How he couldn't consider his life complete without her. Anything other than a string of sentences which sounded suspiciously like an invitation to make sure Maddie and Maggie had a mother figure.

And she wanted a family so badly she could picture easily falling into the role of Mama to those precious babies. At what cost, though?

"You have Hadley for that," she said woodenly. "I'm unnecessary."

"You're not listening to what I'm saying." He held her hand against his chest, and she wanted to uncurl her palm so she could feel his heartbeat. "Hadley is Liam's wife. I want one of my own."

It was the closest thing to a proposal she'd ever gotten. She was certifiably insane for not saying yes. Except he hadn't actually asked her. As always, he couldn't just come right out and say what he meant. That's what had led to the Liam fiasco in the first place, and nothing had changed.

None of this was what she'd envisioned. Kyle was nothing like her father. What about her standards? Her grand romance and fairy-tale life? How in the world would their relationship ever stand the test of time with staged jealousy-inducing ploys and the inability to just talk to each other as their starting point?

"I can't do this, Kyle. I can't—" Her voice broke but she made herself finish. "I thought we were starting something and the moment things get a little rough, you bail. Just like before."

"That's an excuse, Grace." He firmed his mouth, and then pointed out, "I'm here now, aren't I?"

"It's too late," she retorted, desperate to get this horrific conversation over with. "We have too many trust issues. We don't even want the same things."

His green eyes sharpened as he absorbed her words. "How can you say that? I want to be together. That's the same."

"Except that's not what I want," she whispered, and forced herself to watch as his beautiful face blanked, becoming as desolate as a West Texas ravine in a drought. "Goodbye, Kyle."

And before she took it all back in a moment of weakness, she shut the door, dry-eyed. The tears would come later.

Now that Johnny and Slim had a grudging respect for Kyle as the boss, they got on okay.

Which was fortunate, because Kyle drove them all relentlessly. Himself included, and probably the hardest. Spring calving season was in full swing and eighteen-hour days fit with Kyle's determination to never think, never lie awake at night and never miss Grace.

At this point, he'd take two out of three, but the hole where Grace was supposed to be ached too badly to be ignored, which in turn guaranteed he wouldn't sleep. And as he lay there not sleeping, his brain did nothing but think, turning over her words again and again, forcing him to relive them because he deserved to be unhappy. He couldn't be with Grace because she didn't want to be with him. Because she didn't trust him.

All the work he'd done to get over his trust issues, and she'd blindsided him with her own. Because he'd left when life got too difficult. When all he'd wanted was to find his place in the world. And when that place spat him back out, he came back. To forge a new place, put down roots. It had been hard, one of the toughest challenges of his life, and yeah, when it got rough, he dreamed of leaving. But he hadn't. Only to have that thrown back in his face.

If it didn't hurt so bad he'd laugh at the irony.

A week after Operation: Grace had gone down in flames, Liam invited him to the Texas Cattlemen's Club for an afternoon of "getting away from it all" as Liam put it. Curious about the club his grandfather had belonged to, and now Liam, too, apparently, Kyle agreed, with the caveat that they'd only stay a couple of hours tops. The cattle weren't going to tend themselves, after all.

The moment Kyle walked into the formerly men-only club, the outside world ceased to exist. Dark hardwood floors stretched from wall to wall, reflecting the pale gold wallpaper that warmed the place. It was welcoming and hushed, as if the room was waiting for something important to happen. The sense of anticipation was compelling.

Kyle followed Liam to the bar, where some other men sat nursing beers. Kyle recognized Mac McCallum, who'd been Liam's buddy for a long time, and Case Baxter.

"Case is the president of the Texas Cattlemen's Club," Liam said as he introduced everyone around. "And this is Nolan Dane."

"Right." Kyle shook the man's hand. "Haven't seen you in ages."

"I'm back in town, practicing family law now," Nolan explained with a glance at Liam. "Your brother's a client."

Kyle nodded as his lungs hitched. Liam had a legal retainer who practiced family law? Didn't take a rocket scientist to do that math. When Liam had talked about papers and warned Kyle he'd need a lawyer, it hadn't been an idle threat. They hadn't talked about it again, and Kyle had hoped the idea of adoption had been dropped.

Obviously it hadn't.

But why stick it in Kyle's face like this? It was a crappy thing to do after all the hoops Kyle'd been forced to jump through to prove his worth as a father. *Especially* after they'd had their Come To Jesus discussion and Liam had apologized for the Grace thing.

Wasn't that indicative of Kyle's Royal welcome thus far? That's why he shot first. When he didn't, he invariably took a bullet straight into his gut.

Mouth firmly shut as he processed everything, Kyle took a seat as far away from Liam as he could. When the conversation turned to Samson Oil, it piqued his interest sufficiently to pull his head out of his rear long enough to participate. Especially when Nolan Dane excused himself with a pained look on his face.

"More offers for land coming in," Liam affirmed. "Wade Ranch included. I think we've got a problem on our hands."

The other men seemed to share his brother's concern. Kyle leaned in. "What does Samson Oil want? They have to know the oil prospects are slim to none around here. People been drilling for over a hundred years. There's no way Samson will find a new well."

Case Baxter shook his head. "No one knows for sure what they're up to. Fracking, maybe. But the Cline Shale property is mostly bought up already in this area."

"If you've got concerns, I've got concerns," Kyle said as his senses tingled again. "I know a guy in the CIA. Owes me a favor. I'll have him poke around, see what Samson Oil is up to."

The offer was out of his mouth before he'd thought better of it. He didn't owe these people anything. It wasn't as if they'd rolled out the red carpet for the returning war veteran. Or acknowledged that Kyle Wade owned half a *cattle ranch* and wasn't even a member of the Texas Cattleman's Club.

Royal clearly wasn't where Kyle fit, any more than he had ten years ago.

"I knew you'd come in handy." Liam fairly beamed.

"That would be great," Mac threw in. "The more information we have, the better. The last thing we need is to find out they're looking for a site to house a new strip mall after it's too late."

The expectant faces of the men surrounding him settled Kyle's resolve. He couldn't take it back now. And for better or worse, this was his home, and he had a responsibility to it. He shrugged.

"Consider it done." Kyle sat back and let the members

of the club do their thing, which didn't include him. If he kept his mouth shut, maybe everyone would forget about him. It wasn't as if he wanted to be a member of their exclusive club anyway.

But then Liam's phone beeped, and he glanced at it, frowning. When his grave and troubled gaze met Kyle's, every nerve in Kyle's body stood on end.

"We have to go," Liam announced. "Sorry."

Liam hustled Kyle out of the club and into his truck, ignoring Kyle's rapid-fire questions about the nature of the emergency. Because of course there was one. Liam's face only looked like that when something bad happened to one of his prized horses.

Liam started the truck and tore out of the lot before finally finding his voice. "It's Maddie."

All the blood drained from Kyle's head and his chest squeezed so tight, it was a wonder his heart didn't push through two ribs. "What? What do you mean, it's Maddie? What happened?"

Not a horse. His daughter. Maddie.

"Hadley's not sure," Liam hedged. Kyle gripped his forearm, growling. "Driving here. Causing me to have a wreck won't get you the information any faster. I'm taking you to Royal Memorial. Hadley said Maddie wouldn't wake up and had a really high fever. With Maddie's heart problems, that's a really bad sign because she might have an infection. Hadley called an ambulance and left Maggie in Candace's capable hands. We're meeting them there."

The drive couldn't have taken more than five minutes. But it took five years off Kyle's life to be trapped in the cab of Liam's truck when his poor defenseless Maddie was suffering. The baby was fragile, and while she'd been growing steadily, obviously her insides weren't as strong as they should be. His mind leaped ahead to all the ugly possibilities, and he wished his heart *had* fallen out earlier, because the thought of losing one of his daughters—it was far worse than losing Grace. Worse than losing his place on his SEAL team.

Liam screeched into the lot, but Kyle had the door open before he'd fully rolled to a stop, hitting the pavement at a run. It was a much different technique from jumping out of a plane, and his leg hadn't been busted on his last HALO mission.

Pain knifed up his knee and clear into his chest cavity, which didn't need any more stress. The leg nearly crumpled underneath him, but he ignored it and stormed into the emergency room, looking for a doctor to unleash his anxiety on.

The waiting room receptionist met him halfway across the room. "Mr. Wade. Hadley requested that you be brought to the pediatric ICU immediately. Follow me."

ICU? Shades of the tiny room in Germany where Kyle had lain in a stupor for months filtered back through his consciousness, and his stomach rolled involuntarily, threatening to expel the beer he'd been happily drinking while his daughter was being subjected to any number of frightening people and procedures. The elevator dinged but he barely registered it above the numbness. Liam and the receptionist flanked him, both poor wingmen in a dire situation. But all he had.

Finally, they emerged onto the second floor and set off down the hall. Hadley rushed into Liam's arms, tears streaming down her face. They murmured to each other, but Kyle skirted them, seeking his little pink bundle, to assure himself she was okay and Maggie wouldn't have to grow up without her sister. The girls had already been through so much, so many hits that Kyle had already missed.

But he was here now. Ready to fight back against whatever was threatening his family. And that included his brother. The adoption business needed to be put to rest. Immediately.

"Who's in charge around here?" Kyle growled at the receptionist, who must have been used to people in crisis because she just smiled.

"I'll find the nurse to speak to you. Dr. Reese is in with your daughter now."

The receptionist disappeared into the maze of hospital rooms and corridors.

Hadley and Liam came up on either side of Kyle, and Hadley placed a comforting hand on his arm. "Dr. Reese is the best. He's been caring for Maddie since she was born. He'll know what to do."

That was far from comforting. If only he could see her, he'd feel a lot better.

A woman in scrubs with balloon decals all over them emerged from a room and walked straight to Kyle. "Hi, Mr. Wade, I'm Clare Connolly, if you don't remember me. We've got Maddie on an IV and a ventilator. She's stable and that's the important thing."

"What happened? What's wrong with her?" Kyle demanded.

"Dr. Reese is concerned about the effects of her high fever on her heart," Clare said frankly, which Kyle appreciated. "He's trying to bring the fever down and running some tests to see what's happening. The last surgery should have fixed all the problems, but nothing is guaranteed. We knew that going in and, well, we're going to keep fighting. We all want to win this thing once and for all."

This woman genuinely cared about Maddie. He could see it in the worried set of her mouth. Nurses were never emotional about their patients, or at least the German ones weren't.

"Thanks. For everything you're doing. May I talk to the doctor?"

"Of course. He'll want to talk to you, too. We all want to see Maddie running alongside her sister and blowing out candles on her birthday cakes for a long time to come. When Dr. Reese is free, he'll be out," Clare promised, and extended her hand toward the waiting room outside the pediatric unit. "Why don't you have a seat until then."

Clare bustled back into the room she'd materialized from, and Kyle nearly followed her because the waiting room was for people who had the capacity to wait, and that did not describe Kyle.

But Hadley's hand on his arm stopped him. "Let the doctor do his thing, Kyle. You'll only be in the way."

Long minutes stretched as Kyle hovered outside his daughter's room. What was taking so long? Pacing didn't help. It hurt. Everything inside hurt. Finally, another nurse dared approach him, explaining that the hall needed to be clear in case of emergency. Wouldn't he please take a seat?

He did, for no other reason than it would be a relief to get off his leg. Now if only he could find something to do with his hands.

People began filtering into the waiting room. Mac Mc-Callum came to sit with Liam and Hadley, who promptly excused herself to fill out paperwork for Maddie, which she'd offered to do in Kyle's stead so he could be available the moment the doctor came out with news. Hadley's friend Kori came in and took a seat next to Liam.

They all had smiles and words of encouragement for Kyle. Some had stories of how Maddie was a fighter and how many people had sat with her through the night when she was known as Baby Janey. This community had embraced his daughter before they'd even known whom she belonged to. And now that they did, nothing had changed. They still cared. They were all here to provide support during a crisis, which is what the very best of neighbors did.

And then the air shifted, prickling Kyle's skin. He looked up.

Grace.

She rushed into the room, brown curls flying, and knelt by his chair, bringing the scent of spring and innocence and everything good in the world along with her. As he soaked up her presence, he took his first easy breath since Hadley's message to Liam had upended his insides.

"I came as soon as Hadley called me," she said, her brown eyes huge and distressed as her gaze flitted over him.

The muffled hospital noises and people and everything around them faded as they focused on each other. Greedily, he searched her beautiful face for some hint as to her thoughts. Was she getting any sleep? Did she miss him?

She slid her hand into his and held on. "I'm sorry about Maddie. How are you doing?"

"Okay," he said gruffly.

Better now. Much better. How was it possible that the woman who continually ripped his heart out could repair it instantly just by walking into a room?

It was a paradox he didn't understand.

She climbed into the next chair, her grip on his hand never lessening. Her skin warmed his, and it was only then that he realized how cold he'd been.

"What did Dr. Reese say?" she asked.

Did everyone in town know the name of his daughter's pediatrician? "He hasn't been out yet. The nurse, Ms. Connelly, said her fever might be causing problems with her heart, but we don't know anything for sure."

His voice broke then, as sheer overwhelming helplessness swamped him, weighing down his arms and legs when all he wanted to do was explode from this chair and go pound on someone until they fixed his precious little bundle of pink.

"Oh, no." Grace's free hand flew to her mouth in anguish. "That's the one thing we were hoping wouldn't happen."

He nodded, swallowing rapidly so he could speak.

"Thanks," he said. "For coming."

He wouldn't have called her. But now that she was here Grace was exactly what he'd needed, and he never would have taken steps to make it happen. What if she'd said no? But she hadn't, and he didn't care about anything other than sitting here waiting on news about his daughter with the woman he loved. Still. In spite of everything.

If only it made a difference.

Eleven

Grace normally loved being at Royal Memorial because 99 percent of the time, she was there because someone was giving birth. That was a joyous event worthy of celebration. Waiting on news about the health and well-being of Kyle's baby was hands down one of the most stressful things she'd ever done.

At the same time, it was turning into a community event, the kind that strengthened ties and bonded people together. And she hadn't let go of Kyle's hand once. People seemed unsurprised to see them together. Not that they were "together." But they were easy with each other in a way that probably looked natural to others.

Inside, she was a bit of a mess.

How many times had she replayed that last conversation with Kyle in her head, wondering if she'd been too harsh, too unforgiving? If her standards were too high? She'd finally had to shut it down, telling herself ten times a day that she'd stood up for what she wanted for a reason. Kyle wasn't a safe bet for her heart. He'd proven that over and over.

But being here with him in his time of need brought all the questions back in a rush. Because it didn't feel as if they were through. It felt as if they were exactly where they were supposed to be—together.

It was all very confusing. She just hoped that supporting him during this crisis didn't give him the wrong idea—that she might be willing to forget her standards. Forget that he'd stomped on her heart again the moment she'd let her guard down.

Grace had lost track of the hour and only glanced at the clock when Kyle's stomach grumbled. Just as she was about to offer to get him something to eat, Dr. Reese appeared at the entrance to the waiting room, looking worn but smiling.

The entire room ceased to talk. Move. Breathe.

She and Kyle both tightened their grip on each other's hands simultaneously. When he rose, she followed him to the edge of the waiting room, where Dr. Reese was waiting to talk to Kyle privately. She stepped closer to Kyle in silent support, just in case the news wasn't as good as the expression on Dr. Reese's face might indicate.

"I'm Dr. Reese." Parker held out his hand for Kyle to shake. "Your daughter is stable. I was able to bring the fever down, which is a good sign, but I don't know if it adversely affected her heart yet. I need to keep her overnight for observation and run some more tests in the morning after we've both had some sleep. She's a fighter, and I have high hopes that this is only a minor setback with no long-term effects. But I'll know more in the morning."

"Call me Kyle. Formality is for strangers," Kyle said, and his relieved exhale mirrored Grace's. "And any man who saved Maddie's life is a friend of mine. Can I see her?"

Parker nodded instantly. "Sure, of course. She's asleep

right now, but there's no reason you can't stay with her, if you want—"

"Yes," Kyle broke in fiercely. "I'll be there until you kick me out."

That meant Grace wasn't going anywhere, either. If there were rules about that sort of thing, someone could complain to the hospital board, the mayor and Sheriff Battle. Tomorrow. No one was going to stand between her and the man who needed her.

Unless Kyle didn't want her there.

Would be weird to spend the night in the hospital with a man she'd told to get lost?

But then he turned to her, his expression flickering between cautious optimism and fatigue. "I'm glad you're here."

And that decided it. It still might be weird for her to stay, but he needed her, and she could no sooner ignore that than she could magically fix Maddie's frightening health problems.

They gave the others a rundown of the situation and implored them to spend the night in comfort at their homes with a promise to call or text everyone with more news in the morning. With hugs and more murmured encouragement, one by one, the full waiting room emptied out. Kyle smiled, shaking hands and accepting hugs from the women, while Grace watched him out of the corner of her eye to ensure he was doing okay.

What she saw surprised her. His small smile for each person was genuine and he returned hugs easily. For someone who hadn't wanted to come home, he'd meshed into the community well enough. Did he realize it?

Hadley stayed where she was.

"Liam and I will wait with you," she insisted, stubbornly crossing her arms.

Liam quickly hustled Hadley to her feet with a hushed

word in her ear. Whatever he said made her uncross her arms but didn't get her moving out of the waiting room any faster.

"I appreciate that," Kyle said. "But it's not necessary. You've done enough. Besides, I need someone I trust at home with Maggie, so Candace can get back to her house-keeping. That's the most important thing you can do for me."

Grace's heart twisted as she got more confirmation that she'd made the right decision in leaving Maddie and Maggie with Kyle—he clearly had both his daughters' interests in the forefront of his mind.

"Candace is trustworthy," Hadley countered. "She's watched Maggie plenty of times."

Liam captured his wife's hand and pulled on it, his ex-aggerated expression almost comical. "Sweetie, *Grace* is staying with Kyle."

Comprehension slowly leached into her gaze as Hadley finally caught her husband's drift. She started shuffling toward the exit. "Well, if you're sure. We'll be a phone call away."

And then they were gone, leaving Grace alone with Kyle. There was still tension between them but for now, the focus was on Maddie. This was the part where they'd be adults about their issues, just as they should have been all along, and get through the night.

"Guess they thought they'd leave us to our romantic evening," Kyle commented wryly as he nodded after Hadley and Liam. "I'm pretty sure that's why they went to Vail. To give me the house to myself for the weekend in hopes that I'd call you."

Not to get him to step up for his girls. That wasn't even necessary, probably hadn't been from the beginning. Liam and Hadley had gone to Vail for *her* benefit. Hers and Kyle's. And it would have been perfect if she and Kyle had only hashed out their issues before getting involved again, instead of hiding behind their defense mechanisms.

That's why she couldn't give him the slightest false hope that she was here because she wanted to try again. The problem was that she might have given *herself* that false hope.

For all her conviction that she'd made the right decision to walk away from him, something inside kept whispering that maybe it wasn't too late to take a step toward talking about their issues.

"Will you go with me to see Maddie?" Kyle's eyes blinked closed for a moment. "I'm not sure I can go in there by myself."

He'd been stalling. How had she missed that? Because she was busy worrying about what was going on with the state of their relationship instead of worrying about the reason they were here: Maddie. Some support system she was.

Grace smiled as she took his hand again, holding tight. "I'm here. For as long as you need me."

When his eyes opened, he caught her up in that diamond-hard green gaze of his. "Grace," he murmured, "come sit with me."

Meekly, she complied, following him into the hospital room where Maddie lay asleep in a bed with a railing. It looked so much like her crib at home, but so vastly wrong. Machines surrounded her, hooked to wires and tubes that were attached to her tender skin. Grace almost couldn't stand to internalize it.

Clare was checking something on one of the machines and smiled as they came in. "She's doing okay. Worn out from the tests. That couch against the window lies flat, like a futon, if you plan to stay. I have to check on some other patients but we've got Maddie on top-notch monitors, and I'll be back in a couple of hours. Press this button if you notice any change or need anything."

She held up a plastic wand with a red button at the end.

Kyle nodded. "Thanks. We'll be fine."

Then Clare bustled out of the room, leaving them alone with Maddie.

"I would trade places with her in a New York minute," Kyle said softly, his gaze on his daughter. "I would *pay* if someone would let me trade places. She's so fragile and tiny. How is her body holding up under all of those things poked into her? It's not right."

Grace nodded, her throat so raw from holding back tears, she wasn't sure she could speak.

All at once, he spun toward her, catching her up in his desperate embrace, burying his head in her hair. She clung to him as his chest shuddered against hers while they both struggled to get their anguish under control.

"I'm sorry," she whispered, forcing the words out.

"Thank you for staying with me. My life was so empty, Grace," he murmured. "For so long, I was a part of something, and then I wasn't."

"I know." She nodded. "You told me how much the military meant to you."

"*No*. Not that. *You*." Fiercely, he clasped her face in both palms and lifted her head and spoke directly to her soul. "Grace. Please. We have to find a way to make it work this time because I can't do this without you. I need you. I love you. I always have."

And then he was kissing her, pouring a hundred different meanings into it. Longing. Distress. Passion. Fear.

She kissed him back, because *yes*, she felt those things, too. He was telling her what she meant to him, first verbally and then through their kiss, and she was finally listening. But this was how it was with them. She got her hopes up and he dashed them.

What could possibly be different this time? She took

the kiss down a notch, and then pulled back. "Sit down with me and let's talk. For once."

That was *not* what she'd meant to say. She should have said no. Told him flat out that they were not happening again. But the eagerness on his face at her suggestion—maybe talking was that start toward something different than what she'd been looking for.

"We're not so good at the talking, are we?" he asked rhetorically, and let her lead him to the couch. They settled in together and held hands as they watched the monitors beep and shush for a moment. "I'm sorry about Emma Jane."

That was so out of the blue, she glanced at him sideways. "I've already forgotten that."

"I haven't. It was low. And totally unfair to both of you. I apologized to her, too." He stared at Maddie, his gaze uneasy. "I wish I had a better excuse for why I did it. I have a hard time just coming out and saying what's going on with me."

She bit her tongue—hard—to keep from blurting out, *Hallelujah and amen.* She didn't say a word. Barely.

"It doesn't come naturally," he continued, his voice strained, and her heart ached a little as he struggled to form his thoughts. "I'm used to being stomped on by people I trust, and I guess I have a tendency to keep my mouth shut. My rationale is that if I don't tell people what I'm feeling, I don't get hurt."

The tears that had been threatening spilled over then, sliding down her face as she heard the agony in his words. He fell silent for a moment, and she started to give him a pass on whatever else he was about to say, but he glanced at her and used his thumb to wipe the trail of tears from her cheek.

His lips lifted in a wry smile. "Guess what? It doesn't work."

Vehemently, she shook her head, more tears flying. "No,

it doesn't. If I'd just told you how I was feeling ten years ago instead of breaking up with you and then pulling that ridiculous stunt with Liam, we'd be at a different place. Instead, I hurt both of us for no reason."

All of that had been born out of her own inability to tell him what was going on with *her*. They were so alike, it was frightening. How had she never realized that?

"I've already forgotten that," he said, and this time, his smile was genuine and full.

"I haven't," she shot back sarcastically in a parody of their earlier conversation. "I spent ten years trying to forget you, and guess what? It doesn't work."

"For the record, I forgave you way before I ever showed up at your door with those poor flowers."

Chagrin heated her cheeks. That was mercy she didn't deserve. Actually, none of this was what she deserved— which would be for Kyle to walk out of this room with his daughter and never speak to her again.

Instead, it looked as though they were on the verge of a real second chance. *Please, God. Let that be true.*

"I'm sorry about the flowers. I was just so hurt and mad. It never even occurred to me that part of the problem was that I wasn't opening my mouth any more than you were. I don't even have a good excuse. So I'm trying to do things differently this time. Starting now." She covered their joined hands with her other one, aching to touch him, to increase the contact just a bit. "I have a hard time with separating what I think something should look like from reality. I wanted you to be dashing and romantic. Sweep me off my feet with over-the-top gestures and babble on with pretty poetry about how I was your sun and moon. Silly stuff."

Saying it out loud solidified that fact as she took in Kyle's still closely shorn hair that the military had shaped. He'd traveled to the other side of the world in defense of his country, seeing and doing things she could only imagine. What could be more dashing and romantic than *that*?

"I'm sorry I don't do more of that," he said gruffly. "You deserve a guy who can tell you those things. I can try to be better, but I'm—"

"No," she broke in, even as her voice shattered. She wasn't trying to make him into someone different. He was perfect the way he was, and she'd finally opened her eyes to it. "You do something wonderful like bring me flowers, and I don't even take them. I'm just as much to blame for our problems as you are. Probably more. You'd never have left if I had just told you every day what you meant to me."

Kyle was never going to be like her dad, who left notes all over the house for her mother to find and surprised her with diamond earrings to mark the anniversary of their first date. She doubted Kyle even *knew* the anniversary of their first date.

The way Grace felt right now, none of that stuff mattered. She had a man who demonstrated his love for her in a hundred subtle ways if she'd just pay attention.

He tipped her chin up with a gentle forefinger and lightly laid his lips on hers. When he finally pulled back, he said, "But I'm not sorry I left. I gained so much from that. Foremost, the ability to come back to Royal and be a father. I was lost and being a SEAL is how I found myself. I might never have had the courage to enlist if things hadn't shaken out like they did. I'd never have had Maggie and Maddie. There was a higher power at work, and I, for one, am very grateful."

She nodded because her heart was spilling over into her throat, and she wasn't sure her voice would actually work.

Her "standards" had been a shield she'd thrown up to keep other men away, when all along her heart had belonged to this man. And then she'd kept right on using her standards as an excuse to avoid facing her own failures.

There was so much more to say, so she forced herself to open her mouth and spill all her angst about the possibility of Kyle leaving again, which had also been an excuse. It was clear he was here for good—what more proof did she need? But that didn't magically make her fears go away, much as being in love didn't magically make everything work out okay.

He let her talk, holding her hand the whole time, and then he talked. They both talked until Clare came back into the room to check on Maddie, then they talked until Maddie woke up howling for a bottle. When she fell back into an exhausted sleep, they talked some more.

When dawn peeked through the window, they hadn't slept and hadn't stopped talking. Grace had learned more about the man she loved in those few hours than in the entire span of their relationship. Even though Kyle hadn't said *I love you* again—which honestly, she could never hear often enough—and in spite of the fact that he would never be a chatterbox about his feelings, it was hands down the most romantic night of Grace's life.

If only Maddie had miraculously gotten better, it would have been a perfect start to their second chance.

When Clare Connelly came into Maddie's room shortly after dawn, Kyle had to stand up and stretch his leg. With an apologetic glance at Grace, he stood and paced around the hospital crib where his daughter lay.

He didn't want to lose that precious contact with Grace, but she didn't seem to be in a hurry to go anywhere. That could change at a moment's notice. He wished he could express how much it meant to him that she'd stayed last night. His inability to share such feelings was one of the many things that had kept them apart.

"Dr. Reese will be in shortly," Clare told them. "Why

don't you go get some breakfast while I change Maddie. You need to get some air."

Kyle nodded and grabbed Grace's hand to drag her with him, because he wasn't letting her out of his sight. Last night had been a turning point. They were in a good place. Almost. Grace deserved a guy who could spout poetry and be all the things she wanted. But she was stuck with him. If she wanted him. Nothing had been decided, and along with the concern about Maddie, everything weighed on him. He was exhausted and emotional and needed *something* in his life to be settled.

They grabbed a bite to eat and about a gallon of coffee. When they returned to Maddie's hospital room, Liam and Hadley were waiting for them. Perfect.

"Any news?" Hadley asked anxiously. "I hardly slept. I was sure we'd get a text at any moment and have to rush back to the hospital."

"Nothing yet. The doctor will be here soon. I guess we'll know more then," Kyle said.

As if Kyle had summoned him, Dr. Reese strode down the hall and nodded briefly. "I'm going to start some more tests. I'll be out to give you the results in a bit."

The four of them watched him disappear into Maddie's room. What was Kyle supposed to do now? Wait some more to find out what was happening with his daughter?

Liam cleared his throat. "Hadley and I talked, by the way. We ripped up all the adoption paperwork. We're formally withdrawing our bid for custody of your daughters. It's pretty obvious you're the best father they could hope for, and we want you to know we're here for you."

Somehow he managed to blurt out, "That's great."

Grace nodded, slipping her hand into his. "He's an amazing man and an amazing father. I wouldn't have recommended that he retain custody otherwise."

Their overwhelming support nearly did him in. He'd

left Royal to find a new team, a place where he could fit in and finally feel like a part of something, only to learn that there really was no place like home.

"Just like that?" he finally asked Liam and Hadley. "You were going to adopt Maddie and Maggie. It can't be easy to live in the same house and realize what you've missed out on."

He wouldn't take to that arrangement too well, that was for sure. If they'd somehow gotten custody, there was no way he'd have stayed. And he'd have ruined his second chance with Grace in the process. Leaving was still his go-to method for coping. But if things went the way he hoped, he had a reason to stay. Forever.

Hadley shook her head. "It's not easy. It was one of the hardest conversations we've had as a couple, but it was the easiest decision. We both love them, so much, and want the absolute best for them. Which means *you*. They're your daughters. We're incredibly fortunate for the time we've had together, and besides, you're not going anywhere, right?"

"No." Kyle tightened his grip on Grace's hand. "I'm not. Royal is where I belong."

The words spilled from his heart easily, despite never dreaming such a thing would be true.

"Then it will be fine," Liam said. "We're still their aunt and uncle, and we expect to babysit a lot in the future."

"That's a deal." Kyle shook his brother's hand and held it for a beat longer, just to solidify the brotherly bond that they were forging.

Hadley and Liam waited with Kyle and Grace, chatting about the ranch and telling stories about Hadley's cat, Waldo. Finally, the doctor emerged, and Kyle tried to read the man's face, but it was impossible to tell his daughter's prognosis from that alone.

Quickly, he stood.

"She's going to make a full recovery," Dr. Reese proclaimed. "The tests were all negative. The fever didn't cause any more damage to her heart."

Everyone started talking at once, expressing relief and giving the doctor their thanks. Numbly, Kyle shook the doctor's hand and stumbled toward Maddie's room, determined to see her for himself to confirm that she was indeed fine.

After a few minutes, Grace forced him to go home with her so he could get some sleep, but he couldn't sleep. Now that he could stop worrying about Maddie so much, he couldn't get Grace's comments about being swept off her feet out of his mind.

They'd talked, and things were looking up, but no one had made any promises. Of course, it hadn't been the time or place. They'd been in a hospital room while his daughter fought for her life.

But he owed Grace so much. And now he had to step up. This was his opportunity to give her everything her heart desired.

When Hadley called Grace to invite her to a horse show Friday night, Grace actually pulled the phone away from her ear to check and make sure it was really Hadley's name on the screen.

"I'm sorry. Did you say a horse show?" Grace repeated. "There's no horse show scheduled this time of year. Everyone is busy with calving season."

In a town like Royal, everyone lived and died by the ranch schedule whether they worked on one or not. And Kyle had been conspicuously absent for the better part of a week as he pulled calves, worked with the vet and fell into bed exhausted each night.

He always texted her a good-night message, though, no matter how late it was. She might have saved them all, even though not one had mentioned talking about the future. It had been almost a week since the hospital, and she and Kyle had had precious few moments alone together since then.

That's what happened when you fell in love with a rancher.

She'd hoped he might be the one calling her for a last-minute Friday night date so they could talk. It wasn't looking too promising since it was already six o'clock.

"Don't be difficult," Hadley scolded. "Liam is busy helping Kyle and I need some me time. Girls' night out. Come on."

Laughing, Grace said yes. Only Hadley would consider a horse show a girls' night out activity. "Your middle name should be Horse Crazy."

"It is," Hadley insisted pertly. "Says so on my birth certificate. I already asked Candace to watch the girls, so I'll pick you up in thirty minutes. Wear something nice."

Hadley was still acting in her capacity as the nanny, though often, Grace dropped by to spend time with the babies. She and Hadley had grown close as a result. Close enough that Grace felt totally comfortable calling Hadley out when she said something ridiculous.

"To a horse show?"

"Yes, ma'am. I will be dragging you out for a drink afterward, if you must know. Be there soon."

Grace chuckled as she hung up. As instructed, she donned a pink knee-length dress that hugged her curves and made her look like a knockout, if she did say so herself. Of course, she wasn't in the market to pick up an admirer, but it didn't hurt to let the male population of Royal eat their hearts out, did it?

The only arena in Royal large enough for a horse show was on the west end of downtown, and Grace was a bit surprised to see a full parking lot, given the timing.

"How come I haven't heard anything about this horse show before now?" Grace asked, her suspicions rising a notch as even more trucks poured into the lot behind them. This arena was normally the venue of choice for the county rodeo that took place during late May, and it held a good number of people.

"Because it was last-minute," Hadley said vaguely with an airy wave. "Liam has some horses in the show, and that's how I found out about it."

"Oh." There wasn't much else to do at that point but follow Hadley into the arena to a seat near the front row. "These are great seats."

"Helps to have a husband on the inside," Hadley acknowledged with a wink.

The grandstand was already half-full. Grace waved at the continual stream of people she knew, and hugged a few, like Violet McCallum, who was looking a lot better since the last time they'd seen each other. Raina Patterson and Nolan Dane strolled by, Raina's little boy in tow, as always, followed by Cade Baxter and his wife, Mellie. The foursome stopped to chat for a minute, then found seats not far away.

The lights dimmed and the show started. Sheriff Battle played the part of announcer, hamming it up with a deep voice that was so far removed from his normal tenor that Grace had to laugh. And then with a drumroll, horses galloped into the arena, crisscrossing past each other in a dizzying weave. It was a wonder they didn't hit each other, which was a testament to the stellar handling skills of the riders.

Spotlights danced over the horses as they began to fall into a formation. One by one, the horses galloped to a spot in line, nose to tail, displaying signs affixed to their sides with three-foot high letters painted on them. *G-R-A-C—*

Grace blinked. The horses were spelling her name. They

couldn't be. And then the *E* skidded into place. The line kept going. *W-I-L-L*.

Something fluttered in her heart as she started to get an inkling of what the rest of the message might possibly spell out. No. It couldn't be. "Hadley, what is all of this?"

"A surprise," Hadley announced unnecessarily, glee coating her voice. "Good thing you took my advice and wore a pretty dress."

Y-O-U. The last horse snorted as he pranced into place. And then came the next one. *M—*

Holy cow. That definitely was the right letter to start the word she fervently hoped the horses were about to spell. All at once, a commotion to her right distracted her from the horses. The spotlight slid into the stands and highlighted a lone man making his way toward her. A man who was supposed to be in a barn at Wade Ranch. But wasn't, because he was here.

The last horse hit his mark and the sign was complete. *Grace, will you marry me?* It was the most beautiful thing in the whole world, except for the man she loved.

Her breath caught as Kyle arrived at her seat, wearing a devastating dark suit that he looked almost as delicious in as when he was wearing nothing.

She didn't dare look away as he knelt beside her and took her hand. "Hey, Grace."

Tears spilled from her suddenly full eyes, though why Kyle's standard greeting did it when nothing else thus far had was a mystery to her. "Hey, Kyle. Fancy meeting you here."

"Heard there was a horse show. It so happens I own a couple of horses. So here I am." He held up a small square box with a hinged lid. "Okay, I admit I set all this up because I wanted to do this right. I love you, Grace. So much. I want nothing more than to put this ring on your finger right now, in front of all these good people."

Yes, yes, yes. A thousand times yes. There was never a possibility of anything other than becoming Mrs. Kyle Wade. She'd never expected a romantic proposal. She'd have been happy with a quiet evening at home, but this… this took the cake. It was a story for the ages, one she'd recount to Maddie and Maggie until they were sick of hearing it. Because she was going to get to be their mother.

"I'd be okay with that," she said through the lump in her throat.

"Not yet." To her grave disappointment, he snapped the box closed and pocketed it. "You asked to be swept off your feet."

And then he did exactly that. As he stood, he gathered her up in his arms and lifted her from her seat, holding her against his chest as if he meant to never let go.

She'd be okay with that, too.

The crowd cheered. She noted Hadley clapping out of the corner of her eye as Kyle began climbing the stairs toward the exit, carrying Grace in his strong arms.

Kyle spoke into her ear. "I hope you won't be disappointed, but you're missing the rest of the show."

She shook her head, clinging to Kyle's amazingly solid shoulders. "I'm not missing anything. This is the best show in town, right here."

Looked as if she was an excellent judge of character after all.

Once he had her outside, he set her down and pulled her into his embrace for a kiss that was both tender and fierce all at the same time.

When he let go, she saw that a long black stretch limousine had rolled to a stop near them. "What is this?"

"Part of sweeping you off your feet," Kyle acknowledged. "Now that Maddie has fully recovered, I'm whisking you away on a romantic weekend, just you and me, to celebrate our engagement. But I want to make it official."

Then he pulled the box from his pocket and slid the huge emerald-cut diamond ring onto her finger. It winked in the moonlight and was the most beautiful thing she'd ever seen. Except for the man she loved. "Tell me this is forever, Kyle."

He nodded. "Forever. I'm not going anywhere. I'm a part of something valuable. I'm a cattle rancher now with orders pouring in for the calves I've helped deliver. The Texas Cattlemen's Club voted me in as a member earlier today. My daughters are thriving, and I'm going to get the best woman in the world as a wife. Why would I want to leave?"

"Good answer," she said as the tears flowed again. "But if you did decide you wanted to leave for whatever reason, I'd follow you."

"You would?" This seemed like news to him for some odd reason.

"Of course. I love you. I know now I could never be happy without you, so…" She shrugged. "Where you go, I go. We're a team now. Team Wade, four strong. And maybe more after we get the first round out of diapers."

He laughed softly. "I like the sound of that. Keep talking."

* * * * *

A SURPRISE FOR THE SHEIKH

SARAH M. ANDERSON

To Dad, who taught me the importance of never saying "very" when "damn" would do.

Prologue

This was really happening.

Ben's hot body pressed Violet against the back of the elevator. Something hard and long bumped against her hip, and she giggled. Oh, yeah—this was *so* happening.

She was really doing this.

"Kiss me," Ben said in that sinfully delicious accent of his as he flexed his hips against hers. She didn't know where he was from, but his accent made her think of the burning heat of summer sun—because boy, did it warm her up.

Violet ran her hands through his thick black hair and lifted his face away from where he'd been sucking on her neck.

He touched his forehead to hers. "Kiss me, my mysterious, my beautiful V." Then—incredibly—he hesitated just long enough to make it clear he was waiting for her decision.

Power surged through her. This was exactly why she was riding in an elevator in the Holloway Inn up to a man's room—a man who did not know she was Violet McCallum, who did not know she was Mac McCallum's baby sister.

Her entire life, she had been Violet. Violet, who had to be protected from the big bad world. Violet, the lost little girl whose parents died and left her all alone. Violet, who still lived at home and still had her big brother watching over her every move to make sure she didn't get hurt again.

Well, to hell with that. Tonight, she was V. She was mysterious, she was beautiful, and this man—this sinfully handsome man with an accent like liquid sunshine—wanted her to kiss him.

She was not Violet. Not tonight.

So she kissed him, long and hard, their tongues tangling in her mouth, then in his. She did more than kiss him—she raked her fingers through his hair and held him against her. She made it clear—this was what she wanted. He was what she wanted.

She hadn't come to this hotel bar a town away from Royal, Texas, with the intent of going to bed with a stranger. She hadn't planned on a one-night stand. She'd wanted to get dressed up, to feel pretty—maybe to flirt. She'd wanted to be someone else, just for the night.

But she hadn't counted on Ben. "You have beautiful eyes," he said in his sunshine voice, his hands sliding down her backside and cupping her bottom. "Among other things, my mysterious V." Then he lifted, and it was only natural that her legs went around his waist and that the long, hard bulge in his pants went from bumping against her thigh to pressing against the spot at her very center.

Violet's back arched as heat radiated throughout her body. Ben held tight to her, pinning her back against the elevator wall as he pressed his mouth to the cleavage that this little black dress left exposed. One of the hands that was cupping her bottom slid forward, snagging on the hem of her dress as he stroked between her legs. The heat from his hand only added to the raging inferno taking place under her skin.

"If you leave this elevator, you will be mine, you understand? I will lay you out on the bed and make you cry out. This is your last chance to take the elevator down."

A shiver of delight raced through her. Respectable Violet would never let a man talk to her like this. But V? "Is that a promise?"

"It is," he said in such a serious tone that she gasped. "Your pleasure is my pleasure."

That was, hands down, the sweetest thing anyone had ever whispered to her. Her entire life had been one long exercise in telling people what she wanted only to have to listen to the litany of excuses why she couldn't do what she wanted or couldn't have what she wanted. It was too risky, too dangerous. She didn't understand the consequences, she didn't this, she didn't that—every excuse her brother could throw at her, he did.

If Mac knew she was in this elevator with a man whose pleasure was her pleasure—well, there might be guns involved. This was risky and dangerous and all that stuff that Mac had spent the past twelve years trying to shield her from.

She was tired of being protected. She wanted something more than safety.

She wanted Ben.

"Why are we still in this elevator?" she asked in as

innocent a tone as she could muster, given how Ben's body was pressing against hers.

"You are quite certain?"

"Quite. But don't stop talking." The words hadn't even gotten out of her mouth before Ben hauled her away from the wall of the elevator and out into the hall.

"Are you this adventurous in everything?"

He was carrying her as if she weighed nothing at all. She was as light as a feather, a leaf on the wind, in Ben's arms. She was flying and she didn't ever want to come down.

She also didn't want to cop to her relatively limited experiences in the whole "pleasure" department. Every time she got serious about a guy, her brother—her well-meaning, overbearing brother—came down like the hammer of Thor and before Violet could blink, the guy would be giving her the it's-not-you-it's-me talk.

Violet may have had only a couple of boyfriends, but V was knowledgeable and experienced. She could not only handle a man like Ben, she could meet him as an equal. And so help her, no one was going to give her the let's-be-friends talk tonight. "Why don't we find out?"

He growled against her neck.

A door opened. "What's—" an older man, voice heavy on the Texas accent, said.

Ben stopped and, without putting Violet down, turned to stare at the old man in the open doorway. He didn't say anything. He didn't make a menacing gesture. He just stared down the other man.

"Ah. Well. Yes," the older man babbled as the door shut.

"Whoa," Violet said, giggling again. "Dude, you are—wow." So this was what exuding masculinity looked like.

"'Dude,' eh?" Ben said with a sexy chuckle as he

began walking down the hall. Every step made Violet gasp as Ben's hard length pressed against her sex. "For a woman as beautiful as you, you often talk like a man."

"I don't always wear little black dresses."

Ben stopped in front of another door. "Hmm," he said as his hands stayed on her body as he set her down, which effectively meant he hiked her dress up. "Are you sure you won't tell me your name?"

"No," she said quickly. She didn't want this fantasy night of perfection to be ruined by something as mundane as reality. "No names. Not tonight."

He got his key out and opened the door. Then his hands were back on her body, walking her backward into the room. "Who are you hiding from? Family?" He pulled her to a stop and turned her around. His fingers found her zipper and pulled it down, one slow click after another. "Or another lover, hmm?"

"I'm not hiding from anyone," she fibbed. It was a small fib because, no, she did not want Mac to know she'd done something this wild, this crazy. That's why she was in Holloway instead of Royal.

"We are all hiding from something, are we not?" Ben began to pull the dress down, revealing the black bra with the white embroidery that she wore only when she was feeling particularly rebellious. Which, in the last few months, was almost every day.

"I just—look," she said in frustration, taking a step back and pulling free of his hands. "I won't ask about you, you won't ask about me, and we use condoms. That's the deal. If that doesn't work for you…" She grabbed the sleeves of her dress and tugged them back up.

Ben stood there, his sinfully delicious lips curved into a smile. Oh, no—he wouldn't call her bluff, would he?

Because she wanted to strip him out of that suit—and she didn't want to walk out of this room until she was barely able to walk at all.

"I just need a night with you," she said, the truth of that statement sinking in for the first time since she'd walked into the bar at the Holloway Inn and laid eyes on this tall, dark and handsome stranger. She'd thought she just needed a night out, but the very moment Ben had turned to her, his coal-black eyes taking in her lacy black cocktail dress, her wavy auburn hair, her stockings with the seam up the back—then she'd needed him. And she wasn't going to rest until she had him. "That's all I'm asking. One night. No strings. Just…pleasure."

Ben stepped into her, cupping her face in his hands. "That is really all you want from me? Nothing else?"

The way he said it, with a touch of sadness in his voice, made her heart ache for him. She didn't know who he was or why he was here—he wasn't local, that much was obvious. But she got the feeling that in his real life, there were always strings.

She knew the feeling. And for tonight, at least, she didn't want to be hemmed in by other people's expectations of her. Good idea or not, she was going to take Ben to bed. There would be no regrets. Not for her. "No. Your pleasure is my pleasure," she whispered against his lips, turning his words back to him.

"Kiss me," he said against her skin.

So she did. She tangled her hands in his hair and pulled him roughly against her mouth, and then they were flinging each other's clothing off and falling into bed and she couldn't tell where her pleasure began and his ended because Ben was everything she'd ever dreamed a lover could be, only better—hotter, sweeter.

She fell asleep in his arms, listening to him whisper

stories to her in a language she did not know and did not understand, but it didn't matter. She was sated and happy. She'd started this night desperate to do something fun, something for herself.

Ben—no last name, no country of origin—was an answer to her prayers.

One

Four months later

This was *not* happening.

Dear God, please let this not be happening. Violet stared down at the thin strip of plastic. The one that said in digital block letters, *PREGNANT*.

Maybe she'd done it wrong. Peed on the wrong end or something. Yeah, that was it. She'd never taken a pregnancy test before. She hadn't even studied. She'd failed due to a lack of preparation, that was all.

Luckily, Violet had bought three separate tests because redundancy wasn't just redundant. It was confirmation that her night of wild passion four months ago with a stranger named Ben had not left her pregnant.

Crouched in the bathroom off of her bedroom, Violet carefully read the instructions again, trying to spot her mistake. Remove the purple cap: check. Hold the other

end: check. Hold absorbent tip downward: check. Wait
two minutes: check.

Crap. She'd done it right.

So she did it again.

The next two minutes were hell. The panic was so
strong she could practically taste it in the back of her
throat, and it was getting stronger with every passing
second.

The first test was just a false positive, she decided.
False positives happened all the time. She wasn't pregnant. She was suffering from a low-grade stomach bug.
Yeah, that was it. That would explain the odd waves of
nausea that hit her at unexpected times. Not in the morning either. Therefore, it wasn't morning sickness.

And the low-grade bug she was fighting—that's what
caused the positive. It had absolutely nothing to do with
that night in the Holloway Inn four months ago. It had
nothing to do with Ben or V or…

PREGNANT.

Oh, God.

One was a false positive. The second? Considering
that she'd had a wild night of passionate sex with a man
in a hotel room?

What the hell was she going to do?

She didn't have a last name. She didn't have his number. He'd been this fantasy man who had appeared when
she'd needed him and been gone by morning light. She'd
woken up in his room alone. Her dress had been cleaned
and pressed and was hanging on the bathroom door.
Room service had delivered breakfast with a rose and a
note—a note she still had, tucked inside her sock drawer,
where Mac would never see it.

Your pleasure was my pleasure. Thank you for the night.

He hadn't even signed it Ben. No name, no signature. No way to contact him when she had a rapidly growing collection of positive pregnancy tests on the edge of her sink.

She was screwed.

Okay, so contacting Ben was out, at least for the short term. She might be able to hire a private investigator who could track him down through the hotel's guest registry, but that didn't help her out right now.

"Violet?" Mac called out from downstairs. "Can you come down here?"

She was going to be sick again, and this time she didn't think it was because of morning sickness.

How was she supposed to tell her big brother that she'd done something this wild and crazy and was now pregnant? The man had dedicated the past twelve years of his life to keeping her safe after their parents' deaths. He would not react well.

"Violet?" She heard the creak of the second step—oh Lord, he was on his way up.

"Give me a minute!" she called through the door as she grabbed the two used tests and shoved them back in the box. She hid everything under the sink, behind her maxi pads. Mac would never look there.

She needed a plan. She was on her own here.

Violet stood up and quickly splashed some cold water on her face. She didn't normally wear a lot of makeup. She had no need to look pretty when she was managing the Double M, their family ranch. The ranch hands she'd hired had all gotten the exact same message, no doubt—hitting on Mac McCallum's little sister was strictly forbidden. Which irritated her. First off, she wasn't hiring studs for the express purpose of getting it on in the hayloft. Second, she was the boss. Mac ran McCallum Enterprises, the energy company their father had founded, and Violet ran the Double M, and the less those two worlds crossed, the better it was.

Because Mac did not see a ranch manager, much less a damned good ranch manager. He didn't see a capable businesswoman who was navigating a drought and rebuilding from a record-breaking tornado and still making a profit. He didn't see a partner in the family business.

All he saw was the shattered sixteen-year-old girl she'd been when their parents had died. It didn't matter what she did, how well she did it—she was still a little sister to him. Nothing more and nothing less.

Violet had wanted so desperately not to be Mac's helpless baby sister, even for a night. And if that night was spent in a stranger's arms...

And here she was.

She'd just jerked her ponytail out of its holder and started wrenching the brush through her mane of auburn hair when Mac said, "Violet?"

She jumped. She hadn't heard Mac come the rest of the way upstairs, but now he was right outside the door. "What?"

"An old friend of mine is downstairs. Rafe."

"Oh—okay," she said, feeling confused. Rafe—why did that name sound familiar? And why did Mac sound... odd? "Is everything okay?"

Ha. Nothing was okay, but by God, until she got a grip on the situation, she was going to pretend it was if it was the last thing she did.

"No, it's fine. It's just—Rafe is the sheikh, you remember? From college?"

"Wait." She cracked the door open and stared at her brother. Even though she'd hidden the evidence, she intentionally positioned her body between him and the sink. "Is this the guy who had the wild younger sister who tricked you? *That* Rafe?"

"Yeah. Rafiq bin Saleed." Mac's expression was a mix of excitement and confusion.

"What's he doing here right now?" Violet asked. "I mean, correct me if I'm wrong, but didn't he blame you for his sister's—what did you call it?"

"Compromising her innocence? Yeah."

"So why do I have to meet this jerk?"

"He's in town. He's apologized for his behavior years ago."

Violet stared at him. Men and their delicate attempts at friendship. "And you're okay with that?"

"Yeah," Mac said with a shrug. "Why wouldn't I be? It was a misunderstanding. His father was the one who was mad. Rafe is making amends."

After twelve years? That seemed odd. *Men.* "And you're warning me in advance because…"

"Because I know you, Violet. I know you're liable to shoot your mouth off. He's a sheikh—they have a different set of customs, okay? So try to be polite."

She gave him a dull look. "Really? You think I'm so impulsive I can't even make small talk with a man from a different culture?" She shoved the door open. Her hair could wait. "Thanks, Mac. I appreciate the vote of confidence there."

Mac grinned at her. "Said Violet, impulsively."

"Stuff it. Let's get this over with." She pushed past her brother and stomped to the closet, where she grabbed a clean shirt. If she was going to be meeting—wait, what was a sheikh? Were they royalty? Well, whatever he was, the least she could do was make sure she was wearing a shirt that didn't have cow poop on it. "I'll meet your rude sheikh friend and then make myself scarce, okay? I've got stuff to do anyway." Like maybe tracking down her one-night stand and figuring out her due date and, well, her schedule was just *packed*. She started unbuttoning her work jeans.

The wheels of her mind spun. This was going to change everything. She'd had plans—she'd been slowly working on convincing her brother to buy the ranch to the north, the Wild Aces. Violet had loved the Wild Aces for years. She wanted out of this house, out from under Mac's overprotective roof, and the Wild Aces was where she wanted to be.

They were already leasing the land. The Double M's water supply had been compromised by the tornado last year. But Wild Aces had plenty of water. Violet had thought that would be the motivation Mac needed to sign off on the purchase, but because she was the one who'd suggested it instead of his assistant, Andrea Beaumont, Mac had said no. Eventually, the two women had convinced Mac to at least lease the land.

But now? Violet was pregnant. How was she going to manage the Double M, much less the Wild Aces, with a huge belly or a baby on her hip?

Mac didn't say anything for so long she paused and looked up at him. "What?"

"Everything okay?" he asked.

She tensed. "Why wouldn't it be? It's fine. Totally fine."

Mac wrinkled his brow at her but before he could question her further, she said, "Shouldn't you be downstairs with your sheikh friend or something? So I can finish getting changed? Maybe?"

Mac paled. He may have stepped into the role of father figure after their parents' deaths, but he was still a big brother. An irritating one at that.

Okay, so she had a plan. She was going to pretend everything was just hunky-dory for the foreseeable future while she thought of a better plan.

Where was Ben? And even if she could find him, would he be happy to see her? Or would he claim that their night had had no strings attached and a baby was a huge string and therefore, she was on her own?

What a freaking mess.

"Sorry about that," Mac said, strolling back into the room. "Violet's...well, she's Violet."

Rafe sat in the center of the couch, surveying the room and the man before him. Mac had most certainly aged in the past twelve years, but he didn't have the haunted look of someone who had betrayed his best friend.

Rafe was not surprised, not really. At the time Mac compromised Nasira, he had exhibited little regard for Rafe's family's name. He did not look guilty because, more than likely, Mac McCallum was incapable of feeling guilt.

Revenge was a dish best served cold. But Rafe couldn't overplay his hand here. He put on a warm smile and said, "Yes, your younger sister—I remember. She was still in high school when we were at college, correct?"

"Yeah, that's right." Mac shrugged apologetically. If Rafe were capable of being sympathetic with a person such as Mac, he could sympathize over wayward younger sisters. "So," Mac went on, changing the subject. "Tell me about you, man. It's been years! What are you doing in town?"

Rafe shrugged, as if his being in Royal, Texas, were

some sort of happy accident instead of entirely premeditated. "My father is dead," he said.

Mac's cheeks reddened. "Oh, dude—sorry about that."

Rafe smiled—inwardly, of course. The last person to say "dude" to him in such a way had been V, the beautiful woman at the inn a few months ago. It had seemed so odd coming out of her perfect rosebud mouth. It was much better suited to a man like Mac.

Where was V now? That was a question that had danced at the edge of his consciousness for months. He had gotten better at putting the question aside, though. It was almost easy to not think of her. Almost.

"I appreciate your concern, but there is no need for sorrow. He was a…difficult man, as I'm sure you know."

Mac nodded sympathetically. In fact, before Mac's betrayal of Rafe's family, Mac had been one of the few people Rafe had confided in about his "difficult" father. There had been a time, long ago, when Rafe would have trusted this man with his very life.

Rafe did not trust people. He had learned that lesson well. Years spent locked up by his father had taught him that.

"With his passing," Rafe went on, "my older brother Fareed became the sheikh and I became more free to seek my way in the world." He tried to make it sound carefree and, in truth, some of it had been. Fareed had turned his attention to the modernization of their sheikhdom and released Rafe. Fareed had even entrusted Rafe with control of the family shipping business. All things considered, the reversal of fortune had been breathtaking.

But just because Rafe had no longer had to deal with Hassad bin Saleed did not mean he was free. He was still a sheikh. He had his people's honor and pride to preserve.

And if that meant waiting twelve years to exact his revenge, then so be it.

"I had meant to seek you out much earlier," Rafe went on, bending the truth until it was on the verge of breaking. "But my brother gave me the shipping company and I was quite busy turning the business around. You understand how it is. I am expanding my company's holdings and was looking to get into energy. The worldwide demand is rising. Naturally, I thought of you. I remember how fondly you spoke of this area and its many resources."

That was his story. Secretly, Rafe had been buying up land all over Royal, Texas, under the front of Samson Oil, a company he had created ostensibly to purchase the mineral rights and whatever remaining oil existed underground.

But Samson Oil was buying lands that had no more oil and no valuable mineral rights to speak of. The land was good for little else besides grazing cattle, and the entire town knew it. He had hired a Royal native, Nolan Dane, to act as the public face of Samson Oil. The townsfolk had been easily swayed by the outrageous offers and Nolan's down-home charm. They were happy to take his money—except, of course, that no one knew it was *his* money. By the time they figured out his scheme, it would be too late.

Rafe would own this town, and he would do with it as he saw fit.

Mac snorted. "Tell me about it. McCallum Enterprises has completely taken over my life. I can't even run the ranch anymore—Violet handles that for me."

"Your younger sister does a man's job?" But he was not truly surprised. Mac had always spoken of how outlandish his baby sister was—a tomboy, he'd said.

"She does a damn good job, too," Mac said in a thoughtful voice.

"I had thought she was going to follow you to Harvard." That had been the story Mac had told him all those years ago. But had that just been a lie to earn Rafe's trust as they bonded over difficult younger siblings?

"That was before our parents died. They went out for a flight on Dad's plane and..." Mac sighed heavily. "She was so lost after the accident, you know? I hated that I wasn't here for her when it happened."

"I had not realized," Rafe said sympathetically, even though of course he had realized. The McCallum family had suffered a terrible blow when Mac's parents' plane had crashed into an open field. There had been no survivors.

It all happened right after Rafe had been pulled out of Harvard by his father for daring to let his younger sister consort with the likes of Mac. Rafe had not found out the details of the accident for years afterward—after his own father had died and Rafe had suddenly had the means to investigate his enemies.

It had been a missed opportunity. If Rafe had been aware of the McCallums' deaths at the time, he could have moved swiftly to buy Mac's land out from under him or take over McCallum Enterprises. Instead, Rafe had to settle for watching and waiting for his next best opportunity to exact his revenge. He had not rushed. He was, as the Americans often said, playing the long game.

His patience had finally paid off when, last year, a tornado had torn through Mac's hometown of Royal, Texas. The town's economic base was weakened, which was good. But what was better was that Mac's water supply had become compromised.

It was a particularly good scheme. Rafe would not only cut off Mac's water supply and essentially strangle his ranch, but under the guise of Samson Oil, he would also buy up large parts of Royal. Mac had always spoken of his love for his hometown.

When Rafe was done with him, Mac would have nothing. No town, no land. That was what Mac had left Nasira with when he had betrayed Rafe's trust and ruined Nasira.

Thus far, Rafe had been operating in secrecy. But when his scheme came to fruition, he wanted Mac to know it was he who had brought about his destruction.

Which was why he was here, pretending to be concerned for the well-being of his former friend's sister. "Was it hard on her?"

"Oh, man," Mac said with a rueful smile. "I moved back home and tried to give her a stable upbringing, but never underestimate the power of a teenage girl. Hey, listen," he went on, leaning forward and dropping his voice a notch. "I know that things didn't end well between us…"

Rafe tensed inside but outside, he waved this poor excuse for an olive branch of peace away, as if he'd truly left the matter in the past. "It was all a long time ago. Think nothing of it."

"Thanks, man. I never meant to hurt Nasira, but I swear to you, I had no idea she was in my room that night. It wasn't what it looked like."

Rafe's mask of genial friendship must have slipped because Mac's words trailed off. Rafe rearranged his face into one of concern. "It's fine. She was able to marry a man who was more to her liking." It was time for a subject change. "Your sister, Violet? It has been a long time."

"Yeah—that's what I wanted to talk to you about. I

try to keep her out of trouble, but if you, you know, could just keep an eye on her while you're in town, I'd really appreciate it."

Now this was ironic. Here Rafe was, doing everything within his power to avenge the honor of his sister and his family, and Mac, the source of all his troubles, was asking Rafe to look after Violet?

That would be a new layer to Rafe's revenge—corrupting Mac's sister just as Mac had corrupted Rafe's.

"But of course," Rafe said as he bowed his head, trying to look touched that Mac would extend him this much trust. The fool. He was making this too easy.

"My ears are burning." Rafe heard the soft feminine—and familiar—voice seconds before its owner entered the room. "What are you two…talking…"

She stood in the doorway, her mouth open, all the color draining from her cheeks.

Rafe's body responded before his brain could make sense of what he was seeing. His gut tightened and his erection stiffened and one word presented itself in his mind—*mine*. The reaction was so sudden and so complete that Rafe was momentarily disoriented. This woman was lovely, yes, but her body was not the kind that usually invoked such an immediate, possessive response from him.

Then the conscious part of his brain caught up with the rest of him and he realized exactly who she was.

She looked different in the light of day. Rafe had not known her in such mannish clothing—jeans and work shirts. Her hair was pulled into a low ponytail at the nape of her neck and her face was scrubbed clean.

But he recognized her nonetheless.

V.

His mind spun in bewilderment. His mysterious, beautiful V was *here*? The woman he had been unable to put from his mind was…in Mac's home?

Mac stood and Rafe stood with him. This was an… unexpected development. He would have to brazen it out as best he could. "Ah, here you are. Violet, this is my old college friend, Rafe bin Saleed."

"*Bin* Saleed?" she said, her eyes so wide they were practically bursting out of her head. *"Bin?"*

"Um, yeah," Mac said, his gaze darting between the two of them. "Rafe, this is my little sister, Violet."

V was Violet. V was his mortal enemy's younger sister.

Destiny had a twisted sense of humor.

Inwardly, he was kicking himself, as the Americans said. Rafiq bin Saleed did not randomly bring a woman back to his bed. He did not seduce her and strip her and he most certainly did not send her love notes the next morning. He was a sheikh. He had no need for those things. His one night of passion with the exact wrong woman could threaten twelve years of planning.

Outwardly, however, he kept his composure. Years of facing his father's wrath had trained him well in remaining calm in the face of danger. He had to put a good face on this. His scheme had not yet come to fruition, and if Violet placed him in the greater Royal area four months before his "arrival" today, everything could be at risk.

All his schemes could fall apart in front of him, all because he had been unable to resist a beautiful woman.

Unless…a new thought occurred to him. Unless Violet already knew of his schemes. Unless she had been sent by her brother to find him all those months ago. Unless Mac had anticipated Rafe's attack and launched a counterattack while Rafe was distracted by a beautiful smile and a gorgeous body.

But she had insisted on no names. He had never used his real name, just as she had hidden hers. Was it possible that she had really just been looking for a night's passion?

He had no choice but to continue to play the part of the long-lost friend. He couldn't show his hand just because he had accidentally slept with this woman. "Violet," he said, letting the hard *T* sound of her name roll off his tongue, just as so many other things had rolled off his tongue. He bowed low to her, a sign of respect in his culture. "It is an honor to finally meet Mac's beloved sister."

"Is it?" she snapped.

Mac shot her a warning look. "Violet," he said quietly. "We talked about this."

"Sorry," she said, clearly not sorry at all. "I was expecting someone else entirely."

Rafe wanted to laugh. Truthfully, he had been, as well. But he did no such thing. Instead, he said calmly, "Have I come at a bad time?"

Americans had an expression that Rafe had never heard before he'd attended university at Harvard— "If looks could kill." In his sheikhdom of Al Qunfudhah, no one would dare look at a sheikh with such venom— to do so was to risk dismemberment or even death at the hands of Hassad bin Saleed, who had ruled with an iron fist and an iron blade.

But he was no longer in Al Qunfudhah, and if looks could kill, Violet would have finished him off several minutes ago.

He notched an eyebrow at her. He was more than capable of controlling himself. Could she say the same? Or was that why Mac had gone to speak to her privately— were they getting their stories straight?

You were *capable of controlling yourself,* a small voice in the back of his mind whispered. *Until you met her.*

"No, no," Mac said warmly. "Violet, maybe you should get us something to drink."

She turned her wrathful gaze to Mac and Rafe decided that, even if Mac had sent Violet to him, she had not told her brother the truth of their evening together. "Excuse me? Do I look like your maid?"

"Violet!" Mac sent another worried grin toward Rafe. "Sorry, Rafe."

Rafe waved his hand as if Violet's attitude were nothing. "We are not in Al Qunfudhah," he said, trying to set Mac at ease even as he enjoyed his old friend's discomfort. "I remember how things in America are quite different than they are back home. I do not expect to be served by the women in the house."

But even as he said it, he casually sat back in the middle of the sofa, spreading his arms out along the back and waiting to be served by someone. He took up as much space as he could. *I am here*, he thought at Violet, catching her eye and lifting his chin in challenge. *What are you going to do about it?*

Oh, yes. If looks could kill, he would be in extreme pain right now. "That's where you're from?"

The bitterness of her tone was somewhat unexpected. The last time he had seen her, she had been asleep in his bed, nude except for the sheets that had twisted around her waist. Her beautiful auburn hair had been fanned out over her shoulder, and even as she slept, her rosebud lips had been curved into a satisfied, if small, smile. She had looked like a woman who had been thoroughly pleasured, and Rafe had almost woken her up with a touch and a kiss.

But she had only asked for a night, so he quietly let himself out of the room, arranged to have breakfast sent up and then met with Nolan to go over his plans for purchasing more of the land around Mac's Double M ranch. He had tried mightily to put his night of wanton abandon with the beautiful V out of his mind.

Which was not to say he had succeeded. Not for the first time, he replayed their evening together. He had not coerced her—no, he specifically remembered several points where he had given her a respectable out.

It had been her choice to come to his room. Her choice to make it one night. Her choice not to use names or places.

As far as Rafe was concerned, Violet had nothing to be bitter about. He had made sure she had been well satisfied, just as he had been.

"I'll get us something to drink. Violet, can I talk to you in the kitchen?" Mac said, forgoing subtlety altogether.

"I'll take some lemonade," Violet responded, ignoring her brother's request and sitting in a chair across from Rafe. "Thanks."

Of course Rafe knew they were not in Al Qunfudhah anymore, but it was something of a surprise to not only see a woman give a man—her guardian, no less—an order, but to see that man heave a weary sigh and obey.

Perhaps if Nasira had felt freer to assert herself as Violet did...

Well, things might have been different. But knowing his father, things would not have been better.

Rafe pushed away those thoughts and focused instead on the woman before him. Violet was seething with barely contained rage, that much was obvious.

Once Mac was out of the room, Violet leaned toward him. "Rafiq *bin* Saleed?"

He would not let her get to him. She may be a slightly hysterical female, but he was still a sheikh. "It's lovely

to see you again, V. Unexpected, yes, but lovely nonetheless."

"Oh, it's unexpected all right. What the hell?"

He ignored her outburst. "You are well, I trust?"

Her eyes got wide—very wide indeed. "*Well?* Oh,
you're going to care now?"

He bristled at her tone. "For your information, I cared
that night. But it was you who asked for just that—a
night. Just one. So I honored your wishes. No names, no
strings—that was how you put it, was it not?"

She continued to glare at him. "What do I even call
you? Not Ben, I assume."

"Rafe will do for now."

"Will it? Is that your real name? Or just another alias?"

"My name is Rafiq," he said stiffly. He did not enjoy
being on the defensive. "Rafe is a well-known nickname
in my country."

Her nostrils flared, as if she were getting ready to
physically attack him. "Well, Rafe, since you asked, I
am not well."

"No?" Against his will, he felt a plume of concern rise
through his belly. He should be glad she was not well.
That would only cause Mac more suffering.

But Rafe was concerned. He wanted to pull her into
his arms and feel her breath against his skin and make
her well. He was a wealthy man. There was nothing he
could not provide for her. "Not because of something I
have done, I hope."

She was breathing hard now, as if she were standing
on the top of a tall peak and getting ready to jump. "You
could say that. I'm pregnant."

Rafe blinked at her, trying to comprehend the words.
Had she just said—*pregnant*? "Mine?"

She looked much like a lioness ready to pounce on her

prey, all coiled energy and focus. "Of course it's yours. I realize we don't know very much about each other but I don't normally pick up men. That was a one time thing. You're the only man I've been with in the last year and *you* were supposed to use *condoms*!" She hissed the word but quietly. It was for his ears and his ears alone.

Before he could come up with something reasonable to say—something reasonable to think, even—Mac strode back into the room, carrying a tray with a pitcher and glasses. "Lemonade?"

Two

Rafe just…sat there. For Pete's sake, he didn't even blink when Mac walked back into the room. Violet's whole world was falling apart around her and Rafe looked as though she'd announced she liked French fries instead of the fact that she was carrying his child.

She couldn't take it. She needed to go. If she could make it back to a bathroom, where she could throw up in peace and quiet, that'd be great.

"Actually," she said, forcing herself to stand. "I'm not thirsty. Thanks anyway, Mac."

The father of her unborn baby was not just some nameless stranger she'd met in a bar. Oh, no—that would be getting off easy. If that were the case, she'd merely be pregnant and alone. Which was a terrifying prospect, but comparatively?

The father of her child was a sheikh. And not just any sheikh. Her brother's former friend, the one who had blamed Mac for seducing his sister and ended the friendship under no uncertain terms.

Oh, she was going to be so sick.

She willed her legs not to wobble as she stood. Ben or Rafe or Sheikh Saleed or whatever his name was stood with her.

In the past thirty-some-odd minutes, her perfect fantasy night had somehow become an epic nightmare. Had she been dreading telling Mac she was pregnant before? Ha. How the hell was she supposed to tell him now? *I'm expecting and by the way, the father is your old friend. Isn't that a laugh riot?*

Mac already treated her as though she was still a lost little girl of sixteen. What would he do now that she'd proven how very irresponsible she was?

Oh, God—this was going to change everything. It already had.

She turned and headed for the door, but due to her wobbly legs, she didn't get out of the room fast enough. "Violet," Rafe said in his ridiculous voice, all sunshine and honey, and damned if the sound of her name on his lips didn't send another burst of warmth and desire through her. Her head may have been a mess, but her body—her stupid, traitorous body—still wanted this man. Hell.

It didn't matter. She couldn't let his accent melt her from the inside out, because what had happened the last time? She'd ended up pregnant and unmarried. Violet did not often think of her parents—the loss was too painful, even after all these years—but right now, what she wanted more than anything was her mother.

"What?"

Mac winced and Violet could almost hear him adding, *Said Violet, impulsively.*

"I would like to know more about Royal and catch up with my old friends." Something about the way Rafe said *friends* hit Violet wrong, but before she could figure out what it was, he went on, "Would you both join me for dinner tomorrow night?"

What had she done to deserve this? Because the torture of sitting through dinner with both her brother and her former lover at this exact moment of her life and pretending that nothing had changed was right up there with being stepped on by a herd of stampeding cattle.

"Well, damn," Mac said. "I'm going to be out of town. But Violet can go with you."

That was just like Mac, to assume that she spent all her free time painting her nails and listening to Backstreet Boys. She rolled her eyes at Rafe, which must not have been something people in his country did, given the way the color on his cheeks deepened.

Still, Rafe forged on, by all appearances completely unbothered by her impulsiveness or her pregnancy—except for that blush, which only made him look more sinfully handsome. Damn the man.

"Ah, that is acceptable. That way I can keep an eye on you." His gaze never wavered from hers. "Shall we meet tomorrow, say at seven?"

And Mac, the rat bastard, nodded his approval, as if they were having this entire conversation about her without remembering she was in the room.

She was totally going to blame this on hormones, this mix of rage and self-pity and the sudden urge to cry, all folded in together with desire and relief until she was so mixed up she couldn't think straight.

But had Mac already asked this man to keep an eye on her? Violet *so* did not need a babysitter at this point.

In six months or so, yes, she would need a babysitter. But before she had an actual baby, she did not. "I don't—"

"Sure, that'd be great," Mac said warmly, as if Violet were incapable of having dinner on her own without getting into some sort of trouble. "I have a meeting with Andrea scheduled that I can't get out of—Andrea's my assistant," he added, seeing Rafe's quizzical look. "But you two can go on and have a nice time."

A nice time? Oh, she had some things she wanted to say to her brother—about Rafe—but the fact was, she did actually need to talk with Rafe. Alone. "Yeah," she said, trying to sound at least a little bit excited about the prospect. Four months ago, another evening with her mystery man, Ben, would have been too good to be true. But now? "Sure. Dinner."

Rafe gave her a small smile that absolutely did not appease her. She hated him right then, because her entire world had just blown up in her face and the father of her child stood there looking as sexy as he had the night he'd taken her to bed. This pregnancy was going to change everything for her—but for him?

Yeah, they needed to talk. Preferably where no one would interrupt them to offer lemonade. "Tomorrow, then," Rafe said.

"Sounds good." Mac was staring at her, so she dug deep for something polite to say. "I look forward to it."

Rafe tilted his head down but kept his gaze locked on hers. "As do I."

"Say, Rafe, in two nights, I'll be at the Texas Cattleman's Club—we've got a meeting. If you're interested in setting down some roots locally, you could come with me."

Violet started choking. Somehow, the air had gotten

very sharp in her throat. She couldn't have heard that right—could she have? "What?"

Rafe inclined his head at Mac, but he spoke to Violet. "I have been considering branching out into the energy business, so naturally I sought out my old friend."

"Oh, naturally. That makes total sense." She tried to smile, but it must have looked more like teeth baring, because both men recoiled slightly.

Something didn't add up here. But her head was such a hot mess right now that she had no hope of figuring out what it was.

"I shall see you for dinner tomorrow night," Rafe said, and she didn't miss the particular timbre of his voice that seemed designed to send a thrill through her body. Then he turned, giving Mac a big smile that seemed less than sincere, Violet thought. "And I would be delighted to see this club of yours."

"Great," Mac said, clearly missing the forced smile. "It's a plan!"

Morning sickness was a lie. This was what Violet had concluded after a night and a day of suffering with a roiling stomach.

Of course, there was also the possibility that it was not morning sickness. A quick web search revealed that most people were only sick for the first three months, and Violet was safely in her fourth month. After all, she knew the exact date of conception.

Just thinking about that night in Ben's—Rafe's—arms again made her stomach turn. Frankly, she defied anyone to not have an upset stomach in a situation like this.

She stood in front of her meager closet in nothing but her panties and bra—her regular bra, not the black-with-white-embroidery number she'd been wearing when she met Rafe. This was a smooth white T-shirt bra. Not a danged thing sexy about it.

Because that's who she was—functional and dull and not terribly sexy. If Rafe thought she was going to show up for dinner tonight as V again, he had another think coming.

Besides, her one fancy cocktail dress—black with the lacy sleeves—well, it didn't exactly fit right now. She'd already tried it on and she couldn't get it zipped.

All those little changes her body had been experiencing—the slight weight gain, the nausea, the overwhelming urge to nap—she'd written off each and every little bump in the road as exhaustion or a bug or the changing of the seasons or stress or, hell, the phases of the moon. But now?

Not a bump in the road. A baby bump.

She had a plan. She had an appointment with an obstetrician in Holloway in two weeks. It was ridiculous that she felt she had to go to the next town over, but she hadn't exactly decided just yet on how she was going to tell Mac about this "bump in the road." She kind of had it in her mind that once she had a doctor's official... whatever, it would be easier to talk to Mac. But if she went to the local doctor in Royal, word might get back to Mac before she could gird her loins. So she was just buying a little time here.

And as for Rafe...okay, she was still working on that part of the plan. She'd done another quick internet search on his country, Al Qunfudhah. The Wikipedia article had stressed that, compared to some of the neighboring countries and kingdoms, women enjoyed a great deal of freedom in Al Qunfudhah, but the article had hit Violet funny. Why would anyone make such a big deal about women being able to drive as if it were some wondrous gift?

She did not know what Rafe intended to do. He really was, according to that same article, a sheikh. His brother ruled the country. His father had died a few years ago. But beyond that?

It had been bad enough when she'd been pregnant with some random stranger's baby. But a sheikh's baby?

She was getting ahead of herself. Dinner first. And that meant she needed to put on clothes.

She finally settled on one of her few dresses—the fanciest dress she'd owned, until she'd bought the black one on a whim. It was an olive-green cotton dress with tiny pink flowers printed on it, and it had a pink satin bow at the scoop neck. It was just a little bit girlie but also, due to the darker color, not so girlie. Plus, it was a forgiving cut and it still fit. She paired it with her jean jacket and her nice pair of brown boots, the ones with the pointed toe. She twisted her hair up and pinned it into place, but she decided against dangly earrings. This wasn't a date. This was a…negotiation, really.

That didn't stop her from putting on small hoops, as well as mascara and a little blush, though. Not enough that it looked like she was trying, but every little bit helped.

At least Mac wasn't here. If he saw her in any dress at all, he'd start asking questions. Outside of weddings and Easter services, she was not known for busting out the dresses.

She was debating the merits of her regular tinted lip balm versus actual lipstick when the doorbell rang. Crap. Violet started to hurry, but then thought better of it. She was not at Rafe's beck and call. She was pregnant. She would not hurry to accommodate him. He'd better get used to doing the accommodating around here. She slowly applied a light layer of a deep pink lipstick and then grabbed her jacket. She was cool, calm and collected. No reason to be nervous, right? Just dinner with the father of her child. Easy peasy.

But by the time she got downstairs, she was on shaky legs and it only got worse when she opened the door to find Rafe standing there, a devilish grin on his face and a single red rose in his hands. And then he took her in, her dress and her boots and her jacket, and she wished in that moment she'd tried a little harder to get the zipper up on her black dress.

"Ah," he said in a voice that sent a shiver through her. The voice was so unlike the way he'd spoken to her yesterday that she stared at him. This was the man she'd met in a bar. This was the man who'd taken her to bed.

"Hello," she said, feeling unsettled because it was so hard to reconcile this man with the one who'd sat in the living room yesterday and looked at her as if she were a deer and he were a wolf.

He still looked as though he wanted to devour her, but the difference was so startling that she was helpless to do anything but stand there, gaping.

He held out the rose. "A beautiful flower for a beautiful woman."

She couldn't help it: she wanted to kiss him again. She wanted to feel the way he'd made her feel, beautiful and sensual and desirable. But now that they knew who the other was, she didn't think chasing that little bit of happiness was the best idea. "Look—is this a date? What is this?"

There was that hardness in his expression again and she had to fight the urge to step back. She was *not* imagining that. "I would never force you to do something against your will, Violet. If you would like to go to dinner as friends, then we may do that. If you would like to consider this a more romantic evening…" His voice trailed off as his eyes warmed.

She took the rose and set it down on the foyer table. "The last time we had a romantic evening, things went wrong." Two-positive-pregnancy-tests wrong. "I think we should get a few things settled before we do anything else."

"Yes, that is a wise choice. It would be too easy to… well." She could be seeing things but he might have actually blushed. "Shall we? I made reservations at Claire's."

"Oh." Claire's was one of the nicest restaurants in town and she was wearing a jean jacket. Crap. She looked down at her outfit. "Maybe I should change?"

"You look beautiful," he said, stepping toward her. Before she could react, he had cupped her chin in his hand and lifted her face. "You were beautiful that night and you are beautiful now. And anyone who would deign to criticize you will face my wrath."

Wow, that was the sexiest-sounding threat she'd ever heard. Violet was speechless. Even if she could talk, she had no idea what might come out of her mouth. Something impulsive? Something stupid? Both?

Or, worse, would she tell him how much she'd missed him, how much she'd savored their night together?

Because it would be terrible for him to back her into this house and carry her up the stairs the way he'd carried her down the hall of his hotel. It would be awful if he laid her out on her own bed and did all those things he'd done before.

Yup. It would simply be the worst.

"Ah," he breathed, so close to her that she could have tilted her head just a little and brought her lips against his, "you asked me what this evening is about. But now I ask you—what is it you want this evening to be?"

Violet was used to dealing with men. She did a man's work, day in and day out. She dealt with cowboys and her brother, and didn't spend a hell of a lot of time in a beauty salon, gossiping with other women. She could more than hold her own when some jerk got it into his head that she, a delicate female, shouldn't be fixing fences or branding cattle or any of those manly things men liked to think they were the only ones capable of getting done. Men who decided they were alphas and she had to fall into line either got their metaphorical butts handed to them on a platter or a black eye as a souvenir of the experience.

So, really, Violet should not have felt this urge to give in to Rafe, to tell him that whatever he wanted, she wanted. But she was tempted. The masculinity coming off him was so strong, so potent, it was almost as if she could see the air shimmering around him, like heat off a highway.

All those men before—they'd been all talk. They had to tell people they were the boss because otherwise, no one else would know it. But Rafe? Jesus, he was in a different class. This was not just an alpha man, this was a man born to power, a man who breathed it as easily as he breathed air.

This was a sheikh. *Her* sheikh.

But just as she was about to succumb to his sheer machismo, she remembered their situation.

So she forced herself to lift her chin out of his grasp and she forced herself to stare into his eyes—dark and warm and waiting on her to say the word so he could strip her right out of her dress—and she said, "I want to figure out how we got here and what we're going to do next." Dang it all, her voice came out as something closer to sultry than businesslike.

Rafe heard it, too, and his lips curved into a knowing

smile. "Ah, yes. How we got here. I seem to recall carrying a beautiful, mysterious woman to my room and—"

"No, stop." Heat flushed her body, but she was not going to fall for him a second time. She had enough going on right now. "I mean more along the lines of what happened afterward. I'm pregnant. We need to be taking this seriously."

That worked. Rafe straightened and, sighing, nodded. "Would you like to discuss this over dinner or somewhere more private?"

Private was good. Private was great. But private also meant more of those smoldering looks and hot touches from this man and again, she was totally going to blame the hormones on this one, but she didn't know how strong she could be if she had to fend off those sorts of advances all evening long. "Dinner," she said decisively.

Rafe, to his credit, didn't use all of his innate power to overrule her, just as he hadn't coerced her into doing anything she hadn't wanted that night. Instead, with a nod of his head that veered closer to a bow of respect than anything else, he said, "Dinner, then."

Three

Rafe and Violet were shown to a secluded table tucked into a small alcove in the back of the restaurant. Perfect.

He needed this dinner to be in the public eye because he had little doubt that word of it would make its way back to Mac, and Rafe wanted everyone to see him acting like a gentleman. But he also needed to be hidden away enough that he and Violet could discuss things like pregnancy and plans without being overheard.

He held Violet's chair for her, which gave him the opportunity to admire her from the back. There'd been a moment earlier this evening when he'd wanted nothing more than to sweep her off her feet and carry her to a bedroom. Any bedroom would do. In this outfit, she was not the seductress V had been all those months ago, but she was also not the angry cowgirl who, just yesterday, had informed him she was carrying his child.

Yesterday, she had not been so very hard to resist,

between her shell-shocked appearance and her perhaps justifiable anger. But today?

As she sat, Rafe had to physically restrain himself from leaning down and pressing his lips against the exposed nape of her neck, right next to where a tendril of hair had escaped her updo and lay curled against her fair skin like an invitation.

He managed not to kiss her there, but he must have stood too still for too long, for Violet turned and looked up over her shoulder at him and said, "Yes?"

Rafe didn't answer immediately. He took his time circling the table and taking his seat. "I do not think I have told you how glad I am to see you again."

Violet notched an eyebrow at him. "Seriously? You didn't act all that glad yesterday."

"True. But I think that, given the surprising nature of our reunion, we can both be forgiven for being less than enthusiastic at first."

Her eyes narrowed and he got the feeling he'd said the wrong thing. "Oh, really?"

This called for a tactical retreat. A fast one. "Let us plan, as you have requested. How long have you been aware of your impending blessing?"

Because he needed to know that she was being honest—that not only was she expecting, but that it was his child. The four months between that evening and this one left plenty of time for her to have taken other lovers.

Her cheeks colored. "Well, since yesterday. I was in the process of peeing on a stick when Mac came to tell me you were in the living room."

Rafe coughed over her coarse language, which made her eyes narrow again. "I did not realize," he said. "Just... yesterday?"

"Yes." After a pause, she said, "I had been feeling a

little off for a while—super tired all the time, gaining a little weight. I had thought maybe I just had a stomach bug that was hanging on, but then my friend Clare started asking about how I was feeling and suggested…" She swallowed, staring at her water glass. "And I bought a test. A three-pack, just in case, you know?"

"I see," he said, although he was not entirely sure he did. "How many tests were positive?"

"Two. I didn't believe the first one. But two that said the same thing…" Her voice trailed off sadly. "I guess I was maybe a little rude yesterday, but I had gone from suddenly realizing I was pregnant and wondering how the heck I was ever going to find you and tell you, to walking into the living room and finding you. Except you weren't who you said you were."

"Yes," he said sympathetically. "I can see why that would have been a bit of a shock. It was quite unexpected to see you again."

She wrinkled her nose. "Why did you say your name was Ben that night?"

This was dangerous territory because the truth would endanger his scheme. So he turned her question back on her. "Why did you go by V?"

She did not answer immediately and then, just as she opened her mouth to respond, the server came up to take their orders. Rafe did not often drink. In fact, he had not drunk wine since that night. Perhaps that was why he had taken V to bed, because his inhibitions had been lowered.

But tonight, he decided he needed a glass of wine to get through this evening. Otherwise, he might overreact the way he had to Violet's announcement yesterday and if he enraged her again, it would put his whole scheme in danger of collapsing.

He did not know if Violet was his friend or his enemy.

What she was, at this point, was a former lover, and those relationships could go either way. But no matter how this played out, Rafe knew he needed to keep her close.

So he ordered a bottle of sauvignon blanc to accompany his filet mignon and her chicken dish. In the past several months, he had grown quite fond of Texas beef. Even the barbecue was delicious and quite unlike the way beef was prepared in his country.

But when he placed their orders, Violet narrowed those beautiful eyes at him again. It was only when the server was safely out of earshot that she leaned forward and said in a tense whisper, "I can't drink."

"Oh?"

"Because I'm pregnant?" she said, although it was clearly not a question. "I'm not supposed to drink." A look of panic flared over her face. "Do you know anything about pregnancy? About babies?"

Rafe rolled his hand. "Of course not. I do not have any children and, if I did, we would have nannies to care for them. That is how I was raised."

Had he thought this declaration would relieve her anxiety? If so, he had guessed wrong. The color drained out of her face and, if anything, she looked more worried than before. "Nannies? As in, plural? I didn't—I mean, that's not what I had been thinking for our child."

"Let us not get ahead of ourselves," he cautioned, because that look of terror on her face made him strangely uncomfortable. He should be reveling in her panic—thrilled, even, that he was striking such a blow against Mac's sister. This was revenge at its finest.

And yet, it wasn't. If her pleasure had once been his, her terror was also his. It was a weakness he did not like because weaknesses could be exploited.

"Okay," she said softly.

"Let us start at the beginning," he went on, more gently than he had planned to. But it worked because she took a deep breath and sat back in her chair, looking almost calm. "I did not realize who you were that night. And I assume, based on your statement earlier that you were wondering how you'd find me, you did not know who I was?"

"No, I didn't. No names. That was the deal." She cleared her throat and began to fiddle with her silverware, arranging the knife and the fork in perfect alignment. "I was V for the same reason I was out in Holloway instead of Royal. I wanted a night out where word wouldn't get back to Mac." She looked up and he could see in her eyes that she was pleading with him. "He wants what's best for me, I know that. But sometimes…he can be suffocating. I mean, he doesn't think this is a date because he asked you to keep an eye on me, didn't he?"

"This is true," Rafe confirmed.

She exhaled heavily. "That's how he is. Every man is either a threat to my innocence or a babysitter."

"But you have reached your maturity," Rafe noted. "You are not the same little sister he told me about when we were in university twelve years ago."

She snorted. "Try telling him that. He still treats me like I'm sixteen and lost without my parents. But I'm not. I'm a grown woman now and I'm capable of running half the family business and…okay, so getting pregnant wasn't my finest hour, but I can do this, Rafe."

Rafe thought this over as the wine was served. Violet asked for a Sprite instead. "I must ask—your innocence?"

"Lord," Violet said, rolling her eyes toward the ceiling, and Rafe couldn't tell if she was praying for strength or something else. "Fine. No, I was not a virgin. You?"

Rafe almost glared at her because this line of questioning was not something sheikhs had to endure. But as she watched him, he quickly realized that, to Violet, he was not primarily a sheikh. He was, first and foremost, a man to whom she would be forever tied. "No. And before you ask, I am not currently seeing anyone else. In fact, except for our evening together, I have been celibate for some time."

Her lips quirked into something that was almost a smile. "Celibate, huh?"

He shrugged, trying to keep it casual. "I have been busy. My brother is the sheikh of Al Qunfudhah and I run the shipping business owned by our family. While our sheikhdom was originally founded on oil, we have diversified and my shipping business now accounts for thirty percent of the gross domestic product."

"But celibate? You're a sheikh," she said, clearly puzzled. Then her gaze drifted over his face, his shoulders, and down his chest before she looked back at him. "And you're gorgeous."

Rafe felt his face warm. "So I have been told. But just because I could have any woman I want does not mean I should."

"And modest," she added in a mocking tone. But she smiled when she said it. "That's a refreshing attitude, I have to tell you. Most men would take whatever they could get."

"I am not 'most men.'"

"No," she agreed, her smile warming. "You're not."

Rafe was pleased. He should have been pleased because Violet was opening up to him and the more he drew her in, the more complete his revenge would be.

But that was not why he leaned forward and placed his hand on top of hers, stilling it in the middle of adjusting the precise placement of her soup spoon. "And you? Are you involved with anyone?"

"No," she said in a breathy whisper. "Most guys don't last too long before my brother scares them off."

"That must be frustrating."

She tried to shrug off both the sentiment and his hand and, given that they were in public, he had no choice but to sit back in his seat. "It is, but it's also a blessing—I guess. If they can't stand up to Mac, how could I expect them to stand next to me, you know?"

Rafe thought about this. He knew, without a shadow of a doubt, that standing against Mac would not be problematic. "Indeed."

Their meals arrived along with Violet's soda. She sipped at it gingerly and took small bites of her food. "Is it all right?" he asked, concerned. If she was expecting, shouldn't she be eating more?

"It's fine. I just—well, I've been dealing with morning sickness—which is a lie, by the way. My stomach's most upset in the evening. And for a lot of people, it ends after the third month, but I think it's actually getting worse."

This news was alarming. "Have you seen a doctor yet? Do you think everything is all right?"

She looked at him, trying not to smile and not quite succeeding. "I'm fine. According to the internet, this is all normal. I scheduled an appointment with a doctor in Holloway and the quickest they could get me in was in two weeks."

He set his knife and fork down a bit harder than he meant to, given how the beverages danced in their glasses and Violet's eyes widened. "That is not soon enough. I can have a private doctor here tomorrow—Friday at the latest."

"Rafe," she said, her soft Texas accent caressing

his name like a lover's hands. She'd said *Ben* that way, but not *Rafe*. Not like that. It was enough to make him pause as he typed in the password to his phone. "It's fine. There's no danger."

"I merely want what is best for you and the child," he said, his voice getting caught somewhere in the back of his throat. And he was surprised to realize how very much he meant it.

"Yeah," she said in that quiet voice, "about that. Okay, so I'm not seeing anyone and you're not either. Which doesn't mean that we're together."

"I would not make such presumptions," he assured her.

"It just means that, for once, there's one less complication to deal with."

"Agreed. And I would not be outside of bounds if I asked you to refrain from starting a relationship with anyone else while you are carrying my child, would I?"

What started out as a smile progressed into a full giggle. There was simply no other word for it. Violet McCallum was giggling at him. "Out of bounds. Not outside."

He should have been insulted that she was mocking him. What was it about this woman that made him not only accept her teasing, but crave it? "Ah, I see. Thank you. I shall remember 'out of bounds' in the future."

"No," she said, wiping a tear from her eye. "You are not out of bounds. Dating is a challenge in the best of times. Right now, I can't see how it'd be anything but impossible. I am not looking to start a relationship right now."

A new thought occurred to him as Violet settled down and sipped her soda. Rafe's original plan, once he had realized that Violet was V, was to use and discard Violet much as Mac had done to Nasira. That was the ultimate revenge, a sister's honor for a sister's honor.

But now that Rafe was spending more time with Violet, he wondered if he would actually be able to do that to her. She was, after all, carrying his child—if she could be believed. And Rafe desperately wanted to believe her.

What if, instead of treating Mac's beloved little sister as Mac himself had treated Nasira, Rafe instead just *took* Violet? Not a kidnapping—nothing so brutish as that—but Mac had dedicated the past twelve years of his life to protecting his sister. If Rafe were to marry the mother of his child and move her far away, would that not be avenging his family's honor—while preserving his own bloodline? Violet was already tired of Mac and his interference in her life. It would not be that difficult to turn her against her brother completely.

This was an idea that had much merit.

"That is good," he said, trying to keep his voice level. "We should come to an agreement upon what is best for the child."

He must not have kept his voice as level as he would have liked, for Violet's eyes widened. "That sounds…"

He put on his best smile, his American smile. He did not smile like this at home. He had no need for it. But here, in Texas, this situation required finesse. It was tempting to just tell her they would get married and that she would bear his child and live in Al Qunfudhah. If he were at home, that is all he would have to do.

But Violet was not one of his people, and he knew enough about her to know that any such broad proclamation would have the opposite effect. Violet would refuse and, as long as she was in Texas, she *could* continue to refuse him. That was her legal right in this country, he was reasonably sure.

He would ask Nolan, but his lawyer was no longer his lawyer and, at times like this, Rafe missed the man's counsel. He wished mightily that Nolan had not quit Rafe's employ because he had fallen for a local woman— a woman with another man's child, no less. It had been another betrayal, one that stung.

It did not matter. He had promised he would not force Violet to do something she did not wish to do and he would keep that promise, for the sake of his child if for no other reason.

No, what he needed to do was convince her that she wanted to marry him. It should not be difficult. They were attracted to each other and they already had electric chemistry together. All he had to do was push that electric attraction and make her love him.

In the back of his head, he heard the severe voice of his father berating him. There had never been a time when the sheikh had not told Rafe what a worthless son and worthless brother he was. His father had held Rafe personally responsible for the loss of Nasira's innocence and Rafe had been punished accordingly. He had not been allowed to finish his American university studies. He had not been allowed to live abroad. He had been forcibly returned to Al Qunfudhah and confined to the basement of the family compound like a dog that had to be broken. Nasira, at least, had escaped into a marriage that suited her. But not Rafe.

Much like his siblings, Rafe was supposed to have been married off to a bride of his father's choosing, the daughter of another warlord or royal. The marriage would further cement Al Qunfudhah's position in the Middle East, and a suitable bride would bring honor to the bin Saleed bloodlines.

But after Nasira had been compromised by the one man Rafe trusted with his very life, Rafe's father had refused to allow Rafe the escape of marriage. Nasira had been ruined, so their father had not cared when she had married an Englishman and left the country. For all intents and purposes, Nasira had been dead to the old sheikh. Rafe had not been so lucky. He had been stuck in a hell that was not entirely his own making. The only thought that had sustained him during those first years was that of exacting his revenge on Mac McCallum.

It had been a relief for all of them when his father had died.

Now, years after the man's death, Rafe could hear his ominous voice again. *A true sheikh does not play games. A true sheikh would not concern himself with the wants of a woman. A true sheikh would have already carried this woman back to Al Qunfudhah and put her in a harem.*

Not that the bin Saleeds had harems. They did not. But in times past, the sheikh would have kept many women as his concubines. It had always been Rafe's opinion that his father lamented this cultural loss more than anything else.

"You got quiet there," Violet said, pushing what was left of her meal around her plate.

"I was thinking," he said truthfully. "There is something of a cultural gap between us that we need to bridge. My child will be a bin Saleed and I would like him—"

"Or her," Violet interjected.

Rafe let a grin play over his mouth. "Or her," he amended, "to know our people and our ways."

Violet frowned slightly, as if he had once again said something out of place. "I was trying to do a little reading on your people. The article I read made it sound like Al Qunfundaha—"

Now it was his turn to correct her. "Al Qunfudhah."

"Yeah, I'm probably going to screw that up a few more times," she said, forcing a smile onto her face. "But—I mean, what I'm trying to say is, what I've read makes it sound like your country is trying to be progressive toward women and minority rights but…it's still not like it is here."

What was she talking about? Rafe gave her a look and she threw her hands up. "I'm not making sense, am I?"

"Not entirely." He followed this up with another warm smile. This time, it was not as forced. Perhaps the wine was loosening him up. "But you are concerned about your place and the place of our child in my country, no?"

"No—wait, I mean yes. That's exactly what I'm concerned about. I'm not this world traveler like you are. I've hardly left Texas. I was supposed to follow Mac and go to Harvard, but then my parents died and we had to run the business and…" She smiled again, and Rafe thought it looked like an apology. It was. "I'm sorry. I'm just trying to process everything that's happened and I'm hormonal and you're being wonderful, but I'm making a fool of myself—again—and it's still a lot."

He was being wonderful? He should not be pleased with this statement. But he was.

He leaned forward and cupped her face. Her eyes widened but she didn't pull away as she had earlier. Instead, she leaned into his touch. Her skin was soft as silk against his palm, but warmer. "Ah, I am the only fool here."

She looked up at him, her eyes wide and deep and beautiful. "You are?"

"I am." Dimly, he was aware he was leaning in, that her face—her lips—were getting closer. "I find I wish to give you anything your heart desires. Tell me, what is it you want?"

She looked down at her dish. "I like it here. This is my life. But I am so tired of living with Mac, you know?

There's a ranch to the north of us—the Wild Aces. The Double M is leasing it because our water supply got compromised in the tornado, but I wanted to buy it outright. It's a beautiful piece of land and the house on the property is almost a hundred years old—one of those grand old homes. I've always loved it." She looked up at him with much confidence in her eyes. Rafe was certain her bravado was not entirely honest. "If I'm going to have a family—and that does seem to be the plan—I'd love to have my own house, my own land."

"The Wild Aces, you say?" He said it as if he had never heard of such a place before but, in truth, he knew exactly where the property was. The owner had been reluctant to sell to Nolan in large part because she was leasing the water to the Double M. Unlike many of their neighbors, she already had a steady stream of secondary income and was not as tempted by Samson Oil's generous offer.

But the Wild Aces was key to his scheme. If he owned that land, he owned the Double M's water supply. And if he owned that, he owned Mac McCallum. His revenge would be complete and nothing could stop him.

Nothing except a beautiful woman who was carrying his child. "You wish to have this land as your own?"

"I tried to get Mac to buy it, but he always reacts to one of my ideas the same way he reacted back when we were kids—oh, isn't that cute, Violet's trying to think like a big girl!" she said in the high-pitched, nasal voice many Americans used when speaking to small children and animals. Then she rolled her eyes. "It's so frustrating. I have to come at him sideways. He'll at least consider any idea his assistant brings up, so I have to ask Andrea to ask Mac. If I bring it up, he shoots it down, like I'm not smart enough to make wise business decisions on my own."

This was at odds with the way Mac had described Violet's management of the Double M, but Rafe did not show his confusion. "And if you had this land, you would raise our child on it?"

He was very careful not to make it a promise, because he was a man of his word and if he did something foolish like promise Violet the Wild Aces, he would be honor bound to keep that promise and that would mean all of his work was for naught.

Besides, he had no intention of staying in Royal or any part of Texas. And being Mac's neighbor? Out of the question. Rafe had to convince Violet that she belonged with him and that they belonged in Al Qunfudhah.

But making Violet think he would do something so grand as buy her a ranch without actually promising to do so—well, that was tailor-made to his scheme, wasn't it?

"I would love that," she said, her face lighting up with joy.

So much joy, in fact, that Rafe was horrified to hear himself say, "I will see what I can do." Which was not the same as promising her the ranch. He had merely promised to investigate it. He was still operating with honor.

"Really?" Her eyes were wide and she was looking at him with what he could only describe as adoration. "You'd do that for me?"

He had lost control of the situation—of himself—that much was clear. And it became clearer when he said, "I would."

"Rafe…"

And he was powerless to do anything but lean forward, to bring himself closer to her, to see how she looked at him. To be the man she saw, not the man he was. "Violet…"

"Will there be anything else?"

At the sound of the server's voice, Rafe shook himself back to his senses. Had he really been about to kiss Violet? In public? In the middle of this restaurant?

Yes. Yes, he had been. Which was not a part of the plan. He was here as a chaperone to Violet, not a seducer. "No, that will be all," he said, his voice harder than he meant it to be. The server left the bill and hurried off.

Rafe glanced at the bottle of wine—he had consumed perhaps two glasses, at most. This was the problem with abstaining from both women and wine for so long. His tolerance for both was quite low.

"Come," he said, paying the bill with cash. "I shall take you home."

Four

What she would *give* to be able to read this man. That was what occupied Violet's thoughts as she rode in Rafe's very nice sports car. Because he shifted between hard and soft and cold and warm and—yeah, she was going to say it—scary and sexy so fast that she was getting whiplash just watching him.

"This land is quite beautiful," he said conversationally.

Right now was a perfect example. Minutes ago, he'd leaned over and touched her face and told her he wanted to give her whatever she wanted—no, that wasn't right. He wanted to give her *her heart's desires*.

That was the man she'd spent the night with four months ago—sensual and sexy and whispering sweet nothings to her.

But then the waitress had interrupted them—which was good because if word got back to Mac that Rafe had been on the verge of kissing her in public, things would have gotten ugly fast—and all that sensual goodness had flipped off like a switch and suddenly Violet was sitting with an ice-cold man who had terrified the waitress with a few words and a hard look.

Violet didn't know which version of Rafe was in this car with her. But she did know that she vastly preferred the sexy sheikh to the domineering one.

The silence in this car—this very, very nice car that was probably a Lamborghini or a Maserati or some other exclusive brand of vehicle that was expensive and rare and designed to throw other men into a jealous rage—was deafening. She didn't belong here. Not in this fancy sports car, not with a sheikh.

She was just Violet McCallum. Nothing really that special here. She got crap on her boots every day and she was pregnant. Big freaking whoop.

Except…except when Rafe looked at her and spoke to her with that voice of sunshine. She almost felt as if she could do anything she wanted. *Be* anyone she wanted. Which was exactly how she'd gotten into this fine mess in the first place.

He wanted to give her whatever she wanted. Well, what did she want? She knew the answer to that—she wanted the same kind of happy family for her child that she'd grown up with. She'd told him about the Wild Aces—but did she want him there with her? Did she want to go to his country—even if she went as a member of the royal family?

It was all too much, too soon. She wasn't going to do anything stupid like marry Rafe. First things first. Soon she'd be a mother. Which would be wonderful, she had to admit. Now that she and Rafe were getting a few things straight, she was starting to feel more excited about this new adventure. She'd loved her mother—both of her parents, of course, but Violet and her mother had always had a special relationship.

"Now it is you who is silent," Rafe said and thank God, he didn't sound regal about it. "What is the saying? A dollar for your thoughts?"

She grinned, feeling some of her tension melting. "A penny. But you were close!"

Rafe tilted his head in her direction. "I assure you, your thoughts are worth far more than a penny. Do not undervalue yourself."

Coming from anyone else, it would have sounded like a load of manure. And maybe it still was. But the way the words rolled off Rafe's tongue...

"I was just thinking of my mother."

"Ah," he said softly, but he didn't barge into the silence as Mac did every single time Violet had tried to talk about their parents.

Her brother had always had some statement ready to go about how her grief was normal and they were going to get through this together and she was going to be *just fine*. Then, before she could get a danged word in edgewise, he'd pull her into a bear hug and tell her how proud he was of her and how he was going to take care of her and then he'd hurry out of the room, as if she didn't know his eyes were watering. As if they weren't allowed to have feelings in front of each other.

Instead of telling her how she was supposed to feel, Rafe waited for her to talk.

How weird was that?

"I was sixteen when the plane crashed," she said simply. "But I assume you know that?"

"Yes," he replied.

"I mean, I still miss them, but it's been twelve years. Bad things happen and people move on. Or we try," she added, thinking of Mac's overbearing version of love. "But this pregnancy—I was just thinking how much I'd like my mom to be here for this. If that makes sense." If anyone could talk Violet through an unplanned pregnancy, it'd have been Mom.

They'd had their share of fights—Violet had been a teenager, after all. But she'd always known her mom would be there for her. Until she wasn't.

"You were close to your mother?"

What an odd question. "Isn't everyone?"

"Ah," Rafe said, and the regretful tone in his voice made Violet glance over at him. He looked pained—not as though she'd kicked him in the shins, but a deeper pain that spoke of a lifetime of loneliness.

"Oh, right," she hurried to say, remembering what he'd said earlier. "Nannies. I'm sorry."

"I will, of course, defer to you," he said in a not-at-all seductive voice. He sounded more like a businessman and she didn't particularly like it. "If you wish to be more involved, then by all means, I will make that happen."

"How?"

"Excuse me?"

"How?" she repeated. "Look, my life is here. I run the family ranch. I know you told Mac you'd go with him to the meeting at the Texas Cattleman's Club because you were thinking of relocating but honestly? I don't know what your plans are. I don't know why you're here now and I don't know when you'll be leaving. I don't..." Her words trailed off and she suddenly felt like a teenager again, so sure of everything when, in reality, she knew very little. "I don't want to move to the Middle East. Even if your country is progressive."

"I see." Rafe pulled into the driveway of the Double

M. "I can safely say that my plans have recently been revised."

"You want this baby? I mean..." she quickly corrected, because all of a sudden an image of Rafe carrying her child onto an airplane while Violet stood in the terminal, watching them go—powerless to stop them—oh, God. No. "What I'm saying is, you want me to have this baby? Because I want to keep the baby."

"The child will be a bin Saleed. Of course I want you to have the baby," he said with a significant edge to his voice. "I will, of course, need independent verification that I am the father."

"What?" The word rushed out of her like that one time when a bucking calf had caught her in the gut with a hoof. "You don't believe me?"

"I do believe you," he said, the honey back in his voice. "We were together and I can only guess that, at some point, the condoms failed. I did use them because I gave you my word I would. But clearly, something went wrong and my brother, the sheikh of Al Qunfudhah—he will not be satisfied taking the word of an American woman. If the child is to have all the rights and privileges of the bin Saleed family, we must prove that I am the legitimate father."

"Oh." She hadn't considered that. She'd been so focused on what Mac would do when he found out that she hadn't considered Rafe's family obligations.

A family of sheikhs at that. "What will your brother do? When he finds out?"

Rafe slid a sideways smile at her. It was not terribly reassuring. "Calm yourself, my dear. Fareed is not my father and I am no longer powerless. He will most likely insist that the child be cared for and raised to honor our traditions, but," he added with what could only be described as a twinkle in his eye, "I do not think this will spark an international incident."

There was something there, something just below the surface of what he'd said that tugged at her consciousness. But she had a more pressing question she needed answered before she tried to unpack what he'd really meant. "Will you want custody?"

That's what she said. What she meant was, *Will you take my baby away from me?*

Rafe pulled up next to the ranch house and parked before answering. "Ah, yes. We must work out an agreement. This is why my plans have changed. I do not want to be away from my flesh and blood for too long."

So, yes, it was an odd way to phrase it. But the sentiment was what she needed to hear. He wouldn't take her baby and disappear in the middle of a different continent. "Okay, good. I know you said you were interested in expanding into energy—are you thinking of living in Royal? At least part of the time?"

He regarded her for what felt like an eternity. "I am thinking of many things," he said, his voice low. So low, in fact, that she had to lean forward to catch all of his words. "But if I stay here—even part of the time—we would have to have an…understanding, if you will."

"What kind of understanding?"

His gaze traced her face and she felt her cheeks warm. "I know we have agreed not to see other people while you are expecting, but I do not know how I could be around you and see you with another man. It would cut me," he added, placing his hand over his heart.

"Oh," she breathed. What was he saying? If he stayed in Royal, he'd expect them to be a couple? Together? "You mean…what do you mean?" Because if he meant that they were to live together—or get married—she didn't know how she was supposed to feel about that. Panic? Yeah, that was an option. Panic was always a good backup. She was barely coping with being pregnant— how was she supposed to throw a marriage into that mix?

But then another thought occurred to her. Because the one physical thing she hadn't gotten out of Rafe the first time they were together was waking up in his arms. That wouldn't be a hardship, falling asleep with Rafe by her side every night and waking up with him every morning.

Rafe's gaze was burning her in the best way possible. There was so much going on in his eyes—which was at least something to go off, as he was otherwise completely unreadable. Then he reached over and picked up her hand, leaning into her space to press his lips against the back of it. "I have not stopped thinking of you since our night of passion, Violet. I cannot tell you how many times I almost went searching for you. You…" He looked up at her, his voice raw. "You have graced my dreams and haunted my waking hours, a ghost of a woman I could see, but not touch. And it has been torture. The sweetest torture I've ever known."

Oh, my. Was he serious? God, how she wanted to believe he was, that their night together had been more than a one-night stand. "I thought of you, too. I…I still have your note."

He hadn't let her hand go. He was still holding it close to his mouth, where she could feel the warmth of his breath against her skin. Oh, that smile—all of her panic about the future dimmed in the light of his smile. God, Rafe was such a handsome man. "I am pleased to hear that. But I had made a promise to you—one night, no names—and I was honor bound to keep my promise. So I did not search for you. I did not try. I accepted my fate— that one night with my beautiful, mysterious V was all

I would get. And now I have this opportunity to know you—not just as V, but as a woman. As Violet. This is a second chance. I would be a fool to let this—to let you—slip through my fingers a second time."

"Oh, Rafe." She had never heard such a romantic speech in her life—and she'd certainly never been the subject of one. "Is that what you want? A real relationship?"

He turned her hand over and kissed her palm. "I want many things. But you are the one who carries the child. It is you who must be satisfied first." When he looked at her again, she felt as if she were falling into his eyes and she might never want to climb back out. "I think it is time for you to tell me what *you* want."

The air between them suddenly felt very warm, and she had a flashback to the way he'd bought her a drink at the bar at the Holloway Inn and then joined her. At some point between the first drink and the third, he'd leaned over and said those exact words to her. *I think it is time for you to tell me what you want.*

And what she'd wanted then was to be swept off her feet. She'd wanted to have fun; she'd wanted to feel beautiful and special. She'd wanted to be wanted because she was Violet, not because of her brother or her family name or her ranch. Just her.

And she said to him now what she'd said to him on that night. "Why don't we talk about this someplace else?"

One dark eyebrow notched up. "Are you inviting me in?"

She looked back at the dark ranch house. Mac was gone for the next two nights. She knew it. Rafe knew it. She had the run of the place.

"We're not done talking," she said. Although she

wasn't speaking loudly, her voice filled the small space between them.

"Indeed, we are not."

Violet started to undo her seat belt but before she could get her door open, Rafe was out of the car and hurrying around to her side. "Allow me," he said in that honey-and-sunshine voice as he opened her door and extended a hand to her.

She let him pull her to her feet, but he didn't let go of her. Only a few inches separated them. Despite the spring breeze, Violet could feel the warmth of his chest.

"This is just to talk," she heard herself say. "This doesn't mean anything else." Which was possibly the most pointless thing she'd ever said in the history of talking because of course Rafe's coming into her empty home meant something. It might even mean everything.

"I would make no such presumptions," he readily agreed. But his words were directly at odds with the way his thumb was now stroking over her knuckles. She was reading him now, loud and clear. "So tell me what it is you want. What are your dreams for the future? What part do you want me to play?"

"You're being too perfect," she told him. Because it was the truth. Everything he was saying—everything he was doing—was exactly what she needed, when she needed it.

He tilted his head to one side. "Has no one ever asked you what you want?"

"Oh, sure. What do I want for dinner, whether we should castrate the calves today or tomorrow, that sort of thing."

Well, that was some award-winning conversation right there. But Rafe was caressing her hand and looking down at her exactly the way he had when he'd pinned her in an elevator four months ago. Yeah, her mouth and her brain weren't exactly operating on the same wavelength at this point. Heat poured through her body, loosening her limbs as she melted into him, and all she wanted was for him to pick her up and carry her into that house.

"A crime, to be certain," Rafe murmured, cupping her face with his other hand. "I am asking you now. Tell me what you want."

He lifted her face and gazed deeply into her eyes and she was right where she'd been four months ago. She shouldn't do this. She shouldn't have done it last time. She should push Rafe back and cross her legs at the ankle and try, for once, to be the prim and proper sort of girl who was absolutely not swayed by a beautiful man with a beautiful voice.

Rafe was not going to let her go, though. He leaned in closer, so close she felt his breath on her lips, and said, "Because what you want is what I want."

And she didn't want to push him away any more than she had wanted to push him away in the elevator. In his arms, all those months ago, she hadn't been Mac's little sister and she hadn't yet been a future mother. For one glorious night, she'd been who she wanted to be.

It wasn't wrong to be that—to be herself. She could do that with Rafe—and only Rafe.

"Kiss me," she said.

His lips curved into a smile—one that warmed her from the inside out. "Are you sure? Because when it comes to you, I do not know if one kiss will ever be enough."

"I'm sure," she whispered, making her decision. "So kiss me."

Five

Judging from the way Violet threw her arms around his neck and pulled him down roughly into a searing kiss, this was all going perfectly according to his revised scheme. Making Violet fall in love with him would be an easy task. All he had to give her was exactly what she wanted—and, as far as he could tell, what she wanted was a passionate lover and freedom from her overbearing brother. Those were two requirements he could meet easily.

But any thought of revenge went flying out the window as Violet's tongue traced his lips. He had not lied to her—his thoughts had rarely been far from her and to suddenly find her back in his arms was almost more than he could bear.

"Violet," he groaned against the delicate skin of her neck. "Are you quite sure?"

"I want you," she said, her voice practically a growl, which sent an uncharacteristic shiver down his spine.

This was why he had not been able to put Violet from his thoughts—she made him do things that were out of character, such as kiss his enemy's sister because he wanted to do nothing but feel her body against his.

He lifted her against his straining erection and began carrying her toward her house. Every step drove him against her soft heat and there were no thoughts of revenge. There was only this burning need to bury himself in Violet's body, to make her cry out with pleasure.

When they got to the ranch house, he set her down and turned her around so she could open the door. And if she couldn't get it open, he'd break it down. Anything to get inside. But as she fumbled with her keys, the situation grew dire. "Violet," he groaned.

She finally managed to get the door open and then they were safely inside, away from any accidental witnesses. He pulled her back against him, letting her feel what she did to him. "Your room," he whispered against the base of her neck.

"This way." She pulled away and he let her go just enough that she could lead him up the stairs, but he couldn't keep his hands off of her. He traced the outline of her bottom through the thin cotton of her dress, which made her giggle.

When she cleared the top stair, and Rafe was certain they wouldn't tumble to their doom, he gathered her in his arms. All at once she was kissing him and he was kissing her back and pushing her jacket off her shoulders. Dimly, he thought he should be going more slowly, taking his time to savor her—her taste, the small noises she made when he did something she liked.

But he could not take his time. He needed her right now.

He tried to back her toward the right, where an open

door beckoned with the promise of a bed, but she corrected their course and led him left. Then her fingers began to work at the buttons on his shirt as she walked backward into her room.

At least he assumed it was her room. It was dominated by an enormous canopy bed with four tall posts holding up a drape of sheer light blue fabric.

"Kiss me," she said again, grabbing his face in her hands and pulling it down. "Please, Rafe, please."

"I cannot refuse you," he said, carrying her toward the bed. In one swift motion, he peeled her dress off and she was nearly bare before him.

Her hands stilled against his chest. "I've changed. Since that night." She said it as if she were afraid of what his reaction to her body would be.

But Rafe was staring down at the luscious curves. "If anything, you have changed for the better." He lifted her hands away from his chest and guided her back onto the bed until she lay before him. He could not be so thoughtless as to take her roughly, not when she was already nervous. Their first time, she had shared the wine with him and there had been no hesitation. But this time, he knew he needed to reassure her.

"Oh, Rafe," she moaned as he kissed down her neck to the valley between her breasts. Yes, he thought that perhaps they were slightly larger—fuller, he decided as he cupped them in his hands and slid his thumbs over the cups of the bra, right where her nipples should be.

"Take it off," she whispered, threading her hands through his hair and lifting herself up off the bed.

"Your wish is my command," he said, reaching behind her back and deftly removing her bra.

"If anyone else said that to me, I'd think they were full of it," she giggled. "But when you say it…"

"It is because I mean it." He lowered his head to her breast, letting his tongue work her nipple into a stiff peak. "I cannot help myself," he murmured against her skin as he moved to her other breast. "When I'm with you…"

"I know. I feel the same way. I—oh!" That was as far as she got before Rafe kissed his way lower, pulling her innocent white panties down until she was completely exposed to him.

After that, there were no more words to be said because he was busy bringing her to the heights of pleasure with his mouth and she was busy moaning and writhing under his touch. She kept her hands buried in his hair, guiding him in the direction that she most needed him to go.

Their first time, she had climaxed when he slipped his finger inside her. He would hate for her to think that he had forgotten what she liked best, so he repeated the move.

"Rafe!" she cried out as he lapped at her body, her inner muscles tightening around his finger.

And he could not wait anymore, not for her. He could not even do this properly and remove all of his clothing. He unbuckled his pants and grabbed the condom out of his back pocket and somehow managed to get the thing rolled on before he was against her, covering her body with his as he thrust into her warmth.

"Violet," he groaned, wanting to hold himself back—to hold himself apart from her because that was the smart thing to do, the calculated move that would contain whatever emotional havoc she wreaked. But he couldn't, not when she looked up at him with eyes that were glazed with desire, with want—with need.

"Yes," she said in a hoarse whisper as she tried to undo the remaining buttons on his shirt. "Yes, Rafe—*yes.*"

He grabbed her hands and held them against his chest, where his heart beat beyond his control. Then he began to move into her and she began to rise against him, meeting him with her own desire, thrust for thrust.

Mine, he tried to say over and over, but his words had left him and all he could do was hold himself together until she cried out in the throes of her pleasure. When she did, when her body tightened down on him, he gave up all hope of holding himself together. He leaned forward and drove into her harder, deeper, until his climax drained him so completely that he fell forward onto her.

They lay there, breathing hard, their bodies still intertwined. Violet worked her hands free and wrapped her arms around his waist, holding him to her. "Wow, Rafe. Just…wow."

He managed to roll to one side. "A compliment, I hope?"

"Oh, yeah." She giggled again, a light sound of joy.

It made him want to laugh with her. He grinned down at her, tracing the curve of her cheek with the tip of his finger. "When we marry, it will always be like this, I think. You and I…"

His words trailed off because her mouth had twisted off to one side and her eyes had narrowed. "Violet?"

Silently, she sat up, and then stood and walked away from him. Far too late, Rafe realized what he'd said.

Married.

He had overplayed his hand.

Violet sat on the toilet, trying to figure out what had just happened. She found herself reciting the known facts.

Fact: She was pregnant.

Fact: Rafe was the father.

Fact: Sex with Rafe was, unbelievably, even better when she was stone-cold sober than when she'd been mildly buzzed.

Fact: He had just said, "When we marry."

Her brain had gotten stuck on that last word. Okay, Rafe was kind of perfect—sweet words in that liquid sunshine accent of his, hot touches that melted her. He'd even promised to look into the Wild Aces for her. Throw in the sex…

This did not mean she wanted to get married. Even if that vision of her waking up in Rafe's arms every single morning was a warm and fuzzy vision. Even if that meant raising her child—their child—together as a family. Even if…

She dropped her head in her hands, trying to get her muddled thoughts back into some semblance of order.

Not that she got far. Just back to fact number four.

When we marry. It was a statement of fact, a foregone conclusion. There was no uncertainty, no will-she-or-won't-she. Just a fact.

"Violet?"

Oh, God—the concern in Rafe's voice on the other side of the bathroom door was not making this any better.

"Are you well?" he went on.

Violet opened her mouth but closed it again when she realized she had absolutely no idea what she should say. This was all too much, too soon. A mere twenty-eight hours ago, she'd been the same woman she'd always been, one with a fond memory of their rendezvous to keep her warm on cold winter nights. There hadn't been any thought of babies and there hadn't been any thought of marriages.

She put her head between her knees. She didn't want to throw up if he was listening.

"Violet," he said in a whisper that was almost plaintive. "I did not mean…it was just…open this door, please."

"I'm—just a minute," she said, looking around. She didn't even have a robe hanging on the back of the door. Unless she wanted to wrap herself in the shower curtain, she was out of luck. She would feel much better if she could at least cover herself. "Could you go downstairs and get me a Sprite?"

"Ah…yes? Yes," he said again, sounding more sure of himself, and she had to wonder if anyone had ever asked him to fetch anything before. "I can do that for you."

"Thanks."

She exhaled when she heard the familiar creak of the floorboards as he left. Slowly, she opened her door and peeked into her room. Her clothing was scattered all over the place, but aside from that, there was no sign Rafe had been here. That's right. She'd been so turned on, she hadn't even gotten him undressed.

Okay, first things first—she got dressed. She slid her nightgown on and then pulled her light cotton robe over it. Second, she decided to go downstairs. For one thing, the odds of Rafe locating a soda on his first attempt were pretty slim. But more important, it just felt as if it'd be easier to tell him they weren't getting married anytime in the immediate future if they weren't in a bedroom that still smelled of sex.

She padded downstairs to find Rafe staring into the fridge, his eyebrows locked in a confused expression. "Ah," he said in relief when she walked in. "I can't find the Sprite."

"Here," she said, reaching around his body—of course he didn't get out of the way—and plucking the can from behind the eggs.

"Of course," he chuckled. "How did I not see that?"

"I have no idea," she said, trying to be calm.

He shut the fridge door and turned to face her. "Are you well?" he asked, resting his hand on her hip and gently drawing her toward him. His shirt was untucked but still half buttoned.

"Better," she said.

He gave her a hesitant smile, then lifted her free hand up and placed it on his heart. "Your pleasure is my pleasure," he said, pressing her fingers to his chest. "And your pain is my pain. I would never wish to upset you. And if I have done so, I regret that."

"Okay," she said, clutching the cold soda can as hard as she could because the sensation was keeping her grounded in the here and now, preventing her from being swept away by his voice and words again. "Let's get this straight, then, so there's no confusion. It's not really a good idea to tell a pregnant woman that she *will* marry you, okay?"

His eyes crinkled. "That is not done here, I take it?" Then he lifted his hand and kissed her palm again.

She smiled in spite of herself. So he'd freaked her out. But he was also capable of calming her down in a way she couldn't help but be grateful for. "Not really, no."

"Then I shall do better. But there is something between us that makes me lose my head." His eyes twinkled. "Among other things."

She could feel her concerns melting away, but she didn't want him to sweep her off her feet—again—unless things were crystal clear between them. "I don't want to get married, Rafe. I mean, I don't want to say I'll never marry you because, truthfully? You're right. There is something here. But I'm still trying to wrap my head around being pregnant. So can we just agree that we won't talk of marriage for a while?"

He pivoted and leaned back against the fridge, pulling her with him. "I understand, I really do. But you must also understand that it would bring dishonor upon my family and myself if my child were born out of wed-lock."

She shouldn't be surprised by this. And honestly, she wasn't. That didn't mean it was what she wanted to hear seconds after one of the best orgasms of her life. She sagged against his chest, the soda can still in her hands. "Do we—will we have to get married? Is that what happens in your country?"

He paused. "In my family…we do not have a choice. We are married for power. Love…"

She closed her eyes. Love. They had talked about a lot of things, but love wasn't one of them.

Rafe cleared his throat. He began to rub his hands up and down her back. "It is something to consider, yes. But I have made you this promise, Violet, and I will continue to make it. I will not force you to do something you do not wish to do."

"Okay." But honestly, did she know him well enough to believe he'd keep that promise? She had no reason not to trust him. Aside from the fact that he'd used a different name when they met, everything he'd done had been up front. "Will you stay in Royal?"

"I will be here for the foreseeable future," he replied. "But I do not think I could leave Al Qunfudhah perma-nently. It is my home."

She nodded. "I understand."

He leaned her back and stared down into her eyes. "But I would like to suggest that we spend the time getting to know each other. Perhaps," he said gently, pressing his lips to the top of her head for a quick kiss, "it would not be such a bad thing, you and I."

"Perhaps not," she tentatively agreed.

"This is not something I can decide for you," he went on. She wanted to burrow deeper into his chest and feel his honeyed voice surround her. "You must decide that for yourself," he went on. "All I can do is show you that I will be good for you and that I will be a good father to our child."

She leaned back to look at him. "Do you always know the right thing to say?"

That made him laugh. "Based on what happened earlier, I would say the answer is no." He brushed her hair out of her face. "May I stay the night with you?"

She tried to look stern, but didn't think she was successful. "You're not going to propose marriage, are you?"

"Ah, I have many other things I would rather be doing with you," he replied, lowering his mouth to hers.

She sighed into the kiss. Everyone was always telling her what she should do, what was best. When was the last time someone had told her to make the decision?

So Rafe thought they should be married. And given the way he was devouring her, maybe they could be good together. Better than they already were.

She wasn't going to figure it out if she didn't spend some time with him, right? "Stay," she whispered against his skin.

"And tomorrow? I want to know more about you, Violet. I want to know what you do and how you live. I only have a few old stories your brother told me many years ago."

"Mac's out of town for a couple of days. If you wanted, you could ride with me tomorrow." She leaned back and looked at him. "You can ride, can't you?"

That smile—cool and confident, almost cocky. "I can. My family maintains a reputable stable of Arabians, as well as other horses. And I would love to ride with you. But I have some business to attend to in the morning," he said with a rueful smile. "You see, I have made a beautiful woman a promise that I would look into something for her and I would hate to disappoint her."

"Oh." All that languid heat flowed through her again and she thought of how good this could be. "I could meet you here after lunch? We're working calves in the morning, so all we'll have to do in the afternoon is herd the cattle to different pasture."

Something in his smile softened as he touched his fingertips to her cheek. "Mac told me you were a brilliant manager. I would love to see you in your elements, as they say."

She giggled. "In my element," she corrected and he laughed with her.

Oh, yeah, they could be good together. Usually, men said they wanted to "take her away from all this" or some such stupid claptrap, as if she only worked cattle because she had to. As if all she really wanted was to stay home, barefoot and pregnant and baking cakes. As if they could not believe that she, Violet McCallum, might actually be managing this ranch because she wanted to.

And now? Here she was with Rafe, a man who literally could take her away from all of this—away to some distant desert, as the wife of a sheikh—and what did he want? To ride with her. To see her work.

To keep his promise to her.

"Come," he said, taking her hand and kissing it. "The morning is still a long way off."

Six

Rafe, come on in.

Rafe smiled as he pulled the note off the front door and put it in his pocket. Then he walked into Mac McCallum's house as if he owned it.

Soon, he just might.

He had procured the services of a local Realtor, who knew Lulu Clilmer, owner of the Wild Aces. The Realtor had informed Rafe that the Wild Aces, with its 750 acres of prime grazing land, was worth approximately one million dollars but wasn't for sale at this moment in time. She even knew about Mac's leasing arrangements to access the natural springs on the Aces' land.

Rafe had instructed the woman with bouffant blond hair and too-white teeth to offer Mrs. Clilmer two million dollars cash, payable within three days.

Rafe wasn't sure the Realtor trusted him completely.

It would have been better to have a local like Nolan make the offer for Samson Oil instead of Rafe but he was not going to be deterred. And the Realtor was properly motivated by the prospect of an unexpected commission. The only snag was that she wouldn't be able to forward the offer to the owner until tomorrow because she had another closing today.

Which was fine. That gave Rafe another day or so to woo Violet. He made sure he had the box in his pocket— his other errand this morning had been to stop by a local jeweler's. Wedding Violet was almost as important as obtaining the Wild Aces.

In truth, he would prefer to have Violet's promise to wed him secured before he moved on the Wild Aces. His scheme had already undergone enough revisions recently. He did not want to further endanger it.

He stopped inside the front door and listened. Was she upstairs? That was where he had left her early this morning with a kiss and a promise to see her at noon.

Ah, humming—it was coming from the kitchen. And he smelled the scent of fried chicken.

Rafe silently padded down the hall. And there was Violet, assembling their meal. Something in his chest loosened at the sight of her. Her hair was pulled back into a low ponytail. Well-worn blue jeans hugged her hips. She was in her stocking feet and looked smaller, more delicate, than she did when she was in her boots. There was a peace around her that was almost infectious. Most any idiot could see that she was quite happy here.

A series of inexplicable urges hit him. He wanted to be the one that made her that happy. He wanted to walk up behind her and wrap his arms around her waist and kiss her neck and hold her. He wanted…he wanted things he could not put into words, but he could feel, pulling him toward her.

Last night, he had said things that he did not necessarily believe would come to pass. After he exacted his revenge, he had no plans to return to Royal, much less live here. He had told Violet he was considering those options without really meaning it. It had not been a lie—he could consider all his options without choosing to stay.

But this? Coming home at lunch to find her in the kitchen, preparing food? There was something so profoundly normal about it—normal by American standards, at least—that it made him think back to when he was still friends with her brother.

Rafe's childhood had not been one filled with carefree days and playmates. He'd been put through a rigorous education so that he would live up to the iron-fisted expectations of Hassad bin Saleed. And when he failed to meet those expectations, punishment was…harsh. Rafe had quickly learned that failure was not an option, not if he wanted to survive childhood. And although he was unable to save Fareed from any such suffering, Rafe did his best to shield his younger siblings from his father's wrath.

So when Rafe was allowed to venture out of Al Qunfudhah to America to attend Harvard, the freedom had been both sweet and somehow terrifying. It was only when Mac had befriended him that Rafe had started to understand this new world and its expectations.

And those stories… Mac had spoken so often of this house, of the people in it. How his mother still cooked dinner for them all and at least four nights a week, they were expected to sit down as a family and talk. That was such a foreign concept to Rafe. He had only dined with his father during state dinners, when he was expected to follow protocol and remain silent. To imagine a place where the mother and father openly expressed love not only for each other but also their children? Where they did things as a family?

Rafe had so desperately wanted to believe that such a world existed, that such a family existed. And he might have had a better chance to achieve that kind of harmony in his own family if he had not asked Mac to keep an eye on Nasira when she came to visit at Harvard.

In truth, Rafe had thought often of Mac's tales of his home in Royal. But he had not allowed himself to feel this unwanted nostalgia for a dream he had once nurtured and lost.

Not until now. Not until Violet.

Perhaps, if Mac had not betrayed him, this would have been Rafe's destiny. Before the incident with Nasira, they had even made plans for Rafe to make the journey to Royal, Texas, on holiday from university. Rafe would stay with Mac and meet all the people he had heard so many warm stories about—including Violet.

She would have still been in her teens. Would he have felt the beginnings of an attraction for her then? Or would she have just been Mac's irritating little sister?

He would never know. And that thought ate at him.

He slipped up behind her, slid his arms around her waist and leaned down to press his lips to the side of her neck.

"Oh!" She startled in his arms and twisted to look at him. "Rafe! I didn't hear you come in."

"I did not mean to frighten you," he said, pressing another kiss against her lips. "The meal smells delicious."

She grinned and, turning back to her preparations, leaned against him. His hands slid down and cradled her belly. "I hope fried chicken is okay," she said, lifting the chicken out and setting it on a plate to cool. On the counter were a pan of biscuits and a fresh salad.

"It will be wonderful. Here." He pulled the jeweler's box out of his pocket and opened it in front of her. "I brought you something."

She gasped as she saw the pendant. "Rafe—I didn't—I mean—*wow*."

"This is, as I understand, an American tradition. If I have calculated correctly, our child will be born in August," he said, pointing to the light green peridot stone at the center of the pendant. "And you were born in September, correct? So the sapphire is for you."

"And the yellow?"

"Citrine for November, when I was born. It is all set in eighteen-carat white gold."

Violet touched the pendant with a tentative finger. The three stones were strung together with the sapphire first, the peridot in the middle and the citrine on the end. "It's beautiful," she exhaled. "But you really shouldn't have."

"That is nonsense," he said, removing the necklace and opening the clasp. He draped it around her neck and fastened it. "You are carrying my child, a gift I could never hope to match. This is but a small token. There." He adjusted the chain so the pendant lay against her collarbone. "It suits your beauty," he said seriously.

"Rafe," she said and he heard hesitation in her voice. "Is this—I mean, is this really happening? Do you honestly think we can make this work? Or make something work? I mean…well, I don't know what I mean. It's all happening so fast and I just don't want…" Her voice trailed off.

"I take it this was not in your plans?"

"No," she said, giving him a weak smile over her shoulder while she touched the necklace.

"Nor was any of this in my plans. But I think perhaps…" He sighed and let his hands rest against the gentle curve of her stomach again. Within grew his child. No, this was not in his plans at all. "Perhaps this was what was supposed to happen."

"Really?" She didn't bother to conceal her doubt. "You think destiny's been waiting for us to have a one-night stand, huh?"

He grinned against her neck. "Do you know that, at one point, your brother and I had made plans for me to accompany him home on break? We would have met then."

She twisted in his arms, her brow wrinkled. "I would have been, what—fifteen? Sixteen?"

"And I only twenty. Do not mistake me. I would not have made any untoward attempts on you then. I can be very patient. Of that you have no idea. I can wait years for something I want."

Odd, that. He had waited years for revenge on Mac. But what if, instead, he had merely been biding his time for this moment with Violet?

But then, what if he had come home with Mac and Violet had caught his eye twelve years ago? His father would have no sooner allowed a young Rafe to give his heart to a common American girl than he would have allowed Rafe to degrade the bin Saleed name by donning shiny pants and joining a singing group. And if Hassad bin Saleed had discovered that Rafe harbored tender feelings for Violet then, he would have had Rafe married off to the daughter of a political ally within the month and Rafe would never have had the chance to follow his own heart.

But Mac's betrayal had come first.

"I was a different person then," she said, her voice low. "My parents were still alive and I was just a kid, really."

"As was I." She dropped her gaze. He still had her in his arms, but he felt the distance between them. "What is it?"

"Rafe, what happened between you and Mac?"

He supposed that he should appreciate the fact that Violet had phrased it as a question and not an accusation. "It does not signify," he said, his jaw tight. The effort of keeping his voice light was more taxing than he might have anticipated. "What happened was a lifetime ago. I was, as you said, a different person then. It has no bearing on us at this moment."

"But…"

Rafe did the only reasonable thing he could, given the situation. He kissed Violet, hard. She stood stiffly in his arms for a moment but then relaxed into him.

"It does not signify," he repeated, tucking her against his chest. "I am not here for your brother. I am here for you. I am here for our child. Our family."

Odder still that as he said it, it did not feel like a lie.

It felt very much like the truth.

He was surprised to see her eyes fill with unshed tears. "Are you unwell?" he asked hurriedly.

"I'm fine," she said, giving him a watery smile and dabbing at her eyes with the cuff of her sleeve. "It's just the hormones. Okay. Whoo." She exhaled heavily and put on a brighter smile for him. "There."

He was not entirely convinced. "I can still have a private doctor here inside of twenty-four hours."

She waved this suggestion away. "I'm fine," she repeated. "It's just that you have no idea how refreshing it is to know that you don't care about going through my brother."

Ah, yes. His scheme. The one that now hinged on convincing this woman that she wanted to spend the rest of her life with him so that she would turn her back on Mac. He wanted to be impressed that it was going so smoothly, but as she blotted at another stray tear, that was not the emotion that welled in his chest.

"In my country, it is customary to ask permission of a woman's father before you court her," he told her. "Or, if her father is not available, her oldest living male relative."

Violet held her breath. "Oh? You're not going to do that now, are you? I haven't even told Mac about my pregnancy or anything."

"No," he assured her, wrapping his arms around her again and pulling her against his chest. "You forget something."

"What's that?"

"We are not in my country."

Her head lifted and this time, her smile was not forced. "We're not, are we?"

"Not even close. So," he said, cupping her cheek in his hand. "Let us eat this delicious meal and then you can show me what you do. For our child will be a bin Saleed and there are expectations that go along with that, but that child will also be a McCallum and it would be best if they knew how to manage a ranch, would it not?"

Her expression should not make him feel this, well, *good*. Nothing about her except for the sex should make him feel this good. But everything about her did. "It would. And tonight? Will you stay again?"

"I will not leave your side until you tell me to go."

"Good," she said. "Then I want you to stay."

Watching Rafe mount Two Bit was a thing of beauty and quite possibly a joy forever. Good heavens, that man in a pair of blue jeans was the stuff of dreams, Violet decided. She wouldn't have guessed that Rafe could so easily slip into the role of a cowboy but, appearance-wise, he was doing just that. The jeans and the button-down shirt with mother-of-pearl buttons looked completely natural on his athletic form. Hell, he even pulled the hat off with plenty of grit to spare.

Who would have guessed that her sheikh was hiding a cowboy underneath those dark eyes and smoldering gazes? It was hard to disguise the imperial lift of his chin, though.

"Two Bit," he said as he got his seat in the Western saddle. He took up the reins in two hands, but caught himself and switched both to one hand. "That is a quarter of a dollar, correct?"

"Yup. But he's also a quarter horse. All my cutting horses are," Violet said, swinging up onto Skipper's back. Rafe's eyes got wide. "Oh, come on. I'm only a little bit pregnant. Skipper's a good old mare and I've been riding her for years. Trust me, there's nothing dangerous about this. In three or four months, maybe. But I have no plans to ride hell-for-leather today."

"All right," he said doubtfully. "Where are we going?"

"We've been working calves," she explained, gathering Skipper's reins and heading toward the northwest pasture. "We castrate them, brand them and vaccinate them all at one time. But we do that in the morning, when the sun's low and it's still cool. Puts less stress on the animal. So now, we're going to move the calves and the cows from the pasture where we worked them this morning to a different pasture and then round up another group and shuffle them in so they'll be ready to be worked tomorrow morning."

As she talked, she kept a close eye on Rafe's face.

What would he think of her after *that* little lecture? Because thus far, he'd mostly only seen her in dresses at hotels and restaurants. But that wasn't who she really was.

This—crap on her boots, wearing blue jeans and half chaps that covered her thighs—this was who she was.

Could he handle it? Or would his vision of his beautiful, mysterious V be destroyed by a whole lot of cows?

"I gather that being a ranch manager is a hands-on job," he said without wincing at the word *castrate*.

Which was impressive. Most of the men around here—men who castrated plenty of calves on their own—got a look of dread on their faces when Violet said the word out loud.

"It is," she agreed.

"What will you do when you are no longer able to—what is the phrase? Saddle up and ride?"

She shot him a smile. "Good! I've got a good crew. I'll have to hire a few more hands and my crew leader, Dale, will have to take on a bit more responsibility." It wasn't going to be easy to back away from her position like that, but at a certain point when her belly just got too big, she was going to have to accept reality. "We have a Gator, a minitruck I can use to get out into the pastures."

"And when the baby comes?" His tone was not judgmental, nor was he issuing any sort of edicts. Thank heavens for that.

She laughed, but she didn't miss the way it sounded nervous to her own ears. "I'm still working on that. I've only been aware of this pregnancy for a couple of days."

"Ah, yes. I am sorry. One day at a time, correct?"

"Correct."

He was silent for a while and they rode on. Violet pointed out land features as they went. "That's our spring and over there? Those empty concrete pads? That's where our water tanks were," she said. "The tornado ripped our tanks right off their moorings like they were empty pop cans."

"But you could have replaced the tanks, yes?"

"We did. But the spring got messed up. We're not sure what happened—before the tornado, the spring was fine and we had water reserves in abundance. But after the tornado, the cows refused to drink the water and our reserves were gone. Mac thought maybe some fracking that had been happening to our east had something to do with it, but we're not sure."

"But you have water now, correct?"

"Yup. Our tanks are now up on the property line dividing the Double M and the Wild Aces. The Aces has a bunch of springs, including one not that far from the property line. It's the only reason Mac agreed to leasing the Wild Aces—for the water."

Rafe thought this over for a while. "Why did he not allow you to buy the land? You obviously want it."

Violet sighed so heavily that Skipper's ears swiveled back. She leaned forward to pat the horse's neck in reassurance. "I don't know." Rafe turned in his saddle to give her a look. "No, really, I don't. I don't know if he thinks I'm incapable of being on my own or if he just feels more in control of the world if I'm under the same roof. He wasn't here when our parents died and I'm not sure he's ever forgiven himself for it."

"So he did not make a wise business decision because…something might happen to you?" Rafe sounded genuinely confused by this.

"As best I can guess." Rafe was staring at her as if he understood the words, but the meaning was lost on him. "What? Didn't your family try to protect you?"

"Ah," Rafe said in a way that Violet was pretty sure

meant no. "I believe the whole reason my father had children—aside from Fareed, who is the ruler—was to use them to make 'wise business decisions,' as you have said."

Use? Had he really just said *use* like that, like it was this common thing? Sure, her parents expected her and Mac to do their fair share of chores around the ranch, starting when she was three and had the job of making sure the horses' water buckets in the barn were full, but that wasn't the same kind of expectation as being used for business-related purposes. "Really? Didn't your parents love you?"

"My mother, I am sure, felt affection toward us."

Now it was Violet's turn to stare. "'Felt affection'? Didn't she ever tell you she loved you?"

Rafe was silent for far too long and she wasn't sure if the conversation was over or not. Maybe this cultural divide was bigger than she'd thought?

But then Rafe said, "Love is a weakness and weaknesses can be used against you," in such a way that a chill ran down her spine.

"That sounds...awful."

"It was quite normal for us. It is not until you get out into the world and see how other people live that you begin to question your upbringing."

"I never got out into the world," she said quietly. "I've never left home."

"But you will. You will always have a place in Al Qunfudhah as the mother of a royal child."

Another shudder ran through her. Was this what awaited her in this far-off desert country? A royal life with a man who had been raised to believe that showing love—or even affection—to a baby was a weakness?

But how did that mesh with the man who whispered

sweet words in that liquid-honey voice of his, who brought her an expensive necklace symbolizing their birthdays and the future birthday of their baby? A man who had promised he'd look into the Wild Aces for her?

Was that love?

Or was it a wise business decision?

"It was not until I went to Harvard that I saw things could be different," Rafe went on, missing her stunned silence. "I was quite unsure how to understand your brother's closeness to his family, to you."

And then there was that—that unspoken event involving Rafe, his sister and Mac that had destroyed the two men's friendship. Earlier in the kitchen, Rafe had spoken of that time as if it were his fondest memory. It was obvious that Rafe had considered Mac a brother then.

But there were other instances when the mention of Mac's name brought a hard edge to Rafe's eyes—a hardness that Violet couldn't overlook. And she had to wonder what, exactly, Rafe thought of her brother now.

"Were you close to your brothers and sisters growing up?" she asked in a careful tone.

"I did try to protect the younger ones." He gave her a rueful smile. "On that, your brother and I agreed." He turned his gaze away. "To a point."

"And you're not going to tell me what happened? Does it somehow not 'signify'?"

Rafe attempted a careless shrug but, unlike the hat and boots, he couldn't pull it off. She got the feeling that *careless* wasn't in his vocabulary. "In the end, it was for the best. Nasira was promised to a warlord much older than she and, once she was ruined, the warlord released her from her obligations. After that, my father no longer cared what she did, so she was able to leave Al Qunfudhah and marry a man more to her liking."

Ruined. That was, hands down, the ugliest word Violet had ever heard. And Rafe had said it so easily, as if he now thought less of his sister for what she'd done with Mac.

Was that it? Mac and Nasira had taken a liking to each other and Rafe disapproved because he believed Mac had ruined his sister?

Doubt flickered through her mind. This thing with Rafe was happening so fast—was the attraction between them real or was there something else going on here?

"I'm happy for her," she managed to get out in a tight voice. "I'd love to meet her sometime."

"I shall arrange it. But I do not know if she will come to Texas. She resides in England with her husband. They are quite happy, I believe."

They were silent for a bit longer as they approached the pasture where her cows and calves were anxious to begin the trip back out to the wide-open spaces. "Would it be possible to ride out to this other ranch, the Wild Aces, after we are done here? I would love for you to show it to me."

"Yeah."

Rafe looked out over the spring Texas landscape and sighed. There was something in his face—something that looked more relaxed than she'd seen him yet. "It is your dream, is it not?"

"It is." Violet nudged Skipper into a trot. "So let's get moving."

Seven

Violet's workers greeted her warmly and they all tipped their hats to Rafe. No one questioned her statement that Rafe was an old friend of Mac's visiting. And, Rafe noted, no one questioned her skills.

One of the workers swung open a gate and the calves came hurrying out. Rafe watched with interest as the larger cows and smaller calves all paired off. The noise was something new to him. They did not exactly have herds of cattle wandering around Al Qunfudhah. Camels, yes. Arabian horses, yes. Cattle? No.

"Rafe," Violet called. "To your left—we've got a straggler!"

Rafe twisted in his saddle and saw a cow leaving the group as it was herded north. The animal was moving at a good pace and the distance between it and the rest of the cows was quickly growing.

"What should I do?" he called back. He did not miss

the way several of the cowboys laughed under their breath at him.

Embarrassment burned at his ears, but he kept his attention on Violet. "Try to get in front of the cow," she called back. "I'll be right there."

Rafe touched his heels to the horse's side. He may not know the best way to retrieve a wayward cow, but he would be damned if he allowed this beast to outrun him on horseback.

Two Bit leaped into a flat-out run. Rafe held the reins awkwardly in one hand, but the horse responded to his heels wonderfully. Rafe gave the animal his head and trusted his footing.

Behind him, he heard a loud whoop, but he did not know if it was Violet or one of the men who had laughed at him.

Rafe smiled as he leaned over Two Bit's neck. The wind ripped his hat from his head, but he didn't give it a moment's thought.

Oh, how he loved to ride. His father had kept a stable of prizewinning Arabian horses and expected his children to ride and ride well. Anything less than expert horsemanship would have brought shame upon the bin Saleed house.

Rafe's daily rides were the time of his greatest joys, for then, he was free.

Just as he felt free now. The wind ripped at his clothes as he urged Two Bit to go faster. They shot past the stray cow and then, using only his knees, Rafe got Two Bit turned back. The horse stopped and spun, startling the cow to such a degree that the animal froze.

They all stood there, Rafe and Two Bit and the cow, as if none of them were sure what to do next. He had done as Violet had told him—he had gotten ahead of the cow and the animal had stopped. But now what?

Out of nowhere, a looped rope sailed through the air and landed around the neck of the cow. "Gotcha," Violet said, trotting up.

"You roped that cow in one shot? I am impressed," Rafe said, watching as Violet tied the other end of the rope around the horn of her Western saddle and began to pull the stubborn cow back to the herd.

She shot him a smile. "Get up, Bossy," she snapped at the cow, who reluctantly began to move.

When the cow was safely back with its brethren and she had removed her rope, one of the other cowboys rode up to Rafe and said, "Oowee, man—that was some fancy riding! Didn't expect that from a city slicker—no offense."

He looked at the man with a bemused smile. "None taken. I normally ride Arabians, but this is quite a mount." He leaned forward and patted the horse's neck as he glanced at Violet. "I believe Two Bit is worth far more than twenty-five cents."

Everyone laughed at that—but this time, they weren't laughing at Rafe. And he once again had that out-of-time experience where this whole thing could have easily happened twelve years ago, except with Mac by his side instead of Violet.

He was glad, however, that it was Violet by his side now.

"I trained him myself," Violet said as they spread out along the vast herd of cattle to keep any more from wandering off.

"He rode beautifully. I have not spent much time on other horses besides my own—but it was wonderful."

"Cowboy," Violet said, giving him a look that heated

his blood, "any time you want to come back and ride hell for leather, you just let me know."

It was some hours later, with the sun already setting, when Violet said farewell to her workers. The cowboys all departed, but Violet and Rafe stayed out in the pastures on horseback, riding farther away from the Double M.

"You are quite good at this," Rafe said. They were speaking softly. With dusk closing in around them, the sky lighting up in golds and reds like a tapestry woven of the finest silk, Rafe felt as if the world had been made just for them.

"You say that like you're surprised," she teased, a wide smile on her face.

"I would not have guessed that my mysterious, beautiful V could rope and ride half so good as you do."

"Does this mean you're going to stop worrying about me riding a horse?"

"I shall certainly worry less," he promised. "But no, I do not think I can stop worrying about you."

She seemed to consider this. "Will you be able to come to the appointment with me? It's in twelve days. I think I'll be able to hear a heartbeat."

"I would not miss such a chance. But," he added as they began to climb a low rise, "we must consider beyond that."

Even in the rosy evening light, he saw the color drain from her face. "I don't even know where to begin. Can we wait? Until after the appointment? I just feel like if I have a doctor's seal of approval and everything's okay, it'll be easier to decide what to do next."

"We can wait," he promised her. It was a sincere promise because Rafe had no desire to upset her. But it also played into his scheme nicely. The longer Violet withheld this secret from Mac, the more the betrayal would sting when Violet accompanied Rafe to Al Qunfudhah.

But as soon as he had that thought, a sense of discomfort overtook Rafe. After spending the afternoon working and riding with Violet on her well-trained horses, he was having a great deal of difficulty picturing her ensconced in his royal home in Al Qunfudhah, with miles of sand surrounding her instead of a sea of waving grass. She seemed as much a part of this land as the grass and sky. It felt wrong, somehow, to take her away from her home. It would be like caging a wild horse and breaking its spirit.

Could he really do that to her? It went against his every urge to protect her and their child.

What muddled his thinking was that she genuinely appeared to care for him in a way that no one else ever had. What if he never found another woman who felt this way about him? What if, by breaking Violet's spirit, he destroyed his last—his only—chance for happiness?

He shook those thoughts from his head. He was not destined for happiness. The past few days with Violet had been nothing but a…a diversion. A pleasant one, to be sure, but a diversion nonetheless. The only wrong he had to concern himself with here was avenging the wrongs done to his family honor. That was all that mattered.

"Here," she said, breaking him out of his reverie as they crested the hill. She reined her mount to a halt. "That," she said, sweeping her hand out over the vista before them, "is the Wild Aces."

Rafe had, of course, seen a few pictures of it. But the beauty of the land, bathed in the glow of the sunset, took his breath away. He could see how the land differed from the Double M—the trees were larger and more grouped and the grasses were a deeper green, especially around the springs that dotted the land. "It is lovely," he said.

"Down there," she said, pointing south, "those are our tanks. And then there? To the north? That's the house."

Rafe looked in the direction she was pointing and saw a grand old home standing in a grove of tall trees. Clusters of yellow rosebushes crowded around the building's foundation; even at this distance, Rafe could see the blooms. A long drive led away from the house and that, too, had trees planted along it. The home seemed as much a part of the land as everything else.

"I love this place," Violet said with a satisfied sigh. "The house needs to be updated, though. Lulu—that's the current owner—has lived there for close to forty years and she's getting on in age. Renovations haven't exactly been on her radar. Plus, she smokes—a lot—so I'd want the whole house cleaned inside and out before I raise a kid there."

A twinge of an unfamiliar emotion took hold of Rafe so suddenly that he had to rub at a spot in his chest that began physically aching. He needed the Wild Aces to complete his revenge on Mac but...

It would not just hurt Mac, what he was doing. It would hurt Violet, too.

Nonsense, he tried to tell himself. First off, Violet would be joining him in Al Qunfudhah—that was the plan, and he would not allow his sentimental feelings for her to change that plan.

The necklace had merely been the first of such gifts. The day after tomorrow, he would bring her a bracelet of diamonds and rubies and then, a ring—diamond, as required by American tradition. If he were still at home, he would not wait a day to bring her jewels, but Violet had shown enough hesitation over their plan that Rafe did not want to rush her too much. More than he had to, anyway.

And besides, once Rafe had the Wild Aces and had broken Mac, well—Rafe would still have the Wild Aces. And he would also have the Double M. There was nothing that prevented him from keeping the land for Violet, just so long as Mac did not benefit from the arrangement.

This realization made the pain in his chest ease. One way or the other, the Wild Aces would be Violet's. Then she would no longer have to rely on her brother's permission to do anything.

"It will be perfect," he told her in all sincerity. And it would be.

All it required was a little more patience.

Patience was, at this exact moment, something Rafe had in perilously short supply. The last thing he wanted to be doing right now was attending some meeting at some club under false pretenses of perhaps joining the club at some point in the undefined future. He had no intention of settling down in Royal, Texas.

Or at least, he hadn't until two days ago.

He wanted to be back with Violet, and the strength of this feeling was worrisome. He had spent two nights in Violet's arms, in her bed—sharing her body and her dreams. That he had been forced to give that up only because Mac returned from his business trip did not improve Rafe's mood.

Violet was pregnant with *his* child. He felt reasonably certain of that, as certain as a man could feel without blood tests. She had agreed that, at the doctor's appointment, they would get the test that confirmed what they already knew—for Fareed and for Mac.

It bothered Rafe that they both needed to operate in

such a manner to prove to their older brothers beyond a shadow of a doubt that the child was theirs. Rafe had vowed to never again be in a position where Mac held sway over him, and yet now Rafe was sitting next to Mac, pretending as if this situation did not bother him in the least.

The Realtor had been in contact today. She would be making an offer on the Wild Aces in the morning. It was the last piece of the puzzle Rafe had been slowly assembling over the past six months, and he was eager to have it in place.

Violet wanted the ranch not only for land or water but because that was where she wanted to make her home. That was where she wanted to raise their child.

With him?

He was still unclear on that. He had foolhardily mentioned marriage while his head had still been clouded with passion on their second night together—and what a mistake that had been. For a man who was actively trying to convince her to choose him over her brother, it was clear that telling Violet what to do would always be a mistake.

No, if he wanted Violet to abandon Mac, he had to convince her that was what she wanted. And to do that…

Rafe had not often awoken with a woman in his arms. But that was exactly the position he had found himself in the previous two mornings when sleep had left him. He had been on his back and Violet had been curled on her side against him.

It should have felt wrong. Or odd, at the very least. But with Violet exhaling her warm breath against his chest, her breasts pressed against his side, Rafe had felt an unexpected calm. It was almost as if she belonged there.

That feeling had only gotten stronger as he had awoken her with a kiss. With more than one kiss, in fact. He had lost count.

It felt as if a sandstorm had been unleashed upon him and he had no way to protect himself. The facts as he knew them spun faster and faster around his mind until he was dizzy and raw.

"...Started admitting women a couple of years ago," Mac was saying as they drove toward the dim lights of Royal. "It's not the same club my father joined, but I don't have a problem with that."

"Is Violet a member?" Rafe asked. What he needed right now was additional information. He wanted to be absolutely certain that Violet was exactly as she said she was. He could not bear the thought that somehow, the McCallum siblings were working together against him.

The trick was to extract the information without arousing Mac's suspicions. It was possible, however. One of the more applicable lessons his father had taught him was to keep your friends close and your enemies closer. And if your enemy still thought of himself as a friend, well, it made things that much easier.

Right now, all Rafe knew of Violet was a collection of disparate facts that did not necessarily add up. Violet was Mac's baby sister, the one he had worried about, the young girl who'd gotten into all sorts of scrapes and hijinks, forever driving their parents to distraction.

She was a cowgirl who trained horses for cutting and roped cattle and pined for a place of her own.

But Violet was also his V, beautiful and passionate, the rare woman who had made Rafe break his long stretch of celibacy. She was the woman who had haunted the edge of his dreams for months now. The woman who had made him consider breaking his promise of one night,

no strings, and having Nolan, his lawyer, look into finding her.

And she was the woman, soft and tousled with sleep
but still capable of bringing him the greatest of pleasure,
who had cried out his name in the morning. She was the
woman whose rounded belly contained his child growing within.

The thought of Nolan was a source of pain and Rafe
welcomed it. Anything to break his thoughts from Violet.
He had come so far, he could not let this…this infatuation with her destroy his scheme.

Nolan had been his friend, his trusted second here in
America as Rafe set the wheels of his plan into motion.
But Nolan had turned on Rafe just as Mac had all those
years ago—Nolan had found a woman and decided that
love was more important.

Not that what Mac and Nasira had had was love. Even
Rafe understood how lust could drive a man to do things
far outside his normal character. But Nasira…

Rafe struggled to remember what his sister had said
to him at the time, in hidden whispers on the long trip
back to Al Qunfudhah. She had not wanted to marry
the man their father had chosen for her—a much older
man, a tribal warlord with a reputation for cruelty who
had children nearly as old as Nasira herself. She had not
wanted to be forced into a marriage. She had wanted to
choose. And she was sorry—deeply sorry—that Rafe
had been hurt, but his friend had been a better choice
than the warlord.

Which brought Rafe's whirling sandstorm of thoughts
right back to Violet. Was what she wanted so very different from what Nasira had gone to great lengths to get?
The right to choose her husband?

This thought troubled him. It troubled him greatly.

"She hasn't really been interested in joining," Mac was saying. "And truthfully, I haven't really encouraged her. I know what some of those guys are like. They're fine for kicking back and having a beer with in the evening, but I don't want them around my baby sister. They're not good enough for her, you know?"

"You are very protective of her," Rafe said.

"I just don't want anything bad to happen to her, you know? After our parents…" Mac cleared his throat.

Rafe would not allow himself to think fondly of Violet. He would absolutely not allow his baser instincts to override everything else. Instead, he would focus on his reason for being here—avenging his family honor. Nasira. Oh, yes. Rafe was going to make this man pay and pay dearly. How could he sit there and wax poetic about protecting his own flesh and blood after having so callously used Rafe's sister?

"So she does not date among the men from your club?" Mac looked at him sideways and Rafe knew he was treading on dangerous ground. "You did ask me to keep an eye on her. If she is dating someone of whom you approve, I would not want to interfere in that relationship. That is not how things work in my country."

He let the words "in my country" hang in the air. Once, he had tried to explain his culture in general and his family structure in particular to his American friends but it was more difficult than bridging the language divide.

Compared to many other Middle Eastern countries, Al Qunfudhah had an extremely liberal view of women's rights. Women could drive and hold jobs and they had the right to refuse a suitor—well, commoners did, anyway. That had not been true of Nasira or any of the sheikh's children—at least, not under Hassad bin Saleed. His brother Fareed was changing those rules, as well.

But the cultural requirement that a man ask permission of a woman's father or brother before a date in all circumstances did not sit well with most Americans. Perhaps that was one of the reasons Rafe and Mac had been such good friends so quickly—Mac, better than anyone else Rafe had met at Harvard, had understood the impulse to protect sisters.

If Mac believed that Rafe's questions were about Mac's approval or disapproval of his sister's dating, not an effort to ascertain whether or not she engaged with many gentlemen friends, well, that only made Rafe look better. He was supporting his friend's right to rule his family as he saw fit.

"No, no—she doesn't date much. I haven't met the man worthy of her, frankly, and I don't want her wasting her time on losers who are only after one thing."

Well. That certainly lent credence to Violet's claim that in the last year she had only been with Rafe.

This what she was hiding from, the night they spent together. Rafe remembered asking why she was just V—was it family or lovers? And she had not answered the question.

He knew now. She was hiding from family. From the very man Rafe was honor bound to destroy.

This certainly put an interesting twist on things.

Rafe never would have guessed when he made this trip to America that he would be eager to attend a doctor's appointment. His father had never stooped so low as to concern himself with the health of the mother of his children. But Rafe was not his father, thank heavens.

Eleven more days until the appointment, where he

hoped to hear his child's heartbeat, felt a very long time off.

"Here we are," Mac said, pulling up outside a long, low building with immaculate landscaping. "The Texas Cattleman's Club—it missed the worst of the tornado we had last year."

"Mac!" Rafe spun to see a cowboy waving at Mac through the open doors of the clubhouse. "Good to see you, man."

"Hey, Chance. Chance, this is an old friend of mine, Rafe bin Saleed. Rafe, Chance McDaniel."

Rafe shook hands and the two men talked about Chance's new daughter. Rafe looked at pictures of a small, wrinkly baby with rather more interest than he might have otherwise. Was this in his future, a baby like this? "What age?" he asked Chance. He had no experience with babies or even children, for that matter. When his siblings had been younger, they had had nannies and nurses and Rafe had only seen them briefly in the evening, when all the children were brought together and presented for their father's inspection.

"Four months. God, Gabriella's just a natural. I didn't think I could love her more," he said, his gaze fastened on the next picture, which was of a beautiful dark-haired woman holding the baby, who was now wearing a frilly pink dress. "You have any kids, Rafe?"

"Ah, no." He swallowed, uncharacteristically nervous. Until several days ago, there had been no possibility of him having children.

Chance snorted in a good-natured way. "They change everything, kids." He clapped Mac on the back. "I keep telling this guy to settle down, but he's too busy!"

For the first time, the possibility of being a father— outside of wedlock, no less—hit Rafe as a real thing and not just a countermove in his scheme. What would his family think if they found out that Rafe had impregnated Violet? He honestly did not know. His father would have done horrible things in the name of the family honor. Being forced to marry Violet would have been a blessing, compared to what Hassad bin Saleed might have done. But Fareed was a different man and a different ruler.

Still, if Rafe did not marry Violet, he would bring dishonor onto the family, and Fareed would not let that stand.

"Rafe here's thinking about relocating to Royal," Mac said after they had looked at the many pictures of the little girl. "I invited him to a meeting—if he buys some land, he'd be a good member."

"Great," Chance said. Rafe noticed that other men and a few women were all moving back into a larger room. "Oh, shoot—we're late. Come on."

They joined the rest of the group. Mac introduced Rafe around and Rafe shook many hands. Normally, he would be collecting information on each member, examining their connections to Mac. He did recognize several names as people from whom his front corporation, Samson Oil, had purchased land.

But he had trouble focusing because his mind kept returning back to the questions he had yet to answer.

"Case Baxter," a man said, giving Rafe's hand a vigorous shake. "I'll be running the meeting tonight, so if you have any questions, just let me know, okay?"

Rafe nodded and made polite noises of agreement, but his thoughts turned right back to Violet. How could he get her to leave this place with him without breaking her spirit? That was quite a problem—one for which he did not yet have an answer.

"This is my friend Rafiq bin Saleed, a sheikh from

Al Qunfudhah," Mac said to the group. Rafe snapped to attention at the mention of his name. "He's looking to get into the energy business and he might relocate here to Royal. I think it'd be great if we could welcome him into the club!"

There were murmurs, some of approval and some of disapproval. Rafe remembered his American manners and nodded and smiled as warmly as he could while the sandstorm of his mind continued to whirl around winning Violet McCallum.

That would be the ultimate revenge, would it not? First Rafe would destroy Mac's beloved ranch and then his beloved town and then Rafe would marry Mac's beloved sister and whisk her away to Al Qunfudhah, where…

Where Rafe would take her to bed every night. Where her pleasure would be his pleasure.

A voice cut through his reverie. "Rafiq, huh?"

Rafe turned to see a man he did not know standing near the front of the room. His arms were crossed and he looked defensive. More than defensive—he looked dangerous.

This was a challenge, and challenges had to be met head-on. Rafe stood. In times like this, his first instinct was always to do as his father had taught him—rule by force. But Americans were a different breed and Rafe had learned it was best to come at them from the side. "My friends call me Rafe," he said in the congenial tone that worked best with Americans. "And you are?"

"Kyle Wade," the man said stiffly. "Why don't you tell them who you really are?"

Rafe froze. That was the kind of statement that started off badly and only got worse.

Mac interceded on his behalf. "Hey, Kyle—I've

known Rafe since college. We're old friends. He is who he says he is, so maybe ease off a bit on my guest?"

Kyle didn't ease off. Instead, eyes narrowed, he said, "Oh? So you know that Rafiq bin Saleed is the man behind Samson Oil—the company that has been buying up land all around town?" A collective gasp went up from the other members. "Care to explain yourself there, Rafiq? Why have you been buying up property for months?"

Rafe was not the kind of man who panicked. Panicking was a waste of energy that was better spent fixing a situation. Years of enduring Hassad's rages had schooled him well in keeping his features calm and his breathing regular. He resolved to be like the stone that felt nothing.

But if he were capable of panic, he might be feeling it right now. Because suddenly, one huge part of his scheme had exploded in his face, and the feeling of being sucked into a swirling sandstorm was that much stronger. If he were not careful, he would be buried up to his neck in his own lies.

Mac turned to him, confusion and suspicion on his face. At least at the moment, the confusion was winning. "Rafe? Is that true?"

No, he was not panicking. He was a bin Saleed. If anything, he was furious at this Kyle Wade for potentially undermining his plan. Kyle would soon learn not to cross him.

He would, however, prefer not to have any more disruptions to his scheme *today*.

He waved his hand in dismissal and made an effort to look casual. The key to escaping this situation with the bulk of his scheme intact was to play up the cultural differences. "As I said, I'm looking to get into the energy

business. Is this not how it is done in this country? Do
you not buy land for the exploration of mineral rights?"

"None of that land has any oil left on it," shouted a
man from the back of the room. "Why do you think we
sold it to Samson Oil? Only a fool would think they're
going to strike oil on property we've tapped out!"

Rafe gritted his teeth. He was no fool, and to imply it
was to risk his wrath. This was why he had not revealed
himself to Mac and the town earlier. Too late, he saw that
he should have remained in the shadows until his plans
were complete, until he had the Wild Aces and Mac's
water had been cut off completely.

In that respect, the man was right—Rafe was a fool
who had shown his hand too soon. It would be his last
mistake, that was for certain.

But then Mac put his hand on Rafe's shoulder. Odd,
really, how that vestigial touch of friendship could still be
reassuring. "Listen," Mac said loudly over the growing
buzz of people talking. "I vouch for Rafe. They do things
differently in Al Qunfudhah, where he's from. If he says
he's exploring mineral rights, then…" Mac looked at him
and despite this very public declaration of support, Rafe
could see the distrust in Mac's eyes. But then a harder
expression came over his face and he turned back to the
crowd. "Then I believe him," he finished.

Ah, this was excellent. Mac truly had no idea that
Rafe was here to destroy him. And the fact that Mac was
using his influence to convince other people that Rafe
was no danger to them only made the revenge that much
sweeter because when Rafe destroyed Mac, the whole
town would blame Mac for vouching for his "old friend."

Rafe put his best effort into smiling warmly and shaking Mac's hand and looking as innocent as possible.

Which must have been innocent enough because Case

Baxter called the meeting back to order and everyone sat down. While the group discussed club business, Rafe mentally rearranged his plans. Above all else, Rafe had to close the deal on the Wild Aces as soon as possible. The Double M could not survive without the water from the Wild Aces. And if Rafe had a moment of doubt, a moment when he felt guilty about Violet wanting to raise their child on the Wild Aces...

No such doubt existed, and if it did, Rafe pushed it away. Caring for Violet was a weakness and at this late stage, it was a weakness he could not afford.

He had much work to do.

Eight

Violet's phone buzzed. Of course it did. She was in the middle of branding and castrating calves, for God's sake. It was messy work that required her full concentration and she was glad for that because it had been two days since Rafe had slipped out of her bed at six in the morning and kissed her goodbye with a promise that he would see her very soon.

Apparently, very soon meant something different in Al Qunfudhah than it did here in Texas, because there'd been radio silence for the past forty-eight hours and she was starting to get twitchy.

"Here," she said to Dale, her hired hand. "Hold this calf. I've got to take this call." She managed to get loose of the animal without getting kicked.

Hopefully, this was Rafe. No, she didn't really expect another rose or a love note—not when they'd both agreed that they were going to keep their previous acquaintance quiet for the time being, just until they got things settled a little more.

But again—days of radio silence? The only reason she knew that Rafe hadn't skipped town was that he'd gone to that Texas Cattleman's Club meeting with Mac the night before last.

She got out of earshot from her hired hands and pulled out her phone. It wasn't Rafe, dammit. It was, however, Lulu Clilmer, the current owner of the Wild Aces. "Hello?"

"Violet, honey," Lulu began in her gravelly, two-packs-a-day-for-forty-years voice, "I wanted to call you personally."

"Hey, Lulu, what's up? Are you all right? Do you need me to come over?" For years now, Violet had been helping Lulu out, partly because it was the neighborly thing to do but also because Violet wanted the Wild Aces, dang it all.

"I'm fine, honey. Listen, I know that you've always had your heart set on this place..."

Violet smiled nervously—which was pointless, as Lulu wouldn't have been able to video call anyone if her life depended on it. "Yeah. I've been trying to convince Mac to buy you out, but you know how he is."

"Well, honey—I don't know how to say this but..." Violet held her breath. "I've had an offer."

Violet's breath caught in her throat. Was that what Rafe had been doing? Had he spent the past two days "looking into" the Wild Aces for her? For their family? "Oh?" Violet said, not even bothering to sound cool or calm about it. "Who? Anyone I know?" *Please say Rafe. Please.*

Because if it were Rafe, then—finally—the Wild Aces would be hers. She wouldn't have to go through her brother any longer. God, she could hardly wait.

But if it wasn't Rafe...well, if it were someone else, she'd just have to push Mac harder or head down to the bank and see how much of a counteroffer she could scrape together. She was half owner of the Double M, after all. All that land equity had to count for something, right?

"Naw, honey—I'm sorry. It's some outfit that goes by the name Samson Oil."

Violet's heart plummeted down to around her knees.

"I never heard of them before—they're not local, that's for sure," Lulu continued. If it'd been someone local, there was always the chance Violet could reason with the other buyer. But some out-of-towner?

Wait—Rafe wasn't local. "Did you talk with Rafiq bin Saleed? Is he connected with Samson Oil?" She dug deep, hoping that something might ring a bell with Lulu. "Or someone named Ben, maybe?"

"Honey, no. I had been waiting on you, you know—I was happy to lease the land to you in the meantime—but the money this Samson Oil is offering? I can't walk away from this offer. I'm too old to keep this place up and my medical bills..." She trailed off into coughing.

Oh, God. This was, quite possibly, the worst-case scenario. "How much?" she asked weakly, covering her stomach with her hand as a wave of nausea appeared out of nowhere. She was just getting used to the idea of being a mother to Rafe's child. How much more disruption could she take?

There was a pause, which was followed by Lulu coughing some more. "Two," she said when she finally had her voice back.

"Million?" But Violet didn't have to ask. She already knew.

The Wild Aces was worth close to one million dollars.

Lulu had been willing to let Violet have it for $800,000, but Mac had thought that much money for that amount of land was a waste of resources. Lulu had promised that she wouldn't consider selling the Wild Aces out from under Violet for anything less than $1.5 million.

"I sure am sorry, honey," Lulu said again.

Violet put a hand to her head, as if that could get it to stop spinning. It didn't. "What if—what if I come up with a counteroffer?"

"Sweetie, we both know you don't have that much money lying around," Lulu said sympathetically.

She didn't—but McCallum Enterprises did. The company had plenty of capital. "Can you just hold off for a couple of days? Just give me the chance to make a counteroffer, okay?"

There was another long pause; Violet didn't know if Lulu was having trouble breathing again or if she was going to say no. "This Samson Oil—they want the deal done as soon as possible," Lulu said sadly.

"Just two days. A day, even," Violet pleaded. "Let me talk to Mac one more time. If I can get you $1.5 million, would you consider selling the Wild Aces to me?"

Lulu sighed heavily. "Sure thing, honey. I'll give you twenty-four hours."

Violet knew that it was only because she'd spent the past several years helping Lulu out around the house that the older woman was throwing her that small bone. "Thanks, Lulu. I'll be in touch, I promise." She ended the call and stood there, staring at her phone.

Samson Oil? Who—or what—the hell was that? No—wait. It sounded familiar. Hadn't she heard something about Samson Oil buying up a bunch of land around Royal for the oil rights? She remembered people talking about it at the Royal Diner when she'd gone in for coffee one morning a couple of months ago. Some folks had been suspicious, but others had been laughing because some dumb corporation was snapping up nearly worthless land at insane prices.

Like offering Lulu twice what the Wild Aces was worth—that was insane. This whole situation was insane. When had her nice, quiet life gotten so completely out of control? It was as if Violet's reality had been stripped away from her and she'd been thrust into some alternative universe where up was down, left was right and she was living out a soap-opera plot. She looked around, but didn't see J. R. Ewing and his big hat anywhere.

Suddenly, Violet was mad. At her brother, at Rafe, at this Samson Oil—at the universe. What the hell had she done to deserve this? Okay, yes, the one-night stand with Rafe had led to her pregnancy. Fine, she'd earned that one herself. But everything else?

She was tired of doing the best she could with what she got, because what she got was crappy. That's all there was to it. Her parents dying? That was a crappy thing that happened when she was at that age where she needed her mother more than anything. But she went on. She didn't go to Harvard, didn't go out into the great big world and find her own place in it, as Mac had gotten to do. Instead, she stayed home and became a damn fine ranch manager.

But did she get to fall in love? Every boy she'd ever liked had been chased off by Mac. And now there was Rafe. She didn't know if this was love or lust or hormones or what. She liked him. She was definitely attracted to him. And she was going to have his baby. But was that love? Or was this just another crappy thing that was happening to her, another thing she was going to have to muddle through as best she could?

Could she convince Mac that she could handle this,

handle her life? Would he keep trying to shield her from the real world while inadvertently setting her up for the exact heartbreak he was always trying to prevent in the first place?

If he had just bought the Wild Aces when he had the chance...

Angry tears stung her eyes, but the agitated mooing of calves and cows reminded her that she was not, in fact, in the privacy of her room. Instead, she was out on the ranch, surrounded by cows and cowboys, and she was the boss.

That's right, she was the boss. She needed to act like it. She looked up at the sky, trying to get all of her hormone-enhanced emotions under control. She could not fall apart, not now, because if she did, she'd lose the Wild Aces.

Wildly, she thought of Rafe. Where was he? She needed him right now in a way that she wasn't sure she'd ever needed anyone before. For so long, she'd been struggling to show that she was fine, that she could take care of herself. But right now, she wanted Rafe to pull her into his arms and tell her that it was all going to work out, that he'd take care of it—of her. God, she'd never wanted that so much.

And he wasn't here.

"Violet?" Dale asked, worry in his voice. "Everything okay?"

She turned back to where Dale was dusting his chaps off. The other hands were looking at her with confused concern. To them, she was just another cowboy. They didn't treat her like a porcelain doll the way her brother did—but the downside of that was, if she ever had a more emotional moment, they didn't know what to do. It was as if being suddenly reminded that she was, in fact, a woman always freaked them out.

She was not freaking out. She sent a quick text to Rafe, asking him where he was, and then she got her boss face on. Losing the Wild Aces wasn't just a crushing blow to her long-held dream. It could easily be a crushing blow to the Double M. The only reason Mac had agreed to lease the Aces was because they had multiple springs on the property—springs that had remained undamaged from the tornado that swept through Royal last year.

"The Wild Aces might be sold out from under us," she said, keeping her voice level.

Dale whistled and the other cowboys almost visibly relaxed at the revelation that Violet wasn't going to start crying. Because she wasn't. Absolutely no crying in baseball or ranching. "That's gonna put us between a rock and a hard place," Dale said.

"We can…" She had to prepare for the worst-case here—losing the Wild Aces completely. "We can lease Taggert's land and…"

Dale shook his head. "He sold out to Samson Oil a few months back."

"What about—"

"Samson Oil," Dale cut her off. "All of them. The Aces was the last holdout, and Lulu only hung on for as long as she did because she's got a soft spot for you."

"What the hell?" Violet stared down at her phone again, as if it somehow held all the answers. Did Samson Oil own it all? By God, she was so tired of having this crap happen to her. This was the last straw. "I have to talk to Mac."

She would make that man see reason and if they had to shell out $1.5 million damned dollars to get the Wild Aces, then that was his fault for not listening to her the first time. She was the boss. It was high time to show her brother that.

"We've got this," Dale said, motioning her toward her horse. "Go on."

"Thanks, Dale." Violet mounted Skipper and lit out for the house. She was so upset she couldn't even fret about whether or not Rafe would give her a look for riding hell for leather.

They couldn't lose the Wild Aces.

Now she just had to convince Mac of that fact.

"Well, howdy, Violet." Mac's assistant looked up from her desk. "We don't see you during the day much—is everything okay?"

"Andrea—I need help." That was the understatement of the day but Violet's throat closed up and for the second time in the past twenty minutes she was on the verge of tears. Luckily, Andrea Beaumont was one of her closest female friends—not to mention the only person who could get Mac to do anything, basically.

Andrea's face got serious and she stood up, quickly moving around the desk to put her hands on Violet's shoulders. "Oh my God—what?"

As she looked into Andrea's caring face, the corners of Violet's mouth pulled down and her eyes began to water and dammit, she was this close to crying. "I'm going to lose the Wild Aces," she managed to say.

"What? Oh, honey," Andrea said, relief washing over her face. "Good heavens, you scared the heck out of me." Andrea pulled Violet into a quick hug. "I thought there was something seriously wrong. You looked lower than a rattler belly in a wagon rut."

Something was seriously wrong. "I—" *I'm pregnant.* But the words wouldn't come out. She couldn't spill the beans just yet—not without talking to Rafe again. She quickly corrected course. "I'm just worried. We need the Aces for water and if it's sold…"

Andrea sighed. "I wish we could have gotten him to buy it when he had the chance. If you'd come to me first, maybe…"

"Yeah, I know." Mac would never take a suggestion Violet made at face value. He'd only hear her asking for the frivolous things she asked for as a kid—a new pony, new boots, more toys. He never believed that she could have an idea that had merit.

But she'd wanted the Wild Aces so much that, instead of waiting around for Andrea to massage the message, Violet had barged right into all the reasons the Double M should acquire the Wild Aces over dinner. What a mistake that had been.

And now that mistake was going to cost her almost twice the price Lulu would have sold her the Aces for a year ago.

Well, this wasn't all her fault. If Mac wasn't so damned convinced she was nothing but a foolish girl, he'd have seen the logic behind her request and bought the Wild Aces in the first place.

Of course, this was an emergency. There was no time to let Andrea work her magic. She had less than a day to convince Mac that the Aces wasn't just another frivolous thing she wanted—it was part and parcel of the Double M's survival. "Is he in?"

"Yes, let me check." Andrea knocked on Mac's door and stuck her head in. "Your sister is here."

"Come on in," Mac said in the background.

"Good luck," Andrea whispered as Violet edged into the room.

"What's up, sis?" Mac asked without looking up from his computer.

Was there a good way to start this conversation? No, there wasn't. The best she could do at this point was keep quiet about her pregnancy for as long as she could. If Mac found out now—in the middle of this whole thing with Samson Oil—well, the situation would get muddled up beyond all hope. At the very least, she wanted her doctor's appointment to happen before she told Mac.

"We need to buy the Wild Aces," she said without preamble.

Mac sighed heavily, as if she were twelve all over again, an irritating little sister he could barely be bothered to humor. "Again with the Wild Aces, Violet? We don't need to waste money on land we don't need."

"But we need the water, Mac. This isn't about what I want. This is about the Double M. Lulu called—some outfit named Samson Oil offered her two million for the Aces. She'll give me twenty-four hours to come up with at least one-point-five but otherwise, we're out. And if we're out, we'll be out the water."

"Wait—did you say Samson Oil?"

"Yeah, I did. And Dale said they've bought up the Taggerts' land and all the other ranches around ours. If we don't meet Lulu's offer, we're going to be locked out, Mac. We need the water or we'll lose the Double M." She was proud of the way she kept her anger out of it.

Because if he'd just listened to her the first time—or all the other times after that—they wouldn't be in this position.

The blood drained out of Mac's face and he sat back, his full attention on her.

"What?" she demanded. Because he looked a lot more upset right now than he had when a tornado had damaged their wells.

"Samson Oil is—well, it's Rafe. I just found out at the

Cattleman's Club meeting. The other night." He looked flabbergasted. "Kyle Wade told us all."

"Wait—what?" For maybe only the second time in her life, Violet felt faint. The first had been when her parents hadn't come home, but Sheriff Nathan Battle had shown up with some woman Violet had never seen before to tell her that she was now an orphan. It had been perfectly understandable then that Violet had fainted.

But this? Rafe *was* Samson Oil?

Yeah, this was as good a time as any to feel light-headed.

"Hey—hey!" Mac jumped up and hurried toward her. "Geez, Violet—what the heck? Sit down," he said, his voice thick as he caught her under the arms and guided her to the chair in front of his desk. "Andrea, get some water!" he shouted.

"I'm fine," Violet lied, because she wasn't sure of anything anymore, except that she wasn't fine at all. She had just plumb run out of coping, thank you very much. No coping left at all. She couldn't handle one more shock to the system.

Mac grabbed a manila folder off his desk and began fanning her. Andrea rushed in with a glass of water and the two of them hovered over her like protective mother hens. "Should we call an ambulance?"

"For the love of Pete, I'm fine," Violet said, more forcefully this time. She was the boss. Not her emotions and not her hormones. "It's just…he didn't mention Samson Oil when we had dinner."

And that seemed like a rather important fact. When he said he'd look into the Wild Aces for her, for example—that would have been a great time to mention that he was behind the corporation buying up all the land surrounding the Double M at insane prices.

Wait—maybe she was looking at this wrong? What if Rafe had done exactly what he'd said he was going to do?

Hope flared through the mess that was her head. Maybe he was buying the Aces for her, just as he'd said?

"Well, he is Samson Oil," Mac went on. "He didn't deny it at the meeting or anything. Instead, he just said that he was exploring mineral rights." Mac stood back up, frowning. "I don't know, Violet. I mean, it's Rafe—but there's something about this that's not right."

"Dale said we'd be cut off from the water." Just as soon as the hopeful thoughts that Rafe had really bought the Wild Aces for her had emerged, they were sunk under a crushing wave of worry. "Mac," she started, a sense of horror dawning in her mind, "what if he's *not* here because he's checking in with his old friend?"

Just saying those words out loud made her feel ill all over again.

"I don't know if I can believe that either," Mac said, starting to pace. "I mean, he's only been in Texas for, what? A few weeks, tops?"

Violet opened her mouth to correct him because she knew—intimately—that Rafe had been in the area much earlier than that. Four months ago, in fact.

But that's not what she said, at least not directly. "If he's Samson Oil, and Samson has been buying up property all around Royal since last fall, why didn't he come over months ago?"

And that was the $10,000 question, wasn't it? Why had Rafe been in Holloway four months ago? Where had he been since then? And why was he buying up what basically amounted to half the town of Royal, Texas?

"I don't like this," Andrea said quietly. But she wasn't looking at Mac when she said it. Instead, she was staring at Violet.

Oh, no. Andrea wasn't exactly a mother figure, but she was the closest thing Violet had to a big sister. And if anyone could look at Violet and see the little changes that had been happening to her—and put all those little changes together to figure out the one big change—it'd be Andrea. The woman's attention to detail was almost inhuman.

Violet knew her eyes were wide and yeah, she was pretty sure she looked guilty because Andrea's eyes got wide right back. Too late, Violet realized she had covered her stomach with her hands and not in the going-to-be-sick way but the cradling-my-pregnant-belly way. Mac had missed the gesture entirely. But Andrea hadn't.

Oh, *no*. Andrea's mouth opened to say something but Violet cut her off with a shake of her head. They could not have this conversation right now, in Mac's office of all places. Not happening.

Andrea gave her what could only be described as a stern look before quickly nodding her head in agreement. "We'll talk later?" she said quietly.

"Okay," Violet said because really? She wanted to tell someone and of all the people in the world, Andrea was not only the safest option but the one who could most help Violet share her "impending blessing," as Rafe had called it, with Mac with minimal collateral damage. If her mom were here, Violet would have already cried it out on her shoulder. Andrea was the next best thing.

Just not here. Not now.

Her phone buzzed. Numbly, she dug it out of her pocket and saw it was a text from Rafe. When can I see you again?

She stared at the phone. Well, this was awkward. But then, her whole life had become one continuous string of awkward moments. She better get used to it. Where are you?

In Holloway at the inn. Thinking of you.

If she hadn't just been questioning Rafe's every motivation for being in the greater Texas area, she might have been touched by that sentiment. We need to talk.

The problem was how to talk without Mac finding out. It'd been wonderfully convenient that he'd been away on a business trip a few days ago but now? What excuse could she use to get Rafe alone?

Violet looked up at Andrea. "I need Mac to be busy tonight," she said in an urgent whisper.

"Why?"

Violet bit her lip. "I'll explain later."

Andrea gave her that stern look again. "Later, we're going to talk."

"I know. But tonight?"

Andrea sighed heavily, then stood and turned her attention back to Mac. "We need to talk with the other landowners who've already sold to Samson and get an idea of what the terms of the sales were and see if they were all told the same thing or if there are inconsistencies. Once we have a little more information, then we can consider approaching Rafe."

God bless that woman, Violet thought.

Her phone buzzed again. Are you still there?

"Yeah, okay," Mac said, rubbing the back of his neck. "Something doesn't add up, I tell you." He turned his attention back to Violet. She barely managed to get her phone flipped over so her screen was pressing against her thigh before Mac saw. "You going to be okay?"

"I'm fine, really," she said again.

"I want you to go home and take it easy for the rest of the day. Maybe Andrea can come by and fix you some chicken-noodle soup?"

Violet gave Andrea a look, one that Violet hoped said, *Keep him busy.*

"I think I need to come with you," Andrea said carefully. "Violet says she's fine and besides, two heads are better than one. I'll take notes while you talk to people."

"Okay, yeah, that sounds good." When Andrea relaxed into a smile, Violet thought she saw something unfamiliar flicker across Mac's face. "We'll get some dinner and make an evening of it. If," he added, glancing at Violet, "you're sure you're going to be okay?"

Violet stood, casually tucking her phone back into her pocket. "Mac," she said carefully, "I'm not a little girl anymore. If I say I'll be fine, I'll be fine."

For a second, she thought Mac was going to argue with her. But Andrea stepped forward and said, "She'll be fine, Mac."

Mac turned his attention back to Andrea. That look came over his face again and he said, "All right," as if he were physically incapable of taking Violet's word at face value.

God, she loved her brother, but sometimes she just wanted to strangle him.

Violet knew she shouldn't press her luck. She should quit while she was—okay, maybe not ahead, but at least not falling further behind. But they still hadn't resolved the whole reason she'd come here today. "What about the Wild Aces?"

Andrea shot her a warning look. Right. Violet needed to let this drop and she needed to let Andrea work her magic when she and Mac were making an evening of it, so to speak.

"Let me talk to a few people," Mac said, grabbing his hat and firmly cramming it on his head. "But Violet— I won't let it go without a fight. Not if Rafe's got some ulterior motive."

Andrea nodded, and although Violet desperately wanted to remind Mac of how very much they needed the Wild Aces, she let the matter drop.

As soon as Mac and Andrea were safely in his truck, with Andrea already on the phone making calls to everyone who had sold to Samson Oil, Violet texted Rafe back. I'm here. When's good for you?

Now, was the immediate response. Shall I come to you? Or you to me?

She had promised Mac she would go home. And as long as she and Rafe stayed downstairs—with their clothes on—if Mac came home, she could just say, well, Rafe dropped in to chat about all this Samson Oil business.

Can you come to the house? she texted back.

I am on my way.

See you soon.

Soon she would know what he was up to and what part she played and whether or not she was going to get the Wild Aces.

God, she hoped this worked out.

Nine

Rafe paused only long enough to procure another rose for Violet, and even with that small detour, he made it to the Double M in record time.

He did not see Mac's vehicle, which was good. In the two days since he'd left Violet's bed, he hadn't been able to stop thinking about her.

It was discomforting to realize that he missed her. Worse, though, was the fact that he was having conflicting thoughts about the property she wanted, the Wild Aces. The purchase was going according to plan. Despite the issues that kept cropping up, victory was still within his grasp. Once he had the Wild Aces, he could choke Mac McCallum off his property. Revenge served very cold indeed.

Except that he kept thinking back to the grand old home on the Wild Aces, and how Violet wanted to make it over and raise his child there. And how Rafe wanted very much to give her just that—to give her whatever she wanted.

That insidious voice in the back of his head that sounded like his father's angry shouting berated him for even considering letting the Wild Aces—and his entire scheme—fall apart for the sake of one woman.

The family honor. The family name. No one uses a bin Saleed like that and gets away with it.

That was what his father had shouted after he had come to collect Nasira and found her in Mac's bed. Those were the very words he had used to shame Rafe for allowing some common American to take advantage of a bin Saleed.

That was why Rafe was here. That was why he now owned half of this county. He had to avenge the family honor.

In all respects, Rafe had been surprised that his father had not taken even more drastic measures against Mac and his family. But to do so would have continued to draw attention to how Rafe and Nasira had so badly betrayed the family honor. Better to keep the whole incident quiet. At least, that was what Fareed had managed to convince the old man.

Rafe had to do something. The years between when his father had walked in on Mac and Nasira, and the old man's death had nearly killed Rafe in a very real way. All because Mac did not respect Rafe or Nasira enough to keep his lust in check.

Rafe was a bin Saleed.

Honor. Revenge.

Violet…

The diamond-and-ruby bracelet felt heavy in his pocket. It was all part of his new-and-much-improved plan. Wooing Violet away from Mac would complete his revenge in ways he had not even originally considered. He was not letting his scheme fall apart. He was expanding upon it.

As he mounted the steps onto the wide porch, Violet opened the door and he knew immediately that something was not right. "Are you well?" he asked, hurrying to take her in his arms.

"Rafe," she said, not exactly melting into his embrace. Instead, she stayed stiff and he heard the tension in her voice.

And her text came back to him: We need to talk.

He leaned back and looked down at her. And he knew, somehow, that she'd discovered his scheme.

Was it weakness that he wanted to delay that confrontation, even for a moment longer? Was it weakness that had him pressing his lips against hers for one more kiss, because after this kiss, he did not know if he would have another chance to hold her in his arms?

Or was it just the fact that he had failed and he sought the comfort only Violet could provide?

She did not kiss him back. Not as she had kissed him the last time he had seen her.

Suddenly, Rafe was nearly overcome with the urge to fall to his knees and beg her forgiveness. Once, Violet McCallum had been an abstract concept, an afterthought to his scheme. But now? Now she was a living, breathing woman who had shared herself with him, body and soul, and he had been careless with that. With her.

"Who are you?" she said, her voice soft. But that softness did nothing to disguise the anger that she was barely keeping in check. "Who are you, really?"

"Rafiq bin Saleed," he told her truthfully. "I sometimes use Ben. It was…simpler."

"Simpler?" she scoffed, turning away from him.

"Easier to pronounce," he offered, trailing after her as she stalked into her home.

"Or just easier to hide who you really were?"

"That, too."

She spun, her eyes blazing. "Tell me how you're involved with Samson Oil. Tell me why you were here four months ago. Tell me why you suddenly seem to own every single piece of land surrounding the Double M." She began to advance on him and, thankfully, years of conditioned response from being berated by his father had Rafe standing his ground. Cowering was bad enough but to cower before a woman?

"And tell me, Rafe," she went on, her voice getting louder with each word, "*tell me* it doesn't have a damn thing to do with whatever happened between you and Mac back in college. That 'it does not signify.'"

By this point, she was standing directly in front of him and poking him in the chest with one of her fingers.

Tell me you have not failed me. The words were not Violet's but his father's. It had been a trap, because of course Rafe had failed him and Nasira. Rafe had failed the country of Al Qunfudhah by foolishly trusting a duplicitous American.

Some part of him knew that he had failed Violet, that she had had nothing to do with what happened between Mac and Nasira, that she had nothing to do with the hell on earth that had come afterward.

But that part was buried deep beneath Rafe's survival mechanisms. And Violet, while formidable, was not Hassad bin Saleed.

He straightened his back and leveled his best glare at her. He was not the same wayward youth. He would not be dressed down by anyone anymore. Least of all a woman.

Not even *his* woman.

Rafe pushed her finger away from his chest. "Ah, so you have figured it out, have you? I should have guessed that you would put the pieces together before your idiot brother did."

His words had the desired affect—the color drained from her face and, off balance, she stumbled backward. "What?"

Without thinking about it, he caught her around the waist to keep her from falling. He didn't tuck her against his chest, however, nor did he attempt to comfort her. He kept distance between their bodies. "Sit, please. I have no wish to see you hurt."

"Figured *what* out, Rafe?"

"Sit, Violet." This time, it was not a request. It was an order. He backed her up until she hit the chair with the backs of her legs and sat with enough force that Rafe winced. "Take care. Please, think of the child."

Violet looked down at her stomach as if she expected an alien to emerge from her body at any second. "The… child? You still…" Her voice trailed off with the unspoken question.

"Yes, of course I still want the child. The baby will be my flesh and blood just as much as it will be yours." Rafe took the sofa where he had been sitting when she first walked back into his life. She had been ready to flay him alive then. Some things, it seemed, would never change. "Now. Tell me what you know and what your brother knows."

She blinked at him and slowly, he could see her regain her control. "You are Samson Oil."

"That is correct."

"And you've been buying up all the ranches surrounding the Double M for months. That's why you were in Holloway four months ago."

Rafe nodded. "You are correct. I have also bought quite a few other parcels of land."

She looked at him in what he could only call surprise. "Why?"

"So as not to arouse suspicion."

He saw her swallow. "Oh. Of course. And...the Wild Aces? Were you going to buy that, as well, before I told you about it? About how much I wanted it?"

He felt a dull ache spreading in his chest but he held his pose, leg crossed over his knee, arms spread out along the back of the couch. He took up as much space as he could. "Yes."

Pain tightened her features to the point where Rafe fought the urge to stand and pull her into his arms. The jig, as they said, was up. "So you weren't going to buy it for me?"

He let the question hang in the air until he was sure he had his foolish impulses to comfort her under control. "Originally, no."

"Originally?"

"I will keep it for you. In a few years, after this is all settled, you may have it."

He would not have thought it possible for her to get any paler, but she did. "A...few years? And this—what *is* this, Rafe?"

The urge to move was almost overwhelming. No, he did not want to back away or run and hide, but even to stand and pace would be a physical relief. But with his father, any such betrayal of his mental state had always led to not only more beatings, but more severe beatings, as well. So Rafe forced himself to be still. "You are quite bright, Violet. Do not tell me you have failed to guess what 'this' is."

"Mac," she said. It came out almost as a croak.

He nodded his head in acknowledgment. "I can be very patient. Twelve years was nothing to me, not after what your brother did to us."

"But—he didn't," she sputtered. "He told me he found your sister in his bed and that he never even touched her. He always felt terrible about it, but it wasn't his fault!"

Rafe looked at her coolly. "And you believed that, did you?"

Her mouth opened and shut. He could read the doubt in her eyes. "Mac wouldn't lie to me. Not like you do."

"Don't be naive," Rafe said, his tone condescending.

This was not happening. It couldn't be. Maybe… maybe Violet really had fainted in Mac's office. And she was still unconscious. That'd explain this.

The man she was sitting across from looked like the same man she'd met in Holloway months ago. The man she'd taken back to her bed in the past week.

The man she had started to fall for.

But he wasn't. He was nothing but a cold, heartless bastard. "How could you do this to us?" she asked, although she was already starting to get a pretty good idea of the answer. "How could you do this to me?"

Her throat started to close up and her eyes began to water, but she wasn't going to cry. She wasn't going to give him the satisfaction of knowing how upset she was. Besides, she figured a snake of a man like Rafiq bin Saleed wouldn't be moved by a woman crying anyway. That would imply that he was capable of emotions.

He sat looking at her for what felt like a very long time. "Because," he said slowly.

"Don't give me that, Rafe. *Because* isn't an answer. Why are you doing this to me? I never did anything to you or your sister. I never even knew you."

It was only when Rafe exhaled—long and slow, the kind of controlled breath that seemed to say to her he was barely in control—that she realized he might not be quite as calculating as she'd gathered. So she did what she always did—she spoke. Impulsively. "Was this your evil plan all along? Were you waiting for me in Holloway that night for the express purpose of getting me pregnant? Am I nothing but a pawn to you?"

"I understand if you hate me," he said in a much softer voice than she had been expecting.

"Hate you? Jesus, I don't know if I should shoot you or not. And don't think I don't know how," she spat at him. "Talk, damn you."

"You may choose to believe what you wish to, but I have not lied to you."

A bark of laughter escaped her. It was either laugh or start sobbing, and she was the boss of her emotions right now, thank you very much.

"I have, it is true, omitted many things," Rafe went on after she'd settled down. "I did not know who you were—that was the truth. I promised to use a condom, and I did. I promised I would not contact you outside of that evening, and I did not. I promised I would look into the Wild Aces, and I did. Honor is everything to my people, and my family and I have made every effort not to dishonor you through lies."

"You'll excuse me if I don't exactly see the difference between you lying and you carefully not mentioning that the whole reason you were in Holloway and Royal in the first place was to destroy my family."

The infuriating man waved his hand, as if she were

splitting hairs, but he didn't have the energy to argue with her.

"My revenge is complete, with your assistance," he said. He tried to smile, but even in her upset state she could see how forced it was, as if there were something that were pushing him to say and do these awful things. "Surely you can see how Mac and I will be even. He ruined my sister. I merely returned the favor."

Where was her gun? Oh, that's right. Up in her room. She'd never make it up and back before Rafe could get out of range. Dammit.

"For your information, I don't think your sister was ruined just because she chose to get into bed with my brother, and I don't think you ruined me just because I chose to sleep with you—which, by the way, will never happen again."

"As is your choice," he said and there was no mistaking the sorrow in his voice.

"If you think you're ever going to get our baby, you're wrong. I'll fight you every step of the way."

"It does not have to be like that," he said, and it might have been her imagination, but she swore he looked worried.

Well, he could just be worried. She surged to her feet, letting the anger carry her. "The hell it doesn't. I won't let you get the Wild Aces, I won't let you get the Double M, I won't let you get my baby and I sure as hell won't let you get *me*. Now get out."

Rafe stood. "It is too late, you realize. The Wild Aces is as good as mine and soon, your brother will not be able to sustain the Double M."

"It ain't over till it's over," she retorted. "Now leave before I get my gun."

He nodded and walked to the front door. Then he

paused and turned back to her. "You should have been a pawn," he said mournfully. "But you were not. It gives me no pleasure to do this to you."

"Then don't," she said, unable to believe what she was saying. "Don't do it to me. Don't do it to us." And she was horrified to realize that she wanted him to do something—what, she didn't know. Something that would show her that underneath that imperious exterior was the real man she'd almost loved.

"There is no us," he said, turning away from her. "And I have no choice in the matter. I am bound by honor and obligation. But I will hold the Wild Aces for you and for our child. I promise you that, Violet."

She needed to say something—get the last word, put him in his place, but all she could do was watch him open up the door to her house and close it behind him when he went.

Then she sank into the chair and cried.

But not for long. The Double M was her ranch, her home. She was the boss around here. She did not have time for self-pity.

She dialed Mac. "I need you to come home right now," she told him when he answered. "We need to talk."

By the time Mac and Andrea rolled in, Violet had gotten herself under control. She'd texted her best friends, Clare and Grace, because if there was one thing she needed right now, it was backup. She'd splashed her face with water and had a ginger ale and was, all things considered, feeling up to the fight.

"What?" Mac demanded when he walked through the door. Violet stood and faced her brother. "What's so important that you couldn't tell me on the phone? Did you find out something about Samson Oil or Rafe?"

Andrea put a gentle hand on his shoulder and made eye contact with Violet. "What is it, Violet?" she asked, her gaze dropping to Violet's belly.

"Okay, I've got a couple of things to say and I'm going to say them," Violet said, trying to remember to breathe.

"All right," Mac said, looking worried. "What?"

"First off, I'm pregnant."

That might not have been the best way to go about this, but Violet was done tiptoeing around Mac. *"What?"*

"Second off," she said, charging ahead, "Rafe is the father."

"What?" Mac roared. "That bastard! I asked him to keep an eye on you and this is how he repays me? I'm going to—"

Violet held up her hand and Andrea squeezed Mac's shoulder and miracle of miracles, the man shut up. "Third off, I'm four months pregnant. Actually, four months and almost two weeks."

Mac's mouth opened and then shut again. "Wait, what?"

"Rafe was in town months before he showed up here, claiming he wanted to reconnect. I met him at the Holloway Inn in November. That's where…" Mac blanched. Okay, they didn't need to get into the details. "Anyway, I needed a night out. I didn't know who he was and he claims that he didn't know who I was, although obviously we can't exactly take him at his word right now. It was a one-night stand that didn't go quite according to plan."

"Oh, honey," Andrea said.

"I don't think I want to hear anymore," Mac said, looking a little green around the gills.

"Fourth off, he's out to get you and, as near as I can figure, I'm just collateral damage. He made me a lot of promises over the course of the last week and he swears that he'll hold on to the Wild Aces for me and I can have it in a few years after he's put the Double M out of business."

"So this is all—what, exactly?"

"Revenge," Andrea said. "This is revenge."

"She's right. He said he was honor bound to get you back for ruining his sister. Originally, that just meant ruining you. But I guess I provide the ironic twist, don't I?" Her voice cracked and Andrea pulled her into a big hug.

"It's okay, honey," she said softly.

"How the hell is this okay?" Mac shouted. "Some insane sheikh is out to ruin me because his equally insane sister decided the best way to get out of a bad marriage was to be caught in my bed? I had nothing to do with any of this!"

"Mac!" Andrea hissed. "Now is not the best time!"

Mac looked at Violet, who was sniffing violently. "I'm—oh, God, I'm sorry, Violet. I didn't think…"

"It's okay. But I have one more thing I want to say." She straightened up and pushed herself out of Andrea's arms.

Mac eyed her warily. "What's that?"

"This—if you had bought the Wild Aces when I asked you to, if you had listened to me at any point in the last twelve years—we wouldn't be in this position."

The man had the nerve to look hurt. "But Violet—I was just trying to protect you. You've had to deal with more than your share, what with us losing our parents and—"

"It's been twelve years, Mac. I'm not a little girl anymore and I'm not the shell-shocked teenager I was when you got home from college. I'm a grown woman and a ranch manager and soon I'm going to be a mother. Everyone else knows that I can handle myself—even this surprise pregnancy, I can deal with it. But I've spent years tiptoeing around you and asking Andrea to convince you to do things for me because every time I open my mouth, you act like I'm just the cutest little thing playacting at adulthood and I'm sick of it. I don't need your protection. I'm not just your little sister. I am your business partner, dammit, and it's high time you started treating me like it."

Mac gaped at her but, amazingly, didn't tell her he was going to handle it or that it was all going to be okay. "Well, then, what do you suggest?"

Luckily, she'd had enough time to think through the next step. "The only way to cut Rafe off is to buy the Aces out from under him. Lulu said she'd sell it to me for one-point-five million. The very last thing I will ever ask of you is to help me buy it. We need the water and I need my own place to raise my family."

For a second, she thought maybe she'd gotten through to the big lunkhead, but old habits died mighty hard, because Mac's gaze cut to Andrea. Violet rolled her eyes, and she saw Andrea's lips twist into something of a knowing smile.

"She's right," Andrea said. "You know she is."

"Dang it all, I know." Mac took off his hat and rubbed his forehead. "I don't know if we can beat him to the punch. No one knew who was behind Samson Oil at first and the money was too good. He had Nolan Dane doing all his negotiating for him. Kyle Wade is the one who outed him, but I don't think any of us saw this as revenge. Except for you," he added before Violet could correct him. "And why didn't you tell me you were expecting?"

"Because the moment I figured it out is literally the moment Rafe showed back up and I had a lot to deal with, okay?"

Mac put his hands up in the universal sign of surrender. "Okay, okay. Sheesh."

"I need the Wild Aces, Mac."

He nodded—slowly at first, but then more emphatically. "Then I'll go get it for you, partner."

Ten

"I don't know what I'm going to do." It was all well and good for Violet to stand up in front of her brother and tell him she could handle this, but now, far away from Mac, she wasn't so sure.

Which was how she found herself at the Royal Diner, sitting with her best friends, Clare Connelly and Grace Haines, and pouring her heart out while Mac went to try to get the money by liquidating some capital—or something like that. Violet did not handle the money end of things, so Andrea had gently suggested that she get together with her friends for a little girl time.

Violet really did love Andrea. The woman was a peach.

"Honey," Clare said, slinging an arm around Violet's shoulder and giving her a firm hug, "if anyone can handle this, it's you."

"But I'm pregnant." Now that Violet had said the

words out loud, she seemingly couldn't stop saying them. She'd been telling friends, neighbors, Dale—even random people she met in the street. She was pregnant and she was screwed.

"You keep saying that like it's the end of the world, but you know it's not," Grace said. "Heck, I'm suddenly mother to twins. It's a lot but it's *not* the end of the world. You've survived worse, you know."

Violet was too emotionally drained to even wince. "Yeah, but my parents' plane crash was a one-and-done event. This? The father of my child is basically out to destroy the entire town of Royal because he's nursing a grudge against my brother about something that happened over twelve years ago. This isn't a one time trauma. This has the potential to be an ongoing international incident. I mean, he's a sheikh, for God's sake!"

Clare and Grace shared a look. "I'm sure something can be worked out," Clare said. "I mean, look at Grace. First she was Maddie and Maggie's social worker and now she's going to adopt them and marry their father…"

"What Clare is saying is, just because it's complicated doesn't mean you can't find a way to make it work," Grace finished.

"And you know I'll be here with you," Clare said, giving Violet another squeeze. "I love babies! I'll teach you everything you need to know and when your baby gets a little older, we can all have playdates together."

"We?" Violet and Grace both turned to look at Clare. Grace said, "Is there something you're not telling us?"

Clare blushed. "Actually, I'm pregnant. But!" she said quickly, hushing her friends before they could start whooping and hollering. "I'm only a little pregnant. Probably not more than five weeks along, so we're going to keep it quiet for now, okay?"

Now it was Violet's turn to hug Clare. "Oh, honey," she said, and damn the stupid hormonal tears that started up again. At least this time, they were happy tears, right? "I'm so excited for you and Parker!"

As they were comparing due dates, the chimes over the door jingled. All three of them looked up at the newcomer. A woman with long, thick black hair wearing a beautiful gold-yellow suit glided into the diner as if she were walking on rose petals—which was impressive, given her heels. Those suckers had to be at least five inches tall and yet this woman moved in them as if they were a natural part of her feet. The woman paused inside the door and removed her hat—not a cowboy hat, like most of the people here wore, but a short, wide number that was the exact color of her suit, complete with a feather that swept out over the huge brim.

All in all, she looked like someone who might have gotten lost on her way to a royal wedding and wound up in Royal, Texas, completely by accident.

And Violet recognized her immediately.

"Wow," Clare said in a hushed whisper.

"Beautiful," Grace agreed. "Who is that? She's not from around her, is she? I'd remember the hat."

"Rafe," Violet said. Both the women turned to look at her. "I mean, she looks like Rafe. Excuse me."

Her heart pounding, Violet slid out of her booth and approached the newcomer. What was Nasira bin Saleed doing here? Rafe had promised that he would try to arrange a meeting between Nasira and Violet—but Violet was pretty sure Rafe had said he didn't think Nasira would come to America. "Hi—Nasira?"

Because who else could she be? Looking like this woman did—the black hair and olive skin and the same nose and chin as Rafe?

The woman's face registered surprise. "I am sorry," she said in an accent that was similar to Rafe's, but very different. Whereas Rafe's voice always made Violet think of warm sunshine and honey, this woman's voice sounded almost like…like rain and fog and mist. It was not an unpleasant thing, but it was very unexpected. "Do I know you?"

Violet stuck out her hand. "I'm Violet McCallum. I'm Mac's sister. And you're Rafe's sister, Nasira—right? You look like him."

Nasira blushed. "Ah, yes. Violet. Hello. How fortunate I have found you so quickly. I have come to warn you and your brother that—"

"That Rafe's going to buy up the entire town and ruin Mac?" Nasira winced. "Yeah, sorry—it's kind of too late for that."

Nasira clutched at her hat and paled. "Oh, no—I am too late? What has he done?"

Violet decided she liked Nasira immediately. "Why don't you have a seat? Would you like some coffee? Then we can talk."

Clare and Grace introduced themselves and Nasira politely said hello, although she did not shake hands. "Well," Clare said, standing and giving a knowing look to Grace, "we best be running along. But Violet—you call us the moment you need anything."

"Anything at all," Grace added.

And then Violet was alone with Nasira. Once the other women were gone, Nasira sat in the seat Grace had vacated. She sat very stiffly, her back straight and her chin up. She placed her fancy hat on the table next to her and waited silently while Amanda Battle, the owner of the Royal Diner, poured the coffee.

"Anything else I can get you all?" Amanda said, trying not to stare at Nasira.

The Royal Diner was pretty much ground zero for gossip in this town. Violet glanced around. Luckily, aside from a few stragglers, Violet and Nasira had the place to themselves.

"I think we're good," Violet said, smiling warmly at Amanda.

She and Nasira were silent until Amanda was out of earshot. Then, with the most graceful gesture Violet had ever seen, Nasira leaned forward and said, "Tell me what has happened. What has Rafe done?"

So Violet told Nasira what she knew—about Samson Oil, the land grabs, the Wild Aces, everything but her relationship with Rafe. She doubted if just casually blurting out that a person's brother had gotten her pregnant after a one-night stand was "done" in Al Qunfudhah. Violet's life might be a total scandal, but she didn't need to add fuel to the fire if she could help it.

When she'd finished, Nasira sat back—again, her back ramrod straight—lowered her eyes and said, "This is my fault. I am so sorry for the trouble I have caused."

The resignation in her voice alarmed Violet. "What? No way. I mean—okay, so something obviously happened twelve years ago. But I fail to see how that makes you personally responsible for what's going on here."

She was horrified to see Nasira's eyes tear up. "I brought your brother into a family problem without explaining it to him. It was unfair to him and unfair to Rafe."

"Yeah, so what exactly did happen back at Harvard? Mac insists he didn't do anything with you and Rafe won't tell me what he thinks happened either."

Nasira's gaze sharpened, just a little, and she again

looked more like her brother. "Are you and Rafe on good terms, then? Does he talk to you?"

Violet realized she was blushing. "You first," she said, trying to play for time. "Your story happened first, so you tell it first."

"All right," Nasira said again, her voice a little cooler this time.

Oh, yeah, this was Rafe's sister. There was no mistaking it.

After a long pause, Nasira leaned forward again, her voice soft—no doubt to keep anyone from overhearing them. "I chose Mac precisely because I knew him to be an honorable man who would not violate me," she explained. She picked up a packet of sweetener and began to fiddle with it—the first sign of nerves that Violet had seen yet. "I know that may sound unusual to your American ears, but at the time, I felt that letting my father believe I had been compromised by a man such as Mac was the only way I could escape the fate he had chosen for me."

"A man such as Mac? I don't understand—obviously, your father didn't see him as an honorable guy."

A hint of color graced Nasira's cheeks. Really, everything the woman did was grace embodied. "No, he did not. My father barely tolerated Rafe attending an American school, and Mac was not of royal blood. So to be 'defiled' by him—or so my father believed," Nasira hurried to add when Violet opened her mouth to argue with that particular assessment, "was lowering myself even more."

What was it with these people? Ruined? Defiled? No wonder they were so screwed up. Did they ever fall in love and have sex simply because they wanted to?

There had been that night, many months ago, when Violet had gone to bed with Rafe because she wanted to.

She'd wanted one night of fun and freedom and—yes—good sex. And Rafe? He had wanted all those things, too.

But did he now view her as ruined? Defiled? Had he lowered himself by making her pleasure his?

Ugh, she was nauseous again.

Nasira had dropped her gaze to the table, so she missed Violet's reaction. "You must try to understand. I was to be wed to a horrible man, a man I feared greatly. He was well over sixty and had already had two wives who had died in 'accidents' that were not accidents. His first wife died because she only gave birth to girls and his second…well, I do not know why."

Violet gasped. "How could your father marry you off to such a man?"

Nasira looked at her sadly. "I hope you can understand how different our families are. This was all expected when I was a child. I had been promised to the warlord for some time. He was a powerful man and my father wanted to keep him close. It was only when Rafe left for university in America and met your brother…" Her voice trailed off. "Rafe told me such stories, you see. And the way he spoke of his friendship with Mac, of you—of this place—it was almost too good to believe. For the first time in our lives, I envied Rafe."

Violet gave her a confused look. "Wait, what? I mean—you were going to be married off to a monster and you didn't already envy Rafe?" How did that even make sense?

Nasira gave her that sad smile again, one that spoke of pain that Violet could only begin to fathom. "Rafe is second in line for the sheikhdom. In England, he would be the spare, as they say. But we did not grow up in England and my father treated Rafe harshly."

Violet stared at her. Harshly? How harshly?

"But I am getting off the point," she went on. "Rafe was in America and having all of these wonderful adventures, and I was envious. I managed to convince my father that, for my eighteenth birthday, I should be allowed to visit Rafe. Our older brother, Fareed, took my side. It was he who told me what Rafe was doing here in Royal," she added.

"Okay, so Fareed is a decent guy?"

"He is *not* our father," Nasira said emphatically. "He is a just and fair ruler of Al Qunfudhah."

Well, that had to count for something. "So you got to visit Rafe in America and while you were here, you decided to get out of the marriage by... Is *seducing* the right word?"

Nasira's eyes widened in horror and she shook her head. "No, no. I had convinced your brother to kiss me by explaining my situation but, at the last moment, I feared that would not be enough, so I made a foolish choice and snuck into his bed. That was where our father found me." She dropped her gaze again and went back to mangling the sweetener packet. "I regret that choice, but please understand, I also do not regret it. What came after was...terrible." She shuddered and Violet shuddered in sympathy.

"You didn't have to marry that guy, right? That's what Rafe said. He said you were able to leave Al Qunfudhah and marry a man more to your liking."

"Sebastian, yes." There was a note of sorrow to her voice that she tried to hide with a smile. "My life has been much easier than I had ever allowed myself to dream it could be. However, I do not believe Rafe's was." She didn't speak for a moment and, for once, Violet managed not to open her mouth and charge into the gap. "It was a relief when our father died and Fareed took power," Nasira said quietly. "Rafe was allowed to resume life in the outside world."

Violet felt herself gaping at Nasira like a catfish out of water but she couldn't quite get her face under control. "You make it sound like your father imprisoned him because he didn't protect you. Or your honor, anyway."

"It sounds that way because it was that way." Nasira's words were little more than a whisper. "I believe that, in the years between my actions and our father's death, Rafe held one thought that sustained him. And now that he has regained his power and his wealth by his own hands…"

"Revenge."

Nasira set the sweetener packet down and returned her hands to her lap. Violet could see her composing herself. "For a long time, I've wished that there had been another way. It is all my fault."

What Violet needed was a drink. Of course, she couldn't exactly wander over to the bar and do a line of shots, no matter how much she might want to block out the world for a while. "Well. This certainly puts a new spin on things."

"Oh? And what about you, Violet? You speak as if you know Rafe."

"I do. I…" She took a deep breath. "I don't really know how to say this without it sounding bad, so I'm just going to say it. I'm pregnant and Rafe's the father."

She wasn't sure what she expected Nasira to do with that bit of information, but bursting into tears and smiling at the same time wasn't it. "Nasira?"

Amanda Battle hustled over. "Is everything okay?"

"Um—tissues?" Violet said. Just watching Nasira cry was making her tear up, too.

Amanda hurried back behind the counter, bless her heart, and reappeared with a box of tissues. "Thanks,"

Violet said. Amanda got the hint and retreated back to the counter.

"My deepest apologies," Nasira said, grabbing a tissue and blotting at her eyes. "It is just…well, I am very happy that Rafe has opened himself up. I had believed that part of him might have died after…"

"But you're crying," Violet said gently.

"It is nothing," Nasira said, which was pretty obviously a bold-faced lie. "I am quite happy for you and for Rafe," she repeated.

"But…"

Nasira tried to smile but she didn't make it. "I have long wanted a child of my own and we have not been blessed with one. Sebastian is an honorable man. He wishes to have an heir and I…I cannot. I recently lost the baby I was carrying and now he will not…" Her voice trailed off with such hopelessness that it almost overwhelmed Violet.

"Oh." This time, Violet didn't even try to rein in her own tears. "I'm so sorry. This must be—oh," she repeated numbly. Because seriously, the fact that she got pregnant after one time had to be salt in the wound.

"Please," Nasira said, drying her eyes and putting on a good face, "do not apologize. Tell me more of Rafe. You are aware of his scheme, yes?"

"I figured it out. And when I confronted him about it, he told me the rest. I just…look, I get that he blames Mac. But it's been twelve years. And your father—how long has he been dead?"

"Almost seven years," Nasira said.

"Why is he still doing this? I thought…" Now it was her turn to look down at the table. "I thought he cared for me. But when I confronted him, he told me that Mac had ruined you and he was just returning the favor."

Nasira gasped in horror. "He said that?"

Violet nodded. "And I feel like such a fool because he made all these promises that sounded so good, about how I would always have a place in his country and how our child would be both a bin Saleed and a McCallum and…and it was all a trap. He didn't care for me, but I fell for him."

Unexpectedly, Nasira reached across the table and took Violet's hand in hers. "Do not think such things," she said, a harder edge to her voice. "I know Rafe and I know he does not say such things lightly. He does not allow himself to grow close to people in general and women specifically. That was what was so unusual about his friendship with Mac. I do not think that, before that time, Rafe had had many friends"

"Really? But he's so charming. Too charming," she admitted.

"I shall speak to him," Nasira said decisively.

"What? No, you don't have to do that."

"Please," Nasira said, but it wasn't a request. It was an order, and Violet remembered that, touching moments aside, she was technically sitting across from royalty. "This whole thing began with me and will be ended by me. Rafe has no just cause to treat you like this."

"I just don't want my baby to be this rope in a tug-of-war between me and Rafe," Violet said. "I don't want to keep his child from him but I can't live in fear that he'll take my baby and disappear into the desert and I'll never see my baby again."

"I will not allow it," Nasira said. "And if Rafe attempts such madness, Fareed will step in. You will be the mother of a bin Saleed. That affords you certain rights and protections, both in Al Qunfudhah and I assume here in America."

Violet nodded. "I mean, I guess. I haven't even seen a doctor yet. Everything's happened so fast..."

And what she really needed was for things to slow way, way down. At least long enough that she could get a handle on the situation. Honestly, at this rate, she was becoming numb to the shocks. She wouldn't even be surprised if the ghost of Rafe's dad, the old and seemingly really cruel sheikh himself, floated into the diner. It wouldn't faze her at all.

She glanced toward the door. Well, maybe not too much, anyway.

"Do you know where Rafe is?" Nasira asked.

"He's been staying at the Holloway Inn—it's about thirty minutes from here," Violet said. "That's where we met the first time."

Nasira brought up the inn's information on her phone. "Ah, I see."

"What about you? Do you have a place to stay? Do you want to see Mac?"

Nasira blushed, and in that moment, she looked much younger—probably more like the girl who'd been so desperate for a way out that she'd do anything. "He wouldn't be happy to see me, not after what Rafe has done," she said quietly. "I shall take a room at the inn where Rafe is."

"Will you call me and let me know how it goes?"

"Of course."

They exchanged numbers and Nasira stood to go. "Thank you," she said, putting her hat back on her head.

"For what?" Violet asked, trying not to be jealous of Nasira's style and grace. God knew Violet couldn't pull that level of class off. The one time she'd tried, well, she'd ended up pregnant.

"For caring about Rafe. He needs that more than you

could ever know." Her face took on a battle-ready look. It was a beautiful battle-readiness, but still, Violet decided that, in a throw-down, she'd put her money on Nasira. "I will not let him destroy this chance."

"I don't know that I care for him anymore. Not after all of this."

Nasira gave her a smile that sent a shiver racing down Violet's back. "We shall see."

Then Rafe's sister swept out of the Royal Diner just as quickly as she'd arrived. Violet glanced back to where Amanda was trying hard to look as though she wasn't listening. "Not a word to another living soul," she said.

"Not a word!" Amanda held up the Girl Scout sign. "On my honor!"

Violet sighed. She needed to warn Mac that the plot had thickened yet again. But she sat there for a little bit longer, trying to make sense of everything Nasira had shared. Realistically, she knew it was possible that Nasira was here because Rafe had called her, that she was a hedge against damage control. If Rafe's plan blew up in his face, he'd want a soft, beautiful woman to help with the public relations disaster.

Violet had already been a fool more than once, but she couldn't help but feel that Nasira was being honest with her. The woman's reaction to Violet's pregnancy had been too raw, too real.

And if Nasira was being up front, then it followed that…

Rafe's father had gone far beyond punishment. Rafe had spent literal, actual years planning this revenge. He claimed it was for Nasira's honor but…

She wasn't going to care. Rafe's history was tragic, but that didn't excuse his behavior now. He was single-handedly trying to ruin her family, her business and nearly the entire town of Royal, Texas. Violet needed to focus on protecting herself, her assets and, above all else, her child. Rafe wasn't even on that list.

So why did she hope that Nasira could talk some sense into him?

Yup, she was just that big of a fool.

Eleven

The Wild Aces was his.

True, it had cost Rafe an additional million dollars, but three million was nothing when he was worth a thousand times that. Three million dollars was nothing compared to the satisfaction of having finished what he set out to start.

This was a moment of victory. Years of planning and biding his time had finally come to fruition. Rafe had finally, finally avenged his family's name and honor.

He owned the Wild Aces.

He owned Mac McCallum.

Yet...

As Rafe sat in his car outside the Holloway Inn, he could not help but wonder if this was really what victory was supposed to feel like. That dull pain in his chest was back and had been ever since Rafe had dragged the real estate agent away from her family during dinner and driven madly through the countryside to get to the Wild Aces.

That pain had only gotten stronger when, coughing hard, Lulu Clilmer had told him she'd promised Violet McCallum twenty-four hours in which to match Samson Oil's offer. That was when Rafe had made an offer Lulu could not refuse—provided, of course, she signed the papers right then.

It had taken all of his self-control not to order the woman to sign. But in the end, a warm smile and obscene amounts of money had done the job for him. Lulu had signed.

Rafe should celebrate this victory. But the moment that thought occurred to him, his mind turned back to Violet—to meeting V in the bar of this very hotel and taking her to his bed. Promising that her pleasure would be his and then keeping that promise. Taking her to dinner at Claire's and waking up in her arms. Going for a ride across the Texas grasslands and watching her rope a wayward cow and feeling that, for once in his life, he was at peace. He'd glimpsed what happiness could mean for him—not as a distant, undefined thing he would never know, but a real thing he could hold in his hands when he held Violet close.

He was not at peace now. And he wasn't sure why. This was what he wanted, after all. Exacting his revenge upon Mac was the very thought that had kept him going during those dark years. Ruining Mac's life just as Rafe's had been was everything he had been working toward. His work here was about to be done.

Except that Mac had welcomed Rafe back with open arms, even vouching for him to his friends. Except Nolan Dane had been the closest thing Rafe had had to a true friend since Mac's betrayal. Except for Violet and the child she carried.

What was it about these people, this town, that made him doubt himself? No, this was not doubt. He was a bin Saleed. He did not have doubt and he did not question his motives. His motives were pure. The code he lived by—the code that had governed his family for generations—required this. Rafe had damaged the honor of the bin Saleed name. Retribution was the only way to restore that honor.

It was unfortunate that Violet had become a part of the scheme, he thought dimly as he exited his vehicle. And it was unfortunate that Nolan had lost sight of the larger goal and turned his back on Rafe.

It was unfortunate that they had all turned on him, but it did not signify. All that was left to do here was to confront Mac and let him know that Rafe had been the source of his downfall and that justice was finally served.

Then Rafe would be on the family plane, headed back to Al Qunfudhah. Back to the stretches of sand that backed up against the deep blue of the sea. Back to the family home, where Fareed ruled and Rafe was, once again, an unnecessary second. Back to where happiness was an unknown, unknowable thing that was not for him. Never for him.

It was fine. Rafe would turn his full attention back to the shipping business. Piracy was a growing concern and he needed to take measures to prevent his ships from being hijacked. If he could keep his costs low, he could undercut his competition and increase his share of the market, which would in turn increase the standard of living in Al Qunfudhah. That was how his time would be best spent. That was how he was most useful to his people. His personal happiness and sorrows did not signify. He felt nothing.

The pain in his chest was so strong that he paused outside the sliding doors of the Holloway Inn. Had it only been a matter of months since he had walked through these very doors and seen *her* sitting at the bar, the black lace of her dress contrasting with her creamy skin? Since he had taken one look at her wide smile and beautiful face and decided that he needed her in a way that he had not allowed himself to need another person?

Had it only been that long since he had given a part of him to her—a part he had not realized was his to give?

He rubbed at his chest, but it did nothing to help. He needed to leave this accursed place, he decided. In the morning, he would seek Mac out and then he would leave. He needed to be far, far away from Royal, Texas, and the people in it: people who made him want to care about them, people who seemed to care about him.

None of them did. Mac had not cared enough to keep his hands off Nasira. Nolan had not cared enough to stand by Rafe's side when he met a woman. And Violet...

Well, she had cared. Perhaps too much. More than was wise. And he had made her hate him.

At least she hadn't shot him.

One more day. He would be gone by this time tomorrow and then he could begin again. Perhaps Fareed would have selected a wife for him and he could produce legitimate heirs. That had been the purpose he had been raised for, after all. He would visit his wife when appropriate and the children would be shown to him by their nannies in the evening, as was proper. He would hardly know they were there.

And his child here...

Don't do this to me. Don't do this to us, Violet had

whispered, and he had wanted so desperately to turn back to her, to take her in his arms. In that moment, it didn't matter if it was a sign of weakness, but he could not inflict this pain on her. Not willingly.

But really, what choice did he have?

Still, he did not have to keep hurting her. No, he decided, he would not take the child from Violet. Her only crime was being Mac's sister—that and opening herself to him. There was no just cause to hurt her for that.

A voice in the back of his head—a quiet voice that sounded nothing like his father's—whispered that perhaps there was no just cause to hurt her at all. Perhaps, this soft voice suggested, there was no just cause to hurt any of them. Not Mac, not Nolan, not Violet and not the town of Royal.

Rafe pushed this thought aside. That was weakness talking and he had not come this far only to let doubt destroy everything he'd worked for. He'd spent years planning for this moment. This was not the time to have cold feet, as the Americans said. If anyone knew he was filled with this hollow pain, they would use it against him.

Rafe forced himself to breathe regularly. Years of his father's abuse had taught him that the only way to survive was to be as impervious as stone, no matter what Hassad had said or done to him.

Rafe was that stone now. Nothing could hurt him. Not even Violet's stricken face or the way she had cradled her stomach, seemingly without even being aware she was doing it, while she told him she would fight him at all costs.

It did not have to be that way. He had no wish to treat his child as he had been treated. Just the thought of his own flesh and blood having to survive what Rafe had survived at the hands of his father made his stomach turn.

Rafe focused on the movement of each breath in and out of his body. It would not be that way, not if he had anything to say about it. Perhaps, after some time had passed, he could return for a visit or he and Violet and the child could meet somewhere neutral. New York, perhaps. He could give her the deed to the Wild Aces and see his child and that would be enough for him, to get a glimpse of that happiness again, to be near it. He had made do with far less.

Perhaps he could, perhaps he could not. But could he really do that to Violet?

What happened to him did not matter. It never had. But what happened to her—to their child—could he really do this to them?

There had to be a way. He had to do something to protect her and the child, to show her that he cared for her. Something more than just holding the Wild Aces for her.

He could not destroy her. But this was weakness. If his father were still alive, he would beat Rafe for his weakness until he had no more skin left on his back, but he didn't care.

He had to show her she was not the pawn in this game—that she was something more. Much, much more.

This thought calmed him and he was able to straighten up. He would find a way to shield Violet and, until such time as he did, he would continue on. This happiness with Violet was separate from his revenge on Mac.

Besides, it would not do for Sheikh Rafiq bin Saleed to be seen staggering into a hotel as if his heart had been ripped clean of his chest. He was victorious. He had damned well better act like it.

When he was in full control of his faculties, he walked through the sliding doors of the inn. Habit had him scanning the lobby. He had been doing it for months now—

every time he returned to the inn, in fact. And he was always looking for the same thing—his beautiful, mysterious V.

His gaze came to rest on a woman, sitting stiffly in a cushioned armchair facing away from him. With a start, he realized he recognized that posture, that hair, that regal bearing.

Not V. Not Violet.

Nasira.

His sister was here? He had not seen her in several years, although they communicated via email on a regular basis. He was so stunned by her sudden appearance that he had to pause and think—had he called her here? He remembered promising Violet that he would arrange a meeting between the two women. But that was back when Violet was still speaking to him, and Rafe had been so busy in the interim that he was certain he had not had the time to summon Nasira.

Rafe did not allow himself to feel uneasy about this development. There was nothing to feel uneasy about, after all. This was merely his sister, the woman he had promised to protect. The woman he had failed. The woman whose honor he was avenging at this very moment.

"Sister," he said. He had always called her that instead of using her name.

"Ah, Brother, I see you are looking quite well." She rose gracefully to her feet and smiled. "Texas, it seems, agrees with you."

Rafe was immediately on the alert because he certainly didn't feel quite well. "Sister, why are you here?"

If he had offended her, she did not show it. Instead, she tilted her head to one side and gave him a piercing look. "Are you not glad to see me?"

"But of course I am." He stepped forward to wrap his arm around her shoulders and press a kiss to her cheek. "Does Sebastian know you are here? Are you well? Are you…" He glanced down at her stomach.

That got a reaction out of her. As Rafe watched, he saw her eyes grow flat and he knew that his question had caused her pain. For so long, she had been struggling to have a child with her husband. To ask such a question so baldly was in poor form. "Forgive me," he said gently. "That was unkind."

"Never fear." She put that sunny smile back on her face, but it didn't reach her eyes. "We are much the same. He is aware I am here."

Something about that admission sounded off. "Will he be joining you?"

Color bloomed on her cheeks. "Ah, no."

Rafe and Nasira were not children anymore, but to see her embarrassed in public brought back uncomfortable memories, and an old instinct to shield her from attention kicked in. "Shall we continue this conversation in my room? Or your room—are you staying here? I do not even know how long you plan to be in Royal. I intend to leave tomorrow, but if you are here, I do not see why I should not stay with you. I am sure that Sebastian would feel better knowing you are well cared for."

Again, she tilted her head to one side. "I am sure that Sebastian would appreciate that, if he knew you were here. And as for how long I am staying, that depends, I suppose. But yes," she went on before Rafe could ask what, exactly, she meant by that. "It would be best to talk in private, I believe."

"This way." He led her to the elevator. As the doors closed, he felt another unfamiliar stab of panic. "I must ask, Sister—how did you know where I was?"

"Fareed informed me," she said, but she did not elaborate.

"I am glad to see you. In fact, I had thought about calling you several days ago."

"Oh?" She turned to him. "Was there a reason?"

This was his sister, after all. He was not any more comfortable lying to her than he was lying to Violet. "You were in my thoughts," he said, which was both the truth and not exactly the truth.

She tilted her head. "I am honored."

Finally, the elevator came to a halt on his floor. He led the way down to his room and unlocked the door in silence.

Nasira swept into the room, but she did not take the office chair, nor did she sit on the edge of the bed. Instead, she stood in the center of his room as if it were hers, her hands folded in front of her. "So, brother," she said once the door was shut and he was facing her. "Tell me how you came to be here in Royal, Texas."

What had Fareed told her? "I could ask the same of you."

She waved this away. "I am here because Fareed gave me good reason to think that you are here for less-than-honorable reasons."

"I can assure you, sister, my reasons for being here are entirely honorable." It came out harsher than he meant it to. He did not speak harshly to Nasira. He protected her. He tried anyway.

And wasn't that really why he was here? He had tried to protect her and failed.

She sighed heavily, as if his statement had inspired nothing but disappointment. That was how she looked at him—with disappointment. That hollow pain in his chest bloomed again, burning with emptiness. "It is as we feared, then."

"What is?" He was the stone. He felt nothing because feelings were weaknesses and weakness was not tolerated. He was a bin Saleed.

"It began with me, so it shall end with me." She squared her shoulders and fixed him with a fierce gaze. "I was a virgin when I married Sebastian."

"What?" The statement caught Rafe so off guard that he recoiled a step.

"I never slept with Mac McCallum," she went on, as casually as if they were discussing the weather. "Nor did he even know I was in his bed that day. He had agreed to kiss me in front of our father to help me escape the fate that awaited me, but I was young and foolish and impulsive." She favored Rafe with a sad smile. "So foolish. I was afraid that a mere kiss would not be enough to dissuade our father, so I hatched a different plan. I snuck into Mac's bed when I knew you would be showing Father how you lived."

A strange numbness overtook Rafe's limbs as the scene played out in front of his eyes again.

Nasira had been nude under the covers, all of her clothing in a pile on the floor where they would be impossible to miss. Her hair had been freed of its braid. She had looked exactly like a woman awaking in her lover's bed. "We found you there. In his bed."

"Yes, I had been counting on it. My dear brother," she said in a voice that was almost pitying, "you are not the only one in this family who is capable of great schemes."

"Why are you telling me this? Why are you lying for him again?"

There was no mistaking the pity in her eyes this time. "Why do you persist in believing that I am lying for him?

I tried to tell you on the plane ride back. I did not want to marry that monster Father had assigned me to. I did not want to be forced into any marriage against my will. And to that end, the scheme worked perfectly. But I had not foreseen the other consequences. I did not realize what Father would do to you. And worse, I did not realize that you would do this, Rafe. I never dreamed you would even be capable of it."

"You don't know what you're talking about," he snapped at her. "You have no idea."

"Oh?" She was unruffled by his anger. It only made him madder.

"Everything I have done, I have done for you. For your honor. For our family name."

"That is why I have come to stop you."

"Are you quite mad?" he roared.

"Are you? You are the one who has nursed this perceived hurt for years. Years, Rafe. I understand that you are bitter that Father treated you like a prisoner in our home. I regret every day that my choice led to such dire consequences for you. That is a burden I carry with me everywhere I go."

He opened his mouth to say something—what, he did not know, but something, dammit all, that made her realize that *bitter* did not even begin to describe him. But she held up a hand, cutting him off with all the commanding manner of a member of the royal family. "But I have never given up hope for you, Rafe. You are not our father. He is dead and I am glad of it. You no longer have to do as he would do. You no longer have to prove that you are as cruel and heartless as he was."

"This is not cruelty," he shouted, unable to get control of himself. "Cruelty is being thrown in a dungeon and beaten because I allowed my friend to defile my sister."

"Cruelty," she calmly responded, "is destroying a man and an entire town because you were beaten. Cruelty," she said, her voice rising in pitch, "is destroying a woman who cares about you, a woman who carries your child even as we speak." Her voice cracked, the first true sign of emotion since his words had wounded her earlier. She put her hand on her heart. "Cruelty is being given the gift of love, of a child, and doing everything within your power to destroy those gifts."

He would not be moved by her sorrow. "Mac betrayed me!"

"No, Rafe. No." She shook her head and regained her composure. "The only person who has betrayed you is you. Well," she added in a casual tone, as if she had not just swung a hammer of words at his stone heart and broken it to small bits, "you and our father. But then, he betrayed us all, did he not?"

Rafe stared at her, unable to form words in his mind and equally unable to get his tongue to say them.

"Fareed is worried about you," she went on in a quiet voice. "We all are. We had hoped that, with Father's death, you would have been able to find peace. You have a chance for that, Rafe. Do not be the man Father demanded you to be. Be the man you want to be."

She moved a chair out of the way and walked toward him. No, not toward him—toward the door. When she reached him, she said, "Please forgive me for my part in your pain. It was never my intention to see you hurt. But believe me when I say this—I will fight to protect your child from you, if it comes to that. The choice is yours."

She stepped around him. He heard the door open and then shut. He knew, at least on some level, that he was alone.

But he was not. Ghosts of the past—and the present—

cluttered his vision. He saw Nasira in bed, looking shocked to have been discovered. But now he remembered that she had disappeared from their group only a few minutes before that—thirty, at most. Not nearly enough time to have slept with Mac in his bed.

And Rafe remembered Mac's shock at coming into the room and finding all of them there like that—Nasira in his bed, Rafe standing next to it, Hassad raging at both of them. At the time, Rafe had taken that shock as confirmation that Mac had not expected Hassad to find him with his lover but...

Was it possible he had been just as shocked about seeing Nasira in his bed?

And then it had all happened so fast. Within hours, they were on the family jet, flying back to Al Qunfudhah.

"Tell me you have not failed me," Hassad had said in that dank dungeon, in between blows. And Rafe had known there was no hope. He could not defend himself, for his father would call him a liar and beat him more. And he could not admit defeat because his father would beat him for being a coward.

And Fareed—he was there, as well, sneaking down to the dungeon with extra food or wine, with medicines that took the edge off the pain or a blanket to make the stone floor more comfortable or books to read so that Rafe did not go out of his mind. "I will convince him," Fareed had promised. "This is not your fate."

And Rafe had been so beaten down that he had not bothered to correct his brother. This was his fate. He took his father's anger so Hassad did not treat his other children this way. That had always been Rafe's fate, ever since he was a child and had defended Nasira, his closest sibling, from Fareed's teasings and had gotten slapped across the face for daring to speak against the future sheikh of Al Qunfudhah.

Rafe had not gotten to see Nasira get married to Sebastian, a man who did not beat her and did not use her poorly. He had not gotten the chance to meet the man for years.

And Nolan Dane—his ghost was here, as well, looking at Rafe with distrust and something verging on horror.

Then there was Violet—his beautiful, mysterious V, his tough, quick cowgirl. She was carrying his child. She had been haunting his every thought for months. Did he honestly expect that he would return to Al Qunfudhah and not see her everywhere he went?

And woven in with all of these visions were past versions of himself. Of the boy who took the beatings so his siblings would not have to. Of the young man who attended to his tutors closely and dreamed of leaving Al Qunfudhah behind. Of the man who was ripped from his studies and his friends. Of the scarred man who refused to cower in the face of the abuses heaped upon him by the one person who was supposed to have defended him. Of the determined man who watched and waited and schemed.

Of the man who'd seen a beautiful woman who had sparked something in his chest, something that had not been there before. Something that made his heart cry out for pleasure, for something *more*.

Something more. That was what Violet was to him. More than just revenge. More than the stone wall he hid his heart behind. More than what his father expected and demanded.

With a cry of pain, he realized what he had become. Mac, Nolan and Violet—most especially Violet—they had opened their arms to Rafe, embraced him as friend and family. He had never been a sheikh's second son, not to them. He had always been Rafe and, for the first and only time in his life, just being Rafe was enough. More than enough.

Rafe would never be enough for Hassad bin Saleed. He could keep trying and trying and trying but the old man was dead and gone, and just as Nasira had said, Rafe was glad of it.

But he had been wrong. He thought that with Hassad's death, he had been freed of the old man. But he saw now that he had still carried Hassad with him, allowing his father's perverse sense of honor to warp Rafe's thoughts and actions.

Mac had been blameless. And in the name of a dead man's honor, Rafe had bought almost half an American county's worth of land to ruin his old friend.

Nolan had offered Rafe friendship but the moment he got too close, Rafe had shut Nolan out and driven him into the arms of a woman who would love him.

And Violet... She was beyond blameless. Yet Rafe had used her poorly. Cruelly, even.

What had he done? Hassad was dead. Yet he still controlled Rafe. Perhaps that had always been the old man's scheme, his plan to live from beyond the grave.

Well, no more.

Rafe had much work to do.

Twelve

Only one window at the McCallum house spilled light out into the night. It was not Violet's window—of that, Rafe was certain. Did that mean Mac was the only one home?

It did not matter. Rafe was here to make things right and if that meant he had to go through Mac, then that was what must be done.

Rafe shut his vehicle off and got out. Before he even closed the car door behind him, the front door of the McCallum house burst open.

Ah. He would have to go through Mac. Fitting.

But as Mac came down off the porch, Rafe drew back in alarm. He had never seen Mac this visibly angry before. His hands were balled into fists and, for the first time, Rafe thought his old friend could physically harm him.

The question that remained unanswered was, would Mac pummel him for what he'd done to Mac—or to Violet? It did not matter much. Either way, Rafe was deserving of this fury.

Despite the rage that poured off Mac in waves, Rafe held his ground. Years of habit had trained Rafe not to fall back or seek cover. Instead, he awaited his fate.

"Give me one good reason," Mac growled as he advanced in long strides, "why I shouldn't shoot you where you stand." Though he didn't have a gun that Rafe could see, the threat hung heavy in the air between them.

Because if Mac had a gun and pulled the trigger, Rafe would not survive. But he would not fight back.

The family honor, his father's voice whispered insidiously. *No one uses a bin Saleed like that and gets away with it.*

But this time, Rafe pushed the thought away. He did more than push it away. *No one uses a bin Saleed like you used me,* he thought back. *And I am not your instrument any longer.*

Mac was staring at him, rage and confusion blending into one hard mask of hatred. Rafe had earned that. "Well?" Mac demanded.

"You always were a man of honor," Rafe said, not bothering to hide a smile.

"Not like you, you dog. You and Violet? And the land? Why?"

Rafe took a breath. He suspected he had only one chance to get this right. "I have come to beg your forgiveness."

"I'm not buying that load of bullshit." Rafe did not flinch. That instinct had been beaten out of him years ago. "All this happened because you thought I slept with your sister. But I never even touched her, dammit."

"So she has told me."

The confusion in Mac's eyes overtook the rage a bit. "What?"

"She is here. Well, in Holloway. My brother told her

what I was doing. She came to make things right." Odd, that after so many years of trying to protect his siblings, they were now the ones doing the protecting. Except that, instead of protecting Rafe from their father, they were trying to protect him from himself.

"I don't understand."

"She has explained to me what happened the day we found her in your bed," Rafe went on, still trying to make sense of the day's events. "And I have realized something."

Mac fell back a step. "Yeah?"

"I came here for revenge." There was no cushioning that truth with soft words. "But I did not come here to avenge her. I thought I had. I thought I was meting out justice for the shame you brought upon my family's honor and our name. But that was a lie, I see now. A lie that justified my actions."

Mac took another step back. "So why are you here? Why did you come?"

Rafe found himself looking up. The stars were clear and bright here. When his father had him trapped in the dungeon, he had hardly seen the night sky for years. *Years.* "I came here to avenge myself."

"I didn't do a damn thing to you," Mac said. "And I'm not going to let you destroy Violet. I'd sooner rot in prison than see you ruin her."

Rafe smiled at this. "A man of honor," he repeated quietly. "I understand. For, you see, I did the same thing."

"What?"

Rafe had that weird out-of-time sensation again, the same one he felt when he had gone riding with Violet and slept in her bed with her. "I think it was always supposed to be this way," he told Mac.

"I don't know what you're talking about."

He grinned. "I am in love with your sister."

Before Rafe could protect himself, Mac stepped forward and punched him in the jaw. Rafe was knocked sideways as pain bloomed in his face, but he kept his feet underneath him. All told, he deserved that punch.

"You have one hell of a way of showing it. You hurt her, you ass. I've done everything I could to protect her and you waltz in here and…" His voice shook. "And you hurt her. She doesn't deserve that."

Rafe straightened. "No, she doesn't. But you can't get revenge for her." He took a deep breath. This was right. This was peace. "You can only get revenge for yourself."

"What?"

"I have hurt you, Mac. We were friends—I considered you to be a brother. Which makes the way my entire family acted toward you all the worse." Rafe bowed his head before Mac. "Please accept my apologies on behalf of my sister, my father—and myself. You did not deserve to be used like you were."

Mac stood there, his mouth open wide as he gaped at Rafe. "I—you—"

"I would like to speak to Violet now." Rafe reached for the deed to the Wild Aces. "I want to give this to her and tell her I love her."

But as he moved, Mac tensed and reached behind his back. Someone screamed.

And a gun went off.

"That bastard is here." Those had been Mac's exact words as he'd grabbed his pistol, shoved it in the back of his waistband and run out the door before Violet could do anything else.

Rafe had come back? That man must have a death wish. If Mac didn't get him, Violet would.

Lulu had called. She was sure sorry, but three million—well, she knew that Violet would never be able to come close to that. The money was too good. She'd signed the papers.

Tears silently streaming down her face, Violet had ended the call.

Gone. It was all gone. All because Rafe had his facts wrong.

Bastard wasn't a strong enough term.

Still, she didn't exactly want Mac to shoot Rafe. At the very least, he shouldn't kill Rafe. A flesh wound might be okay.

No, that was just the anger talking because if Mac shot Rafe, Mac would wind up in prison and Rafe's family would want to know why and there would be an international incident. And the very last thing Violet wanted right now was an international incident.

So she hurried out through the kitchen and crept along the side of the house, sticking to the shadows. When she could peek around the porch, she saw that Rafe and Mac were standing only a few feet away. Oddly, Mac wasn't holding his gun. Odder still, the two men were talking.

"...And tell her I love her," she heard Rafe say as he reached into his pocket.

Mac tensed and reached around his back—for his gun.

Oh, God—he was going to shoot Rafe. And Rafe had just said that he loved her? Hadn't he?

One thing was clear. Mac couldn't kill Rafe. He couldn't even wound him.

But that wasn't stopping Mac. He had the gun out of his waistband. She tried to shout a warning—but she couldn't even get the words, "Don't kill him!" out before a shot was fired into the darkness.

Violet screamed so loudly that the world went blue on the edge of her vision and then, just as it was going black, she saw both men turn in her direction.

Rafe was the last thing she thought about before she blacked out.

"Violet," she heard a silky voice say. For some reason, it made her think of sunshine and honey, warm and sweet. "Are you well? Please open your eyes," the voice pleaded. "Please be well."

"Here," another voice said. This one was gruff and tight. It was her brother, Mac.

"Ah," said the liquid sunshine voice. *Rafe*. Rafe was here. Oh, thank God.

Then something wet splashed on her face and she startled. Her eyes flew open and she saw the night sky and Rafe's face close to hers and Mac's hovering behind him. "What happened?"

"Someone scared the hell out of me," Mac said. He sounded mad, but she could see the worry lines on his face. "And I pulled the trigger."

"I fear the car will never be the same," Rafe said. He managed a small grin at her.

"You're not dead? I'm not dead?"

"No one is dead," he assured her. "You, however, fainted."

"Dammit." This was embarrassing.

"Yeah," Mac replied. "She's shooting her mouth off again. She's fine. Help me get her up."

"I have her," Rafe said. He pulled Violet into his arms and cradled her against his chest. Then, as if she weighed nothing at all, he stood. "If you could be so kind as to find the paper I dropped..."

"Sure. What is it?"

"The deed to the Wild Aces." He said it casually as he carried her into the house.

"What?" she gasped.

"The Wild Aces. It is yours." He sat down on the couch, but he did not let her go. Instead—in the middle of the living room, in full view of her brother and anyone else who might wander through—he pulled her onto his lap. "Whatever you choose, I will accept. But the land—and the water—it is yours."

She blinked up at him. "Are you serious? You're just going to *give* me the Aces? You spent three million dollars on it!"

"I would pay twice that if that was what it took to give you a beautiful home where you can raise our child. I want you to give him or her the kind of life that you have had, surrounded by family and love."

"I don't understand." It came out confused and weak, and she didn't want to be weak in front of him. She tried to shove herself off his lap, but his arms closed around her and there was no escaping him.

"I am sorry," he said. "I beg your forgiveness, Violet." He gave her an oddly crooked smile. "If my father could see me begging a woman for forgiveness…"

"Don't," she said. "I don't want to ever hear his name again."

"A sheikh of Al Qunfudhah does not ask for forgiveness. And begging is unthinkable. But that is what I am doing now, Violet. I treated you poorly and there is no excuse."

There was something else going on here and it wasn't just that he'd been crazy enough to tell an armed-and-dangerous older brother he was in love with her.

It was the same *something else* that Violet had seen in Nasira's eyes when Nasira had said that their father had imprisoned Rafe. At the time, she had hoped that the other woman was speaking metaphorically or Violet had misunderstood because of the language and cultural differences between them, even though Nasira spoke perfect, if British, English.

What if…what if she hadn't been speaking metaphorically?

Rafe bowed his head over her. "My father was…a difficult man."

Violet waited. She had the feeling that he was getting to the truth of the matter and she could not rush him.

"He held me responsible for what had happened to Nasira. He washed his hands of her and she was able to move to London. In that, I had succeeded in protecting her. Her life has been much better for it. But as for my father, I had failed him. And he made me pay for that failure."

"What do you mean, he made you pay? Nasira said…"

The sorrow on Rafe's face made her tear up. "He locked me in the dungeons."

"Oh, God." She blinked, but the tears refused to go away.

"For years, until he died, I was a prisoner in my own home." His voice wavered and he closed his eyes, but only for a moment. When he opened them again, he looked almost unmoved by what had happened. But she could see now that it was a lie. He wasn't incapable of emotions. He was just hiding the pain. "Fareed is the only reason I am still alive. He snuck me food and medicines and did his best to convince our father to free me—or at least treat me better."

Violet's heart about broke. *Oh, Rafe.*

"It does not excuse my behavior," he said sternly. "But during those years, there was but one thought that sustained me. I had lost everything. My freedom, my life, my friend. And I believed that it was because of Mac that everything I loved had been taken from me."

She didn't know what to say. So instead, she hung her arms around his neck and held him to her, as if that could take the pain away.

Rafe went on, "I told myself that I had to avenge the family name, I had to make us even for Nasira's honor. That was what my father beat into me. But I see now that it was never that. I suffered greatly. And I wanted to make Mac feel the same hopelessness I had felt."

Violet's throat closed up and she had to choke down a sob. So that was it. His father hadn't delivered a meta-phorical beating—hell, it wasn't even a single beating. The horrible man had treated Rafe like a whipping boy.

She couldn't stop the tears that traced down her cheeks. All those times when a shadow had crossed his face—was he remembering what his father said or did to him?

This wasn't fair. He was making her feel things for him and she didn't want to. She didn't want to feel any-thing but hate because he had been prepared to take ev-erything she loved away from her. She absolutely did not want to feel this urge to pull him into her arms and hold him tight and tell him that as long as she lived, no one would ever do that to him again. A silly girl's silly promise—Rafe was a man now, and more than capa-ble of taking care of himself. But, as silly as it was, she wanted to say it to him. She wanted to tell him that she would never let anyone treat their child like that either.

She wanted to keep him safe. After all these years of being guarded and protected, this sudden urge to defend Rafe was almost overwhelming.

Stupid pregnancy hormones. She had no idea if she was mad or sad or upset or so, so happy because Rafe really did love her and he had come back to apologize. He wasn't going to destroy her.

He wasn't going to destroy the two of them.

"All those years ago, Mac had entranced me with stories of your happy family and your beautiful ranch and your town. And for years, I waited for a way to destroy those things. But when I was with you, it all came back to me. And I felt like... I feel like I had finally come home again."

"Oh, Rafe," she gasped. "Why couldn't you see it sooner? I would have been your family. We all would have been. This could have been your home—with me." She lifted his hand and put it against her stomach. "With us."

That look of sorrow passed over his face again, then he cupped her cheeks in his hands and touched his forehead to hers. "I understand. My treatment of you has been unforgivable and I will regret until my dying day that I hurt you so. The Wild Aces is yours, but I know that it can never truly make up for my actions. I will leave tomorrow and I will not trouble you again."

She froze, a feeling of horror building in her chest. "Wait—what?"

Rafe gave her a sad smile. "I wish to stay—I wish to be with you. You are my only happiness. But to do so would bring dishonor upon my family name. But more than that, it would dishonor you and your family. I cannot do that, not anymore. I cannot destroy what I love."

"I swear to God, if you ever talk about doing something stupid out of honor again, I'm going to shoot you myself."

At this announcement, Rafe's eyebrows jumped up so high they almost cleared his forehead. "What?"

"You keep talking like it's too late—well, I've got news for you, buster. Just because you hold a grudge for over a damned decade doesn't mean I have to."

"But—my actions—I have hurt you."

"You're damn right you have." She glared at him, trying to put her thoughts into something that resembled order. "But you've also faced down my brother to apologize. You survived a horrific childhood and yet here you are, trying so hard to do the right thing that you're about to go and screw it up again." She threw her hands up, almost hitting him in the chin. "God! Men!"

Rafe was staring at her, a puzzled look on his face. "What are you saying?"

"You begged my forgiveness. That's what you said, right?" He nodded. "Well, I forgive you. I forgive you, Rafe."

The impact of these words hit Rafe as hard as if she'd actually shot him. He fell back against the couch, clutching at his chest. His eyes went wide and he turned a scarily pale color.

Violet panicked. "Rafe? Are you okay?"

"You—you forgive me?" He said it in such a way that it was clear that the thought had never crossed his mind. Forgiveness hadn't been an option. "I nearly ruined your life!"

"But you didn't," she reminded him. This was right, she decided. She could hold this misguided attempt to rule the world against him—but that would be punishing the son for the sins of the father. And Rafe was more than that.

He was the father of her child. And she would not let those sins ruin them all. "I forgive you, Rafe. I hope you can forgive yourself."

He was physically shaking. She really had no choice but to wrap her arms around him and hold him tight— tighter than she'd ever held anyone before.

"I do not deserve you, Violet. I am not worthy of your love."

"Is that what *he* told you—that bastard of a father of yours? Because it was a lie, Rafe. You are the man I want—when you're not trying to be what *he* wanted you to be."

Rafe looked at her with so much longing and pain in his eyes that she had trouble breathing. "Violet…"

"Found it," Mac said, walking into the room. He took one look at the two of them curled up on the couch together and groaned. "Am I going to have to shoot you or not?"

"In my country," Rafe said without flinching at all, "when a man wishes to marry a woman, he would ask permission of her father or her oldest male relative."

Mac's mouth opened, but Rafe didn't let him get a word in. "However," he said, his gaze never leaving Violet's face, "we are not in my country, are we?"

Violet's heart—the same heart that had very nearly stopped beating only a few minutes ago—began to pound. "No," she said, quietly. "We aren't."

"Lord," Mac scoffed. "I will shoot you if you do anything stupid to deserve it ever again."

Rafe laughed. "I have a feeling you won't have the chance."

"You're nuts," Violet said. "Both of you. Now, Mac—if you don't mind, I think Rafe was trying to ask me something?"

"I don't want to know," he muttered, turning on his heel and stalking out of the room. The last thing Violet caught before the front door slammed was, "…little sister—gross!"

She laughed and Rafe laughed with her. "I'm sorry my brother almost killed you."

"I deserved it. I have no right to ask this of you and you have no obligation to say yes—but Violet McCallum, would you do me the honor of becoming my wife?"

She wasn't sure she remembered how to breathe, but it didn't matter. All that mattered was Rafe was here and there were no more lies between them. "Are you sure we can make this work? You've got to admit that nothing about this has been a normal relationship."

"You have shown me there is another way." Rafe rested his hand on her belly. "I want nothing more than to spend my days riding by your side and my nights in your bed. I want to hear our child's heartbeat and be there when you bring him or her into this world. I want to do all the things my parents did not do, all the things Mac spoke of that gave me hope. Dinners and birthday parties and movies with popcorn and love. I want your love, Violet. I do not deserve it but—"

He didn't get to say anything else because Violet had pulled him down to her and covered his mouth with hers.

"Do you love me?" she asked, pulling away before she lost what little control she still had. "Really?"

"I have never loved anyone before, but I love you. You grace my thoughts during the day and haunt my dreams at night, my beautiful, mysterious Violet. I love you more than I can hold inside me. I think I always have," he whispered against her forehead.

"It was always supposed to be this way," she said, remembering his words. She leaned into his touch, curling her hands into the fine cloth of his shirt and holding him to her.

"I was always supposed to be yours," he agreed. "I just did not realize it until it was too late."

"It's not too late," she told him, throwing her arms

around his neck and hugging him. "But no more shocks, okay?"

"No more shocks. You know the worst of me. All I can hope to do is show you the best of me. Your pleasure is my pleasure," he said into her hair. "And I swear I will spend the rest of our lives giving you nothing but pleasure."

"I'm going to hold you to that," she cautioned him. "Because your pleasure is my pleasure, too."

He cupped her face in his palm and stared into her eyes. "I love you, Violet McCallum. Marry me. Be my family. Because I want there to be an *us*."

Us. He might have torn them apart, but he was going to put them back together. "I love you, too. Stay with me, Rafe. Let me protect you."

"Only so long as I can protect you. This is your last chance, Violet. If you say no, I will leave, peacefully and quietly. I will support our child, but I will not interfere with your life again."

For some reason, she thought of their conversation in the elevator their first night together. He'd given her a chance to say no then, too—but she hadn't. "And if I say yes?"

His grin grew wicked. "If you say yes, you will be mine, you understand? And I will be yours. For always and forever."

"Then I better say yes. I am yours, Rafiq bin Saleed."

He touched his forehead to hers. "I am yours, Violet McCallum."

And that was all either of them said for quite some time.

* * * * *

LET'S TALK

Romance

For exclusive extracts, competitions
and special offers, find us online:

f facebook.com/millsandboon

🐦 @MillsandBoon

📷 @MillsandBoonUK

Get in touch on 01413 063232

COMING SOON!

We really hope you enjoyed reading this book. If you're looking for more romance, be sure to head to the shops when new books are available on

Thursday 21st March

To see which titles are coming soon, please visit

millsandboon.co.uk/nextmonth

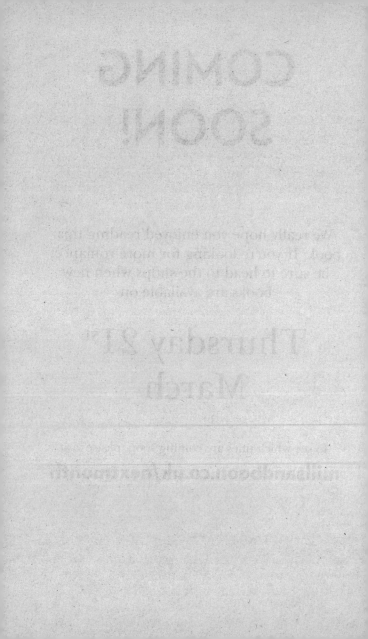